Writer's Choice

COMPOSITION AND GRAMMAR

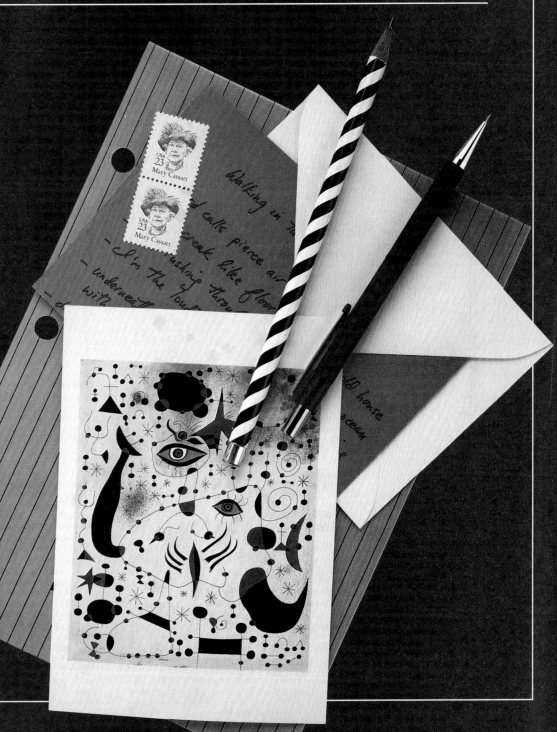

Case Studies: Writers at Work

Melanie McFarland
Movie Reviewer

Sandra Cisneros
Poet and Fiction Writer

Gary Ross
Screenwriter

Lisa Twyman Bessone
Sportswriter

Suzanne Winckler
Science Writer

Lorenzo Chavez
Feature Writer

Student Advisory Board

Michael Kim

Rachel Hansen

Charles Dayton

Claire Monty

David Ojeda

Maritza Pagán

Yahna Awazu

Maurice Phifer

Chris Fickes

Writer's Choice

COMPOSITION AND GRAMMAR

Vincent van Gogh, *The Starry Night*, 1889

Consulting Author for Composition
William Strong

Grammar Specialist
Mark Lester

Visual-Verbal Learning Specialists
Ligature, Inc.

GLENCOE

Macmillan/McGraw-Hill

Lake Forest, Illinois   Columbus, Ohio   Mission Hills, California   Peoria, Illinois

Front cover includes Joan Miró, *Chiffres et constellations en amoureux de sa femme*, 1941.

Back cover includes a letter in Spanish, which translated reads: "Agustín and I went today to the drugstore to buy paper to build kites. Agustín told me that in his country they call them *papalotes*. I already have the wood sticks and the cord needed to build my kite. Agustín asked his father to bring him some wood from work tomorrow. Between Agustín and me we are going to build the most beautiful kites in the entire neighborhood."

Send all inquiries to:
GLENCOE DIVISION
Macmillan/McGraw-Hill
15319 Chatsworth Street
P.O. Box 9609
Mission Hills, CA 91346-9609

ISBN 0-02-635201-X
(Student's Edition)
ISBN 0-02-635202-8
(Teacher's Wraparound Edition)

Printed in the United States of America

1 2 3 4 5 6 7 8 9 10 AGH 96 95 94 93 92

Consulting Author for Composition

William Strong is Professor of Secondary Education at Utah State University, Director of the Utah Writing Project, and a member of the National Writing Project Advisory Board. A nationally known authority in the teaching of composition, he is the author of many volumes, including, most recently, *Writing Incisively: Do-It-Yourself Prose Surgery* (McGraw-Hill, 1991).

As Consulting Author, Dr. Strong helped to develop the structure and content of Part 1: Composition. He reviewed and edited all Composition units. Dr. Strong also conceived and wrote Unit 8: Style Through Sentence Combining. He collaborated on *Sentence Combining Blackline Masters*, which accompanies *Writer's Choice*.

Grammar Specialist

Mark Lester is Professor of English at Eastern Washington University. He formerly served as Chair of the Department of English as a Second Language, University of Hawaii. He is the author of *Grammar in the Classroom* (Macmillan, 1990) and of numerous professional books and articles.

As Grammar Specialist, Dr. Lester reviewed student's edition material from Part 2: Grammar, Usage, and Mechanics. He collaborated on *Grammar Reteaching Blackline Masters*, which accompanies *Writer's Choice*.

Associate Consultant in Writing

Bonnie S. Sunstein is Associate Professor of English and Director of the Master of Arts in Teaching Program at Rivier College in Nashua, New Hampshire. Dr. Sunstein has taught extensively in New England in colleges and secondary schools, as well as in the New Hampshire Reading and Writing Program. She has published in the area of writing and teaching and is the coeditor of *Portfolio Portraits* (Heinemann, 1992) and the author of a forthcoming book about teachers and writing (Boynton/Cook).

As Associate Consultant in Writing, Dr. Sunstein established the theoretical framework for integrating writing portfolios into *Writer's Choice*.

Contributing Writers

Larry Beason is Assistant Professor of English at Eastern Washington University. Dr. Beason is the writer of *Grammar Reteaching Blackline Masters*, which accompanies *Writer's Choice*.

Willis L. Pitkin Jr. is Professor of English at Utah State University. Dr. Pitkin is the writer of *Sentence Combining Blackline Masters*, which accompanies *Writer's Choice*.

Visual-Verbal Learning Specialists

Ligature, Inc., is an educational research and development company with offices in Chicago and Boston. Ligature is committed to developing educational materials that bring visual-verbal learning to the tradition of the written word.

As visual-verbal and curriculum specialists, Ligature collaborated on conceiving and implementing the pedagogy of *Writer's Choice*.

Acknowledgments

Grateful acknowledgment is given authors, publishers, photographers, museums, and agents for permission to reprint the following copyrighted material. Every effort has been made to determine copyright owners. In the case of any omissions, the Publisher will be pleased to make suitable acknowledgments in future editions. *Continued on page 806*

Composition Advisers

The advisers reviewed Composition lesson prototypes. Their contributions were instrumental in the development of the Writing Process in Action lessons.

Michael Angelotti
Head of Division of Teacher
    Education
College of Education
University of Oklahoma

Charles R. Duke
Dean of the College of Education
    and Human Services
Clarion University

Carol Booth Olson
Director
University of California, Irvine,
    Writing Project

Judith Summerfield
Associate Professor of English
Queens College, City University of
    New York

Denny Wolfe
Professor and Associate Dean
Darden College of Education
Old Dominion University
formerly Director, Tidewater Writing
    Project

Educational Reviewers

The reviewers read and commented upon manuscripts during the writing process. They also critiqued early drafts of graphic organizers and page layouts.

Lenore Croudy
Flint Community School
Flint, Michigan

John A. Grant
St. Louis Public Schools
St. Louis, Missouri

Vicki Haker
Mead Junior High School
Mead, Washington

Frederick G. Johnson
Georgia Department of Education
Atlanta, Georgia

Sterling C. Jones Jr.
Detroit Public Schools
Detroit, Michigan

Barry Kincaid
Raytown School District
Kansas City, Missouri

Evelyn G. Lewis
Newark Public Schools
Newark, New Jersey

M. DeAnn Morris
Crescenta Valley High School
La Crescenta, California

Anita Moss
University of North Carolina
Charlotte, North Carolina

Ann S. O'Toole
Chesterfield County Schools
Richmond, Virginia

Suzanne Owens
Glendale High School
Glendale, California

Sally P. Pfeifer
Lewis and Clark High School
Spokane, Washington

Marie Rogers
Independence High School
Charlotte, North Carolina

Barbara Schubert
Santa Clara County Office of
    Education
San Jose, California

Ronnie Spilton
Chattahoochee High School
Alpharetta, Georgia

Robert Stolte
Huntington Beach High School
Huntington Beach, California

Student Advisory Board

The Student Advisory Board was formed in an effort to ensure student involvement in the development of *Writer's Choice*. The editors wish to thank members of the board for their enthusiasm and dedication to the project.

The editors also wish to thank the many student writers whose models appear in this book.

Thanks are also due to Miami University of Ohio for help in the selection of models from student portfolios and to *Merlyn's Pen* for cooperation in providing student models.

Writer's Choice

COMPOSITION AND GRAMMAR

Writer's Choice was written for you, the student writer. You're the writer in the title, and real students like you contributed to the materials you'll study. The book is organized into three main parts: (1) Composition; (2) Grammar, Usage, and Mechanics; and (3) Resources and Skills.

Part 1 Composition

The lessons in Composition are designed to give you help with specific writing tasks. You can use the units and lessons in order from beginning to end or select just the ones that help with your own writing needs.

Part 2   Grammar, Usage, and Mechanics

In the unique Troubleshooter you'll learn to identify and correct the most common student writing problems. Throughout the rest of Part 2, you'll find plenty of practice to reinforce what you learn.

Part 3   Resources and Skills

You can use these resources and skills not just in English class but wherever you need to communicate effectively. The tone and approach are user-friendly, with many opportunities to practice and apply the skills you learn.

Contents

CONTENTS

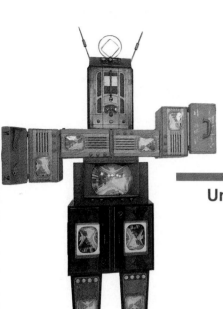

Unit 3   Descriptive Writing: *Real Toads in Imaginary Gardens*   *123*

Unit 4   Narrative Writing: *The Basic Tale*   *165*

Unit 5   Expository Writing: *Planet Earth*   *213*

CONTENTS

Part 2 Grammar, Usage, and Mechanics

CONTENTS

xiii

CONTENTS

Part 3 Resources and Skills

Literature

Each literature selection is an extended example of the mode of writing taught in the unit.

Literature Models

Excerpts from outstanding works of fiction and nonfiction exemplify specific writing skills.

Workshop Literature

Each workshop uses an excerpt from a novel or long work of nonfiction to link grammar, usage, or mechanics to literature.

Case Studies

Each case study focuses on a real writer working on a real-life writing project. Come on backstage!

Fine Art

Fine art—paintings, drawings, photos, and sculpture—is used to teach as well as to inspire.

Writer's Choice

COMPOSITION AND GRAMMAR

*W*elcome *to Writer's Choice! Your writing and your choices are what this book is all about. The modular format of the book allows you to choose quickly the lesson or handbook section that will help you with a writing problem or task. With this big picture in mind, take a few minutes to get to know each of the main parts of the book, which are illustrated on the upcoming pages.*

Part 1   Composition

Unit Opener

Case Study

Part 2   Grammar, Usage, and Mechanics

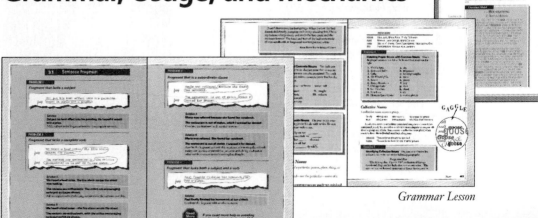

Troubleshooter

Grammar Lesson

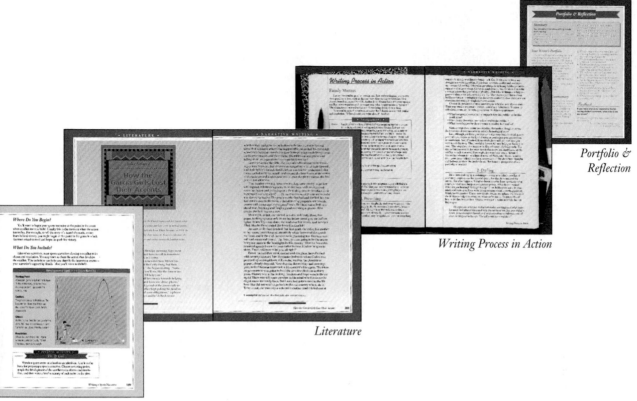

Portfolio & Reflection

Writing Process in Action

Literature

Composition Lesson

Part 3   Resources and Skills

Unit Review

Workshop

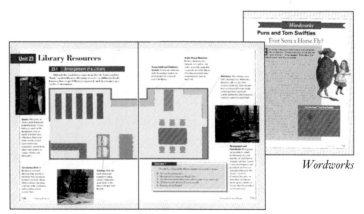

Wordworks

Resources and Skills Lesson

Inside Composition

The basic building block of the Composition units is the four-page lesson. Each lesson clearly focuses on a specific writing problem or task. You will always find clear and specific instruction, models of effective writing, and a variety of writing activities.

Literature Models help you learn from the pros by showing you how published authors have met the writing challenges you face.

Student Models present writing by students like you to help you achieve your own writing goals.

Writing Process Tips help you connect the skills you're learning to other stages of the writing process.

How Do You Tell the Story?

After you've chosen a sports event, determined your starting point, and charted the action, you're ready to draft your sports narrative. Begin by considering your lead. A lead is a strong opening sentence that grabs the reader's attention and gets the story moving. Examine your story's starting point. Is there anything dramatic, amusing, or surprising about it? If so, you might use that for your lead. Remember, however, that if you're writing a sports feature or news article, a narration of the event will only make up part of your article. (For tips on how to write a sports feature, see the Unit 4 Case Study on sportswriting on pages 166–171.)

State the Facts Clearly   Be sure that you have presented the sequence of events and all the facts in your narrative clearly. Double-check quotations for accuracy, and make sure each source is clearly identified.

Use Vivid Language   Wherever possible, show your readers the action rather than telling them about it. Vivid action verbs and sensory details can help bring your story to life and hold your readers' interest.

Read the following selection from baseball writer Roger Angell's book *Season Ticket*, which contains a series of narratives about baseball games the writer has attended. Notice how Angell makes even a seemingly actionless stretch of a game interesting.

Prewriting Tip

When prewriting about a sports event, try list making to generate details. Use the significant details to develop your narrative.

Literature Model

Angell uses precise, vivid verbs to show the reader the action.

A base runner leads cautiously away from first, then trots back as the pitcher steps off the rubber. The third-base ump walks seven steps out toward left field, turns, and strolls back again. Another foul ball, bounced softly past first base

4.5   Writing a Sports Narrative

Making Points

Student Model

The conflict in a sports narrative is often person against person, as each athlete struggles to win the sports event.

What is the climax in this sports narrative? How is it resolved?

The pop of the gun sets the swimmers' legs in motion and arms flawlessly scooping pockets of water. Their heads bob rhythmically, each straining to reach the end of the pool. At the end of each lane, fellow swimmers stand and cheer their teammates, with a single exception. One blond-haired swimmer receives cries from teammates who lean close to the water, straining to show the swimmer their enthusiasm and their lips. The swimmer is deaf, and the encouraging motions of her friends urge her to go faster.

The race is close. The blond head edges out in front, neck and neck, with another swimmer beside her. However, with a last, powerful stroke, the blond swimmer breaks the tie and hits the timer seconds before her competitor. As she rests against the wall of the pool, accepting the congratulations of her teammates, an ear-to-ear grin appears across her face.

Charissa Adelman, Quartz Hill High School, Quartz Hill, California

Most sports news articles report the results of a game, but they also recount the gripping action in the event itself. Sporting events involve all the elements so essential to a good narrative: character, setting, and a conflict that develops to a climax and resolution.

188   *Narrative Writing: The Basic Tale*

Writer's Choice Activities give you a full page of writing options to help you apply what you have learned in the lesson. You'll also find fine art or a special feature on using computers in writing.

· ACTIVITIES ·
Writer's Choice

The following are some writing options to help you apply what you have learned.

1. Guided Assignment   The editor of your school newspaper has asked you to write a sports narrative based on an important basketball game. Use the following information to write the narrative. Remember to begin at the point at which the conflict starts to build, and use transitions to guide your readers through the action. Be sure, too, to enliven the story with action verbs.

> West High and East High, long-standing rivals, face each other in the state basketball finals. The game is close until the fourth quarter, when East High pulls ahead with a 78 to 70 lead. Finally West High comes from behind to win the game 82-80, with a basket in the final seconds of the fourth quarter.

PURPOSE To narrate an exciting sports event for a school newspaper
AUDIENCE Student and teacher sports fans
LENGTH 1–2 pages

2. Open Assignment   Imagine you're a freelance sports writer on assignment for an important sports magazine. Choose one of the following topics or one of your own as the subject for your sports narrative. Identify the major characters, plot, and setting in your narrative. Then chart the action on a graph like the one shown on page 189. Use the graph to help you write your narrative.

- An older tennis player plays the match of his life against the current best player in the world—a much younger man. The older player wins in an exciting fifth set.
- After trailing seven runs throughout most of the game, a baseball team makes a surprising comeback in the ninth inning.

...tive
...Use the
...his page to
...ports nar-
...k in small
...rainstorm
...tory. Agree
...rs, setting,
...hart the
...n have
...member
...count of
...ake turns
...ur narrative
...p, and
...rent
...to the

Where Do You Begin?

You'll want to begin your sports narrative at the point in the event when conflict starts to build. Usually this is the moment when the action intensifies. For example, to tell the story of a team's dramatic, come-from-behind victory, you might begin at the point in the game in which the team seized control and began its push for victory.

What Do You Include?

Like other narratives, most sports narratives develop a conflict to its climax and resolution. You may want to chart the action that develops the conflict. This technique can help you identify the important events—your narrative's supporting details—that you'll want to include.

Visual/Verbal Instruction combines words with images and graphics to help you visualize ideas and master the skills of writing.

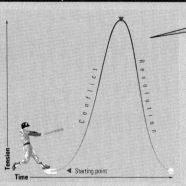

Development of Conflict in a Sports Narrative

Starting Point:
A baseball game is tied at the bottom of the ninth inning, with two outs. A runner on third represents the winning run.

Conflict:
The pitcher stares at third base. The base runner, determined to break the record for stolen bases, boldly stares back.

Climax:
As the pitcher fires the ball over home plate, the base stealer makes a dash for home and plows into the catcher.

Resolution:
When the dust clears, the umpire waves his arms and yells, "Safe!" The crowd roars with delight.

· JOURNAL ACTIVITY ·
Try It Out

Watch a sports event at school or on television. Use it as the basis for preparing a sports narrative. Choose a starting point, graph the development of the conflict to its climax and resolution, and then write a brief summary of each point in the plot.

Journal Activity, at the bottom of the second page of every lesson, gives you a chance to reflect and respond to the lesson material.

Writing a Sports Narrative   **189**

Inside Grammar

This grammar handbook works for you, not the other way around. You'll learn how to find and fix errors in your writing. Two special sections—the Troubleshooter and the Workshops— help you expand your grammar skills.

The Troubleshooter presents in one place the solutions to the twelve errors most frequently made by student writers. Your teacher may refer you to the Troubleshooter by marking errors in your papers with the abbreviations shown down the far left side of the page.

Unit 9 Troubleshooter

Research on thousands of student papers has identified the errors most frequently made by students and marked by teachers. This Troubleshooter is based on that research and is designed to help you correct these errors.

Use the Table of Contents below to locate quickly a lesson for a specific error. Your teacher may mark errors with the handbook codes in the left-hand column.

9.1 Sentence Fragment

PROBLEM 1
Fragment that lacks a subject

frag   Sal put his best effort into his painting. Hoped it would win a prize.

Solution
Sal put his best effort into his painting. He hoped it would win a prize.
Add a subject to the fragment to make it a complete sentence.

PROBLEM 2
Fragment that lacks a complete verb

frag   We heard a loud noise. The fire alarm across the street.

frag   The reviews are enthusiastic. The critics encouraging us to put on future shows.

Solution A
We heard a loud noise. The fire alarm across the street was wailing.

The reviews are enthusiastic. The critics are encouraging us to put on future shows.
Add a complete verb or a helping verb to make the sentence complete.

Solution B
We heard a loud noise—the fire alarm across the street.

The reviews are enthusiastic, with the critics encouraging us to put on future shows.
Combine the fragment with another sentence.

378   *Troubleshooter*

PROBLEM 3
Fragment that is a subordinate clause

frag   Maria was relieved. Because she found her notebook.

frag   The restaurant is out of melon. Which I wanted for dessert.

Solution A
Maria was relieved because she found her notebook.

The restaurant is out of melon, which I wanted for dessert.
Combine the fragment with another sentence.

Solution B
Maria was relieved. She found her notebook.

The restaurant is out of melon. I wanted it for dessert.
Rewrite the fragment as a complete sentence, eliminating the subordinating conjunction or the relative pronoun and adding a subject or other words necessary to make a complete thought.

PROBLEM 4
Fragment that lacks both a subject and a verb

frag   Paul finally finished his homework. At ten o'clock.

Solution
Paul finally finished his homework at ten o'clock.
Combine the fragment with another sentence.

Need More Help?   *If you need more help in avoiding sentence fragments, turn to 13.9.*

Sentence Fragment   379

Each of the twelve errors is explained in detail in the Troubleshooter Unit.

For each common error, Troubleshooter shows you the solution. If you need more help, Troubleshooter also refers you to the appropriate lesson.

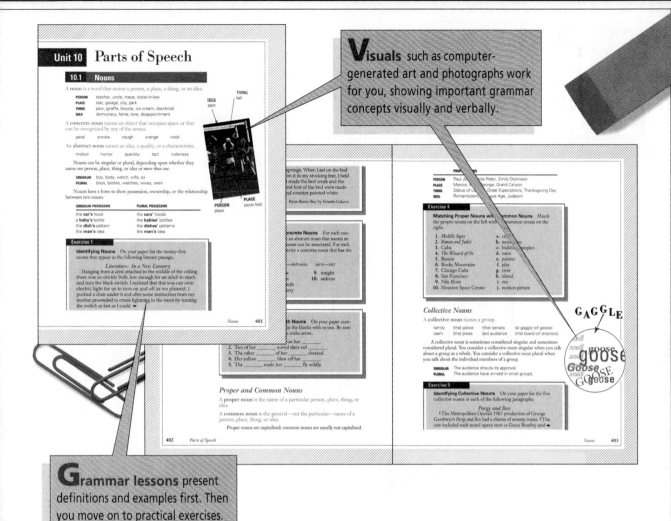

Visuals such as computer-generated art and photographs work for you, showing important grammar concepts visually and verbally.

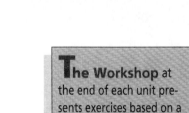

Grammar lessons present definitions and examples first. Then you move on to practical exercises.

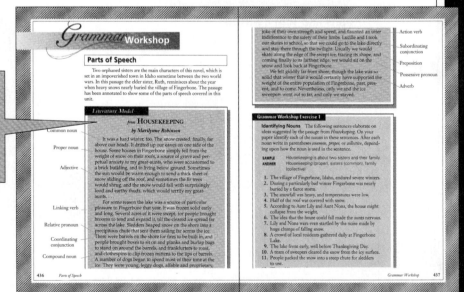

The Workshop at the end of each unit presents exercises based on a selection from a novel or other work of literature.

Inside Resources

The lessons in this unit give you the skills necessary to prepare and deliver a speech, take a test, use a dictionary, and find books in the library. Each lesson is complete, concise, and easy to use.

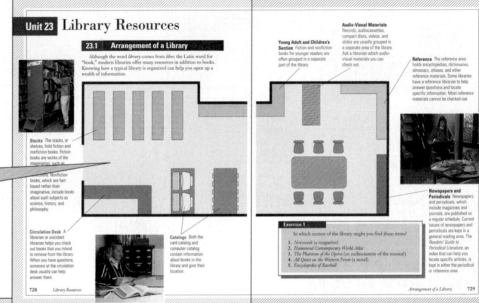

Graphics help you comprehend complex information at a glance.

Wordworks pages like this one provide a humorous look at how we use and misuse our language. These features appear in the first unit in Resources, which puts you in command of basic facts about the English language.

Part 1

Composition

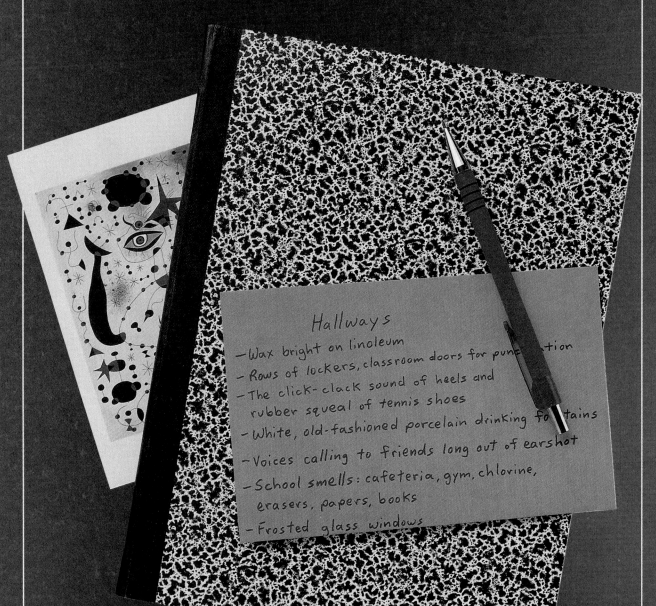

Hallways
— Wax bright on linoleum
— Rows of lockers, classroom doors for punctuation
— The click-clack sound of heels and
   rubber squeal of tennis shoes
— White, old-fashioned porcelain drinking fountains
— Voices calling to friends long out of earshot
— School smells: cafeteria, gym, chlorine,
   erasers, papers, books
— Frosted glass windows

Part 1 Composition

Personal Writing

Who Am I?

Chuck Close, *Cindy II*, 1989

A Letter from
Sandra Cisneros

"I could call people, but I just love to write letters. When I write a letter I'm forced to shine my shoes and capture my experiences in the most accurate way possible for someone who's not present. It takes me a long time to write a letter. I want to write something very beautiful to give as a gift, the way an artist would give a sketch."

Sandra Cisneros

On a windy spring day, Sandra Cisneros stole some time from her busy schedule to write a letter to her friend, Pulitzer prize-winner and poet laureate of Illinois, Gwendolyn Brooks. Cisneros had just published a new book of fiction called *Woman Hollering Creek*. She says, "This was right before my book tour began. For some reason, I always tour with Brooks's book *Maud Martha*. That morning I'd read one of the stories. I thought, 'I should tell Ms. Brooks how much I like her book.'"

Cisneros had not written to Brooks for a long time, but she says, "I wanted her to know how happy her book made me at this moment and how important it's been to me. I'm sure I'll get a response from her further down the line."

Cisneros learned how to write a proper letter in the fifth grade, but she has struggled all her life to forget that lesson. The writer recalls, "In

Writing a Letter

  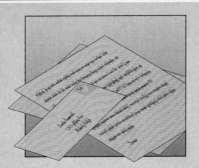

1. An Invitation to Follow **2.** The Heart of Who You Are **3.** Runways

FOCUS

Writing letters can help you communicate with someone, can teach you something new about yourself, and can stimulate new writing ideas.

school they gave us all the parts of a model letter to a friend—and they taught us to write it as if it were an essay. It was a lesson in how to sound like someone we're not."

Now Cisneros only writes letters in which she is free to be herself. The author says her letters are "not the kind of conversations you have when you're dressed in your suit, but the kind you have sitting at your kitchen table wearing your pajamas, talking to someone who's very dear to you."

Cisneros often writes her letters on "pretty paper, that delicious creamy kind with texture. Not intimidating paper, but paper you can do anything on. I'm very fussy about my pens and my papers. But then I need to get to a

typewriter; I need to see it typed to do the editing."

For her letter to Gwendolyn Brooks, Cisneros sat at her typewriter for a couple of hours. She says, "When it's someone as special as Gwendolyn Brooks, you can't just dash off a postcard."

Gwendolyn Brooks's novel Maud Martha *was published in 1953.*

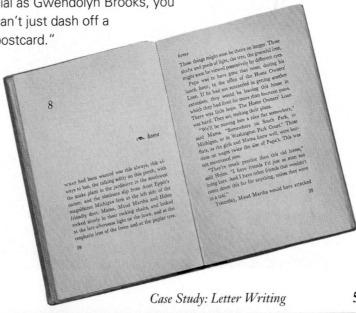

Case Study: Letter Writing   **5**

1. An Invitation to Follow

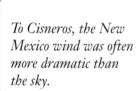

When you write a letter to a dear friend, says Cisneros, "You are blessing your recipient with your confidence, allowing [her or him] to follow your inner meanderings and showing a part of you that perhaps no one else has seen."

Cisneros had recently moved to New Mexico when she began her letter to Gwendolyn Brooks. "When I get to a new place, I like to sift through the events that are affecting me. I don't know how I feel about them until I write letters. Now, [people] talk about the sky in New Mexico, but they never mention the wind. The wind here just rolls out and bangs porch doors open. I've never seen anything like it."

So Cisneros opened her letter to Gwendolyn Brooks by talking about the wind in New Mexico. As Cisneros says, "People don't realize that you can start a letter from whatever comes into your head."

INTERFACE *You are about to write a letter to a good friend you haven't seen for several years. Identify something in your surroundings (such as the wind) that could stand for your feelings and provide a lead-in to your letter.*

To Cisneros, the New Mexico wind was often more dramatic than the sky.

2. The Heart of Who You Are

Writing letters can reveal hidden or private aspects of yourself. Cisneros calls letter writing her "way of meditating, of listening inside my heart to how I'm being affected by the outside world. The heart of who you are comes out when you truly write."

This writer considers her letters to be a much more accurate reflection of her life than any other kind of record, including her journal, which she uses primarily as a place to write "shorthand" notes to herself.

Cisneros says, "In my letters, I can plunge right into that deeper level where my poems come from. Unless you talk for a very long time to someone you know very well, you can't reach that level. I often surprise myself by what I pull up. Then I make copies of my letters and they become longer journal entries."

A copy of Cisneros's letter to Gwendolyn Brooks will probably end up in Cisneros's journal under the title, "The Windy Day—Letter to Gwendolyn Brooks."

INTERFACE *Sandra Cisneros ends her letter with a Spanish phrase— un abrazo fuerte, fuerte—that literally translates as "a big hug, strong, strong." Think of several original phrases you could use to substitute for the commonly used "love" or "sincerely."*

March 5th, 1991

Dear Ms. Brooks,

It is what Winnie the Pooh would call a blustery day here. Or what Miss Emily would designate a wind like a bugle. From over and over the mesas, snapping dust and terrifying trees.

I am in my pajamas though it's past mid-day but I like my leisure to dream a little longer when I am asleep, and continue dreaming on paper when I am awake. I am rereading your wonderful MAUD MARTHA again, a copy you gave me, and which I am very grateful to have. I remember when I first discovered that book, in the American library in Sarajevo, across from the famous river where the archduke was shot that started a world war. And it was there too that I read T.S. Eliot's collected poems. If you go to Sarajevo, and look at the chapter on PRACTICAL CATS you'll see a cherry stain on one of the pages--because I was reading the book on the opposite bank of the river, under a row of cherry trees in front of my American friend Ana's apartment house, and at the moment I was reading about one of Eliot's cats--the Rum Tum Tigger?--a wind shook a cherry loose that landed with a startled plop on the page. And my heart gave a little jump too because the book wasn't mine. A wine-colored stain against the thick creamy pages.

In the letter's second paragraph, Cisneros tells Brooks about the cherry that the wind shook loose from the tree.

7

3. Runways

When Cisneros is teaching, she advises her students to write a personal letter to an intimate friend as a "runway" to the creative writing process. Cisneros uses her own letters to give flight to her writing in several ways.

She says, "Sometimes I'll go through copies of my letters and I'll underline with a marker some nugget I'm going to save to reuse. When I'm stuck with a story, I might go through all my old letters and just read. I'll ask, 'Where can I put this?' Sometimes I start by writing a letter and then realize I've got a story. Other times, as I'm writing a story, I'll have a character rant or rave or whine or howl or laugh or swoon, and I'll realize that was really a letter to someone, but it's not going to get sent and it doesn't matter."

She continues, "I might use part of this letter to Gwendolyn Brooks in an essay that would include the anecdote of the cherry stain. What this letter particularly sparked for me was how I would like [to teach] the book *Maud Martha* in a course."

INTERFACE *Consider how a writer's tools influence the writing process. Which way of writing would allow you to feel most comfortable expressing yourself in a letter—writing it out in pen, typing it on a typewriter or word processor, or dictating it into a tape recorder for later transcription? Why?*

Cisneros often revises and edits her letters on a typewriter.

In the second page of the letter, Cisneros tells Brooks how she wants to teach Maud Martha *in a class.*

> I mean to teach it one day along with other books that use a series of short inter-related stories. Perhaps with Ermilo Abreu Gomez's CANEK and Nellie Campobello's CARTUCHO albeit the translation of both is crooked. The form fascinates. And I'd done as much with MANGO STREET, though I hadn't met your MAUD yet. Perhaps I was "recollecting the things to come."
>
> Ms. Brooks, please know I haven't quite disappeared altogether from the land. I've been migrant professor these past years, guest writer-in-residence at UC Berkeley, UC Irvine, the Univ. of Michigan at Ann Arbor and now here for one semester. All for the sake of protecting my writer self. Some years dipped low and some reeled to high heaven. But now the days are good to me. I have a new book due out from Random (see enclosed reviews) and I have sold my little house on Mango to the big house of Vintage. Both books slated for this April. And it seems my life is in a whirl like the wind outside my window today. Everything shook and snapped and wind-washed and fresh, and, yes, that is how it should be.
>
> I only wanted to say this to you today. That your book gives me such pleasure. That I admire it terribly. I think of you often, Ms. Brooks, and your spirit is with me always.
>
> un abrazo fuerte, fuerte,
>
> Sandra Cisneros

ON ASSIGNMENT

1. Sandra Cisneros advises her students to write a letter as if they were sitting at a kitchen table in their pajamas. In this setting or another that feels even more comfortable to you, write a one-page letter to your best friend. You don't need to mail the letter unless you wish to. Compare the experience of writing a letter to that of talking with your friend on the telephone. Which do you prefer? Why? How do you express yourself differently?

2. Literature Connection
Sandra Cisneros wrote her letter to Gwendolyn Brooks to express her admiration for Brooks's book *Maud Martha.* You have probably read a book, poem, or story that moved you deeply or raised questions in your mind. Write a one-page letter to the author to explain how you felt about what you read. If you like, mail your letter to the author in care of the publisher of the book (a librarian can give you the publisher's name and address). Many authors are surprised and delighted to hear from their readers.

3. Cooperative Learning
Form groups of two. For a period of one week, communicate back and forth to one another entirely by letter. During this time period, you can't speak to each other; you need to say everything you want to say in your letters. The letters can be whatever length you wish, from a few sentences to a few pages. At the end of the week, look over your collection of letters, and talk about how letter writing is different from speaking. Did this difference affect what you wanted to say? How? Were there some things you could or could not say in a letter that you might or might not have said aloud? Why?

What Makes Me Me?

John Lennon, *Self Portrait*, 1968

Former Beatle John Lennon expressed his identity in this self-portrait. You can express yourself by drawing, like Lennon did, or by writing, as N. Scott Momaday does below. And you can make discoveries about yourself, as Momaday does in this personal writing he published.

Literature Model

> *What uncertainties does Momaday give voice to here? Who is this writing for, in your opinion?*

> *Recalling specific details of sights and sounds helps Momaday deal with his uncertainties.*

Oh I feel so dumb . . . I don't know how to be a Kiowa Indian my grandmother lives in a house . . . only it doesn't have lights . . . and you have to carry wood in from the wood pile . . . but that isn't what makes it Indian its my grandma the way she is the way she looks her hair in braids the clothes somehow yes the way she talks she doesn't speak English so well . . . wait I know why it's an Indian house because . . . there is Indian stuff all around blankets and shawls bows and arrows everyone there . . . talks Kiowa and the old people wear Indian clothes . . . and there is laughing Indians laugh a lot and they sing oh yes they love to sing . . . there are drums too and it goes on through the night *that's* Indian . . .

N. Scott Momaday, *The Names*

Learning by Writing

Momaday sets out to discover something about himself through writing. He begins by wondering, somewhat confused, about his Kiowa heritage and then simply starts to write. Answers come as he recalls experiences, feelings, observations.

Asking personal questions like the ones that follow can help you get started on writing about yourself, or you can get started by reviewing your experiences, feelings, memories, observations, and reactions, as the diagram on this page illustrates.

Personal Questions Chart (with Sample Answers)

Q. What are some of the central things that make me *me*?
A. African American, teen-ager, oldest kid in my family, member of soccer team

Q. How do I feel as a typical day goes on?
A. I usually feel pretty good; too much homework gets me down, though. I feel warm and secure at home but free and more myself with my friends.

Q. What kinds of lessons have I learned recently?
A. I've learned about friendship, about dating, and about being a good loser in soccer.

Q. What do I enjoy most lately?
A. Hanging out with friends, playing soccer, vegging out to dumb TV shows, and, believe it or not, my world history class

Observations
Our dog, Sparky, is getting pretty old. He sleeps most of the time and doesn't play catch anymore.

Reactions
I get so angry when Mom expects me to babysit my little sister, Mandy.

Some sources for personal writing

Memories
Oatmeal always reminds me of breakfasts with my family.

Experiences
The first time Alissa and I went downtown alone we got lost.

Feelings
I feel completely in control when I strike out a batter.

• JOURNAL ACTIVITY •
Try It Out

John Lennon's self-portrait emphasizes three features: his hair, his nose, and his eyeglasses. In your journal, draw a simple sketch of yourself emphasizing three simple attributes, either physical or personality traits. Then write to answer this question: What does your self-portrait reveal about who you are?

Writing About Yourself

Whatever your sources, though, often the easiest way to begin personal writing is simply to begin—let your thoughts run free and write whatever comes to mind. Don't worry about spelling or grammar. Set a definite time limit—say, ten minutes—and keep writing until the time is up. If you get stuck, write anything, even "I'm stuck!" Just keep going. Before you know it, a word will spark a memory or another idea, and you'll be on your way. In the process, you may clarify your thoughts and even discover something about yourself. The chart below shows how this might happen.

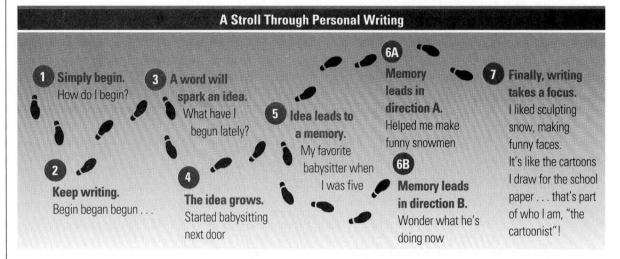

A Stroll Through Personal Writing

1 Simply begin. How do I begin?

2 Keep writing. Begin began begun . . .

3 A word will spark an idea. What have I begun lately?

4 The idea grows. Started babysitting next door

5 Idea leads to a memory. My favorite babysitter when I was five

6A Memory leads in direction A. Helped me make funny snowmen

6B Memory leads in direction B. Wonder what he's doing now

7 Finally, writing takes a focus. I liked sculpting snow, making funny faces. It's like the cartoons I draw for the school paper . . . that's part of who I am, "the cartoonist"!

Your experiences, feelings, memories, observations, and reactions are your best sources for personal writing. Student Vallery McCann took her own stroll through personal writing and learned about herself in the process.

Student Model

How would you assess the honesty of Vallery's writing? Does it sound authentic?

This journal entry helps Vallery think about plans for her future. What plans might you write about?

W ell, today is a milestone in my life. Yeehah. Three years ago today I was ending an old life and beginning a new one, & I didn't even know it. The freedom I have today is incredible. I am not ashamed of me. I have gotten to know myself. I was thinking on my way to school today maybe the difference between a romantic relationship & a friendship is that in a friendship the only commitment is unconditional love. I'm getting ready to graduate. Life looms ahead. I'm finding myself believing in education. I want to teach and give that opportunity of freedom to others. So today is my third anniversary drug free! I will not back down! I am free!

Vallery McCann, Hamilton Heights High School, Arcadia, Indiana

The following are some writing options to help you apply what you have learned.

1. Guided Assignment   Create a piece of personal writing aimed at self-discovery. Use freewriting to get yourself started, but unlike other freewriting you will do, this time go through the following specific steps:

- Begin with a declaration of how you feel or what you think about yourself.
- Explain your opening statement. Tell why you feel or think this.
- Next, present a perplexing issue or problem that you would like to investigate to learn more about yourself.
- Freewrite about the issue or problem, utilizing any personal experiences, observations, feelings, reactions, and memories.
- Try to arrive at some kind of conclusion, even if it's not a final answer.
- Share your writing with the class if you wish.

PURPOSE Self-discovery
AUDIENCE Yourself
LENGTH 1–2 pages

2. Open Assignment   Practice focused freewriting. Choose one of the following opening phrases, or use one of your own, to write about freely for five minutes. Remember, keep writing. If you get stuck, repeat a word over and over until something else comes to you.

- If only I could . . .
- The one word that best describes me is . . .
- I would never give up my . . .
- No one knows that I . . .
- The one thing I would like to change about myself is . . .

When you are finished, review what you have written. Underline any parts that help you learn about yourself. Did you discover anything new? Then circle phrases or ideas that you might want to use in a composition and save them for future reference.

3. Social Studies   Spend about five minutes writing about your town, city, or community, and how it has contributed to making you who you are. For example, think about the following points:

- How does the size of your community affect you? Do you live in a crowded city, always surrounded by other people, or in an isolated rural environment?
- Do your friends and neighbors share a similar cultural background, or is it a very mixed neighborhood? What have you learned from this?
- How have the schools in your neighborhood affected you?
- How do the characteristics of your community contribute to making you the kind of person you are? Do you think you might have been a different person if you came from somewhere else?

Summarize your answers to these and any other questions you can think of in a paragraph or two. If you like, share your answers with others in your class.

COMPUTER OPTION

Your computer should have the graphic capability to allow you to develop a table. Consider creating a table that shows the positive and negative ways your community has affected you. Some computer programs allow you to convert existing text into a table. Or you may prefer to enter the text as a table from the very beginning. Use the Help function on your computer to direct you.

Your Own Place

Wouldn't it be great to have a place to examine your feelings, take risks, try out new ideas, express wonder, even dare to ask embarrassing questions? Many writers find just such a place in their journals. Anne Frank was one such writer. During World War II, thirteen-year-old Frank and her family were forced into hiding in a cramped attic to avoid capture by the Nazis. Frank's journal became her refuge—a place to explore her deepest thoughts and feelings.

Literature Model

Notice that Frank dates the journal entry.

Frank is first inspired to write by thoughts of sensory details—"cold on their faces," "smelling fresh air."

Frank uses this brief journal entry to ask important questions, give herself advice, and vent her feelings. What is the value of such expression, in your opinion?

Friday, 24 December 1943

When someone comes in from outside, with the wind in their clothes and the cold on their faces, then I could bury my head in the blankets to stop myself thinking: "When will we be granted the privilege of smelling fresh air?" And because I must not bury my head in the blankets, but the reverse—I must keep my head high and be brave, the thoughts will come not once, but oh, countless times. Believe me, if you have been shut up for a year and a half, it can get too much for you some days. . . . Cycling, dancing, whistling, looking out into the world, feeling young, to know that I'm free—that's what I long for; still, I mustn't show it. . . . I sometimes ask myself, "Would anyone, either Jew or non-Jew understand this about me, that I am simply a young girl badly in need of some rollicking fun?" I don't know, and I couldn't talk about it to anyone.

Anne Frank, *The Diary of a Young Girl*

Why Keep a Journal?

Keeping a journal is like thinking out loud—on paper. In your journal you might record daily events, but you also are free to follow an idea wherever it leads. By writing about your experiences, reactions, and observations, you can make discoveries about yourself and the world.

Freewriting can go wherever the writer's mind goes. Notice how Kimberly even makes up a word—"teen-agism."

Kimberly expresses an important lesson about growing up and moving on. Perhaps she'll develop this idea more fully later.

You can choose from a number of different kinds of journals, each with a different purpose. A diary, for example, is a personal record of daily events that the writer doesn't usually plan to share. A student may also keep a learning log to record thoughts and impressions of school courses and what's going on in those courses.

Your journal can also serve as a writer's journal—that is, a source for ideas to inspire your writing. These might be brief notes on writing ideas, a collection of words or phrases, even news clippings, jokes, or photographs. Here's a story idea that came from one student's journal.

Student Model

I was thinking about something rather funny the other day. I wondered what it would be like to have grown old overnight and pass up all the hardships of life (develop this as the opening of my story). I would already be retired and I wouldn't have to worry about finishing school or getting a job. . . . I would be able to go places and do things without having to worry about getting somewhere on time (give examples and go into more detail). . . . (All of this could be developed into a story about a boy who has grown old and finds out . . . that he has missed the best parts of life.)

Matthew Porter, Jefferson Davis High School, Montgomery, Alabama

Do you find Matthew's idea for writing interesting?

Notice how Matthew uses his writing to come up with a concrete idea for a story. This can work for you, too.

• JOURNAL ACTIVITY •
Think It Through

Compare the two student models on this page. What do they reveal about their writers? What kinds of materials are included in each? Record your reactions in your own journal.

How Do You Keep a Journal?

Journal writing has no set rules. You just need to find a system that works for you. Here are some tips that might help you get started on your own journal.

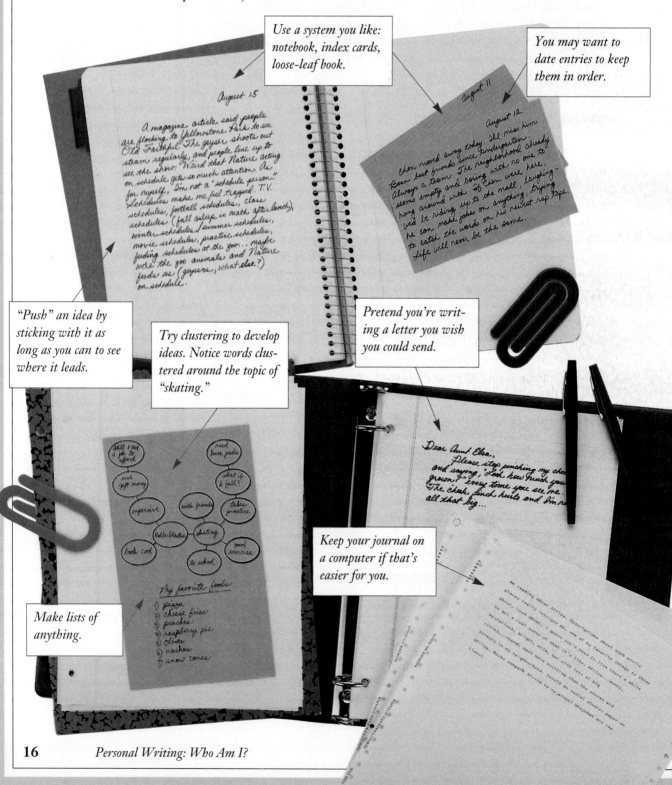

Use a system you like: notebook, index cards, loose-leaf book.

You may want to date entries to keep them in order.

"Push" an idea by sticking with it as long as you can to see where it leads.

Try clustering to develop ideas. Notice words clustered around the topic of "skating."

Pretend you're writing a letter you wish you could send.

Keep your journal on a computer if that's easier for you.

Make lists of anything.

Writer's Choice

The following are some writing options to help you apply what you have learned.

1. Guided Assignment   Photographs are a popular way to capture and remember special moments. They can also be good additions to your journal. Find a photo from a special moment in your life. If you have no photos, think back to recapture a memory. Then write a journal entry about the event in the photo or memory. You might include the following:

- a description of the event
- your feelings about what was going on
- your observations about other people in the photograph or memory
- some things you might have learned about yourself from the event
- any writing ideas the event might bring to mind

PURPOSE   To remember special moments
AUDIENCE   Yourself
LENGTH   1–3 paragraphs

2. Open Assignment   Take a familiar phrase, and use it as the subject of a journal entry. Concentrate on your own personal feelings, and write as much as you can about the phrase you choose. Then go back, and underline parts that might be interesting to explore in future compositions. You could write about the phrase "inner space" or "looking back" or "homework blues" or another phrase that you choose.

3. Art   Look at the painting on this page. Create a writer's journal entry based on this painting. Write, for example, about what you see in the painting. Does it evoke any memories of your own, of you engaging in similar activities, or of watching others from a distance?

Berthe Morisot, *The Cherry Tree*, c. 1891

4. Cooperative Learning   In a small group brainstorm about travel experiences that have helped you discover things about yourself. Think and talk about places you have seen, people you have met, experiences you have had away from home, or places you would like to visit if you had the opportunity. Let others take notes as you each talk. Use the notes from the brainstorming session to complete your own travel journal entry.

Writing a Personal Essay

Law?
Medicine?
Getting Married?
Paying Bills!
Buying a Car?
Killing Bugs Myself!

On Becoming an Adult

The young woman to the left is thinking some serious thoughts—thoughts about what growing up and becoming an adult might involve. What are your views on the subject? Would you believe that being an adult involves cleaning up all sorts of gunk? That's what Robert Fulghum thinks. To see what he says on the subject, read his personal essay below.

Literature Model

After the dishes are washed and the sink rinsed out, there remains in the strainer at the bottom of the sink what I will call, momentarily, some "stuff." A rational, intelligent, objective person would say that this is simply a mixture of food particles too big to go down the drain. . . . But any teenager who has been dragooned into washing dishes knows this explanation is a lie. That stuff in the bottom of the strainer is toxic waste—deadly poison—a danger to health. In other words, about as icky as icky gets.

One of the . . . reasons I had . . . respect for my mother when I was thirteen was because she would reach into the sink with her bare hands—BARE HANDS—and pick up that lethal gunk and drop it into the garbage. . . .

Never mind what any parent or objective adult might tell me, I knew that the stuff in the sink drainer was lethal. . . .

But now. Now, I am a grown-up. And have been for some time. And I imagine making a speech to a high school graduating class. . . . I would give them this list of things that grown-ups do: clean the sink strainer . . . clean up the floor when the baby throws strained spinach, clean ovens and grease traps and roasting pans. . . . I'd tell the graduates that when they can do these things, they will be adults. Some of the students might not want to go on at this point. But they may as well face the truth. . . . Being an adult *is* dirty work.

But someone has to do it.

Robert Fulghum, *It Was On Fire When I Lay Down On It*

What effect do words like "toxic" and "icky" have on you? What other words contribute to Fulghum's vivid, humorous picture?

Why do you suppose Fulghum saved the main point for the end of his piece?

What Is a Personal Essay?

A personal essay expresses your viewpoint about a subject you have experienced—a subject other than yourself. The personal essay is not directly about you. You may write your personal essay in a traditional essay format—introduction, body paragraphs, and conclusion—or you may write it in a freer way, following your own train of thought. As you write your essay, you can follow Fulghum's example and use humorous anecdotes and exaggeration to express your views.

What Can I Write About?

If you have an assigned topic, explore the aspects that especially intrigue you. Otherwise, write about whatever interests you. You can write on just about anything—friendship, homework, school cliques. . . .

Coming Up with a Topic   Your journal, newspapers, and magazines are sources of essay ideas. Here are two other ways to find a topic.

Freewriting

Write freely to find a topic.
Write on whatever we
want...write on write on write
on...right on! Old slang
phrase. Not totally awesome or
even groovy--more tubular?
Slang words mean different
things "Bad" means good (drove
Dad crazy with that one!)
Where did all those words come
from? (requires research) What
does slang do for me? Why
slang? with friends? with
adults? It'S LANG uage isn't
it? TOPIC!

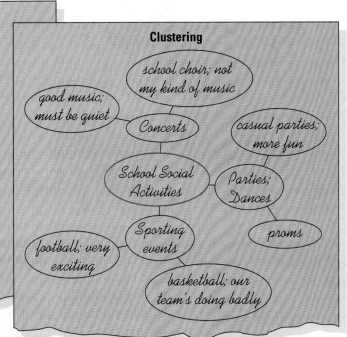

Clustering

school choir; not my kind of music

good music; must be quiet

Concerts

casual parties; more fun

School Social Activities

Parties; Dances

football; very exciting

Sporting events

proms

basketball; our team's doing badly

• JOURNAL ACTIVITY •
Try It Out

In your journal, try creating a cluster diagram to think of an essay topic. Begin with a base word about something that interests you and see where you end up. If you need help getting started, look around the room and write the name of an object you see.

Coming Up with a Thesis Statement   A thesis statement conveys your main point clearly. It may also explain the ways you intend to support your main point. To develop a thesis statement, ask yourself some questions about your topic—about your feelings, problems, hopes. These questions will help you focus on a specific aspect of the subject and condense it to a basic statement. Consider Fulghum's thesis statement: "Being an adult *is* dirty work."

How Can I Make My Essay Come to Life?

By letting your enthusiasm for your topic influence your choice of words and details, you can make your essay lively. Support your thesis with vivid details and examples. These tips and model might help.

How Can I Make My Essay Interesting?	
Tip	**Example**
Answer offbeat questions about the subject.	What might views on this subject have been a hundred years ago? A hundred years ago, people might have thought that . . .
Include personal anecdotes.	I won my first carnival goldfish when . . .
Pretend to be a reporter covering a news story.	We are at the local video arcade to . . .
Compare your topic to something familiar and fun.	Doing algebra problems is a little like working out crossword puzzles.

Student Model

D on't You Know Me?
   Our smiles are simple smiles. As we both sit down next to each other we realize that smile that was shared will probably be the first and last between us. Even though we go to the same school and have the same classes, we're two different people with two different images to uphold. Hers is the jet set world of witty conversation, the latest styles, and dates. The purse, the walk, and the friends she keeps tell her lifestyle and identity. The buzzing in the halls, the shared glances between them let you know you are the outsider looking in.
   As we step off the bus we put on our "masks" for the stage we'll be on. One's mask is a little bit brighter, the other one's dull, but each a character just the same.

Keshia White, Hyde Park Career Academy, Chicago, Illinois

Notice how Keshia expresses herself by following her own train of thought instead of using traditional essay form.

Like Fulghum, Keshia first presents her main point at the end of the essay.

The following are some writing options to help you apply what you have learned.

1. Guided Assignment   You have been asked to write a personal essay for the teen section of your town's newspaper on how teen-agers spend their weekends. To help organize and focus your thoughts, you may use some or all of the information provided below, or you can come up with your own details. Be sure to make clear what kind of weekend you are writing about and what it is that you wish to convey.

The Busy Weekend   painted the front porch; fixed the broken gate; went shopping at the mall for running shoes and a sweatshirt; went bowling Saturday night with friends; ate out afterward; went to soccer game on Sunday afternoon; met friends downtown for dinner

The Lazy Weekend   lounged on the hammock in the yard; watched videos; took a few naps; didn't go out much; made some phone calls

PURPOSE   To describe an aspect of teen-age life in a personal essay
AUDIENCE   Adult and teen-age newspaper readers
LENGTH   2–3 pages

2. Open Assignment   Use one of the following topics or one of your own choosing to write a personal essay that could be published in your school or hometown newspaper:

- how becoming a teen-ager changed my life style
- what one U.S. teen-ager thinks about the future of the country
- what I wish someone had told me when I was five

3. Cooperative Learning   In a small group study the painting on this page. Discuss similarities and differences between your neighborhood and that shown in the painting. When you were a child, were you curious about the adults who were your neighbors? Consider how the artist might have painted your street if he had used you or your neighbors as subjects, and write an essay about this topic. Use the group discussion to help you write your individual essays. Then regroup, and consider how you might present the essays to the class as a whole.

Allan Crite, *Harriet and Leon*, 1941

Writing Autobiography

The Week I Explored a Dream

Exploring outer space—what could be more exciting? That's what Lynn Griffey dreamed of for her future. Then, when she was sixteen, she got the chance to explore her dream.

Students at Space Camp

Notice how Lynn introduces the subject, setting, and main idea early on. Where do you first sense what might happen? Which words help to create this sense?

Lynn concludes by relating how her experience changed her perception of herself as well as her goals and expectations.

Student Model

*E*ver since I was a child, I've been fascinated with space. So in the fall of my junior year my parents sent me to the United States Space Camp. I was so excited; I thought this was going to be the beginning of great things to come. This was my dream come true. I always had dreams of me in space, and I always knew I could do it.

Immediately after I got there, I looked around. I saw how every one of those kids had the same dreams and feelings I had. It was incredible.

After sitting through lecture after lecture, and going through experiment after experiment, I realized that I wasn't so sure of my feelings anymore. I knew I was having a great time learning and exploring, but I also knew that I didn't have the same look in my eye that one boy did. He was having more than just a "good time"; he lived to be doing this.

I began feeling guilty because I started thinking of all the money my parents had spent for me to go there. Then I realized they want me to be happy. That's why they spent all the money, to see if this was what I wanted to do for the rest of my life.

I think I learned a lot about myself that week. I discovered that at sixteen it's not necessary to know precisely what the future holds. Maybe I'll still want to be in space some day. However, right now I just want to be sixteen and explore all the exciting careers I have to choose from.

Lynn Griffey, Hamilton Heights High School, Arcadia, Indiana

What Is an Autobiography?

An autobiography is a person's written account of his or her own life—experiences, thoughts, feelings. An autobiographical sketch, like Lynn's, is personal writing about a significant event or period in the writer's life. It should give readers a sense of who the author is, how the author came to be that way, and what the author has experienced.

How Do You Find Autobiographical Material?

Your autobiographical material comes from your life—anything you have done, felt, thought, dreamed, experienced, or learned.

Flip Through Your Mental Files We all have mental files of our experiences. Each of us uses a variety of different filing systems. We file events by emotional content—happy, sad, exhilarating. We file them according to the time in our lives they occurred—before school age, during elementary school. We even file them according to the areas in our lives they relate to—school, family, friends.

To search through your mental files, start by making a list of general categories, or file labels, you might find in each of the filing systems listed below. Then brainstorm, freewrite, or use other prewriting techniques to retrieve some of the specific experiences to be found in these files. Refer to Lesson 2.2, pages 64–69 for other prewriting techniques.

Your Autobiographical Files		
Filing System	**Sample File Labels**	**Sample Experience**
By emotional content	Happy, sad, afraid, angry	Getting a new bicycle
By time they occurred	Early childhood, junior high	Beginning junior high school
By area in life they relate to	Family, friends	Taking car trips with my family

Follow Your Nose Scientific evidence suggests that smells are powerful triggers of memory. You might put this belief to the test by trying to "sniff out" your material. Wander through familiar places with a pen and paper and try to notice the smells you find there. Freewrite to discover and explore the memories you associate with these odors.

• JOURNAL ACTIVITY •
Try It Out

In your journal, create a "life map." From left to right, draw or write important events from your life in chronological order. Shape your map any way—straight line, peaks and valleys, loops.

How Do You Present Your Material?

There are many ways to present autobiographical material. You can begin with "I remember" and then recount a particular event. You can structure your story as an interview. You can "flashback" to a past experience and then relate that experience to something in the present. Or you can present an experience in a series of journal entries. Whatever you decide, remember that readers don't know as much about your life as you do. So you may want to explain what is significant about a particular experience, as Kareem Abdul-Jabbar does in the model below.

Two Ways to Present Your Material

	Present	Past	Present
Flashback	Shopping with Gloria today, we both loved the same clothes.	Even as 4-year-olds she and I wanted the same toys.	I hope that we don't start to like the same boys now.
Successive Journal Entries	**Feb. 8** Nelsons asked me to go skiing with them —sort of scared.	**Feb. 9** Best day ever! I skied great—for my first time out.	**Feb. 10** Couldn't get out of bed. It hurt to walk.

Literature Model

Abdul-Jabbar sets the scene and presents the main idea immediately.

What kind of words does Abdul-Jabbar use to create a vivid picture of the event?

In the final sentences of this autobiographical sketch, Abdul-Jabbar sums up the significance of this event.

*I*t was that summer [after seventh grade] that I grew so many inches and started at least to *look* like a basketball player. I started to be able to do things like palm a basketball and touch the rim, and it was soon obvious that the long frame could be put to use in places other than the baseball diamond. Around this same time, one event changed my view of basketball and how to play it dramatically. I went to see a high school all-star game at the Brownsville Boys Club in Brooklyn. Guys like Connie Hawkins, Roger Brown, Billy Burwell, and other All-City players were on the court doing their thing, and I was awestruck. I had never seen people dunk and soar and change direction in midstride the way these guys did. . . . The warm-up was awe-inspiring, and I feel that evening in Brooklyn changed my concept forever of what is possible on the court. Baseball would remain close to my heart, but here was a game that was best played by individuals with *my* physical attributes. The possibilities seemed endless.

Kareem Abdul-Jabbar with Mignon McCarthy, *Kareem*

Writer's Choice

The following are some writing options to help you apply what you have learned.

1. Guided Assignment Develop an outline for an autobiographical sketch about the first day of school. (You can choose any year.) Once your outline is completed, write an essay about yourself, using the information outlined as a guide. Use the following outline form to note the information:

   I. Introductory statement
      A. State the time in your life.
      B. Tell why this time was important.
  II. Body of the sketch
      A. Tell what happened first (paragraph 1 of body). Include details to support this statement.
      B. Tell what happened next (paragraph 2 of body). Again, include details to explain and expand the story.
      C. Continue with paragraphs like those above until the story is complete.
 III. Conclusion
      A. Express your feelings about the events you have related.
      B. Show how these events have influenced your life in the present.

PURPOSE To tell something about yourself
AUDIENCE Classmates and teacher
LENGTH 2–4 pages

2. Open Assignment Write an autobiographical sketch in the form of a letter, interview, or poem. One of the following ideas might help get you started, or you can focus on an incident or time of your own choosing:

- You would know me if you saw my room because . . .
- I dress like a rock star because . . .
- No one would ever guess that I . . .
- If I were a color I would be . . .

COMPUTER OPTION

You may wish to consider sharing your autobiographical sketch with family members. If so, your computer's page makeup capability can assist in helping you to design a professional-looking document. You might design the page with the title of the essay or poem as the headline, in boldface type. A laser printer will also make your final copy more attractive. If you or your school does not have a laser printer, check with your local quick-print copy center on what they charge for using their equipment.

3. Social Studies Use personal questions to explore possibilities for an autobiographical sketch about an experience you have had with someone quite different from yourself. For example, you might write about a friendship with someone from an ethnic, economic, or age group different from your own. Include such questions as these:

- When did I first encounter this person?
- What were my initial reactions to and impressions of him or her?
- What happened during our encounter?
- How did I feel about what happened?
- What did I learn?

4. Cooperative Learning In a small group take turns acting as a reporter, each selecting someone from within the group to interview. Ask questions that will allow you to find out some outstanding or unusual skill that person possesses. Use his or her responses to write an essay and read your essay to the group. Ask the others whether additional questions need to be answered. Use their suggestions to revise your essay, and ask the person interviewed to read it over for accuracy. As a group decide how best to present your essays to the class.

Writing a Poem

Eyes Like the Stars

Langston Hughes wanted to express his feelings about his people—African Americans. Notice how powerfully, almost magically, he does so in the brief poem below. As you read it, think about why poems can express so much in so few words.

> ### Literature Model
>
> *My People*
>
> The night is beautiful,
> So the faces of my people.
>
> The stars are beautiful,
> So the eyes of my people.
>
> Beautiful, also, is the sun.
> Beautiful, also, are the souls of my people.
>
> Langston Hughes

This free-verse poem does not have regular rhyme or rhythm patterns, but the repetition gives it a rhythmic feeling.

Expressing Yourself in a Poem

In this simple poem, Hughes has put together words to create sounds and images that express much more than what the words alone actually say. Such sounds and images help poets actively engage their readers' memories, emotions, and imagination. And, quite often, poets stretch the usual rules of grammar, usage, and mechanics in order to create unique and effective sounds and images.

Using Traditional and Free Verse

Many poets write traditional forms of poetry that follow set patterns of rhythm and rhyme. In free verse, though, there are no set patterns of rhyme or rhythm. Compare the following humorous poem with the Hughes poem. Notice the regular rhyming and rhythmic patterns in "Song of the Open Road" and the freer form and style of "My People." One thing both poems have in common, though, is a strong central image.

Song of the Open Road

I think that I shall never see
A billboard lovely as a tree.
Indeed, unless the billboards fall
I'll never see a tree at all.

Ogden Nash

Speaking the Language of Poetry

The language of poetry is one of vivid sounds and images. Just think of how Langston Hughes's images of night, stars, and sun linger and overlap with the images of his people's faces, eyes, and souls. Poets create such memorable pictures with a variety of techniques such as those explained in this chart.

Some Poetic Devices		
Device	**Definition**	**Example**
Sensory detail	A detail that appeals to one of the senses: sight, touch, taste, smell, or hearing	Slivers of frosty grass crunched underfoot.
Simile	A comparison between two unlike things, using the words *like* or *as*	Sleep, like a soft, dark blanket, comforted him.
Metaphor	A comparison between two unlike things, without using the words *like* or *as*	Her dress was a pink cloud of crepe.
Personification	The giving of human qualities to objects, animals, or things	Flowers saluted the morning sun.
Sound effect	A pattern of sound (e.g., rhyme, rhythm, repetition) used to help create an image	The raspy snarl of a motorcycle awakened him.

• JOURNAL ACTIVITY •
Try It Out

Find a single word in one of the poems in this lesson or in the list of examples above to use as the center for brainstorming. Generate associations, in the form of words or phrases, with this word as fast as you can. Then use some of your associations to create a brief poem.

Experimenting with Poetry

Literature Model

There was a young person from Perth
Who was born on the day of his birth.

He was married, they say,
On his wife's wedding day

And died when he quitted this earth.

Anonymous

Like most limericks, this one begins "There was a . . ." and ends with a funny or unusual rhyming line.

Like most traditional haiku, this one has five syllables in lines 1 and 3 and seven in line 2.

Literature Model

Butterfly, these words
from my brush are not flowers,
only their shadows.

Soseki

In the above poems, notice the limerick's rhyming pattern and the haiku's syllable pattern. Following is a free verse poem.

Student Model

Intimate Calm

There—
With the soft rays of the lamp
Resting on the pallid walls
And the earthen carpet—
With the falling leaves and the dark, dewy dusk
Enveloping me
Like my grandmother's familiar afghan—
With the comforting sounds of the television
Capturing my attention with its witty charm—
With the beautiful willowing wisps
Of my brother's laughter in the kitchen
With my body
Propped against my favorite pillow
Sunken into the billowing cushions
Curled like the kitten
Asleep in my lap
Underneath that familiar yarn
Which conceals the memories of my mother's mother—
I lay
With a peaceful mind—
Eating refried beans

Heather Robertson, Jefferson Davis High School, Montgomery, Alabama

Why do you suppose Heather chose to repeat the word "with" at the beginning of several lines?

The repetition of the k and hard c sound provides a rhythm to these two lines.

Writer's Choice

Rufino Tamayo, *Hombre Ante el Infinito (Man Contemplates Infinity)*, 1950

The following are some writing options to help you apply what you have learned

1. Guided Assignment For an upcoming school production you've been asked to write and read an original limerick to the assembly. Review the limerick on page 28 before you begin to write one of your own. As you write, pay special attention to rhythm and rhyme patterns. Remember to end with a humorous line. Try one of these first lines, or use one of your own:

- There once was a student named Fred . . .
- There once was a maiden from Dover . . .
- There once was a poet like me . . .

PURPOSE To write an original limerick
AUDIENCE Students and teachers
LENGTH 5 lines

2. Open Assignment Try freewriting for a few minutes to come up with an idea for a poem. Begin by focusing on a subject about which you have strong feelings and then write whatever comes to mind. Write about wandering aimlessly on the beach, revisiting a place from your past, or looking through a telescope at the stars. Or write about a subject of your own choosing. Next, underline any words or phrases you have used that are especially descriptive of your topic or your feelings about it. Use some, or all, of the underlined items in your poem.

3. Art The painting above is Rufino Tamayo's *Hombre Ante el Infinito (Man Contemplates Infinity)*. Using some of the poetic techniques discussed in this lesson (similes, metaphors, and personification), write a poem that expresses your impression of the painting. To help you get started, imagine that you are the central figure in the painting. What do you see? What are you thinking about? What do you picture when you think about infinity? The poem may be free verse or one following a regular pattern of rhyme and rhythm.

Writing About Literature
Keeping a Reader-Response Journal

A Letter to Kezia

When Mitchell Kittlaus finished Katherine Mansfield's story "The Doll's House," he was so impressed by the kindness of one character that he decided to "write her a letter" in his reader-response journal.

Student Model

Dear Kezia,

I admire you greatly for the courage you displayed. . . . You took a big risk by inviting the Kelvey girls into your courtyard to see the doll house. Do not be intimidated by your aunt's punishment. Although you should obey your elders, it was right of you to question their negative opinion of the Kelveys. If you do not understand their attitude, take the initiative to talk with your parents and relatives, so that together you can discuss their views. You may not agree with what they believe, but it is important that you fully comprehend their feelings.

I also respect you for the kindness that you showed to Lil and Else Kelvey. It is always easier to hurt someone's feelings by acting in an inconsiderate way, especially when such thoughtless behavior is encouraged by one's peers. . . .

I encourage you to continue to keep an open mind in your relations with others. People should only be judged by the content of their character. Hopefully, you can set a positive example for others to follow.

Mitchell Kittlaus, Evanston Township High School, Evanston, Illinois

What word choices in Mitchell's letter suggest the degree of his involvement in the story?

Mitchell expresses his personal feelings about the story's main incident.

Responding Personally

A reader-response journal can be a special section in a larger personal journal or a journal in itself. In this kind of journal, you record your reactions to whatever you are reading—a novel, short story, poem, play, or other work of literature. The journal can help you keep track of what's going on in the work. But, more importantly, keeping a reader-response journal can help you see how your reading relates to your own life. For example, you might write about similarities you find between a character's view of life and your own. In a reader-response journal you can write about what interests, delights, puzzles, worries, angers, or even bores you about your reading.

Responding Creatively

Think up some new ways to respond to your reading. Maybe you'll decide to write a letter of encouragement (or complaint) to the main character. Or perhaps you'll rewrite a scene from a play to make it take place in your home town. You might like some of these ideas.

Responding to What You Read	
Idea	**Sample**
1. Write a news flash.	Flash! Three local children disappeared last night from their backyard. Relatives say the three had been talking about time travel just prior to their disappearance. (response to *A Wrinkle in Time* by Madeleine L'Engle)
2. Imagine yourself as a main character.	Here I am shipwrecked on a deserted island with just a bunch of other boys my own age. I'd better make a plan for survival. (response to *Lord of the Flies* by William Golding; the photo on the right is from a movie based on that novel)
3. Write about the character visiting your home.	As Mrs. Luella Bates Washington Jones came through the door, she filled our living room with her powerful presence. (response to "Thank You M'am" by Langston Hughes)

In your reader-response journal, you could suggest what might have happened if two characters had never met, or if one event hadn't taken place. What if the setting were changed? Feel free to be as creative as possible in finding ways to write about your reading.

• JOURNAL ACTIVITY •
Try It Out

In your journal create a list of five stories, novels, or poems for which you might like to create a reader-response entry. Next to each selection, explain why you have chosen this particular piece about which to write a personal response.

Responding to Learn About Yourself

An important part of any story, novel, play, essay, or poem is what you, the reader, bring to it. When you reflect on it in light of your personal experiences and impressions, literature can actually change you.

Keeping a reader-response journal gives you a chance to think more about a work of literature—a chance to get at the relevance of the story or poem to your own life. How is it the same as your life? How is it different? What do you think about . . . ? How would you change it to make it more real? What if . . . ? Would you have done what the characters did?

By considering these kinds of questions, you come to a new, deeper understanding of the story. Michelle Kalski learns about herself by responding to Shel Silverstein's poem "Reflection" in two different ways: with a poem of her own and with a letter.

REFLECTION

Each time I see the Upside-Down Man
Standing in the water,
I look at him and start to laugh,
Although I shouldn't oughtter.
For maybe in another world
Another time
Another town,
Maybe HE is right side up
And I am upside down.

Shel Silverstein

Student Models

Just a reflection of myself.
Or so it seems.
What stares back is a person
Full of peace and at ease.
A backward image of me.

Dear Mr. Silverstein,

Finally, someone has managed to step into the world of a reflection. As a curious youngster, I was always fascinated with reflections and looked for ways to prove that the person in the pool of water or the mirror was somehow different than me. I thought it was wonderful of you to reveal the idea of a reflection being in the world right side up.

Michelle Kalski, Evanston Township High School, Evanston, Illinois

Notice how Michelle relates Silverstein's poem to her own life by telling of a childhood fascination of hers.

Writer's Choice

The following are some writing options to help you apply what you have learned.

1. Guided Assignment In *The Adventures of Huckleberry Finn*, Mark Twain recounts the story of a boy who has spent most of his childhood living on his own in a shack by a river. By the time of the excerpt below, however, Huck has been living in town with the Widow Douglas. In this passage Huck talks about how he is adjusting to school and "new ways." Read the passage, and then respond according to one of the suggestions that follow it. Or come up with a response of your own.

> At first I hated school, but by and by I got so I could stand it. Whenever I got uncommon tired I played hookey, and the hiding I got the next day done me good and cheered me up. So the longer I went to school the easier it got to be. I was getting sort of used to the widow's ways, too, and they warn't so raspy on me. Living in a house and sleeping in a bed pulled on me pretty tightly mostly, but before the cold weather, I used to slide out and sleep in the woods sometimes, and so that was a rest to me. I liked the old ways best, but I was getting so I liked the new ones, too, a little bit. The widow said I was coming along slow but sure, and doing very satisfactory. She said she wasn't ashamed of me.

Imagine you're giving tips to Huck on coping in today's society. Write about how you could make him more comfortable if he were to visit you in your school or town. Include tips on how he might adjust to the "new ways" of adults today.

PURPOSE To explore your reactions to Huck Finn
AUDIENCE Yourself
LENGTH 1–3 paragraphs

2. Open Assignment Read the poem presented here or one of your own choosing. Then respond to it in a creative way as you would in a reader-response journal. You may try one of the formats listed after the poem or make up a response of your own.

> *Old Mary*
>
> My last defense
> Is the present tense.
>
> It little hurts me now to know
> I shall not go
>
> Cathedral-hunting in Spain
> Nor cherrying in Michigan or Maine.
>
> Gwendolyn Brooks

Rewrite the poem as a prose statement from Brooks to her editor. Or, in a letter to a friend, describe your impressions of the poem and tell how you think Brooks might address teens in an advice column.

3. Cooperative Learning In a small group select a poem in this book. Write your own individual response-journal entry about the poem. Then meet again to share your entries. Discuss the differences in your responses. Finally, return to your response journal, and write a second entry, recording what you learned from other students.

COMPUTER OPTION

If you are entering your reader-response entries into a computer file, you will need some way to identify your entries for retrieval. A good plan is to date each entry. Or you might add a code word, such as *poems* or the author's name. Then you can use the Search function to retrieve a particular entry.

Amelia Earhart and Me

In the last lesson you learned about keeping a reader-response journal. Now take a look at Shella Calamba's personal response to a specific form of literature, a biography.

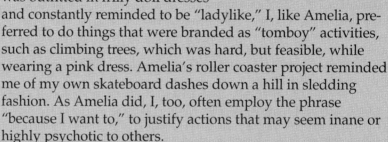

Amelia Earhart, 1933

Student Model

I never thought Amelia Earhart and I could have so much in common. Although, as a little girl, I was outfitted in frilly doll dresses and constantly reminded to be "ladylike," I, like Amelia, preferred to do things that were branded as "tomboy" activities, such as climbing trees, which was hard, but feasible, while wearing a pink dress. Amelia's roller coaster project reminded me of my own skateboard dashes down a hill in sledding fashion. As Amelia did, I, too, often employ the phrase "because I want to," to justify actions that may seem inane or highly psychotic to others.

Not only did Amelia's childhood remind me of mine, she also made me think of a friend from grammar school who dreams of becoming a pilot. She will undoubtedly be forced to deal with sexism in pursuing her goal, but I think reading Amelia's biography would prevent her from being discouraged in achieving her ambitions. Even by today's standards, what Amelia accomplished was remarkable and unprecedented by any man or woman. However, Amelia is not someone to be admired exclusively by pilots. Her courage, determination, and persistence set an inspiring example for anyone with a dream.

Shella Calamba, Lincoln Park High School, Chicago, Illinois

What words signal the many comparisons between Shella and Amelia in the first paragraph?

Shella shows the relevance of the biography to others in today's world, moving from personal meanings to more general ones.

Responding Personally to a Biography

Shella responded personally to the story of Amelia Earhart's life. When you respond personally to a biography, you are responding to the subject of the biography and to his or her world. You have a chance to get to know the subject by focusing your reader-response journal entries on the subject's attitudes, values, and behavior. Try to find out what the subject cares about and what motivates her or him in life. Relate your discoveries to your own life. Do you care about the same kinds of things as the subject? What qualities does the subject have that you admire? Are your motivations similar to or different from the subject's? What do the subject's accomplishments teach you about your own life?

The chart below shows some ways you can respond personally to a biography. Try any of the following suggestions or come up with other ways of thinking about a biography's subject.

Some Formats for Responding to Biography	
Format	**Example**
Write a skit showing how the person might act in a new and unusual situation.	Ben Franklin at an electrical plant
Write an encouraging letter helping the subject with a problem.	To Mohandas Gandhi encouraging his efforts to win independence for India
Write an editorial endorsing the person for public office.	Michael Jordan for mayor of your town
Bring a historical figure into the modern-day world.	Queen Isabella visiting NASA and learning about space exploration
Write a diary entry from a crucial day in the person's life.	Amelia Earhart's diary from the day her plane was lost over the Pacific Ocean
Rewrite an incident from the subject's life, changing one part slightly.	Abraham Lincoln not going to the theater where he was assassinated
Enact an on-the-spot news story with your subject.	A news interview with Clara Barton immediately after a Civil War battle

• JOURNAL ACTIVITY •
Think It Through

Create your own chart like the one above, but on yours show other formats for a personal response to a biography. Or, if you choose, develop a different type of chart or any other kind of graphic to show your ideas. Be as creative as you can. Then copy your chart into your journal.

Interviewing Your Subject

One way to get to know the subject of a biography is through an imaginary interview. If you want to develop such an interview, a good way to begin would be to work with a classmate and role-play. One of you should take the role of the interviewer and the other portray the subject of the biography. In your interview, don't be satisfied with questions like, "What did you do then?" Instead, ask questions that get at the whys and hows of the person's life. Remember to tailor your questions to your particular subject. Then base the subject's responses on what you know from your reading.

Feel free to be creative and have fun with the interview. You might choose the form of a late-night talk show discussion, such as Jay Leno interviewing Leonardo da Vinci. Or pose as a confused math student in Albert Einstein's class. Or pretend that a historical character is visiting the present-day world, as in Elizabeth Chen's write-up of an imaginary interview with Dr. Martin Luther King Jr. for a made-up newspaper, the *Chronicle*.

Sample Interview Questions

- What was the accomplishment you were most proud of?
- What was your greatest challenge?
- What surprises you most about today's world?
- If you could tell the people of today one thing, what would it be?

Student Model

Chronicle: Dr. King, what you did for the civil rights movement in the 1950s and 1960s obviously had an enormous impact then, but do you think it affects society today?

MLK: What the people did then, promoting the cause of civil rights through peaceful means, has led the way toward a day of equal rights for all people.

Chronicle: Do you think there is equality now?

MLK: Under the law, yes, but in the hearts and minds of some Americans, no. I cannot say there is equality when I hear of racial violence every day. There will not be equality until everyone is treated the same in practice as well as under the law.

Chronicle: But how can we change that?

MLK: Through education. Through the help of all people—black, white, red, and yellow—to show that the only difference between us is skin color. By showing that all people can achieve the same success if given an equal opportunity.

Elizabeth Chen,
Downers Grove North High School, Downers Grove, Illinois

Writer's Choice

The following are some writing options to help you apply what you have learned.

1. Guided Assignment   Read the following passage from M. S. Handler's introduction to *The Autobiography of Malcolm X*. Handler, a *New York Times* reporter, is recalling his wife's observation after her first encounter with civil rights leader Malcolm X.

> "You know, it was like having tea with a black panther."
>
> The description startled me. The black panther is an aristocrat in the animal kingdom. He is beautiful. He is dangerous. As a man, Malcolm X had a physical bearing and the inner self-confidence of a born aristocrat.

Imagine that a reporter from your school or local newspaper is writing an article about you. Write a few paragraphs describing what you think the reporter's first impressions of you might be.

PURPOSE   To explore how you might be perceived by others
AUDIENCE   Yourself
LENGTH   1–3 paragraphs

2. Open Assignment   Choose a major event or decision in the life of the person whose biography you have read. Then rewrite the event as it might have happened if something had been changed. You may use one of the changes listed here, or make up a change of your own:

- Change the setting to one hundred years in the future.
- Leave out one detail that was important to the event or the decision.
- Put yourself in the story as a trusted friend of and adviser to the subject.

3. Social Studies   Read the biography of a historical American political figure—anyone from a city mayor to a signer of the Declaration of Independence. Then write a series of reader-response journal entries about the biography. Use some of the following suggestions, or think up questions of your own:

- What would I have done in some of the crucial situations this person faced?
- How might this leader change my city, town, or community if he or she were in charge?
- What would I most want to tell this leader about political life in the United States today?
- What question would I most want to ask this person about how his or her childhood influenced later actions?

4. Cooperative Learning   In a small group select a famous scientist, artist, or author whose work is familiar to everyone in the group. Divide up the task of researching the person's life, one member of the group taking the person's childhood, another the person's early career, and so on. Write a paragraph on the area you researched, and share your paragraph with the others in the group. Combine the paragraphs into group essays, with individual writers adding their own beginning and concluding paragraphs.

COMPUTER OPTION

As you begin to collect biographical information for your writing assignment, use your computer to store data. Type in the information along with the boldface heading to identify the subject. Then use the computer to draw lines around your data to give it the appearance of a note card. Organize the notes just as you would if they were on actual three-by-five-inch cards. As you begin to draft your essay, copy the information from your electronic file and insert it into the essay.

Maya Angelou

from

I Know Why the Caged Bird Sings

Maya Angelou, best known for her autobiographies I Know Why the Caged Bird
Sings *and* Gather Together in My Name, *has also been a poet, playwright, movie and
television writer, journalist, dancer, actress, director, composer, and civil rights worker. In this
autobiographical sketch Angelou relates a turning point from her childhood.*

For nearly a year, I sopped around the house, the Store, the
school and the church, like an old biscuit, dirty and inedible.
Then I met, or rather got to know, the lady who threw me my
first life line.

Mrs. Bertha Flowers was the aristocrat of Black Stamps. She had
the grace of control to appear warm in the coldest weather, and on
the Arkansas summer days it seemed she had a private breeze which
swirled around, cooling her. She was thin without the taut look of
wiry people, and her printed voile[1] dresses and flowered hats were as
right for her as denim overalls for a farmer. She was our side's
answer to the richest white woman in town.

Her skin was a rich black that would have peeled like a plum if
snagged, but then no one would have thought of getting close

---

1 voile (voil) a thin, sheer fabric; often made of cotton

enough to Mrs. Flowers to ruffle her dress, let alone snag her skin.
She didn't encourage familiarity. She wore gloves too.

I don't think I ever saw Mrs. Flowers laugh, but she smiled often.
A slow widening of her thin black lips to show even, small white
teeth, then the slow effortless closing. When she chose to smile on me,
I always wanted to thank her. The action was so graceful and inclu-
sively benign.[2]

She was one of the few gentlewomen I have ever known, and has
remained throughout my life the measure of what a human being
can be.

Momma had a strange relationship with her. Most often when she
passed on the road in front of the Store, she spoke to Momma in that
soft yet carrying voice, "Good day, Mrs. Henderson." Momma
responded with "How you, Sister Flowers?"

Mrs. Flowers didn't belong to our church, nor was she Momma's
familiar. Why on earth did she insist on calling her Sister Flowers?
Shame made me want to hide my face. Mrs. Flowers deserved better
than to be called Sister. Then, Momma left out the verb. Why not ask,
"How *are* you, *Mrs.* Flowers?" With the unbalanced passion of the

2 benign (bi nīn') good-natured

Harriet Powers, *Pictorial Quilt*, c. 1895–1898

I Know Why the Caged Bird Sings

young, I hated her for showing her ignorance to Mrs. Flowers. It didn't occur to me for many years that they were as alike as sisters, separated only by formal education.

Although I was upset, neither of the women was in the least shaken by what I thought an unceremonious[3] greeting. Mrs. Flowers would continue her easy gait up the hill to her little bungalow,[4] and Momma kept on shelling peas or doing whatever had brought her to the front porch.

Occasionally, though, Mrs. Flowers would drift off the road and down to the Store and Momma would say to me, "Sister, you go on and play." As I left I would hear the beginning of an intimate conversation. Momma persistently using the wrong verb, or none at all.

"Brother and Sister Wilcox is sho'ly the meanest—" "Is," Momma? "Is"? Oh, please, not "is," Momma, for two or more. But they talked, and from the side of the building where I waited for the ground to open up and swallow me, I heard the soft-voiced Mrs. Flowers and the textured voice of my grandmother merging and melting. They were interrupted from time to time by giggles that must have come from Mrs. Flowers (Momma never giggled in her life). Then she was gone.

She appealed to me because she was like people I had never met personally. Like women in English novels who walked the moors (whatever they were) with their loyal dogs racing at a respectful distance. Like the women who sat in front of roaring fireplaces, drinking tea incessantly from silver trays full of scones and crumpets. Women who walked over the "heath"[5] and read morocco-bound[6] books and had two last names divided by a hyphen. It would be safe to say that she made me proud to be Negro, just by being herself.

She acted just as refined as whitefolks in the movies and books and she was more beautiful, for none of them could have come near that warm color without looking gray by comparison.

It was fortunate that I never saw her in the company of powhitefolks. For since they tend to think of their whiteness as an evenizer, I'm certain that I would have had to hear her spoken to commonly as Bertha, and my image of her would have been shattered like the unmendable Humpty-Dumpty.

One summer afternoon, sweet-milk fresh in my memory, she stopped at the Store to buy provisions. Another Negro woman of her health and age would have been expected to carry the paper sacks

---

3 **unceremonious** (un' ser ə mo' nē əs) impolite

4 **bungalow** (buŋ' gə lō') a small house, usually one story high plus an attic

5 **heath** (hēth) an expanse of wasteland, especially in Britain, covered with heather and shrubs

6 **morocco-bound** (mə rä' kō) having a leather cover

Beverly Buchanan, *Bogart, Georgia*, 1989

home in one hand, but Momma said, "Sister Flowers, I'll send Bailey up to your house with these things."

She smiled that slow dragging smile, "Thank you, Mrs. Henderson. I'd prefer Marguerite, though." My name was beautiful when she said it. "I've been meaning to talk to her, anyway." They gave each other age-group looks.

Momma said, "Well, that's all right then. Sister, go and change your dress. You going to Sister Flowers's."

The chifforobe[7] was a maze. What on earth did one put on to go to Mrs. Flowers' house? I knew I shouldn't put on a Sunday dress. It might be sacrilegious.[8] Certainly not a house dress, since I was already wearing

---

7 **chifforobe** (shif′ ə rōb′) a combination of wardrobe and chest of drawers

8 **sacrilegious** (sak′ rə lij′ əs) involving the violation of something holy

a fresh one. I chose a school dress, naturally. It was formal without suggesting that going to Mrs. Flowers' house was equivalent to attending church.

I trusted myself back into the Store.

"Now, don't you look nice." I had chosen the right thing, for once.

"Mrs. Henderson, you make most of the children's clothes, don't you?"

"Yes, ma'am. Sure do. Store-bought clothes ain't hardly worth the thread it take to stitch them."

"I'll say you do a lovely job, though, so neat. That dress looks professional."

Momma was enjoying the seldom-received compliments. Since everyone we knew (except Mrs. Flowers, of course) could sew competently, praise was rarely handed out for the commonly practiced craft.

"I try, with the help of the Lord, Sister Flowers, to finish the inside just like I does the outside. Come here, Sister."

I had buttoned up the collar and tied the belt, apronlike, in back. Momma told me to turn around. With one hand she pulled the strings and the belt fell free at both sides of my waist. Then her large hands were at my neck, opening the button loops. I was terrified. What was happening?

"Take it off, Sister." She had her hands on the hem of the dress.

"I don't need to see the inside, Mrs. Henderson, I can tell . . ." But the dress was over my head and my arms were stuck in the sleeves. Momma said, "That'll do. See here, Sister Flowers, I French-seams around the armholes." Through the cloth film, I saw the shadow approach. "That makes it last longer. Children these days would bust out of sheet-metal clothes. They so rough."

"That is a very good job, Mrs. Henderson. You should be proud. You can put your dress back on, Marguerite."

"No ma'am. Pride is a sin. And 'cording to the Good Book, it goeth before a fall."

"That's right. So the Bible says. It's a good thing to keep in mind."

I wouldn't look at either of them. Momma hadn't thought that taking off my dress in front of Mrs. Flowers would kill me stone dead. If I had refused, she would have thought I was trying to be "womanish" and might have remembered St. Louis. Mrs. Flowers had known that I would be embarrassed and that was even worse. I picked up the groceries and went out to wait in the hot sunshine. It would be fitting if I got a sunstroke and died before they came outside. Just dropped dead on the slanting porch.

There was a little path beside the rocky road, and Mrs. Flowers walked in front swinging her arms and picking her way over the stones.

Charles Alston, *Girl in a Red Dress*, 1934

She said, without turning her head, to me, "I hear you're doing very good school work, Marguerite, but that it's all written. The teachers report that they have trouble getting you to talk in class." We passed the triangular farm on our left and the path widened to allow us to walk together. I hung back in the separate unasked and unanswerable questions.

"Come and walk along with me, Marguerite." I couldn't have refused even if I wanted to. She pronounced my name so nicely. Or more correctly, she spoke each word with such clarity that I was certain a foreigner who didn't understand English could have understood her.

"Now no one is going to make you talk—possibly no one can. But bear in mind, language is man's way of communicating with his fellow man and it is language alone which separates him from the lower animals." That was a totally new idea to me, and I would need time to think about it.

"Your grandmother says you read a lot. Every chance you get. That's good, but not good enough. Words mean more than what is set down on paper. It takes the human voice to infuse them with the shades of deeper meaning."

I memorized the part about the human voice infusing words. It seemed so valid and poetic.

She said she was going to give me some books and that I not only must read them, I must read them aloud. She suggested that I try to make a sentence sound in as many different ways as possible.

"I'll accept no excuse if you return a book to me that has been badly handled." My imagination boggled at the punishment I would deserve if in fact I did abuse a book of Mrs. Flowers'. Death would be too kind and brief.

The odors in the house surprised me. Somehow I had never connected Mrs. Flowers with food or eating or any other common experience of common people. There must have been an outhouse, too, but my mind never recorded it.

The sweet scent of vanilla had met us as she opened the door.

"I made tea cookies this morning. You see, I had planned to invite you for cookies and lemonade so we could have this little chat. The lemonade is in the icebox."

It followed that Mrs. Flowers would have ice on an ordinary day, when most families in our town bought ice late on Saturdays only a few times during the summer to be used in the wooden ice-cream freezers.

She took the bags from me and disappeared through the kitchen door. I looked around the room that I had never in my wildest fantasies imagined I would see. Browned photographs leered or threatened from the walls and the white, freshly done curtains pushed against themselves and against the wind. I wanted to gobble up the room entire and take it to Bailey, who would help me analyze and enjoy it.

"Have a seat, Marguerite. Over there by the table." She carried a platter covered with a tea towel. Although she warned that she hadn't tried her hand at baking sweets for some time, I was certain that like everything else about her the cookies would be perfect.

They were flat round wafers, slightly browned on the edges and butter-yellow in the center. With the cold lemonade they were sufficient for childhood's lifelong diet. Remembering my manners, I took nice little lady-like bites off the edges. She said she had made them expressly for me and that she had a few in the kitchen that I could take home to my brother. So I jammed one whole cake in my mouth and the rough crumbs scratched the inside of my jaws, and if I hadn't had to swallow, it would have been a dream come true.

As I ate she began the first of what we later called "my lessons in living." She said that I must always be intolerant of ignorance but understanding of illiteracy. That some people, unable to go to school, were more educated and even more intelligent than college professors. She encouraged me to listen carefully to what country people called mother wit. That in those homely sayings was couched the collective wisdom of generations.

When I finished the cookies she brushed off the table and brought a thick, small book from the bookcase. I had read *A Tale of Two Cities* and found it up to my standards as a romantic novel. She opened the first page and I heard poetry for the first time in my life.

"It was the best of times and the worst of times . . ." Her voice slid in and curved down through and over the words. She was nearly singing. I wanted to look at the pages. Were they the same that I had read? Or were there notes, music, lined on the pages, as in a hymn book? Her sounds began cascading gently. I knew from listening to a thousand preachers that she was nearing the end of her reading, and I hadn't really heard, heard to understand, a single word.

"How do you like that?"

It occurred to me that she expected a response. The sweet vanilla flavor was still on my tongue and her reading was a wonder in my ears. I had to speak.

I said, "Yes, ma'am." It was the least I could do, but it was the most also.

"There's one more thing. Take this book of poems and memorize one for me. Next time you pay me a visit, I want you to recite."

I have tried often to search behind the sophistication of years for the enchantment I so easily found in those gifts. The essence[9] escapes but its aura[10] remains. To be allowed, no, invited, into the private lives of strangers, and to share their joys and fears, was a chance to exchange the Southern bitter wormwood[11] for a cup of mead[12] with

---

9 **essence** (es′ 'ns) the basic nature or most important quality

10 **aura** (ôr′ ə) the atmosphere or feeling that seems to surround a certain person or thing

11 **wormwood** (wʉrm′ wood′) a bitter oil

12 **mead** (mēd) a drink made of honey and water

Wilmer Angier Jennings, *Landscape*, 1945

Beowulf or a hot cup of tea and milk with Oliver Twist. When I said aloud, "It is a far, far better thing that I do, than I have ever done . . ." tears of love filled my eyes at my selflessness.

On that first day, I ran down the hill and into the road (few cars ever came along it) and had the good sense to stop running before I reached the Store.

I was liked, and what a difference it made. I was respected not as Mrs. Henderson's grandchild or Bailey's sister but for just being Marguerite Johnson.

Childhood's logic never asks to be proved (all conclusions are absolute). I didn't question why Mrs. Flowers had singled me out for attention, nor did it occur to me that Momma might have asked her to give me a little talking to. All I cared about was that she had made tea cookies for *me* and read to *me* from her favorite book. It was enough to prove that she liked me.

For Discussion

1. Do you share Marguerite's admiration for Mrs. Flowers? Explain.

2. From what you learn about Marguerite in this selection, how would you describe her to a friend?

Readers Respond

This selection from *I Know Why the Caged Bird Sings* was about a special relationship a young girl has with a woman whom she looks up to and admires. What I liked best about the passage was Mrs. Flowers' poetic words of advice about how the human voice can express words better than paper can. What I remember best was a small part about ice: Marguerite was thinking about how it figured that Mrs. Flowers had ice on any ordinary day, when most people just had it on Saturdays. In a few short sentences the author described how special Mrs. Flowers was to Marguerite.

The story made me realize more about how it was to grow up then, and I think this would be a good selection for anyone to read.

Claire Monty

I liked the fact that Mrs. Flowers opened Marguerite's eyes to speech and literature. I would recommend this selection to a friend because I think there's a point in everyone's life when someone they like has taken them aside to teach them something good.

David Ojeda

Did you notice?

☞ Did you notice the imagery Angelou uses to describe Mrs. Flowers and her importance to Marguerite? How do these images make Angelou's writing personal?

☞ Is there a Mrs. Flowers in your life? If there is—or if you can imagine what she would be like—try writing about her importance to you in your journal. This personal writing could become the basis for a more extensive piece of writing later.

Writing Process in Action

Lifelines

Have you ever moped around, feeling lost and blue, until one day, unexpectedly, someone or something came along and snapped you out of it? Maya Angelou recounts just such an experience in the excerpt from *I Know Why the Caged Bird Sings,* on pages 38–46. Specifically, Angelou tells about the momentous day when Mrs. Bertha Flowers threw her a "life line," taking Angelou into her home for the first of many "lessons in living."

Now you are invited to write an autobiographical sketch about an interaction that made a difference in your life—perhaps one that involves a lifeline thrown to you by a Mrs. Flowers of your own.

• Assignment •

CONTEXT   You stumble across the current issue of *Everyday People,* a magazine founded on the belief that every person—not just the movie stars, athletes, and politicians—has a story to tell that's worth hearing. While you leaf through the magazine, a special note addressed to students in grades 9–12 catches your eye. It reads: "Attention, students! We are devoting an upcoming special issue to autobiographical sketches written by everyday people just like you. Specifically, we want to publish accounts of incidents and personal interactions that have made a difference in your lives." The note goes on to explain that the difference should be a positive one because the editors believe that people prefer uplifting stories to discouraging ones.

PURPOSE   To write a brief autobiographical sketch that shows how an incident or interaction changed your life for the better

AUDIENCE   Everyday people: students, parents, teachers, and other townspeople

LENGTH   2–3 pages

For more advice on how to approach this assignment, you will find the next few pages helpful. But don't feel that you have to remember all of what follows. You can come *back* to these pages as you write, getting help where and when you need it. You're in charge of your own writing process.

1. Prewriting

The first step is to find an incident or interaction to write about. Did anything personal come to mind when you read Angelou's story or the assignment? If not, try some of the suggestions at the top of the next page.

- Look at the writing you did for this unit. Are there any journal entries, autobiographical sketches, or poems that contain the seeds of an idea for this assignment?
- Get personal. Lesson 1.1, page 11, can help you ask personal questions.
- Search your mental files, using Lesson 1.4, page 23, for help.
- Freewrite to discover your thoughts. Lesson 1.3, page 19, can help you with this technique.

Once you have an idea in mind, try to recall what happened as fully and vividly as possible. A good way to start is to write down your answers to *who*, *what*, *where*, *when*, *why*, and *how* questions.

For this assignment, your goal is not just to retell the incident or interaction. You also need to get across the significance of the event. One way to explore your thoughts on this is to create a "Before and After" chart. Divide a piece of paper into two columns, with "before" at the top of one column and "after" at the top of the other. In the "before" column, list key traits that describe yourself, your outlook, and your circumstances before the incident or interaction took place. In the "after" column, note any ways in which you, your outlook, and your circumstances differed after the incident or interaction took place. Then compare and contrast the descriptions in your "before" and "after" columns to zero in on the significance of your experience.

Next, try freewriting to see if you can come up with a statement that summarizes what the experience meant to you, how it changed you, or what you learned from it. This statement can become the focus of your sketch—that is, the key point you want to convey, something along the lines of a thesis statement in a personal essay. For more help in writing this summary statement, see the material on writing thesis statements in Lesson 1.3, page 20.

Remember, however, that you are supposed to write an autobiographical sketch—not a personal essay. An autobiographical sketch is personal writing about a significant event or period in your life that gives your readers an idea of who you are, how you came to be this way, and what you've experienced.

2. Drafting

Start with the statement you wrote to summarize the significance of your chosen incident or interaction. Then, with the aid of your prewriting notes, begin adding sentences and paragraphs to back up this statement. That's essentially what Angelou does. Her first paragraph tells us what was significant about Mrs. Bertha Flowers: she was "the lady who threw me my first life line." Then Angelou creates a portrait of Mrs. Flowers that explains why she was a remarkable woman and why she had such an influence on the young Angelou. Starting with your summary statement can help you focus your thoughts, impressions, and other details as you write. It also will prepare your readers for what they are about to read. In so doing, it helps ensure that they will understand your subject as you intend it to be understood.

Next, tell your story. Write freely, referring to your prewriting notes as you go, but do try to get your thoughts down in some sort of logical order.

For example, if your experience consists of a clear sequence of events, the most logical way to organize your sketch is probably by putting these events in chronological order—that is, in the order in which they occurred. Angelou uses this approach; after establishing Mrs. Flowers's significance, Angelou retells the story of her first "lesson in living" as it happened, step by step.

You can, however, use any means of organization that works for you. You might consider structuring your sketch in one of these ways:

- as an interview between yourself and the significant person
- as a flashback
- as a series of journal entries

As you write, look for ways you can make your sketch come to life. Are there anecdotes, descriptions, comparisons, figures of speech, or other details that you can use to make your story more vivid? Look at what Angelou does. Instead of merely giving a physical description of Mrs. Flowers, for example, she uses comparisons to create a portrait that captures something of Mrs. Flowers's personality as well as Angelou's idolization of her.

> *She had the grace of control to appear warm in the coldest weather, and on the Arkansas summer days it seemed she had a private breeze which swirled around, cooling her.*

Also consider using dialogue to help bring your characters to life. Angelou gives readers a feeling for the proper, educated Mrs. Flowers and her own casual, uneducated grandmother with just a few words of dialogue from each.

> *She spoke to Momma in that soft yet carrying voice, "Good day, Mrs. Henderson." Momma responded with "How you, Sister Flowers?"*

Lesson 1.3, page 20, contains additional tips for enlivening writing.

3. Revising

To begin revising, look back at the assignment, and then read your draft to see if you have met the goals of this assignment. The following questions can help you evaluate your work:

- Does my writing qualify as an autobiographical sketch?
- Is my sketch easy to follow?
- Is my sketch vivid and accurate?
- Does my writing show how this incident or interaction changed my life for the better?
- Is my writing appropriate for my audience?

If you have trouble answering any of these questions, you may find that returning to the prewriting or drafting stages can help you improve your work. For example, you can

- expand upon the prewriting chart of "before" and "after" details to include more personal details; then rework your sketch to include new details;

- insert some transitional words and phrases to make the connections between ideas clearer;
- reconsider your organization, devising a new plan for arranging your details; then completely redraft your sketch according to this new plan; or
- start all over again with a different topic.

As part of the process of revising, you may also want to exchange drafts with some of your peers. Then share your reactions to each other's work and use the feedback to evaluate your draft.

4. Editing

Now think about your choice of words and phrases. Since this is a personal story, your words and phrases should sound like they're coming from you. Read Angelou's story aloud, and you can almost hear her talking. Now read your sketch aloud. Have you captured the way you speak—the rhythms of your sentences, your figures of speech? If not, try drafting your account as a letter to a friend. Or try telling your story to a friend while paying attention to the way you tell it. Then make your written account sound more like your oral one.

After you've personalized your words and phrases, it's time to get down to the nitty-gritty—the grammar, usage, and mechanics of what you've written. Review your work with the following questions in mind:

Criteria
1. *Focuses on an incident action that improved yo*
2. *Conveys the significanc incident or interaction*
3. *Answers the who, what, when, why, and how qu*
4. *Reflects your spoken rhy and phrases*
5. *Uses verb tenses accurate consistently*
6. *Follows correct grammar, usage, and mechanics*

- Do my sentences express complete thoughts?
- Do my subjects and verbs agree?
- Have I chosen precisely the right words to express my meaning?
- Are my spelling, capitalization, and punctuation correct?

Also, make sure your verbs signal the proper time frame. Paying attention to verb tenses is especially important if you include flashbacks in your account.

5. Presenting

Are you ready to send your manuscript to the magazine editors? This is an autobiographical piece, so you may choose to keep it to yourself if you think it's too personal to share. However, should you decide to keep it private, put it with your journal, and look at it when you're searching for new writing ideas or when you want to see how you are progressing as a writer.

• Reflecting •

What did you discover in writing this sketch? Did you learn anything about yourself or about the process of writing? Record any thoughts that come to mind in your journal. In fact, try to make a regular practice of writing about your writing process whenever you finish an assignment.

Portfolio & Reflection

Summary

Key concepts in personal writing include the following:

• Personal writing is a way of making discoveries about oneself.
• A personal journal is a place for recording experiences, thoughts, and feelings and so can serve as a valuable source of writing ideas.

• Strategies for exploring ideas for personal essays include freewriting and clustering.
• Flashbacks and journal entries are methods of presenting autobiographical materials.
• Poets use poetic devices such as sensory language to create memorable word pictures.
• A reader-response journal is a place to respond personally to literature.

Your Writer's Portfolio

Look over the personal writing you have done during this unit. Select two pieces of writing to put into your portfolio. Each piece should demonstrate that you have worked with one or more of the preceding concepts. In other words, look for a piece of writing that does one or more of the following:

• records a valuable self-discovery, or something special that makes you *you*
• can serve as an idea source for a personal essay in the future
• is based on ideas generated by freewriting, clustering, or creating an idea map
• expresses your own personal thoughts and feelings in poetic form
• relates a piece of literature to your life

Reflection and Commentary

Now write one page in which you demonstrate that you understand what this unit asked of you. Use your two selected pieces of writing as evidence while you consider the following numbered items. Respond to as many numbered items as possible. Label the page "Commentary on Personal Writing," and include it in your portfolio.

1. What element reveals something important about what you are like? Where did you take risks you'd take only in a journal?
2. What specific elements grew out of freewriting or clustering? What elements make your essay interesting?
3. What autobiographical details grew out of your memories?
4. What lines in a poem represent experiments with poetic devices? In your opinion, is your poetry successful? Why or why not?
5. What personal writing would you like to reshape later for others to read, and how?
7. What part of your writing process worked well? What goals will you set for personal writing, including keeping a journal?

Feedback

If you had a chance to respond to the following student comment, what would you say or ask?

Only when I'm writing do I express my true feelings. I'm a very quiet and shy person. Writing is sort of an outlet for me.

Indrani Sen, Edison High School,
Edison, New Jersey

The Writing Process

Snapshots

Jane Ash Poitras, *Family Blackboard*, 1989

Chavez and the Quest for

Human-Interest Stories

"The feature story tries for a more humane point of view, to draw in the reader, to get the reader to see that people are not statistics. . . . A feature story can make us more sensitive to what's really happening."

Lorenzo Chavez

E veryone knows what a news story is. The papers brim with fast-paced accounts of the day's international tensions, business ups and downs, personal triumphs and tragedies. But what's a feature story?

One quick way to answer that question is to scan a fifteen-foot magazine rack in a big grocery store. Almost every magazine carries feature stories—information pieces that are "softer, more personable, less direct . . . and that lean more toward entertainment," according to Lorenzo Chavez, a free-lance writer and writing teacher. Chavez writes on subjects as diverse as Latin America, the arts, education, and business for newspapers and for *Vista*, a magazine for Hispanic readers inserted in about twenty Sunday newspapers nationwide.

Writing the Feature Story

1. Researching the
Feature Story

2. Drafting the
Feature Story

3. Revising the Draft
for Publication

FOCUS

Writing a can't-put-it-down feature
story takes careful research, creative
writing, and hard-nosed editing.

As Chavez will tell you, feature stories can cover anything: sports stars, science breakthroughs, tips on buying cars—even tracing your family history, or genealogy, a subject Chavez covered for *Vista*.

Chavez will also tell you that ideas for feature stories are everywhere; in fact, there are "just too many," laughed Chavez. And, of course, you have to be alert and open to ideas. The idea for Chavez's story on family histories, "The Quest for Hispanic Roots," came from *Vista* readers. Over the years, hundreds of *Vista* readers had written into "Rootsearch," a popular genealogy column devoted

to tracing family histories. In this case, with so many readers writing in to the column, the *Vista* staff decided to run an article that could help people do family research on their own. But before Chavez could help others with their research, he had to go through his own research. Chavez began his writing process by narrowing his focus and doing some research.

rootsearch

From Abadia to Zúñiga,
Hispanic surnames tell the
story of a people in a restless
migration over the centuries
from the Old to the New World.
Every month VISTA traces the
history of Hispanic family
names to help its readers in
their quest for beginnings.

ALARCON

This surname comes from the village of Alarcón in Cuenca, Spain. When the town was recaptured from the Moors by Fernán Martínez de Ceballos in 1176, King Alfonso IX allowed Martínez to change his surname to that of the city as a reward. After that he was known as Fernán Martínez de Alarcón, and his descendants spread throughout the Spanish-speaking world.

The Alarcons from Cuba trace back directly to the village in central Spain. Don Lope de Alarcón, mayor of the town, had a daughter named Teresa who married Gonzalo de Ocaña in 1492. When he died, the children were given the right to use their mother's maiden name as their primary surname. One descendant, Antonio de Alarcón-Ocaña, took the name to Havana, where he died in 1664, leaving many

1. Researching the Feature Story

Before Chavez could start researching the article on genealogy, he had to narrow his original idea to a few key points—no more than he could cover in the allotted space of 1,500 words, or about six pages in *Vista* magazine. Ultimately, he chose to write about the biggest and most active genealogical societies and libraries in Texas and California, states from which the majority of reader letters had come.

With story idea in hand, Chavez had to gather the facts, and he began by listing a few questions to direct his research: Why do people search for their pasts? What libraries or associations can help?

It took Chavez about a week to get the answers. Some information came from newspaper clippings, but most of it came from thirty or forty phone calls he made to libraries and researchers.

Lorenzo Chavez interviewed many genealogists as part of his research for this feature.

INTERFACE *You've volunteered to write a weekly social issues story for your community newspaper, and the editor has accepted your proposal. What social issues interest you? How will you begin to collect ideas for your weekly stories?*

2. Drafting the Feature Story

After his interviews, Chavez had twenty pages of notes, several taped conversations, a few newspaper clips, and a head full of ideas. Before sitting down at the computer, though, Chavez reminded himself of one key thing: He had to picture the people he was writing for, a "middle-aged to older generation, people of Mexican descent, mostly retirees, who have spare time and an interest in history and politics." To engage his readers, Chavez had to put himself in their shoes and anticipate questions they might ask.

Now Chavez was ready to write. To grab the reader, he used an anecdote about Mickey Garcia, a Texas genealogist who researches family histories. He portrayed Garcia as a treasure hunter. "She's searching for a valuable thing, not gold, but a family history," Chavez said. "I used that [approach] because I didn't want to frighten the reader by saying this was a long, time-consuming, arduous task."

From there Chavez stitched the story together in a clever way. Using quotes, descriptions, and explanations, he told readers what sparked people's interest in genealogy, introduced top researchers, described huge family reunions, and explained how to find family records.

To close the story, Chavez quoted researcher George Ryskamp, who said: "To be a good genealogist, you have to be a good detective. You never know what you're going to find."

INTERFACE *You're a staff writer for* **Modern Music,** *and your editor tells you to write a 1,000-word feature on trends in rock. Who do you think your audience will be? How will this knowledge focus your writing?*

Human interest is a key element in a good feature story. In his feature story Chavez included a photo of the Vela family reunion, which boasted nearly 1,500 participants.

3. Revising the Draft for Publication

After writing for three days, Chavez had a rough draft. "It was messy, but I knew I had everything I wanted there," he said. Now he was ready to revise.

At this stage, Chavez worked on a printout of his story, not on the computer. On hard copy he could see problems more clearly. "Problems pop up more. You can see poor structure [when there are] too many prepositions. If the lead is too long, you can see it—

How do you know if your copy is dull or lively? If your story excites you, it will probably excite the reader.

the paragraph is all gray. No one is going to get through that first paragraph," he explained.

Before printing out a copy of his story, Chavez checked the length on the computer so he knew if he needed to cut sentences or paragraphs. Then he checked his facts, spelling, and grammar. "If you have poor spelling and grammar or the facts are wrong, the reader will ask, 'Why should I read this guy? He doesn't know what he's talking about.'"

After that, Chavez worked to improve his style. He rewrote dull sentences to make them bold and active. He varied sentence lengths to create rhythm, so the story sounded interesting, not monotonous. Finally, he checked to be sure the story had some mystery. "You can't put all the information at the top or the reader doesn't have anything to look forward to," Lorenzo said. "You have to have some suspense, something pushing the reader forward."

Finally Chavez turned his copy over to staff editors, who reviewed his work before publication. His editors, he said, catch mistakes and other problems because they have a fresh point of view and different experiences.

ON ASSIGNMENT

1. Clip a feature story on a favorite subject from a newspaper or magazine. Review the story and rate its success. What strategies did the writer use to grab your interest? Did the writer begin the feature with an anecdote or lively quote? If the writer did not grab your interest, what do you think the writer should have done differently?

2. Collect a series of feature stories that appeal to you for various reasons, and assemble them into a small book. The topic of your nonfiction book can be anything that interests you, as long as the writing is engaging. Write a brief introduction to your book, pointing out the strengths of each story.

3. **Cooperative Learning**
Form small writing teams of three or four people. Brainstorm subject ideas for a 1,000-word feature story on one topic related to your town, city, or school. Once you've selected your subject, collaborate on ideas for focusing your topic. Who will your audience be? What interviews will you need to conduct? Have each team member select someone to interview. Review each other's questions. Be sure the questions reflect both your subject focus and audience. Assemble all the interviews into one article. Assign two people to write lead and end paragraphs.

Case Study: Feature Writing **59**

Overview of the Writing Process

Discovering Your World

Take a look at this fresco by Michelangelo, which he painted on the ceiling of the Sistine Chapel in Rome in the 1500s. Centuries later, art historians X-rayed it and found earlier drawings that Michelangelo had sketched beneath it. After the artist began painting, new ideas emerged, and he decided to resketch and repaint based on these new ideas. The many sketches and the layers of paint reveal the artist's process of exploration.

A writer works in much the same way. He or she may explore an idea in a rough draft, refine it, or even discard it and search for a new idea. Like life itself, writing can be a voyage of discovery.

Michelangelo, detail of the Sistine Chapel Ceiling, 1508–1512

Stages in the Process

When you let your mind wander, what do you think about? Your plans for baseball practice after school, the lyrics to your favorite song, a memory of your grandmother telling you a bedtime story when you were very young? Images flash vividly through your mind like snapshots. These snapshot images are raw material for the writer within you.

Writing is a way for you to explore those pictures and help others clearly and fully see them. It is also a way for you to discover more about yourself and about the people and experiences that have helped make you who you are. Although no two writers approach the writing process in exactly the same way, most writers go through five basic stages: prewriting, drafting, revising, editing, and presenting.

Prewriting During prewriting, you generate and explore ideas and decide what you want to write about. You might start by looking at your own thoughts, feelings, and memories. At this stage, you also begin to think about your audience—those who will read your work—and your purpose. Your audience may be a friend, a teacher, or the readers of a national magazine. Your purpose is what you hope to accomplish through your writing.

Drafting Writing a draft, or turning your ideas into paragraphs, is not only a stage in the writing process, it is a tool in itself. For as you compose your draft, you find links between ideas and new meanings in your words and phrases.

Revising When you begin revising, one of your goals is to make sure that your writing is clear and well organized. Does it accomplish your purpose? Does it reach your audience? If not, look for ways to cut or add to your writing to improve it. Mark these changes right on your draft, and then incorporate them. Compare the writer's revised draft with her earlier draft to see what changes she incorporated during revising.

Editing This is when you get picky. You make sure that you've chosen the best possible words to communicate your ideas and that your sentences are grammatically correct. Finally, you proofread your writing and correct mistakes in capitalization, punctuation, and spelling. Note the editorial changes this writer has marked on her revised copy.

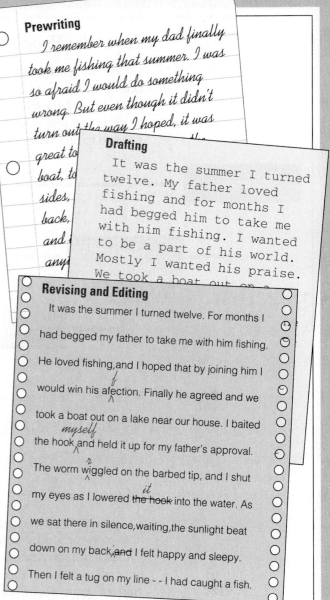

Prewriting

I remember when my dad finally took me fishing that summer. I was so afraid I would do something wrong. But even though it didn't turn out the way I hoped, it was great to... boat, to... sides,... back,... and... any...

Drafting

It was the summer I turned twelve. My father loved fishing and for months I had begged him to take me with him fishing. I wanted to be a part of his world. Mostly I wanted his praise. We took a boat out on a...

Revising and Editing

It was the summer I turned twelve. For months I had begged my father to take me with him fishing. He loved fishing, and I hoped that by joining him I would win his afection. Finally he agreed and we took a boat out on a lake near our house. I baited the hook myself and held it up for my father's approval. The worm wiggled on the barbed tip, and I shut my eyes as I lowered ~~the hook~~ it into the water. As we sat there in silence, waiting, the sunlight beat down on my back, and I felt happy and sleepy. Then I felt a tug on my line - - I had caught a fish.

Presenting This is the stage at which you share your work with others. You might read what you've written aloud in class, submit it to the school newspaper, or give it to a friend to read. There are many avenues for presenting your work.

· JOURNAL ACTIVITY ·
Think It Through

What stages do you go through when you write? Describe the stages you went through on a recent writing assignment. How do they compare with the stages described above?

How the Process Works

At any point in the writing process, you may return to any of the preceding stages. For example, if you're having trouble drafting a paragraph, you may go back to the prewriting stage and outline it first. If you get stuck as you revise, you may redraft some of your writing. You may even need to gather more information or reevaluate your purpose.

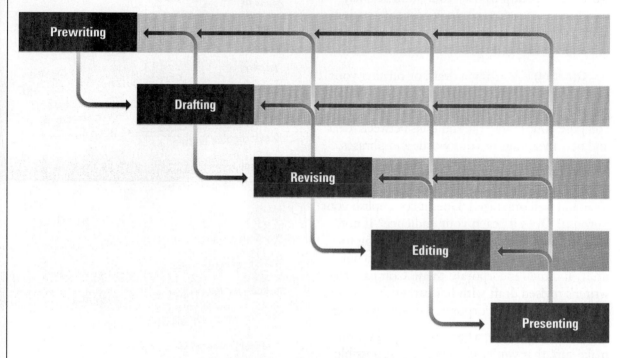

Remember, too, that because writing is a process of discovery, you may be surprised by what you find when you write. Through writing, you can explore your ideas, your feelings, your memories—anything that interests you. Like Alice Walker, you may discover something new about yourself, your world, and the forces that have shaped your life.

What did Walker discover about her mother through her writing?

After years of listening to her mother's stories, Walker decides she wants to write about them.

Literature Model

So many of the stories that I write . . . are my mother's stories. Only recently did I fully realize this: that through years of listening to my mother's stories of her life, I have absorbed not only the stories themselves, but something of the manner in which she spoke, something of the urgency that involves the knowledge that her stories—like her life—must be recorded.

Alice Walker, *In Search of Our Mothers' Gardens*

The following are some writing options to help you apply what you have learned.

1. Guided Assignment Study the photo of the painting on page 60. How is the process of painting a picture similar to the writing process? Write a paragraph in your journal in which you compare the two processes.

To help you begin, compare the following stages in the artistic process with what you have learned about the writing process:

- A painter may generate ideas by drawing on personal experience, studying the work of others, or observing the outside world.
- A painter may begin exploring an idea by making sketches or early paintings of it.
- As new ideas emerge—or in order to correct mistakes—the painter may choose to resketch or repaint.
- A painter often shares a completed work by displaying it in a gallery.

PURPOSE To compare the writing process to the painting process
AUDIENCE Yourself
LENGTH 1–2 paragraphs

2. Open Assignment Writer Lawrence Osgood noted that "Writing is like exploring. . . . As an explorer makes maps of the country he has explored, so a writer's works are maps of the country he has explored." Use Osgood's analogy to suggest to you how writing is like another process (not including painting). Consider sculpting, ceramics, needlework, photography, building bridges, or another of your own choice. Consider each stage of the two processes. Write a paragraph or two explaining what the two have in common. If there are ways in which the two processes are not alike, be sure to point that out as well.

COMPUTER OPTION

Whenever you are comparing two things or two processes, as in assignments 1 and 2, a visual diagram may help you. You can use your computer or PC to put the information into a comparative chart or, using a series of boxes, into a cluster diagram. Consult the Help function on your machine to find out how to create such visual aids on your machine.

3. Civics Sometimes the more you know about something the more questions you can think of to ask. Take out an assignment you have written earlier this year or in a previous year for a civics class, and reread it. Have recent current events changed your understanding of anything you have written? Are there ideas in your essay that you would like to explore now in greater detail? Do you know more about the subject now that changes the conclusions you came to earlier? Spend five minutes freewriting about the essay, then outline in detail how you might revise the essay. If you feel you need to do additional research, note that in your outline. Finally, if you like, revise the essay according to your new outline.

4. Cooperative Learning In a small group, share problems you have had in writing. These might include writer's block—the inability to put anything down on paper; disorganized paragraphs; the lack of information; or too much information. Choose one, and write a "Dear Abby" letter (as if to an advice columnist) detailing the problems you are having. Exchange letters within the group. Answer the letter you have received, using what you have learned in the lesson about the writing process to help you. Finally, share the letters and the responses with other members of the group, and ask for additional comments.

Prewriting: Getting Started

Set Your Imagination Loose

Where do writers' ideas come from? As Lorenzo Chavez points out in the Case Study on pages 54–58, ideas for writing are everywhere. You may find them in a conversation, a TV show, a book, a memory, or even a photo from the family album.

You can begin to generate ideas for writing through prewriting. During prewriting, you unleash your imagination to allow promising writing topics to emerge. You might start with what is close at hand, writing about yourself and your family, and see where your ideas lead you.

How Do I Begin?

Poet Donald Hall once said, "Writing begins with invention." To begin inventing, all you need is something to set your mind wandering. Among the techniques that writers find useful for generating writing ideas are freewriting and collecting.

Freewriting   When you freewrite, you choose a topic and a time limit and then just start writing. Don't worry about grammar, spelling, punctuation, or logic. Just write down your ideas as they come to you. If you run out of ideas, you can repeat the same word over and over until a new idea occurs to you. When the time is up, review what you've written. The ideas that most interest you are likely to be the ones that will be most worth writing about.

Take a look at the freewriting generated by one writer. Note how many ideas she came up with in just a few minutes.

Model

Is the writer more interested in the quick flow of ideas or in following grammar or punctuation rules? How do you know?

I love spending time with my uncle Edward. He always has stories to tell—like how he used to roller-skate to work when he first got out of college. And stories about my father—his little brother—that make me laugh but that seem like they're about somebody else because I can't imagine my dad as a kid but I can imagine Uncle Edward as a kid, even though he's a lot older than my dad. Probably because he's ➡

so easy to talk to—he's more like my friend than my uncle. I told him that I wanted to be a writer someday, but he didn't laugh—he said I should start now. I wonder if I could write a story about Uncle Edward on skates.

Collecting Writers also find ideas by collecting. You can collect information from books, magazines, newspapers, radio programs, movies, even from conversations with other people. A good place to collect all this raw material is your journal. Based on a journal entry, Moses Thomas Greene II wrote the following reaction to a TV show.

Student Model

*A*s a young person in America, I think of death as something that will occur when I am in my eighties or older. However, an episode of *A Different World* made me realize that I can't take this longevity for granted anymore.

In this episode, a group of college students in a public speaking class were given a unique assignment: they were asked to deliver their own eulogy. Although most of the students gave humorous speeches, one student took the assignment more seriously because she had Acquired Immune Deficiency Syndrome, or AIDS. Up until then, the student had kept her condition a secret, but she decided to tell her classmates the truth when she delivered her eulogy. As a result, the rest of the students began avoiding the young woman and didn't want to hear about how she was dealing with her condition.

What I liked best about the episode was that it handled the issue realistically. The students' reactions reflected the attitude of many "real" people toward the disease—ignore it and it will go away. However, the episode made me see that AIDS is a problem that needs to be dealt with and that can't be ignored.

Moses Thomas Greene II,
Brentwood High School, Brentwood, New York

How does Moses "hook" you in the first paragraph of his essay?

Writing about this difficult subject helped Moses sort out his feelings about it.

· JOURNAL ACTIVITY ·
Try It Out

Pick one idea you find interesting from your own collection of raw material and freewrite about it in your journal. What new ideas did your freewriting generate? Note these in your journal.

How Can I Explore My Ideas?

Once you have generated some writing ideas, you need to explore them further. Exploring your ideas should help you clarify your thinking and find a focus for your writing. Two useful techniques for exploring ideas are making lists and asking questions.

Making Lists   You've probably made shopping lists and lists of things to do, but making a list can also be a powerful tool for exploring writing ideas. Start with a key word or idea, and list other ideas as they occur to you. Don't worry about the order; just let your ideas flow freely from one to the next. This kind of free-association activity is also often referred to as brainstorming.

One writer used the technique of list making to generate the ideas shown below. What other ideas come to mind as you read through each list?

Memorable Events

Eighth-grade graduation

Visiting my dad last summer

When I got my first bicycle

Mom's graduation from college

Grandfather in the hospital

Favorite Places

My grandmother's house

The mall

The park down by the waterfront

My room

The basketball court behind the school

Embarrassing Moments

When I forgot my lines in the school play

When I struck out in the playoff game

When I marched the wrong way during the band's halftime performance

When I tripped on my dress at my sister's wedding

Earliest Memories

Falling down the basement stairs when I was three

A family trip to Yellowstone Park

Fingerpainting in kindergarten

Building a snow fort with my best friend in first grade

Listening to my grandfather tell stories

Making lists can help you figure out what you want to write about. Once you've finished, look over your lists and underline the ideas that seem most interesting to you. Draw lines between related ideas. Did any unexpected ideas appear? Did you recall events you had not thought about for a long time? Did you learn something new about yourself? These ideas may be worthwhile writing topics.

Asking Questions   You can also explore a topic by asking and answering questions about it. News reporters begin with six basic questions when they explore a subject: *who? what? where? when? why?* and *how?* In the chart below, the writer explored an idea generated through list making by asking and answering questions based on these six questions.

Questions to Explore Ideas

Who
Q. Who or what do I want to write about?
A. My seventy-three-year old grandfather, who grew up in Vietnam and came to the United States after the Vietnam War.

What
Q. What happened to my subject?
A. During the war he was separated from his family. He finally escaped from Vietnam. He spent a long time in a refugee camp, until family members in the United States could arrange for him to come here.

Where
Q. Where did this happen?
A. In a small village in Vietnam and later in a refugee camp just across the border of Thailand.

When
Q. When did this happen?
A. He escaped in 1973 and lived in a makeshift tent in Thailand until 1978.

Why
Q. Why did it happen?
A. Because of the war. Many people left Vietnam because they were afraid of the new Communist leaders. They fled to nearby Thailand because it wasn't under Communist rule.

How
Q. How did my grandfather survive?
A. He survived partly because of his determination to see his family again and partly because of luck.

• JOURNAL ACTIVITY •
Think It Through

Choose a family member you might like to write about. In your journal pose *who, what, where, when, why,* and *how* questions to explore your subject. Do your questions differ from those posed above? Why couldn't you ask the same questions?

How Do I Narrow My Focus?

Once you've chosen a general topic to write about, you need to narrow its scope. You can use a network tree to help you narrow your writing topic. Start by listing your general topic at the top of the tree. Then use the same free-association technique that you used in list making to generate ideas to fill out the tree. Narrow your focus further each time you move to a new level on the tree. Note how many writing ideas one writer generated in the network tree below.

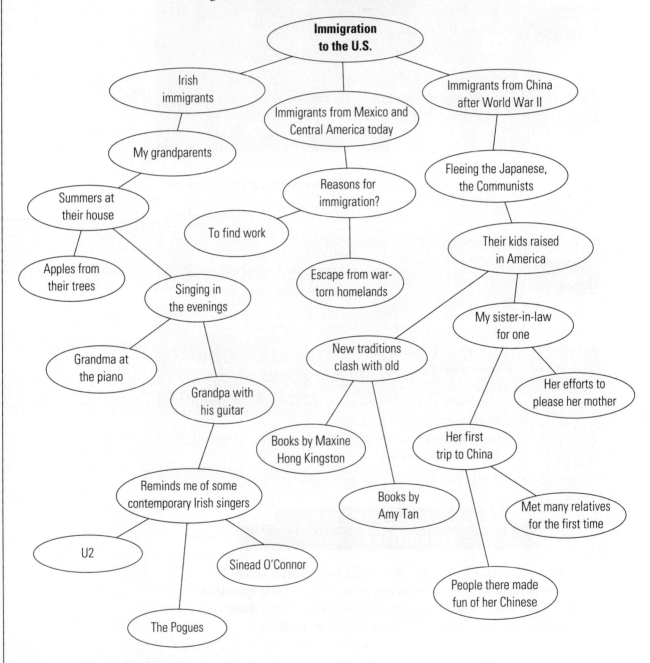

Writer's Choice

The following are some writing options to help you apply what you have learned.

1. Guided Assignment   Using any one of the methods learned in this lesson, take five minutes to explore writing topics based on the painting below. Consider the woman's facial expression and her pose as well as the objects laid out on the table. Remember to keep writing during the entire five minutes. If you get stuck, you can repeat the same word over and over until a new idea occurs to you. After your time is up, look over your prewriting. Select an idea you would like to develop further, and then write a brief paragraph about it.

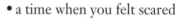

PURPOSE	To explore writing topics
AUDIENCE	Yourself
LENGTH	1 paragraph

2. Open Assignment   Writer Willa Cather once said, "Most of the basic material a writer works with is acquired before the age of fifteen." Think back over your own life experiences. Then choose one of the topics in the following list or one of your own, and explore it further. If, as you explore your topic, you discover another topic that interests you more, feel free to change direction and explore the new topic. Use the material you develop to write a paragraph on the topic of greatest interest to you.

Janet Fish, *Kara*, 1983

- a time when you felt scared
- a favorite toy from childhood
- how you're different from your parents
- a grandparent
- a family heirloom

3. Cooperative Learning   In a small group discuss several families that you have come to know through television shows, movies, or books. How do the family members relate to one another? What makes each family unique? What do you know about each family's history?

Choose one family with which all group members are familiar. Have each group member freewrite for about five minutes about a different person in that family. Read each piece of freewriting aloud. Are there any ideas that could be developed as writing topics? Have each member write a paragraph using a different topic suggested in the discussion. Then combine the paragraphs to create a "family portrait."

Prewriting: Getting Started   **69**

Prewriting: Identifying Purpose and Audience

Reaching Out

When you write a letter, you usually have a clear idea of why you're writing (your purpose) and whom you're writing to (your audience). For example, you might write to an older sister who is away at college to tell her about life at home. Or you might write to the director of your school's study-abroad program to explain why you want to be a foreign exchange student.

Whether you're writing a letter or a research paper, establishing your purpose and audience can help you focus your writing. Here's how one writer narrowed her writing topic. How will her choice of audience help her focus her topic further?

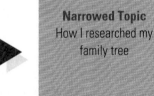

| **Broad Subject**
Genealogy | ▶ | **Narrowed Topic**
How I researched my
family tree | ▶ | **Purpose**
To explain to readers
how they can research
their own family
histories |

Determining Purpose

When you write, you usually have one primary purpose in mind: to inform or explain, to persuade, to amuse or entertain, to narrate, or to describe. For example, you might write a humorous short story to entertain or amuse your classmates. Sometimes, however, you may be writing to accomplish more than one purpose. For instance, suppose you write a letter to the editor of your school newspaper praising a campaign to raise money for a shelter for the homeless. Your primary purpose in writing the letter might be to inform your fellow students about the campaign and the shelter. Your secondary purpose might be to persuade students to help with the campaign. So, how do you determine the primary purpose of your writing? Answering the questions on the next page may help.

1. Do I want to narrate, or tell, a story?

2. Do I want to describe someone or something?

3. Do I want to inform my readers about the topic or to explain something about it?

4. Do I want to persuade them to change their minds about something or take some action?

In the following paragraphs, writer Yoshiko Uchida explains her purpose in writing about the lives of Japanese Americans during World War II. At that time, the United States was at war with Japan. Many Japanese-American families were forced to leave their homes and live in camps run by the U.S. government. Uchida often speaks to schoolchildren about her own experiences in one of the camps.

Literature Model

I always ask the children why they think I wrote *Journey to Topaz* and *Journey Home*, in which I tell of the wartime experiences of the Japanese Americans. "To tell about the camps?" they ask. "To tell how you felt? To tell what happened to the Japanese people?"

"Yes," I answer, but I continue the discussion until finally one of them will say, "You wrote those books so it won't ever happen again."

And that is why I wrote [*Desert Exile*]. I wrote it for the young Japanese Americans who seek a sense of continuity with their past. But I wrote it as well for all Americans, with the hope that through knowledge of the past, they will never allow another group of people in America to be sent into a desert exile ever again.

Yoshiko Uchida, *Desert Exile*

What is Uchida's primary purpose? Do you think Uchida believes that "the pen is mightier than the sword"?

Uchida considers the needs of her two audiences: Japanese Americans and all other Americans.

• JOURNAL ACTIVITY •
Think It Through

Choose a topic that appeals to you. How might you approach that topic if your purpose were to inform? To persuade? To entertain? To narrate? To describe? In your journal, jot down ideas about different ways to approach the same topic.

Addressing Your Audience

Writing is communication. So when you write, you want to make sure that your writing will be understood by your audience—those who will read what you've written. Your audience may be your teacher, your classmates, a friend, or the readers of your school newspaper.

To be sure that your audience will understand your writing, try to put yourself in their place. First, think about what your readers would need or want to know about the subject. Second, think about the language that would best communicate your ideas to them.

Finding the Right Level   Before you begin writing, think about how much your audience already knows about the subject you've chosen. You probably get impatient when someone explains something to you that you already know. You probably feel frustrated when someone talks about something that you don't understand. Your readers will feel the same way.

In addition, you need to think about what aspect of the subject will most interest your readers. For example, an audience of tennis enthusiasts may enjoy reading about the specific shots a player used to win a game. However, an audience that is less familiar with the sport may be more interested in reading about the player's personality.

Finding the Right Language   Your choice of words should also be appropriate to your audience and purpose. For a research paper or a letter to the principal, you would use formal English, paying attention to rules of standard grammar and usage. For a letter to a friend, conversational, or informal, English would be more appropriate.

One way to make sure that your writing will reach its intended audience is to ask yourself several questions. The questions below helped one writer determine how to address his audience. The writer chose to write on the following topic: "How My Sister Ann Drives Me Crazy." The basic purpose of the piece of writing was to entertain.

Questions to Help You Address Your Audience	
1. Who am I writing for?	My English class, other ninth-graders
2. How much do they know about Ann?	Not much. I'll have to present a vivid description and character sketch of my sister.
3. What writing style should I use?	I'll use a humorous, informal, conversational style to help keep them interested in what I'm saying.
4. What vocabulary is appropriate?	Words they understand, especially some contractions and slang to get across the way my sister talks.

Writer's Choice

The following are some writing options to help you apply what you have learned.

1. Guided Assignment   Pick one of the writing topics listed below.

- a family reunion
- coping with family conflicts
- what parents don't understand about your favorite kind of music
- getting your first job

Narrow the focus of your topic, and decide on a primary purpose for your writing. Pick one of the audiences listed below, and answer questions similar to those listed on the opposite page. Your answers will help you develop the topic for the audience you've chosen. Use your answers to help you write a paragraph or two on your chosen topic.

- family members
- school officials or teachers
- a good friend or classmate
- an older friend who lives far away

PURPOSE As selected
AUDIENCE As selected
LENGTH 1–2 paragraphs

2. Open Assignment   Look at the sculpture on this page. What would you say about it if you were explaining it to a younger child, reviewing it for an arts magazine, or describing it to a friend who has little interest in art? Choose one topic, and identify a purpose and audience of your choice for your writing. Use the questions on the facing page to help you determine how you would approach the topic. Answer the questions and then write a paragraph on your topic.

3. Cooperative Learning   In a small group brainstorm to come up with some ideas for ways to make school life more enjoyable or to

Keith Haring, *Untitled*, 1985

encourage greater student involvement in school policy. Ideas might include safety concerns or recycling. Agree on one idea. Then, using the questions on the opposite page, each of you write a letter to the person (principal or teacher) or persons (students) you want to persuade. Regroup, and read and respond to one another's letters. Consider sending the final letters.

Prewriting: Gathering Information

What's the Story?

Suppose you've stumbled upon a box of old photographs in your grandmother's attic. Most of the photos are faded, but one has been carefully preserved behind glass in a silver frame. It shows a girl sitting on a young woman's lap. Who are these people? What is the story behind the photo?

To find out, you might have to do some research. Similarly, for some writing projects you'll need to gather additional information. But don't worry—there are plenty of sources. You can find out most of what you need to know at the library or by interviewing people.

Using the Library

For some writing projects, your own thoughts and experiences can provide all the information you need. Other projects, however, require research, and your local library is a good place to start.

To locate books on your topic, you can use the card catalog or the on-line computer system. You can use both cataloguing systems to search for a book by title, subject, or author. Each listing also contains subject headings, which can serve as cross-references to related material. You may want to search under these headings to look for additional information on your topic. When you are looking for a particular book, you may also want to browse among the others you find in the same section. You might find something useful there.

After you locate a particular book, be sure to make a note of its author, title, and call number so that you can find it easily next time. It's also a good idea to keep a record of the books that don't provide helpful information on your topic. That way you won't waste time searching for them again.

As you look through each book, don't forget to examine its bibliography for other related titles. Other books by the same author may provide useful material.

Remember to ask the librarian if you need help at any point in your search. Also, see pages 728–739 in Resources and Skills for more information on using library resources.

Conducting Interviews

The library is not your only source of information. Some of your best resources are people. You can find out about a person's ideas, feelings, and experiences in an interview.

Informational Interviews In an informational interview, you ask a person to speak about a subject he or she knows well. The interview may be informal—that is, a casual conversation—or formal—that is, one for which you need to make an appointment.

Whether your interview will be formal or informal, you should prepare for it carefully. Learn as much as you can about your subject and about the person you are going to interview. Think about what your readers will want to know. Then write down at least four or five major questions that will help you get at this material. Use *who, what, where, when, why,* and *how* questions so that you get answers that provide information, not just a yes or no response.

During the interview, listen carefully so that you can ask intelligent follow-up questions. Often the most interesting information emerges in response to a question you had not planned to ask. Take notes or tape record the interview.

As soon as possible after the interview, write up a full account of it, based on your notes or your tapes. Write down everything you remember. If necessary, contact the person you interviewed to clarify any confusing ideas or questionable facts.

Before the Interview
- Make the appointment.
- Research your topic and find out about your source.
- Write out four–five basic questions.

During the Interview
- Ask informational questions (*who, what, where, when, why,* and *how*).
- Listen carefully.
- Ask follow-up questions.
- Take accurate notes (or tape record).

After the Interview
- Write a more detailed account of the interview.
- Contact source for any needed clarification or to double-check facts.

• JOURNAL ACTIVITY •
Try It Out

Imagine that you are researching services for senior citizens in your community for a class assignment. In your journal, write down four or five informational questions you might ask a senior citizens' program director during an interview.

Oral Histories   If you want information about an event in recent history, you might interview someone who lived through it. Suppose you are writing about the impact of the Vietnam War on American society. You might interview people who grew up during that era about their memories of the war. Or imagine you want information about your family history. You might interview a relative who can tell you about the lives of other family members. These "spoken memories" are called oral history.

Family stories can tell you a great deal about both the story-teller and life in the past. The following is an excerpt from the oral history *Hannah's Daughters*. Hannah Lambertson Nesbitt, who lived from 1876 to 1974, describes life on her grandfather's farm.

Literature Model

*I*n my grandaddy's time it was different than it is now. It was all hand labor, and men could support their families. . . . We had poorhouses, yes. A lot of men lived on a poor farm. I used to know a portion of a song about a son who persuaded his parents to deed him their farm. Well, they yielded to him and he turned them out. They had to go "over the hills to the poorhouse." That's what the song was called. There's many children did that to their folks. But I'm talking about what *my* folks done. They looked after those that needed help. If a man took sick or died, they looked after his family. Grandaddy sent Grandma to different places; she had several families she used to keep. She'd clothe them and everything else. She'd just go to visit and see what they had to have. . . .And if they needed a barrel of flour, they got it. . . .The farmers just did it. They helped those that needed it. Not like it is today.

Dorothy Gallagher, *Hannah's Daughters*

Life on Farms
Most of the work on farms was done by hand. Some farmers had enough to get by. Others ended up on a poor farm. (Need to find out more about this.)

Family Life
Men were responsible for supporting their families. Some children treated their parents badly. Grandaddy seems to have been the head of the family.

Farm Communities
Some farm families took care of others, giving them clothing, food, and wood, when they needed it. Farm communities were close-knit.

Writer's Choice

The following are some writing options to help you apply what you have learned.

1. Guided Assignment Collect information for your own family history. Begin by interviewing two relatives who can tell you something about your family's past. You might ask some questions about your own childhood, such as the following:

- What is your first memory of me?
- What was I like as a child?
- What other relative do I remind you of?
- Is there a story behind my name?

Or you might ask questions about their memories of family life:

- Where did the family originally come from?
- How were special occasions, such as birthdays, weddings, or holidays, celebrated?
- Who took care of the children?
- Who took care of elderly family members?
- What kinds of jobs did family members have?
- What did family members do for fun?
- How did major historical events, such as wars, elections, or economic hard times, affect the family?
- How did technological advances (the first telephone, car, television) affect family life?

After you have finished interviewing your family members, write a few pages on what you have learned about yourself or your family.

PURPOSE To gather information for a family history
AUDIENCE Yourself and other family members
LENGTH 1–4 pages

2. Open Assignment Suppose you worked as a researcher for a popular news magazine. You are required to identify five library sources and two people whom you could interview for every story. Pick one of the topics below, or choose one of your own. First list the sources you will use, and then proceed to collect the information. Finally, write a page or two on the topic of your choice, based on the notes you took while researching.

- comparing popular music from an earlier era to popular music today
- making home videos
- immigration to the United States during the last twenty years
- the changing role of women today
- protecting the environment for future generations

3. Social Studies Select a well-known historical figure, and pretend that you are able to interview this person today. Prepare a list of interview questions asking for eyewitness views on historical events, and exchange lists with a classmate. Assume the role of the historical figure to answer the questions on your classmate's list, and then again exchange papers. Finally, write a page based on the answers your classmate gave to your questions.

COMPUTER OPTION

Your computer can be an excellent tool to save valuable information for research projects. You can use it when compiling a family history or any research project for which you will want to continue to gather information over a long period of time. Place your interview notes in a file for easy retrieval. Establish a classification system, and use it to list the information you've obtained, the source, and the date. As you gather additional data, create subheads to classify, store, change, and retrieve information as needed.

Drafting: Turning Prewriting into a Paragraph

Something to Say

Family ties, sometimes I feel like I've got so many responsibilities to my family I don't have a life of my own. Babysitting my brothers. If I have to do that again next weekend I'll just scream. And when they do something wrong, I get the blame. Can't Mom see I need to have some time to myself? Wasn't she ever my age? Life must have been so different when she was growing up.

Swimming

First experience—nearly drowned when I fell into a pond when I was four years old

Learning to swim was a nightmare for me

If we were meant to swim, we'd have gills and fins

The time my uncle taught me how to tread water—he was so patient, didn't laugh at me

Overcame fears

Wonder what a wave-action pool is like . . .

Like the examples above, your own prewriting is rich with possible writing ideas. You've got something to say. But how can you develop that raw material into something you can share with your readers?

In the drafting stage you take your ideas and shape them into paragraphs. A paragraph is a group of related sentences that develop or support one main idea. For instance, based on the freewriting above, the writer may choose to develop a paragraph about a family member's responsibilities. The brainstorming selection may lead to a paragraph about how the writer overcame her fear of the water and learned to swim.

The Structure of a Paragraph

A paragraph consists of a main idea—or controlling idea—and supporting details. Often the main idea is stated in a topic sentence. The supporting details develop the main idea by proving, clarifying, or expanding upon it. Like building blocks, the supporting details provide the foundation on which the main idea rests.

CONTROLLING IDEA

| Supporting Detail | Supporting Detail | Supporting Detail |

Literature Model

No one was particularly glad that Mary Fortune looked like her grandfather except the old man himself. He thought it added greatly to her attractiveness. He thought she was the smartest and the prettiest child he had ever seen and he let the rest of them know that if—IF that was—he left anything to anybody, it would be Mary Fortune he left it to. She was now nine, short and broad like himself, with his very light blue eyes, his wide prominent forehead, his steady penetrating scowl and his rich florid complexion; but she was like him on the inside too. She had, to a singular degree, his intelligence, his strong will, and his push and drive. Though there was seventy years' difference in their ages, the spiritual distance between them was slight. She was the only member of the family he had any respect for.

Flannery O'Connor, *A View of the Woods*

Why do you suppose O'Connor puts a topic sentence up front and reinforces it at the paragraph's conclusion?

Details reveal physical resemblance and point out similarities in personality traits.

The Process of Writing a Paragraph

There is no magic formula for writing a paragraph. You may write your supporting sentences first to help you determine your main idea and then write a topic sentence to express that idea. Or you may want to come up with the topic sentence first. Keep in mind that you can revise any part of your paragraph at any point in the writing process.

• JOURNAL ACTIVITY •
Try It Out

Look through your journal for possible main ideas for paragraphs. Pick one idea, and list supporting details that you might use to develop that idea in a paragraph.

Writing a Topic Sentence   A topic sentence may be a statement or a question. Whatever its form, a good topic sentence expresses the main idea clearly and makes the reader want to keep reading. Your choice of topic sentence also helps determine how you will develop the paragraph.

Try out several possible topic sentences before choosing the one that best expresses your main idea. Each of the following topic sentences is based on the painting shown here. Note how each would take a paragraph in a different direction.

Eastman Johnson, *The Hatch Family*, 1871

- Just a century ago, several generations of a family often lived together under one roof.
- Although a frail man, my grandfather still ruled the family.
- The dark wood paneling glowed in the firelight.

Organizing Supporting Details   Before you begin writing, you may find it helpful to organize your details in an outline. One way to outline your ideas is to sort them into categories, as shown below. If an idea doesn't seem to fit anywhere, leave it out. If a new idea occurs to you while you're sorting, put it in if it fits. Once you have sorted out all the ideas, number them within each column in the order that seems most logical. Here's how one writer organized her ideas based on the topic sentence "I always liked my aunt Alicia best."

Organizing Ideas in an Outline

- My aunt Alicia
- Her mysterious apartment in the city
- Apartment filled with books and the little clay animals she found in Mexico
- I got lost once on my way there
- Her embroidered jeans jacket
- Her flashy jewelry
- Long dark hair, held up with a comb
- Treated me like a person, not just her niece
- Listening to her old rock-and-roll records

Introductory Material	Body	Concluding Material
1. My aunt Alicia	**1.** Her mysterious apartment in the city	**2.** Treated me like a person, not just her niece
3. Her flashy jewelry	**3.** Listening to her old rock-and-roll records	**1.** One place in the world I felt at home
4. Her embroidered jeans jacket	**2.** Apartment filled with books and the little clay animals she found in Mexico	
2. Long dark hair, held up with a comb		

The following are some writing options to help you apply what you have learned.

1. Guided Assignment   Write several different topic sentences based on the collage shown below. Focus on aspects that intrigue you. You might consider individual figures, including the dog. Or you might pose a question about what is not shown in the collage, such as the stove that goes below the skillet. Or you might want to discuss colors, moods, and people's interior and exterior lives. Choose one topic sentence that you can develop into a paragraph with several supporting sentences. Then draft your paragraph.

PURPOSE   To proceed from drafting topic sentences to drafting a paragraph

AUDIENCE   Teacher and classmates

LENGTH   1 page

2. Open Assignment   For a school newsletter you are asked to supply one paragraph about a topic selected from the list given below, or a topic of your own choosing. Brainstorm to develop a list of details that support the topic you selected, and organize your details as suggested by the chart on the opposite page. Write three possible topic sentences. Choose one of the three topic sentences, and write a paragraph using the supporting details.

- what it's like to be the oldest (youngest, middle, only) child in a family
- the day I grew up overnight
- a family member who was important to me during my childhood

3. Cooperative Learning   In a small group brainstorm to create a list of statements that express the most common attitudes toward the elderly in U.S. society today. Ask one group member to write down the statements into topic sentences. Discuss possible supporting details for each one. Then have each group member write a paragraph using a different topic sentence. Put the paragraphs together to form a group essay. Have each person create his or her own version of the essay by writing a beginning and concluding paragraph for it.

Romare Bearden, *Blue Interior, Morning,* 1968

Drafting: Turning Prewriting into a Paragraph   **81**

Drafting: Writing Unified Paragraphs

Getting It Together

Does your family tell stories about a relative you never knew? Do you see any similarities between yourself and that relative? In Sandra Cisneros's book *The House on Mango Street*, a young woman named Esperanza relates some of the stories she's heard about her great-grandmother and thinks about her own life.

Literature Model

The narrator, Esperanza, uses details from her great-grandmother's life to support the selection's main idea.

My great-grandmother. I would've liked to have known her, a wild horse of a woman, so wild she wouldn't marry until my great-grandfather threw a sack over her head and carried her off. Just like that, as if she were a fancy chandelier. That's the way he did it.

And the story goes she never forgave him. She looked out the window all her life, the way so many women sit their sadness on an elbow. I wonder if she made the best with what she got or was she sorry because she couldn't be all the things she wanted to be. Esperanza. I have inherited her name, but I don't want to inherit her place by the window.

Sandra Cisneros, *The House on Mango Street*

Do you like the way Cisneros has delayed stating the main idea until the last line? Why or why not?

The literature model above is unified by a main idea: Esperanza has inherited her great-grandmother's name, but she does not want to inherit her fate. All sentences and details in the selection work together to support this main idea. This quality in a paragraph is called unity.

The Main Idea

Usually each paragraph has just one main idea. You can express that idea in a direct statement—that is, in a topic sentence. Or you can imply the main idea by suggesting it indirectly through your choice of supporting details.

Stated in a Topic Sentence There are several advantages to stating your main idea in a topic sentence. First, providing a clear statement of what the paragraph is about helps give your writing direction. Second, the sentence tells the reader what to focus on.

A topic sentence may appear anywhere in the paragraph. When a topic sentence appears at the beginning of a paragraph, it lets the reader know what's to come. When the topic sentence appears at the end, it summarizes the preceding supporting details and ensures that the reader has understood the main idea.

Implied   In some paragraphs, the main idea is only implied, or stated indirectly. This is often true of descriptive or narrative paragraphs. In such cases, the supporting details are so strongly linked by a main idea that this main idea shines through without having to be stated directly. Thus, a narrative writer might choose to describe a character's emotions rather than state, for example, "June Woo was happy to be home."

The Supporting Details

In a unified paragraph, each sentence provides one or more details that support the main idea. Supporting details include sensory details, examples or incidents, facts , statistics, and reasons. Your purpose in writing will help you determine which kinds of supporting details to use.

Sensory Details   Words that describe how things look, sound, smell, feel, or taste provide sensory details. Vivid sensory words draw your readers in and help them experience the scene or subject.

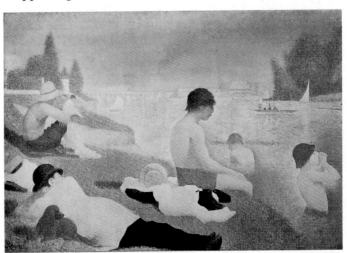

To develop sensory details, try to visualize the scene you are describing and think about each of the senses in turn. For example, how would you use sensory details to describe the scene in this painting? First think about what you would see, hear, smell, feel, and taste if you could step inside it. Then try to make the scene come alive for your readers.

Georges Pierre Seurat, *The Bathers at Asnières*, 1883–1884

Drafting: Writing Unified Paragraphs   **83**

Examples or Incidents   Sometimes you'll find that the best way to develop a main idea is through describing examples or incidents. Suppose you want to develop the main idea that "starting high school was one of the hardest things I've ever done." You might support this idea by telling about something that happened when you started high school. Then, to explore a specific incident, ask yourself *who, what, where, when, why,* and *how* questions.

Facts and Statistics   Sometimes facts and statistics are the best way to support a main idea. A fact is a statement that has been proved by observation, experience, or study—for example, "Washington, D.C., is the capital of the United States." Statistics are facts that involve numbers —for example, "The average American sees 300 ads a day."

Suppose you wanted to write a paragraph with the following topic sentence: "There's not enough free time in the average high school student's life." Here's how one student used a timeline to organize the facts and statistics that could help support this topic sentence.

Facts and Statistics Organized on a Timeline

Algebra: 25 word problems due tomorrow.	Track practice: 1 hour.		Eat dinner: 30 minutes. Then spend 30 minutes cleaning up, taking out the garbage.				Begin practicing lines for drama club play.
1 P.M. **2 P.M.** **3 P.M.**	**4 P.M.** **5 P.M.**	**6 P.M.**	**7 P.M.**	**8 P.M.**	**9 P.M.**		
English: essay assigned. Get 85% on quiz.	Go home. Take care of brother until Mom gets home in 1.5 hours.		Start homework.				

Reasons   If your topic sentence expresses an opinion or gives an explanation, you can back it up with reasons. Suppose you wanted to write a paragraph to support your opinion about the importance of equality in the home. Your topic sentence might be "Husbands and wives should undertake an equal share of the housework and child care." You might use a graphic organizer like the one below to help you develop and outline the reasons that support your topic sentence. You could even use the graphic organizer as an outline to help you draft your paragraph.

The notion that taking care of the home and children is "women's work" is sexist.

An equal relationship between parents presents a good model for their children.

Why should husbands and wives undertake an equal share of the housework and child care?

Spending more time together benefits both fathers and their children.

It is unfair to expect women employed outside the home to shoulder all of the domestic responsibilities as well.

The following are some writing options to help you apply what you have learned.

1. Guided Assignment   Psychologist Erik Erikson observed that young people are often more concerned with what others think of them than with what they think of themselves. Free-write for five minutes in response to this statement, focusing on coming up with observations and examples. Do your experiences support or contradict Erikson's assertion? Whose opinions matter to you? Your family's? Your peers'? Your teachers'? Your own? When are you most concerned with how you look or behave? Whose opinions seem to be important to those around you? Do your peers act and dress a certain way out of concern for how other people view them?

Once you have a response to Erikson's theory, draft it as a topic sentence. Use the examples you have identified in your freewriting to support your topic sentence as you develop it into a paragraph. Revise and edit your work, and if possible, share your conclusions with your peers by reading your paragraph aloud to the class.

PURPOSE   To use examples to support a topic sentence
AUDIENCE   Yourself and your peers
LENGTH   1 paragraph

2. Open Assignment   Choose one of the topic sentences below—or one of your own—and write a paragraph in which you support the topic with examples or incidents. Be sure to ask yourself *who, what, where, when, why,* and *how* questions to help you think of details about the examples or incidents.

- I learned something about my father (mother) this year.
- There are more people in my family than just those with my last name.
- My grandmother was a stubborn (shy, strong, forgiving, etc.) woman.

- My family isn't like the families I see on television and in the movies.

3. Science   A person using scientific method states a theory, or hypothesis, and then either proves or disproves by experimentation. You will be performing a simple experiment. Equally fill two glasses nearly to the top with water. Drop one paper clip at a time into one of the glasses and ten paper clips at a time into the other glass.

Compose a hypothesis as to how many paper clips you will have to drop into each glass before any water spills. Explain whether you think there will be a difference and why. Then conduct the experiment, counting the paper clips as you drop them into the water.

Take notes as you observe what happens. Was your hypothesis correct? Do the two glasses spill from the same number of paper clips? Why or why not? Might you have a new hypothesis to make based on your conclusions? Draft a paragraph, using your initial hypothesis as your topic sentence. Use your observations to support or refute your topic sentence. Include any reasons you can provide for your results.

COMPUTER OPTION

You might like to make a small chart based on your experiment from the exercise above. Use a drawing or charting program to create a bar graph, showing the number of paper clips you guessed would be needed to spill the water in each glass, as compared to the actual number of paper clips it took to spill the water. You may even be able to cut and paste the graph into your word processing program so that both the paragraph and the chart can be printed out on the same page. Go back and revise your paragraph so that you refer to the graph in your analysis of the experiment.

Drafting: Writing Unified Paragraphs   **85**

Drafting: Ordering the Details

Details, Details

When novelist Edward Hannibal begins working on a book, he draws "a train of linked boxes, beginning with the central event in the middle of the page, then building the Super Chief in both directions." Hannibal's Super Chief helps him organize his details in chronological order—the order in which the events occurred.

The computer screen below lists various methods of organizing supporting details and the most common purposes for which these methods are used. However, don't feel that you have to limit the organization of your writing to what is shown here.

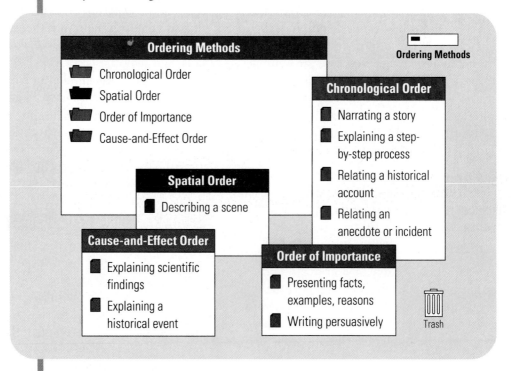

Chronological Order

Chronological order is one of the most common ways of organizing narrative writing. Notice how writer Jim Barnes uses chronological order—giving events in the order that they happened—to narrate the details of a frightening incident.

A deep, low moan—ghostly but unmistakably human—rolled up from the bowels of the black earth. There was for a moment, my brother recalls, a stillness like doom upon all of them. Then everybody was running, running. . . . A great shadow passed beside my brother. It was a horse. The moan persisted, even over the sound of thumping boots and racing hoofs. Now my brother passed the horse, and burst through the barbed wire fence at the edge of the field with one wild bound. He flung himself down the lane and plunged through the doorway of our house and hugged himself close to the dying coals in the fireplace. An hour passed before he began to cry.

Jim Barnes, *On Native Ground*

How many major events are signaled by transitions like "then," "now," and "an hour passed"?

Because the writer describes the action almost minute by minute, the reader feels drawn into the events.

Spatial Order

Spatial order is the order in which objects appear in a physical place. When you use spatial order, you may describe these items as they appear from left to right, from top to bottom, from back to front, or in any other logical combination. Clue your readers in on the relationships among items by using words like *above*, *below*, *behind*, and *next to*. Such clues will help them "see" the scene you are describing.

For example, if you wanted to describe the scene shown here, you might begin by identifying the chessboard in the middle of the room. From that starting point, you might go on to describe the two men on either side of the chessboard. Then you might move behind the men to the fireplace against the wall. Finally, you could describe the women on either side of the hearth.

Henri Matisse, *The Painter's Family*, 1911

• JOURNAL ACTIVITY •
Try It Out

Describe your favorite room using spatial ordering. Identify a starting point in the room and use words like *above* and *next to* clearly indicate the placement of each object in the room.

Order of Importance

When your supporting details are facts, statistics, incidents, or examples, you may want to organize them according to their importance. For example, if you want to make an immediate impact on your reader, start with your most important detail. If you want to leave your reader thinking about your strongest point, build up to the most important detail.

Cause-and-Effect Order

When you want to show that one event took place because of another, you can use cause-and-effect order. In a cause-and-effect paragraph, the topic sentence may state the cause and the supporting details identify the effects. Or the topic sentence may state the effect and the supporting details present the causes. This method works well whether you are writing about science, history, or even about yourself.

In the paragraph below, Ginger Lumpkin examines something that happened to her and the effects that event had on her life.

Student Model

The topic sentence prepares the reader for a cause-and-effect ordering of the supporting details.

A teacher who once doubted me ironically became a source of inspiration. In the seventh grade, I wrote a poem entitled "Lost on a Desert." After my teacher read my poem, she asked me who I had copied it from—she didn't believe that I had written it. Her remarks hurt me, but the experience made me feel determined to prove my creative writing abilities. As a result, I began to write a variety of poems, short stories, and plays, all of which my teacher praised. In the end, I not only showed my teacher that I could write well, but through my writing, I also gained a better understanding of myself.

How do these details support the topic sentence?

Ginger Lumpkin, Hyde Park Career Academy, Chicago, Illinois

The graphic below shows the cause-and-effect relationships presented in the paragraph. Note that most of the effects in turn act as causes.

I wrote a poem for my seventh-grade teacher.

My teacher read the poem but didn't believe I had written it.

Hurt but determined to prove my abilities, I continued to write.

The teacher liked my new work; I gained new self-knowledge.

Writer's Choice

The following are some writing options to help you apply what you have learned.

1. Guided Assignment Use the glazed ceramic bowl on this page as a source of details for a paragraph. Decide on a topic sentence, and then write your paragraph. For example, you might want to speculate on the relationship between the king and his attendant on the left and the petitioners on the right. Or you could describe the animals in relation to each other and to the people in the picture. Use chronological order, spatial order, order of importance, or cause-and-effect order to organize your supporting details.

> **PURPOSE** To order details about a work of art
>
> **AUDIENCE** Yourself and your teacher
>
> **LENGTH** 1 paragraph

Iranian glazed ceramic bowl, c. 1200

2. Open Assignment Imagine that you are writing a paragraph for a column in a teen magazine. You may use one of the topic sentences given below or one of your own choice. Use one of the ordering methods discussed in this lesson to organize your details.

- Parents and children will never see eye to eye on certain subjects.
- The house where I grew up holds very special memories for me.
- Ending high school is really only a beginning.

3. Social Studies You have been assigned by your social studies teacher to write three or four paragraphs on the American family today.

You are asked to answer one of the following questions:

- What constitutes a family today?
- What are the responsibilities of family members to one another?
- How have family roles changed? Are there any definable roles? Should there be? Why or why not?

Use one of the organizing methods discussed in this lesson to order your details. After you have drafted your paragraphs, exchange papers with a classmate for peer editing. Use the comments of your peer editor to finalize your paper.

Drafting: Writing Coherent Paragraphs

Building a Better Paragraph

"A novel is a piece of architecture. . . . It's a building—it has to have walls and floors and the bathrooms have to work." That's how author John Irving describes it anyway.

But how does a writer build a piece of writing? What holds the sentences together and keeps the building standing? Transitions, repeated words, synonyms, and pronouns are the "glue" or "mortar" you can use to link your sentences and build a better paragraph.

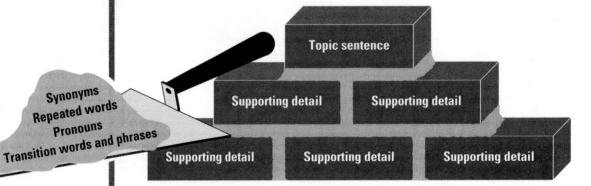

Synonyms
Repeated words
Pronouns
Transition words and phrases

Topic sentence

Supporting detail   Supporting detail

Supporting detail   Supporting detail   Supporting detail

As you write, you want to build paragraphs that are both unified and coherent. In a unified paragraph, each of the sentences supports the topic sentence or main idea. In a coherent paragraph, all the sentences are clearly and logically connected to one another. You can use the following checklist to help make sure your paragraphs are coherent.

Checklist for Writing Coherently
1. Are all the sentences linked clearly and logically to one another?
2. Can I repeat any words to help show the connections between ideas?
3. Have I used synonyms that my readers will be able to understand?
4. Does each pronoun refer back to some antecedent noun?
5. Are there any transitions I can use to link the sentences better?

Using Transition Words and Phrases

Transitions—words or phrases that show relationships between ideas—can help you write coherent paragraphs. Transitions create logical links between sentences in a paragraph and help the reader follow your train of thought. The chart below shows some common transitions.

Transitions			
Kinds	**Examples**		
Time	after first	before meanwhile	finally then	next when
Place	above below	beside here	next to near	there opposite
Importance	first primary	second mainly	more important	most important
Cause and effect	as a result so	consequently therefore	for that reason	because
Comparison and contrast	although similarly	in contrast however	on the other hand like	in the same way unlike
Example	for example together with	for instance along with	namely likewise	that is

You can also use transitions to link paragraphs in a longer piece of writing such as an essay. An essay consists of an introductory paragraph, body paragraphs, and a conclusion. Transitions such as *first, second,* and *most important* can help readers understand the relative importance of each paragraph in the body. Other transitions clue the reader in on different relationships between body paragraphs. Transitions such as *finally* and *therefore* often create a successful link to the concluding paragraph.

• JOURNAL ACTIVITY •
Try It Out

Look through your journal, and select a paragraph you have developed in a draft. Then use the list of questions on page 90 to make sure the paragraph is coherent. Insert transitions listed in the chart above to create links between your sentences.

Using Repetitions and Synonyms

Another way to link sentences is to repeat the same word from sentence to sentence. But be careful: too much repetition will bore your readers. One way to check your writing is to read it aloud. If you hear the same word too often, it's probably time to look for a new one.

One way to avoid too much repetition is to use synonyms—words that have similar meanings. Synonyms can lend interest and freshness to your writing. Keep your audience in mind, however. Unfamiliar synonyms may make your ideas more difficult to follow.

In the paragraph below, N. Scott Momaday repeats words and phrases and uses synonyms to link his sentences.

Literature Model

My grandmother lived in a house near the place where Rainy Mountain Creek runs into the Washita River. Once there was a lot of sound in the house, a lot of coming and going, feasting and talk. The summers there were full of excitement and reunion. The Kiowas are a summer people; they abide the cold and keep to themselves, but when the season turns and the land becomes warm and vital they cannot hold still; an old love of going returns upon them. The old people have a fine sense of pageantry and a wonderful notion of decorum. The aged visitors who came to my grandmother's house when I was a child were men of immense character, full of wisdom and disdain. They dealt in a kind of infallible quiet and gave but one face away; it was enough. They were made of lean and leather, and they bore themselves upright. They wore great black hats and bright ample shirts that shook in the wind. They rubbed fat upon their hair and wound their braids with strips of colored cloth. Some of them painted their faces and carried the scars of old and cherished enmities. They were an old council of war lords, come to remind and be reminded of who they were.

N. Scott Momaday, *House Made of Dawn*

Repetition of words such as "they" and "there" helps link sentences.

What effect does the use of synonyms have?

Effective repetition of "they" results in parallel structure.

Using Pronouns

You can also substitute pronouns for a word, a group of words, or an idea that appears in a preceding sentence. Pronouns can help you avoid the boring repetition of specific nouns. Note the use of pronouns in the literature model above. As an experiment, mentally substitute nouns for the pronouns. How does the selection sound?

The following are some writing options to help you apply what you have learned.

1. Guided Assignment   You have been asked to write about Amy Tan for a column on writers in a magazine for teen-agers. Select from the following details about Tan's life to draft your paragraph. Check your use of pronouns and transition words in maintaining coherence.

- Childhood: Wanted to be an artist, but winning an essay contest at the age of eight inspired her to write; her parents didn't encourage her in this pursuit
- Father: Baptist minister; died when Tan was a teen-ager
- Mother: Chinese immigrant; introduced Tan to her Chinese heritage
- Early career: Received an education in English and linguistics; spent four years working with disabled children; next became a copywriter and free-lance writer; then decided to devote herself full time to writing fiction
- Now: Has published two successful novels and started research for a third book

PURPOSE To write a coherent paragraph about a writer
AUDIENCE Teen-age readers
LENGTH 1 paragraph

2. Open Assignment   Your class is preparing a booklet introducing the ninth-grade class to the rest of the school. Your assignment is to write a paragraph about the ways your ethnicity defines you or enriches you or about something else that defines who you are. Use the tools that were discussed in this lesson to keep your writing coherent.

3. Art   The painting below is the work of Aaron Douglas, one of the foremost artists of the Harlem Renaissance. Douglas liked most to work with images of people of African descent. What might this painting be saying about the creation of huge historically significant structures? Why title it as he did? Why also do you suppose Douglas included the smaller structure in the lower left-hand corner? Write a paragraph that expresses what you feel this painting is trying to convey. Use repetition to keep your paragraph strong and coherent. Remember to employ synonyms where excess repetition threatens to make your work boring.

Aaron Douglas, *Building More Stately Mansions*, 1944

Drafting: Writing Coherent Paragraphs   **93**

Revising: Improving Paragraphs

Getting the Words Right

Sometimes you don't get the words quite right the first time. For instance, it may have taken General MacArthur several tries before he came up with his memorable farewell line: "I shall return."

Even professional writers don't always get the words right the first time they try. For example, novelist Ernest Hemingway rewrote the ending to *A Farewell to Arms* thirty-nine times. "What had you stumped?" asked an interviewer. "Getting the words right," answered Hemingway.

Like Hemingway you'll want to get the words right. That's where revising comes in. Revising is the stage of the writing process in which you improve your first draft. You evaluate your work, perhaps ask others for comments, and then rewrite your draft to solve any problems.

March 16, 1942: The night before he leaves the Philippines, Gen. MacArthur works on his farewell address.

Reading Over Your Work

One useful strategy for revising is to break the process down into three parts—three different readings of your work. During the first reading, you go through the draft quickly to check for meaning. You make sure that the main idea is clear and that you've provided plenty of details to support it. During the second reading, you go a bit slower and check for unity. You make sure that the supporting details are organized logically and that they all support the main idea. During the third reading, you read more closely, revising line by line for coherence. You make sure that the sentences flow and that you have chosen words that clearly communicate your meaning.

As you revise, you may learn something new about your piece of writing. You may clarify its meaning, find a way to say it more effectively, or even discover entirely new ideas. It can be fun and satisfying to see a piece of writing take shape. As writer Donald Murray puts it, revising can give a writer "the satisfaction of craft, the feeling we have when we lean our weight into the corner and make our bicycle swing gracefully where we want it to go."

Checking for Meaning

After you finish your first draft, set it aside for a few hours or even a few days. Then when you pick it up to revise it, you'll see it with fresh eyes. You'll read it more the way your readers will.

Read it through once quickly and jot down notes or ideas in the margins. Don't worry about word choices, grammar, spelling, or punctuation. Use the following checklist to help you focus on the big picture—the meaning.

Meaning Checklist
1. Have I presented the main idea clearly? What is the main idea? (Hint: If you cannot easily answer the question after reading your writing, chances are you have not presented it clearly enough.)
2. Have I achieved my purpose through my writing?
3. Who is my audience? Have I written this piece with their needs in mind?
4. Do I need to give my readers more information?

If you have trouble answering any of these questions, you may need to return to the prewriting or drafting stages to rework your ideas. Don't be discouraged. Going back and forth between the stages is part of the writing process. Even writers like Joan Didion rework their ideas: "My writing is a process of rewriting, of going back and changing and filling in. In the rewriting process you discover what's going on."

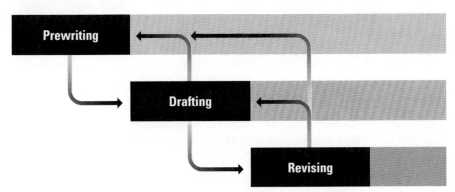

Prewriting

Drafting

Revising

• JOURNAL ACTIVITY •
Think It Through

Suppose you have used the Meaning Checklist to review a paragraph you have written and you discover that its content is too difficult for your intended audience. What prewriting or drafting techniques might help you rework your paragraph?

Checking for Unity

Now read through your draft a second time, focusing on organization and unity. Read relatively quickly and make brief notes in the margins. Refer to the following checklist as you read.

Unity Checklist
1. Does every detail I have selected support the main idea?
2. Have I organized the supporting details in the most logical way?
3. Have I included any sentences that are unnecessary because they simply restate the main point without adding any new information or meaning?
4. Have I made the relationships between my ideas clear?

One way to check for unity is to outline your main idea and supporting details. If some details don't support your main idea, throw them out.

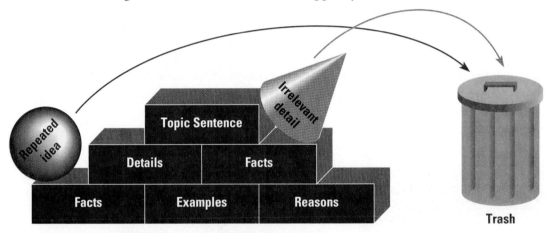

Checking for Coherence

Finally, read your draft a third time. Read more slowly now, line by line, to make sure that your writing is coherent. Check that all sentences are clearly and logically linked to one another. Make sure, too, that you've chosen the best possible words to communicate your meaning. Try reading your draft aloud. If you stumble over some words or lose your place in the middle of a sentence, you've probably identified some trouble spots in your writing. Use this checklist as you read.

Coherence Checklist
1. Have I written sentences that flow logically and clearly?
2. Would repeated words, pronouns, synonyms, or transitions improve the flow of my writing?
3. Have I made appropriate word choices?
4. Have I used specific nouns and active verbs?
5. Have I deleted all unnecessary words?

Writer's Choice

The following are some writing options to help you apply what you have learned.

1. Guided Assignment   Revise the following paragraphs, using the checklists on pages 95 and 96 to help you identify problems. After writing out the revised version, let it sit for twenty-four hours. Reread for any additional revisions. Mark the changes on your copy.

Against all odds, Venus Ebonistarr Williams is on her way to becoming a tennis star. In 1991, when she was just ten years old, she was ranked number one in southern California in the girls' 12-and-under division. This is one of the toughest divisions in the country. Venus is a really excellent player.

Venus lives in a poor neighborhood in Compton, California, near Los Angeles. The tennis courts where Venus practices are sometimes the scene of gang warfare. Venus has had to learn how to drop to the ground in the middle of a game and get away from the crossfire. It hasn't been easy, though.

Venus's father, Richard, coaches her. Her mother is a nurse. Her father taught himself to play tennis by reading books, watching videos, and practicing. Her entire family, including her mother and four sisters, plays tennis.

Venus's father has great faith in his daughter's ability. Venus also hopes to become an astronaut someday. Every day her father takes her to the local tennis courts and gives her lessons in tennis. Since Venus was seven years old, her father has kept a journal of the important events in her life. Many tennis coaches and pros think this young tennis player will one day be a major star.

PURPOSE   To revise an existing passage
AUDIENCE   Yourself and your teacher
LENGTH   4 paragraphs

2. Open Assignment   Write a paragraph about one of the following topics or one of your own. Then use the checklists presented in this lesson to revise your paragraph for meaning, unity, and coherence.

- your earliest memory
- how to survive ninth grade
- an imaginary ancestor
- your first experience speaking before a group

3. Social Studies   For a class project you are helping to compile a paper describing family life styles in different cultures. Use the checklists presented in this lesson to help you evaluate the following paragraph about families in the Minangkabau culture of western Sumatra in Indonesia. Then, on a separate piece of paper, revise the paragraph.

Minangkabau society is matrilineal. All inherited property and family names are handed down from mother to daughter. Most Minangkabau are rice farmers. The grandmother is the most powerful member of the family. Children are given the name of their mother's family. All the descendants of one grandmother live together in one big house. Up to thirty family members live in one house. A woman marries and the husband moves in with his wife's family.

COMPUTER OPTION

Many word-processing programs have a Search (or Find) and Replace feature that can help you correct mistakes quickly and easily. Suppose you realize that you've misspelled the name *Minangkabau* over and over in your paper. Using Search and Replace you can tell your PC to find every use of the name and to correct the spelling.

Editing: Checking Words and Sentences

Editor Catches Dangling Modifier

COMPLAINTS ABOUT NBA REFEREES GROWING UGLY

It is bad manners to break your bread and roll in your soup.

Plunging 1,000 feet into the gorge, we saw Yosemite Falls.

GRANDMOTHER OF EIGHT MAKES HOLE IN ONE

TUNA BITING OFF WASHINGTON COAST

No bear feet allowed.

Imagine how embarrassed you'd be if you were the one who let these headlines and sentences get by. Mistakes slip into everyone's writing, but careful editing can help you catch and correct many of them. Can you spot the headlines above that contain modifiers?

When you edit, you make sure that you've used words correctly. You also check your writing for errors in grammar, word usage, punctuation, capitalization, and spelling. The goal of editing, like the other stages in the writing process, is to communicate your ideas clearly to your readers.

Editing Your Draft for Sense

When you edit for sense, you make sure that your words and sentences say what you want them to say. You make sure that your sentences make sense and your words are right. Use the following checklist to help identify and correct errors in your writing.

Editing Checklist

Question	Example
1. Are all words used correctly?	She could ~~of~~ *have* waited.
2. Do subjects and verbs agree?	Each of my brothers drive*s* a truck.
3. Are verb tenses correct?	If you wanted it, you should ~~say~~ *have said* so.
4. Are pronoun references clear and correct?	~~Ann~~ *The* called her mother every day, *W*hen ~~she~~ *Ann* was away at camp.
5. Have I corrected all run-ons and fragments?	She turned on the radio*, but* she heard only static. ~~W~~hich was annoying.

Self-Editing To edit your own writing, you need to approach your work objectively and critically. Reading your work aloud is crucial. Note the changes Rachelle Netkow chose to make.

Student Model

My family is *a* typical ~~of a~~ family *of* ~~in~~ the 1990s. Both of my parents work, which means many of the household responsibiliti*e*s are left to my brother and ~~I~~ *me*. We do them, of course, even though we don't like ~~it~~ *the extra work*. Since *everyone in* my family is busy with *various* activities, it is unusual for all of us to be home at the same time. ~~But~~ *O*ccasionally though, we try to do special things *together*. My family is very close even if we don't see each other ~~all that~~ *very* often.

Rachelle Netkow, Centennial High School, Pueblo, Colorado

Change makes pronoun reference grammatically correct.

Why did Rachelle add "everyone in" here?

• JOURNAL ACTIVITY •
Think It Through

How can you make sure that your changes in one sentence do not alter the meaning of the following sentence? Write down a few general tips that will help you edit any writing project.

Peer Editing   As a peer editor, focus on the ideas and organization of a piece of writing rather than on its grammar and mechanics. Be honest, but respect the writer's feelings. Identify strengths as well as weaknesses. Offer suggestions for improvement, not just criticisms. For example, note the peer editor's comments on the paragraph below.

> *Avoid repetition of pronouns.*
>
> *Good transition!*
>
> *Expand — tell us what she talked about.*
>
> *Rearrange sentences.*
>
>   Last fall, my family drove my older sister Shana to college. It was her freshman year, and even though she didn't say so, I could tell ~~she~~ *Shana* was scared and sad to leave home. <u>For one thing</u>, she talked more during the drive than she has for the past three years. She didn't even yell at me when I helped carry her stereo equipment to her room. Normally, ~~She~~ *Shana* has a fit if I so much as touch one of her records. It really was a day full of surprises. When it was time to go, she even hugged me.

Marking Your Draft

Once you've edited the structure and wording of your draft, you're ready to proofread. Proofreading is reading closely to find errors in spelling, punctuation, and capitalization. For marking corrections, use a set of basic proofreading symbols. The chart below shows a few.

Proofreading Marks		
Mark	**Meaning**	**Example**
∧	Insert	My granmother is eighty-six years old.
✗	Delete	She grew up on a dairry farm.
#	Insert space	She milkedcows every morning.
◡	Close up space	She fed the chickens in the barn yard.
≡	Capitalize	times have changed.
/	Make lower case	Machines now do the Milking.
⟳ sp	Check spelling	Chickens are fed automatically.
⁀	Switch order	Modern farms are like more factories.
¶	New paragraph	Last year I returned to the farm.

Writer's Choice

The following are some writing options to help you apply what you have learned.

1. Guided Assignment   Imagine you are an editor for the school newspaper. The following draft paragraph was submitted to you by a rookie reporter. Use the editing checklist presented in this lesson to determine what changes should be made. Incorporate your corrections and write out a clean, finished copy of the paragraph for publication.

Actor Lou Diamond Phillips has very multicultural roots. He is part native American, Filipino, Hawaiian, Scotch-Irish, and Hispanic. He was born in the phillipines, but grew up in Corpus Christie, Texas. There, for the first time, Phillips faces racial discrimination because of his brown skin. It hurt him, he survived. He graduated from the University of Texas drama department. His first big break as an actor came. When he was choosen to play the part of 1950s Hispanic rock star Richie Valens in the hit movie, La Bamba. Recently Phillips decided to learn more about his native American roots. He was inducted into the Sioux nation. and given a sioux name, Starkeeper.

PURPOSE   To edit a paragraph for the school paper
AUDIENCE   Readers of the school paper
LENGTH   1 paragraph

2. Open Assignment   Choose a paragraph or two you have written or are currently writing for another class. The paragraphs may be part of a larger essay. Proofread the paragraphs for errors, using the proofreading marks shown on page 100. Use a dictionary to check your spelling. Read the paragraphs aloud to ensure they make sense. Then rewrite the paragraphs, incorporating the changes you have marked.

3. Foreign Languages   The most difficult task in translating from a foreign language is getting the translation to convey the meaning and flavor of the original. Find a paragraph in your foreign language textbook, and translate it into English. Use a translation dictionary to help you identify words. Get help from a language teacher if you are having trouble. Once you are done translating the words, look at the paragraph. You will probably find errors in word order, word choice, noun-verb agreement, and pronoun reference. Edit the paragraph so that it makes sense in English, and write out a clean, finished copy.

4. Cooperative Learning   Find as many newspaper or magazine articles as you can about a celebrity you admire. In what city did the person grow up? What can you discover about this celebrity's heritage? Summarize in a single paragraph what you discover about the person's cultural and family background.

Then, in a small group, trade papers with a peer, and give comments with regard to content, unity, and coherence. Revise your paper, and trade with a different group member. This time check each other's papers for grammar, spelling, punctuation, and capitalization.

COMPUTER OPTION

The spell-checker in your word-processing program will most likely identify your name as an error every time you check a document for spelling. Try adding your first and last name into your computer's spelling dictionary. The spell-checker may offer you the option of doing so whenever it identifies an error. Otherwise, consult your manual to discover how to add new words to the spelling dictionary. Once the computer recognizes your name, you can concentrate on the real spelling and typographical mistakes you have made.

Going Public

What will you do with your writing? Toss it in the trash after a quick look at the grade? Think again. You've worked long and hard on it. In fact, you're rather proud of it. Why not share it with others?

Cain Claxton wrote the following for the sports section of his school newspaper, the *Peninsula Outlook*. A school newspaper is just one of the many places, or forums, in which you can present your writing.

---

10 SPORTS

The Peninsula Outlook November 20, 1990

Forever a Seahawk: Erstwhile PHS football great shines with Seattle Seahawks

by Cain Claxton

Twelve years have passed since Paul Skansi played split end for Peninsula High School.

Since Skansi played football in high school, he has gone on to play the sport for the University of Washington Huskies, the Pittsburgh Steelers, and the Seattle Seahawks. Along the way he impressed many people: his coaches, his friends and relatives, and even people who have never met him.

"In the sixth grade you could see that he was a blue chipper," Key Peninsula Middle School teacher John Leverett said. Leverett, who taught Skansi in the sixth grade at Goodman Middle School, threw passes to him before any professional quarterbacks did.

"That was one of the funnest years I've had growing up," Skansi said, adding that Leverett "was a teacher that I'll never forget. We did a lot of math, a lot of social studies, and played a lot of football."

Skansi's small size worried his parents, Nick and Patti Skansi. They were concerned that he might get injured playing against larger players. They didn't let Skansi play his freshman and sophomore years, and were reluctant to let him play his junior year.

"He was engaged in all the other athletic events

Photos courtesy of Corry Trewin (Seattle Seahawks)
CATCH AND CELEBRATION—Seattle Seahawk Paul Skansi (#82) in the end zone after catching the game-tying touchdown pass from teammate Dave Krieg between Kansas City Chief players Pearson (#24) and Martin (#57). Seahawk John L. Williams (#32) looks on. After Seahawk kicker Norm Johnson lifted Seattle over the Chiefs, 17-16, Skansi and Krieg (#17) revel over the come-from-behind win.

that were offered," Skansi's father said. "I just thought that was enough."

When Skansi finally got a chance to play his junior year, 1977, former Head Football Coach Larry Lunke, now coaching Anacortes High School, already had Mike Bos, a star receiver in his senior year. Lunke needed Skansi to play in other areas and placed him at

---

Skansi's Collegiate Records

Paul Skansi

Bowl Play...   1978

Written Presentations

At any point in the writing process, you can begin thinking about how to present your work. However, presentation often depends on your particular audience. As a result, you may want to begin thinking during the prewriting stage about where you'd like your writing to appear. You have many options for presenting your work to others: at school, in your community, and in the wider world.

School Forums   The diagram below shows some of the presenting options that may be available at your school. Often, the nature of your writing project will help determine its forum. For example, a short story or poem might be ideal for a class anthology. A movie review might appear in a school newspaper.

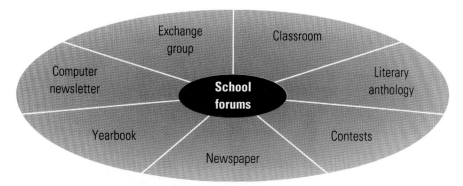

Community Forums   If you'd like to reach a wider audience, find out what's being published in your community. Community newspapers may print feature stories about local people and events. Community groups, too, may publish newsletters that accept student work.

Contests   Magazines, such as *Redbook*, *Seventeen*, and *Merlyn's Pen*, and organizations, such as the National Council of Teachers of English, often sponsor writing contests. The winners may receive prizes and have their work published.

• JOURNAL ACTIVITY •
Think It Through

In your journal, create a diagram like the one shown on this page. Put a check mark next to each of the school forums in which you currently present your work. Then circle those you would like to submit your work to. Find out more about each new forum you have circled. For example, if you've always wanted to write for the school newspaper, find out how to submit a piece for publication.

Open-Market Forums If you've got your sights set on an even wider audience, you might try the big time—writing for the open market. If you're interested in writing for periodicals, you might target magazines aimed at teen-agers, such as *Seventeen*, *Sassy*, or *'Teen*. Or you might choose special-interest magazines, such as *Bicycling* or *American Photo*.

You can start with something you've already written and try to find a market for it. Or you can find a magazine first and then write a piece for that publication. Either way, you'll need a reference book, such as the *Writer's Market*. The *Market Guide for Young Writers* lists publications that accept material from young writers. The guide describes the type of material each publication accepts and explains how to prepare a manuscript for submission. It also tells about writing contests.

The first paragraph lists the name of the publication, the publisher's name and address, and a description of the publication and its audience.

* **PURPLE COW,** Signa Publications, 3423 Piedmont Road N.E., Ivy Place Suite 320, Atlanta, GA 30305. Monthly tabloid (ten issues) covering any subject of interest to 13 to 18 year olds.

The second paragraph describes the type of material published.

Publishes: General articles of interest to teens; book, movie, and record reviews; humor; interview/profile; sports (general and anecdotal—no "How to Play Soccer"); personal experience: coping with problems (drugs, sex, etc.); and seasonal interest material.

The third paragraph explains how to submit material. Note that "SASE" stands for "self-addressed stamped envelope."

Submission Info: All manuscripts must be typed and accompanied by SASE. Articles should be 500–3,000 words. Pays $5–$40. Maximum length for fillers is 150 words. Pays $5–$10 for fillers and photos. Send complete manuscript or query with published clips of published work. Buys one-time rights. Submit seasonal and holiday material three months in advance. Simultaneous, photocopied, and previously published submissions are okay. Sample copy $1. Pays on acceptance. Address to: Margaret Anthony, Editor.

Oral Presentations

You can also present your work orally. The most common forum is the classroom, where you may give an oral report or your teacher may read your writing aloud. A high school drama club may perform a play written by a student. You may present a speech or a story as part of a competitive speech tournament. You may even videotape your presentation. A school or community radio station may also welcome student work.

The following are some writing options to help you apply what you have learned.

1. Guided Assignment For each of the following pieces of writing, suggest three possible forums for presentation. Keep in mind that presentations may be written or oral. Consider school, community, contest, and open-market forums. If possible, look for ideas in *Writer's Market*, the *Market Guide for Young Writers*, or any other sources you can locate at the library. Then, explain what you would have to do to present one of the pieces of writing listed here in a forum you proposed.

- a poem about winter
- an account of an overnight bicycling trip
- an essay on freedom
- a science-fiction story
- a play about an immigrant family
- a news article about a local photography or art exhibit

PURPOSE To explore possible forums for presentation
AUDIENCE Yourself
LENGTH A list of eighteen forums

2. Open Assignment Write a letter responding to something you have read in one of the publications below, or another you choose. Carefully draft, revise, and edit your letter so that your point is clearly stated. Then send your letter to the publication. The mailing address for letters should be printed in the publication. Ask a teacher for help if you have trouble finding it.

- your school or city newspaper
- a rock music magazine
- a weekly news periodical
- a celebrity fan magazine
- a comic book
- a science magazine

3. Civics Research to find new ways your student government might contribute to making your school or the surrounding community more environmentally friendly. Perhaps you'll want to suggest a recycling program for plastic bottles, or you may wish to consider starting a student tree-planting program. Write a short speech that you could deliver to your student government in which you state your proposal. Be sure to include specific ideas for how the students at your school could make your proposal work. Then, if you are feeling enthusiastic, talk to your class representative to find out how to actually present your speech before the student council.

4. Cooperative Learning Write a two- or three-minute skit about a generation gap between two characters. Then, in a group, give copies of your script to two people. Do not direct them. Listen as they read your skit aloud to the group. Talk about each script after you read it. Try to focus on the writing, instead of the performance of the readers, as you discuss each script. Make any revisions to your skit you think are appropriate. Meet in the group again to read and discuss the revised scripts. If your group has one or two favorite skits, talk to your teacher about performing them for the entire class.

COMPUTER OPTION

When reading a play script, you may have noticed that the stage directions are typically in italic type. When stage directions are visually distinguished, a reader can better focus on the dialogue. If you include instructions for action, costumes, or props in your skit, use your word processor to italicize the type. Your actors and anyone who reads your script will be able to follow it more easily.

Writing About Literature
Explaining Theme

What's It All About?

Have you ever read a piece of literature that seemed to speak directly to you? Did you ever identify so strongly with a character that you felt as if you were reading your own thoughts? Did you ever feel as if you were seeing your own life unfold on the page?

If so, you may want to use the stages in the writing process to help you analyze and clarify your understanding of a piece of literature. In the brief essay below, Tad Burton discusses a poem by Louise Erdrich entitled "Indian Boarding School." Erdrich's poem is about the situation of a group of Native American girls at a boarding school, but it is also about something more. What is the main idea of Tad's essay? What details does he present to support the main idea?

Student Model

Tad states the main idea in his topic sentence: freedom does not depend upon physical restrictions but is a state of mind.

Tad uses specific details as well as lines from the poem to support his main idea.

How does Tad broaden his theme? How does he link this theme to his original one?

In Louise Erdrich's poem "Indian Boarding School," the poet suggests that freedom is a state of mind. Although the Native American girls who live in the boarding school are subjected to physical abuse and are forced to deny their heritage, their will is not crushed. The girls imagine what a real home would be like and visit it in their dreams. In addition, even though they really have no chance to escape from their captors, some of the boarding school's inmates feel free when they hide out for a brief time in the enclosed boxcar of a train.

The idea that freedom is in one's mind is also extended to encompass a broader scope. In the last line of the poem, speaking about "the old injuries of the past," Erdrich compares the girls' situation with the experience of the Native American people at the hands of the early settlers. Like the girls in the school, the Native Americans underwent much suffering. They were taken away from their homes and placed on reservations. Nonetheless, the poet believes that the Native American people ultimately remained free because no one could manipulate their thoughts.

Tad Burton, Rangeview High School, Aurora, Colorado

Identifying a Theme

When you write an analysis of a piece of literature, you first identify a theme, or underlying meaning, in the work. In the student model on the preceding page, Tad identified a theme in the Erdrich poem—the meaning of freedom—and used that theme to analyze the piece.

What Is a Theme?   A theme is a generalization about life or human nature that the writer communicates through the piece of literature. For example, one theme in the novel *To Kill a Mockingbird* by Harper Lee is that prejudice often leads to injustice. One of the themes in Shakespeare's play *Macbeth* is that evil eventually destroys the evildoer.

How Do You Identify Themes?   To discover a theme in a piece of literature, you need to see what messages the writer is trying to communicate. One way to discover a theme is to use prewriting techniques, such as freewriting. You might begin with the line "What [title of work] tells me" and freewrite for five minutes. You might also try brainstorming to close in on a theme. In a small group, take turns completing the following: "I think one of the author's messages is . . . ." Discuss each group member's answer.

Freewriting

What <u>Romeo and Juliet</u> tells me is that love can spring up in the most unlikely circumstances, that love can triumph over hate, that love and hate are closely related, that strong emotions can lead to violent ends.

Brainstorming

Maria: I think one of Shakespeare's messages is that hatred can destroy lives.
Jamal: I think one of Shakespeare's messages is that even though hatred can destroy lives, love can triumph over hatred.

• JOURNAL ACTIVITY •
Think It Through

What other strategies—besides the freewriting and brainstorming techniques described above—might you use for discovering the themes in a piece of literature? Write down your ideas in your journal.

Supporting a Theme

Once you have identified a theme, you need to look for details from the piece of literature that reflect or support that theme. You need to provide evidence to convince your readers that the message you have discovered is indeed one that the author was trying to convey.

The basic elements of any piece of narrative literature are character, setting, and plot. Use prewriting techniques to examine each of these elements as you seek evidence to support your analysis. Your evidence may include quotations, descriptions, summaries of key events, and explanations of passages in the text.

Characters   To support your analysis of a theme, study the characters' physical descriptions, thoughts, actions, words, and relationships with other characters. Suppose you want to show that one of Shakespeare's themes in *Romeo and Juliet* is that love can triumph over hate. In that case, you might describe Romeo's impulsive behavior at the masked ball, where he falls in love with Juliet, the daughter of his sworn enemies, the Capulets. Despite her family, he vows to pursue her.

Setting   The setting—time of day, place, mood, and other details—can also help develop a theme. Try to determine what message the author is conveying through the choice of setting. For example, Romeo and Juliet first meet at a masked ball. Perhaps, in choosing this setting, Shakespeare is saying something about the senselessness of a feud based only on appearances and one's last name.

Plot   The plot—the sequence of events in the story being told—can also reveal the theme. Generally the plot begins with a central conflict and develops it to its climax and resolution. Romeo and Juliet's meeting at the ball triggers the central conflict—that is, the conflict between their love and the hatred between their families.

A scene from the movie *Romeo and Juliet*

Writing About a Theme

Once you have identified a theme and have gathered the details to support it, you're ready to draft your paragraph. Like any other paragraph you write, your analysis should be unified and coherent. Generally you will want to state the theme in your topic sentence and then present the supporting details in a logical order—perhaps in order of importance. As you revise your work, be sure to use transitions to help the reader understand relationships between ideas.

The following are some writing options to help you apply what you have learned.

1. Guided Assignment   Freewrite to help you identify a theme in the following poem.

If There Be Sorrow

If there be sorrow
let it be
for things undone
undreamed
    unrealized
       unattained

to these add one:
love withheld
    restrained

    Mari Evans

State the theme you discover in the form of a topic sentence. From that central idea, draft a paragraph analyzing and exploring the poem's theme. Use examples from the poem or from your own experience as supporting details for your topic sentence.

PURPOSE   To explain a poem's theme
AUDIENCE   Your teacher
LENGTH   1 paragraph

2. Open Assignment   Choose one of the following pieces of literature or another one with which you are familiar. Freewrite for five minutes to try to discover a theme that you can then write about in a paragraph. Use quotations, descriptions, and summaries of events in the story to support your analysis.

- *The Odyssey* by Homer
- *The Old Man and the Sea* by Ernest Hemingway
- *The Call of the Wild* by Jack London
- *The Joy Luck Club* by Amy Tan

3. Art   What details attract your interest or attention in the painting at left? Do the bright colors and sunny images spark any memories in you? Freewrite or use a cluster map to help you identify a theme in the painting. Remember that theme has to do with what a piece of art is able to communicate to you. Although they are not explicit, elements of character, setting, and plot are given in the painting. Use details from the painting and from your response to it to support a paragraph or two about the painting's theme.

Beatrice Whitney Van Ness, *Summer's Sunlight*, c. 1936

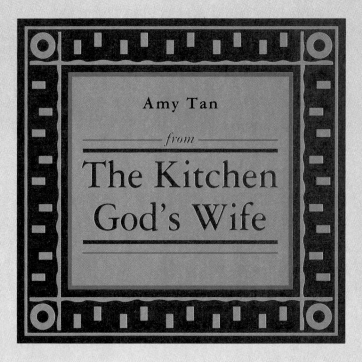

Amy Tan

from

The Kitchen God's Wife

Amy Tan uses incidents from her own family history as the raw material of her writing process. In her books The Joy Luck Club *and* The Kitchen God's Wife, *Tan, who was born of Chinese parents in the United States, explores her Chinese heritage. Notice that the following selection depicts four generations of a Chinese-American family—from Grand Auntie Du to Pearl's three-year-old daughter, Cleo. As this selection opens, Pearl and her husband Phil have just brought Pearl's mother home after a weekend visit with them. Then they drive off, but they return because their two children need to use the bathroom.*

My mother is standing outside the house when we return. "I tried to chase you, but you were too fast," she says as soon as I get out of the car. "And then I knew you would remember and come back." Tessa and Cleo are already racing up the stairs.

"Remember what?"

"Grand Auntie's farewell gift. Remember? Two three days ago I told you not to forget. Yesterday I said, Don't forget. You forgot?"

"No, no," I say. "Where is it?"

"In back, in the laundry room," she says. "Very heavy, though. Better ask your husband to carry it." I can just imagine what it must be: the old vinyl ottoman Grand Auntie used to rest her feet on, or perhaps the set of chip-proof Melmac dishes. As we wait for Phil to come back with the girls, my mother hands me a cup of tea, waving off my protests. "Already made. If you can't drink it, I only have to throw it away."

I take a few quick sips. "This is really good." And I mean it. I have never tasted tea like this. It is smooth, pungent, and instantly addicting.

"This is from Grand Auntie," my mother explains. "A few years ago she bought it for herself. One hundred dollars a pound."

Tomie Arai, *Laundryman's Daughter*, 1988

"You're kidding." I take another sip. It tastes even better.

"She told me, 'If I buy myself the cheap tea, then I am saying my whole life has not been worth something better.' So she decided to buy herself the best tea, so she could drink it and feel like a rich person inside."

I laugh.

My mother looks encouraged by my laughter. "But then she thought, If I buy just a little, then I am saying my lifetime is almost over. So she bought enough tea for another lifetime. Three pounds! Can you imagine?"

"That's three hundred dollars!" I exclaim. Grand Auntie was the most frugal[1] person I knew. "Remember how she used to keep all the boxes of See's candies we gave her for Christmas, telling us they were too good to eat? And then one year, she gave a box back to us for Thanksgiving or something. Only it was so old—"

My mother was nodding, already laughing.

"—all the candies were white with mold!"

"Bugs, too!" my mother adds.

"So she left you the tea in her will?" I say.

"Already gave it to me a few months ago. She was thinking she was going to die soon. She didn't say, but she started to give things away, good things, not just junk. And one time we were visiting, drinking tea. I said, 'Ah, good tea!' same as always. This time, Grand Auntie went to her kitchen, brought back the tea. She told me, ' *Syau ning*, you take this tea now.' That's what she called me, *syau ning*, 'little person,' from the old days when we first knew each other.

"I said, 'No, no! I wasn't saying this to hint.' And she said, '*Syau ning*, you take this now so I can see how happy you are to receive it while I am still alive. Some things can't wait until I'm dead.' How could I refuse? Of course, every time I came to visit, I brought back her tea."

Phil returns with Cleo, Tessa is right behind. And now I am actually sorry we have to leave.

"We better hit the road," says Phil. I put the teacup down.

"Don't forget," my mother says to Phil. "Grand Auntie's present in the laundry room."

"A present?" Cleo says. "Do I have a present too?"

Phil throws me a look of surprise.

"Remember?" I lie. "I told you—what Grand Auntie left us in her will."

He shrugs, and we all follow my mother to the back.

"Of course it's just old things," says my mother. She turns on the

---

1 frugal (froo′ gəl) thrifty

light, and then I see it, sitting on the clothes dryer. It is the altar for Grand Auntie's good-luck god, the Chinese crèche.[2]

"Wow!" Tessa exclaims. "A Chinese dollhouse."

"I can't see! I can't see!" Cleo says, and Phil lifts the altar off the dryer and carries it into the kitchen.

The altar is about the size of a small upturned drawer, painted in red lacquer. In a way, it resembles a miniature stage for a Chinese play. There are two ornate[3] columns in front, as well as two ceremonial electric candles made out of gold and red plastic and topped by red Christmas tree bulbs for flames. Running down the sides are wooden panels decorated with gold Chinese characters.

"What does that say?" I ask my mother.

She traces her finger down one, then the other. *"Jye shiang ru yi.* This first word is 'luck,' this other is another kind of luck, and these two mean 'all that you wish.' All kinds of luck, all that you wish."

"And who is this on the inside, this man in the picture frame?" The picture is almost cartoonlike. The man is rather large and is seated in regal splendor, holding a quill[4] in one hand, a tablet in the other. He has two long whiskers, shaped like smooth, tapered black whips.

"Oh, this we call Kitchen God. To my way of thinking, he was not too important. Not like Buddha, not like Kwan Yin, goddess of mercy—not that high level, not even the same level as the Money God. Maybe he was like a store manager, important, but still many, many bosses above him."

Phil chuckles at my mother's Americanized explanation of the hierarchy of Chinese deities.[5] I wonder if that's how she really thinks of them, or if she's used this metaphor[6] for our benefit.

"What's a kitchen god?" says Tessa. "Can I have one?"

"He is only a story," answers my mother.

"A story!" exclaims Cleo. "I want one."

My mother's face brightens. She pats Cleo's head. "You want another story from Ha-bu? Last night, you did not get enough stories?"

"When we get home," Phil says to Cleo. "Ha-bu is too tired to tell you a story now."

But my mother acts as if she has not heard Phil's excuses. "It is a very simple story," she says to Cleo in a soothing voice, "how he

---

2 **crèche** (kresh) a display representing the birth of Jesus

3 **ornate** (ôr nāt') heavily decorated and ornamented

4 **quill** (kwil) a pen made from the stem of a feather

5 **the hierarchy of Chinese deities** (hi'ə rär' kē) (dē'ə tēz) the order of importance of all the Chinese gods

6 **metaphor** (met'ə fôr) a comparison of two unlike things used to clarify the more unfamiliar one

The Kitchen God's Wife   113

became Kitchen God. It is this way."

And as my mother begins, I am struck by a familiar feeling, as if I am Cleo, again three years old, still eager to believe everything my mother has to say.

"In China long time ago," I hear my mother say, "there was a rich farmer named Zhang, such a lucky man. Fish jumped in his river, pigs grazed his land, ducks flew around his yard as thick as clouds. And that was because he was blessed with a hardworking wife named Guo. She caught his fish and herded his pigs. She fattened his ducks, doubled all his riches, year after year. Zhang had everything he could ask for—from the water, the earth, and the heavens above.

"But Zhang was not satisfied. He wanted to play with a pretty, carefree woman named Lady Li. One day he brought this pretty woman home to his house, made his good wife cook for her. When Lady Li later chased his wife out of the house, Zhang did not run out and call to her, 'Come back, my good wife, come back.'

"Now he and Lady Li were free to swim in each other's arms. They threw money away like dirty water. They slaughtered ducks just to eat a plate of their tongues. And in two years' time, all of Zhang's land was empty, and so was his heart. His money was gone, and so was pretty Lady Li, run off with another man.

"Zhang became a beggar, so poor he wore more patches than whole cloth on his pants. He crawled from the gate of one household to another, crying, 'Give me your moldy grain!'

"One day, he fell over and faced the sky, ready to die. He fainted, dreaming of eating the winter clouds blowing above him. When he opened his eyes again, he found the clouds had turned to smoke. At first he was afraid he had fallen down into a place far below the earth. But when he sat up, he saw he was in a kitchen, near a warm fireplace. The girl tending the fire explained that the lady of the house had taken pity on him—she always did this, with all kinds of people, poor or old, sick or in trouble.

" 'What a good lady!' cried Zhang. 'Where is she, so I can thank her?' The girl pointed to the window, and the man saw a woman walking up the path. Ai-ya! That lady was none other that his good wife Guo!

"Zhang began leaping about the kitchen looking for some place to hide, then jumped into the kitchen fireplace just as his wife walked into the room.

"Good Wife Guo poured out many tears to try to put the fire out. No use! Zhang was burning with shame and, of course, because of the hot roaring fire below. She watched her husband's ashes fly up to heaven in three puffs of smoke. Wah!

"In heaven, the Jade Emperor heard the whole story from his new arrival. 'For having the courage to admit you were wrong,' the Emperor declared, 'I make you Kitchen God, watching over everyone's behavior. Every year, you let me know who deserves good luck, who deserves bad.'

"From then on, people in China knew Kitchen God was watching them. From his corner in every house and every shop, he saw all kinds of good and bad habits spill out: generosity or greediness, a harmonious nature or a complaining one. And once a year, seven days before the new year, Kitchen God flew back up the fireplace to report whose fate deserved to be changed, better for worse, or worse for better."

"The end!" shouts Cleo, completely satisfied.

"Sounds like Santa Claus," says Phil cheerfully.

"Hnh!" my mother huffs in a tone that implies Phil is stupid beyond words. "He is not Santa Claus. More like a spy—FBI agent, CIA, Mafia, worse than IRS, that kind of person! And he does not give *you* gifts, you must give *him* things. All year long you have to show him respect—give him tea and oranges. When Chinese New Year's time comes, you must give him even better things—maybe whiskey to drink, cigarettes to smoke, candy to eat, that kind of thing. You are hoping all the time his tongue will be sweet, his head a little drunk, so when he has his meeting with the big boss, maybe he reports good things about you. This family has been good, you hope he says. Please give them good luck next year."

"Well, that's a pretty inexpensive way to get some luck," I say. "Cheaper than the lottery."

"No!" my mother exclaims, and startles us all. "You never know. Sometimes he is in a bad mood. Sometimes he says, I don't like this family, give them bad luck. Then you're in trouble, nothing you can do about it. Why should I want that kind of person to judge me, a man who cheated his wife? His wife was the good one, not him."

"Then why did Grand Auntie keep him?" I ask.

My mother frowns, considering this. "It is this way, I think. Once you get started, you are afraid to stop. Grand Auntie worshipped him since she was a little girl. Her family started it many generations before, in China."

"Great!" says Phil. "So now she passes along this curse to us. Thanks, Grand Auntie, but no thanks." He looks at his watch and I can tell he's impatient to go.

"It was Grand Auntie's gift to you," my mother says to me in a mournful voice. "How could she know this was not so good? She only wanted to leave you something good, her best things."

"Maybe the girls can use the altar as a dollhouse," I suggest. Tessa nods, Cleo follows suit. My mother stares at the altar, not saying anything.

"I'm thinking about it this way," she finally announces, her mouth set in an expression of thoughtfulness. "You take this altar. I can find you another kind of lucky god to put inside, not this one." She removes the

Ch'ing dynasty, Porcelain teapot and beaker, c. 1700

picture of the Kitchen God. "This one, I take it. Grand Auntie will understand. This kind of luck, you don't want. Then you don't have to worry."

"Deal!" Phil says right away. "Let's pack 'er up."

But now I'm worried. "Are you sure?" I ask my mother. She's already stuffing the plastic candlesticks into a used paper bag. I'm not exactly superstitious. I've always been the kind who hates getting chain letters—Mary used to send them to me all the time. And while I never sent the duplicate letters out as instructed, I never threw the originals away either.

Phil is carrying the altar. Tessa has the bag of candlesticks. My mother has taken Cleo upstairs to find a plastic neon bracelet she left in the bathroom. And now my mother comes back with Cleo and hands me a heavy grocery sack, the usual care package, what feels like oranges and Chinese candy, that sort of thing.

"Grand Auntie's tea, I gave you some," my mother says. "Don't need to use too much. Just keep adding water. The flavor always comes back."

For Discussion

1. Did you enjoy Pearl's mother's story of the Kitchen God? Explain.

2. Pearl and her husband Phil were unsure whether to accept the gift of the altar and picture of the Kitchen God. Would you have accepted the gift? Why or why not?

Readers Respond

I enjoyed the story because it informed me of another religion and culture. I thought the facts and details surrounding the story of the Kitchen God's origin, however, seemed very far-fetched. I would have made Phil's doubts of the grandmother's story more critical so that there would have been a logical response to a story that seems illogical.

Michael Kim

The matriarch, or grandmother, of the story was my favorite character because of her good attitude, her belief in her culture, and her talent for telling stories. She seemed very confident and wise, too. I felt the matriarch's wisdom and attitude were great assets. The scene that I remember most clearly was when Zhang went before the Jade Emperor, who decided that Zhang should be Kitchen God to look over people's households and to see whether they were decent people. The writer kept my attention because of the interesting story of the Kitchen God and the wonderful detail in the story.

I enjoyed the portrayal of the Chinese-American family, where the husband was Caucasian and his wife and her family were Chinese and very loyal to their culture. The story showed how cultures relate and clash at the same time.

Rachel Hansen

Do you agree?

☞ Do you agree with Michael that the story of the Kitchen God is far-fetched? Explain your answer.

☞ Have stories been passed down within your family or culture? Write in your journal about the time you first heard one of these stories. What significance did the story have for you then? What significance does it have now?

Writing Process in Action

The Stories We Inherit

"'In China a long time ago,' I hear my mother say, 'there was a rich farmer named Zhang, such a lucky man. . . .'" So begins the tale of the Kitchen God. In the excerpt on pages 110–116 that includes the retelling of this tale, Amy Tan shows how stories are passed from one generation to another—along with fine tea, traditions, and other treasures. These stories, like the tea and traditions, are part of one family's rich cultural heritage. What stories have you inherited from previous generations?

You are invited to retell a story a family member has told you—whether the story has been in your family for generations or is a new addition to your family's collection of favorites.

• Assignment •

CONTEXT   After reading *The Kitchen God's Wife*, your cousin has decided to create a written collection of memorable family stories, one through which future generations will be able to know their ancestors and their past. To achieve this end, she has sent letters to relatives near and distant asking them to send her their favorite family tales. In the letter your family received she writes, "The stories in this collection, like the photographs in a photo album, should capture something of the essence of the people in our family and our experiences." Inspired by Tan, she adds, "Ideally, the 'flavor' of these people and experiences will return upon reading about them just as the flavor of fine tea comes back when you add hot water."

PURPOSE   To write a story that was originally told to you by a family member

AUDIENCE   Family members, friends, and future generations

LENGTH   2–3 pages

For more advice on how to approach this assignment, you will find the next few pages helpful. But don't feel that you have to remember all of what follows. You can come *back* to these pages as you write, getting help where and when you need it. You're in charge of your own writing process.

1. Prewriting

Perhaps a story came to mind as soon as you read this assignment: the story your uncle used to tell again and again (and again), one of your grandma's favorites, or maybe a story about you yourself that your parents are fond of repeating. But if you're still looking, consider these suggestions.

- Check your journal. Have you written about memories, family members, or other personal experiences that shed light on your own heritage?
- Ask your family. Brainstorm with family members to make a list of the tales that are your family's greatest hits.
- Look at family albums. What clues to your past do you find in the faces and places in the photographs?

Once you've found a tale that interests you or a likely subject for a tale, use freewriting, collecting, list making, or questioning to explore the tale or subject further. Try to discover its essential qualities. For help in using these techniques, see Lesson 2.2.

Then take some time to think about your purpose. Your main purpose is to tell a memorable family story, but is there anything else you want to accomplish? Do you want to inform readers of your family's cultural background? Make your readers laugh? Persuade them to be proud of their roots? Describe an unforgettable relative, place, or family possession? If you do have a secondary purpose, identify it in a sentence so that you can keep it in mind as you draft. Lesson 2.3 may help you identify your purpose.

Next, consider your audience. Since your readers will be family, friends, and future generations, you may choose to write in a rather informal or personal way. For instance, you may use slang, include intimate family details, and even address your readers directly now and then. However, friends and future generations might lack your and your family's current familiarity with your subject. So you might add to your prewriting notes any information these readers would need to understand and appreciate your story as you do. Try to strike a balance between explaining too much (which might bore some readers) and too little (which might confuse others). See Lesson 2.3 for help.

Finally, gather any remaining details you may need to provide a full and accurate account of your chosen tale. Presumably you will have already noted your own recollections of the tale. So now ask family members to retell the story while you take notes on what *they* say. Note the sensory details and bits of dialogue they use to bring their accounts to life. If differences arise between accounts, note them and ask questions to clarify these points. If you need help jogging people's memories, try asking them questions based on your own recollections. For other interviewing tips, see Lesson 2.4, pages 75–76.

2. Drafting

Once you have your story firmly in mind, you're ready to start drafting. A good way to start is just to jump in. Let the story tell itself, flowing naturally from beginning to end. You can go back and make changes later.

But don't just rush through it. As you draft, refer to your prewriting notes for details that will make your story stick in your reader's mind. For example, look at how Tan describes Zhang and Lady Li. She doesn't just state that they were rich and wasteful. She provides these memorable details: "They threw money away like dirty water. They slaughtered ducks just to eat a plate of their tongues." Lessons 2.5–2.8 can help you build paragraphs that will tell

Writing Process in Action   **119**

your story clearly and completely. And, if you ever find yourself at a loss for details, you can fill in these gaps by going back to prewriting activities such as freewriting, list making, and interviewing.

If you have trouble beginning your story, you might want to set it up in some way. Tan frames the story about the Kitchen God within a story about the day the family picked up Grand Auntie's good-luck altar. This larger story gives her a logical reason for relating the mother's tale about the Kitchen God. In fact, Tan leads into the tale by having her characters ask for it.

> *"What's a kitchen god?" says Tessa. "Can I have one?"*
> *"He is only a story," answers my mother.*
> *"A story!" exclaims Cleo. "I want one."*
> *My mother's face brightens. She pats Cleo's head. "You want another story from Ha-bu? Last night, you did not get enough stories?"*
> *"When we get home," Phil says to Cleo. "Ha-bu is too tired to tell you a story now."*
> *But my mother acts as if she has not heard Phil's excuses. "It is a very simple story," she says to Cleo in a soothing voice, "how he became Kitchen God. It is this way."*

If you decide to lead into your story like Tan does, once you've finished telling your story within a story, you may want to come back to your context-setting story and bring it to some sort of closure as well. The suggestions in Lesson 1.4 on writing a story as a flashback can help you reach that closure.

3. Revising

To make sure your story will have a place in the family collection, look back at the assignment. Ask yourself these questions:

- Does this story match the one in my head?
- Does it "capture something of the essence of the people in our family and our experiences"?
- Does the "flavor" of the people or experiences come through?

If your answer to any of these questions is no, think about what may be missing. For additional help in determining what's missing, review your prewriting notes, freewrite about the question, or share your draft with a family member who is familiar with the story.

Next, think again about your purpose. Your primary purpose is to tell a memorable family story. Have you done so? What about your secondary purpose—to inform, explain, entertain, or describe? Have you accomplished that as well? If not, you might want to consider whether you have accomplished a different secondary purpose. If that is the case, perhaps all you need to revise is your understanding of your secondary purpose. If that isn't the case, however, you may want to revise your story to make it more informative, entertaining, or descriptive. To see how you might make your tale more informative, peek ahead to Lessons 4.4 and 5.1–5.4. To learn how to make your story more entertaining, look at Lessons 4.4, 4.6, 5.1, and 5.3. For tips on making it more descriptive, see Lessons 3.1–3.4.

Then consider the needs of your audience. Are there references in your story a reader might not understand? Tan knew that her American readers would not be very familiar with Chinese gods, so she used analogies that would make sense to these readers. First, to explain the Kitchen God's importance in the hierarchy of Chinese gods, she compared him to "a store manager, important, but still many, many bosses above him." Later, to explain the Kitchen God's powers, she compared him to "a spy—FBI agent, CIA, Mafia, worse than IRS, that kind of person!" Can you use comparisons to explain any key references?

Finally, revise your sentences and paragraphs to improve their unity and coherence, as necessary. Use the checklists in 2.9 for help.

4. Editing

Now it's time for the final polishing of your tale. The checklist in Lesson 2.10 can help you review your grammar, usage, and mechanics. But you may also need to consider some special items.

- If you used any foreign words, check to make sure you spelled and capitalized them correctly.
- Check the spellings and capitalizations of all names.
- If you used any family expressions, dialect, or slang, make sure your readers will be able to understand them.

Finally, make a clean copy of your story, and proofread it.

5. Presenting

Although for this assignment you have responded to a letter from a fictional cousin, there's no reason you can't use the story you wrote to start a family collection of your own. To do so, send your tale along with a letter similar to the one from your "cousin" to members of your family, asking them to send you *their* favorite family tales in return. Another way to present your story is to tell it at the next family gathering. Look at Lesson 2.11 for additional ideas for presenting your work.

• Reflecting •

You have just retold a tale that probably was familiar to you. In fact, you may have heard or even told it yourself countless times before. Did that make it easy to write? Or did you stumble over points that had never troubled you when you listened to or told the tale before? What are some of the differences between orally telling a story and writing one? Which experience do you prefer? Why?

Criteria
1. Focuses on a tale about a family member or experience
2. Hooks interest by establishing its relevance to the reader early on
3. Uses vivid sensory details, realistic dialogue, and effective figurative language
4. Provides any explanations needed to understand the story and its significance
5. Follows correct grammar, usage, and mechanics

Portfolio & Reflection

Summary

Key concepts in the writing process include the following:

- Prewriting involves finding, exploring, and narrowing a topic, deciding on a purpose and audience, and sometimes researching the topic.
- Drafting means turning prewriting notes into paragraphs, with the writer's purpose determining the organization.
- Revising means reworking a piece for meaning, unity, and coherence.
- Editing means correcting grammar, usage, spelling, punctuation, and capitalization.
- Presenting means sharing your writing.
- Writing is a five-stage process in which a writer may return to any previous stage at any time.

Your Writer's Portfolio

Look over the writing you have done during this unit. Select two pieces of writing to put into your portfolio. Each piece should demonstrate that you have worked with one or more of the preceding concepts. In other words, look for a piece of writing that does one or more of the following:

- grows out of ideas generated by using techniques such as freewriting
- contains words and ideas chosen with a particular audience in mind
- has a clear topic sentence that controls appropriate supporting details
- reflects careful revising and editing
- grows out of all five stages of the writing process, including presenting

Reflection and Commentary

Write one page that demonstrates you understand what this unit asked of you. Use your two selected pieces of writing as evidence while you consider the following numbered items. Respond to as many items as possible. Label the page "Commentary on the Writing Process," and include it in your portfolio.

1. What elements in your writing show the value of specific prewriting techniques? Which technique will you handle differently in the future?
2. What details show that you wrote with a specific purpose and audience in mind?
3. What paragraph has an effective topic sentence and supporting details?
4. Which stage of the writing process has helped you the most with your writing? Which stage do you need to work on?
5. What would you need to do to get your writing ready for an audience?

Feedback

If you had a chance to respond to the following student comment, what would you say or ask?

I write late at night on my computer. I type as fast as the ideas enter my head. The night gives me a feeling of solitude—like I'm alone at the top of the world.

Sandra Emch, Quartz Hill High School,
Quartz Hill, California

Descriptive Writing

Real Toads in Imaginary Gardens

James Christensen, *Vanity*, 1989

Ross Scripts

Big

"Every child says, 'I wish I were a grown-up.' The screenplay for Big came out of wondering what would happen if that wish were ultimately fulfilled."

Gary Ross

Writing a screenplay about a boy who got his wish to be big seemed like a natural transition to Gary Ross. The screenwriter explains, "I grew up in Los Angeles, and my father is a screenwriter. I'd written novels and a couple of other scripts that people hired me to do. I realized I wanted to do something I cared about."

Ross worked on the *Big* script with his friend Anne Spielberg. Describing their process, he says, "First, we outlined the whole movie. We planned out every scene in

Scripting a Movie

1. Outlining the Whole Movie

2. Detailing a Scene

3. Choosing the Right Words

Final Script

F O C U S

Screenwriters depend upon descriptive writing to let the director know exactly how they envision the finished movie.

---

detail, and we each wrote our own scenes. Then we'd discuss and rewrite each other's scenes until the script was unified into one voice."

As they worked their way through the writing process, they needed to make each scene vibrant and alive on the page. They could achieve this goal to some extent through dialogue, but detail and description are key to providing actors and directors with a script that conveys a real sense of mood.

Ross says, "Every image you describe must be chosen to bolster a particular point." Ross puts it another way: "The screenwriter has to take the reader to the movie before it's made."

In this Case Study, Gary Ross talks in detail about three scenes with vivid descriptions that gave the director a clear idea of the story he and Spielberg had imagined.

Descriptive passages in a movie script generate specific images that help to establish mood.

Your Wish is Granted

1. Outlining the Whole Movie

Before the Zoltar machine was built for the film, Zoltar originally appeared as a detail in the outline and then as a descriptive paragraph in the script.

Even in the early stage of outlining the movie, Ross and Spielberg were aware of the mood they wanted the finished film to evoke. This awareness helped them select appropriate details and develop them into descriptive paragraphs in the script.

Ross recalls the scene near the beginning of the movie, when the main character, Josh, goes to an amusement park on the shore with his family. Earlier, the twelve-year-old has been thwarted by not being grown-up enough to have a date with the girl he likes or even being big enough to go on the roller coaster.

As Josh walks alone near the beach, he hears a huge wave. Ross says, "That wave is meant to be a little ominous. It isolates Josh from the carnival, and it also serves as a portent of what's coming."

The boy walks past "the most modern games" to get to the machine that will eventually change him into an adult. This antique fortune-telling machine, "Zoltar Speaks," contrasts sharply with the newness of the video games.

Ross and Spielberg's vivid description of Zoltar provided a blueprint for the invention of the Zoltar machine featured in the finished movie. Ross says, "We wrote this description to give a dangerous, timeless, and lonely feeling. Of course, that's very much what the journey from childhood to adulthood is about. It's mysterious to embark on that, and these are the qualities we wanted to evoke."

2. Detailing a Scene

Another of Ross's favorite scenes shares the seaside carnival setting of the Zoltar scene. Now Josh has been transformed to an adult.

As Josh and his girlfriend stand on the boardwalk, they hear music coming from an old dance pavilion. "The pavilion is shown for only a couple of seconds in the film," Ross says, "but I'm proud of our description. I was inspired by something I'd read in an F. Scott Fitzgerald book, about life on the French Riviera. We wanted to evoke the same romance and magic but also the decline and the sadness that's coming."

Ross and Spielberg had a particular, real-life amusement park in mind for this scene. Ross says, "After writing this description, we lobbied for this particular location. We asked them to shoot it there, and they did."

INTERFACE *Select any topic that you feel strongly about. Now, make a list of details that accurately describe the topic. How do your feelings for the topic come through in your descriptive details?*

```
WIDER SHOT — INCLUDING MACHINE

Josh reaches out tentatively and grasps the brass handles.
He hesitates for a moment then squeezes them tightly. The
red lights start to flash. Josh looks up at the blinking
bulbs, then suddenly lets go of the levers.

THEIR POV

A single red light burns on top reading "DANGEROUS."

JOSH AND SUSAN

They look at it awkwardly for a moment, then glance at
each other. It seems like each of them is about to say
something, but neither one does. They stay like that for a
second, when Susan cocks her head to the side.

                    SUSAN
        You hear that?

                    JOSH
        What?

                    SUSAN
        Music.

EXT. BOARDWALK

The sounds of Big Band Music drift out of the old dance
Pavilion. Built near the turn of the century, it is part
Mosque, part Opera Hall, part Seaside Pleasure Palace. All
the obelisks have flagpoles for the banners that have long
since gone away. The sound of Moonlight Serenade echoes up
the boardwalk as the ocean pounds in the distance.

EXT. ARCADE

Josh and Susan walk out of the arcade onto the nearly
deserted boardwalk. Towering above them is the dark metal
hulk of a roller coaster, closed for the winter. Further
on is the latticework of an empty Ferris wheel.
```

Ross and Spielberg's description of the old dance pavilion in the script creates a mood of faded grandeur.

3. Choosing the Right Words

EXT. BASEBALL FIELD

It's late afternoon as the sun turns the field a
light gold. Two boys stand alone on the grass,
shagging flies in the fading light. There is
silence, then the crack of a bat, then the distant
pop of a ball hitting leather. Josh watches
silently from the side of the field leaning back
in his business suit. There is no conversation as
the ritual continues between them — just the swing
of the bat and the long lazy arc of a fly ball as
it goes from one boy to another. Josh loosens the
knot of his tie as he stares at the boys in front
of him. A light breeze ruffles his hair.

This paragraph from the script describes a scene Josh revisits from his childhood.

When editing the script to unify it into one voice, Ross and Spielberg were aware that the words would need to be precise to evoke a particular mood in a scene. For example, near the end of the film, Josh revisits a scene from his childhood; the mood needed to be nostalgic. Ross says, "We knew if we wrote this scene poetically, the director would end up putting the poetry into the film. Usually you have to write lean for the screen, but this time we really pulled out all the stops and went for it. We even used a poetic device, alliteration, to describe the 'long lazy arc' of the fly ball."

This scene takes place in what Ross calls "that mystical, magical, temporal instant between day and night. The sun turns the field gold for only a few minutes a day, so there's a fragile, fleeting quality of something that's there for only an instant and then is lost."

Ross continues, "The fact that the two boys stand alone gives the scene a beautiful, isolated quality. There's nothing in the world except them." For a while the scene is shot from Josh's point of view. Ross says, "Josh is privy to this scene, but he's lost the beauty of it because of his wish to be big. Showing Josh in a business suit emphasizes that he's constrained by being an adult. And when he loosens his tie, he shows that being big is constricting him. That's what I mean by writing description that bolsters a point. When the light breeze ruffles his hair, it harkens back to the magical wind that blew when he first wished to be big. This time the wind shows he's drawn back to the world of childhood."

INTERFACE *Gary Ross chose to describe a scene of baseball because, as he says, "I love it, and I've lived a lot of my life around it." If you wanted to write a scene to evoke happy memories of your own childhood, what descriptive details would it include?*

ON ASSIGNMENT

1. Details are critically important in a screenplay of a fantasy because writers are creating pictures that may exist only in their own minds. From a writer's words the director must be able to "see" how the film will look. Imagine a scene that conveys a specific mood. If you can't imagine a scene, look at the painting printed below. Write a paragraph describing either the painting or an imaginary scene in clear detail so that it could be used by a director in a movie. Does every image in your scene work to bolster the mood you are trying to convey?

2. **Literature Connection**
Gary Ross says that a particular paragraph from F. Scott Fitzgerald's *Tender Is the Night* sparked his description of the dance pavilion in *Big.* Find an evocative description in a literary work of your choice, and use it as a springboard to write a descriptive paragraph of your own.

3. **Cooperative Learning**
Gary Ross and Anne Spielberg worked independently on their scenes and then reworked each other's scenes to achieve a unified voice. Choose a partner to work with on creating a description of a person, place, or thing that evokes a particular mood for you both. Decide together what you will describe, who your audience is, and what feeling you want to get across. After you each write your descriptions individually, meet to discuss and unify them into one piece.

Joan Miró, *Carnival of Harlequin*, 1924–25

Case Study: Fantasy Writing   **129**

Beholding the Mountain of Fire

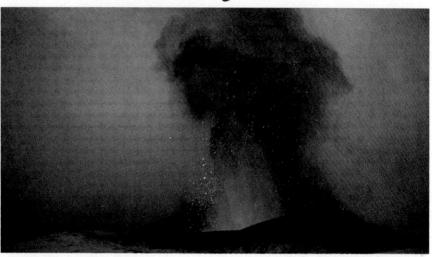

Ahead of Sam lies the perilous path to Orodruin, the Mountain of Fire. But can you, the reader, really picture the danger, the horror, that Sam's eyes behold? In fact, you can, as author J. R. R. Tolkien uses his descriptive skills to transport you to the eerie scene.

Literature Model

Tolkien's first sentence conveys the overall impression of the scene.

What is Tolkien's writing strategy, as indicated by words like "before his feet," "on the further side," and "far beyond it"?

H ard and cruel and bitter was the land that met his gaze. Before his feet the highest ridge of Ephel Dúath fell steeply in great cliffs down into a dark trough, on the further side of which there rose another ridge, much lower, its edge notched and jagged with crags like fangs that stood out black against the red light behind them: it was the grim Morgai, the inner ring of the fences of the land. Far beyond it, but almost straight ahead, across a wide lake of darkness dotted with tiny fires, there was a great burning glow, and from it rose in huge columns a swirling smoke, dusky red at the roots, black above where it merged into the billowing canopy that roofed in all the accursed land. ➡

> Sam was looking at Orodruin, the Mountain of Fire. Ever and anon the furnaces far below its ashen cone would grow hot and with a great surging and throbbing pour forth rivers of molten rock from chasms in its sides. Some would flow blazing toward Barad-dûr down great channels; some would wind their way into the stone plain, until they cooled and lay like twisted dragon-shapes vomited from the tormented earth. In such an hour of labor Sam beheld Mount Doom, and the light of it, cut off by the high screen of the Ephel Dúath from those who climbed up the path from the West, now glared against the stark rock faces, so that they seemed to be drenched with blood.
>
> J. R. R. Tolkien, *The Return of the King*

Creating an Overall Impression

There are many ways to begin putting together a description. One way is to think of the overall impression, or mood, you want to communicate. Then when you write your topic sentence, use words and phrases that will help convey this mood to your reader.

Mood   Your descriptive paragraph will have greater impact if it evokes a particular mood than if it just describes details that aren't unified. Perhaps you want to express horror or inspire fear, as Tolkien does. Or maybe you intend to communicate a happy, light-hearted feeling or a sad, nostalgic one. Whatever impression you choose, carefully write your paragraph to present that impression clearly.

Remember, in writing a descriptive paragraph, don't try to express too much at once. Concentrate on conveying a single, effective picture to the reader. In the Tolkien model, for example, the author creates a picture of a forbidding, polluted, "accursed land." He appeals to the reader's senses with images of dull fires, smoke, jagged rocks like fangs, and a "lake of darkness." The overall impression in the reader's mind is of a grim, tormented, and frightening landscape.

• JOURNAL ACTIVITY •
Try It Out

Go through some art books and magazines at the library until you find a few scenes that interest you. For each scene decide on the overall impression, or mood, you think the artist wanted to convey. Next, make a list of details in each scene that supports the overall impression.

Topic Sentence   In a descriptive paragraph the topic sentence should "overview" the scene and summarize the content of the paragraph. In doing so, it can also help establish the paragraph's mood. The rest of the paragraph should then contain details that support the topic sentence.

A topic sentence at or near the beginning of a paragraph lets the reader know what's coming. For example, the topic sentence of the literature model on page 130 is at the very beginning of the paragraph. A topic sentence at or near the end of a paragraph, as in the model below, can summarize what you have described and help the reader pull together all the parts of the paragraph. Whatever its placement, the topic sentence serves to tie together the paragraph's supporting details. You might want to envision the parts of your paragraph like this.

Revising Tip

In the revising stage of your work, check to make sure the details you have used actually support your topic sentence.

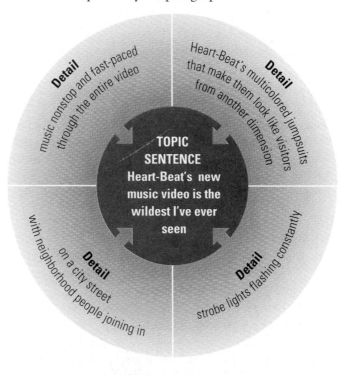

Detail music nonstop and fast-paced through the entire video

Detail Heart-Beat's multicolored jumpsuits that make them look like visitors from another dimension

TOPIC SENTENCE Heart-Beat's new music video is the wildest I've ever seen

Detail on a city street with neighborhood people joining in

Detail strobe lights flashing constantly

Now read this paragraph in which the writer sums up the details with a topic sentence at the end.

In what order are details mentioned in this description? Does the writer rely only on visual details?

Model

Ambassador Aleesa Aguilar entered the control room of the Galavian spacecraft, guided wordlessly by two of the craft's security officers. As the first earthling to meet the Galavians and to see a Galavian craft, she instinctively did a quick scan of her surroundings. A whirring sound directed her eyes to the far left of the brightly lit, cavernous white room. There she saw the "pilots," actually two androids—robots—who ➡

monitored the ship's course. Her experienced eyes next followed a series of about fifteen "space windows," computer screens that simulated the view off into space in fifteen directions. At five of these "windows" sat groups of Galavians, as expressionless as the androids, rapidly making calculations and plotting courses. Then a sharp voice to her right blared "All rise," as the craft's commander entered. In these few seconds, the savvy Ambassador Aguilar learned much about these hard-working, severe, highly regimented aliens.

The topic sentence at the end summarizes the importance of this brief description.

Getting Oriented

Your goal in writing a descriptive paragraph is to transport the reader to the scene. You do this with your topic sentence and supporting details. Yet to transport the reader, you must also help to orient him or her—to provide a sense of direction and where things are. Describing items in spatial order is one way to help your reader get oriented.

Spatial Order There are many kinds of spatial orders. For example, the Tolkien model on pages 130–131 uses near-to-far spatial order. The author begins by describing what lies nearest the character and proceeds to describe things farther and farther away. In fact, he follows the order your own eyes might move in if you were looking at the scene. Other ways your eyes might move include left to right (or right to left), as in the model on pages 132–133, and top to bottom (or bottom to top).

Prewriting Tip

Before you begin drafting, refer to Grammar, Usage, and Mechanics, pages 469–470, to get some ideas for prepositional phrases you can use in your description.

Left to right

Near to far

Top to bottom

• JOURNAL ACTIVITY •
Think It Through

What are some other ways to look at and describe a scene? In your journal suggest two alternatives to spatial order. Then write a description of your room, the street you live on, or your school, using spatial order or one of the alternatives you suggested.

Using Transitions   Transitions are words that connect one sentence or idea to the next and help show the relationship between the two—words like *before, then, next, under, in front of, to the right of,* and *inside.* In descriptive writing, transitions can help readers keep track of where things are. Look at the picture below to determine the transitions you might use in describing a scene.

Notice how Mary Stewart ties together her description with spatial-order transitions in this excerpt, taken from a story about the days of the legendary King Arthur.

Literature Model

Stewart uses the following spatial-order transitions: "behind," "against," "over," "around," "in front," "a few paces away," "between," "above," "beyond," "to the peak," "at," "where we had seen."

At first, after the blaze of the guard-room, I could see nothing. I shut the door behind me and leaned back against the damp wall, while the night air poured over me like a river. Then things took shape around me. In front and a few paces away was a battlemented wall, waist high, the outer wall of the castle. Between this wall and where I stood was a level platform, and above me a wall rising again to a battlement, and beyond this the soaring cliff and the walls climbing it, and the shape of the fortress rising above me step by step to the peak of the promontory. At the very head of the rise, where we had seen the lighted window, the tower now showed black and lightless against the sky.

Mary Stewart, *The Crystal Cave*

The following are some writing options to help you apply what you have learned.

1. Guided Assignment Describe a room with which you are familiar in a paragraph or two. Write your description so that you could read it to a sightless person who needed to know where everything in the room was located. Include more in your description than simply what is needed to navigate the room. For example, if you are describing a classroom, include the location of the pencil sharpener in case the person needs to use it. Pay close attention to the spatial order and transition words you employ. Everything in the room will need to be described in some relation to the location of something else.

  PURPOSE To describe a room
  AUDIENCE A person without eyesight
    LENGTH 1–2 paragraphs

2. Open Assignment In a paragraph describe a place you would like to visit, either real or imaginary. Be sure all your details support both the main idea and the mood conveyed in the topic sentence. Write two versions of your paragraph. Structure one so that the topic sentence is at the beginning of your paragraph, and the other so that it falls at the end. How is the mood affected by each version?

3. Art Look closely at James Doolin's *Last Painter on Earth*. How do the title and the shadow add to the mood of the painting? What effect do the colors and the form of the landscape have on the painting's mood? Identify specific details in the painting, and write a paragraph describing the scene. Be as vivid as you can. Create a mood such that a different artist reading your paragraph could render a painting with a mood similar to this one.

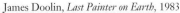

James Doolin, *Last Painter on Earth*, 1983

Using Descriptive Language

To the Fifth Dimension and the Planet Uriel

Meg Murray and her friends have just made an abrupt trip from her backyard through the fifth dimension to the planet Uriel. What words does Madeleine L'Engle use to capture your attention and help you imagine Meg's experience?

Literature Model

What is the combined effect of such phrases as "delicious fragrance," "when the sun's touch is gentle," and "golden with light"?

With the words "tender," "new," and "tiny," L'Engle suggests that the world of Uriel is innocent, unsullied, and young.

She looked around rather wildly. They were standing in a sunlit field, and the air about them was moving with the delicious fragrance that comes only on the rarest of spring days when the sun's touch is gentle and the apple blossoms are beginning to unfold. She pushed her glasses up on her nose to reassure herself that what she was seeing was real.

They had left the silver glint of a biting autumn evening; and now around them everything was golden with light. The grasses of the field were a tender new green, and scattered about were tiny, multicolored flowers. Meg turned slowly to face a mountain reaching so high into the sky that its peak was lost in a crown of puffy white clouds. From the trees at the base of the mountain came a sudden singing of birds. There was an air of such ineffable peace and joy all around her that her heart's wild thumping slowed.

Madeleine L'Engle, *A Wrinkle in Time*

Choosing Words for Their Connotations

In the model you have just read, L'Engle seems able to choose just the right word to convey a feeling or a vision. She writes of a "delicious fragrance," for example. Why didn't she use the word *odor*, since *odor* and *fragrance* have the same basic meaning—smell? The answer is simple: most readers associate *odor* with an unpleasant smell and *fragrance* with an appealing one.

In choosing words for your descriptive writing, remember that many words come loaded with such connotations. Connotations are the feelings and values readers usually associate with any given word, associations that go beyond the simple dictionary definition of the word. So just as L'Engle chose "delicious fragrance," you should choose the best words you can find to re-create your vision.

Using Precise Nouns

Precise, vivid nouns are an important tool for re-creating your vision and making your writing more lively. By choosing nouns that are specific (*cloak*, for example) instead of general (*clothes*), you convey a clearer, more complete picture to your reader. Which of the above words, for example, best describes the literature model on page 136? The chart below shows some examples of nouns going from general to specific.

Drafting Tip

When drafting a description, you can refer to the material about concrete nouns on pages 401–402 of Lesson 10.1 in Grammar, Usage, and Mechanics.

Nouns		
General	**Specific**	**More Specific**
monster	vampire	Count Dracula
animal	amphibian	bullfrog
rain	storm	hurricane

• JOURNAL ACTIVITY •
Try It Out

How specific can you get? In your journal write the words *plant*, *machine*, *person*, *music*, *art*, *sport*, and *game* down the left side of one page. Then, after each word, write as many nouns as you can think of that are increasingly specific examples of the general word.

Selecting Vivid Modifiers

Vivid modifiers—that is, adjectives and adverbs—can bring your descriptions to life. With modifiers, as with nouns, make sure each word's connotation fits the impression you want to create. For example, a *shining* sword gives a different impression from a *blazing* one. For help finding more colorful and appropriate words, refer to a thesaurus, a listing of words with their synonyms and antonyms.

Don't settle for dull, overused modifiers, like *good* or *bad*. Instead, select more colorful and original modifiers, such as *honorable* and *wicked*. Sometimes you may even want to use exaggeration to make your description more colorful. For example, "My date last night was horrendous—everything went wrong." Notice how the modifiers on the right, below, convey a more vivid picture than the ones on the left.

Making Your Modifiers More Lively

funny	amusing	hilarious
heavy	weighty	ponderous
well	adequately	expertly

Here's how one student used precise nouns and lively modifiers to re-create an eerie scene from her imagination.

Student Model

Notice the dramatic effect of words and phrases like "nightmarish," "looming shadow," and the narrator "flattened . . . against the far wall."

What is the effect of the words "massive claws"? What impact does this effect have on the ending?

It was after me again. I kept on running, my heart beating wildly. But it kept on coming, more determined than ever to catch me. I ran into a small hut near the end of the village, hoping I could find protection there; but the hut was empty and that horrible, nightmarish creature grew closer with every step. When I saw its looming shadow in the doorway, I flattened myself against the far wall. It came toward me, my screams for help growing louder with every step it took. Finally, it was but mere inches from my face. I closed my eyes and prayed for a quick demise. It reached slowly with its massive claws toward me and said, "You're it!"

Nikki Phipps, Hamilton Heights High School, Arcadia, Indiana

The following are some writing options to help you apply what you have learned.

1. Guided Assignment   You have just written the following descriptive paragraph as part of a story you are writing for a literary journal:

> They entered the woods at night. Trees stood all around and blocked out the sky. The air smelled. As they walked farther on, they could hear noises behind and beside them. The ground under their feet felt soft. Lights flickered ahead of them, then died. Something flew into one girl's face. Then they heard another sound and tried to run out of the woods.

Rewrite this paragraph, substituting precise nouns and adding vivid modifiers to help make your nouns more specific. For example, change the word "noises" to "unsettling noises," or "scratching sounds," or "squeaks." Keep revising the paragraph until you feel you have created the most vivid and scary word picture you can.

PURPOSE   To revise a paragraph for vivid description
AUDIENCE   Readers of a journal
LENGTH   1 paragraph

2. Open Assignment   Imagine you will write a story in which you wake up one day in an imaginary world. Write a paragraph describing the 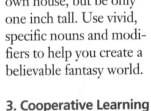 place you might be. Perhaps you are inside a television and have the freedom to jump from channel to channel. Or you could be in your own house, but be only one inch tall. Use vivid, specific nouns and modifiers to help you create a believable fantasy world.

3. Cooperative Learning
In a small group brainstorm about the painting at left. Identify specific details, such as the heart in the man's palm. Work together to come up with vivid and specific nouns and modifiers to describe these details. Then describe the scene in a paragraph. As a group, decide how best to present the paragraphs to the class.

Marc Chagall, *Paris Through the Window*, 1913

Using Descriptive Language   **139**

To the Farthest Reaches, to the Darkest Depths

Where would you travel if you could go anywhere in the universe? In the following selection science-fiction writer Ray Bradbury's rich imagination takes him and his readers to the planet Mars.

Literature Model

They had a house of crystal pillars on the planet Mars by the edge of an empty sea, and every morning you could see Mrs. K eating the golden fruits that grew from the crystal walls, or cleaning the house with handfuls of magnetic dust which, taking all the dirt with it, blew away on the hot wind. Afternoons, when the fossil sea was warm and motionless, and the wine trees stood stiff in the yard, and the little distant Martian bone town was all enclosed, and no one drifted out of their doors, you could see Mr. K himself in his room, reading from a metal book with raised hieroglyphs over which he brushed his hand, as one might play a harp. And from the book, as his fingers stroked, a voice sang, a soft ancient voice, which told tales of when the sea was red steam on the shore and ancient men had carried clouds of metal insects and electrical spiders into battle.

Mr. and Mrs. K had lived by the dead sea for twenty years, and their ancestors had lived in the same house, which turned and followed the sun, flower-like, for ten centuries.

Mr. and Mrs. K were not old. They had the fair, brownish skin of the true Martian, the yellow coin eyes, the soft musical voices. Once they had liked painting pictures with chemical fire, swimming in the canals in the seasons when the wine trees filled them with green liquors, and talking into the dawn together by the blue phosphorus portraits in the speaking room.

Ray Bradbury, *The Martian Chronicles*

"Fossil sea," "motionless," "stiff," "bone town"—what is the overall feeling created by this description?

How does the order in which various activities are described contribute to the overall effect of the description?

Creating Your Own Imaginary Place

You might have an idea for an imaginary place already. If not, try brainstorming, freewriting, or clustering to come up with an idea. A few words that might help you focus on imaginary places include *beneath*, *beyond*, *inside*, *before*, and *after*. Let your mind wander. Or simply let yourself wonder, "What would it be like there?" Look at something familiar, like your school, from a different point of view—such as through the eyes of a bug. Maybe one of the following ideas will start you on the way to your own imaginary place:

fantasy lands	future societies	glacial caves
under the sea	behind the wall	a laboratory
an ancient castle	inside a chrysanthemum	alien planets

Exploring Your Imaginary Place

Exploring your imaginary place will help you see it in greater detail. And these details will enable you to share your vision. One good way to explore a place in detail is by asking and answering questions about it. What are its inhabitants like, if there are any? What do I see, hear, smell, feel, and taste here? Does any part of this place seem familiar? What, if anything, does it resemble? Don't be afraid to ask creative questions. For example, you might come up with some like the ones below.

Creative Questions and Answers

Q: What colors are most common there?
A: Neon-green atmosphere, acid-yellow swampland, and orange vines

Q: What do the inhabitants do for fun?
A: March stiffly in long lines around the main swamp

Q: What presents the greatest danger there?
A: Deadly purple vapors from the swamp

Q: What do the inhabitants eat?
A: Yellow vapors that spray from the swamp vines

• JOURNAL ACTIVITY •
Try It Out

In your journal put together a list of creative questions you could use to explore any imaginary place. Try to come up with questions about specific, even unusual, details of the place. Keep the list, and use it when you begin planning and creating your own imaginary world or place.

Determining the Mood of Your Place

The details you discovered as you explored your place probably already suggest a specific mood, or feeling. Nevertheless, you may still want to heighten this feeling to make your description more effective. Or if none of your details suggests a particular feeling, you may want to decide upon one and add details to convey it.

A chart like the one below can help you come up with sensory details for your description. Some of the most effective details are those that appeal to a reader's senses. What details can you add to the ones below?

Using Details to Create a Mood	
Feeling	**Sample Details**
Loneliness	utter silence, dusty furniture, ticking clock, dead air, musty odors
Mystery, horror	secret passages, distant moaning, creaking floors
Excitement	fast pace, lively music, bright colors, laughter
Warmth, safety	glowing lights, crackling fire, steaming tea kettle, soft cushions

Organizing the Details of Your Place

After you explore and analyze your imaginary place, the next step is to arrange the relevant details into a first draft. Remember, your goal is to choose the method of organization that best conveys your description to the reader. What is the most important feature of the scene—a castle, a tree, clouds of purple mist? How does that feature relate to other details? You can organize not just objects but other descriptive elements, as Bradbury does when he describes actions in a "winding-down" form in the literature model on page 140.

As you draft your description, follow the spatial order that works best for your scene. If, for example, a tree or tall building dominates the picture, top-bottom spatial order might work best. What kind of organization would you choose to describe the place pictured to the left?

The following are some writing options to help you apply what you have learned.

1. Guided Assignment Imagine you are a mystery story writer. Private investigator Todd Kim has just entered an apartment located in a high-rise building in your city. He is hoping to find clues to a murder, before the apartment's occupant returns. Write a paragraph describing the apartment and what Todd finds there. Select the time of day and the season. Create a feeling of urgency, emphasizing that the person who lives there may appear at any moment. Be sure to include details that evoke all the senses.

Exchange papers with a classmate for peer editing. When reviewing one another's papers, identify specific details and how they function. What details help make the apartment more real? What details add to a sense of suspense or urgency? Suggest missing details that a trained investigator might look for or notice about the apartment. Offer ideas for heightening a sense of mood.

Finalize your paper after making sure you understand all the suggestions from your peer editor. Incorporate the suggestions with which you agree. Attach the draft with the editing suggestions of your partner to your final draft.

PURPOSE Description of an imaginary place, evoking suspense and urgency
AUDIENCE Readers of mystery novels
LENGTH 1–2 pages

2. Open Assignment Write a paragraph describing one of the following imaginary places or a scene from your own imagination:

- a backyard barbecue, from the point of view of a fly
- the bedroom in your dream house
- a baseball field, from the point of view of an alien visitor
- the recreation room on an orbiting space station
- a city too polluted for humans to live in

In your description, include details that appeal to each of the five senses—sight, hearing, touch, taste, and smell. Taken together, the details should convey a single, specific mood or idea.

3. Geography An important element of geography is the interaction between people and their environment. One of the basic questions this field of study asks is, How have people changed the landscape? Plan and write a description of a landscape, real or imagined, in which you give a sense of the original, natural setting and the ways in which people have altered that setting. For your prewriting technique, develop a spider diagram to come up with sensory details about the physical and human landscape. Try to think of as many details as possible for each of the five senses. Then write the description, using the details to help you decide on the overall feeling you want to communicate.

4. Music Music can evoke a scene or setting in one's imagination. Listen to a piece of classical or other instrumental music with your eyes closed. Then write a paragraph describing the setting the music evokes for you. Use specific sensory details in your description.

COMPUTER OPTION

The line spacing function in your word processor can help make peer editing easier. Set your line spacing to double or even triple spacing for your draft. When you print it out, your peer can make notes and suggestions immediately underneath your text. Wide margins all around your text can achieve a similar effect.

Describing an Imaginary Place **143**

From Heroes to Monsters

Nam June Paik, *Family of Robot: Grandfather*, 1987

Superheroes, alien beings, fearsome monsters—each is the product of someone's rich imagination. Look at the character on this page. Called *Family of Robot: Grandfather*, it was created by Nam June Paik from a radio cabinet, televisions, and videotapes. At almost eight-and-one-half feet tall, this "robot" surely towers over anyone you have ever seen.

Think about this enormous imaginary character for a moment. What kind of personality would you attribute to it? How do you think it might communicate? What might it say?

Imagining a Character

Your own imaginary character can be based on just about anything—from your wildest fantasy to someone you observe on the bus. Just begin by deciding on the type of character you want to create. Then ask yourself some creative questions to help develop details about your character. Questions like the following might help.

Questions for Developing Character Details

1. What are my character's most prominent features?

2. How does my character move and communicate?

3. What trait or traits set my character apart from others?

4. Does my character's appearance fit his, her, or its personality?

Read the model below to meet an aged woman of the imaginary town of Gont who is trying to help a child recover from severe burns. The observer, Tenar, has doubts about this woman known as Aunty Moss.

Literature Model

Tenar was not at all sure what she wanted Aunty Moss to be, finding her unpredictable, unreliable, incomprehensible, passionate, ignorant, sly, and dirty. But Moss got on with the burned child. Perhaps it was Moss who was working this change, this slight easing, in Therru. With her, Therru behaved as with everyone—blank, unanswering, docile, in the way an inanimate thing, a stone, is docile. But the old woman had kept at her, offering her little sweets and treasures, bribing, coaxing, wheedling. "Come with Aunty Moss now, dearie! Come along and Aunty Moss'll show you the prettiest sight you ever saw. . . ."

Moss's nose leaned out over her toothless jaws and thin lips; there was a wart on her cheek the size of a cherry pit; her hair was a gray-black tangle of charm-knots and wisps; and she had a smell as strong and broad and deep and complicated as the smell of a fox's den. "Come into the forest with me, dearie!" said the old witches in the tales told to the children of Gont. "Come with me and I'll show you such a pretty sight!" And then the witch shut the child in her oven and baked it brown and ate it, or dropped it into her well, where it hopped and croaked dismally forever, or put it to sleep for a hundred years inside a great stone, till the King's son should come, the Mage Prince, to shatter the stone with a word, wake the maiden with a kiss, and slay the wicked witch. . . .

"Come with me, dearie!" And she took the child into the fields and showed her a lark's nest in the green hay, or into the marshes to gather white hallows, wild mint, and blueberries.

Ursula K. LeGuin, *Tehanu: The Last Book of Earthsea*

LeGuin contrasts unpleasant aspects of Moss's appearance with her good side, both here and later in the selection.

What is the picture of Aunty Moss created by such details as "toothless jaws," "thin lips," and "gray-black tangle"?

By contrasting Moss's behavior with that typically associated with witches, LeGuin helps us to see her more as an individual than as a stereotype.

· JOURNAL ACTIVITY ·
Think It Through

In your journal describe a fantasy or science-fiction character with whom you are familiar. Explain how the character's personality does or does not fit his or her appearance.

Making a Character Come to Life

Drafting Tip

When you are ready to draft your character sketch, you might begin by describing the character's most vivid or outstanding trait.

If you were to describe your best friend, you would probably mention your friend's looks and personality, noting in particular the unique strengths that draw you to him or her. You might also note some of your friend's unique quirks or habits. Such details would help other people to envision your friend as the real live person he or she is.

When describing an imaginary character, you want to include these same kinds of details. Such details will help you make your character come to life. Note, too, that the details that are most unusual or most inconsistent with the rest of the description will do the most to bring your character alive. Such details will help give your character a three-dimensional quality that a character with no inconsistencies might lack. In addition, inconsistencies will tend to arouse your reader's interest and curiosity. A truck driver who writes poetry, for example, or a shy person who joins a comedy group will seem more notable by virtue of his or her inconsistencies. Similarly, Aunty Moss is interesting because she seems to look like a witch, but she does not behave as we might expect a witch to behave.

Here's a character description from the imagination of student Todd Crusey. How does he bring life to his character? Think about what inconsistencies you might add to make the character more interesting, yet still believable.

How would you describe the overall impression created by sensory details such as sweat rolling down his forehead "like an avalanche" and "the carved stones he called hands"?

Todd holds our interest by waiting until the very end to reveal who the character really is.

Student Model

S weat rolled like an avalanche down his broad, sloping forehead. It collected on the ledge of his square jutting brow and was then absorbed by the dense brown forest of his eyebrows. Slowly the perspiration dripped down into the large sockets that housed his squinting onyx eyes. From his hollow temples ran a flood of exhaustion that made his whole face glisten in the dark amber light of the prison wall. His nose was a wide, flat wedge, beaten down by the fists of over a hundred men. From his broad shoulders to the carved stones he called hands, he was a warrior. He had done battle in countless brawls and riots and had the scars to show for it. His only reward was his heartbeat; he had survived. This mean and relentless beast of a man always prevailed and was feared by all sane men. That's why they brought him here. Within these prison walls he reigned. He was truly a giant; he made the rules and he had the power to enforce them. That's why they called him warden.

Todd Crusey, Jefferson Davis High School, Montgomery, Alabama

The following are some writing options to help you apply what you have learned.

1. Guided Assignment   You are writing a movie script for a Hollywood producer. You have one character already, Tanya Behnia, a twenty-eight-year-old paralegal in a profitable law firm. She has expensive tastes and dresses extremely well. She is dependent upon technology, including the cellular phone she carries in her purse. Tanya has severe allergies and suffers from constant sneezing fits. She likes to sing songs she makes up, although she cannot carry a tune.

Write a description of the other character in the movie, who will accompany Tanya on an adventure that may take them anywhere. Create someone who will help make your movie interesting, whether your character is Tanya's best friend, a romantic interest, or someone she hates. Refer to the questions on page 144 to help you define your character.

PURPOSE To describe a character in a movie
AUDIENCE A movie producer
LENGTH 1–2 paragraphs

2. Open Assignment   Observe someone from one of the places described below or a place you choose. Take notes on the person's appearance, and use your notes to create a description of an imaginary person you could write a short story about. Let the personality grow out of the person's appearance, but try to make it contrast with the appearance.

- while you are riding on a bus
- looking outside your window
- in line for a movie
- from a park bench

3. Cooperative Learning   Brainstorm in a group to come up with details for a description of the character in this painting. What does the environment add to your perception of the character? Each person should write a one-paragraph description. Select those details you most liked, and add any details of your own. Return to the group, and compare your paragraphs.

Remedios Varo, *Useless Science or the Alchemist*, 1958

Describing an Imaginary Person   **147**

Analyzing Character Descriptions

Of Wizards and Dragons

What can you learn from a description of a character? To get an idea, read Arthur Housinger's analysis of a character called both Mr. Underhill and Yevaud from the story "The Rule of Names" by American writer Ursula K. LeGuin.

Student Model

*O*ne common desire links one living being to another, to be happy. Some find happiness with friends and money. In this respect, the dragon in "The Rule of Names," Yevaud, was no different from a man. He was a slightly egocentric being who just wanted some friends and some treasure.

Yevaud showed his egocentricity several times. As Blackbeard told Birt, Yevaud attacked the island of Pendor and killed many men just so he could have a treasure all for himself. After one hundred years, he ran away from the island with the treasure. He locked it in his inner chamber at Sattins Island.

Yevaud knew that this would not be enough to ensure happiness, but he had a few more tricks up his sleeve. First, he changed his appearance. Yevaud knew the unfortunate truth that people often judge a book by its cover; therefore, he changed his cover to a "little fat man of fifty who waddled along with his toes turned in." By changing his appearance, Yevaud, also known as Mr. Underhill, not only made a few friends, but he covered his tracks as the thief of the treasure. Blackbeard accurately called him a "wise, cunning monster, full of strength and subtlety."

Yevaud's tricks lacked perfection, though, just as many of his elixirs did. Since Yevaud was constantly showing a false ➡

Arthur notes the importance of this character's change in appearance.

front, a barrier came between him and the villagers. His smiles were even false and made the village girls feel nervous. Yet since he was such a bumbling wizard, the townspeople simply treated Mr. Underhill as a fellow villager. This too was a falsehood, as was shown when Yevaud used his great powers to fight Blackbeard.

Here Arthur shows the villagers' reactions to Yevaud/Underhill.

Yevaud tried to be something he wasn't, a friendly, inept wizard called Mr. Underhill. Once this barrier of deceit disappeared, Yevaud's true self, along with his true name, could spread its wings. Although Blackbeard's description of Yevaud was accurate, it was not complete. Yevaud was also a friendly being who found a home where he felt comfortable, one who wanted friends and treasure.

Arthur next analyzes Yevaud/Underhill's actions and how these actions affected other characters.

Arthur Housinger, Rich East High School, Park Forest, Illinois

A Character's Appearance

When you write about a literary character, you may want to pay particular attention to the details of that character's physical appearance. These details can suggest a great deal about the nature and background of the person. In "The Rule of Names," for example, the details of the main character's appearance are especially significant, since they hint at his true nature and background.

You may also want to consider the order and way in which these physical details are presented. An author may put the most important facts about a character first or describe them in the greatest detail so as to impress them upon you. In *Robin Hood: Prince of Thieves,* for example, novelist Simon Green first describes Robin Hood's friend Azeem as follows: "Tall and heavily muscled, he had dark skin covered with intricate tattoos. Even his shaved head was ornamented with them."

Thus, Green emphasizes Azeem's strength and his exotic quality, suggesting that these are important features of this character. As the story unfolds, readers learn that these are, in fact, among the most important things to know and remember about him.

• JOURNAL ACTIVITY •
Think It Through

Find a description of a favorite literary character. In your journal note what the author describes first about that character and what features the author describes in the most detail. From what you know about the character, are these the most important features? If so, explain their significance.

A Character's Thoughts, Words, and Actions

When you analyze a character, it is important to consider everything about him or her, especially since a character's thoughts, words, and actions might not always be in line with his or her appearance. For example, Azeem looks like a powerful and exotic person. Yet through his thoughts, words, and actions, readers also learn that he is a loyal, honorable, and loving friend.

Thoughts		Words		Actions		Conclusion
"Not for the first time, Azeem realized he was a long way from home, and those he had loved."	**+**	"It is because I love them so dearly that I cannot dishonor them by breaking my vow."	**+**	"Azeem examined Fanny's swollen belly... and then looked at her compassionately." He then delivered Fanny's baby.	**=**	These thoughts, words, and actions indicate that Azeem is a loving, loyal, and compassionate man.

When you begin to analyze a character's thoughts, words, and actions, you may want to ask yourself how you feel about what the character says and does. You might also ask such questions as these: How would I feel around this person? Would I react the same way the character did? What qualities does this character have that I admire or dislike? Asking and answering such questions will help you get to know the character personally and will help make your writing about the character fresh and stimulating.

Revising Tip

When you revise, look for places your draft might be strengthened by adding actual excerpts from the literature to convey details of a character's appearance, thoughts, words, and/or actions.

Reactions of Other Characters

An author can also reveal much about a character by showing how other people react to that character. Be aware of these reactions as you analyze a character, but be sure to consider the nature of the person who is doing the reacting, too. The character's enemies would naturally dislike him or her, while the character's friends would be biased in his or her favor. So the reactions of neither would be completely accurate. Yet you can interpret them and learn about the character. The chart shows two reactions to Azeem. Which do you think shows the truest picture?

Reaction A
Robin Hood tells his men his opinion of Azeem, "I trust him."

Reactions to Azeem

Reaction B
Friar Tuck and the others distrust Azeem and call him a savage because his ways are so different from their own.

Writer's Choice

The following are some writing options to help you apply what you have learned.

1. Guided Assignment   Read the following description of a Lut from the story "The Odd Ones" by R. Gordon Dickson:

> The Lut, on the other hand, was built more on the model of an earthly tiger, except that he was longer—being fully as long as the Snorap—and thicker, with an almost perfectly round body, rather like a big sewer main. He was tailless, his head was big and flat of face, and he possessed an enormous jaw which could crunch boulders like hard candy. His eyes had a fierce green glint to them and he was covered with very fine, but incredibly tough, small glassy scales which would have permitted him to take an acid shower every morning and never notice it at all.

How might you react if you were to meet a being who looked like this? Now read the rest of the paragraph describing the Lut.

> But in spite of his appearance, he was just as civilized, just as intelligent, and just as much a gentleman as the Snorap; which put them both, as a matter of fact, several notches above the two humans they were watching, in all those respects.

Write a description of the Lut that a human space traveler might read in a guide to alien races. Structure your description so that a reader, upon encountering a Lut, would not immediately fire a weapon or run away in the opposite direction. Feel free to expand upon what you know of the Lut from the descriptions above.

PURPOSE   To describe an alien being beyond its fearful appearance
AUDIENCE   A human encountering that being
LENGTH   2–3 paragraphs

2. Open Assignment   Select a character from one of the books or stories below or another with which you are familiar:

- *When the Legends Die*, by Hal Borland
- *Great Expectations*, by Charles Dickens
- *To Kill A Mockingbird*, by Harper Lee
- *A Wizard of Earthsea*, by Ursula K. LeGuin

Imagine the character was a dinner guest in your home last night. Write in your journal about your family's reactions to the character. Describe any discussions or activities that may have happened during the evening.

3. Social Studies   Do some research about a significant person you admire in history. Treat that person as a character in literature. Find information you can put into three lists: one describing the person's appearance; one recording the person's thoughts, words, and actions; and a third noting public perceptions of the person, both when alive as well as today. Use your notes to create a profile of the person that could be used as a single-page feature in a history book. As you write, focus more on the "character" of the person as shown in the lists you've made than on the specific dates and places associated with the person.

COMPUTER OPTION

Save a step in the note-taking process by conducting your research with the aid of your word processor. Bring your books with you to the computer, and type in each significant detail you discover about the person. Hit the return key after each note you type, so that you can later rearrange your details into the three lists. Then you won't have to type the pieces of information into your file again as you develop your writing structure.

Writing About Literature: Analyzing Character Descriptions   **151**

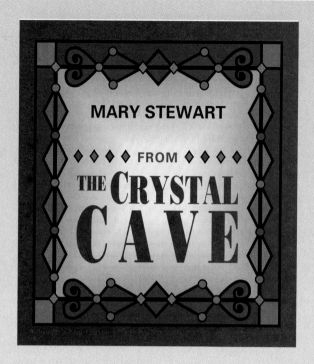

MARY STEWART

◆ ◆ ◆ FROM ◆ ◆ ◆

THE CRYSTAL
CAVE

Until 1970 Mary Stewart wrote popular mystery thrillers in her native England. That year, Stewart began publishing historical fiction, especially novels about King Arthur's sixth-century England through the eyes of the magician Merlin. These novels included The Crystal Cave, The Hollow Hills, *and* The Last Enchantment. *In these works, Stewart vividly describes the world of Arthur and Merlin in imaginative stories she calls "somewhere between legend and truth and fairy tale and known history."*

This was bigger than had appeared from outside. Only a couple of paces inside the archway—and my paces were very short— the cave opened out into a seemingly vast chamber whose top was lost in shadow. It was dark, but—though at first I neither noticed this nor looked for its cause—with some source of extra light that gave a vague illumination, showing the floor smooth and clear of obstacles. I made my way slowly forward, straining my eyes, with deep inside me the beginning of that surge of excitement that caves have always started in me. Some men experience this with water; some, I know, on high places; some create fire for the same pleasure: with me it has always been the depths of the forest, or the depths of the earth. Now, I know why; but then, I only knew that I was a boy who had found somewhere new, something he could perhaps make his own in a world where he owned nothing.

Next moment I stopped short, brought up by a shock which spilled the excitement through my bowels like water. Something had moved in the murk, just to my right.

I froze still, straining my eyes to see. There was no movement. I held my breath, listening. There was no sound. I flared my nostrils, testing the air cautiously round me. There was no smell, animal or human; the cave smelt, I thought, of smoke and damp rock and the earth itself, and of a queer musty scent I couldn't identify. I knew, without putting it into words, that had there been any other creature near me the air would have felt different, less empty. There was no one there.

I tried a word, softly, in Welsh. "Greetings." The whisper came straight back at me in an echo so quick that I knew I was very near the wall of the cave, then it lost itself, hissing, in the roof.

There was movement there—at first, I thought, only an intensifying of the echoed whisper, then the rustling grew and grew like the rustling of a woman's dress, or a curtain stirring in the draft. Something went past my cheek, with a shrill, bloodless cry just on the edge of sound. Another followed, and after them flake after flake of shrill shadow, pouring down from the roof like leaves down a stream of wind, or fish down a fall. It was the bats, disturbed from their lodging in the top of the cave, streaming out now into the daylight valley. They would be pouring out of the low archway like a plume of smoke.

I stood quite still, wondering if it was these that had made the curious musty smell. I thought I could smell them as they passed, but it wasn't the same. I had no fear that they would touch me; in darkness or light, whatever their speed, bats will touch nothing. They are so much creatures of the air, I believe, that as the air parts in front of an obstacle the bat is swept aside with it, like a petal carried downstream. They poured past, a shrill tide of them between me and the wall. Childlike, to see what the stream would do—how it would divert itself—I took a step nearer to the wall. Nothing touched me. The stream divided and poured on, the shrill air brushing both my cheeks. It was as if I did not exist. But at the same moment when I moved, the creature that I had seen moved, too. Then my outstretched hand met, not rock, but metal, and I knew what the creature was. It was my own reflection.

Hanging against the wall was a sheet of metal, burnished[1] to a dull sheen. This, then, was the source of the diffused[2] light within the

1 **burnished** (bʉrʹ nish'd) polished
2 **diffused** (di fyoozʹ 'd) spread out in every direction

cave; the mirror's silky surface caught, obliquely,[3] the light from the cave's mouth, and sent it on into the darkness. I could see myself moving in it like a ghost, as I recoiled[4] and let fall the hand which had leapt to the knife at my hip.

Behind me the flow of bats had ceased, and the cave was still. Reassured, I stayed where I was, studying myself with interest in the mirror. My mother had had one once, an antique from Egypt, but then, deeming such things to be vanity, she had locked it away. Of course I had often seen my face reflected in water, but never my body mirrored, till now. I saw a dark boy, wary, all eyes with curiosity, nerves, and excitement. In that light my eyes looked quite black; my hair was black, too, thick and clean, but worse cut and groomed than my pony's; my tunic and sandals were a disgrace. I grinned, and the mirror flashed a sudden smile that changed the picture completely and at once, from a sullen young animal poised to run or fight, to something quick and gentle and approachable; something, I knew even then, that few people had ever seen.

Then it vanished, and the wary animal was back, as I leaned forward to run a hand over the metal. It was cold and smooth and freshly burnished. Whoever had hung it—and he must be the same person who used the cup of horn[5] outside—had either been here very recently, or he still lived here, and might come back at any moment to find me.

I was not particularly frightened. I had pricked to caution when I saw the cup, but one learns very young to take care of oneself, and the times I had been brought up in were peaceful enough, at any rate in our valley; but there are always wild men and rough men and the lawless and vagabonds to be reckoned with, and any boy who likes his own company, as I did, must be prepared to defend his skin. I was wiry, and strong for my age, and I had my dagger. That I was

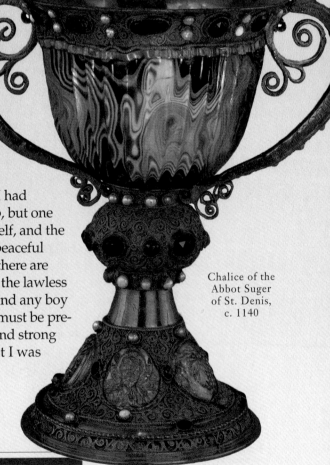

Chalice of the Abbot Suger of St. Denis, c. 1140

3 **obliquely** (ə blēk′ lē) indirectly

4 **recoiled** (ri koil′ ′d) fell back

5 **cup of horn** a cup made from an animal's horn

Descriptive Writing: Real Toads in Imaginary Gardens

barely seven years old never entered my head; I was Merlin, and, bastard or not, the King's grandson. I went on exploring.

The next thing I found, a pace along the wall, was a box, and on top of it shapes which my hands identified immediately as flint and iron and tinderbox,[6] and a big, roughly made candle of what smelled like sheep's tallow.[7] Beside these objects lay a shape which—incredulously and inch by inch—I identified as the skull of a horned sheep. There were nails driven into the top of the box here and there, apparently holding down fragments of leather. But when I felt these, carefully, I found in the withered leather frameworks of delicate bone; they were dead bats, stretched and nailed on the wood.

This was a treasure cave indeed. No find of gold or weapons could have excited me more. Full of curiosity, I reached for the tinderbox.

Then I heard him coming back.

My first thought was that he must have seen my pony, then I realized he was coming from further up the hill. I could hear the rattling and scaling of small stones as he came down the scree[8] above the cave. One of them splashed into the spring outside, and then it was too late. I heard him jump down on the flat grass beside the water.

It was time for the ring-dove again; the falcon was forgotten.[9] I ran deeper into the cave. As he swept aside the boughs[10] that darkened the entrance, the light grew momentarily, enough to show me my way. At the back of the cave was a slope and jut of rock, and, at twice my height, a widish ledge. A quick flash of sunlight from the mirror caught a wedge of shadow in the rock above the ledge, big enough to hide me. Soundless in my scuffed sandals, I swarmed on to the ledge, and crammed my body into that wedge of shadow, to find it was in fact a gap in the rock, giving apparently on to another, smaller cave. I slithered in through the gap like an otter into the river-bank.

It seemed that he had heard nothing. The light was cut off again as the boughs sprang back into place behind him, and he came into the cave. It was a man's tread, measured and slow.

If I had thought about it at all, I suppose I would have assumed that the cave would be uninhabited at least until sunset, that whoever owned the place would be away hunting, or about his other business, and would return only at nightfall. There was no point in wasting

---

6 **tinderbox** (tin' dər bäks') a metal box holding the materials to make a fire

7 **tallow** (tal' o) animal fat used to make candles

8 **scree** (skrē) a slope covered with rock fragments

9 **It was time for the ring-dove again; the falcon was forgotten.** Unlike the ferocious falcon, the ring-dove was a bird that kept quiet and knew when to run away. While Young Merlin was often called "falcon," one character had told him that he was still a ring-dove.

10 **boughs** (bouz) tree branches

candles when the sun was blazing outside. Perhaps he was here now only to bring home his kill, and he would go again and leave me the chance to get out. I hoped he would not see my pony tethered[11] in the hawthorn brake.[12]

Then I heard him moving, with the sure tread of someone who knows his way blindfold, towards the candle and the tinderbox.

Even now I had no room for apprehension,[13] no room, indeed, for any but the one thought or sensation—the extreme discomfort of the cave into which I had crawled. It was apparently small, not much bigger than the large round vats they use for dyeing, and much the same shape. Floor, wall and ceiling hugged me round in a continuous curve. It was like being inside a large globe; moreover, a globe studded with nails, or with its inner surface stuck all over with small pieces of jagged stone. There seemed no inch of surface not bristling like a bed of strewn flints, and it was only my light weight, I think, that saved me from being cut, as I quested about blindly to find some clear space to lie on. I found a place smoother than the rest and curled there, as small as I could, watching the faintly defined opening, and inching my dagger silently from its sheath into my hand.

I heard the quick hiss and chime of flint and iron, and then the flare of light, intense in the darkness, as the tinder caught hold. Then the steady, waxing[14] glow as he lit the candle.

Or rather, it should have been the slow-growing beam of a candle flame that I saw, but instead there was a flash, a sparkle, a conflagration[15] as if a whole pitch-soaked beacon was roaring up in flames. Light poured and flashed, crimson, golden, white, red, intolerable into my cave. I winced back from it, frightened now, heedless of pain and cut flesh as I shrank against the sharp walls. The whole globe where I lay seemed to be full of flame.

It was indeed a globe, a round chamber floored, roofed, lined with crystals. They were fine as glass, and smooth as glass, but clearer than any glass I had ever seen, brilliant as diamonds. This, in fact, to my childish mind, was what they first seemed to be. I was in a globe lined with diamonds, a million burning diamonds, each face of each gem wincing with the light, shooting it to and fro, diamond to diamond and back again, with rainbows and rivers and bursting stars and a shape like a crimson dragon clawing up

11 **tethered** (teth′ er′d) tied with a rope or chain

12 **brake** (brāk) a thicket

13 **apprehension** (ap′ rə hen′ shən) dread

14 **waxing** (waks′ iŋ) slowly growing larger

15 **conflagration** (kän′ flə grä′ shən) an enormous fire

the wall, while below it a girl's face swam faintly with closed eyes, and the light drove right into my body as if it would break me open.

I shut my eyes. When I opened them again I saw that the golden light had shrunk and was concentrated on one part of the wall no bigger than my head, and from this, empty of visions, rayed the broken, brilliant beams.

There was silence from the cave below. He had not stirred. I had not even heard the rustle of his clothes.

Then the light moved. The flashing disc began to slide, slowly, across the crystal wall. I was shaking. I huddled closer to the sharp stones, trying to escape it. There was nowhere to go. It advanced slowly round the curve. It touched my shoulder, my head, and I ducked, cringing. The shadow of my movement rushed across the globe, like a wind-eddy[16] over a pool.

The light stopped, retreated, fixed glittering in its place. Then it went out. But the glow of the candle, strangely, remained; an ordinary steady yellow glow beyond the gap in the wall of my refuge.

"Come out." The man's voice, not loud, not raised with shouted orders like my grandfather's, was clear and brief with all the mystery of command. It never occurred to me to disobey. I crept forward over the sharp crystals, and through the gap. Then I slowly pulled myself upright on the ledge, my back against the wall of the outer cave, the dagger ready in my right hand, and looked down.

He stood between me and the candle, a hugely tall figure (or so it seemed to me) in a long robe of some brown homespun stuff. The candle made a nimbus[17] of his hair, which seemed to be grey, and he was bearded. I could not see his expression, and his right hand was hidden in the folds of his robe.

I waited, poised warily.

He spoke again, in the same tone. "Put up your dagger and come down."

"When I see your right hand," I said.

He showed it, palm up. It was empty. He said gravely: "I am unarmed."

16 **wind-eddy** (wind′ ed′ ē) a current of wind

17 **nimbus** (nim′ bəs) a bright cloud or aura surrounding a person
    or object

Frankish, Dagger, c. 600 A.D.

"Then stand out of my way," I said, and jumped. The cave was wide, and he was standing to one side of it. My leap carried me three or four paces down the cave, and I was past him and near the entrance before he could have moved more than a step. But in fact he never moved at all. As I reached the mouth of the cave and swept aside the hanging branches I heard him laughing.

The sound brought me up short. I turned.

From here, in the light which now filled the cave, I saw him clearly. He was old, with grey hair thinning on top and hanging lank over his ears, and a straight growth of grey beard, roughly trimmed. His hands were calloused and grained with dirt, but had been fine, with long fingers. Now the old man's veins crawled and knotted on them, distended[18] like worms. But it was his face which held me; it was thin, cavernous almost as a skull, with a high domed forehead and bushy grey brows which came down jutting over eyes where I could see no trace of age at all. These were closely set, large, and of a curiously clear and swimming grey. His nose was a thin beak; his mouth, lipless now, stretched wide with his laughter over astonishingly good teeth.

"Come back. There's no need to be afraid."

"I'm not afraid." I dropped the boughs back into place, and not without bravado[19] walked towards him. I stopped a few paces away. "Why should I be afraid of you? Do you know who I am?"

He regarded me for a moment, seeming to muse. "Let me see you. Dark hair, dark eyes, the body of a dancer and the manners of a young wolf . . . or should I say a young falcon?"

My dagger sank to my side. "Then you do know me?"

"Shall I say I knew you would come some day, and today I knew there was someone here. What do you think brought me back so early?"

---

18 distended (dis tend′ ′d) swollen

19 bravado (bre vä′ dō) pretended confidence or courage

For Discussion

1. What parts of Stewart's descriptions in this piece stand out most vividly in your memory? Why?

2. When you read the line "Then I heard him coming back," what did you feel? What did you expect to happen next? Why? What descriptive words have helped to create this effect?

Readers Respond

The owner of the cave had an easy-going, relaxed feeling about him. He laughed when he saw the kid running out instead of being angry for his being there. Stewart made the old man seem real by giving such a detailed description of his face and of what he did each moment. I also liked the description Stewart gave of the moment when the man lit the candle and the "diamonds" were sparkling brightly. I would like to read beyond this selection to find out what happens next.

Yahna Awazu

I always enjoy exploration-type scenes, so the scene during which the boy explores the cave was the one I liked most. The dominant mood was one of curiosity and suspicion. The writer created that mood by making all things very odd or at least out of the ordinary. The meeting of the old man and the boy seemed for a second to be the end for one of them.

The old man is the sort of character I usually enjoy. He laughs at the over-inventive and imaginative people. He is quite likely a cynic. The scene in which the boy, Merlin, met the old man was by far the most memorable. I have already recommended this selection to a friend. It is very good, and the subject matter—the Merlin and King Arthur legends—is fascinating.

Charles Dayton

Did you notice?

☞ Did you notice, by the end of the first paragraph of the selection, that this description of a child's experience is told from an adult's memories of that experience? How does this perspective affect the telling of the story?

☞ Have you ever explored an unfamiliar or unusual place? Write a descriptive paragraph about the place and your experience, using sensory details to enliven your description.

Writing Process in Action

A Traveler's Companion

Using her descriptive powers, Mary Stewart—author of _The Crystal Cave_, excerpted on pages 152–158—takes readers into a cave that until she wrote about it existed only in her imagination. What if you wanted to transport readers to a place only you have imagined? Do you think your descriptive powers would be up to the challenge? In this lesson, you are invited to find out. You may choose to depict a familiar kind of place that could exist somewhere in this world. Or you can attempt to take readers a step further to an entirely fantastical place—possibly one that's out of this world.

• Assignment •

CONTEXT You are a staff writer for _Vicarious Voyager_, a magazine devoted to publishing descriptive writing that lets "even dedicated couch potatoes expand their horizons." Now you need to write a description of an imagined place for the magazine. This place can be a familiar one that could exist somewhere in this world. Or it can be an entirely fantastical place. The editors expect you to write from your own point of view and to focus on describing your personal impressions of the place and your sensations in it rather than on speculating about _why_ the place may be as it is. The editors believe that this type of writing best enables readers to voyage vicariously—that is, to experience your feelings and sensations just by reading about them.

PURPOSE To write a first-person description that so vividly conveys your impressions of a place you've imagined that it helps readers to feel transported there

AUDIENCE Imaginative teen-agers who want the experience of visiting new places without ever actually leaving home

LENGTH 2–3 pages

For more advice on how to approach this assignment, you will find the next few pages helpful. But don't feel that you have to remember all of what follows. You can come _back_ to these pages as you write, getting help where and when you need it. You're in charge of your own writing process.

1. Prewriting

Where might you want to go—an exotic country, an alien wilderness, a landscape that might exist on the head of a pin? If you've got a place in mind, begin with that. If not, try rereading the literature models in Lessons 3.1–3.4

Descriptive Writing: Real Toads in Imaginary Gardens

to get some ideas. Look also at Lesson 3.3, page 141, for help in coming up with an imagined place.

Then start exploring your place by mentally wandering through it. Asking and answering questions like those in Lesson 3.3, pages 141–142, or like the ones below can help guide your wanderings.

- What details would I use to describe my sensations here? (I see . . . , I smell . . . , I hear . . . , I taste . . . , I feel . . .)
- What type of place is it? (city, forest, ocean, home, factory?)
- How does it compare with places like it that I know? (more advanced, cleaner, dirtier, older, newer?)
- Who or what lives here—if anything? (plants, big insects?)
- What do the inhabitants do here? (dance, sing, work?)
- Do the natural laws of our known world hold true in this imagined one? (Is there gravity? Is there just one sun?)

As you wander, write down what you find. Note, in particular, your personal impressions and sensations. To get an idea of what you might jot down, note the kinds of sensory details Mary Stewart includes here:

> I froze still, straining my eyes to see. There was no movement. I held my breath, listening. There was no sound. I flared my nostrils, testing the air cautiously round me. There was no smell, animal or human; the cave smelt, I thought, of smoke and damp rock and the earth itself, and of a queer musty scent I couldn't identify. I knew, without putting it into words, that had there been any other creature near me the air would have felt different, less empty. There was no one there.

Once you have generated a page or two of prewriting notes, review your notes to see whether you've included enough details to enable your readers to see, smell, hear, taste, and touch the place you are describing. Consider also what mood these details, taken together, may suggest. If they don't suggest a mood, you may want to work on developing one. For help in doing this, see Lesson 3.1. If they do suggest an overall impression, Lesson 3.1 can also provide tips on heightening this mood. A place that has a particular mood is more likely to leave a lasting impression than a place that doesn't.

Characterizing a place by exaggerating one particular detail can also help you create a strong impression. Think about your place logically to see what detail(s) may be appropriate to accentuate. Since caves tend to be dark places, Stewart logically accentuates this darkness. She does so both by limiting visual details and by providing more input from other senses:

> There was movement there—at first, I thought, only an intensifying of the echoed whisper, then the rustling grew and grew like the rustling of a woman's dress, or a curtain stirring in the draft. Something went past my cheek, with a shrill, bloodless cry just on the edge of sound. Another followed, and after them flake after flake of shrill shadow, pouring down from the roof like leaves down a stream of wind, or fish down a fall.

2. Drafting

To begin drafting, think of a likely point of entry to your place. This will probably be the point from which you began envisioning your place during prewriting. But it doesn't have to be. You might want to choose a spot from which you can easily orient your readers to their surroundings. For instance, you could begin crouched behind a door. Or, you could choose a point that affords your readers an overview, such as a hilltop. Stewart begins just inside the entrance to the cave. For help in orienting readers, review spatial organization in Lesson 3.1, page 133.

Then, visualizing the place from your chosen point of entry, begin drafting your description. Refer to your prewriting notes for words and details that convey your sensations and that contribute to the overall mood of your place. But don't stop writing in order to find "just the right word." At this stage, it's more important to keep your words flowing.

How you proceed through your place will both depend upon the mood of the place and reinforce it. The fact that Stewart's narrator explores the cave cautiously both makes logical sense and enhances the mysterious mood of the place. How might the mood of her description have been affected had the narrator simply marched confidently into the cave?

As you may have done during prewriting, you can let your "journey" be guided by your reactions to various sensations. Or, you can describe details either by spatial arrangement or order of importance.

- To organize details spatially, describe all of the elements in a place by their location as you perceive them. This may be from top to bottom, left to right, or front to back.
- To organize details by order of importance, start by describing the key details and then move on to less important ones. This method works well if your readers need to grasp certain important details before they can understand the rest of your world. Alternatively, you can build suspense by starting with the minor details and leading up to the most important ones.

Once you think you've got everything down on paper—even if you're not totally happy with how you've said it—put your draft aside. Stepping away from it for a few hours or even a day can help you to see its strengths and weaknesses more easily when you next read it.

3. Revising

Describing an imagined place can be tricky, since this place exists only in your mind. After all, how do you know that your readers will be able to picture your world as you intend? One of the best ways to find out is to ask peer editors to read your draft and then describe your world back to you. If they do an accurate job, your description is probably clear. If not, you may improve upon your description by revising those aspects of it your peer editors miss or confuse. For help revising your description, review it while asking yourself the questions at the top of the next page.

- Have I used details consistently to establish and maintain a believable reality? (An inconsistency can destroy your world's believability.)
- Might I order the details here in a more logical way? (Review Lesson 2.7 for suggestions on ordering details.)
- Would adding transitional words and phrases help orient my readers better? (See Lessons 2.8 and 3.1 for some ideas on transitions and on orienting readers.)
- Could using figurative language make my description more vivid? (To develop similes and metaphors ask yourself questions such as, "What is it like?" "To what can I compare it?")

Next, consider your peer editors' reactions in light of your assignment. Do they find your place interesting? If not, you may need to revise your description to make it more interesting. This task may involve eliminating details—often a writer's favorite ones—that are excessive or irrelevant. So, check your favorite bits of description for unnecessary details. Then eliminate unnecessary details from the rest of your description as well.

Criteria
1. *Focuses on an imagined place*
2. *Orients readers by presenting details in a logical order*
3. *Uses vivid sensory details and figurative language*
4. *Maintains readers' interest by creating suspense and empathy and by avoiding the use of excessive or irrelevant details*
5. *Uses first-person point of view consistently*
6. *Follows correct grammar, usage, and mechanics*

4. Editing

Once you are comfortable with the basic content and structure of your description, look at your paragraphs and sentences. Are they unified and coherent? Lesson 2.9, page 96, can help you check unity and coherence.

Next, look at the words you have used. If you have included any invented or adapted terms, make sure that you have used, spelled, capitalized, and punctuated them in a consistent manner. Consider whether you can make your description more vivid and precise by adding or replacing words. Look to Lesson 3.2, pages 136–138, for suggestions on choosing words for their connotations and using precise nouns and vivid modifiers. When you're satisfied with your description, make a clean copy and proofread it one more time.

5. Presenting

Although you have written a description for a fictional magazine, you can use the descriptions you and your classmates wrote to create a magazine of your own. To do so, form an editorial board to read, discuss, and select the best descriptions based on the criteria provided in the text. As a group, create a cover, a table of contents, and an introduction to these descriptions. Then combine these items, and make the collection available for others to read.

• Reflecting •

Description can add life to all types of writing. Look at another piece you have written to see if you could improve it with description. Then, in a brief paragraph, tell what you discovered about your powers of description.

Portfolio & Reflection

Summary

Key concepts in descriptive writing include the following:
- An effective descriptive paragraph conveys a single overall impression.
- The overall impression is stated in a topic sentence and supported with details.
- Descriptive language is chosen for its connotations, precision, and vividness.
- Describing an imaginary place means choosing details to convey a mood.
- Describing an imaginary person means conveying the person's uniqueness.

Your Writer's Portfolio

Look over the descriptive writing you have done during this unit. Select two pieces of writing to put into your portfolio. Each piece should demonstrate that you have worked with one or more of the preceding concepts. In other words, look for a piece of writing that does one or more of the following:
- contains descriptive details that create a strong overall impression
- contains precise, vivid language that has the appropriate connotations
- describes a place by creating a mood
- describes a person by conveying the person's uniqueness

Reflection and Commentary

Now write one page in which you demonstrate that you understand what this unit asked of you. Use the two pieces of writing you've selected as evidence while you consider the following numbered items. Respond to as many numbered items as possible. Label the page "Commentary on Descriptive Writing," and include it in your portfolio.

1. Which details create a strong overall impression?
2. Where did you orient your reader by presenting details in spatial order? What transitions help your reader see exactly what you saw or imagined?
3. What words did you choose for their positive or negative connotations? What precise nouns and vivid modifiers did you use?
4. What descriptive techniques worked especially well for you? What details did you generate through a technique such as creative questioning?
5. What details give life to your description of a place or person? How will you change and improve your process for writing description?
6. Explain why you think readers could picture a place or person you described. How could you describe a place or person better the next time?

Feedback

If you had a chance to respond to the following student comment, what would you say or ask?

The best thing about writing is the elusive, satisfying final result. All writers ache for this.

Mathew Isaac, Rich East High School,
Park Forest, Illinois

Narrative Writing

The Basic Tale

Jan Vermeer, *Servant Handing a Letter to Her Mistress,* c. 1665

Bessone Profiles a

Winner

"Sports are about games, but they can be a metaphor for so much more. When I write sports stories, I try to look beyond to something that's not readily apparent. I really want to tell a story, not just who won. And when I empathize with the person I'm writing about, I can make my readers feel something, too."

Lisa Twyman Bessone

L isa Twyman Bessone grew up in a family that took its sports seriously. Her father, Jack Twyman, played basketball for the Cincinnati Royals, and the whole family traveled to many of his games. At Dartmouth, Bessone became the captain of the rowing crew. The "incredibly unbiased" sports stories she wrote about her team helped her land a job on a suburban paper in Cincinnati. A few years later, in 1981, Bessone joined the staff of *Sports Illustrated*.

"You start as a fact checker," Bessone recalls. "You're trying to get the story exactly right before it's published." Later, when

Writing the Sports Story

1. Finding the Narrative

2. Researching the Narrative

3. Writing the Narrative

4. Publishing the Narrative

FOCUS

Most sports narratives focus on character and conflict—conflict between players or between teams, or an individual's struggle to overcome personal limitations.

she started actually writing stories for *Sports Illustrated*, Bessone sharpened her interest in "what's going on behind the field. You try to get to know what motivates the athlete, what makes these people so driven and so disciplined."

1. Finding the Narrative

Lisa Bessone knew she'd found a great story when she watched a triathlon in 1989. She recalls, "A couple of my friends were running. Along comes this guy running with a prosthesis [artificial leg] and doing incredibly well. We all remarked on how amazing it was. A small feature appeared in the paper the next day about this football player, Jim MacLaren, who had lost his leg in a motorcycle accident and was now running triathlons in excellent times." So Bessone's idea for the nonfiction narrative came from her observation of MacLaren running in the triathlon and from reading the newspaper feature story about him later.

Once she got the idea for the narrative, Bessone sent a query letter to her editor at *Sports Illustrated* requesting approval to pursue the story. Bessone's editor gave her an enthusiastic go-ahead. Now she was ready to research her narrative.

2. Researching the Narrative

Armed with a tape recorder, Bessone flew to New England to interview Jim MacLaren. Before an interview Bessone always writes down questions she calls "touchstones to remind myself of the direction I want to go. Usually one question will spark a half-hour discussion."

At first, MacLaren didn't want to talk about the injury that destroyed his leg and nearly took his life. Bessone was willing to wait. "As a sportswriter, you learn the art of hanging out. The more people know you, the more they trust you. After a while Jim told me about the accident. . . . It was obviously traumatic that he'd lost his leg, but most of the other aspects of his story were really upbeat."

An interviewer's tools often include a tape recorder and a notebook of key questions.

In addition to interviewing MacLaren, his mother, and several of his friends, Bessone sought statistics from the Triathlon Federation: "You need that kind of stuff to give your story a factual basis. Instead of just saying MacLaren is a really good runner, for example, I could say he finished the race only twenty-four minutes behind the winner. And the triathlon is a grueling race with two legs, let alone one." Even as she was collecting information, Bessone considered how best to arrange those crucial elements of character and conflict into a compelling narrative.

INTERFACE *You've been invited to accompany Lisa Bessone as she interviews Jim MacLaren. Make a list of five questions you'd like to ask this athlete.*

The Ironman Triathlon is a race consisting of a 2.4 mile swim, a 112-mile bike ride, and a 26-mile run.

3. Writing the Narrative

Lisa Bessone listened to her tapes, noting the things she wanted to include in her narrative. The sportswriter usually has some idea of the organization she's going to use. "That's like a road map you're following the whole time," Bessone says. "Once you have the organization down, the whole piece works." Bessone's "road map" for this narrative was MacLaren's progression from his accident and rehabilitation to competing in races.

After Bessone had completed her first draft, however, MacLaren ran the 1989 Ironman Triathlon, and Bessone decided to revise her story. At this triathlon, held annually in Hawaii, MacLaren bested the previous amputee record by almost two hours. Bessone also wanted to include an anecdote MacLaren later told her about an incident that occurred during the marathon leg of the Triathlon;

Bessone decided to use this anecdote in her lead paragraph.

This lead paragraph sets a scene that arouses curiosity, creates drama, and then reels the reader in with its last sentence. Bessone comments, "At first you don't know why you're reading; then you find out. It's like holding a card back. Then in the next paragraph, I explain why MacLaren merits this story." Bessone also used her conclusion to drive home the message of her narrative, that there are no limits on any of us.

In the marathon leg of the 1989 Ironman Triathlon in Hawaii, Jim MacLaren, a 27-year-old professional triathlete and a former linebacker for Yale, fell in step with 41-year-old Ken Mitchell, who played the same position for the Atlanta Falcons from 1972 to '75. Given the demands of the race (a 2.4-mile swim, a marathon run, and a 112-mile bike ride), conversation had to be minimal, but the two talked a bit about Mitchell's 11 knee operations, the result of his football career. After about a mile MacLaren decided to pull ahead. "I'm saying a little prayer for you, Jimmy," Mitchell called out as he dropped farther and farther behind. MacLaren, you see, was running with a prosthesis on his leg.

4. Editing and Publishing the Narrative

A newspaper sportswriter's story usually appears almost exactly as it is written. But it's the rare magazine story that gets published without being changed. Bessone explains, "I try to tell the whole story, but you have to submit to the editing process. Of course, when your story is well edited, you look smarter.

"The editors cut this piece a lot. The main section they cut was about why it's so phenomenal that MacLaren does what he does. A biophysicist I talked to said that the fact MacLaren runs so fast defies medicine. In the original story I also had him coming back, finishing the Ironman with tears in his eyes. I was sad to see these things go. But there are space constraints on any magazine piece."

The magazine editors and designers wrote the heading and subheading for the story and sent a photographer to take pictures of MacLaren. One of the two photographs they used shows MacLaren with his wife. "She, too, played a larger role in my original story," Bessone says. "But the editors decided to let the visual carry that part of the story."

In response to her article about MacLaren, Bessone says she got many telephone calls, including one from someone who wanted to do a movie about Jim MacLaren. "He's a heroic figure," says Bessone. "It was a happy story."

INTERFACE *Study the two photos on this page. How do they enhance the story? What other photos would you include to tell MacLaren's story? Why?*

ON ASSIGNMENT

1. Choose a school or community sports event to cover. Interview a player, coach, or parent to get background information before or after the event. Write a brief feature that includes elements of narrative writing and tells an interesting story about the event.

2. **Literature Connection**
   Many sports stories include elements of narrative writing such as character and conflict. Select a sports story from a newspaper or magazine to review. Who are the characters? What is the conflict, and how is it resolved?

3. **Cooperative Learning**
   As a group, select a sports event to cover. Each member of the group should pick a different way to tell the story of the event. One person might write a factual report, another might write a feature, one might take photographs, and another might write a poem or prepare an edited videotape. Determine as a group how best to put together a presentation for the rest of the class.

Case Study: Sportswriting

Telling a Story

"Guess what happened to me today!" These words often begin a narrative, that is, a story relating a sequence of events with a beginning, a middle, and an end. The story may be true—nonfiction—or imagined—fiction. In the following narrative, Jamaica Kincaid tells the true story of how her mother came to live on the Caribbean island of Antigua.

Literature Model

W hen my mother, at sixteen, after quarreling with her father, left his house on Dominica and came to Antigua, she packed all her things in an enormous wooden trunk that she had bought in Roseau for almost six shillings. She painted the trunk yellow and green outside, and she lined the inside with wallpaper that had a cream background with pink roses printed all over it. Two days after she left her father's house, she boarded a boat and sailed for Antigua. It was a small boat, and the trip would have taken a day and a half ordinarily, but a hurricane blew up and the boat was lost at sea for almost five days. By the time it got to Antigua, the boat was practically in splinters, and though two or three of the passengers were lost overboard, along with some of the cargo, my mother and her trunk were safe.

Jamaica Kincaid, "The Circling Hand"

Notice that the story has a beginning—the departure from Dominica; a middle—the journey; and an end—the safe arrival in Antigua.

What vivid images help you "see" Kincaid's story?

Understanding the Basics

All narratives contain characters, setting, and plot. Characters are the individuals in a story. In the story above, the characters include Kincaid's mother and grandfather. Setting establishes a story's time and place, such as the boat bound for Antigua in Kincaid's story. Finally, the events that occur in a story make up its plot. Kincaid narrates a sequence of events from her mother's journey to Antigua.

Narratives may contain a conflict, a struggle that triggers the action. The conflict in Kincaid's story is between the mother and the hurricane.

Generating Ideas

The best narratives contain believable characters and situations. Therefore, it's a good rule of thumb to base your narratives on what you know, drawing on the ordinary and not-so-ordinary experiences that shape your life. A family trip, for example, probably contains all the basic elements of a narrative. To get started, try to generate some writing ideas by talking with friends or family about your experiences or theirs, or by freewriting about your experiences.

Talking   Talking about what you've done and where you've been can help you discover what you want to say in writing. In addition, reaction to your stories can help you gauge their audience appeal. Listening to other people's stories might also trigger writing ideas.

Freewriting   You can also freewrite as a way to generate a topic for a story. Then, when you come up with an idea that interests you, use freewriting again to explore it. Write down whatever comes into your mind about your topic for about five minutes. In the following model of freewriting, a writer decided to explore an everyday experience: a routine trip to the dentist.

Model

*T*error. What else do you feel when you go to the dentist? Sitting in that waiting room, trying to read a magazine. Muffled groans and screams—and some not so muffled—foretell the horrors awaiting me. If only I'd flossed regularly, not just two or three days before this torture session. That doesn't fool anybody. Certainly not my dentist. I think he enjoys poking around in my mouth, making me squirm. He puts on his gloves, snapping the elastic loudly to watch me jump. Then grinning sadistically like the crazed dentist in *Little Shop of Horrors*, he says the most frightening words in the English language: "Open wide."

> *Note that as the writer loosens up, ideas flow more freely.*

> *This freewriting contains some narrative elements. Can you identify them?*

• JOURNAL ACTIVITY •
Try It Out

Look through your journal to find ideas for a story. Underline any incidents that seem significant or interesting to you. Then freewrite about each incident to try to generate more story ideas.

Building on Your Ideas

You can build on your ideas by answering questions about your story's basic elements and by constructing a framework of your story's events. Remember, however, that you may not even discover your story until you begin writing it. As writer Flannery O'Connor once said, "I write because I don't know what I think until I read what I say."

Answering Questions   If you want to flesh out the basic elements in your narrative before you begin drafting, try answering the following questions. If you would prefer to just begin drafting, you may want to refer to these questions as you write your draft.

Questions to Flesh Out the Basic Narrative Elements

1. Who are my characters? About whom do I want to write?
2. What conflict(s) will my characters be involved in?
3. When does my story take place?
4. Where does my story take place?
5. Why do my characters get involved in their conflict(s)?
6. How does the setting affect my characters? How do they overcome their conflict(s)?
7. Do my characters change in any way during the course of the story? If so, in what ways and why?

Constructing a Framework   Many narratives are organized in chronological order, the order in which the events happened. To organize the events in your narrative, try plotting them in chronological order along a timeline. As you do so, keep asking yourself the question, What happened next? This will help you keep track of the events and write them down in their proper order.

1:30 P.M. First Event	4:45 P.M. Second Event	9:00 P.M. Third Event	7:00 A.M. Fourth Event	8:00 A.M. Final Event
Paul and Carlos set off to ride their mountain bikes through the woods near their home.	They become confused by the many logging trails and take a wrong turn. As night falls, they are hopelessly lost.	They try to keep warm and build a shelter with tree branches. They spend a cold, miserable night in the woods.	The next day, they continue to try to find their way back home.	They come upon old railroad tracks. They follow the tracks back to town and safety.

Writer's Choice

The following are some writing options to help you apply what you have learned.

1. Guided Assignment   Imagine that you've been asked to write a narrative for your school's literary anthology. Use the basic elements detailed below to help you write your story. Freewrite and use the questions on page 174 to flesh out these narrative elements. Before you begin writing, plot the sequence of events in your narrative along a timeline. Concentrate on the events that directly lead up to and resolve the conflict. Then write your story and, if you wish, submit it for publication in your school's literary anthology.

> *Main Characters:*   Rhonda and Monica—teammates and star players on the Jets, their high school's basketball team
>
> *Setting:*   The Jets' home court during a game against their arch rival, the Sharks
>
> *Plot:*   During the game, which is very close, Rhonda twists her ankle.
>
> *Conflict:*   Rhonda denies that she is in pain and wants to continue playing. Monica, who is jealous of her teammate, tells the coach that Rhonda's injury will weaken her performance and cost their team the game.

PURPOSE   To write a narrative for your school's literary anthology
AUDIENCE   Schoolmates, parents, and teachers
LENGTH   2–3 pages

2. Open Assignment   You've decided to enter a writing contest sponsored by a national teen magazine. The contest rules state that you may choose one of the following topics or one of your own as the basis for a one-page narrative. Use the prewriting techniques described in this lesson to help you explore your topic and build on your narrative's basic elements. Refer to your prewriting samples as you draft your narrative, but don't feel limited by the ideas you came up with at that stage in the writing process.

- a situation or place in which you felt like a stranger
- a time when you risked something
- an experience that did not turn out as you had expected

COMPUTER OPTION

If your word processor has an outlining feature, you can use it to outline the paragraph you write for the Open Assignment. As you create your outline, this feature simultaneously creates a skeleton draft of your paragraph. In addition, as you come up with new ideas and enter the changes on your outline, the draft also changes. After you have completed your outline, "flesh out" your skeleton draft. Then use the cut-and-paste feature on your computer to help you revise and edit the draft.

3. General Science   Write a narrative about a scientist or team of scientists who made an important scientific discovery or breakthrough. For example, you might tell the story of Marie and Pierre Curie's discovery of radium. Or you might write about Galileo's experiments and use of the scientific method. If you like, freewrite and answer questions to develop your narrative's characters, setting, plot, and conflict before you begin writing.

4. Cooperative Learning   Think about the factors that have helped shape your life. Are there any specific incidents that show how these factors have affected you? Get together in a small group and have each member share such an incident. Be sure to include characters, setting, and plot.

After each story has been told, invite group members to discuss their reactions. Then have each group member write his or her story, keeping in mind the comments of group members.

The Main Event

Imagine you've just seen a great movie, and you want to tell a friend about it. You'd probably begin by explaining the movie's plot—its sequence of events. More often than not, what set these events in motion was conflict, a struggle involving the main character. In the movie *Jaws*, for example, three men struggle to kill a shark that is, itself, a fearsome killer. The uncertain outcome of this conflict makes for a gripping story.

The Role of Conflict

As long as a reader wants to find out how a conflict will be resolved, he will keep reading a story. Conflict engages a reader's interest. Additionally, conflict plays the same role in a narrative that a main idea plays in other types of writing. Just as all supporting details help develop a main idea, all events in a narrative help develop its conflict.

As a character grapples with the conflict, the plot builds to a climax, the high point of the story. The resolution, in which the aftermath of the climax is revealed, brings the narrative to an end. The graph on the opposite page shows how the development and eventual resolution of a conflict form the basis for the plot in a narrative.

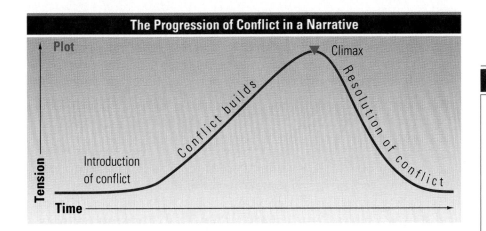

The Progression of Conflict in a Narrative

Plot

Tension ↑

Time →

Introduction of conflict

Conflict builds

Climax

Resolution of conflict

Drafting Tip

As you draft the conflict in your narrative, remember that a conflict with a less predictable climax and resolution is more likely to involve your readers.

The Menu of Conflicts

Conflicts fall into two basic categories: external and internal. External conflicts involve the character and an outside force. Internal conflicts occur within a character. The chart below lists four types of conflict.

Four Types of Conflict	
Conflict	**Examples**
Person Against Person The narrative pits one character against another.	One character exposes a flaw in another. One character attempts to harm another. One character opposes the beliefs of another.
Person Against Nature A character struggles against a dangerous animal, place, or illness.	A character is attacked by a rampaging elephant. A character tries to scale a dangerous peak. A character is threatened by a hurricane.
Person Against Society Society or tradition stands in the way of a character's desires.	Society prevents a character from doing something. An ethnic or religious group imposes its beliefs on a character who no longer wants to follow them.
Person Against Self The conflict is within the character's mind.	A character struggles with a lack of ambition. A character seeks to achieve an unrealistic goal. A character tries to overcome a fear of flying.

• JOURNAL ACTIVITY •
Think It Through

Think about a narrative you've read in which you identified with a character (or characters) facing a particular conflict. How did the writer of the narrative make you care about what happened to the character(s)? Write your answer in your journal.

Ways to Develop Conflict

To identify a conflict for a narrative, start with what you want to write about and use prewriting techniques to explore this topic further. For example, freewrite to discover the types of conflicts that would most challenge your main characters. Or use list making to determine the conflicts likely to occur in a particular setting.

Once you have identified a main conflict, use prewriting techniques to generate a list of events that might be used to develop or eventually resolve such a conflict. If you think an event might affect the characters or forces involved, try listing some of its possible effects. As you write, keep pushing yourself to answer the question What happens next? until your story is complete. See how writer Russell Baker presents two conflicts in the following selection.

Literature Model

Baker sets up two types of conflict: Baker versus his own fear of deep water and Baker versus the Navy instructor.

Baker uses dialogue to develop the conflict between himself and the Navy instructor.

What is the climax of each conflict? How are the conflicts resolved?

On the first day in the pool an instructor with a voice like a bullhorn ordered fifty of us to climb a high board and jump in feet first. . . . A line was formed to mount the ladder and jump. I drifted to the end of the line, then stepped out when the splashing started and introduced myself to the instructor.

"I'm a nonswimmer," I said. "You want me to go to the shallow end of the pool?" At City College I'd spent four years in the shallow end of the pool.

"This pool doesn't have a shallow end," the instructor said.

"Well, what am I going to do?"

"Get up on that platform and jump," he said.

The pool depth was marked as fifteen feet at that point.

"I'm not kidding. I can't swim a stroke."

"Up! Up!" he shouted.

"But I'll drown."

"This pool's got the best lifesaving equipment in the Navy," he said. "Don't worry about it."

"Come on."

"I'm giving you an order, mister. Up!" . . .

I stepped to the edge, closed my eyes, and walked into space. The impact of the water was like being smacked on the bottom by a two-by-four, then I was sinking, then—my God! —I was rising irresistibly to the surface. My head broke water. The water was actually supporting me, just as everybody had always said it would.

Russell Baker, *Growing Up*

Writer's Choice

The following are some writing options to help you apply what you have learned.

1. Guided Assignment   Your teacher has asked you to write a story, using the conflict, climax, and resolution supplied below. Begin your assignment by plotting these elements on a graph. Then freewrite or brainstorm to come up with specific events or details to flesh out each element. Plot these events and/or details on the graph. Then use the graph as an outline as you write your narrative.

> *Conflict:*   Julia wants to break up with her boyfriend, Raphael, who wants to stay together.
>
> *Climax:*   The couple have a serious argument.
>
> *Resolution:*   Julia decides to give their relationship one more chance.

PURPOSE To write a narrative, using the person-against-person conflict given above
AUDIENCE Your teacher
LENGTH 1–2 pages

2. Open Assignment
You've decided to contribute a three-page narrative to a booklet entitled *Common Conflicts Encountered by Teens.* The booklet is prepared by and designed for students at your school. Choose one of the following conflicts to develop into a narrative, or select one of your own:

- A student is afraid to speak out when her friend is jeered at by fellow classmates.
- A student wants to try out for a part in the school play but isn't sure if he's good enough.
- A student feels pressured by her friends to remain at a party after her curfew.

3. Art   Study the self-portrait below by César A. Martinez. The drawing, entitled *Mestizo*, shows the artist flanked by a jaguar, which is native to the Americas, and a Spanish bull, which represents Europe. The drawing reflects Martinez's struggle to come to terms with his own cultural identity, rooted in North America and in Spain. Freewrite about the artist's internal conflict. Then generate events that might be used to develop or eventually resolve the conflict. Finally, write a brief narrative based on the drawing.

César A. Martinez, *Mestizo*, 1987

Developing Conflict in Narrative   **179**

He Said, She Said

"Of course not, Calvin."
"Mom, can I drive on the way back?"

"No, Calvin."
"Can I just steer then? I promise I won't crash."

"No, Calvin."
"Can I work the gas and brakes while you steer?"

"You never let me do anything."

What's going on in the cartoon strip above? It's hard to tell without the dialogue—the conversation between the characters—because dialogue is such an essential element of a comic strip. It brings the characters to life and makes you feel as if you're witnessing the events depicted. Dialogue serves the same purposes in narrative.

The Uses of Dialogue

You can use dialogue to help advance a narrative's plot. For example, if the plot involves an argument between two characters, you can let the characters speak for themselves rather than summarizing their dispute.

You can also use dialogue to reveal your characters' personality traits or to show the relationships between characters. For instance, instead of just telling the reader, "Robert was shy," let Robert reveal his shyness through his own actions and words: "Robert shuffled uneasily, looked at his feet, and mumbled, 'Nice to meet you.' "

Additionally, you can use dialogue to make the reader feel closer to the action. The reader sees the story as it unfolds rather than hearing about it from a narrator. This effect is one reason writers often use dialogue to develop important moments in a story. Early in a narrative, dialogue can help establish character and conflict. At the climax, dialogue can make a conflict more powerful and real to the reader.

Ways to Develop Dialogue

When you're writing dialogue for a story about something that really happened, try to remember as closely as possible what each person said. If your story is fictional, you'll need to invent dialogue. To do so, you might try to imagine that you are one of the characters and freewrite about the conflict from the character's point of view. Keep in mind the character's age, background, and personality and the ways that those qualities may be reflected in speech.

Editing Tip

When you edit your dialogue, be sure to use correct punctuation. For help with punctuation, see Lesson 21.9 in Grammar, Usage, and Mechanics, pages 684–687.

> *Sometimes my mother makes me want to scream. Why won't she let me get an after-school job? All my friends are working and making their own money. Why does Mom still treat me like a kid?*

If the conflict involves two characters, you might try freewriting a letter from each character to the other. Each letter should reflect the character's point of view and feelings about the conflict.

Dear Angela,

I know you're angry with me because I won't let you work after school. But I'm afraid a job would interfere with your studies. You know you won't get into a good college if your grades are poor. Besides, I'd worry when you'd be coming home after dark.

Dear Mom,

I promise you a job won't hurt my grades. I'll be home every day by 7:00, which gives me tons of time to do my homework. And Carla's already said she can give me a lift home after work. Best of all, I'll be able to buy that winter jacket I saw at the mall with my own money.

Dialogue should sound like real speech—the way real people talk to each other. In real speech, people often interrupt each other, ignore each other's comments, speak in fragments, and break the rules of grammar. To test your dialogue, read it aloud. Dialogue should sound natural for each character's age, background, and personality.

• JOURNAL ACTIVITY •
Think It Through

In your journal write down three pieces of dialogue that you have overheard and that struck you as interesting. Why do you think you remembered these particular conversations? What made them interesting? Write down your ideas in your journal.

Dialogue in Action

Dialogue can bring your writing to life. At the beginning of Matthew Cheney's short story "The Nauga Hunters," Hank invites his younger brother Chucky to hunt for a nauga, an imaginary beast. Note how, in the following selection from the story, Matthew uses dialogue to develop believable characters and to advance the story.

Student Model

Dialogue effectively reveals the story's central conflict and its climax: the boys' parents are getting a divorce.

Chucky stood next to his brother without saying anything. Then he asked quietly, "Is it about Mom and Dad?"

"Jus' beat it!"

"What's gonna happen? Is Dad gonna leave?"

"You wanna know? You really wanna know, you little jerk? Las' night I heard Mom and Dad talkin'."

"Fightin'?"

"Nope, jus' talkin'. Dad said he's gonna leave and go ta New York and take me, and Mom can have you. So I brought you out here jus' ta be nice 'cause I may never really be able ta do anythin' like this again. Okay? Satisfied?"

"You sure yer tellin' the truth?"

How does Matthew use dialogue to convey Hank's anger and confusion?

Hank stood up and jumped on his brother; they fell to the damp ground. His eyes were sparkling and his lips were unfirm. "Would I lie about that, you little . . ." His voice faded as he pulled his arm up to punch Chucky. Chucky was crying now. Hank stood up. "Forget it," he said. "Supper'll be almost ready." Chucky was still on the ground. "You comin'?"

Chucky pulled himself up and brushed off his rear end. His face was streaked with tears. "Yup," he said softly.

Matthew Cheney, New Hampton School, New Hampton, New Hampshire.
First appeared in *Merlyn's Pen: The National Magazine of Student Writing.*

Prewriting Tip

To develop your ability to write realistic dialogue, watch a favorite television show, and note how the dialogue reflects the ages, backgrounds, and personalities of the characters.

Try to make your dialogue as realistic as possible. As you write dialogue, keep the following guidelines in mind.

Dialogue Guidelines

- Use language that reflects the age, background, and personality of each character.
- Make sure your dialogue has a purpose—to advance the action, reveal a character's personality or relationships between characters, or show the conflict.
- Begin a direct quotation with a capital letter, and enclose it in quotation marks.
- Begin a new paragraph each time the speaker changes.

Writer's Choice

The following are some options to help you apply what you have learned.

1. Guided Assignment   You've been chosen to write the dialogue in a skit that your school's theater group plans to perform. Information on the skit's characters, setting, and plot is given below. Before you begin to draft dialogue for the skit, freewrite about each character's age, personality, and background. Then freewrite about the conflict described in the information below from each character's point of view. Be sure to write dialogue that reveals the characters' personalities as well as the relationship between the characters.

Chen and Kirby are best friends, but their personalities are exact opposites. Chen is the optimist, always able to see the bright side. Kirby is the pessimist, who always assumes the worst. Chen and Kirby are both on the track team. For the first time in years, the team has a chance to win the state title. As they warm up before the championship race, Kirby admits to Chen that he wants to withdraw. He's afraid he'll cause the team to lose. Chen inspires Kirby with his own enthusiasm. By the time the starting signal sounds, both friends are ready to give their personal best.

PURPOSE   To write dialogue for a skit to be performed by your school's theater group

AUDIENCE   Your school's student body

LENGTH   2–3 pages

2. Open Assignment   Your teacher has asked you to use dialogue to develop the conflict in a narrative for a class assignment. She has supplied you with several narrative situations. Choose one of the situations given below or one of your own, and develop its conflict with one or two pages of dialogue.

- A junior in high school loves to work on cars and wants to become an auto mechanic. The girl's father, a businessman, doesn't approve of her career choice and one night at the dinner table tells his daughter so.
- Two fourteen-year-old boys find a wallet with fifty dollars inside it on the sidewalk. One of the boys wants to keep the money. The other argues that they should hand the wallet over to the police.
- A favorite sweater is missing. A fifteen-year-old sister accuses her twelve-year-old sister, who is always "borrowing" her clothes, of taking it and losing it. The younger sister denies the accusation.

3. Cooperative Learning   In a small group, choose a dramatic scene from American history and dramatize it. First discuss the personalities and backgrounds of the characters. Do research if necessary. Then meet with your group to write dialogue that develops the action and accurately reflects each character's personality and background. Each group member should be responsible for one character's speeches. Once all the dialogue has been written, present your group scene to the rest of the class.

COMPUTER OPTION

If you need to conduct research to gather information on the event you've chosen to dramatize, you can use your personal computer as an electronic notebook. Record all of the notes you take in a file. Use a separate file, if you wish, for the historical figure you research. When your research is complete, print out your notes, photocopy them, and distribute to your group members.

Did I Ever Tell You About the Time . . . ?

When James Thurber, the American humorist, was still a young newspaper reporter, his editor complained that Thurber's stories lacked drama. "Write short, dramatic leads to your stories," urged the editor. Thurber took the advice to heart and turned in a murder story with the following lead: "Dead. That's what the man was when they found him with a knife in his back at 4 P.M. in front of Riley's Saloon at the corner of 52nd and 12th streets."

The above story is an anecdote, a short narrative used to illustrate a point or reveal character. This particular anecdote reveals Thurber's wry sense of humor. Most anecdotes entertain or instruct, and they often contain dialogue. Although anecdotes can stand on their own, they are frequently used as supporting details in longer pieces of writing.

In the following model, biographer Arnold Rampersad uses an anecdote about the poet Langston Hughes to reveal something of Hughes's character. Rampersad describes how Hughes dealt with Jim Crow laws, which established separate facilities and services for whites and blacks, during a cross-country speaking tour in 1945.

This anecdote contains a plot—Hughes is trying to get served dinner; characters—Hughes, the steward, the naval officer; and a setting—a train's dining car.

How is dialogue used to reveal Hughes's fearless scorn of the Jim Crow laws?

Literature Model

*B*y this time he unquestionably had become bolder in confronting Jim Crow. Always now he entered the dining car at the first call, instead of shrinking back and waiting for the last as blacks were supposed to do.

Picking a center table, he usually tried to brazen it out before incredulous but discreetly supportive black waiters and often indignant, but often yielding, white stewards. "Are you a Puerto Rican?" a steward demanded in Alabama. "No, hungry!" The man handed over a menu. "Are you Cuban?" a curious white Navy officer then asked. "No, American," Langston coolly replied. "Are you Cuban?"

Arnold Rampersad, *The Life of Langston Hughes, Volume II: 1941–1967*

How to Generate Anecdotes

You can generate anecdotes by drawing on real-life experiences or by using prewriting techniques to invent them. Keep in mind that you will use the anecdote to illustrate a point in a longer piece of writing.

Anecdotes Based on Fact Some anecdotes are based on incidents that actually happened. To generate true-life anecdotes, think about significant or entertaining incidents from your own life. You might want to look through your journal for ideas. Then think about the point each anecdote could make in a longer piece of writing.

Drafting Tip

When you draft your anecdote, be sure to present the events of the story in chronological order.

Factual Anecdotes	
Anecdote	**Point**
The time I stood up for myself even though my friends disagreed	To show that you should voice your opinions, even if they are unpopular
The time my brother first went away to college	To show that life is a process of change
The time I struck out and lost the game	To show that true friends stand by you even when you fail

Invented Anecdotes When you're writing a fictional narrative, you can invent anecdotes. First decide on the point you want to make. Then freewrite to come up with an anecdote that could illustrate that point.

Invented Anecdotes	
Point	**Anecdote**
To show a character's selfishness	A character thinks only of himself or herself at the expense of others
To show that two characters have different values	An argument between two characters
To show that you have to confront a fear to overcome it	A character confronts his or her fear of heights by climbing a mountain

• JOURNAL ACTIVITY •
Try It Out

Look through your journal for incidents that could be written up as possible anecdotes. Then list the incidents, and identify the point each could make in a longer piece of writing.

Where and How to Use Anecdotes

Once you have an anecdote, you need to consider whether or not to use it to make a specific point in a longer piece of writing. To help you decide, ask yourself the following questions.

Questions to Determine the Usefulness of an Anecdote

1. Does this anecdote make the point I want to make?
2. Does the anecdote advance the narrative?
3. Is the anecdote brief, yet meaningful?
4. Does the anecdote instruct or entertain?

In her short story entitled "My Grandmother's House," Jennifer Tuck used an anecdote to make a point about dealing with a loved one's death. After her grandmother dies, the narrator of the story dreads returning to her grandmother's house. As a little girl, she had been afraid of the house because it was so large and dark. On one particular occasion, however, her grandmother helped her overcome her fears.

Student Model

What does the anecdote reveal about the narrator's grandmother?

I had been sitting on the porch for nearly an hour when my grandmother came out, quietly letting the screen door creak on its old rusty hinges and then sigh as it came to rest against the crooked door frame Grandpa was always saying he would fix.

"Why don't you come inside?" she said. "We are going to eat dinner soon and I would hate to think of sitting at the table without you."

"I'm afraid." I barely whispered this shameful feeling, and stared straight down at my untied shoes.

Notice that the anecdote could stand on its own as a brief narrative, complete with plot, setting, and characters.

"That's OK. I was afraid when we first moved here, too. You just have to remember that this house is a lot like your house, only there's love from many families here instead of just our own. Did you ever stop to wonder who could have lived here before? There must be so many memories within these walls!"

We talked on and on and gradually my fear began to fade. When my mother called us inside, I didn't hesitate for an instant before following my grandmother inside.

Jennifer Tuck, Central High School, Manchester, New Hampshire.
First appeared in *Merlyn's Pen: The National Magazine of Student Writing*

The following are some writing options to help you apply what you have learned.

1. Guided Assignment   You're writing the life story of a famous actor for a big publishing house. Before the book can be released, however, the actor wants to read part of your manuscript to see how you handle a particular anecdote that illustrates a key episode in his life. The anecdote reveals the actor's determination to pursue an acting career. All the information you need to write the anecdote is given below. Be sure the anecdote instructs or entertains, and use dialogue to enliven the piece.

The actor's first role was in a high school production of *Our Town*, playing the part of the stage manager. In the first scene, the actor forgets his lines and is mortified by his failure. A girl in the cast helps him see that it's not the end of the world, however, and the actor decides that he loves acting too much to be discouraged by this setback. He does well in the rest of his scenes and at play's end is met by thunderous applause from the audience.

Joan Brown, *After the Alcatraz Swim #3*, 1976

PURPOSE   To write an anecdote that illustrates a key episode in an actor's life

AUDIENCE   The actor and general readers of his biography

LENGTH   1–2 pages

2. Open Assignment   Your English class is collecting an anecdote from each class member for a get-to-know-your-classmates project. The collection will be distributed to all of the students in the class. Write a one-page anecdote that reveals something about your personality. Use one of the ideas below for an anecdote, or choose one of your own:

- a time when you made a fool of yourself in front of someone you wanted to impress
- a time when your persistence paid off
- a time when your sense of humor helped relieve an unpleasant situation

3. Art   Works of art often tell stories. Look at the painting above. What ideas for anecdotes does it suggest to you? Freewrite or make a list to come up with one anecdote idea and details of character, setting, and plot based on the painting. Then decide what point your anecdote could make. Finally, draft your anecdote, using dialogue.

Writing a Sports Narrative

Making Points

Student Model

The conflict in a sports narrative is often person against person, as each athlete struggles to win the sports event.

The pop of the gun sets the swimmers' legs in motion and arms flawlessly scooping pockets of water. Their heads bob rhythmically, each straining to reach the end of the pool. At the end of each lane, fellow swimmers stand and cheer their teammates, with a single exception. One blond-haired swimmer receives cries from teammates who lean close to the water, straining to show the swimmer their enthusiasm and their lips. The swimmer is deaf, and the encouraging motions of her friends urge her to go faster.

What is the climax in this sports narrative? How is it resolved?

The race is close. The blond head edges out in front, neck and neck, with another swimmer beside her. However, with a last, powerful stroke, the blond swimmer breaks the tie and hits the timer seconds before her competitor. As she rests against the wall of the pool, accepting the congratulations of her teammates, an ear-to-ear grin appears across her face.

Charissa Adelman, Quartz Hill High School, Quartz Hill, California

Most sports news articles report the results of a game, but they also recount the gripping action in the event itself. Sporting events involve all the elements so essential to a good narrative: character, setting, and a conflict that develops to a climax and resolution.

Where Do You Begin?

You'll want to begin your sports narrative at the point in the event when conflict starts to build. Usually this is the moment when the action intensifies. For example, to tell the story of a team's dramatic, come-from-behind victory, you might begin at the point in the game in which the team seized control and began its push for victory.

What Do You Include?

Like other narratives, most sports narratives develop a conflict to its climax and resolution. You may want to chart the action that develops the conflict. This technique can help you identify the important events—your narrative's supporting details—that you'll want to include.

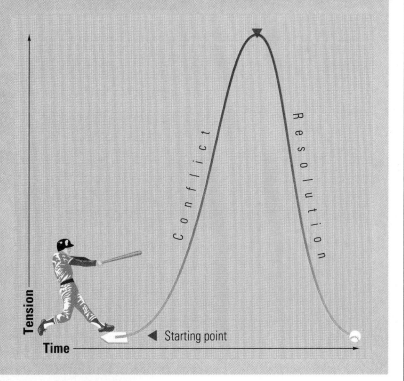

Development of Conflict in a Sports Narrative

Starting Point:
A baseball game is tied at the bottom of the ninth inning, with two outs. A runner on third represents the winning run.

Conflict:
The pitcher stares at third base. The base runner, determined to break the record for stolen bases, boldly stares back.

Climax:
As the pitcher fires the ball over home plate, the base stealer makes a dash for home and plows into the catcher.

Resolution:
When the dust clears, the umpire waves his arms and yells, "Safe!" The crowd roars with delight.

Tension / Time / Conflict / Resolution / ◄ Starting point

· JOURNAL ACTIVITY ·
Try It Out

Watch a sports event at school or on television. Use it as the basis for preparing a sports narrative. Choose a starting point, graph the development of the conflict to its climax and resolution, and then write a brief summary of each point in the plot.

How Do You Tell the Story?

After you've chosen a sports event, determined your starting point, and charted the action, you're ready to draft your sports narrative. Begin by considering your lead. A lead is a strong opening sentence that grabs the reader's attention and gets the story moving. Examine your story's starting point. Is there anything dramatic, amusing, or surprising about it? If so, you might use that for your lead. Remember, however, that if you're writing a sports feature or news article, a narration of the event will only make up part of your article. (For tips on how to write a sports feature, see the Unit 4 Case Study on sportswriting on pages 166–171.)

State the Facts Clearly   Be sure that you have presented the sequence of events and all the facts in your narrative clearly. Double-check quotations for accuracy, and make sure each source is clearly identified.

Use Vivid Language   Wherever possible, show your readers the action rather than telling them about it. Vivid action verbs and sensory details can help bring your story to life and hold your readers' interest.

Read the following selection from baseball writer Roger Angell's book *Season Ticket*, which contains a series of narratives about baseball games the writer has attended. Notice how Angell makes even a seemingly actionless stretch of a game interesting.

When prewriting about a sports event, try list making to generate details. Use the significant details to develop your narrative.

Prewriting Tip

When prewriting about a sports event, try list making to generate details. Use the significant details to develop your narrative.

Literature Model

Angell uses precise, vivid verbs to show the reader the action.

What details does Angell use to help the reader "hear" the sounds of the ballpark?

A base runner leads cautiously away from first, then trots back as the pitcher steps off the rubber. The third-base ump walks seven steps out toward left field, turns, and strolls back again. Another foul ball, bounced softly past first base. "Throw it *straight*," somebody in the press box mutters. There are spatters of applause in the stands, but they die away for lack of hope. . . . I can see some fans getting up, in twos and threes, and heading up the aisles for home and dinner. The park is half empty by now. Out in the sloping right-field sector of the seats, there is a thin, a-cappella rendering of "Happy Birthday," for somebody—her name is Ella, it turns out—and other fans around the park join in on the last "happy birthday to you-ooo!" and Ella gets a little round of applause, too. But that ends as well (a coach is out talking to the pitcher now), and even the everyday noises of the baseball park—the hum of voices, the undercurrent of talk and cheers and laughter and vender cries—drop and fade, and Fenway Park is almost silent, just for a minute.

Roger Angell, *Season Ticket*

Writer's Choice

The following are some writing options to help you apply what you have learned.

1. Guided Assignment The editor of your school newspaper has asked you to write a sports narrative based on an important basketball game. Use the following information to write the narrative. Remember to begin at the point at which the conflict starts to build, and use transitions to guide your readers through the action. Be sure, too, to enliven the story with action verbs.

West High and East High, long-standing rivals, face each other in the state basketball finals. The game is close until the fourth quarter, when East High pulls ahead with a 78 to 70 lead. Finally West High comes from behind to win the game 82-80, with a basket in the final seconds of the fourth quarter.

PURPOSE To narrate an exciting sports event for a school newspaper
AUDIENCE Student and teacher sports fans
LENGTH 1–2 pages

2. Open Assignment Imagine you're a freelance sports writer on assignment for an important sports magazine. Choose one of the following topics or one of your own as the subject for your sports narrative. Identify the major characters, plot, and setting in your narrative. Then chart the action on a graph like the one shown on page 189. Use the graph to help you write your narrative.

- An older tennis player plays the match of his life against the current best player in the world—a much younger man. The older player wins in an exciting fifth set.
- After trailing seven runs throughout most of the game, a baseball team makes a surprising comeback in the ninth inning.

3. Cooperative Learning Use the image on this page to develop a sports narrative. Work in small groups to brainstorm ideas for a story. Agree on characters, setting, and plot. Chart the action. Then have each group member write an account of the story. Take turns reading your narrative to the group, and discuss different approaches to the story.

Elaine de Kooning, *Campy at the Plate,* 1953–1980

Writing a Sports Narrative **191**

Writing About Literature
Writing About Suspense

On the Edge of Your Seat

A sleek black car passes another car, just as it rounds a curve at the crest of a hill. Unseen by the driver of the black car, a speeding truck approaches the top of the hill from the opposite direction. Will the black car be able to swerve at the last moment and escape disaster? Who is driving the black car? Why is he or she taking such a chance?

In the image to the left, the artist Grant Wood effectively creates suspense, or anxiety about what will happen next. A writer can create suspense with words and often may do so to heighten the reader's interest in a story's conflict and how that conflict will be resolved.

Grant Wood, *Death on the Ridge Road*, 1935

Creating Suspense

A writer may create suspense through foreshadowing—giving the reader clues about what is going to happen later in the story. Or a writer may withhold information from the reader in order to build suspense. By withholding information, the writer keeps the reader guessing—and reading—until the end of the story.

Foreshadowing The distinctive theme music in the movie *Jaws* is played each time the killer shark draws near its next victim. Similarly, foreshadowing often prepares the reader for an ominous turn of events in a story. The writer causes the reader to anticipate what is to come by giving the reader clues. The clues may include details of setting, characters, or plot. In the example on the opposite page, note how writer Mario Vargas Llosa uses a character's fearful imaginings to foreshadow events to come.

A fter swimming for a few minutes Miguel felt the cold that had momentarily vanished coming over him again, and he speeded up his strokes because it was in his legs, especially in his calves, that the water had a greater effect, first making them insensitive, then stiffening them. He was swimming with his face in the water, and each time his right arm rose out of it, he turned his head to expel air and breathe in another supply, at which he submerged his face and chin once more, just barely, so as not to hinder his own progress but, on the contrary, to split the water like a prow and make his forward movement easier. With each stroke he glanced at Rubén swimming smoothly, effortlessly on the surface, not splashing now, with the delicacy and ease of a seagull gliding. Miguel tried to forget Rubén and the sea and the breakers, which must still be far off, for the water was clear and calm, and they were swimming only through newly risen surf. He wanted to remember nothing but Flora's face and the down on her arms that sparkled on sunny days like a little forest of golden threads. But he could not prevent another image from succeeding to that of the girl—the image of a mountain of raging water . . . in a real ocean stirred by inner cataclysms in which were thrown up unusual waves that could have swamped an entire ship and upset it with astonishing rapidity, hurling passengers, lifeboats, masts, sails, sailors, porthole covers, and flags into the air.

Mario Vargas Llosa, "Sunday"

> *The writer builds suspense by describing Miguel's progress, stroke by stroke. As a result, the reader feels the character's weariness and fear.*

> *What image does Vargas Llosa use to foreshadow the possible dangers ahead for Miguel?*

Withholding Information   In withholding information from the reader, a writer creates a puzzle with a few pieces missing, a mystery to be solved. Curious to find out what will happen, the reader reads on to unravel the mystery's solution. Mystery writers often withhold some key piece of information until the final scene when the mystery is solved.

• JOURNAL ACTIVITY •
Think It Through

Sometimes a writer withholds information from the character(s) in a story but reveals it to the readers. What effect does this have on the reader? Write your ideas in your journal.

Writing About a Suspenseful Story

When you analyze a suspenseful story, focus on the ways in which the writer creates suspense. Provide examples from the text to support your ideas. As you read, consider how the writer uses narrative elements to build suspense, asking yourself the following questions.

Questions to Determine How a Writer Creates Suspense

1. What details in the descriptions of the characters help build suspense?
2. Which events in the plot help build suspense?
3. What aspects of the setting build suspense?
4. What are the characters' reactions as suspense builds?
5. What atmosphere or mood does the writer create? How does the mood change?
6. In what ways does the writer foreshadow events to come?
7. What information does the writer withhold from the characters?

By exploring your answers to the above questions through freewriting or brainstorming, you can develop a focus for an analysis of a suspense story. In the model below, Elizabeth Chen analyzes some of the techniques writer Richard Connell uses to build suspense in his short story "The Most Dangerous Game."

Student Model

Elizabeth uses specific examples from the story to develop the focus of her essay.

Richard Connell uses foreshadowing to heighten suspense in "The Most Dangerous Game." When Rainsford falls off his yacht and swims to General Zaroff's island, he is relieved to reach its "dense jungle." However, the narrator states, "What perils that tangle of trees and underbrush might hold for him did not concern Rainsford just then." This statement suggests that the character will soon be in danger. By foreshadowing this future event, the author creates a sense of anticipation in the reader and compels him to read on.

At the end of her essay, how does Elizabeth herself withhold information in order to pique the reader's interest in the story?

Connell also draws the reader into the story by withholding information. When Zaroff asserts that he hunts "the biggest" game on his island, he does not at first reveal what that game might be. As a result, Rainsford and the reader are forced to guess. The diabolical answer, which directs the course of the rest of the story, becomes clear to both at about the same time.

Elizabeth Chen,
Downers Grove North High School, Downers Grove, Illinois

The following are some writing options to help you apply what you have learned.

1. Guided Assignment Imagine that you've been asked to write about suspense in Edgar Allan Poe's short story "The Pit and the Pendulum" for your school's Mystery Club newsletter. Specifically, the editor would like you to explain what details in the story's setting create an atmosphere of suspense. Read the following selection from the story. Then use the questions from page 194 to help you write your piece.

> So far I had not opened my eyes. I felt that I lay upon my back, unbound. I reached out my hand, and it fell heavily upon something damp and hard. There I suffered it to remain for many minutes, while I strove to imagine where and *what* I could be. I longed, yet dared not, to employ my vision, I dreaded the first glance at objects around me. It was not that I feared to look upon things horrible, but that I grew aghast lest there should be *nothing* to see.

Edgar Allan Poe,
"The Pit and the Pendulum"

PURPOSE To identify the details in a story's setting that help create suspense
AUDIENCE Members of a school's Mystery Club
LENGTH 1–2 paragraphs

2. Open Assignment A publishing company has asked you to write a book jacket blurb discussing a suspenseful short story. Choose one of the short stories below or another suspenseful short story that you have read. Then, in a brief paragraph, identify the ways in which the writer creates suspense.

- "The Lottery" by Shirley Jackson
- "A Good Man Is Hard to Find" by Flannery O'Connor
- "Quitters, Inc." by Stephen King

3. Art Study the painting below. Details in the painting create anxiety about what is going on. For example, the figure hiding behind the tree may make you feel uneasy. Is someone looking for him? Or is he waiting for some unsuspecting person to come along? Determine what details in the painting help create an atmosphere of suspense. Then briefly discuss them in a paragraph.

Patricia González, *Fountain View*, 1985

Consider the Source

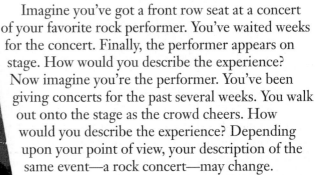

Imagine you've got a front row seat at a concert of your favorite rock performer. You've waited weeks for the concert. Finally, the performer appears on stage. How would you describe the experience? Now imagine you're the performer. You've been giving concerts for the past several weeks. You walk out onto the stage as the crowd cheers. How would you describe the experience? Depending upon your point of view, your description of the same event—a rock concert—may change.

The writer of a narrative also chooses a point of view, or a perspective, from which to tell the story. The point of view is reflected in the author's choice of a narrator—someone to tell the story. The author's choice of narrator determines how the story will be told, which, in turn, affects the reader's understanding of the story.

Identifying Point of View

There are three basic points of view an author may choose in telling a story. In a story told from a first-person point of view, the narrator is a character in the story. This type of narrator uses first-person pronouns, such as "I" and "we" in telling the story. A first-person narrator knows only what he or she is thinking and describes only the events he or she witnesses.

In a story told from a third-person limited point of view, the narrator stands outside the story. This type of narrator uses third-person pronouns such as "he," "she," "it," and "they." The third-person limited narrator describes the actions and words of all the characters but the thoughts and feelings of only one character.

In a story told from a third-person omniscient point of view, the narrator stands outside the action but knows all and sees all. The third-person omniscient narrator can relate everything that happens in the story, including the thoughts and feelings of all the characters.

Examining the Effect of Point of View

After identifying the point of view of a narrative, you need to find out why the author chose it. First examine the narrative to see what effect the choice of point of view has on the presentation of the story. Then use examples from the text to support your written opinion.

First-Person Narrator Stories told by a first-person narrator tend to draw the reader into the action. The reader identifies with the "I" who is telling the story. Keep in mind, however, that the narrator may be a biased or unreliable witness. As you evaluate the effect of a point of view on a narrative, try to determine how much you can trust the first-person narrator. In the following selection from Eugenia Collier's short story "Marigolds," the first-person narrator recalls how she felt after hearing her father cry for the first time.

Drafting Tip

When writing about point of view, be sure to refer to the narrator rather than the author of the narrative. Don't assume that the narrator expresses the author's point of view.

Literature Model

*T*he world had lost its boundary lines. My mother, who was small and soft, was now the strength of the family; my father, who was the rock on which the family had been built, was sobbing like the tiniest child. Everything was suddenly out of tune, like a broken accordion. Where did I fit into this crazy picture? I do not now remember my thoughts, only a feeling of great bewilderment and fear.

Eugenia Collier, "Marigolds"

Notice that the narrator only reports her pain and confusion. She does not consider how her father must be feeling.

Do you identify with the child telling the story? If so, why?

• JOURNAL ACTIVITY •
Think It Through

Choose a piece of narrative writing told by a third-person limited narrator. Now imagine the same piece told by a first-person narrator. What effect might the change in point of view have on the story? Write down your ideas in your journal.

Third-Person Limited Narrator A third-person limited narrator stands outside the story but relates events as if he or she were looking over the shoulder of one of the characters. Because the narrator is so close to this one character, the reader tends to identify with and sympathize with the character. Be aware, however, that this narrator may withhold information or tell more than the character would tell.

In the following example, Mathew Isaac analyzes the effect of a third-person limited narrator in O. Henry's "The Gift of the Magi."

Mathew maintains that O. Henry used a third-person limited narrator to make the story's ironic ending more effective.

What specific examples and quotations from the story does Mathew use to support his opinion?

I n O. Henry's "The Gift of the Magi," a third-person limited narrator primarily relates the actions, thoughts, and feelings of the character Della. The narrator withholds information from the reader about her husband, Jim, and thereby sets up the story's final, ironic twist.

The story's narrator is also used to comment ironically on the characters themselves. For example, when Della cries because she doesn't have enough money to buy Jim a present, the narrator remarks that "life is made up of sobs, sniffles, and smiles, with sniffles predominating." Later, the narrator compares Jim and Della to King Solomon and the Queen of Sheba. The wealth of these Biblical figures contrasts ludicrously with the poverty of the story's two characters.

Although we are encouraged to laugh at Della and Jim, at the story's end, the reader is the object of the narrator's irony. There it is implied that the reader who only laughs at the pair, without recognizing their deep love, is the real fool.

Mathew Isaac, Rich East High School, Park Forest, Illinois

Third-Person Omniscient Narrator The third-person omniscient narrator also stands outside the action of the story but relates the thoughts, feelings, words, and actions of all the characters. Keep in mind, though, that although this narrator seems objective, he or she still tells only as much or as little as the author wants to reveal.

In the selection below, the narrator relates the action as Ethan and his daughter Becky ride a ski lift. As you read, consider what the narrator does and doesn't tell about the story's events and characters.

The narrator doesn't reveal what happens to the out-of-control skier. What effect does this have on the reader?

What words and phrases suggest that the narrator may not be telling the reader everything about the characters' thoughts?

A dark figure with spreading legs veered out of control beneath them, fell forward, and vanished. Ethan cried out, astonished, scandalized; he imagined the man had buried himself alive. Becky was barely amused, and looked away before the dark spots struggling in the drift were lost from sight. As if she might know, Ethan asked, "Who was that?"

"Some kid." Kids, her tone suggested, were in plentiful supply; one could be spared.

John Updike, "Man and Daughter in the Cold"

Writer's Choice

The following are some writing options to help you apply what you have learned.

1. Guided Assignment   Your teacher has asked you to read the following paragraphs from the short story "Metamorphosis" by Franz Kafka. Your assignment is to analyze the effect of point of view on the narrative. The story is told by a third-person limited narrator who reveals the main character's state of mind when he discovers that he has been transformed into an insect. However, the narrator does not explain why or how the character has been transformed. What effect does this limited narration have on the reader? Be sure to use specific examples from the text to support your ideas.

> As Gregor Samsa awoke one morning from uneasy dreams he found himself transformed in his bed into a gigantic insect. He was lying on his hard, as it were armor-plated, back and when he lifted his head a little he could see his domelike brown belly divided into stiff arched segments on top of which the bed quilt could hardly keep in position and was about to slide off completely. His numerous legs, which were pitifully thin compared to the rest of his bulk, waved helplessly before his eyes.
>   . . . [T]here came a cautious tap at the door behind the head of his bed. "Gregor," said a voice—it was his mother's— "it's a quarter to seven. Hadn't you a train to catch?" That gentle voice! Gregor had a shock as he heard his own voice answering hers, unmistakably his own voice, it was true, but with a persistent horrible twittering squeak behind it like an undertone. . . .
>
> Franz Kafka, "The Metamorphosis"

PURPOSE   To analyze the effect of point of view on the narrative
AUDIENCE   Your teacher
LENGTH   1–2 paragraphs

2. Open Assignment   Write a letter to a friend in which you discuss a short story you have read recently. Tell your friend about the story by analyzing its point of view. Choose one of the following short stories or another that you have read:

- "Raymond's Run" by Toni Cade Bambara
- "Sonny's Blues" by James Baldwin
- "A Geronimo Story" by Leslie Marmon Silko
- "Best Quality" by Amy Tan
- "A Worn Path" by Eudora Welty
- "An Occurrence at Owl Creek Bridge" by Ambrose Bierce

COMPUTER OPTION

When you're ready to edit your paragraph, use the spelling checker on your computer to help you proofread your work. Remember, however, that the checker can't catch correctly spelled words that are used incorrectly. If you write *their* when you meant to say *there*, for example, the checker won't recognize the error. Therefore, it's a good idea to use the checker to catch obvious spelling errors. Then proofread your work yourself line by line to find the less obvious mistakes.

3. Literature   Read O. Henry's short story "The Gift of the Magi." Then imagine that the story had been narrated from Jim's point of view. What effect would this change in the point of view have on the story? What information would the reader gain? What would the story lose? Analyze the effect of the different point of view in a paragraph.

Julia Alvarez
· · · · · · · · · *from* · · · · · · · ·

How the García Girls Lost Their Accents

Born in the Dominican Republic, Julia Alvarez came to the United States with her family when she was ten. In college, Alvarez studied literature and writing and later went on to teach poetry. She published her first book of fiction, How the García Girls Lost Their Accents, *in 1991. In this selection from "Daughter of Invention," one of the short stories in Alvarez's collection, she presents a simply structured narrative with characters and setting intimately familiar to her.*

The weekend before the assembly Monday morning Yoyo went into a panic. Her mother would just have to call in tomorrow and say Yoyo was in the hospital, in a coma.

Laura tried to calm her down. "Just remember how Mister Lincoln couldn't think of anything to say at the Gettysburg, but then, bang! *Four score and once upon a time ago,*" she began reciting. "Something is going to come if you just relax. You'll see, like the Americans say, *Necessity is the daughter of invention.* I'll help you."

That weekend, her mother turned all her energy towards helping Yoyo write her speech. "Please, Mami, just leave me alone, please," Yoyo pleaded with her. But Yoyo would get rid of the goose only to have to contend with the gander. Her father kept poking his head in the door just to see if Yoyo had "fulfilled your obligations," a phrase he had used when the girls were younger and he'd check to see whether they had gone to the bathroom before a car trip. Several times that weekend around the supper table, he recited his own high school valedictorian speech. He gave Yoyo pointers on delivery, notes on the great orators and their tricks. (Humbleness and praise and falling silent with great emotion were his favorites.)

Laura sat across the table, the only one who seemed to be listening to him. Yoyo and her sisters were forgetting a lot of their Spanish, and their father's formal, florid diction was hard to understand. But Laura smiled softly to herself, and turned the lazy Susan at the center of the table around and around as if it were the prime mover, the first gear of her attention.

That Sunday evening, Yoyo was reading some poetry to get herself inspired: Whitman's poems in an old book with an engraved cover her father had picked up in a thrift shop next to his office. *I celebrate myself and sing myself. . . . He most honors my style who learns under it to destroy the teacher.* The poet's words shocked and thrilled her. She had gotten used to the nuns, a literature of appropriate sentiments, poems with a message, expurgated[1] texts. But here was a flesh and blood man, belching and laughing and sweating in poems. *Who touches this book touches a man.*

That night, at last, she started to write, recklessly, three, five pages, looking up once only to see her father passing by the hall on tiptoe. When Yoyo was done, she read over her words, and her eyes filled. She finally sounded like herself in English!

As soon as she had finished that first draft, she called her mother to her room. Laura listened attentively while Yoyo read the speech out loud, and in the end, her eyes were glistening too. Her face was soft and warm and proud. "*Ay,* Yoyo, you are going to be the one to bring our name to the headlights in this country! That is a beautiful, beautiful speech I want for your father to hear it before he goes to sleep. Then I will type it for you, all right?"

Down the hall they went, mother and daughter, faces flushed with accomplishment. Into the master bedroom where Carlos was propped up on his pillows, still awake, reading the Dominican papers, already days old. Now that the dictatorship had been toppled, he had become interested in his country's fate again. The interim government was going to hold the first free elections in thirty years. History was in the making, freedom and hope were in the air again! There was still some question in his mind whether or not he might move his family back. But Laura had gotten used to the life here. She did not want to go back to the old country where, de la Torre or not, she was only a wife and a mother (and a failed one at

---

1 expurgated (eks′ pər gāt′ ′d) with objectionable passages removed

that, since she had never provided the required son). Better an independent nobody than a high-class houseslave. She did not come straight out and disagree with her husband's plans. Instead, she fussed with him about reading the papers in bed, soiling their sheets with those poorly printed, foreign tabloids. "*The Times* is not that bad!" she'd claim if her husband tried to humor her by saying they shared the same dirty habit.

The minute Carlos saw his wife and daughter filing in, he put his paper down, and his face brightened as if at long last his wife had delivered the son, and that was the news she was bringing him. His teeth were already grinning from the glass of water next to his bedside lamp, so he lisped when he said, "Eh-speech, eh-speech!"

"It is so beautiful, Cuco," Laura coached him, turning the sound on his TV off. She sat down at the foot of the bed. Yoyo stood before both of them, blocking their view of the soldiers in helicopters landing amid silenced gun reports and explosions. A few weeks ago it had been the shores of the Dominican Republic. Now it was the jungles of Southeast Asia they were saving. Her mother gave her the nod to begin reading.

Yoyo didn't need much encouragement. She put her nose to the fire, as her mother would have said, and read from start to finish without looking up. When she concluded, she was a little embarrassed at the pride she took in her own words. She pretended to quibble with a phrase or two, then looked questioningly to her mother. Laura's face was radiant. Yoyo turned to share her pride with her father.

The expression on his face shocked both mother and daughter. Carlos's toothless mouth had collapsed into a dark zero. His eyes bored into Yoyo, then shifted to Laura. In barely audible Spanish, as if secret microphones or informers were all about, he whispered to his wife,"You will permit her to read *that*?"

Laura's eyebrows shot up, her mouth fell open. In the old country, any whisper of a challenge to authority could bring the secret police in their black V.W.'s. But this was America. People could say what they thought. "What is wrong with her speech?" Laura questioned him.

"What ees wrrrong with her eh-speech?" Carlos wagged his head at her. His anger was always more frightening in his broken English. As if he had mutilated the language in his fury—and now there was nothing to stand between them and his raw, dumb anger. "What is wrong? I will tell you what is wrong. It show no gratitude. It is boastful. *I celebrate myself? The best student learns to destroy the teacher?*" He mocked Yoyo's plagiarized words. "That is insubordinate.[2] It is

2 **insubordinate** (in' sə bôr' d'n it) disobedient

improper. It is disrespecting of her teachers—" In his anger he had forgotten his fear of lurking spies: each wrong he voiced was a decibel[3] higher than the last outrage. Finally, he shouted at Yoyo, "As your father, I forbid you to make that eh-speech!"

Laura leapt to her feet, a sign that *she* was about to deliver her own speech. She was a small woman, and she spoke all her pronouncements standing up, either for more projection or as a carry-over from her girlhood in convent schools where one asked for, and literally, took the floor in order to speak.

Diego Rivera, *Tina Modotti*, 1927

She stood by Yoyo's side, shoulder to shoulder. They looked down at Carlos. "That is no tone of voice—" she began.

But now, Carlos was truly furious. It was bad enough that his daughter was rebelling, but here was his own wife joining forces with her. Soon he would be surrounded by a houseful of independent American women. He too leapt from the bed, throwing off his covers. The Spanish newspapers flew across the room. He snatched the speech out of Yoyo's hands, held it before the girl's wide eyes, a vengeful, mad look in his own, and then once, twice, three, four, countless times, he tore the speech into shreds.

"Are you crazy?" Laura lunged at him. "Have you gone mad? That is her speech for tomorrow you have torn up!"

"Have *you* gone mad?" He shook her away. "You were going to let her read that . . . that insult to her teachers?"

"Insult to her teachers!" Laura's face had crumpled up like a piece of paper. On it was written a love note to her husband, an unhappy, haunted man. "This is America, Papi, America! You are not in a savage country anymore!"

---

3 **decibel** (des′ ə bel′) a numerical measure of the loudness of sound

Meanwhile, Yoyo was on her knees, weeping wildly, collecting all the little pieces of her speech, hoping that she could put it back together before the assembly tomorrow morning. But not even a sibyl[4] could have made sense of those tiny scraps of paper. All hope was lost. "He broke it, he broke it," Yoyo moaned as she picked up a handful of pieces.

Probably, if she had thought a moment about it, she would not have done what she did next. She would have realized her father had lost brothers and friends to the dictator Trujillo. For the rest of his life, he would be haunted by blood in the streets and late night disappearances. Even after all these years, he cringed if a black Volkswagen passed him on the street. He feared anyone in uniform: the meter maid giving out parking tickets, a museum guard approaching to tell him not to get to close to his favorite Goya.

On her knees, Yoyo thought of the worst thing she could say to her father. She gathered a handful of scraps, stood up, and hurled them in his face. In a low, ugly whisper, she pronounced Trujillo's hated nickname: "Chapita! You're just another Chapita!"

It took Yoyo's father only a moment to register the loathsome nickname before he came after her. Down the halls they raced, but Yoyo was quicker than he and made it into her room just in time to lock the door as her father threw his weight against it. He called down curses on her head, ordered her on his authority as her father to open that door! He throttled that doorknob, but all to no avail. Her mother's love of gadgets saved Yoyo's hide that night. Laura had hired a locksmith to install good locks on all the bedroom doors after the house had been broken into once while they were away. Now if burglars broke in again, and the family were at home, there would be a second round of locks for the thieves to contend with.

"Lolo," she said, trying to calm him down. "Don't you ruin my new locks."

Finally he did calm down, his anger spent. Yoyo heard their footsteps retreating down the hall. Their door clicked shut. Then, muffled voices, her mother's rising in anger, in persuasion, her father's deeper murmurs of explanation and self-defense. The house fell silent a moment, before Yoyo heard, far off, the gun blasts and explosions, the serious, self-important voices of newscasters reporting their TV war.

A little while later, there was a quiet knock at Yoyo's door, followed by a tentative attempt at the doorknob. "Cuquita?" her mother whispered. "Open up, Cuquita."

"Go away," Yoyo wailed, but they both knew she was glad her mother was there, and needed only a moment's protest to save face.

---

4 **sibyl** (sib′ ′l) a fortune teller

Together they concocted a speech: two brief pages of stale compliments and the polite commonplaces on teachers, a speech wrought by necessity and without much invention by mother and daughter late into the night on one of the pads of paper Laura had once used for her own inventions. After it was drafted, Laura typed it up while Yoyo stood by, correcting her mother's misnomers[5] and mis-sayings.

Yoyo came home the next day with the success story of the assembly. The nuns had been flattered, the audience had stood up and given "our devoted teachers a standing ovation," what Laura had suggested they do at the end of the speech.

5 **misnomers** (mis nō′ mərz) errors in naming persons or places

Adrián Luis González, Painted pottery typewriter, c. 1980

She clapped her hands together as Yoyo recreated the moment. "I stole that from your father's speech, remember? Remember how he put that in at the end?" She quoted him in Spanish, then translated for Yoyo into English.

That night, Yoyo watched him from the upstairs hall window, where she'd retreated the minute she heard his car pull up in front of the house. Slowly, her father came up the driveway, a grim expression on his face as he grappled with a large, heavy cardboard box. At the front door, he set the package down carefully and patted all his pockets for his house keys. (If only he'd had Laura's ticking key chain!) Yoyo heard the snapping open of locks downstairs. She listened as he struggled to maneuver the box through the narrow doorway. He called her name several times, but she did not answer him.

"My daughter, your father, he love you very much," he explained from the bottom of the stairs. "He just want to protect you." Finally, her mother came up and pleaded with Yoyo to go down and reconcile[6] with him. "Your father did not mean to harm. You must pardon him. Always it is better to let bygones be forgotten, no?"

Downstairs, Yoyo found her father setting up a brand new electric typewriter on the kitchen table. It was even better that her mother's. He had outdone himself with all the extra features: a plastic carrying case with Yoyo's initials decaled below the handle, a brace to lift the paper upright while she typed, an erase cartridge, an automatic margin tab, a plastic hood like a toaster cover to keep the dust away. Not even her mother could have invented such a machine!

But Laura's inventing days were over just as Yoyo's were starting up with her school-wide success. Rather than the rolling suitcase everyone else in the family remembers, Yoyo thinks of the speech her mother wrote as her last invention. It was as if, after that, her mother had passed on to Yoyo her pencil and pad and said, "Okay, Cuquita, here's the buck. You give it a shot."

___

6 reconcile (rek′ ən sīl′) to make up; to settle a disagreement

---

For Discussion

1. How might this story have been different if your own family had been involved?

2. Have you ever feared something the way Yoyo fears giving her speech? Compare your way of overcoming fear with Yoyo's.

Readers Respond

My favorite character was Laura, the mother, because she was kindhearted and open-minded. She reminded me of my mother. The writer made Yoyo's mother seem real by making her passionate.

The scene I remembered most clearly was when the father ripped up Yoyo's speech. His reaction seemed so unjust and unfair.

Maritza Pagán

My favorite character was Laura. I really enjoyed her enthusiasm for her daughter's speech and how she stood up to her husband, a forbidden act in the Dominican Republic. The author set up the conflict by telling how the family's life had been in the Dominican Republic and then contrasting that culture with the American culture.

I would have written the story in first person. Maybe the author wrote it in third person because it was based on a personal experience and brought back too many memories, so she had to distance herself by writing in third person.

Rachel Hansen

Did you notice?

☞ Did you notice that the speech Yoyo presents to her father is not printed in the story? Why do you think Alvarez does not include the speech?

☞ Have you ever had a similar conflict with a parent or another adult? Write a narrative paragraph in which you tell an event from your point of view. Then try writing about the same event from the adult's point of view.

Writing Process in Action

Family Matters

Just as fires tend to produce smoke, conflicts and resolutions tend to produce good narratives, such as the one from *How the García Girls Lost Their Accents*, found on pages 200–206. Author Julia Alvarez bases this story upon a conflict between parent and teen-ager over what is appropriate or "proper." The characters then resolve this conflict to bring the story to a close.

Now you're invited to write a narrative that is based on a central conflict and resolution. What should you write about? Read on.

• Assignment •

CONTEXT   Imagine that the editors of *Writer's Choice* are putting together a companion anthology of student writing called *Family Matters*. Their aim is to publish a book of realistic, compelling stories that will appeal to students your age and provide insights into family life in the 1990s—stories like Alvarez's. The editors hope to collect a wide range of stories—happy, serious, bizarre, thought-provoking—all emerging from family conflicts. Now the editors have contacted your class to ask you and your classmates to submit stories based on real incidents you have experienced or know about. They have explained that you can fictionalize the account, changing details about characters, setting, and events from your actual experience. You can even change the way the conflict is resolved to suit yourself. They have also said that they want the stories to be written from the third-person point of view.

PURPOSE   To write a short narrative for an anthology of student writing

AUDIENCE   High school students and teachers throughout the nation

LENGTH   3–5 pages

For more advice on how to approach this assignment, you will find the next few pages helpful. But don't feel that you have to remember all of what follows. You can come *back* to these pages as you write, getting help where and when you need it. You're in charge of your own writing process.

1. Prewriting

What to write about—the time you fought the undertow to save your sister, worked with your whole family to dig the car out of a snowbank, or competed against your mom in a local 10k run? Your first task is choosing a problem or incident in which members of your family—or someone else's—were faced with a conflict. The conflict may be against someone or something outside the family or within the family itself. Conflict in a narrative is any struggle to resolve a problem. If you want to review conflict and resolution, see Lessons 4.1 and 4.2. Otherwise, just plunge in by listing incidents that you experienced or know about. Glance through your journal for ideas. Freewrite about situations that you feel strongly about. For other techniques to help you generate ideas, refer to Lessons 1.1 and 2.2. Then narrow your list to those incidents that are meaningful to the characters involved in them and that these characters can resolve through their own actions.

Choose the incident that most interests you to be the basis of your story. Then map out the sequence of events involved in this incident. To come up with these events, try freewriting to answer the following questions.

- What background events had to happen before this problem or incident could occur?
- What do my characters have to do to resolve the problem?
- What has to happen for the characters to resolve their conflict?

Next, arrange these events on a timeline. Remember, though, that you don't have to tell your narrative in strictly chronological order.

Last, although you know you must write this story from the third-person point of view, decide on the kind of narrator you're going to use—limited or omniscient. And, if limited, from which character's point of view you want to tell the story. The material in Lesson 4.7 may help you decide this issue. Thinking about the narrator in Alvarez's story might also help. The omniscient narrator in this story reveals the nature and significance of the conflict to each character. How might the story have been different if Alvarez had chosen to use a limited narrator? Now, what do you want to do in your story: help the reader to understand all the characters' thoughts and feelings, or show the reader the conflict from the perspective of one particular character?

2. Drafting

Move into drafting by envisioning the scene in which the conflict of your story erupts or reaches its crisis point. See the characters and the setting. See what happens. If you've chosen to write from a particular character's point of view, imagine you are that person. What do you notice? What are you hearing? Feeling? Seeing? Then, holding the scene in your mind, start writing as if you were telling someone about it—writing partner, friend, family member. Use sensory details, similes, metaphors, and whatever else it takes to help this person see what you're seeing. To get an idea of how to do this, look at how Alvarez presents the scene in which the conflict erupts:

> The expression on his face shocked both mother and daughter. Carlos's toothless mouth had collapsed into a dark zero. His eyes bored into Yoyo, then shifted to Laura. In barely audible Spanish, as if secret microphones or informers were all about, he whispered to his wife, "You will permit her to read that?"

Of course what you've just read here is probably the product of many hours, days, or even weeks and months of revising and editing. So, if your first draft pales by comparison, don't worry. At this point, you just need to focus on putting what you're envisioning into words—any words.

Next, working backward from the central paragraph, try to fill in the information about characters, setting, and events the reader needs to know to understand what leads up to this scene.

- Who appears in the scene?
- Why are these characters there?
- How did these characters get there?
- Where does this scene take place?
- Why does it take place in this particular setting?

Then, working forward from the central scene, write about the events that resolve the complication. Be sure to note what the characters do and any ways in which they change. If you get stuck, focus on answering "What happens next?"

Once you have drafted the pieces of your story, refer to your timeline to arrange them. You don't have to begin at the beginning. For instance, to provide background information you could use a flashback. Lesson 1.4, page 24, shows some different ways to relate events.

Next, look for good places to add dialogue or anecdotes. Lessons 4.3 and 4.4 can help you identify these. Alvarez's story can also give you some ideas for where you might want to insert dialogue or anecdotes. When Alvarez includes choice bits of the advice that Laura gives Yoyo, she reveals details about Laura's character and her relationship to her daughter. Alvarez also uses dialogue in moments of crisis and conflict to bring these scenes to life.

3. Revising

Nothing is more useful at the revising stage than presenting. Go ahead and present your work to an audience of one or two peer editors. But first share with them the details of your assignment, and ask them to listen to your narrative—or read it—the way your intended audience is likely to do. Then pay attention to their responses. They may have not only good suggestions but also questions and reactions that help show you what to work on.

If a peer editor is confused by what happens, you might need to add transitions to make the order of events clearer. You might even need to reconsider the order in which you present these events. Confusion can also indicate that you've left out important details. So, you might also want to double-check that you've included all the essential information. Refer to your timeline: Is it complete? Did you include in your draft all the events you had arranged on it?

If a peer editor can't clearly remember an important event, character, or setting, you might need to add specific sensory details and images. If a peer editor gets bored, you might need to withhold some information to create suspense. On the other hand, if a peer editor is surprised by an event you didn't intend to be a surprise, you might need to add details to foreshadow it.

Next, refer back to the assignment to make sure you have met its requirements. If you haven't, note what you'll need to revise so that your story meets these requirements.

Then, when you get down to making the nitty-gritty changes in your draft, keep looking for ways to bring your story to life. Consider, for example, the connotations of your words—that is, their subtle shades of meaning, the feeling they create. You might want to choose words that work together to create a particular mood. Look at how Alvarez uses nouns, verbs, and adjectives to make this scene vividly convey an overall feeling of an angry outburst.

> *He too leapt from the bed, throwing off his covers. The Spanish newspapers flew across the room. He snatched the speech out of Yoyo's hands, held it before the girl's wide eyes, a vengeful, mad look in his own, and then once, twice, three, four, countless times, he tore the speech into shreds.*

If you get stuck at any point during your revising, go back to visualizing as you did during the drafting stage. Visualizing the moment you're working on can help you pick up the thread of your story.

Criteria
1. *Focuses on an interesting family conflict*
2. *Hooks interest by establishing setting, characters, and conflict early*
3. *Uses dialogue, anecdotes, and figurative language effectively*
4. *Evokes emotional response to resolution*
5. *Uses third-person point of view consistently*
6. *Follows correct grammar, usage, and mechanics*

4. Editing

When your story is ready for editing, you might begin by focusing on dialogue. Although dialogue can bring your characters and their conflicts to life, it can also confuse your readers if it's paragraphed and punctuated incorrectly or not identified sufficiently. If you need to review how to paragraph and punctuate your dialogue, see Lesson 21.9.

Then use the checklists in Lessons 2.9 and 2.10 to edit your sentences and paragraphs for unity and coherence. Proofread for other errors in grammar, usage, and mechanics. Finally, create a clean copy of your narrative.

5. Presenting

Although for this assignment you have written a narrative for a fictitious anthology, there's no reason why you can't submit it to a real anthology. If you decide to do so, you may want to create a few other items. You might write a letter to the editors in which you explain a little bit about yourself and your story and provide them with an address and phone number at which you may be reached. If you would like your narrative returned after the editors review it, you should prepare a self-addressed, stamped envelope (SASE) to send them.

• Reflecting •

In the process of writing this narrative, what, if anything, did you learn about Alvarez's story? What did you learn about writing narratives? And what, if anything, did you learn about your writing process in particular?

Portfolio & Reflection

Summary

Key concepts in narrative writing include the following:

- Characters, setting, plot, and conflict are basic elements of narrative.
- The basis of a plot is the development and resolution of a conflict.
- Dialogue enlivens narrative, advances plot, and reveals character.
- Anecdotes are brief narratives used to make a point, often in another narrative.
- Sports narratives usually focus on character and conflict.

Your Writer's Portfolio

Look over the narrative writing you have done during this unit. Select two pieces of writing to put into your portfolio. Each piece should demonstrate that you have worked with one or more of the preceding concepts. In other words, look for a piece of writing that does one or more of the following:

- contains the basic narrative elements—characters, setting, plot, and conflict
- involves a character in a conflict that leads to a climax and a resolution
- uses dialogue to advance plot, reveal character, or bring the story to life
- is or contains an anecdote

Reflection and Commentary

Now write one page in which you demonstrate that you understand what this unit asked of you. Use the two pieces of writing you've selected as evidence while you consider the following numbered items. Respond to as many numbered items as possible. Label the page "Commentary on Narrative Writing," and include it in your portfolio.

1. In a narrative where did you use characters and events from your life?

2. Which elements of your narrative grew out of talking, freewriting, answering questions, or constructing a framework?
3. Which element—characters, setting, plot, conflict—did you handle best?
4. Which element of your narrative do you think needs work? What will you do to improve that element the next time?
5. Why will your story's conflict interest readers? Is the outcome uncertain?
6. Do all your narrative events develop the conflict, leading to a resolution? What could you do to make the conflict and its resolution more interesting?
7. Did you experiment with dialogue? Does your dialogue sound real? How would you change it if you could?
8. What prewriting steps gave you an idea for your anecdote?

Feedback

If you had a chance to respond to the following student comment, what would you say or ask?

Writing allows a person to make dreams a reality for a character.

Damaris Ortiz, Brentwood High School,
Brentwood, New York

Expository Writing

Planet Earth

Vincent van Gogh, *The Starry Night*, 1889

Winckler Tracks

CACTUS

"I started out by watching birds, and then I followed birds into nature and found a larger, more complicated world there—a world that is being compromised by our behavior. I wanted to write about that."

Suzanne Winckler

The day of the big cactus hunt started early, at 4:30 A.M. actually, when a group of Cassin's kingbirds set up a racket outside Winckler's tent. "I lay there thinking how they sounded like a pack of overindulged miniature poodles. . . ," she later wrote.

Annoying as they were, the kingbirds provided the perfect indecorous start to a slightly wacky day in nature study: the first and perhaps the only big day in cactus.

Big day? Winckler, a free-lance writer and passionate bird watcher, got the idea from the big day tradition in the bird world. In bird watching a "big day" means choosing teams, heading into the field, and trying to spot as many feathered species as possible in twenty-four hours. "I wanted to take that idea, poke a little fun at it, and apply it to another organism, in this case cactus," she explained. For Winckler, this particular big day would result in a piece of writing published in a national magazine.

"I selected cacti as my subject because I love them, although I didn't know a great deal about them," Winckler said. "I also love

Writing the Cactus Story

1. Stalking the Facts

2. Crafting the Story

3. Revising the Prickly Details

F O C U S

The expository writer informs and explains and must keep in mind what the audience needs to know.

the landscape they're in and the fact that they're sort of the antithesis of birds: they don't fly, and except for their gorgeous flowers, they're retiring. I was also attracted by the strong conservation angle, the greedy way people will go in and steal these cacti. I wanted to make a point about that."

Winckler's first step was to approach Dr. Allan Zimmerman to see if he'd participate in her wry adventure. "Allan is one of the premier taxonomists in the world of cactus," Winckler explained, "but he's also an avid birder, so he immediately understood what the joke was."

Then Winckler called an editor she knew at *Audubon,* an environmental magazine, and talked the idea through, a common practice for her. With the go-ahead, Winckler got a deadline and a limit on the number of words she could write—about 2,000. Assignment in hand, Winckler readied herself for the field.

An Elf Owlet sits on a saguaro cactus that blooms with red, edible fruit.

1. Stalking the Facts

Southwest Texas

NEW MEXICO

TEXAS

Pecos R.

• Odessa

• Fort Stockton

Marathon

• Sanderson

Rio Grande

• Del Rio

Big Bend National Park

Eagle Pass

MEXICO

These pages of Winkler's journal reveal some of her detailed notes.

The setting for Winckler's big day was, appropriately, Big Bend, a vast desert area in southwest Texas. In this region of varied soils and terrains, the team could find the biggest number of species in the world with the least amount of driving. Winckler staged her big day over a long weekend and invited Zimmerman and three other biologists.

On the day of the hunt, the team started out before daylight and worked intensely until after dark. They searched dry arroyos, grassy pastures, and searing desert flats, using the characteristic field posture of the cactologist—running around in circles with heads bowed in close exploration. In the end, they got better acquainted with

forty-three species, from chollas and prickly pears to living rocks and barrel cacti.

For Winckler, the day was a juggling act—stalking rare cacti with the team, then stepping back to record the experience as a writer for a magazine. Winckler jotted information in a hard-bound record book, about five by seven inches. She also sketched each cactus and asked Zimmerman to tell her their names. "He was excellent about scientific names," Winckler said. "He spelled and respelled for me that day."

When Winckler got back home, she interviewed several more cactus experts by phone. "I talked to some people who not only grow rare cacti but are also involved in the legal aspects of protecting rare species. I used that information as background— as a larger landscape to set this piece in."

INTERFACE *You're a staff writer for an environmental magazine, and you want to do a story about air pollution. Many articles have been written already, quoting statistics on the amount of pollutants in the air and citing the damaging effects of air pollution. Some angry articles have also appeared. Think of a different approach to inform readers and get them involved.*

2. Crafting the Story

Before Winckler began to write, she organized her notes and transcribed tapes from a friend, who had carried a recorder on the hunt. Because the article would be short and personal, Winckler didn't develop an outline, something she works from for longer stories. But she did map out a rough structure for the piece in her mind. Then she "sat down, took a deep breath, and started writing." It would take her about about five mornings at the computer to craft the story, working slowly to create two or three pages of solid copy a day.

Winckler led off her story with the noisy kingbirds. "I wanted to emphasize that what I was picking up on in the landscape was birds— not cacti—and the sense that it was an incredible experience in the tent. I think that not many people are aware of how alive the world is at unexpected hours of the day," she said. "I also didn't want anyone to think I was an expert on cacti, because I wasn't."

From there, Winckler worked to entertain readers, teach them about Big Bend and rare cacti, and leave them caring about the place and its garden of obscure, strange plants. How did she do it?

By comparing unfamiliar cacti to everyday things, Winckler helped readers experience the spiny plants firsthand. Chollas, readers learned, "grow out on the desert like enormous cande-

labras," while *Echinocereus viridi-florus davisii* look like "a tiny hair-ball." A blooming *Coryphantha vivipara* smelled like "floor pol-ish" to Winckler, old tuna-fish cans to someone else.

With all her descriptions, Winckler resisted the urge to go overboard. "In describing an organism, a landscape, or an organism in a landscape, you must not get carried away in a purple sense," she said. "I mean you shouldn't be too flowery, too cute, too gorgeous for what the situation really is."

As a nature writer, Winckler also stressed the importance of going beyond beautiful description. "It's very easy to love nature and get sentimental about it," she said. "But you can't do that if you're really going to be scientific about it. You can use description to get readers involved in an exposi-tory article. But you can't just ride on that. You have to introduce the science of nature so people will understand how things function in the larger planetary sense."

To convey scientific informa-tion, Winckler developed simple, clear examples. For instance, she pointed out how every cactus is

There are about sixty species of cactus in west Texas out of a family total of two or three thousand. Some of them, like the chollas, which grow out on the desert like enormous candelabras, are quite common and widespread, while other species ex-hibit a fierce partiality to small and scattered plots of certain soils. Need-less to say these finicky ones are, first, rare and, second, highly prized by cactus fanciers, a situation that has helped put them on that old proverbial brink. One finds these rare cacti by knowing something about the Mix-

Even though Winckler conveys much technical information about cacti in her article, she makes the subject lively and enjoyable through her first-person point of view and informal style.

adapted to a special location and soil: "We drove hither and yon that day from a hummock of limestone to a hill of gypsum, each of which harbored its own brand of cactus."

Winckler closed her story with an update on laws protecting cacti. Though far from perfect, Winckler explained, the laws have had some effect. "I am told that cacti are no longer leaving the Trans Pecos by the tons as they used to," she wrote. That was good news for Winckler—and readers, newly concerned about *E. v. davisii* and all the others.

INTERFACE *You're an environmental writer preparing a story on nocturnal desert animals, and you want to lead your story with a description of approaching darkness. How could you use comparison-contrast in your lead to set the stage for your discussion of the animals?*

3. Revising the Prickly Details

Once Winckler finished her first draft, she began to revise—adding some details, deleting other information. She also finished working on her sentence structure. "I spend a lot of time writing a sentence and then turning it on its head, putting something in the middle. I play at it a lot."

That kind of effort resulted in strong, clear sentences, like the one Winckler used to begin a paragraph on pink, neon-colored cactus flowers. "One complaint I have about birds is that too few of them are pink," she wrote.

Once Winckler's editor read the story, she had relatively few changes to suggest because the story had little complex detail and touched on no major legal issues. Most of Winckler's larger pieces do take more editing and fact checking, however, something she appreciates. "I wish I were edited more heavily," Winckler observed. "The world needs more editors. I'm aware of how much other people can help your writing."

Winckler loves working at her computer, where she plays with the language, revising and editing each sentence until it's just what she wants.

ON ASSIGNMENT

1. Find a copy of *Audubon, Natural History*, or *Discover* magazine in your library. Select an article about a plant, an animal, or an ecosystem. Write a paragraph explaining the main point of the article. Did the writer make the issue clear? Was the writing sufficiently vivid to help you care about the living things involved?

2. **Literature Connection** Read one chapter or essay from a nature book such as *Arctic Dreams* by Barry

Lopez or *A Book of Bees* by Sue Hubbell. Write a one- to two-page letter to the writer of the book on the following question: How did the writing move you to see the natural world in a new way?

3. **Cooperative Learning** Divide into environmental reporting teams of three or four persons each. Choose a specific natural area that is threatened in some way, such as a national park, the Arctic tundra in Alaska, or the Amazon rain forest.

Your job as a reporting team is to explain the natural systems at work in the place you've chosen and the threats to those systems. Divide your research questions into three or four categories, one per person. Consider for example, how the sun, soil, water, plants, and animals work together to keep the system going; what threats exist to upset the system; what can be done to save the system; and why it is important to save the system. Each individual writer should research and write a 500- to 1,000-word report on his or her question. Then all writers should pool their information for a presentation to the class. Perhaps one of the team members would like to create a poster including magazine photographs and illustrations as part of the team's presentation.

Case Study: Nature Writing **219**

Explaining and Informing

What Really Happens When You Get Out of Bed?

Your alarm clock resonates through your room. You reach over to turn it off and slowly sit up, preparing to get out of bed. You probably give little thought to these first motions of the morning. But as science writer David Bodanis explains, stepping out of bed causes some strange and jarring events.

Literature Model

Bodanis introduces the cause of the surprising chain of tiny, imperceptible events that follow the simple act of getting out of bed.

Whack thump bam! The man's foot extends out of bed and lands on the floor. The floorboards jam down and their vibrations travel sideways like pond waves to the wall. The whole house compresses in the new loading—bricks where the floor fits into the wall shrinking smaller by 1/100,000 inch from the weight.

What are some items in your own room that might "lift up and bounce down" as you step out of bed?

Any impact that doesn't get lost in the walls stays quivering in the floor. The chest of drawers starts lifting up and down, as does the bed, the chair, the table with its plant on top, the stack of magazines and Sunday papers in the corner, and even the old coffee cup left down on the floor. All lift up and bounce down, rebound up and crash down again as the floor reverberates to get rid of its buzzing energy. In a particularly energetic leap out of bed this bouncing of furniture can be seen (lampshades especially are prone to being knocked over in such moments), but even with a softer landing the furniture shaking takes place.

Then the second foot touches down, the waker stands up, and he steps to the double-glazed window to see what is happening outside.

David Bodanis, *The Secret House*

The Nature of Expository Writing

Bodanis's description of what happens on a microscopic level when a person gets out of bed is an example of expository writing—writing that explains and informs. He shows a clear linkage between a cause and its effects. The student model below shows another type of expository writing. It describes the step-by-step process of a flower sprouting, growing, and blooming. Although there are different kinds of expository writing, all writers of exposition share one goal: to present a clear, concise explanation that readers will find interesting and informative.

Student Model

The flower, one of nature's many miracles, is created through a series of complex steps. With an embryo, a supply of stored food, and a protective covering, the seed begins the process. Most seeds remain dormant at first, usually because conditions are not favorable for growth. Seeds have been known to stay dormant from one week to fifty years and still germinate properly. Germination occurs when there is an abundant supply of water, an adequate amount of oxygen, and the proper temperatures. Crucial to the plant's life, water begins the next step in the process. The seed absorbs large amounts of water, causing the protective coating to soften. The internal tissues then swell and break through the coating. This new life, this plant, immediately begins to burn food by taking in oxygen and giving off carbon dioxide, and it produces the energy necessary for growth. The vulnerable plant now becomes susceptible to sunlight. Too much or too little can harm it. However, the sun helps make the food for the plant to burn and receive energy. This process continues even after the first leaves develop. The plant grows stronger and more mature each day. Finally, the full-grown plant is ready to receive its crowning glory—the flower.

Billy McKnight, Jefferson Davis High School, Montgomery, Alabama

Billy McKnight introduces this paragraph with a clear statement of what he will explain.

Billy ties his process explanation together with transitions that show chronological order. What are some of these transitions that he uses?

• JOURNAL ACTIVITY •
Try It Out

Look through some books and magazines for five expository paragraphs on different topics—for example, the development of a frog or the construction of a house. In your journal briefly explain why each is an expository paragraph and what it accomplishes.

The Varieties of Expository Writing

Drafting Tip

For help with drafting a topic sentence, see the chart on this page and Lesson 2.5, page 80.

The essay is one of the most common forms of expository writing. This short composition consists of an introduction, body, and conclusion. The introduction includes a thesis statement, which is a one-sentence summary of your purpose for writing. The body consists of one or more paragraphs of details that support the thesis. The conclusion summarizes or gives the implications of what you've said in your essay.

You probably use other forms of expository writing quite often without even realizing it. You are using expository writing if you write out instructions for a neighbor on taking care of your cat while you are on vacation, or if you jot down directions for a friend to pick you up at an after-school job.

The chart below presents the various *kinds* of expository writing, the basic purpose of each kind, and an example of each. While each variety has a distinct purpose, you can use two or more varieties in combination to explain and inform whether you're writing an essay or some other form of exposition.

Kinds of Expository Writing		
Kind	**Basic Purpose**	**Example**
Definition	To define a term or give the basic tenets of theory	A supernova is a star that explodes, becoming extremely bright before fading and leaving a huge cloud of dust and gas.
Process	To give the steps in a process or explain a sequence of events	To locate their prey, bats use a process called echolocation, in which they send out high-pitched sound waves. These waves bounce off insects and echo back to the bat.
Cause and Effect	To explain how or why one or more events or actions cause other things to happen	The rubbing and grinding of the earth's crustal plates against one another causes earthquakes.
Classification	To break down a broad topic into narrower categories	There are two main types of whales: toothed whales and baleen whales.
Comparison-Contrast	To discuss similarities and differences between two related phenomena or events	Venus' flytraps and pitcher plants are both meat-eating plants. Venus' flytraps trap insects in their leaves. Pitcher plants capture insects that drown in their jug-shaped leaves.

The following are some writing options to help you apply what you have learned.

1. Guided Assignment   Imagine you're a third-grade teacher. Use the following facts to write an explanation of the cause of thunder that your students will understand:

- The electrical charge of lightning heats the air through which it passes.
- The heat causes air molecules to move outward in every direction.
- The heated molecules crash into cooler air.
- The crash creates an air wave that makes a thundering roar.

PURPOSE   To explain the cause of thunder
AUDIENCE   A class of third graders
LENGTH   1–3 paragraphs

2. Open Assignment   Imagine that you are writing a column for your school newspaper in which you answer perplexing questions students have on just about any topic.

Choose one of the following questions or make up one of your own, and write an expository paragraph giving the answer. Use any reference book you need.

- Why does the moon seem to change shape?
- How and why did a sculptor carve four President's faces onto Mount Rushmore?
- What is a black hole?
- What must an immigrant do to become a United States citizen?

3. Cooperative Learning   The fresco on this page is *The Making of a Fresco Showing the Building of a City* by Diego Rivera. In a small group discuss possible topics for one- to three-page expository papers about the fresco. Then have each group member write and research a different kind of expository paper. For example, one student might write about the art of fresco painting; another might explain what's going on in the fresco; and a third might compare and contrast Rivera's work with Michelangelo's frescoes.

Diego Rivera, *The Making of a Fresco Showing the Building of a City*, 1931

A Lemon a Day . . .

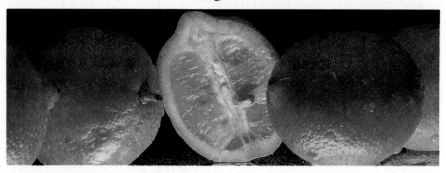

Did you know that smells can change your behavior? One Japanese company, Shimizu, wafts odors into the air to make its workers more efficient. Science writer Judith Stone takes a somewhat lighthearted look at this phenomenon.

Literature Model

Here Judith Stone provides statistics to illustrate her point.

W e have already developed a system to control the environment by fragrance," says Junichi Yagi, vice president of S. Technology Center-America, a subsidiary of Shimizu, Japan's largest architectural, engineering, and construction firm. . . . Experiments in Japan with thirteen keypunch operators, monitored eight hours a day for thirty days, showed that the average number of errors per hour dropped by 21 percent when office air was scented with lavender (it reduces stress) and by 33 percent when laced with jasmine (it induces relaxation); a stimulating lemon scent reduced errors by 54 percent. . . .

Stone adds two scents to the list. Which smells might you add?

Shimizu researchers also find that orange, peppermint, eucalyptus, chamomile, and Japanese cypress are soothing, while scarlet sage and rosemary are stimulating. (I would add Play-Doh and Rockin' Roger's Bar-B-Q Sauce to the stimulating list.)

Judith Stone, *Light Elements*

Kinds of Supporting Details You Can Use

Supporting details give expository writing its strength. Stone's paragraphs about odor and human behavior are clear because of their facts and statistics. Note the types of supporting details listed in the chart.

Supporting Details for Expository Writing	
Kinds	**Example of Use in Exposition**
Facts	Alligators live largely in fresh water, while crocodiles live mostly in salt water or in at least slightly salty water.
Statistics	The world's largest tree is a giant sequoia called the General Sherman tree. It measures 101.5 feet at the base, is 272.4 feet tall, and weighs about 12,334,000 pounds.
Examples/ Incidents	The chimpanzee is an example of an animal that makes and uses tools. Chimpanzees cut pieces of grass to specific lengths for fishing termites out of termite mounds.
Sensory details	The aurora borealis appears as a glimmering curtain of light flashing in the night sky.
Reasons	One reason some people think penguins are mammals rather than birds is that their feathers are short and fluffy and, from a distance, resemble hair.

• JOURNAL ACTIVITY •
Think It Through

Read a magazine article. Next, without reviewing the article, list in your journal the supporting details you recall. What makes these details memorable? Write your ideas.

Some Criteria for Selecting Supporting Details

Common sense will help you select supporting details. For example, if you are explaining a process, you will want to present all the steps. The following factors are the most important for selecting types of supporting details for a particular exposition:

- the type of exposition you are writing
- your purpose for writing, especially your secondary purpose (see examples of secondary purpose in the following chart)
- the level of knowledge or expertise of your audience

Prewriting Tip

To help come up with supporting details, you can brainstorm with other students. To learn more about brainstorming, see Lesson 2.2, page 66.

The chart below shows two situations and how you might analyze key factors in order to help you select appropriate supporting details for exposition.

Using Supporting Details		
Factor	Situation #1	Situation #2
Main purpose and type of your exposition	To explain the cause and effects of a natural phenomenon	To compare two theories about a natural phenomenon
Your secondary purpose	To interest your audience in the topic	To show your knowledge of the theories
Level of knowledge of your audience	Audience unfamiliar with the topic	Most of targeted audience (scientists) familiar with the topic
Kinds of supporting details you might rely on most heavily	Incidents and interesting sensory details	Facts and statistics that provide convincing support

A Note on Organizing Supporting Details

How you organize your supporting details depends in part on the type of exposition you are writing. For example, if you are writing about a cause and its effects, you might present the least important effect first and the most important effect last.

Model

In what order does the writer list her supporting details?

The writer concludes with a prime example of one urban gardener.

Urban gardens—plots overflowing with juicy red tomatoes, shiny green cukes, crisp beans, and myriad flowers—have been popping up in greater numbers all over our neighborhood since spring. You've probably seen them in backyards, empty lots, even on rooftops. Rising vegetable prices, up 35 percent from last year, are surely one reason behind the spread of these garden plots. Even more important reasons include the desire for healthful, pesticide-free vegetables and for the better taste of the home-grown vegetables. Delia Jackson exemplifies this trend. She even took a course called City Gardens at the local community center. Soon after the class ended, she began a roof garden atop the high-rise where she lives. "My friends joked about it at first," she says, "but now the same ones are coming over for my vine-ripened tomatoes."

Writer's Choice

The following are some writing options to help you apply what you have learned.

1. Guided Assignment   Rearrange and use the following details to write an explanation of the term *hurricane*. Imagine you are writing for a television newscast, so your audience is made up of nonexperts. In addition to explaining what a hurricane is, you also want to impress the audience with a hurricane's great destructive power.

- In 1983 a hurricane hit Galveston, Texas, causing two billion dollars in damage and killing twenty-one people.
- The winds of a hurricane can exceed seventy-five miles per hour.
- Hurricanes develop over warm tropical ocean waters.
- The winds and rain produce massive waves, called a storm surge, which bring floods.
- A hurricane is a powerful, swirling storm.
- The most destructive part of the hurricane is the area of wall clouds that surround the eye, where winds may reach 150 miles per hour.
- A hurricane may cover an area of 200 to 300 miles in diameter.
- At the center of a hurricane is the eye, an area of calm about twenty miles in diameter.

PURPOSE   To explain what a hurricane is and to demonstrate its destructive power
AUDIENCE   Television viewers
LENGTH   2–3 paragraph TV news script

2. Open Assignment   Imagine that you are a columnist for a teen magazine writing an explanation in answer to a reader's question. You want to create a well-written explanation for an audience of nonexpert high school students. Choose one of the following topics or a topic of your own. Look through magazines and reference books to find an example of each of the kinds of supporting details listed on page 225 that relate to the topic. Then write two to five paragraphs that include these details.

- What causes waterfalls?
- What is a fossil?
- What is the life cycle of a butterfly?

3. Geography   Imagine you're a writer for a sixth-grade social studies textbook. Choose a city, and use an encyclopedia or other reference book to find out about the natural geography of the location. Then write one page telling, in an impartial way, why this geographic location is or is not a good one for a city. Incorporate facts, statistics, examples, and reasons as supporting details. Give your piece to a peer editor to edit and revise. Include your references, so your peer editor can check your facts just as a real textbook editor would do.

COMPUTER OPTION

Perhaps your peer editor will find that you have misspelled a word or name throughout your textbook page. Once you have the correct spelling, check and see if your word-processing program has a Search (or Find) and Replace feature. Using such a feature, you can tell your PC to find every use of the misspelled word or name so you can correct the spelling.

4. Cooperative Learning   Imagine you need to explain a natural process, such as soil erosion, to an ESL (English as a second language) class. Work with a small group, some of whom, if possible, are studying the languages spoken by your ESL class members. Together, make a list of the supporting details you will use to explain the process. Then individually write a draft of your explanation in English. Your audience does not speak English well, so write your exposition as clearly as possible and define difficult terms.

The Art of Getting Lost

Do you think getting lost in the woods is easy? Think again. According to humorist Patrick McManus, getting lost takes careful preparation and planning. Here are his instructions.

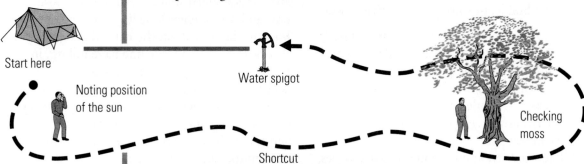

Start here

Noting position of the sun

Water spigot

Shortcut

Checking moss

In his introductory sentence, McManus identifies the process he will be explaining.

McManus gives tips to help a camper get lost. Have you gotten lost anywhere besides the woods? What tips would you give to get lost where you did?

Literature Model

N ow how should you go about getting lost? . . . If you are camped in a public campground, simply say that you are going to take a shortcut to the communal spigot [water faucet] to fill the water bucket. . . . Shortcuts rank number one among ways to get lost quickly and thoroughly. . . . Before starting your shortcut, take careful note of the position of the sun. This will give the impression that you know what you're doing. . . . [Also,] always study on which side of the trees the moss is growing. Guides and other experienced woodsmen are fond of giving this advice, because looking at moss helps even them to get lost.

Patrick McManus, *Rubber Legs and White Tail-Hairs*

Thinking About a Process

Although many people do not need expert advice on how to get lost in the woods, they may need instruction on how to do other things. How do you steer a canoe? How do you feed a pet snake? You can teach any of these skills as a series of steps, or a process.

You may also choose to explain a process just to share knowledge. For example, if you write to explain how fireflies make their flashing lights, your primary purpose is to share knowledge rather than to teach your readers how to make flashing lights themselves.

Now suppose you wanted to write an exposition on how to bathe a dog. The chart below shows the steps you would use during the prewriting stage.

Drafting Tip

Some transitions useful in process writing are *after, always, as soon as, before, first, following, in order to, now, soon, so that, then, until.*

Planning a "How to" Paper

1. Choose topic: how to bathe a dog.

2. Define audience: first-time dog-owners.

3. Gather information: read manuals, interview, observe.

4. List steps of the process in chronological order.

   a. Set up safe bathing area—rubber mat in the tub, nonskid rug on floor.

   b. Gather shampoo, sponge, bucket or shower head, towels, comb or brush, and other equipment you need.

   c. If you don't have a hand-held shower head, fill tub half-full with lukewarm water.

   d. Plug dog's ears with cotton to prevent water from entering. (Remember to take cotton out after bath.)

   e. Wet dog all over with lukewarm water.

   f. Shampoo dog, using your fingers to scrub.

   g. Rinse dog with water, using bucket or shower head.

   h. Wash dog's face with sponge dipped in clear water.

   i. Let dog shake off excess water.

   j. Rub dog dry with towels, or use hair dryer.

   k. Comb dog when coat is dry.

5. Note any special instructions.

6. Tell result of process: clean, happy dog.

• JOURNAL ACTIVITY •
Think It Through

In your journal list five possible topics for a process explanation. Then write a brief statement explaining whether the purpose of each would be to teach a skill or simply to share knowledge.

Writing About a Process

You can use the chart you made during the prewriting stage to help you write the first draft of your exposition. First, make sure the steps in the process are clear. You may need to combine steps for simplicity, as illustrated in the diagram below. Next, show the relationships between these steps with appropriate transitional words and phrases. The diagram indicates some transitions you might use to create a smooth chronological flow for the exposition.

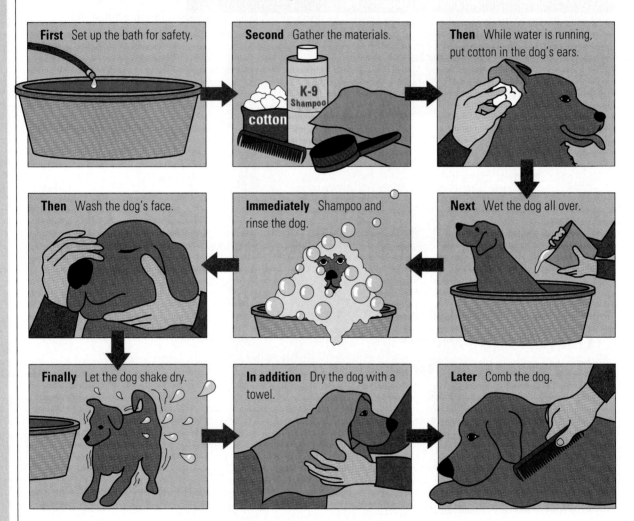

First Set up the bath for safety.

Second Gather the materials.

Then While water is running, put cotton in the dog's ears.

Then Wash the dog's face.

Immediately Shampoo and rinse the dog.

Next Wet the dog all over.

Finally Let the dog shake dry.

In addition Dry the dog with a towel.

Later Comb the dog.

Exposition needs an introduction and conclusion. In your introduction state the process you are explaining and the relevance of the process. This will help capture your reader's interest. Also, you can often use humor to engage your readers. In your conclusion emphasize the importance of the process you have explained, identifying its benefits to your audience. This will help you to leave your reader with a strong impression.

Writer's Choice

The following are some writing options to help you apply what you have learned.

1. Guided Assignment   The list below gives the steps in the process of planting carrot seeds. However, the steps are not in order. Read the steps, and put them in the correct order. Then write a brief report for science class explaining the process. Your goal is to make the process clear enough so your fellow students will be able to plant successfully their own carrots from your instructions. Be sure that your explanation has an introduction, transitions between the steps, and a conclusion.

> a. Pile the soil in a mound over the planted seeds. Lightly pat down.
> b. Place seeds one-eighth to one-sixteenth of an inch apart.
> c. Lightly water.
> d. Dig a half-inch-deep trough.
> e. Thin the sprouted carrots. Leave an inch or more between each.
> f. Dig up the soil in your vegetable garden. Turn over the top eighteen to twenty-four inches to loosen and add air to the soil.

PURPOSE   To explain a process
AUDIENCE   Classmates in science class
LENGTH   1–3 paragraphs

2. Open Assignment   Select one of the following processes or a process of your own choosing, and write an exposition to describe the process:

- how to study for a social studies exam
- how to avoid getting called on in class
- how to shoot three-pointers in basketball
- how to find fossil rocks
- how to do the backstroke
- how to ask someone out on a date
- how to make granola
- how to get a driver's license

3. General Science   Think of a process you have learned about in your science class. Write an explanation of the process for students in a fifth-grade science class. Assume that the students have little or no background knowledge about the subject. Make sure to define all the unfamiliar terms you use. Use short, simple sentences that fifth-graders will be able to understand. Use transitions, so the readers can understand where they are in the process. If you wish, include a diagram or other illustration to help explain the process. Then present your paper to a fifth-grade science class.

4. Social Studies   At the beginning of this lesson, you read a selection by Patrick McManus about camping, a favorite leisure activity of many Americans. Write a short article for a student newspaper explaining a process involved in some other popular leisure activity. You can write about anything from "how to throw a knuckle ball" to "how to go on a family Sunday drive." Your piece can be serious or humorous, like McManus's. If your article is serious, your goal will be to teach your student-readers how to accomplish the process. If your article is humorous, your goal will be to entertain and amuse them.

COMPUTER OPTION

Your explanation of a leisure-time process (and the other process explanations on this page) could probably be enhanced by illustrations. If you have access to drawing or illustration software programs, you can create original images on the computer for your process explanation. Even without such software, most word-processing programs will enable you to create simple process diagrams to accompany your explanation.

Why the Earth Is Round

Could our planet have a mountain taller than Everest? Or does the earth have limits on how much it can vary from a perfect sphere? In explaining the surprising effects of gravity, science writers Carl Sagan and Ann Druyan answer these questions.

Literature Model

Sagan and Druyan describe a general effect and explain its cause in the first sentence.

Sagan and Druyan use this simple comparison to help make their point.

Do you think Sagan and Druyan's hypothetical example of Mount Everest is effective? Explain why or why not.

T he Earth and the other planets tend to be almost perfect spheres because, as Newton showed, gravity is a central force—it pulls everything equally toward the center of the world, itself held together by the force of gravity. The mountains sticking up above the spherical surface of the Earth represent less of a deviation from a perfect sphere than does the layer of paint or enamel on the surface of a typical globe that represents the Earth. If you were able to pile a sizable mountain on top of Mount Everest, it would not just sit there, poking in solitary magnificence into the stratosphere. The additional weight you had added would crush the base of Everest, and the new composite mountain would collapse until it was no larger than Everest is today. The Earth's gravity severely limits how much deviation from a perfect sphere our planet is permitted.

Carl Sagan and Ann Druyan, *Comet*

Writing About Causes and Effects

Cause-and-effect writing helps a reader understand the relationships between events or facts. In other words, it explains how one event causes another. This type of exposition can focus either on effects, as does the literature model above, or on causes, as shown in the diagram on the next page. Note how each effect listed on this diagram serves as the cause for the next effect.

Cause

Massive plates that make up the earth's surface move, putting great pressure on the rocks at the plates' edges. Sometimes the pressure becomes too great for the rocks to bear.

Effects

Rocks along the edges break and shift when pressure becomes too great, creating an earthquake.

▼

The earthquake releases energy in the form of waves, or vibrations.

▼

The waves shake the earth's surface, buildings, bridges, sometimes causing great damage.

Not all cause-and-effect writing is based on a complex series of causes and effects. Some exposition may deal with only one cause and only one effect, giving a clear, detailed explanation of the relationship.

Beware of false cause-and-effect relationships. If one event follows another, the second wasn't necessarily caused by the first. Consider the sentence "The moon eclipsed the sun; then clouds covered the sky." This sentence does not show cause and effect, only sequential events. The eclipse did not cause the clouds to cover the sky. Also remember that cause-and-effect relationships have different degrees of certainty. For example, an earthquake certainly will cause the ground to shake; it may or may not cause property damage.

An important way to make a true cause-and-effect relationship clear is with a thesis statement—a clear statement of your main idea—presented in a topic sentence. A thesis statement for an essay on earthquakes might be the following: "Great pressure along the edges of the earth's moving plates causes rocks to break and shift, creating an earthquake that can bring its destructive shock waves to the earth's surface."

• JOURNAL ACTIVITY •
Think It Through

If the relationship between events or facts makes sense when you connect them with the word *because*, the relation is causal, not just sequential. In your journal write possible causal relationships, such as effects caused by TV watching or causes for earning good grades, and try the "*because* test" on them.

Organizing Causes and Effects

Revising Tip

As you revise your cause-and-effect piece, decide whether you are placing proper emphasis on the causes or the effects or both to achieve your purpose.

Once you have a thesis statement, you can begin organizing your draft. You can follow either a cause-to-effect pattern or an effect-to-cause pattern. For example, you might organize a piece about the greenhouse effect by listing and explaining the many causes and concluding with the possible effects. A piece on the tides might first describe tides and the changes they bring to coastlines and then discuss their cause.

Whichever form of organization you use, you will need to connect your events, facts, and ideas with effective transitions. The chart below shows two types of transitions you may need to use.

Some Transitions for Cause-and-Effect Writing		
Cause and Effect	as a result because consequently	due to if, then since	so therefore thus
Degrees of Certainty	certainly likely maybe	necessarily possibly probably	undoubtedly unquestionably of course

Your exposition will also need an introduction and a conclusion. In your introduction you should catch the reader's attention and give your purpose. Your thesis statement can serve as your introduction. Then you can conclude by summarizing the cause-and-effect relationship or extending the information you have presented. Note the introduction, transitions, and conclusions in the selection below by Eric Koszyk.

Eric begins with a topic sentence that clearly states the causal relationship he plans to explain.

What are some words in addition to "believe" that Eric uses to stress the uncertainty of the theory?

In his conclusion Eric restates his cause-and-effect relationship but again stresses its uncertainty.

Student Model

An ice age usually occurs every couple of million years or so, but some scientists now believe that the current warming of the earth is likely to speed up this process. They believe that the warming of the planet will melt the polar ice caps. This, then, will change the level of water in the planet's oceans, which, therefore, will change the salt composition of the oceans. This altered salt composition would bring about a change in the jet stream winds that circle the earth. And this change in the jet stream would bring about the cooling trend that could well speed up the coming of the next ice age. Some scientists disagree, but a large number of other scientists and environmentalists believe in this theory.

Eric Koszyk, Quartz Hill High School, Quartz Hill, California

Writer's Choice

The following are some writing options to help you apply what you have learned.

1. Guided Assignment For a talk at an Earth Day assembly, you want to explain why whales are endangered. Use the list below to help you write one cause-and-effect paragraph for your talk. Include a topic sentence and a conclusion.

- overhunting by whalers
- noise pollution preventing whales from communicating, thus disrupting breeding
- ocean pollution killing some whales before they have a chance to breed
- depletion of fish (important food source for whales) by fishing crews

PURPOSE To explain why whales are endangered
AUDIENCE High school students
LENGTH 1 paragraph

2. Open Assignment Choose one of the following pairs or a pair of your choice, then research and write two to three paragraphs discussing the cause-and-effect relationship between the items.

- hours of study and good grades
- gravity and the moon's orbit

3. Art Study the painting below. Write a brief cause-and-effect paragraph explaining what has occurred in this scene, presenting at least two causes and two effects.

4. Cooperative Learning In a small group research the effects of recycling. Have each group member write about the effects of a different aspect of recycling. For example, individual students may research glass recycling, paper recycling, or recycling laws. The group can act as peer editor for each paper and then decide by discussion on the best way to present these papers to the class as a report on recycling.

Henry O. Tanner, *After the Storm*, c. 1880

Classifying a Subject

Hoots, Wails, and Other Loon Calls

You're walking in the woods, all alone, when you suddenly hear haunting laughter. For a moment you freeze in panic, then you recognize the "laugh" for what it is—one of the many calls of a loon. In the passage below, Sue Hubbell classifies loon calls according to purpose and structure.

Literature Model

What does Hubbell tell the reader in her first sentence?

Hubbell describes the hoot, the wail, the tremolo, and the yodel as the four basic types of loon calls.

What do you learn from Hubbell's conclusion?

I n recent years, loon calls have been studied by researchers and it is now generally accepted that there are at least four basic calls in the loon's vocabulary, with gradations and combinations and shading to refine the meanings. Within a family, loons call to one another with a soft hoot. The wail, the cry with which the nightly chorus commences, is used when one loon is trying to establish contact with other loons. The tremolo calls that are supposed to sound like a madman's laughter are alarm calls. . . . The yodel is the song of the male loon, a complex series of rising notes followed by an undulation [pulsating tone]; it is gorgeous to human ears but a loon uses it to define and defend his territory. Very recently, researchers have discovered that male loons' yodels are distinctive, each from the other, and can be used as aural tags to study and follow individuals.

Sue Hubbell, "For the Love of Loons," *Smithsonian*

What Is Classification?

When you classify, you group items into categories based on common attributes, or qualities. In the diagram on page 237, one writer has classified clouds according to their general shapes. She has done so to help organize her ideas about clouds. With that type of classification, she will be able to provide a clear overview of the topic, make information accessible, and better inform or instruct her audience.

Classification is a basic part of thinking. Don't you have ideas about the types of stores in your neighborhood, for example, or different kinds of bicycles? Take a minute to think about some of the ways you classify things.

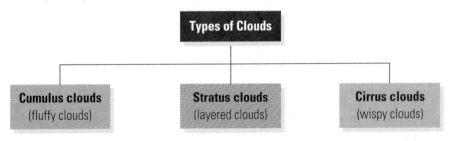

Drafting Tip

When drafting your classification, you may want to use some of the following terms: *categories, classes, groups, kinds, types, varieties, divisions, branches,* and *subclasses.*

How Do You Plan a Classification?

Your most important task in planning a classification is to create meaningful categories appropriate for your purpose and audience. One way to make categories meaningful is to be sure they are mutually exclusive; that is, that you can place any item in one and *only* one category. Meaningful categories should also be based on common features. Look at the common feature that ties together each category of trees in the chart.

Three Ways of Classifying Trees		
Audience	**Classification**	**Common Feature**
Scientists	• Cone-bearing trees • Seed-bearing trees • Spore-bearing trees	Reproduction
Landscape Architects	• Shade trees • Trees for windbreaks • Ornamental trees	Usefulness
Wild-food Collectors	• Trees that bear edible nuts • Trees that bear edible fruits • Trees that have edible sap	Source of food

• JOURNAL ACTIVITY •
Try It Out

Think of a subject for which you will plan a classification, such as types of writing in your journal or students in your class. In your journal create a diagram like the one at the top of this page in which you classify your subject. Make sure your categories are mutually exclusive and based on a common feature.

How Do You Write a Classification?

As you draft your classification, follow the organization shown in the chart below, just as Alli Arnold has in the model.

Revising Tip

As you revise your classification, make sure your thesis statement is clear. For advice on writing thesis statements, see Lesson 7.2, pages 322–325.

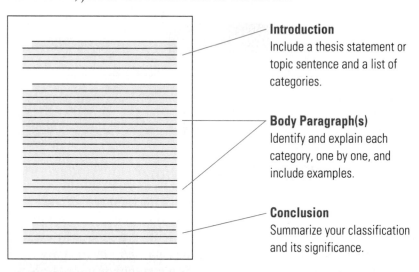

Introduction
Include a thesis statement or topic sentence and a list of categories.

Body Paragraph(s)
Identify and explain each category, one by one, and include examples.

Conclusion
Summarize your classification and its significance.

Student Model

On what feature does Alli base the categories she introduces in her first sentence?

Wildflowers, admired for their beauty and magnificence, include flowers from woodlands, mountains, prairies, deserts, and swamps.

Woodland flowers rely on humus, the product of decaying leaves and wood, for food. Unable to grow in bright sunlight, they favor early spring for growth. Typical woodland flowers include rhododendron and violets. Mountain flowers flourish on any high mountaintop, but grow only after the ice and snow melt. Examples are alpine roses and saxifrages. Prairie flowers are voluptuous and plentiful; their bright colors represent the stereotypical wildflower. Masses of globemallows, sunflowers, and beardtongues clothe the prairie. The beauty of desert flowers is only temporary, as they quickly grow and flower after infrequent rains, then wither in the blinding sun. They have thorny branches, no leaves or very few, and thick, fleshy, water-holding stems. Desert plants include octillos and cacti. Finally, swamp flowers, such as lizard's-tails and willows, love wet meadows and ponds. Others, including pitcher plants and spider lilies, thrive in marshes.

Their simple dignity and elegance make wildflowers an unequaled natural phenomenon and a worthy topic of study.

Alli's body paragraph includes images such as "beardtongues clothe the prairie."

From reading her conclusion, how would you explain Alli's own attraction to this topic?

Alli Arnold, Henry Clay High School, Lexington, Kentucky

Writer's Choice

The following are some writing options to help you apply what you have learned.

1. Guided Assignment Imagine you are teaching a class at a local community center on the care of lightweight bikes. You are writing a classification of lightweight bicycles to hand out to your pupils, inexperienced bike owners. You will want to begin by explaining what a lightweight bike is and what kinds there are. Use the following facts:

- The gears on a lightweight bike make it possible to pedal at a number of speeds with little difficulty.
- Racing bikes weigh about twenty pounds.
- Lightweight bikes are constructed for speed, maneuverability, and comfort.
- Touring bikes vary in weight from about twenty-three to twenty-eight pounds.
- Most racing bikes have gear systems with ten to twelve speeds.
- Touring bikes, designed for long trips, have fifteen to eighteen speeds.

PURPOSE To explain and classify lightweight bicycles

AUDIENCE Inexperienced bike owners, all ages

LENGTH 1 or 2 paragraphs

2. Open Assignment Choose one of the following groups or a group of your own, and work out a way of classifying the items in that group. Then write a paragraph classifying the items.

- rocks and minerals
- friends
- movies
- popular music groups
- precipitation

3. Art Study the painting at the bottom of the page. Then write a classification explaining the contents of the painting. In your classification categorize items according to common features; for example, if you categorize the people, you might categorize them according to what they are doing or what they are wearing. Be sure that your categories are mutually exclusive; that is, no item can fit into more than one category.

Pablita Velarde, *Old Father Story Teller*, 1960

Comparing and Contrasting

The Gawky Dodo and the Graceful Blue Pigeon

In the 1500s Europeans first came to Mauritius, an uninhabited island in the Indian Ocean. There they saw many birds they had never seen before, including the large, flightless dodo and the smaller, colorful blue pigeon. These birds share certain similarities but also have some notable differences as the diagram below shows.

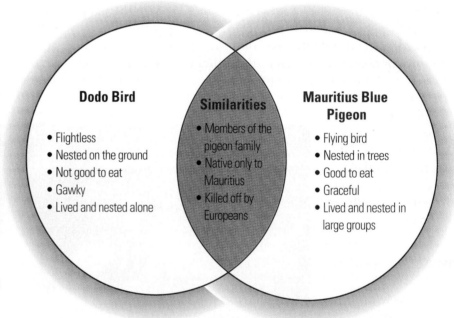

Dodo Bird

- Flightless
- Nested on the ground
- Not good to eat
- Gawky
- Lived and nested alone

Similarities

- Members of the pigeon family
- Native only to Mauritius
- Killed off by Europeans

Mauritius Blue Pigeon

- Flying bird
- Nested in trees
- Good to eat
- Graceful
- Lived and nested in large groups

A writer could use a diagram like the one above to sort out similarities and differences between the two subjects when preparing to write a paragraph comparing and contrasting the dodo and the blue pigeon. Comparing involves discussing similarities between two or more related things. Contrasting involves discussing differences between such items. Comparison-contrast writing is an effective way to explain many subjects. Note how nature writer David Day uses comparison and contrast to present information about the two extinct birds.

*T*he Dodo was not the only pigeon to suffer extinction on Mauritius. There was also the striking crested Pigeon Hollandaise, which is commonly called the Mauritius Blue Pigeon *(Alectroenas nitidisima).* Like the Common Dodo, it was endemic [native only] to Mauritius. This exotic Blue Pigeon did not suffer from the Dodo's inability to fly, nor did it nest on the ground. It was a graceful forest bird that fed on fruit, berries and seeds. It lived in large flocks and nested communally in trees. Again, unlike the Dodo, this bird was delicious to eat. "Shooting parties" were often organized by the resident Europeans for sport and food.

David Day, *The Doomsday Book of Animals*

In the first sentence the writer introduces the main idea—that two related birds suffered a similar fate on Mauritius.

Do you have a stronger reaction to the fate of one of these birds, or is your reaction the same toward each? Explain.

Thinking About Similarities and Differences

When planning a comparison-contrast, you need to pick two or more items that are related somehow. For example, a comparison between an elephant and a water purifier would be nonsensical. But a comparison between an elephant and a hippopotamus might reveal some interesting similarities and differences between these animals.

One technique you can use to explore similarities and differences between two subjects is a Venn diagram, like the one on page 240. Follow the steps below to set up a Venn diagram.

Drafting Tip

Transitions like the following help you organize a comparison-contrast: *but, however, in the same way, like, unlike, similarly.*

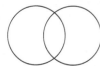 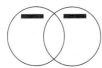 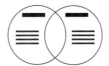 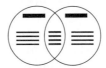

1. Draw two intersecting circles.

2. Title the circles with the subjects to be compared.

3. List unique features of each subject.

4. List the similarities of the two subjects in the space where the circles intersect.

• JOURNAL ACTIVITY •
Try It Out

What are some other tools you could use to explore similarities and differences between two subjects, such as you and your best friend? In your journal try creating a chart or other tool to help you compare two subjects of your choosing.

Organizing a Comparison-Contrast

Once you have explored similarities and differences between two subjects, you can organize your comparison-contrast. The chart below shows two methods of organization: (1) subject by subject and (2) feature by feature. Notice how the writer organized the essay in the model below.

Editing Tip

When you edit your comparison-contrast, make sure that your comparisons are complete. See Lesson 18.4, page 607.

Comparison-Contrast: Elephants and Hippos

Subject by Subject

Subject 1: Elephants	Subject 2: Hippos
Feature A: Anatomy	Feature A: Anatomy
Feature B: Size	Feature B: Size
Feature C: Habitat	Feature C: Habitat
Feature D: Endangered	Feature D: Endangered

Feature by Feature

Feature A: Anatomy	Feature C: Habitat
Subject 1: Elephants	Subject 1: Elephants
Subject 2: Hippos	Subject 2: Hippos
Feature B: Size	**Feature D: Endangered**
Subject 1: Elephants	Subject 1: Elephants
Subject 2: Hippos	Subject 2: Hippos

Model

Does the writer's use of subject-by-subject organization successfully create a vivid comparison between elephants and hippos? Explain.

Note the writer's use of visual details in this comparison-contrast.

Two of the world's most wondrous and enormous animals, the elephant and the hippopotamus, may one day disappear. Just think of the majestic elephant, the largest land-dwelling animal. A typical African bull, or male, measures eleven feet tall at the shoulders and weighs about four tons. African cows, or females, and Asiatic elephants are only slightly smaller. And, as you picture an elephant, you probably think of its thick gray skin, long trunk, fan-shaped ears, and great ivory tusks. The valuable ivory of the tusks presents the greatest danger for elephants, as ivory-seeking hunters kill thousands each year.

Not quite as massive as the elephant, the hippo is the third largest land animal, just behind the rhino. A typical hippo weighs about 2,500 to 3,000 pounds and is about five feet tall at the shoulders. Besides its huge body, among the hippo's most recognizable features are its bulging eyes, allowing it to submerge most of its head yet still keep its eyes above water. Farmers and hunters kill many hippos each year to protect farmlands and to sell the animals' meat, hide, and tusklike ivory canine teeth.

Writer's Choice

The following are some writing options to help you apply what you have learned.

1. Guided Assignment   You are a sports reporter for your school newspaper, writing a feature about the girls' volleyball team. In one part of the story, you want to compare and contrast the team's two best players. Create a Venn diagram to sort out the similarities and differences between the two players described below. Then use your diagram to write a comparison-contrast paragraph.

Eliza Romero
- cowinner of team Most Valuable Player award
- tall (six feet, two inches) and thin
- slow moving but a good scorer and spiker
- shows little emotion as she plays

Detriece Bankston
- cowinner of team Most Valuable Player award
- short (five feet, one inch) and stocky
- moves quickly around court, sets up others
- very animated, emotional player—talks, laughs, cheers, cries during games

PURPOSE	To compare and contrast two volleyball players
AUDIENCE	Readers of high school newspaper
LENGTH	1 paragraph

2. Open Assignment   Choose one of the following pairs or a pair of your choice, and write a paragraph comparing and contrasting the items:

- Joshua trees and saguaro cactuses
- board games and video games
- the North and the South during the Civil War

3. Art   Study the painting below, and look again at the painting *After the Storm* on page 235. Each depicts a different mood of the sea. Write a two- to five-paragraph comparison-contrast of the two paintings in the form of a paper for art class.

Katsushika Hokusai, *The Great Wave off Kanagawa*, c. 1830

Comparing and Contrasting   **243**

Writing with Graphics

A Map Soaked in Oil

Sometimes words alone can't convey enough information about a topic. Notice how the map and text work together in this magazine feature, a piece of exposition.

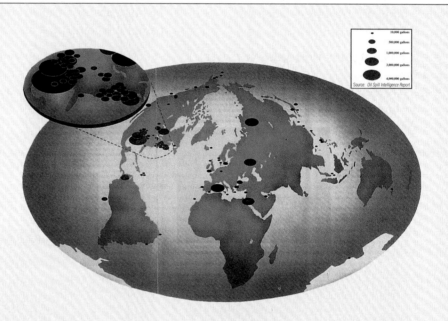

Why do you think the writer uses the term "oil-soaked map"?

Here the writer explains to the reader what the map shows.

In March 1989 the world watched in horror as the *Exxon Valdez* disgorged 10.8 million gallons of North Slope crude [oil] into the pristine waters of Prince William Sound. It was the largest spill ever off the United States. But whatever lessons may have been learned about preventing spills were not effectively applied in 1990. Hardly a week passed without news of yet another disturbing spill. The first ten months of the year saw an estimated 28 million gallons of oil discharged around the world, which makes 1990 a typical year. . . . On our oil-soaked map you'll see the spills that reached at least 10,000 gallons, whether from tanker accidents caused by human error . . . or storage tanks struck by lightning.

"Another Crude Year," *Discover*, January 1991

Your Basic Options

Graphics come in four main forms: maps, diagrams, tables, and graphs. Each type of graphic can help illustrate your expository writing in specific ways.

Maps A map is a graphic most commonly showing all or part of the earth's surface. Maps often show what might take many paragraphs to describe. For example, a map can show how far south the glaciers extended during the last ice age. Whenever you use a map in your writing, be sure your readers understand the map's legend, which explains the symbols on the map.

Diagrams Diagrams use one or more pictures to clarify the relationship among parts of a whole or to show how something works. For example, the diagram to the right shows how the water cycle works. Such a diagram can help your reader visualize what you are trying to convey.

Tables In a table, information is organized in a concise, systematic way. By examining the information in the rows and columns of a table, you can see how a subject changes under different conditions, such as time or location. The table on page 246, for example, compares temperature range and precipitation among four of the world's biological zones, or biomes (regions divided according to climate and soil conditions).

Graphs Often the best way to convey numerical information will be a graph. Graphs can reveal patterns of information, which in turn may show relationships among different numerical facts or statistics. They can thus be a useful tool in comparison-contrast writing. A bar graph, for example, may compare the wealth of three nations. Graphs can also show how something develops over time. The line graph to the right shows how the number of sunspots changes over thirty-six years.

Editing Tip

Make sure you label all parts of any graphic clearly and accurately. Labels help the reader recognize and understand information.

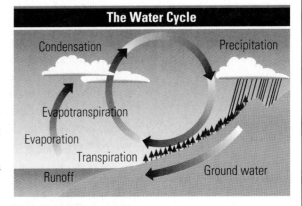

The Water Cycle

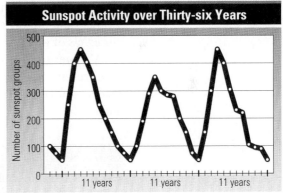

Sunspot Activity over Thirty-six Years

• JOURNAL ACTIVITY •
Try It Out

For each type of graphic discussed above, in your journal list writing situations or subjects for which that type of graphic might be useful. Then note which type of graphic aid you feel most comfortable creating for a composition, and explain why.

How to Use Graphics

Whenever you use graphics in your writing, place them and refer to them so they make the greatest impact on the reader.

Positioning Graphics   Where you place a graphic depends on the function of the graphic and your purpose for using it. For example, to capture the reader's attention and establish a basic framework, you could put a graphic at the beginning of your piece. Imagine you're writing a piece of exposition about cells. You might use a diagram of a basic cell, with all its parts labeled, as part of the opening paragraph.

In the middle of the essay, you might include graphics that convey a great amount of information in a concise way, reinforce information, or serve as a handy reference for the reader. In the example of an essay on cells, a table showing the variation in sizes of different types of cells might appear in the middle.

At the end of your piece of exposition, you will probably want to summarize your main points. For example, in the conclusion of an essay on cells, you could include a table comparing and contrasting plant and animal cells. Wherever and however you use graphics, you need to let the reader know why they are there and when to look at them.

Referring to Graphics   In referring to a graphic, you might simply tell the reader to look at it when the graphic helps illustrate a point you are making. For example, with a table of cell sizes, you might write, "Different kinds of cells vary in size, as shown in the table." You can also instruct the reader to use the information from a graphic in a specific way. If you were using the table below in a piece of exposition about biomes, you might tell the reader to use the table to compare the different levels of precipitation in each biome.

Whatever your purpose, though, title graphics clearly when you present more than one. In that way you will be sure that the reader is not confused and can refer to the appropriate graphic quickly and easily.

Revising Tip

As you read your first draft, check all references to graphics to be sure that they are helpful to the reader, that is, that they really add to the exposition.

Four Biomes: Temperature and Precipitation		
Biome	Avg. Yearly Temperature	Avg. Yearly Precipitation
Deciduous forest	6°C to 28°C	75 to 125 cm
Grassland	0°C to 25°C	25 to 75 cm
Desert	24°C to 34°C	less than 25 cm
Tropical rain forest	25°C to 27°C	200 to 400 cm

Writer's Choice

The following are some writing options to help you apply what you have learned.

1. Guided Assignment Read the paragraph below describing the formation of a glacier. Then write a brief suggestion for a graphic that might be used to illustrate this topic for each of the following writers and audiences: a third-grade teacher for a science class, a high school student for a class assignment, and a scientist as a prelude to presenting a new theory to her peers.

If the average temperature of a land area is at or below the freezing point, water falling to that surface freezes and becomes solid ice. Over a period of years, snow falls in thick layers on the ice. The pressure from the great weight of the snow, combined with melting and freezing, eventually produces a mass of solid ice. As more and more snow falls, the ice mass increases in size. When the weight of this ice mass becomes great enough, the mass begins to move slowly across the land, and a glacier has been created.

PURPOSE To select audience-appropriate graphics
AUDIENCE A third-grade class; a high school science teacher; fellow scientists
LENGTH 3 paragraphs

2. Open Assignment Choose one of the following topics or a topic of your own. Do some research to find one or more graphics (maps, graphs, tables, and diagrams) you could use to enhance a piece of expository writing on that topic. Then write one or two paragaphs that you will supplement with the graphic or graphics to support your main idea. Next, exchange your draft and your sources with a peer editor. Each of you should make suggestions for revising and also check the facts. Carry out those revisions suggested by your peer editor

with which you agree, and clip both sets of papers together for your teacher's review.

- tornadoes
- baseball fields
- giant tortoises
- disappearing wetlands
- the President's veto power
- sound waves

3. Cooperative Learning In a small group meet to decide how to create a brief group report about your community, using each of the following types of graphics: maps, tables, graphs, and diagrams. In your group meeting, try to determine what facts about your community each type of graphic might show. For example, a map might show important places, a graph might show population changes, and a diagram might show how the local government works. Each of you should then choose one graphic to research and to create or find. Write two to five paragraphs about that particular aspect of your community, using the graphic to aid your explanation. Be sure to title your graphic and to include in your written text a reference to the graphic. Share your work with your group. You may wish to combine the final products into a pamphlet about your community.

COMPUTER OPTION

Once you complete your reports, you might want to use a page layout computer program to give your pamphlet a professional look. Some graphics can be created using your word-processing program. Or you might use illustration software to create graphics. If you want to use a laser printer to create an even more finished look, you might be able to use a printer in a neighborhood print and copy shop for a small fee.

The Stories Behind the News

RAIN FOREST PLANTS MAY CURE DISEASE
MAYOR PROMISES EXTRA FUNDS FOR CITY PARKS
POWER OUTAGE CAUSES SCHOOL, BUSINESS CLOSINGS

You probably see headlines like these on the front page of your local newspaper each day. Such headlines grab your attention and lead into news articles—stories of immediate relevance that tell who did what, when, where, how, and why. A news story on the rain forest might begin, "Environmentalists today threatened to block next week's opening of a new highway construction project in Brazil's vast tropical rain forest area."

As you page through the newspaper, though, you begin to see another kind of story—the feature story. Usually longer than a news article, the feature story presents in-depth information behind the news. The feature writer may try to capture a mood, a moment, a place; to focus on a person, a problem, a process. Feature writers try to bring out issues of general human interest, often on topics related to current news articles. And since feature writers use description, narration, and exposition, their stories tend to be both entertaining and informative. The photograph above shows a scene from just such a story. Notice how Donald Dale Jackson opens his feature story, "Searching for Medicinal Wealth in Amazonia," from *Smithsonian* magazine with a detailed description of the rain forest and a scientist.

An hour and a half had passed since we had seen any human scratches on the great green kingdom below us, the rain forest of southern Suriname at the northern fringes of Amazonia. Since then our Cessna six-seater had droned over an unforgiving landscape of jungle dotted with cloud-shadow puddles and tree-choked arroyos [stream beds] streaked by brown rivers. Even at 4,000 feet I could feel the oppressive heat, and we were beginning to descend. The lumpy carpet of rain forest gradually metamorphosed into a canopy of high trees that hid the ground.

Mark Plotkin leaned forward and squinted. Three plumes of smoke stained the horizon ahead. A few seconds later a clearing suddenly materialized, dun-colored and impossibly puny amid the green sea. Now I saw a village of about 80 thatched huts clustered beside a chocolate river. . . . Plotkin grinned. "Welcome to Kwamalasamutu," he said. "The first time I came here I thought I'd found paradise. I still think it's as close as we're apt to get."

Plotkin—New Orleans born, Harvard trained and Washington based—was coming home, in a sense, to this tiny settlement in Amazonia. . . . Plotkin has assigned himself the task of collecting and documenting the plants the Tiriós [Amazonian Indians] use before the mixed blessings of creeping civilization supplant the tribal medicine men and their wisdom. . . .

As a field ethnobotanist who doubles as a conservation stump speaker, Plotkin is the most visible exponent of a discipline that has only recently come into its own. Where ethnobotany was once mainly concerned with plant identification, it is viewed today as a potential lifesaver. The chemical components of plants that medicine men use in healing rites could conceivably be building blocks for new drugs or even cures for such scourges as cancer and AIDS. It is this flickering hope that gives ethnobotanical work its urgency.

What do you learn from the opening sentence of Jackson's feature article?

The writer's direct quotes and sensory details give the reader an intimate view of people and places.

How would you define "ethnobotany" and explain its importance, based on Jackson's fourth paragraph?

• JOURNAL ACTIVITY •
Think It Through

Look through a newspaper to find an interesting feature story. In your journal note what about the story interests you and how this information is conveyed. In a sentence or two, summarize your discoveries.

Planning a Feature Article

Feature writers face two basic challenges. First, they must identify current topics that will interest their readers. Then they must gather the information and uncover the details to bring that topic to life and give readers important background to the news.

Thinking Up a Topic   Feature articles can be on just about anything. Many, but not all, feature articles focus on current news stories, casting them in new light with important background or interesting approaches. Feature writers may also provide information not related to the news. For example, they might tell of intriguing people or share personal experiences.

Coming up with a good topic for your own feature article requires insight into your audience. You need to know their general age, their interests, what they might hope to learn, and what it might take to capture their imaginations.

The best way to find an interesting topic is to think about things in the news or in your own life that are of special interest to you. What are you curious about? If an idea seems intriguing to you, it may also fascinate your audience. The following tips may help you think of fresh feature ideas.

Some Ways to Get Ideas for Your Feature Story

- Take a different route to school. What new things do you see?

- Go someplace you don't usually go. Listen to conversations. Watch what people do. What questions do these people spark?

- Sit in a familiar spot, and note anything that seems out of the ordinary about the people or the place. What did you see that you didn't expect to see?

- Put yourself in the place of someone in the news, a character in a book, a person you see on the street. What ideas do you get from looking at the world through their eyes?

- Leaf through a type of book or magazine you don't generally read. What new topics spark your interest?

After trying one or more of these methods, some idea is likely to hit you. Then it's just a matter of "fine-tuning," or narrowing down, your topic.

Unearthing Information   Once you have settled on an idea for a feature story, you need to gather information. Reading will give you background. Visiting places related to your topic may help you write descriptions with greater detail and authority and even re-create a mood. But interviewing a person who has firsthand knowledge of your topic— an expert in the field, a witness to an event—will provide the most valuable information for your feature story.

You might want to review Lesson 2.4, pages 74–77, for some tips on interviewing. The following list presents some questions a writer might ask when interviewing a scientist such as Mark Plotkin about the rain forest.

Some Questions for a Rain Forest Scientist
• How did you first become interested in rain forests?
• How would you summarize the importance of your work in the rain forest?
• In what parts of the world do you think the rain forest is most likely to survive? Why?
• What is the most surprising thing you have seen on all your trips to the rain forest?

Drafting a Feature Article

After you have gathered information for your feature, you can begin writing a draft of your article. Construct an outline to organize your ideas. Then use the following advice to create a lively article.

A Lead That Pulls   Journalists use the term *lead* to describe the opening of a story. An effective lead sets the story in motion and draws the reader into the writing. The chart below lists some ways to create a successful lead.

A Lead for Your Feature Story
• a surprising detail
• an anecdote that gets at the story's essence
• a revealing image that indicates the direction of the story
• a vivid description of the place
• a summary of the central conflict
• a portrait of one of the main people
• a lively quote
• an event that kicks off the story

Revising Tip

When you revise, have a friend look for places where your story lacks supporting details (see Lesson 5.2, pages 224–227) or doesn't flow smoothly.

Presenting Tip

Make sure your quotes are accurate and you have been fair to everyone. You might phone the people involved in the story to read them the final version.

• JOURNAL ACTIVITY •
Try It Out

Look through newspapers and magazines for feature stories. Clip some leads that catch your attention. Tape these clippings into your journal. Then try writing leads for your own story that are like these.

Lively Details   The details you include in your feature will make or break your story. Pick details that make your main points vivid and memorable. Include anecdotes that create empathy for your subject. Include quotes that let the reader hear your subject speaking in his or her own voice. Craft explanations that give your audience a clear understanding of the history, significance, or inner workings of a topic. Notice how Jackson includes such details in the excerpt from "Searching for Medicinal Wealth in Amazonia" below.

Jackson uses sensory details to make this scene come to life.

What do you learn about the people in this article from the quotations Jackson presents?

Literature Model

The Indians mobbed him [Plotkin] as he climbed out of the plane. Boys tugged at his arms and grabbed his luggage. Speaking Sranan tongo, the trading language of Suriname, Plotkin had a smile or joke for each of them. "We thought you forgot us," one boy said—he hadn't been there for two years. "We were crying." Here in this exotic outpost light-years removed from his own culture, in a remote corner of a country that few Americans can identify or pronounce, the kid from New Orleans was among friends. "It feels terrific," he said.

An Effective Ending   The ending of your feature should be as fresh and vigorous as the lead. It should tie the feature together and, if possible, leave the reader with a new thought to ponder.

Some of the best ways to begin a feature are also good ways to end it. Quotes, humorous anecdotes, close-up portraits, lively details, and vivid scenes work well at the end of a story as well as at the beginning. Why do you suppose Jackson concludes his article with an image of the rain forest as seen from the airborne Cessna?

Jackson uses strong sensory details to help bring his ending to life.

Note Jackson's use of adjectives to tell his story, especially the string of adjectives in the concluding sentence.

Literature Model

The Cessna finally appeared in the northeast sky and touched down five minutes later. Thirty tense minutes ensued before the pilot could get the engine started for the return trip. The plane's cabin felt like a broiler. . . .

A few minutes later we were airborne. The dust-brown clearing that was Kwamalasamutu became smaller and smaller until it was a tiny brown speck lost in the great green, and then it was gone and there was only the green, the endless, timeless, pitiless, life-giving, suffocating green of the rain forest.

Writer's Choice

The following are some writing options to help you apply what you have learned.

1. Guided Assignment   Imagine that you are a student who has spent three weeks of your summer vacation as a volunteer at a dig in North Dakota. Write a lead and a paragraph or two for a feature article in the school newspaper about your experiences. Use any of the details below. Feel free to use a quotation you yourself might have said about your experience in your lead.

- who: shirt-sleeved paleontologists and sunburned student volunteers
- what: sifting soil, hour after hour
- when: three weeks during summer vacation
- why: looking for dinosaur fossils
- conditions: hot, dusty, stifling

PURPOSE To catch readers' attention and make them want to read the rest of the feature
AUDIENCE High school students
LENGTH 1–2 paragraphs

2. Open Assignment   You are a feature writer for a local newspaper. Choose one of the following topics or a topic of your own choice, and write a one- to two-page feature article. Do library research, and, if possible, conduct interviews to gather information for your newspaper story.

- beachcombing
- collecting plants of the rain forest
- nature photography
- Isaac Asimov
- wildlife preserves

3. Cooperative Learning   Look at the sculpture shown in the photograph below. In a small group meet to discuss members' individual impressions of the sculpture. Use this discussion to generate about ten quotations on the work. Then have each member write a feature story about how viewers react to the sculpture. Use one or more of the group's quotations in the lead. The following facts, along with those provided under the photo, will help you write the story:

- The sculpture is painted steel plate, fifty-three feet high.
- Sculptor Alexander Calder lived from 1898 to 1976.
- Calder's stationary sculptures, like this one, are called stabiles; his movable sculptures are called mobiles.
- The sculpture stands in the Federal Center Plaza in Chicago, Illinois.

Alexander Calder, *Flamingo*, 1974

Answering an Essay Question

Why Do Cats Purr?

Fortunately, when you take an essay test you don't have to answer the crazy kinds of questions that columnist Cecil Adams has to address every week. But a look at Adams's answers can give you an idea of what it takes to respond to an essay question successfully.

Adams begins his answer by explaining one thing he knows for sure about cats' purring: when they do it.

What does Adams mean when he says purring "seems to be a kind of homing device"? Does this hypothesis make sense to you?

Adams concludes with a theory that highlights all that we don't know about cats' purring.

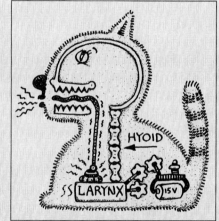

Cats don't purr just when they're feeling chipper—they also purr when they're frightened or badly hurt. Purring doesn't have any specific emotional connotation; rather it seems to be a kind of homing device. Cats learn the signal in the first few days of kittenhood, when they can't see, hear, or smell very well. The mother cat purrs to call the kittens to nurse—unable to hear the sound, the kitten can feel the vibrations.

There are two schools of thought on exactly *how* a cat purrs. One theory traces the vibrations to a set of "false vocal cords," a bundle of membranes that lies above the genuine vocal cords and seems to have no other clear function. The other opinion locates the purr in the vibrations of the hyoid apparatus, a series of small bones connecting the skull and the larynx that nominally serves to support the tongue. Since it's very difficult to induce a cat to purr while you are examining his hyoid apparatus, the truth may never be known.

Cecil Adams, *The Straight Dope*

Cecil Adams has all week to research and write an answer to an essay question. But you may have less than forty-five minutes when you are working on a test. Nevertheless, essay tests don't have to give you the jitters. If you budget your time so that you can answer each question, and if you follow the tips in this lesson, you can compose an answer that effectively presents your knowledge about a subject.

How Do You Know What the Question Is Asking?

Answers to essay questions follow a basic format—the format of the essay. The introduction contains a thesis statement, a one-sentence summary of the thrust of your answer. The body of the answer supports the thesis statement with facts, examples, details, and reasons. The conclusion summarizes or gives the implications of your answer. The essay question itself often gives strong clues as to how the answer should be structured. The chart below can help you decipher the clues essay questions give you.

What Essay Questions Tell You

Clue Verb	Action to Take
Describe	Paint word pictures by providing precise details of an event, a process, or a person.
Explain	Tell why or how by using facts, examples, or reasons, and emphasize cause-effect relationships or step-by-step processes.
Compare	Show how two or more subjects are alike.
Contrast	Highlight the differences between two or more subjects.
Classify	Group and label the important features of a subject, and discuss the different categories into which you have grouped them.
Analyze	Break something down into the parts that compose it, show the relationship between the parts and the whole, and tell the function or significance of each of the parts.

• JOURNAL ACTIVITY •
Think It Through

For each clue verb in the chart above, identify one or more prewriting tools, such as a Venn diagram, that can help you answer that particular kind of essay question efficiently. List each tool in your journal next to the corresponding clue verb.

How Do You Generate Your Answer?

By taking time to identify and organize your information, you can avoid the common mistake of writing down everything you know about a subject in a haphazard, disjointed fashion.

Organize Your Information   The following diagram details the process you might use to answer a "take home" essay question.

Answering an Essay Question

Question
Describe hail, and explain how and when hailstones form.

Underline clue verbs and other key words.
Describe <u>hail</u>, and <u>explain</u> how and when hailstones form.

List notes.
- Hail: form of precipitation made up of lumps of ice
- Begins as tiny ice crystal in thundercloud
- Strong winds in cloud toss crystal up and down; water condenses around crystal and freezes, forming layers of ice on the crystal, thus creating a hailstone and making it grow larger and heavier.
- Hailstone becomes too heavy to remain aloft, falls to ground.
- Size of stone depends on strength of wind, length of time in cloud.
- Most hailstones smaller than one inch in diameter, but some larger than a baseball
- Large hailstones smash windows, dent cars, destroy crops.
- Hailstorms usually occur in summer, when thunderstorms are more frequent, violent.

Develop thesis statement.
Hail is a form of precipitation made up of lumps of ice that form within thunderclouds.

Outline answer and develop conclusion.
Organize your answer into main points and supporting details. The conclusion might summarize the answer.

Hail: What is it and how and when does it form?

What? ——————————————————— *When?*

How?

- *A form of precipitation made up of lumps of ice*

- *Begins as crystal in thundercloud*
- *Strong winds toss it up and down*
- *Water condenses around crystal, freezing into layer of ice*
- *Layers of ice build up around crystal, creating a hailstone, which continues to get larger and heavier*
- *Hailstone becomes too heavy to stay aloft, falls to ground*

- *Usually forms in summer, when thunderstorms are more frequent and violent*

Write Your Answer   If you follow a process like the one just laid out, writing an answer to an essay question will become a much easier task. Your plan for your answer will help you focus your ideas, write quickly, and avoid including unnecessary information. Follow the steps below when writing your answer to an essay question.

Prewriting Tip

Before working on a question, read the directions and all the questions to find out what the essay exam involves. Budget time by the number of points each question is worth.

Writing Your Essay Answer

1. Express your thesis in the opening sentence to show that you understand the question. Writing your thesis at the beginning will also help you focus your answer.

2. Use your notes, thesis statement, and organizational plan to develop your major points and supporting details. You can draw additional supporting details from your notes.

3. Include transitions between each major point.

4. Do not stray from your plan unless you realize some point is incorrect or unworkable. Do not add information that does not support your thesis.

5. Provide an ending that reflects the basic answer you have written.

• JOURNAL ACTIVITY •
Try It Out

In your journal copy five essay questions from your science textbook, or make up five sample questions. For each question do some research to list enough notes to form an answer, and then write a thesis statement to help focus your answer.

Revise and Edit Your Answer   Leave time to read over your answer once you have finished. Make sure that your thesis statement is clear and that you have covered all important points. Correct any content errors first. Omit unnecessary details simply by crossing them out. Add details by inserting sentences where necessary. You can clarify a relationship between ideas by adding or changing a transitional word. Budget time so that you can proofread to check your grammar and spelling. Make corrections neatly, so that your answer is legible.

Now look at Jason Larmore's essay answer to the question "Into what three general classes do astronomers group stars? What are the characteristics of each class of stars?"

Student Model

How does Jason's first paragraph demonstrate that he understands the question?

What supporting details does Jason use to point out the characteristics of the stars in each of the three groups?

In his conclusion Jason stresses the relationship among the different classes of stars.

Astronomers group stars into three general classes: the main-sequence, the giant and supergiant, and the white dwarf. Each class has its own characteristics; size, brightness, and color all help determine a star's group. Of these three factors, size is the most important because size differences between classes are dramatically obvious.

Main-sequence stars are the most common. The yellowish main-sequences form an average between the white dwarves and the "red" giants, but because of the giant's immensity, everything seems microscopic in comparison.

The enormousness of the giant-class stars can be shown by comparing them to our own solar system. A single supergiant, placed where our sun is, would engulf all of the inner planets and some of the outer planets. Because the giant stars are so massive, they sometimes are unable to burn gases at a normal temperature. A decrease in this temperature causes them to have a reddish color, common to many giants. There are, however, exceptions to the "red" giant pattern. Deneb is a giant that shines with a blue light. This indicates an extremely high temperature. These exceptions comprise the brightest stars in the night sky.

The final class of stars is the white dwarf. These stars are the result of giant stars that collapsed because they couldn't maintain their mass. The white dwarves are very dense and shine white. These stars are much smaller than our sun, yet they outweigh it exponentially. The fact that white dwarves come from giant stars shows that even though stars are divided into classes, they are in some ways related.

Jason Larmore, Henry Clay High School, Lexington, Kentucky

The following are some writing options to help you apply what you have learned.

1. Guided Assignment Imagine that you are a student taking a final exam in general science. Use the notes below to write a one-paragraph essay answer to the following question: How do fish breathe under water? Allow fifteen minutes to write and five minutes to revise and edit.

- Fish takes in water through mouth.
- Water contains oxygen.
- Water passes to gills.
- Gill chambers on each side of head contain filaments.
- Gill filaments absorb oxygen into blood through tiny extensions called *lamellae*.
- Blood gives off carbon dioxide.
- Water, carbon dioxide exit through gill openings—slits on sides of fish's head.
- Fish begins next breath with another gulp of water.

PURPOSE To write an answer to an essay exam in general science
AUDIENCE Your general science teacher
LENGTH 1 paragraph

2. Open Assignment Write an answer to an essay question using the process described in this lesson. Show all your work, including your notes, thesis statement, outline, and revisions that you make on your essay. Choose one of the following essay questions or an essay question of your own (for which you will not need to do research):

- Compare and contrast "Earth Day" of 1970 with "Earth Day" of 1990.
- Diagram a food web, and explain how energy flows within the food web.
- How do red blood cells differ from white blood cells?

3. Geography Leaf through your geography or social studies textbook to find an essay question on the subject of geography. Write out the question so you can underline the key words and clue verbs. Read the appropriate chapter to answer the question, taking notes as you read. Then make an outline of your proposed answer. Finally give yourself about twenty-five minutes to write, revise, and edit your answer.

COMPUTER OPTION

Remember that creating an outline is an important part of putting together an essay answer. Many word-processing programs include an outlining feature that allows you to create an outline and a "skeleton draft" at the same time. If you change your outline, the draft also changes. When the outline for your essay answer is complete, you can fill in the draft with the appropriate sentences and details.

4. Cooperative Learning Work together in a small group, and brainstorm your own list of "imponderables," questions about the natural world like those Cecil Adams might answer in his column. (See the model on page 254.) What parts of the natural world puzzle or mystify you? Here's your chance to have someone else find the answers for you. When you have finished, exchange lists with another group. Select one question from their list for your group to research and answer. Each group member should research and write the answer individually. After all of you have written your answers, meet and read aloud what you have learned. If necessary, revise your answers based on what you learn from other members of your group. When you have completed the final version of your answer, return it to the other group. They may wish to grade your paper based on how well you have answered their question.

Writing About Literature
Comparing and Contrasting Two Myths

The First Humans, Two Myths

According to a myth of the Sioux, Native Americans of the Plains, the first man sprang from the soil of the Great Plains. As he emerged, he saw only the sun. The mountains, rivers, and forests had not yet been formed. After freeing himself from the clinging soil, he began to take halting steps. The sun shone on his body, toughening his skin and making him strong. He began to leap and dance with joy at being alive. The Sioux descended from this man.

A myth of the Zulu people of Africa describes how the sky god created the first people. After his marriage to the earth goddess, the sky god walked through a swamp. He broke off reeds of different colors and fashioned a man and a woman from each different colored reed. A different tribe descended from each pair of reed people.

Student Mathew Isaac read these ancient stories and pondered their similarities and differences. Here's what he came up with.

Student Model

Mathew finds a central point of comparison between the two myths— the fertile soil.

What central difference does Mathew find between the two myths?

The Sioux and Zulu myths attempt to explain the creation of mankind. The setting and the characters in the myths reveal a great deal about these groups. Both deeply revered their soil, for their pastoral life styles revolved around it. This reverence may be inferred from the fertile land, the setting for both myths. The Sioux man emerged from the soil, while the Zulu were created from reeds in a swamp. The Zulu people recognized a god as their creator. The Sioux did not, at least according to this myth, although their myth notes the importance of the sun for continued life.

The beliefs and values of the Sioux and Zulu, some of which were shared, are visible in their creation myths.

Mathew Isaac, Rich East High School, Park Forest, Illinois

What Is a Myth?

A myth is an age-old story that offers an explanation for why the world, especially the natural world, is the way it is. Myths may also offer explanations for why things happen as they do. Science provides one kind of explanation, but myths offer alternative views. The Ancient Romans explained the seeming movement of the sun across the sky as the work of a heavenly charioteer circling the earth daily. The ancient Japanese explained the creation of their islands with a myth about the spear of a god named Izanagi. In fact, there are probably as many distinctly different mythologies as there are different cultures.

How Can I Compare Two Myths?

Although myths may offer widely different explanations for the same thing, they still have many points of comparison. They have common concerns and possess elements common to most literature. The chart below shows the common elements of literature, which all myths share. You can cite these elements to compare myths from different cultures.

Drafting Tip

In a comparison of two stories, use a feature-by-feature comparison. This form will help you weave together your points of comparison. See Lesson 5.6, page 242.

Common Elements of Literature	
Element	**Definition**
Setting	The place and time in which the action of the story occurs The location can be real or imaginary. In a myth, the time is usually the past.
Characters	The people, animals, or gods that participate in the action of the story
Conflict	The struggle that is central to the story It can be a struggle between characters or forces.
Plot	The story's sequence of events A plot revolves around a conflict and builds to a climax that is later resolved.
Theme	The message or main idea of the story The theme may or may not be stated directly.

• JOURNAL ACTIVITY •
Try It Out

Think about a myth with which you are familiar. In your journal write a brief summary of the myth, and then, in a short list, identify each of the literary elements in that myth.

How Can a Comparison Frame Help Me?

How did the sun and the moon get into the sky? Here are two answers in the form of myths, one ancient Mexican and one ancient Nigerian.

According to the Mexican myth, the gods were arguing about who among them should light the earth by day and who should light the earth by night. After four days of arguing, two gods volunteered. One of the gods was rich and strong, and the other was poor and feeble. The gods then built a huge bonfire, and the two volunteers stepped toward it. The rich and powerful god was afraid of the flames and drew back from the fire. But the poor god jumped right into the fire and was catapulted high into the sky. This god became the sun. The bonfire began to die. But the rich god still wanted a share of the glory. He leaped into the embers and then sailed into the sky. This god became the moon.

According to the Nigerian myth, before there were people, the sun and the moon were married and lived on earth. The sun was good friends with the water and one day invited him to his village to meet his wife. The water flowed into the village, with the fish, the crabs, the whales, and all the other living things swimming in the seas. Soon the sun and the moon had to climb on top of the village huts because of all the water. But the water kept coming and began lapping the rooftops. The sun and the moon had to flee their homes. They each took a bounding leap into the sky, and that's how they came to be in the heavens, so far away from earth.

The comparison frame below will help you compare and contrast the two myths.

Comparison of Two Myths		
Element	**Mexican Myth**	**Nigerian Myth**
Setting	A long time ago on earth	A long time ago on earth
Characters	The Mexican gods	The sun and moon, a married couple, and the water
Conflict	Which of the gods will get to be the sun and which the moon?	Water threatens to drown the sun and moon when he visits.
Plot	The gods argue. Two gods volunteer, one rich and strong, the other poor and feeble. . . .	The sun invites water to his village. Water flows into the village, rising up to the rooftops. . . .
Theme	Bravery, not wealth, brings great glory.	Some guests can't be accommodated in one's home.

The following are some writing options to help you apply what you have learned.

1. Guided Assignment   Imagine that you are writing a paper entitled "Some Common Themes in World Mythology" for your literature class. Make a comparison frame to compare and contrast the two myths summarized below. Then use the comparison frame to help you write a comparison-contrast of the two myths, but focus more on what the myths have in common than on how they differ.

Iroquois myth: Four animals, bound on leashes by a giant, are responsible for the winds. A strong, fierce bear brings on the north winds of winter. A gentle fawn brings on the south winds of summer. An angry panther brings on the west winds that accompany storms and whirlwinds. A moose brings on the east winds with their chilling mists. The giant unleashes these animals to match his moods. But he tries to keep to his duty and unleash each wind in its proper season and time.

Italian myth: The north wind is a woman who at one time wanted to marry the south wind. But the south wind was lazy and comfortable in his bachelorhood. When the north wind proposed they get married, the south wind told her that he couldn't marry her without a dowry [the riches a woman brings to a marriage]. To make her dowry, the north wind blew for three days and nights. When she stopped, the land was covered with a blanket of silver snow. This she presented as her dowry. The south wind, not wanting to get married anyway, blew for three days and nights. His hot breath melted all the snow. The north wind's dowry disappeared completely. She decided that she no longer wanted to marry the south wind,

because of the way he frittered away her entire dowry in only three days.

PURPOSE   To compare two myths
AUDIENCE   Your high school literature teacher
LENGTH   1–2 paragraphs

2. Open Assignment   Look in an encyclopedia or other books to find two myths of your own choosing. You might consider the Greek and Roman myths of Hercules (called Heracles by the Greeks), the Native American myths of animals, or the Incan myths of the sun. Find two myths you can compare and contrast, and make a comparison frame for them. Review the selection by Mathew Isaac on page 260, and then write out your own comparison-contrast.

3. Literature   Choose two pieces of literature (other than myths) that have something in common. You may choose two poems, two short stories, or two novels. Then, use what you have learned in this lesson about comparison frames to help you write a comparison-contrast essay about your two selections.

COMPUTER OPTION

Use the Copy feature of your word-processing program to preserve the first draft of your comparison-contrast essay as you work to improve it. When your first draft is complete, save it. Then, make a copy of it (either as a new file or as a new page on the existing file), and continue to work on improving your comparison-contrast of the two pieces of literature. Continue to do the same with each successive draft. In this way, you'll always have a record of your earlier ideas and the changes you've made. Thus you will be able to reinstate previous ideas and even earlier drafts if later changes in your comparison-contrast don't work.

Barry Holstun Lopez

from

Of Wolves and Men

Barry Lopez writes about natural history and the environment in books, short fiction, articles, and essays. Among his books are Of Wolves and Men, Crossing Open Ground, *and* Arctic Dreams, *which was listed among the "Best Books for Young Adults" by the* New York Times Book Review. Of Wolves and Men *grew out of a 1974 article on wolves that Lopez wrote for* Smithsonian *magazine. One reviewer called this informative book "one of the most complete sources of information on these animals ever published."*

Imagine a wolf moving through the northern woods. The movement, over a trail he has traversed many times before, is distinctive, unlike that of a cougar or a bear, yet he appears, if you are watching, sometimes catlike or bearlike. It is purposeful, deliberate movement. Occasionally the rhythm is broken by the wolf's pause to inspect a scent mark, or a move off the trail to paw among stones where a year before he had cached[1] meat.

The movement down the trail would seem relentless if it did not appear so effortless. The wolf's body, from neck to hips, appears to float over the long, almost spindly legs and the flicker of wrists, a

---

1 **cached** (kashd) stored up

bicycling drift through the trees, reminiscent of the movement of water or of shadows.

The wolf is three years old. A male. He is of the subspecies *occidentalis*, and the trees he is moving among are spruce and subalpine fir on the eastern slope of the Rockies in northern Canada. He is light gray; that is, there are more blond and white hairs mixed with gray in the saddle of fur that covers his shoulders and extends down his spine than there are black and brown. But there are silver and even red hairs mixed in, too.

It is early September, an easy time of year, and he has not seen the other wolves in his pack for three or four days. He has heard no howls, but he knows the others are about, in ones and twos like himself. It is not a time of year for much howling. It is an easy time. The

Nancy Schutt, *Encroachment*, 1987

weather is pleasant. Moose are fat. Suddenly the wolf stops in mid-stride. A moment, then his feet slowly come alongside each other. He is staring into the grass. His ears are rammed forward, stiff. His back arches and he rears up and pounces like a cat. A deer mouse is pinned between his forepaws. Eaten. The wolf drifts on. He approaches a trail crossing, an undistinguished crossroads. His movement is now slower and he sniffs the air as though aware of a possibility for scents. He sniffs a scent post, a scrawny blueberry bush in use for years, and goes on.

The wolf weighs ninety-four pounds and stands thirty inches at the shoulder. His feet are enormous, leaving prints in the mud along a creek (where he pauses to hunt crayfish but not with much interest) more than five inches long by just over four wide. He has two fractured ribs, broken by a moose a year before. They are healed now, but a sharp eye would notice the irregularity. The skin on his right hip is scarred, from a fight with another wolf in a neighboring pack when he was a yearling. He has not had anything but a few mice and a piece of arctic char[2] in three days, but he is not hungry. He is traveling. The char was a day old, left on rocks along the river by bears.

The wolf is tied by subtle threads to the woods he moves through. His fur carries seeds that will fall off, effectively dispersed, along the trail some miles from where they first caught in his fur. And miles distant is a raven perched on the ribs of a caribou the wolf helped kill ten days ago, pecking like a chicken at the decaying scraps of meat. A smart snowshoe hare that eluded the wolf and left him exhausted when he was a pup has been dead a year now, food for an owl. The den in which he was born one April evening was home to porcupines last winter.

It is now late in the afternoon. The wolf has stopped traveling, has lain down to sleep on cool earth beneath a rock outcropping. Mosquitoes rest on his ears. His ears flicker. He begins to waken. He rolls on his back and lies motionless with his front legs pointed toward the sky but folded like wilted flowers, his back legs splayed,[3] and his nose and tail curved toward each other on one side of his body. After a few moments he flops on his side, rises, stretches, and moves a few feet to inspect—minutely, delicately—a crevice in the rock outcropping and finds or doesn't find what draws him there. And then he ascends the rock face, bounding and balancing momentarily before bounding again, appearing slightly unsure of the process—but committed. A few minutes later he bolts suddenly into the woods, achieving full speed, almost forty miles per hour, for forty or fifty yards

2 **char** (chär) a kind of trout
3 **splayed** (splād) spread out

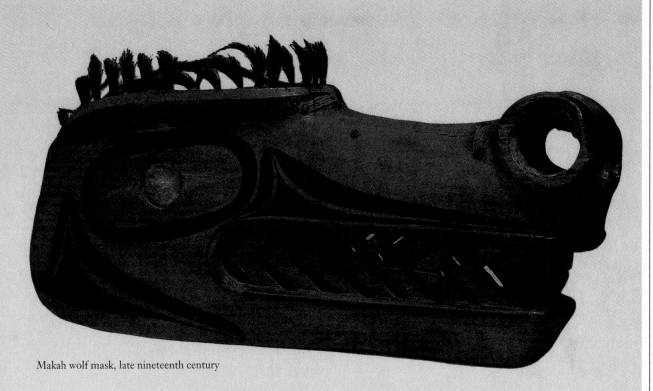

Makah wolf mask, late nineteenth century

before he begins to skid, to lunge at a lodgepole pine cone. He trots away with it, his head erect, tail erect, his hips slightly to one side and out of line with his shoulders, as though hindquarters were impatient with forequarters, the cone inert in his mouth. He carries it for a hundred feet before dropping it by the trail. He sniffs it. He goes on.

The underfur next to his skin has begun to thicken with the coming of fall. In the months to follow it will become so dense between his shoulders it will be almost impossible to work a finger down to his skin. In seven months he will weigh less: eighty-nine pounds. He will have tried unsuccessfully to mate with another wolf in the pack. He will have helped kill four moose and thirteen caribou. He will have fallen through ice into a creek at twenty-two below zero but not frozen. He will have fought with other wolves.

He moves along now at the edge of a clearing. The wind coming down-valley surrounds him with a river of odors, as if he were a migrating salmon. He can smell ptarmigan[4] and deer droppings. He can smell willow and spruce and the fading sweetness of fireweed. Above, he sees a hawk circling, and farther south, lower on the horizon, a flock of sharp-tailed sparrows going east. He senses through his pads with each step the dryness of the moss beneath his feet, and

4 ptarmigan (tär′ mə gən) a kind of northern or alpine bird

the ridges of old tracks, some his own. He hears the sound his feet make. He hears the occasional movement of deer mice and voles.[5] Summer food.

Toward dusk he is standing by a creek, lapping the cool water, when a wolf howls—a long wail that quickly reaches pitch and then tapers, with several harmonics,[6] long moments to a tremolo.[7] He recognizes his sister. He waits a few moments, then, throwing his head back and closing his eyes, he howls. The howl is shorter and it changes pitch twice in the beginning, very quickly. There is no answer.

The female is a mile away and she trots off obliquely through the trees. The other wolf stands listening, laps water again, then he too departs, moving quickly, quietly through the trees, away from the trail he had been on. In a few minutes the two wolves meet. They approach each other briskly, almost formally, tails erect and moving somewhat as deer move. When they come together they make high squeaking noises and encircle each other, rubbing and pushing, poking their noses into each other's neck fur, backing away to stretch, chasing each other for a few steps, then standing quietly together, one putting a head over the other's back. And then they are gone, down a vague trail, the female first. After a few hundred yards they begin, simultaneously, to wag their tails.

In the days to follow, they will meet another wolf from the pack, a second female, younger by a year, and the three of them will kill a caribou. They will travel together ten or twenty miles a day, through the country where they live, eating and sleeping, birthing, playing with sticks, chasing ravens, growing old, barking at bears, scent-marking trails, killing moose, and staring at the way water in a creek breaks around their legs and flows on.

5 **voles** (vōlz) field mice

6 **harmonics** (här män′ iks) overtones

7 **tremolo** (trem′ ə lo′) a pulsating tone

For Discussion

1. Does this selection hold your interest? Why or why not? What is the most interesting piece of information Lopez presents here? What makes it interesting?

2. If you could meet Barry Lopez, what questions would you ask him about wolves?

Readers Respond

The writer chose third-person point of view for an unbiased examination of the wolf's actions. The dominant mood of the selection was one of solemnity, which the writer created by always making the episode serene, not bringing out action.

Chris Fickes

What I liked best about this selection from *Of Wolves and Men* was all the details the author used. Lopez's words made me realize exactly what the wolf was feeling. The mood was calm, but as a reader I still felt a sense of danger. The writer created that mood by carefully detailing the wolf's life—the danger that he had been through and that was yet to come.

I think Lopez's choice of third person was appropriate because it makes the reader an observer, watching the wolf and his movements rather than seeing the scene from the wolf's point of view. I would recommend this selection to a friend because it teaches you in an interesting way about the life of a wolf.

Claire Monty

Do you agree?

☞ Do you agree that this selection provides an unbiased examination of a wolf? In what ways could this selection be biased?

☞ Think of an animal or a natural phenomenon that interests you, and write a brief piece of exposition in your journal. Talk about your subject from an objective or unbiased point of view.

Writing Process in Action

Natural Dignity

Look at the wolf through gun sights or fables such as "Little Red Riding Hood" or "The Three Little Pigs," and chances are you will perceive it to be a cunning and threatening creature. But *see* the wolf in its own world, and you may perceive it very differently.

In the selection from *Of Wolves and Men* on pages 264–268, author Barry Lopez portrays the wolf as he *sees* it, in its own right and its own world, "tied by subtle threads to the woods he moves through." In so doing, Lopez enables us to actually see the wolf too—instead of looking at it as a potential threat.

Now you are invited to *see* a creature and to help others see it by presenting it in its own right and natural habitat.

• Assignment •

CONTEXT A science teacher has a problem: this year most of his sixth-grade students—as well as a number of his younger students—seem to be afraid of or disgusted by the creatures about which he wants to teach them. In fact, whenever he brings one of these critters to class, his students shriek and run to all corners of the room. This makes teaching about them nearly impossible. So he has come to your class for help. He wants your class to write brief articles about insects, animals, and other creatures people typically label "bad" that will help his students appreciate these creatures.

PURPOSE To write a brief article about a creature people often label "bad" that will help children experience and appreciate this animal in its own right—instead of looking at it merely as a threat to themselves

AUDIENCE Sixth-grade science students or younger science students

LENGTH 2–3 pages

For more advice on how to approach this assignment, you will find the next few pages helpful. But don't feel that you have to remember all of what follows. You can come *back* to these pages as you write, getting help where and when you need it. You're in charge of your own writing process.

1. Prewriting

What would you like to write about—wolves, sharks, spiders, bats? Any of these creatures are fair game, but see what other creepy animals you can come up with. Brainstorm with classmates to generate a list of "vicious," "evil," "disgusting," or just misunderstood creatures. From this list select a subject that both interests you and that is likely to repel or intrigue your audience.

Once you've identified something to write about, freewrite or brainstorm to create an inventory of what you think you know about this creature. The following questions can help get you started on this:

- If you were to experience it at close range, what would you see, hear, smell, feel, or otherwise notice? (a sweet odor; rough, scaly skin?)
- How does *it* perceive the world? (mostly by smell, in two colors?)
- How does it interact with others of its kind? (fights to defend its territory, hunts with others in its pack, plays with its cubs?)
- How does it find a mate? (produces a certain sound, does a dance?)
- How does it obtain its food? (hunts for it in packs, scavenges?)

Next, do research to get the facts. Start by checking encyclopedias, magazines, and videotapes to determine the validity of each item you listed in your initial inventory. Then work on expanding your inventory by doing more research in the library or by conducting interviews with authorities on your particular creature. These might include zoo keepers, animal trainers and handlers, pet store owners, farmers, or rangers. See Lesson 2.4, pages 74–76, for help in using the library and conducting interviews. Refer also to Lesson 5.8, pages 250–251, for additional tips on unearthing information.

Lesson 7.1 will also introduce you to the idea of gathering information about a subject by observing it firsthand. Such observation may yield enough details about one particular individual to enable you to focus your exposition on that individual. Focusing on one individual would be to your advantage. You can almost always create more empathy and understanding for an individual than you can for a group in general. Think, for example, about Lopez's exposition. Would you have acquired as much appreciation and understanding for wolves if he had written about wolves as a general group instead of focusing on one particular wolf? Do you think such general exposition would have been as involving as Lopez's more narrowly focused account?

Once you have a few pages of prewriting notes, evaluate these notes with your purpose and audience in mind. Ask yourself the following questions:

- Do I have enough sensory details to bring my subject to life?
- Do I have enough details about this creature's perceptions and motives to help my readers understand the way *it* experiences the world?
- Do I have enough information about a particular individual to create a personal account?
- Do I have details that will help readers overcome their negative reactions to this creature?
- Do I have details likely to interest and appeal to my audience?
- With this information can I explain everything my readers need to know?

You might want to do a little extra brainstorming or information gathering at this point to fill out your prewriting notes. You may also want to refer to Lesson 2.3, page 72, for help in meeting the needs of your audience.

Then look over your notes to determine how you can best organize your information. The notes themselves may seem to suggest a particular kind of organization. However, if they don't, look for a main idea or focus, and consider weeding out all details not related to that focus. Pick out your most interesting details to use in your lead, or introduction, and then try to determine what would most naturally follow from that. Or, consider these possibilities:

- Proceed in chronological order from the subject's birth to its death.
- Reveal what you *saw* as you discovered it, along the lines of what Lopez does in the excerpt from *Of Wolves and Men*.
- Frame your article with a beginning and ending something like Donald Dale Jackson's (see Lesson 5.8, pages 249 and 252).
- Write your article as a series of journal entries (see Lesson 1.4, page 24).
- Use a flashback format (see Lesson 1.4, page 24).

2. Drafting

For this assignment, you need to grab and hold your readers' attention. So you might want to start with a fact or myth that is likely to intrigue young readers. Lopez begins with a gentle description of a wolf that stands in sharp contrast to the vicious reputation of wolves. Notice how he uses terms usually reserved for people—*neck, hips, wrists*—to show his appreciation for the animal:

> *The movement down the trail would seem relentless if it did not appear so effortless. The wolf's body, from neck to hips, appears to float over the long, almost spindly legs and the flicker of wrists, a bicycling drift through the trees, reminiscent of the movement of water or of shadows.*

As you write, be sure to support the points you want to make with specific details. Try also to bring your subject to life with the facts, analogies, and other evidence you present. Look at how Lopez both explains and brings to life the relationship between the wolf and his habitat:

> *The wolf is tied by subtle threads to the woods he moves through. His fur carries seeds that will fall off, effectively dispersed, along the trail some miles from where they first caught in his fur. And miles distant is a raven perched on the ribs of a caribou the wolf helped kill ten days ago, pecking like a chicken at the decaying scraps of meat. A smart snowshoe hare that eluded the wolf and left him exhausted when he was a pup has been dead a year now, food for an owl. The den in which he was born one April evening was home to porcupines last winter.*

When you've accomplished the purpose for your feature, you're ready to conclude your article. Your conclusion may be a natural outgrowth of the rest of your draft. For instance, if you chose to present the story of one animal's life from birth to death, your conclusion might focus on the end of this individual's life. If you wrote your feature as a flashback, your conclusion would need to bring your readers back to the present. Whatever else your conclusion does, it should also give your feature some sense of closure or completeness. You can create this sense of closure by summarizing the points you've made, tying up loose ends, or by "coming full circle"—that is, by returning to imagery or ideas you introduced in your lead.

3. Revising

Look again at the assignment to be sure your feature is doing what the science teacher hoped it would. Consider these questions:

- Will my article grab and hold the attention of my readers? (If not, try making it more engaging by adding specific and vivid nouns and modifiers or by finding an entirely new lead.)
- Is my feature easy to follow? (If not, try cluing your readers into the relationships between ideas by adding transitional words and phrases. If this doesn't work, however, you may want to go back to the prewriting stage to figure out a more logical or natural way to organize your information for presentation.)
- Is my article likely to get my readers to understand and appreciate my subject? (If not, try "humanizing" your subject somewhat by describing it with terminology usually reserved for people. Or, devote more space to aspects of your subject's appearance and behavior likely to appeal to people. For example, show it at play or taking care of its family.)

Then refer to Lesson 2.9, page 93, for additional suggestions on checking your draft for meaning. Use the checklists in that lesson to improve the unity and coherence of your writing.

Criteria

1. *Focuses on a creature likely to repel young students*
2. *Fosters an appreciation for the subject in its own right and habitat*
3. *Develops in a logical, natural way*
4. *Possesses an engaging lead and a satisfying ending*
5. *Supports points with specific details that bring the subject to life*
6. *Follows correct grammar, usage, and mechanics*

4. Editing

At this stage, in addition to concerning yourself with the correctness of your grammar, usage, and mechanics, think once again about your audience.

- Is the vocabulary appropriate? (If not, explain or replace difficult terms.)
- Is the level of knowledge I am assuming my audience has appropriate? (If not, you may need to provide some background information.)
- Is my writing style appropriate? (If not, you may need to simplify or shorten some of your sentences or make your tone more informal.)

5. Presenting

Think about how you can make your essay easy for sixth-graders to read and understand. Would a map help you explain your animal's habitat? Would a graph help you present statistical information about your subject? See Lesson 5.7 to learn how you might use graphics to enhance your presentation.

• Reflecting •

Note in your journal the ways in which audience concerns influenced your writing process for this assignment. Then think about the role audience plays in your writing in general. What assumptions do you make about different audiences? How do they affect your writing and writing process?

Portfolio & Reflection

Summary

Key concepts in expository writing include the following:

- The strength of an exposition is its use of supporting details such as facts, statistics, and examples.
- Process writing explains step by step how something happens or is done.
- Cause-and-effect writing explains how one event or fact causes another.
- Classifying means grouping items in categories based on common attributes.
- Comparing and contrasting means exploring similarities and differences.
- Feature articles present interesting in-depth information behind the news.

Your Writer's Portfolio

Look over the expository writing you have done during this unit. Select two pieces of writing to put into your portfolio. Each piece should demonstrate that you have worked with one or more of the preceding concepts. In other words, look for a piece of writing that does one or more of the following:

- has a clear expository purpose
- uses supporting details appropriate for its purpose and audience
- grows out of a prewriting chart that shows the steps in a process
- illustrates a clear cause-to-effect or effect-to-cause organization
- classifies a subject into categories based on common features
- explains similarities and differences examined by means of a Venn diagram

Reflection and Commentary

Now write one page in which you demonstrate that you understand what this unit asked of you. Use your two selected pieces of writing as evidence while you consider the following numbered items. Respond to as many numbered items as possible. Label the page "Commentary on Expository Writing," and include it in your portfolio.

1. What were your expository purposes in the two pieces you selected?
2. Which stage in your writing process taught you the most about effective expository writing? How will your process be different in the future?
3. What element in your writing shows the result of a prewriting technique you used for the first time?
4. Where does your expository writing show a topic and details chosen with a particular audience in mind?

Feedback

If you had a chance to respond to the following student comment, what would you say or ask?

Writing helps teach a person to think for himself or herself. Through writing we gain perspective on ourselves and on our world.

Mitchell Kittlaus, Evanston Township High School, Evanston, Illinois

Persuasive Writing

I Know What I Like

Lili Lakich, *Mona*, 1981

★ ★ ★ ★ ★ ★ ★ ★ ★ **AT THE** ★ ★ ★ ★ ★ ★ ★ ★ ★

MOVIES

"When you see an advertisement for a movie, whether it's Out of Africa *or the* Garbage Pail Kids, *it's going to try to sell you on how good this movie is. And that's what a movie reviewer is for—to tell people, this is a really good movie, go see it, or this is terrible, stay away, don't waste your money."*

Melanie McFarland

The houselights dim, the crowd settles back, and after a few previews, *Dances with Wolves* begins. Minutes later, a wounded man's terror and the noise and confusion of combat have swept viewers onto a Civil War battlefield.

The high-voltage scenes grip everyone, including movie reviewers like Melanie McFarland, a high school senior at Morgan Park Academy in Chicago. But McFarland is working, too. She's looking for original scenes, believable characters, a high-quality experience. Her reviews, which appear in a monthly teen newspaper called *New Expressions,* help shape the opinions of Chicago-area high school students. The effect of these reviews can be as direct as determining readers' weekend movie-viewing plans.

Writing a Movie Review

Behind the Scenes

In the Theater

On Deadline

FOCUS

Like all persuasive writers, movie reviewers rely on facts, examples, logic, and strong feelings to sway a reader's opinion.

McFarland is a young reviewer, but her intense love of film puts her in the company of superb critics. Among them are reviewers who evaluate films for the consuming public—Roger Ebert of the *Chicago Sun-Times* and Roger Corliss at *Time.*

These and other top reviewers and critics share certain traits. They love films. They're film experts, having viewed and thought about thousands of performances. And they're skilled persuasive writers, who bolster their points of view with vivid examples pulled from a broad knowledge of actors, directors, and moviemaking.

One thing critics don't always share, however, is their opinion of an actor or a film. "Every critic's verdict is going to be different because everyone has different tastes," McFarland observed.

What, then, does McFarland think of the films she's seen in the last few years? In her opinion, *Dances with Wolves* was the best film of 1990 because of its quality and its compassionate depiction of Native Americans. On the other hand, she finds most films aimed at teens disappointing, especially films that stereotype teens. "I'd like to see more films that deal with the real, everyday problems kids have to deal with growing up," she said.

Read about your peers' ideas and opinions in a monthly teen magazine.

1. Behind the Scenes

All of McFarland's behind-the-scenes preparation enables her to focus on the film when she sees it. Before McFarland ever sets foot in a movie theater, she does her homework. In part, that means gleaning information from the press kit that film companies send to reviewers and critics.

The press kit is a thick, glossy notebook-sized folder filled with background information, including biographies of the actors, writers, producer, and director. "I read the biographies of the actors so I can see what other work they've done," McFarland explains. "If I'm not familiar with

Knowing film inside and out—that enables reviewers to spot clichés and innovations.

[their work], I'll go out and rent some films."

Watching movies that constitute an actor's body of work is crucial for reviewers. By knowing an actor's skill and range—the huge variety of characters played by Meryl Streep, for example—reviewers can spot new achievements or the lack of them in an actor's current work.

INTERFACE *You have just been hired as the movie reviewer for a national news magazine. Your first assignment: Review the latest film by a well-known director. Write a plan of action, listing the sources you'll tap to build up your knowledge of the director's work before seeing the film. What information will you look for in each source?*

2. In the Theater

Reviewers strive to capture the high points—and low points—of their viewing experience for their readers.

Reviewers begin their real work as they walk into the movie theater. "When you go to the movie, you should have some expectations [of the genre]," McFarland said. "For instance, if you're going to see *Naked Gun,* you don't expect to see great acting because this is a campy film. You watch for how good the gags are."

During the film, reviewers look for original writing. "The lines should be imaginative," McFarland said. "They should make the actors glow." Reviewers also watch for strong directing and acting that's natural, not contrived. In a comedy McFarland notes how much of the audience is laughing—"the entire audience, not just the [person] in front of you." In a drama or action film, she considers the "grip factor"—how much the film grabs your emotions.

McFarland also makes a point of taking a friend to the movies "to get another opinion of the film," she said. After the film McFarland jots down notes about key scenes, dialogue, acting, plus her insights and reactions. These prewriting notes will help McFarland to focus her ideas when she sits down to write.

3. On Deadline

Never gush. Quoted dialogue, colorful descriptions of characters and scenes—proof of your viewpoint gets readers to listen.

Before McFarland writes her review, she mulls over her reactions for a day. She jots down any important insights and reviews her background information and press kits.

When she's ready to write, McFarland imagines her audience—a few teen-agers who want an intelligent opinion of the film she's seen. "I imagine what I would say to an audience right in front of me," McFarland said. "And then I write it down."

Like professional critics and reviewers, McFarland strives to grab readers with a strong lead. "I tend to set up scenarios in the opening paragraphs that lead into the actual critique."

Once McFarland finishes drafting the review on the computer and proofreading for

spelling, grammar, and punctuation, she gives the review to one of her peer editors or supervising editors. In addition to proofreading, the peer editor checks the review for completeness, logic, and style. The supervising editor usually makes minor copyediting changes and, if there are major revisions needed, returns the manuscript to McFarland. After McFarland writes the final draft, the copy is imported from one computer system to another, and dummy electronic pages are created.

McFarland is always curious to see the layout and often returns to the office for one last check. A common error, she says, occurs when the copy is imported; text can "disappear" during the process, and she wants one last chance to proofread before press time.

ON ASSIGNMENT

1. Read two movie reviews of the same film in news magazines or newspapers. You can also watch reviewers on television. Then write a summary of each review, explaining its position on the film and its supporting evidence. At the end of your summary, explain which review was more persuasive and why.

2. **Literature Connection**
   Rent a video of a film based on a book you've read, such as *Field of Dreams, Out of Africa,* or *Lord of the Flies.* Then write a review of the film, paying special attention to how well the film captured the book's plot and characters. Use examples, facts, and your own opinions to persuade readers to see the film or avoid it.

3. **Cooperative Learning**
   Divide into groups of three or four, and decide on a movie you'll all see. After the film, each of you write your own review and support your written opinion with specific details from the film. Exchange your reviews with one another, and peer edit for punctuation and spelling.

Take turns reading your reviews aloud before the group and respond to the reviews with suggestions to help clarify ideas. Assemble the final reviews in a binder, and circulate them among your classmates.

281

OK, OK, You Convinced Me

Suppose your parents believe that all rock stars set a bad example for young people, but you strongly disagree. How would you convince them of your point of view? You might inform your parents that many rock stars donate their time to worthwhile causes, such as Farm Aid. You might also point out that the lyrics of rock songs such as Bruce Springsteen's "Born in the U.S.A." and John Mellencamp's "Small Towns" celebrate national pride. In any case, your parents are more likely to be convinced if you use sound evidence to support your point of view.

Using Persuasive Writing

Persuasive writing is writing that tries to influence a reader to accept an idea, adopt a point of view, or perform an action. You might use persuasive writing to ask your principal to relax your school's dress code. You might also use persuasive writing to create an effective movie review for your school newspaper or to advertise a school dance. Even filling out an application for a summer job may involve persuasive writing. After all, you're trying to persuade an employer to take a particular action: to hire you.

Constructing a Logical Argument

When you write to persuade, you present an argument, the body of evidence used to support your point of view. Your readers are more likely to respect your point of view if you support it logically.

When you present your evidence logically, you take your readers step by step through your argument. You clearly and reasonably show your readers why they should accept your point of view as their own. The chief stages in the construction of a logical argument are detailed on the following pages.

Identify Your Purpose   Before you begin constructing your argument, decide why you want to write your persuasive piece. What do you want it to accomplish? For instance, suppose you want to write a letter to your principal about the lack of sports opportunities for girls at your school. In that case, your purpose might be to ask the principal to help develop a girls' soccer team.

State Your Central Claim   A claim is a statement that asserts something. In persuasive writing your central claim usually makes clear your main purpose for writing, that is, what you're writing to accomplish. You might want to begin your argument by presenting this claim. For example, the letter requesting increased sports opportunities for girls might begin, "Our school should organize a girls' soccer team." Identifying your claim at the beginning of your argument will help keep you focused.

Identify Supporting Evidence   Of course, your claim can't stand on its own. You need to support it with sound evidence. One way to start identifying your evidence is by asking yourself questions that begin, "What evidence do I have that . . . ?" Then look for answers to your questions.

For example, to support the claim that her school should organize a girls' soccer team, one writer asked herself, "What evidence do I have that . . ."

- enough girls are interested in joining a soccer team?
- the team would benefit the girls and the school?
- there is a need for additional sports activities for girls?
- the school can provide the necessary staff?

To get answers to these questions, the writer then conducted a survey of the girls at her school. As a result, she discovered overwhelming interest in a soccer team. She also talked to the coach of the girls' soccer team at a nearby high school and some of the gym teachers at her own school. As authorities on the subject, these people supplied the writer with expert testimony to support her claim. By using these kinds of sound evidence in her persuasive writing piece, the writer will improve her chances of persuading her audience.

• JOURNAL ACTIVITY •
Think It Through

Try to recall a situation in which you were persuaded to do something. What do you think got you to do it? In your journal, note the evidence and tactics that were most effective in persuading you to take action. Then explain why these tactics may have been so effective.

Explain How the Evidence Supports Your Claim   After you have identified your evidence, determine how this evidence supports your claim. If the link between your claim and the evidence you use to support it is obvious, you don't need to state it. If, however, the connection is not clear, you must explain how the evidence supports your claim and why the reader should accept your evidence.

Read the following model, in which the writer presents her case for a girls' soccer team in a letter to her high school principal. Notice how the evidence supports her claim.

Model

The link between the survey results and the claim for a soccer team is obvious. The connection does not need to be stated.

Dear Mr. Lopez,

   I strongly believe that our school should organize a girls' soccer team, and I am not alone in this belief. After conducting a survey among the junior and senior girls at our school, I found that fifty girls would be interested in trying out for a soccer team.

   To discover how similar teams have worked out at other schools, I talked to Ms. Young, the girls' soccer coach at Fairfax High. When I asked her how the team has benefited the girls and the school, she said: "The girls on my team have become close friends. They help each other with everything—homework, personal problems." She added, "Their grades have improved— they've become all-around better students—and that's always good for a school."

What is the logical link between the girls at Fairfax High and the writer's claim?

   A soccer team would be of equal benefit to the girls at our school. Just like the girls at Fairfax, many of the girls here have trouble making friends. A soccer team might help them adjust to school life.

   Moreover, it would be simple to start a team. I've already talked to my gym teacher, Ms. Jordan. She's willing to take on the responsibility of coaching the team. The question of where to practice isn't a problem either, since the playing field isn't used after three o'clock on Tuesdays and Thursdays. All we need now is your support.

Reaffirm Your Claim   After you have presented all your evidence, conclude your argument by reaffirming your claim. You might suggest that, given the evidence you have presented, your claim is the logical conclusion. You might also explain how your claim could be put into action. In the model above, for example, the writer explains where and when the soccer team could meet and identifies a teacher who is willing to coach it.

The following are some writing options to help you apply what you have learned.

1. Guided Assignment   As the curator of a large museum, you have just received on loan from another museum the bronze plaque from the former kingdom of Benin, in present-day Nigeria, shown below. Half of your museum's board of directors believes that the metalwork does not belong in the art section because it is not beautiful according to European standards. They also claim that, because the plaque was among many works of art seized by the British in 1894, it should be treated as a historical artifact.

The other half of the board believes the plaque belongs in the art section because it is beautiful according to Benin standards. The heavy neck rings are symbols of royalty. Also, the craftsmanship is of a very high order.

Decide where you, as curator, would place the work of art. Then write a report to the board in which you state your position and support it logically with sound evidence.

PURPOSE   To persuade a museum's board of directors that an exhibit should be treated as art or as a historical artifact

AUDIENCE   A museum's board of directors

LENGTH   2–3 paragraphs

2. Open Assignment   Write to the letter-to-the-editor section of your school newspaper to call attention to some aspect of school life that you'd like to see changed. Be sure to construct a logical argument to support your claim. Select one of the following topics for your letter, or choose one of your own:

- The school cafeteria should serve food from a popular fast-food chain.
- Students should place recycling bins beside the school's soft drink and snack machines.
- Teachers should reduce subject workloads for graduating seniors.

3. Cooperative Learning   In a small group talk about the summer jobs that you might like to apply for. Discuss the kinds of experience necessary for each particular job. Then write a job application in which you explain why your prospective employer should hire you, using your previous experience and other qualifications as evidence. Finally, have each member present his or her application orally to the rest of the group, who represent the hiring board for the job. Based on the evidence, the board should determine whether or not they would hire the applicant.

Bronze plaque from Benin, date undetermined

Using Evidence Effectively

Prove It

When a prosecuting attorney argues her case before a judge in a court of law, she needs to present sound evidence that supports her claim beyond a reasonable doubt. Weak evidence won't prompt a conviction. A judge won't even pay attention to unreliable or irrelevant evidence. So, too, when you set out to support a claim in a piece of writing, your audience will expect you to use strong, reliable, and relevant evidence to prove that claim.

Defining the Evidence

The following chart lists the most common kinds of evidence used in persuasive writing: facts, statistics, examples or incidents, opinions, and reasons. You can gather these kinds of evidence by freewriting, clustering, or list making about your issue. You can also gather evidence by reading about your issue and by interviewing people. Keep in mind that the more kinds of evidence you use to support your claim, the stronger your argument will be.

Evidence Used in Persuasive Writing

Kind	Definition	Example
Fact	Something that is known to be true	Prehistoric dancers pictured on rock surfaces in Africa and southern Europe prove that dancing is one of the oldest forms of human expression.
Statistic	A fact that is expressed in numbers	When the musical *A Chorus Line* closed on Broadway in 1990, it had achieved a record of 6,137 performances.
Example or Incident	A particular case or event	In some societies, dancing plays a role in courtship. For example, in the United States, many high school students get to know one another at high school dances.
Opinion	A personal judgment based on what the person believes or feels to be true	A famous dancer once claimed, "The dance is a poem of which each movement is a word."
Reason	A logical argument	Many ballet dancers protest the use of toe shoes because the shoes cause permanent damage to the wearer's feet.

• JOURNAL ACTIVITY •
Think It Through

What do you think are the most reliable kinds of evidence you can use to support a claim? Why do you think this may be so? Write down your ideas in your journal.

Assessing the Accuracy of the Evidence

To assess the accuracy of your evidence, verify it in up-to-date sources. Check facts and statistics by consulting current encyclopedias, atlases, and other reference sources. Consult an expert on your subject to clarify something you don't understand or to obtain information that printed sources cannot provide. If you have trouble verifying a statement, or if the only source available to you is out-of-date, you may want to omit the statement from your argument. Your position will be greatly weakened if your readers spot inaccuracies in your argument.

Before you include other people's opinions in your writing, be sure that they are authorities on your subject. Resist using the opinions of well-known persons who have no connection to your subject. So-called testimonials do not have the validity of opinions supplied by authorities. They may cause your audience to question the reliability of the evidence you use throughout your argument. Before quoting someone's opinion, ask yourself what connection the person has to your subject. If he or she has no logical connection, don't use the opinion.

Assessing the Relevance of the Evidence

After you have verified your evidence, examine each detail and ask yourself if it helps develop the point you want to make. If not, you should probably discard the detail as irrelevant to your argument. Relevant details help unify a piece of persuasive writing and ultimately make it more convincing. Irrelevant details, on the other hand, interrupt the flow of your writing and confuse your readers. For example, if you wanted to convince your audience that Spike Lee is a great movie director, you wouldn't include a statement naming his favorite restaurant. The statement has nothing to do with Lee's ability as a director and would only distract your readers from your central point.

Now read the following selection by commentator Anthony Lewis. Notice that Lewis uses sound, relevant evidence to support his claim that the nicotine in cigarettes is as addictive as heroin or cocaine.

Literature Model

D r. C. Everett Koop, the Surgeon General, was only spelling out in scientific terms what we all have observed about cigarette smoking. Users become dependent on the habit, and breaking it can be extremely difficult.

Of those who try to give up smoking, 80 percent have relapsed by the end of a year. Heroin users who try to give up their addiction have the same rate of failure.

"The pharmacologic and behavioral processes that determine tobacco addiction," the Koop report concluded, "are similar to those that determine addiction to drugs such as heroin and cocaine."

There is one profound difference between heroin and nicotine addiction. Tobacco kills 80 times as many people in this country. About 320,000 Americans die every year as a result of using tobacco products, while 4,000 die from the effects of heroin and related drugs.

Anthony Lewis, "Merchants of Death," *New York Times*

Lewis cites facts and statistics from a highly respected source, the U.S. Surgeon General, to support his claim.

In what way is each point Lewis uses in his argument relevant to his claim?

The following are some writing options to help you apply what you have learned.

1. Guided Assignment   As an art expert, you would like a local art gallery to exhibit the fur cup and saucer shown below. The gallery owners, however, aren't convinced and ask you to explain why they should exhibit the work. Use some of the following evidence to write your persuasive piece. Be sure, however, to evaluate this evidence first to make sure it is accurate and relevant to your claim.

- Méret Oppenheim, the woman who created the piece, is a talented but neglected artist who deserves to be introduced to art lovers.
- According to the art critic for your local newspaper, "The fur cup is a fine example of surreal art. In fact, it is often mistaken for a work by Salvador Dali."
- The cup isn't useful, since it can't hold tea.
- Because the work will excite controversy, many people will be curious to see it.
- Your brother, a dentist, said, "The cup left me with a furry taste in my mouth."
- Since the cup's first exhibition in 1936, most artists and critics have praised the object because it challenges expectations.

PURPOSE   To convince an art gallery to exhibit a particular work of art
AUDIENCE   Owners of an art gallery
LENGTH   1–2 paragraphs

2. Open Assignment   As principal of your school, you've been asked to express your point of view about the rights of teachers before your community's superintendent of schools. Choose one of the following claims, or select one of your own. Then support your claim with reliable, relevant evidence.

- Teachers deserve higher salaries.
- Teachers shouldn't be allowed to strike.
- Teachers should be given regular semester-long leaves of absence.

3. Cooperative Learning   Get together in a small group, and discuss television shows that feature teen-agers. Talk about the ways you think each show could be improved. Then have each group member choose one show and write a letter to its producers in which he or she proposes ideas for change. Finally, take turns presenting each letter to the rest of the group, who will act as the show's producers and assess the relevance of the evidence.

Méret Oppenheim, *Object (Luncheon in Fur)*, 1936

Don't Be a Fuzzy Thinker

When you're writing persuasively, you may be tempted to use any means to convince your audience. As a result, some fuzzy or dishonest thinking may sneak into your writing and weaken an otherwise sound argument. For example, suppose you want that outfit you saw in the mall yesterday. How do you persuade your parents to buy it for you? You might point out that it's on sale and that your parents will save if they buy it now. However, your parents could counter that they'd save even more money if they didn't buy it at all.

Learning to recognize the logical flaws in an argument can help you eliminate these flaws from your own writing. It can also help you identify weaknesses in your opponent's argument.

Eliminating Faulty Logic

Once you've chosen your evidence, you need to make sure that the conclusions you draw from that evidence are logical, or follow correct reasoning. If your conclusions are illogical, your readers may reject your entire argument—no matter how compelling your evidence and no matter how well written your argument. As you write, watch out for three of the most common errors in reasoning: red herrings, either/or thinking, and cause-and-effect errors.

Red Herrings   The term *red herring* derives from the practice of dragging a strong-smelling fish across a trail to confuse hunting dogs and throw them off the scent. In writing, a red herring is a topic or statement introduced to distract the reader's attention from the central issue or to hide a weak argument.

Read over your argument to check for red herrings. Make sure that each of your points is directly related to your claim. Anything that sends your reader in a different direction may be a red herring. For example, suppose you are defending your claim that students at your school be given more of a voice in determining the curriculum. If in your argument you bring up your belief that the food in the cafeteria could be better, you've got a red herring on your hands.

Either/Or Thinking If you oversimplify your argument by assuming that the issue has only two sides, you are guilty of either/or thinking. For example, a writer might make the following claim: "Schools should eliminate computer instruction and return to teaching students the basics—reading, writing, and arithmetic." This position, however, fails to take into account the possibility that computers may aid in teaching these basic subjects.

To make sure that you have not used either/or thinking in your writing, look for other reasonable positions between the two sides presented in the argument. If you find them, you are probably oversimplifying the issue.

Cause-and-Effect Errors Just because one event precedes another in time does not mean that the first event is the cause of the second. To make sure that you have identified true cause-and-effect relationships, plot your evidence on a cause-and-effect diagram. Ask yourself if each effect is the direct result of the cause you have listed. If not, you need to rethink your argument.

In the cause-and-effect diagram shown below, one writer plots the evidence supporting her argument that the demand for ivory jewelry has endangered African elephants. Is each effect the direct result of its preceding cause? Read about the "*because* test" described on page 233 in Lesson 5.4 for another way to check an argument for cause-and-effect errors.

Revising Tip

Use limiting words to eliminate either/or thinking. Useful limiting words include *some, frequently, may, most, often, rarely,* and *usually.*

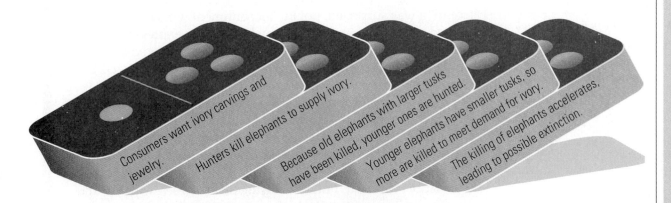

Consumers want ivory carvings and jewelry.

Hunters kill elephants to supply ivory.

Because old elephants with larger tusks have been killed, younger ones are hunted.

Younger elephants have smaller tusks, so more are killed to meet demand for ivory.

The killing of elephants accelerates, leading to possible extinction.

• JOURNAL ACTIVITY •

Try It Out

Select an argument you have begun to write. In your journal plot its evidence on a cause-and-effect diagram like the one shown above. Then ask yourself if each effect you have listed is the direct result of the preceding cause. Correct your argument if it is not.

Analyzing Your Opponent's Logic

You can strengthen your argument by identifying and eliminating its logical flaws. You can also strengthen your position by pointing out flaws in the opposing argument. To find the logical flaws in the opposing argument, evaluate the information presented, point by point. If the argument contains a red herring, identify it and explain how it distracts readers from the central issue. If the opposing argument oversimplifies the issue, identify the flaw and explain why it involves either/or thinking. Likewise, note any faulty cause-and-effect relationships .

If, on the other hand, you find points in the opposing argument that are difficult to disprove, you may need to concede their worth, or admit that those points are valid. If your argument is strong, making a few concessions will not weaken it. In fact, making reasonable concessions may make your argument more convincing. It gives the reader the impression that he or she is reading a well-researched, unbiased argument.

In the following selection, Yona Zeldis McDonough points out some logical flaws in the argument against wearing fur coats. However, she also concedes some points to the opposition. Is her argument strengthened by the concessions she makes?

Literature Model

Notice that McDonough evaluates key points in the opposing view and points out their flaws.

As I walked along 57th Street in Manhattan, a woman hissed, "A lot of animals were tortured to make that coat!" I was surprised, not by her sentiment, which I understood and even respected, but by her need to express it, unsolicited, in public. In the following weeks, I discovered that my outspoken critic was not alone. . . . Like it or not, I realized I was going to have to defend my coat against detractors.

I understand the arguments against wearing fur and have decided to wear one anyway. Not only does fur solve, more efficiently than any other substance known to man, the need for warmth, it has also been with us for hundreds if not thousands of years.

What points does McDonough concede? How does she use them to expose weaknesses in her opponents' argument?

Since I eat meat, I find the distinction between wearing and eating arbitrary. Animals don't care whether their flesh is consumed or their skins are worn; the point is, they have died and we have killed them. This may sound cruel, but it is honest.

I would like to ask those women who keep shouting at me just how consistent they are: What about wearing leather and suede? Animals must be killed for those skins, too. Do all these women wear only sneakers and carry canvas bags?

Yona Zeldis McDonough, "Sisters Under the Skin," *New York Times*

Writer's Choice

The following are some writing options to help you apply what you have learned.

1. Guided Assignment As head of the dress-code committee at your school, you have been asked whether or not you believe the code should be relaxed. You must bring your ideas before a panel composed of teachers and school administrators. Use some of the following evidence to persuade the panel to accept your ideas. Make sure you analyze the logic of the evidence before you build your argument, however. Some of the evidence contains red herrings, either/or thinking, and cause-and-effect errors.

- The way students dress is one of the few things teen-agers can control, and that independence shouldn't be restricted.
- After the dress code at a nearby school was relaxed, the students' grade averages rose.
- The dress code should be stricter because too many students concentrate on their looks rather than on their schoolwork.
- Some students' dress expresses their ethnic and cultural diversity.
- If students aren't given total freedom in determining their dress, they will strike.
- In addition to determining the dress code, students should also have a voice in choosing the books they read in class.
- Dress should be regulated only if what the student wears creates a disturbance or poses a danger.

PURPOSE To persuade a panel to accept ideas regarding a school's dress code

AUDIENCE A panel composed of teachers and school administrators

LENGTH 2–3 paragraphs

2. Open Assignment Imagine that you write a weekly editorial for your school newspaper in which you express your views on popular culture. Write a one-page editorial in which you take a position on one of the following issues or on another issue about which you feel strongly. Use the methods detailed in the lesson to check your argument for errors in reasoning.

- Is there too much violence in films?
- Is television really "bubblegum for the eyes"?
- Should comic books be considered an art form?
- Will pay-per-view television eventually replace most network programming?

3. Civics Every election year, a large percentage of the population does not vote. Do you think voting is a privilege and people should be encouraged to exercise it? Or do you think that many people choose not to vote in order to express their dissatisfaction with the candidates? Develop an argument in which you define your position on this topic. Make sure the evidence you use does not contain red herrings, either/or thinking, cause-and-effect errors, or other kinds of faulty logic. Also, if you think the opposition has some valid points, be sure to concede them.

COMPUTER OPTION

Some software programs can search a piece of writing for subject-verb agreement problems, overly wordy sentences, and other errors in grammar, usage, and mechanics. You might want to use such a program as you write your argument for the Civics activity above. However, although the program can effectively aid the revising process, don't expect it to point out all of your errors. Remember that you are responsible for finding and correcting errors in reasoning—not your computer.

Getting Words to Work for You

Of course, you can't always persuade your audience to accept your argument. As the comic strip above demonstrates, empty adjectives and wild promises fool no one. You stand a better chance of persuading your readers if you use precisely the words that express your meaning. You can make your writing more precise by using limiting words, by replacing general words with specific ones, and by understanding the connotations of the words you use.

Using Limiting Words

One way to add precision to your persuasive writing is to use limiting words. Limiting words are words that allow you to account for exceptions when you state your point of view. You can use limiting words to avoid overgeneralizations. An overgeneralization is an oversimplification or gross exaggeration of the facts. Readers who spot an overgeneralization may dismiss your entire argument as biased or poorly supported. For example, if you said, "Today's rock singers depend on sophisticated sound equipment to make up for their lack of musical talent," many of your readers would read no further. They'd recognize that your point of view is a gross overstatement. On the other hand, if you said, "*Some* of today's rock singers depend on sophisticated sound equipment to make up for a lack of musical talent," you'd probably stand a better chance of holding your audience's attention. *Some* is a limiting word. The following chart lists some common limiting words you can use to avoid making overgeneralizations.

Limiting Words		
almost never	in most cases	occasionally
a minority of	less than half	often
as a rule	many	rarely
certain	more than half	seldom
few	most	several
frequently	mostly	some
half	nearly all	sometimes
hardly ever	nearly always	the majority of
in general	not all	usually

Using Specific Words

You can also make your persuasive writing more precise by replacing general words with specific ones whenever you can. A general word is fairly vague, while a specific word provides more definite information and so may express your meaning more exactly. For example, compare the following two sentences:

> "Certain types of television programs have really bad effects on young children."
> "Violent television shows cause violent behavior and nightmares in young children."

Notice that the second sentence tells you much more than the first about the types of television programs and the effects they have on young children. The specific words in the second sentence also bring more vivid thoughts and images to mind. Thus, they are more likely to hold the reader's attention, which is a major concern in persuasive writing. After all, you'll never convince your readers of anything if you can't hold their attention.

Revising Tip

During revising, try using a thesaurus to help you find precise words that express your meaning exactly. See Resources and Skills, pages 744–745, for tips on how to use a thesaurus.

• JOURNAL ACTIVITY •
Think It Through

What strategies might you use to help you identify overgeneralizations? What strategies might you use to help you identify general words that could be replaced with more specific ones? Write down your ideas in your journal.

Considering Connotations

Leonardo da Vinci, *Mona Lisa*, 1503–1505

Another way to make sure you're using words precisely is to choose words that not only express your specific meaning but also have the right feeling, or connotation. The connotation of a word is an idea or notion suggested by the word beyond its exact meaning. Suppose, for instance, that you describe the famous smile in Leonardo da Vinci's painting, the *Mona Lisa*, as *weird*. The word weird implies that there is something unpleasant about her smile. If, on the other hand, you refer to Mona Lisa's smile as mysterious, you suggest that it is interesting and attractive.

Some words have highly emotional connotations. These words, called emotionally loaded words, cause strong negative or positive responses. For example, how would you react if someone referred to you as bold? How would you react if someone called you reckless? Although the words have similar meanings, they prompt very different emotional responses. *Bold* excites positive feelings because it suggests a daring, confident spirit. *Reckless*, on the other hand, stirs up negative feelings because it implies irresponsibility.

In the following model, the writer uses the connotations of words to praise the candidate he supports and to establish arguments against the opposition.

Model

Words such as "heroic" imply that Edwards nobly defends lost causes.

How would the tone of the piece be affected if you substituted the phrase "level charges" for "make petty allegations"?

What other words used in the model convey particular notions about Edwards and the candidate opposing him?

I heartily encourage you to vote for Don "Bud" Edwards for mayor, a man of action and notable accomplishments. As a former alderman, Bud battled tirelessly against the bureaucrats on the city council to guarantee inexpensive housing for the underprivileged. Furthermore, his heroic efforts on behalf of the elderly have been chronicled by prominent journalists across the country.

On the other side of the coin, we have Bud's opponent, Gus Badenough. Gus is notorious for his waffling stands on the issues and for his vicious opposition to Bud. In fact, he has attempted to obstruct Bud's valiant work for the homeless more than once. Now Gus has begun to make petty allegations, which our candidate will not lower himself to address.

Are we going to allow these smear tactics to succeed? I hope not. On election day, I believe that there will still be enough upstanding citizens to vote for a true gentleman and statesman, Bud Edwards.

Writer's Choice

The following are some writing options to help you apply what you have learned.

1. Guided Assignment   Your local art museum is going to exhibit the painting shown at the right, Pablo Picasso's *Two Acrobats with a Dog.* You've been asked to rewrite a paragraph describing the painting for the museum's newsletter. As it stands now, the paragraph makes Picasso's work seem unappealing. Rewrite the paragraph so that it might inspire potential museum visitors to come see the painting. Pay particular attention to the connotations of the words you choose.

Pablo Picasso, *Two Acrobats with a Dog*, 1905

Picasso's painting of two young circus tumblers is depressing. The children's colorful costumes contrast pathetically with the miserable expressions on their faces. Gloom issues from their downturned mouths and staring eyes. The older boy holds a tiny pack over his shoulder—probably containing both boys' meager rags of clothes. Perhaps the circus is traveling to yet another town, and the pair must move on, like homeless orphans seeking shelter. Even the dog looks wretched.

PURPOSE   To make an unappealing description of a painting more appealing and intriguing
AUDIENCE   Potential art museum visitors
LENGTH   1 paragraph

2. Open Assignment   Imagine you've entered a school contest in which you are to write an essay on one of the following topics or on one of your own. A panel of teachers will select the winning essay. Be sure to avoid overgeneralizations and to use specific words.

- Explain why your favorite teacher should receive a teacher-of-the-year award.
- Make a case for offering Latin (or some other subject) at your school.
- Explain why there should be more parental involvement on school councils.

3. Music   Write a brief review of a record or song you have heard recently. Use connotative words to evoke either a positive or negative reaction in your readers and to persuade them to accept your opinion of the song.

Writing an Editorial

Speaking Your Mind

Literature Model

Yesterday's announcement of a plan for U.S. and Soviet Olympic committees to test athletes for drugs is welcome news. It's also overdue. Sports organizations are fighting a losing battle against anabolic steroids, and the reason is that most don't have their hearts in the struggle. Only a handful of competitors, including Ben Johnson, the Canadian sprinter, were expelled from the Seoul Olympics for using the forbidden drugs. Yet, according to *The Times*'s recent series on drug use, probably half or more of the 9,000 athletes at Seoul had used steroids or similar drugs during training.

Steroid use has long been rampant, yet sports bodies from Olympic committees downward have been failing in their responsibility to deter it. Drug-using athletes set a dispiriting example to a society trying to fight drug abuse, especially to young people who are at grave risk of injury from the drugs. "The system is saying, do whatever it takes to win," says Bill Curry, football coach at Alabama.

. . . [D]iet and exercise are accepted ways of enhancing physical ability; drugs are not. Many athletes apparently take steroids not because they want to but from peer pressure or fear of losing to others who do. . . . Once the message is out that sports organizations are really serious about steroids, most athletes will probably abandon them with relief.

"Winking at Steroids in Sports," November 22, 1988, *New York Times*

The writer uses comments such as "It's also overdue" to express his stand on the use of steroids.

What pieces of evidence does the writer use to support his opinion?

Speaking your mind—that's what an editorial is all about. In an editorial, a writer expresses an opinion about a current news event or issue. An effective editorial is direct and absorbing and can move its readers to take a stand on or reevaluate an issue.

In the editorial above, the writer expresses his opinion that sports organizations should become more serious about deterring athletes from using steroids. Do you think the argument is effective?

Choosing an Issue

The New Television Season:
Another Winning Lineup

Fair Fare for Films

What's Right with Rap

Whatever it is,
it isn't art

Why do dancers
always have to be
on their toes?

Captive Audiences

Support your
local drama club

To get a sense of controversial issues in your community, read the editorial page and the letters to the editor in local newspapers and magazines. Listen to talk shows on the radio or watch them on television. Talk to people you know about what's on their minds.

Once you've collected several ideas for editorials, choose one issue about which you feel strongly. You might state the issue in the form of a question. Then brainstorm to generate evidence you could use to support your viewpoint. In the following example, two writers with opposing viewpoints answered this question: "Are rock musicians who lip-sync at live concerts cheating their fans?"

Prewriting Tip

If you are having trouble coming up with evidence to support your argument, try to imagine a conversation on the subject with someone who holds an opposing view.

Yes, because...	Fans who pay a lot of money for concert tickets deserve to hear live music. People go to live concerts to hear live music. It's not as exciting for the fans; they might as well listen to a record.
No, because...	Today's concerts offer more than just singing. It's exciting just to be there at a live performance. The audience gets more for its money because shows are so extravagant.

• JOURNAL ACTIVITY •
Try It Out

Generate a list of currently controversial issues that interest you, and choose one that could be the topic of an editorial you might write. Then brainstorm to generate evidence that you could use to support your viewpoint.

Appealing to Your Audience

Once you've chosen an issue, select evidence that will persuade your audience to take your stand. Keep in mind that a striking image can often speak more powerfully than a list of facts and statistics. For example, rather than saying "Thousands of people thronged the concert," you might say, "So many people attended the concert that the crowd that night formed the third largest city in the state."

Since editorial writers try to get their readers on their side, you might also want to consider injecting some humor into your editorial. When you make your readers laugh, they open up to what you have to say. They may feel that they share common ground with you and so may be more disposed to agree with what you're saying.

Summing Up

Because many editorials try to persuade readers to take some action, editorial writers often save their strongest reason for last. A good conclusion sums up the argument and spurs the reader to action. In the editorial below, Eugene Weresow makes his strongest point at the end.

Student Model

Eugene makes concessions to his opponents but counters their objections by discussing the intentions of the authors.

What is Eugene's strongest point? What action does he encourage his readers to take?

Hanging on my classroom wall is a long list of books that have been banned from certain schools. As I scanned the list, I recognized several that were among the best I've ever read, including *Catcher in the Rye*, *1984*, and *Brave New World*. Although these books contain controversial language and situations, I believe it would be a mistake to ban them.

Admittedly, some of the characters in *Catcher in the Rye* use words that would be inappropriate in the classroom. But real people often swear and use slang expressions; the author is just trying to make his book realistic. Similarly, *1984* and *Brave New World* portray situations that some may consider unacceptable for political or social reasons. But the authors mean to convey a message with these works; the extreme situations they use make a more lasting impression upon the reader than would more acceptable situations.

I don't believe it is dangerous to expose students to the controversial material in these books. On the contrary, I believe the books should be valued for the ideas they express. Rather than protect impressionable students, those who ban these books do us a disservice: they deny us access to ideas.

Eugene Weresow, Edison High School, Edison, New Jersey

Writer's Choice

The following are some writing options to help you apply what you have learned.

1. Guided Assignment   You have been asked to deliver an editorial on *Teen Say*, a television program for teen-agers. As a guest on the program, you will be allowed three minutes to discuss whether the school year should be extended. Begin preparing your editorial by stating the issue in the form of a question: "Should the academic school year be extended through July?" Then brainstorm to generate evidence to support your argument. Use the following to help you get started:

> Yes, because . . .
> The U.S. school year is one of the shortest among schools in industrialized nations. If U.S. students want to compete successfully with young people from other countries, they need to spend more time in school.

> No, because . . .
> Students need a full summer in which to relax and just be kids.
> It isn't the quantity of time students spend in school but the quality of the education they receive there that's important.

As you write your editorial, remember to keep your audience in mind. Inject some humor into your editorial if possible, and use striking images to convey your meaning. Conclude your editorial by summing up your argument and calling your audience to action.

PURPOSE   To persuade your audience to accept your views on extending the school year
AUDIENCE   Teen-age TV viewers
LENGTH   1–2 pages

2. Open Assignment   Imagine you are the editor of an arts magazine written by and for teen-agers. Write an editorial, choosing one of the following issues or another issue in which you are interested. Then brainstorm to generate evidence for your editorial.

- Should certain books be banned from school libraries?
- Are special effects being overdone in movies?
- Should companies be allowed to promote their products by paying fees to have the products appear prominently during movie scenes?
- Do television programs reflect or help shape our lives?
- Should admission to public museums be free?

3. Art   In some cities, a certain percentage of the budget for new buildings must be set aside for the purchase of public art. Sometimes disputes arise when members of the public dislike the art chosen. Who should decide what art is displayed in public spaces? Take a position on the issue, and decide on a purpose for a newsletter editorial. What arguments would be most persuasive if your audience were a group of gallery owners? A local citizens group?

COMPUTER OPTION

Suppose you wanted to send the newsletter containing your editorial on the purchase of public art to one of the audiences suggested above. In addition, suppose you wanted to include each person's address on the newsletter. Instead of typing multiple copies of your piece, use the Mail Merge feature of your word-processing program. Just type a list of the addresses where you want to send the newsletter. Then use Mail Merge to print as many newsletters as you want, each addressed to a different person.

Two Thumbs Up

The movie critic for *Rolling Stone* magazine called *Dances with Wolves* "heartfelt and engrossing." The critic for the *New Yorker* magazine found the film "childishly naive." She felt that the Native Americans who befriended director and star Kevin Costner should have named him "Plays with Camera" instead of "Dances with Wolves."

Although movie reviewers may differ widely in their opinions, they all do essentially the same thing: evaluate the movie. Read the Case Study at the beginning of this unit to find out how one student reviewer approaches her work.

Provide Background Information

Most reviewers begin by expressing their opinion of the film. They then provide background information on the film by briefly summarizing the plot and identifying the characters, actors, director, and scriptwriter. If the film you're reviewing is popular, you may be able to provide a minimum of background information. If, however, the film is not well known, you will need to give more detail. To determine how much background information to include, ask yourself how much your audience already knows about the film and what they need to know to understand your review of it.

Examine the Movie's Elements

When you write a movie review, you do more than tell if you liked it. You evaluate certain elements of the film and measure the film's success by specific criteria. These criteria differ somewhat for different types of films. For example, if a film is a comedy, you judge it by how funny it is. But, if it's an action film, you might measure its success by how exciting it is. There are, however, some criteria by which you may judge most movies. These are outlined on the chart below.

The Elements of a Movie	
Plot What happens in the film	Does it hold your interest? Does it seem plausible or contrived?
Theme What the film means	Is the movie's theme significant, worth pondering? Does the film develop the theme, or does it oversimplify a complex issue?
Characterization The way the characters are developed by the scriptwriter and the director	Do the characters seem real, believable? Are their motivations and actions true to their backgrounds and personalities?
Acting The way the actors portray their characters	Do the actors create believable characters? Do they evoke the intended responses in the audience—laughter, fear, sorrow?
Special Effects Techniques used to create illusions	Do the effects create the desired illusions? Do they enhance or overpower the story?
Sound Track The music that accompanies the visuals	Is the music appropriate to the scene in which it is used? What is the quality of the music? Is the sound track well recorded, clear?

• JOURNAL ACTIVITY •
Try It Out

Think about a movie that you have seen recently. When you have one in mind, use the questions in the chart above to examine the movie's elements and help you generate details that you could use in a movie review.

Evaluate the Movie Critically

You can approach a movie review in many ways. The questions below may help you think of new angles to use for evaluating a movie critically.

Prewriting Tip

If you compare or contrast one movie with another movie or with a novel, use a comparison frame (see Lesson 5.10 on page 262) to help organize your details.

A Critic's Checklist

1. Can I compare or contrast this film with another that explores the same theme?
2. Is this film adapted from written work, such as a novel or a play? If so, can I compare it to the original work?
3. Can I compare my reactions with those of the audience?
4. Can I critique the film from a particular social or political perspective? Am I well informed enough to do so?

Notice which elements of *Terminator 2* student reviewer Lina Chern chooses to focus on in the following movie review.

Student Model

What elements of T2 *does Lina examine in her review?*

What is Lina's opinion of the movie? Why do you think she compares T2 *with the original* Terminator *to express her opinion?*

I must admit that I was not expecting terrific results from *Terminator 2: Judgment Day*, the most eagerly awaited sequel of the summer. After all, its predecessor was one of the most thoughtful, understated action movies ever made, while *T2* was promising to be a typical overblown summer blockbuster. I was only half-correct—the story has lost some thought and subtlety and gained a great deal of special effects, but is still interesting and definitely entertaining.

Arnold Schwarzenegger (too marketable now to play the bad guy) stars as a reprogrammed Terminator cyborg that is ordered to go back in time to protect the still-adolescent John Connor (Edward Furlong); the boy is to become a key figure in the future war between humans and machines. After John and the Terminator rescue John's mother, Sarah (Linda Hamilton)—now a tough, hell-bent warrior—from a mental hospital, the three set out to prevent the coming nuclear holocaust, or Judgment Day. Meanwhile, they have to deal with another, more advanced Terminator that has been sent back to kill John.

In general, *Terminator 2* is engaging and creative, but in a more conventional way than the original. It is a clean, slick moneymaker, which should not deter anyone from seeing it.

Lina Chern, Maine East High School, Chicago, Illinois

The following are some writing options to help you apply what you have learned.

1. Guided Assignment   You have been chosen to participate on a panel made up of teenagers that reviews films once a week for your community newspaper. Think about the movies you have seen in the last few months and prepare a written review of the one you liked the best. Provide brief background information on the film, and then choose one or two specific elements to evaluate. For instance, if you believe that the film presents an unrealistic picture of the life of a teen-ager, you might give examples from the plot or the characterization to support your opinion. Finally, use the critic's checklist of questions on page 304 to help you prepare your review.

PURPOSE   To write a movie review
AUDIENCE   The teen-age, movie-going readers of a community newspaper
LENGTH   1–2 pages

2. Open Assignment   Some people believe that special effects have overshadowed and indeed replaced the need for a strong plot and convincing characters in movies. Other people believe that special effects are an indispensable part of film. Select one of the following films known for its special effects or one of your own choosing. Then write a review of the movie for the readers of your high school newspaper. Base your review on an evaluation of the movie's use of special effects. Be sure to explain whether or not you think the special effects overshadow the other elements of the film, or discuss how they enhance the film.

- *Star Wars* (original or sequels)
- *Terminator* (original or sequel)
- *Back to the Future* (original or sequels)
- *Star Trek* (original or sequels)
- *Jaws* (original or sequels)

3. Literature   Choose one of the films listed below or another you have seen that is based on a work of literature. Then prepare a written review of the film in which you compare it with the original work of literature. If you like, submit the review for publication in your school's literary journal.

- *Wuthering Heights*
- *A Raisin in the Sun*
- *The Grapes of Wrath*
- *Great Expectations*
- *The Color Purple*

4. Cooperative Learning   Have each member of a small group give a brief oral review of the movie of his or her choice. If any of the other group members are familiar with the movie under discussion, invite them to share their impressions of the film. Then have each group member write a review of his or her chosen film. Be sure to state your overall opinion of the movie, and then use specific details from the film to support it. Use the checklist of questions on page 304 to help you determine your critical approach. Finally, collect the finished reviews as a movie guide, and share them with the other students in your class.

COMPUTER OPTION

After your group has completed the Cooperative Learning activity above, consider using your PC and a simple page-layout program to make your movie guide look like the work of a professional group. Some word-processing software is sophisticated enough to do the job as well. If available, use drawing software programs to create images representing the movies and/or the reviewers, and add them to your writing. Finally, for a polished look, print out your movie guide on a laser printer.

Clara Spotted Elk

• • •

Skeletons in the Attic

Clara Spotted Elk has worked to help her fellow Native Americans regain the skeletal remains of their ancestors from museums, collectors, and federal agencies. In September of 1989, thanks in part to persuasive efforts such as hers, the Smithsonian Institution began returning some of these remains to their Native American descendants. In the following article, Spotted Elk expresses her point of view on this cultural issue.

Millions of American Indians lived in this country when Columbus first landed on our shores. After the western expansion, only about 250,000 Indians survived. What happened to the remains of those people who were decimated by the advance of the white man? Many are gathering dust in American museums.

In 1985, I and some Northern Cheyenne chiefs visited the attic of the Smithsonian's[1] Natural History Museum in Washington, D.C., to review the inventory of their Cheyenne collection. After a chance inquiry, a curator[2] pulled out a drawer in one of the scores of cabinets

---

1 **Smithsonian** the Smithsonian Institution, a research organization administered by the United States government
2 **curator** (kyoo rāt′ ər) a person in charge of a museum

that line the attic. There were the jumbled bones of an Indian. "A Kiowa,"[3] he said.

Subsequently, we found that 18,500 Indian remains—some consisting of a handful of bones, but mostly full skeletons—are unceremoniously stored in the Smithsonian's nooks and crannies. Other museums, individuals, and federal agencies such as the National Park Service also collect the bones of Indian warriors, women, and children. Some are on display as roadside tourist attractions. It is estimated that another 600,000 Indian remains are secreted away in locations across the country.

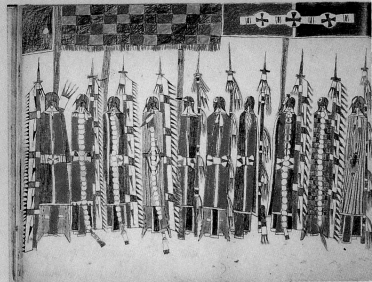

Howling Wolf, Untitled drawing, 1876

The museum community and forensic[4] scientists vigorously defend these grisly[5] collections. With few exceptions, they refuse to return remains to the tribes that wish to rebury them, even when grave robbing has been documented. They want to maintain adequate numbers of "specimens" for analysis and say they are dedicated to "the permanent curation of Indian skeletal remains."

Indian people are tired of being "specimens." The Northern Cheyenne word for ourselves is "tsistsistas"—human beings. Like people the world over, one of our greatest responsibilities is the proper care of the dead.

We are outraged that our religious views are not accepted by the scientific community and that the graves of our ancestors are desecrated.[6] Many tribes are willing to accommodate some degree of study for a limited period of time—provided that it would help

---

3 **Kiowa** (kī' ō wä) a tribe of Plains Indians formerly of Colorado, Oklahoma, Kansas, New Mexico, and Texas

4 **forensic** (fə ren' sik) able to apply medical knowledge to legal matters

5 **grisly** (griz' lē) horrible; ghastly

6 **desecrated** (des' ə krāt' 'd) treated something considered holy in an inappropriate manner

Indian people or mankind in general. But how many "specimens" are needed? We will not accept grave robbing and the continued hoarding of our ancestors' remains.

Would this be tolerated if it were discovered that it affected other ethnic groups? (Incidentally, the Smithsonian also collects skeletons of blacks.) What would happen if the Smithsonian had 18,500 Holocaust victims in the attic? There would be a tremendous outcry in the this country. Why is there no outcry about the Indian collections?

Indians are not exotic creatures for study. We are human beings who practice living religions. Our religion should be placed not only on a par with science when it comes to determining the disposition of our ancestors, but on a par with every other religion practiced in this country.

To that end, Sen. Daniel K. Inouye (D.-Hi)[7] will soon reintroduce the "Bones Bill" to aid Indians in retrieving the remains of their ancestors from museums. As in the past, the "Bones Bill" will most likely be staunchly resisted by the collectors of Indian skeletons—armed with slick lobbyists,[8] lots of money, and the mystique[9] of science.

Scientists have attempted to defuse this issue by characterizing their opponents as radical Indians, out of touch with their culture and with little appreciation of science. Armed only with a moral obligation to our ancestors, the Indians who support the bill have few resources and little money.

But, in my view, the issue should concern all Americans, for it raises very disturbing questions. American Indians want only to reclaim and rebury their dead. Is this too much to ask?

7 **(D.-Hi)** Democrat, Hawaii

8 **lobbyists** (läb 'ē ists) people who work to influence laws and government decisions in favor of one special-interest group

9 **mystique** (mis tēk') a set of mysterious feelings and attitudes surrounding a person, group, or activity

For Discussion

1. How did you react to the author's revelation of the Native American skeletons being kept by museums, individuals, and federal agencies?

2. Does the author win you over to her viewpoint? Why or why not? Do you think this piece could change the minds of "collectors" or of legislators? Why or why not?

Readers Respond

The writer kept my attention by giving statistics of the wrong that was being done to her people. The dominant tone of this article was sympathetic. Clara Spotted Elk made us sympathize with and feel sorry for her people. She showed us what was happening and opened our eyes to the facts. I would recommend this article because it is important for everyone to be aware of what has happened to the Indians.

Yahna Awazu

This selection was about how one American Indian feels about scientists using her ancestors' bones for research. The article had an angry tone, which the author created simply by telling what the scientists are doing. I don't like the fact that scientists think they have a right to use Indian bones for research. They seem to have no respect for the dead. Because I am part Indian, this selection held my attention. I would definitely recommend it to a friend.

Maurice Phifer

Do you agree?

☞ Do you agree that the tone is sympathetic, or do you think it is angry? Or is it neither? What effect does the tone have on your reading of the article?

☞ Do you agree with Clara Spotted Elk's article? In your journal make a list of defenses for or arguments against the claims and opinions in the article. Give evidence to support your opinion.

Writing Process in Action

Taking a Stand

In "Skeletons in the Attic," reprinted on pages 306–308, journalist Clara Spotted Elk not only reveals that there are quite literally hundreds of thousands of skeletons—Native American skeletons—hidden in America's "attics" but also takes a stand on this issue. She states that these remains should be returned to their rightful resting places. Spotted Elk then argues persuasively to rally her readers in support of legislation to aid Native Americans in retrieving the remains of their ancestors from museums.

Now you are invited to expose a problem—perhaps even an injustice—in your school or community and to take a stand in favor of whatever corrective action you think is appropriate.

• Assignment •

CONTEXT You have promised to submit an editorial or other short piece of persuasive writing to *Student Voices*, a monthly newsletter some friends of yours publish. You can write about anything you want to see changed in your school or community, be it an irritating problem or a deeply disturbing injustice. This is your opportunity to get through to the people who make the policies and decisions that affect your life but who otherwise might not listen to you. It's also your chance to speak your mind to other students.

PURPOSE To write a brief persuasive article or editorial that exposes a problem or injustice and rouses readers to take corrective action

AUDIENCE Teen-agers, teachers, school administrators, and community members

LENGTH 1 page

For more advice on how to approach this assignment, you will find the next few pages helpful. But don't feel that you have to remember all of what follows. You can come *back* to these pages as you write, getting help where and when you need it. You're in charge of your own writing process.

1. Prewriting

What problems or injustices are on your mind? Are you upset because your favorite deli just put up a sign stating "No More Than Five Students Allowed at a Time"? Here are some suggestions for exploring your thoughts:

- Review your journal writing to find problems and disagreements.
- Check school and community newspapers and magazines for possible topics. See also Lesson 6.5, page 299, for ways to find controversial issues.

- Freewrite to discover problems and injustices. Start by writing "It bothers me that . . ." Then see how many ways you can complete the sentence.
- Brainstorm with your classmates to create lists of problems and injustices under the headings "School" and "Community."

Once you have identified some problems or injustices, select the two or three that concern you most, and devote five minutes of freewriting to each. Begin by clearly stating the problem or injustice. Then rant, rave, try out arguments, test defenses. Get anything and everything to do with that topic down on paper. By the time you've finished freewriting about these topics, the one you most want to write about will probably be obvious to you. However, if you're still undecided, ask yourself these questions:

- About which problem or injustice do I care the most? (Hint: Usually this is the one about which you have the most to say.)
- What claim do I feel the most confidence in making? (Hint: Usually this is the one for which you have the strongest evidence and for which you have provided the most logical argument.)
- About which topic are my readers most likely to share my concern? (Hint: Usually this is the one that is most personally relevant to your readers.)

Once you've narrowed down to one particular topic, look more critically at the freewriting you did about it. In particular, zero in on your purpose. If you wish, you may use Spotted Elk's purpose as a model for your own. Spotted Elk's purpose may be seen as twofold. She writes to convince her audience that her central claim (Native Americans should be allowed to reclaim and rebury their dead) is valid. She also writes to convince her readers to take the corrective action (supporting Senator Inouye's "Bones Bill") she recommends. Following this model, your purpose would be to persuade your audience to believe in the validity of your central claim *and* to take the corrective action you recommend.

Sometimes the second purpose may be combined with the central claim into a single statement (We should support the passage of the "Bones Bill" to enable American Indians to reclaim and rebury their dead). Lesson 6.1, pages 283–284, can tell you more about combining the two. Note, however, that if you combine the second purpose with your central claim, then essentially your purpose in writing becomes to support your central claim.

Next, take some time to think about your audience. How much are your readers likely to know about your topic? Will you need to provide background information or explain key concepts? Consider their attitudes. Are your readers likely to agree or disagree with you? Do they already care about the issue, or must you persuade them to care? Determining the needs and attitudes of your audience is very important since persuading readers to act upon your argument may require meeting their needs and overcoming their attitudes.

Finally, start building your case by gathering and evaluating evidence that will help you achieve your purpose. Notice how Spotted Elk uses a mix of statistics ("18,500 Indian remains—some consisting of a handful of bones, but mostly full skeletons—are unceremoniously stored in the Smithsonian's nooks and crannies"), opinions ("Our religion should be placed not only on a par with science when it comes to determining the disposition of our ancestors, but on a par with every other religion practiced in this country"), comparisons ("Would this be tolerated if it were discovered that it affected other ethnic groups?"), and other kinds of details to back up her central claim. Look at Lesson 6.1 for suggestions on identifying supporting evidence through questioning. Also see Lesson 6.2, pages 286–289, for ideas about the types of evidence you might gather and considerations for evaluating it.

2. Drafting

You've identified your purpose, stated your claim, sized up your audience, and gathered your evidence. Now it's time to prove your case. When you write persuasively, you want to present your information in a way that will have a strong impact on your readers. To achieve that goal means using language that is forceful and direct. Look at what Spotted Elk does. Her tone is confident, yet respectful, and she uses specific words with strong connotations to plead her case. For example, she doesn't say her people are upset because their religious views are not accepted and the graves of their ancestors have been dug up. She writes as follows:

> *We are* outraged *that our religious views are not accepted by the scientific community and that the graves of our ancestors are* desecrated [emphasis added].

See Lesson 6.4, pages 294–297, for help in using language to advantage.

Next, think about how you want to present your evidence. Sometimes you want to build up to a central claim, which you state last. That's the approach Spotted Elk uses. She starts with the fact that remains of Native Americans are "gathering dust in American museums" and then presents her evidence, piece by piece, leading up to her central claim: "American Indians want only to reclaim and rebury their dead. Is this too much to ask?"

An alternate approach is to hit your readers with your big guns first. State your claim forcefully at the start, present your evidence, and then reinforce it with a strong conclusion. Experiment to see what works best for you.

As you write, try to address opposing viewpoints. Each valid counterargument you ignore is a potential excuse for readers to dismiss your position. So if you can't prove an opposing argument to be false, at least acknowledge and respond to it in some way. That's what Spotted Elk does when she responds to the argument that "specimens" are needed for analysis.

> *Many tribes are willing to accommodate some degree of study for a limited period of time—provided that it would help Indian people or mankind in general.*

Lesson 6.3, page 292, may provide you with additional suggestions for responding to opposing arguments.

Once you have finished stating your case, write a conclusion that will leave a strong impression. Summarize your main points, state your central claim, or urge readers to take action. Lesson 6.5, page 300, can help you sum up your appeal.

3. Revising

Now that you've gotten everything down on paper, check to see how well you have stated your case. Consider these points:

- Have you clearly presented your central claim? (Lesson 6.1 can help you with this.)
- Is all of your evidence accurate and relevant to your central claim? (Lesson 6.2 can help you determine the quality and relevance of your evidence.)
- Is your reasoning sound? (See Lesson 6.3 to make sure you have avoided faulty logic.)
- Have you stated your case in a way that will appeal to your audience of teen-agers, teachers, school administrators, and community members? (Refer to Lesson 6.5, page 300, for help in appealing to your audience.)

You also might ask a peer to read your draft and think of arguments to challenge your position. Use the arguments to help you identify possible weaknesses in your reasoning and give you ideas for responding to opposing viewpoints.

Criteria

1. *Focuses on a school or community problem or injustice*
2. *Contains a central claim and identifies a main purpose for writing*
3. *Supports its central claim with accurate and relevant evidence*
4. *Uses sound reasoning and addresses counterarguments*
5. *Uses limiting words, specific words, and connotations to advantage*
6. *Follows correct grammar, usage, and mechanics*

4. Editing

At this stage look closely at your writing, paying special attention to your use of language. Check to see if you employ limiting words to avoid overgeneralizations. Notice that Spotted Elk doesn't accuse *all* scientists and museums with hoarding skeletal remains. Instead, she states, "*With few exceptions*, they refuse to return remains . . . [emphasis added]." Also check to make sure you have used specific words and phrases to present your evidence in its strongest light. Note how such powerful and evocative phrases as "the jumbled bones of an Indian" enhance the persuasiveness of Spotted Elk's message. Look at Lesson 6.4 for other ways you can use language to your advantage. Then use the checklist in Lesson 2.10 to complete your edit.

5. Presenting

Submitting your work to the student newsletter is one way to take your stand, but it isn't the only way. Think about using your article as the starting point for a campaign in support of your position. Could you rework your writing to make it into a speech? A petition? A leaflet? If your writing is truly persuasive, it may have a great deal of impact.

• Reflecting •

Was it easy for you to take a particular stand, or did you see equal validity to a variety of different positions? Record in your journal any insights your reflecting yields about your writing process and persuasive writing.

Portfolio & Reflection

Summary

Key concepts in persuasive writing include the following:

- Persuasive writing involves supporting a claim with a logical argument and accurate, relevant evidence.
- Persuasive writers should avoid red herrings, either/or thinking, or cause-and-effect errors.
- Persuasive language contains limiting words, specific words, and words with appropriate connotations.
- Editorial writers use strong evidence, striking images, and humor.
- Movie reviewers rely on facts, examples, logic, and strong feelings.

Your Writer's Portfolio

Look over the persuasive writing you have done during this unit. Select two pieces of writing to put into your portfolio. Each piece should demonstrate that you have worked with one or more of the preceding concepts. In other words, look for a piece of writing that does one or more of the following:

- supports its claim by presenting logical, accurate, relevant evidence
- uses limiting words, specific words, and words with appropriate connotations
- appeals to an audience by using strong evidence, a striking image, or humor
- uses facts, examples, logic, and strong feelings in reviewing a movie

Reflection and Commentary

Now write one page in which you demonstrate to your reader that you understand what this unit asked of you. Use the two pieces of writing you've selected as evidence while you consider the following numbered items. Respond to as many numbered items as possible in your one-page commentary. Label the page "Commentary on Persuasive Writing," and include it in your portfolio.

1. In your persuasive writing, where did you use strong evidence or logic?
2. What elements show that you were writing for a particular audience?
3. Where does your evidence include the opinion of a reliable authority?
4. Where do you point out logical flaws in an opposing argument?
5. Did you take any risks in your persuasive writing, such as supporting an unpopular idea? If you could do it over, would you take the same risks?
6. What part of your process worked best? What part gave you trouble? How will you work differently in the future?

Feedback

If you had a chance to respond to the following student comment, what would you say or ask?

[Writing is] the most coherent, imaginative, and expressive way of voicing your opinions and being heard.

Sandeep Gangadharan, Edison High School, Edison, New Jersey

Roy Lichtenstein,
Mural with Blue Brushstroke, 1986

A Blueprint for Success

George W. G. Ferris, the man who dreamed up the Ferris wheel, had a great challenge ahead of him: he had to turn his idea into a solid, working structure. After quite a bit of sketching and planning and a step-by-step approach, Ferris finally created this fantastic new contraption, the likes of which the world had never seen before.

In much the same way—with careful planning and a step-by-step approach—you can create a successful and engaging research paper.

Understanding the Research Paper

First of all, what is this project called the research paper? The research paper differs from many other kinds of writing because it includes factual information from a variety of sources. These sources may be primary (records of the people who took part in the event or period you are studying, such as journals, documents, or photos) or secondary (books and articles written about the event or period). And whatever the sources, you can write one of four basic kinds of research paper.

Four Types of Research Paper	
Summary	The writer explores a topic by summing up the opinions of other writers and researchers.
Evaluative	The writer states an opinion and backs it up with evidence found in primary and/or secondary resources.
Original	The writer does original research on a topic and reports on his or her findings.
Combination	The writer combines approaches in one paper, such as summarizing opinions, then conducting original research.

Choosing a Good Topic

One of your first decisions is what to write about. Try to find a topic that interests you, one that you really want to learn about. If your teacher assigns a subject area, go to the library and skim some general articles covering that area in an encyclopedia. Look for any aspects of the subject that relate to your own interests and activities, or any personalities or events that sound intriguing and exciting. These can become topics to explore in the paper.

Also, keep in mind how much information will be manageable given the length of your research paper. If the topic is very broad, you'll have too much information, too many ideas to cover. If the library has a number of books on that particular topic, say, five to ten, or if the encyclopedia gives it more than two pages, the topic is probably too broad for a typical paper. On the other hand, some topics are so narrow that you won't be able to uncover enough material. If you write about such a topic, your paper will probably lack substance (unless you do original research). If you can only find one or two articles on the topic, for example, and if the encyclopedia doesn't cover it, you will almost certainly not have enough to write about.

Too narrow: The gear mechanisms of a Ferris wheel

Appropriate: The history of the Ferris wheel

Too broad: Amusement parks and carnivals

Britta Waller, who wrote the model paper in Lesson 7.6, pages 342–347, was instructed to write about technology in history. She wanted to avoid run-of-the-mill topics but had to choose a subject on which there was enough information to write an adequate paper. After some brainstorming and a trip to the library, she decided to write about the construction of the first Ferris wheel. It seemed an appropriate topic, since authors have devoted sections of books to it, and since she found articles on different aspects of the topic.

Finding Information on Your Topic

Once you have a topic, you need to figure out what you want your paper's central idea to be—the idea that will guide your thinking and your selection of questions to research. You might try to identify three to seven research questions, each question focusing on one aspect of the topic. Ask the *what*'s, *why*'s, and *how*'s about your topic (for example, "Why was this considered so important? What effect did it have on different groups in society? How did it come into being?"). As you begin to find answers, you'll come up with more sharply focused questions. Feel free to modify your central idea as you learn more and more about the topic.

The chart below lists and describes various sources of information for answering your research questions in one area—science and technology.

Basic Sources of Science and Technology Information		
Type	**Description**	**Examples**
Periodicals	Newspapers, magazines, journals, and other sources that are published on a regular basis, either for general readers or for more specialized audiences	*Washington Post* *Scientific American* *National Geographic* *Science Digest* *Discover*
Government Agencies	Branches of federal, state, and local governments that publish reports, statistics, and other information on scientific topics	National Aeronautics and Space Administration U.S. Wildlife Service State and local departments of health
Nonprofit Organizations	Private groups that study certain scientific areas or topics and publish reports and statistics	World Wildlife Fund American Cancer Society American Dental Association Sierra Club
Computer Data Bases	General science information available through computer linkup for a fee	*Applied Science and Technology Index* *General Science Index* *Magazine Index*

Taking Notes

Once you have found some sources, you can begin taking notes and collecting information. Taking notes efficiently and accurately is one of the most important steps in writing a good research paper. You will probably take many more notes than you end up using, but don't worry—so do professional writers and researchers.

Developing a Working Bibliography   As you begin your research, assemble a record of the books, articles, and other sources you consult. This record is your working bibliography. When you find a useful source, record the publishing data on a three-by-five-inch index card, and number it. This way you can find and use the information more easily later. With complete bibliography cards you will also be able to write your final list of works cited more easily.

Different kinds of sources need different data on their bibliography cards, as the samples below illustrate. Notice also that the writer identifies each bibliographic source with a number on its card. This number will serve as an easy way to identify the sources of information on note cards later on.

Editing Tip

When you edit your paper, you can check the accuracy of your spelling, punctuation, and capitalization of titles and authors by referring to your bibliography cards.

Kinds of Bibliography Cards

Book

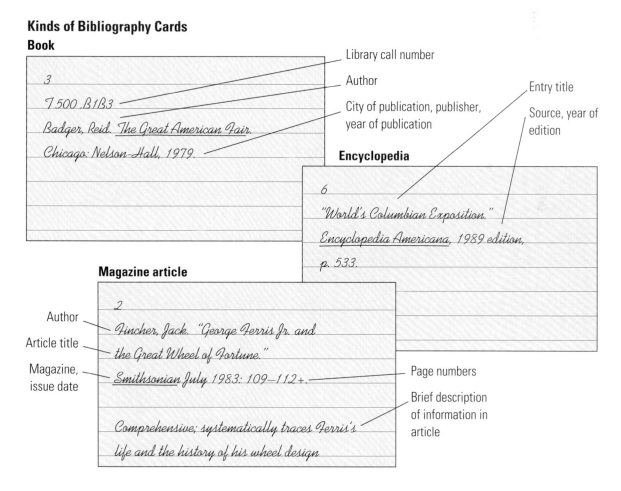

Library call number

Author

City of publication, publisher, year of publication

3

F 500 .B1B3

Badger, Reid. The Great American Fair.

Chicago: Nelson-Hall, 1979.

Encyclopedia

Entry title

Source, year of edition

6

"World's Columbian Exposition."

Encyclopedia Americana, 1989 edition,

p. 533.

Magazine article

Author

Article title

Magazine, issue date

2

Fincher, Jack. "George Ferris Jr. and

the Great Wheel of Fortune."

Smithsonian July 1983: 109–112+.

Comprehensive; systematically traces Ferris's

life and the history of his wheel design

Page numbers

Brief description of information in article

Recording Information   Read your sources thoroughly for information, ideas, statements, and statistics that relate to your research topic. When you find something you can use, write it on a three-by-five card, with one piece of information per card, and record the number of that source's bibliography card. When making these note cards, you can either paraphrase, summarize, or quote the source directly.

International expositions are of recent origin. The first was the Great Exhibition held in London in 1851 which was the scene of Joseph Paxton's Crystal Palace—the first large-scale, prefabricated iron and glass building—which alone attested that fair's significance. From then until 1893 there were several European expositions, probably the most famous being that held in Paris in 1889, celebrated for its Eiffel Tower. The United States had hosted several trade fairs but only one full-scale international exposition, that held in Philadelphia in 1876, the celebration of the centennial of American independence. The World's Columbian Exposition would be the fifteenth world's fair and the second American one. But it was of greater scope than any of its predecessors. Early simply of one large exhibition hall, or of such a hall augmented with the main hall might be artfully devised to lay out the surround-lish the buildings with sculpture Exhibition of 1867 originated both

To paraphrase, you rewrite the information in your own words.

Previous fairs   6
1. London, Great Exhibition, 1851
2. Philadelphia, 1876
3. Paris, 1889
Columbian Exposition was of a much larger scale.

6
Previous fairs
While it was built on the model of the other world's fairs, the 1893 Columbian Exposition was the grandest fair yet.

To summarize, you write down only the main ideas and key supporting material.

To use a passage exactly as written, write the direct quotation as it appears, and put it in quotation marks on your card.

Previous fairs   6
"The World's Columbian Exposition would be the fifteenth world's fair and the second American one. But it was of vastly greater scope than any of its predecessors."
                                        page xii

Reading Sources Critically As you read and research, try to think about sources critically. A source may be biased; that is, the writer may be prejudiced toward one particular viewpoint over others. Using a biased source without recognizing it as such can hurt your argument. To detect bias, ask yourself questions such as, "Does this writer have a hidden purpose?"

When you get to taking specific notes, pay attention to each idea's context, or relation to ideas before and after it. You may even want to note this context on your card. If you use information out of context, you may mislead the reader. For example, a particular nation's political leader might have supported a shift to military rule—but only during wartime. If you don't mention that last fact, you are presenting that leader's position out of context.

Avoiding Plagiarism Presenting someone else's ideas or statements as your own is plagiarism. You must avoid plagiarism—even accidental plagiarism. Writers sometimes accidentally plagiarize when they begin to paraphrase but instead present an idea almost as it was originally written and then take credit for it. The best way to avoid plagiarism is to read your sources critically, keep very complete and well-documented notes, and credit other writers when you should. (See Lesson 7.4, "Citing Sources.") If you have doubts about whether you may be plagiarizing, try rewriting the passage again in your own words, or cite your source.

• ACTIVITIES •
Writer's Choice

The following are some writing options to help you apply what you have learned.

1. From the list of topics below, write an explanation of why each is too broad, too narrow, or about right for a five-page research paper:

- effects of the car on the United States
- 3-D movies—invention and refinement
- latest developments in contact lenses
- building the Great Pyramid of Giza

2. Suppose you wanted to write a report about the development of new, high-definition televisions. Which of the following sources do you think might have useful information on this topic? Choose the two best and the two worst sources, and include a sentence or two explaining each choice.

- *Newsweek* magazine
- *Encyclopaedia Britannica*, 1965
- *TV Guide*
- *Scientific American*
- *The Great Old Movies on TV*
- *Video Technology Review*, this year's annual edition

3. Select a topic for your own research paper—something you really want to know about. Choose any appropriate field for your paper. This will be the paper you will work on throughout the unit. And even though this unit uses examples from science and technology, the basic methods you learn will apply to the writing of any research paper. Begin by writing three to seven research questions. Then prepare bibliography cards, and begin taking notes for your research paper.

Bringing Order to Chaos

WHAT PURE CHAOS! might be your thought, facing your mounds of research notes. But your notes are probably not any more impossible to sort out than is the pile of hardware shown here. All you need to bring order to the chaos is an organizing principle. For example, if you examine the hardware with the idea of function in mind, you might see that you could place all the items that hold things together in one pile, all the items that prevent leaks in another, and so on. Not only can an organizing principle help you bring order to your notes, it can help you develop an outline, which is a particularly useful tool for writing a research paper.

Creating an Outline

If you develop a working outline—one that you continue to write and revise as you conduct your research, you will be better able to think about your topic critically and make your research efficient. The following tips will help you create such an outline.

Tips on Outlining

1. Look for similarities among notes: group note cards on similar topics together. Use each group as a main topic in your outline.

2. Within groups cluster similar note cards into subgroups that elaborate on the larger and more general main topic. Use these subgroups as the subtopics in your outline.

3. Arrange main topics to build on your central idea. And, under each main topic, arrange subtopics so they elaborate on the main topic in a logical way.

4. As you continue your research and learn more, revise and elaborate in your outline, subdividing information in subtopics into outline entries as well.

5. Set aside note cards that don't fit under any heading.

6. Before you begin your first draft, prepare a final outline.

```
                  Title of Paper
     I. Main Topic
        A. Subtopic
           1. Division of a subtopic
              a. Subdivision of a subtopic
              b. Subdivision of a subtopic
           2. Division of a subtopic
              a. Subdivision of a subtopic
              b. Subdivision of a subtopic
        B. Subtopic
    II. Main Topic
```

Number main topics with Roman numerals.

Notice the lettering, numbering, and indentation systems for subtopics and their divisions and subdivisions.

A subtopic doesn't have to have any subdivisions. But if you list any at all, you must list at least two.

How can you decide on the best way to arrange the ideas in your notes? Since ideas can be divided up many different ways, you have a number of options, depending on the nature of your information. In a history paper you might arrange ideas chronologically. In a science paper you might arrange ideas in causal order to show how one idea or event directly determines another, or in logical order to show how the presence of one item or idea makes another reasonably predictable. Britta Waller, writing on a topic that combines history and technology, creates an outline that proceeds from general to specific.

```
                George W. G. Ferris
        The Man Who Re-invented the Wheel

     I.  Background of 1893 Columbian Exposition
         A. Continued tradition of big fairs
            1. Previous world's fairs
               a. London and the Crystal Palace,
                  1851
               b. Philadelphia, 1876
               c. Paris and the Eiffel Tower, 1889
            2. Chicago fair to be larger than
               earlier fairs
         B. Emphasized cultural achievements
            1. Planners D. H. Burnham and
               F. L. Olmsted
            2. Nation's top artists, inventors,
               industrialists
         C. Reflected values of the era
    II.  Background of George W. G. Ferris
```

Britta provides a chronological account of the years leading up to the 1893 fair.

In what order does Britta present her topics? Is this a good way to arrange this paper?

Developing a Thesis Statement

So far, you have guided your research and outline according to your central idea, or the basic questions you've been exploring. You've probably rethought this idea as you have learned about the topic. Now, as you get ready to begin your first draft, it's time to turn that central idea into a thesis statement—that is, a concise idea that you try to prove, expand on, or illustrate in your writing. This statement gives your writing a focus from start to finish.

To create a thesis statement, look at your central idea critically. Is it as clear as it can be? Does it include all important aspects of your topic? Does it include historical background or new developments if these are relevant? Does it make the significance of your topic clear?

After asking these and other similar sorts of questions, write the idea again as a single sentence that describes your topic more precisely. This time include a mention of your approach to the topic. Are you comparing one topic with another, exploring a single topic in depth, trying to prove or disprove any common notions?

Now follow the chart below as it progresses from central idea to thesis statement.

Revising Tip

Thesis statements are often compound sentences. To review how to create compound sentences, see Lesson 13.3 in Grammar, Usage, and Mechanics, pages 490–491.

Example of a central idea:
The Ferris wheel was a unique engineering feat when it was constructed.

Examples of revising a central idea:
1. The Ferris wheel, a unique engineering feat in its day, came on the scene in time to help assert American superiority over Europe and became the most popular attraction at the Columbian Exposition.
2. The Ferris wheel, a unique engineering feat, was conceived at a time when America needed to show its superiority over Europe, but the wheel became the most popular attraction at the Columbian Exposition, overshadowing the many cultural exhibits.

Example of a thesis statement:
The unique engineering feat of the Ferris wheel was one of many assertions of American pride at the World's Columbian Exposition, but its huge popularity overshadowed the fair's other cultural attractions.

The chart below explains the four basic kinds of thesis statements you can use and shows you an example of each.

Four Types of Thesis Statements		
Type	**Description**	**Example**
Original	Describes the background and results of original research to be presented in the paper	My survey of students and teachers at Lincoln High School has uncovered a desire for more and better computers and more instruction in computer science.
Evaluative	Identifies an issue and evaluates opinions on the issue that the writer will convey through the paper	Solar power provides our best option for future energy needs, taking into account both economic and environmental concerns.
Summary	Introduces the different perspectives on a topic for a paper that primarily summarizes the work of others	High-speed trains, traveling at speeds greater than 125 miles per hour, have revolutionized intercity travel in both France and Japan.
Combination	Combines any two or all three of the above approaches	Interviews with music-store salespeople and compact disc owners lead me to believe that the CD represents the future of the recording industry.

• ACTIVITIES •
Writer's Choice

The following are some writing options to help you apply what you have learned.

1. Organize the following pieces of information into three different categories. Then supply an outline heading for each, with subheadings. The outline should be appropriate for a six- to ten-page paper explaining lasers to a nonexpert audience.

- Laser stands for *l*ight *a*mplification by *s*timulated *e*mission of *r*adiation.
- Lasers can be used in surgery.
- CD players use lasers to "read" compact discs.
- A laser creates a narrow beam of monochromatic and coherent light.
- Holograms rely on laser technology for their effects.

- Stores use lasers to ring up purchases.
- Lasers help guide some "smart" bombs to their targets.
- Laser light is the result of a chain reaction of atoms discharging photons.
- Manufacturing industries use lasers to inspect the quality of their products.

2. Rewrite the following into a concise, single-sentence thesis statement:

The race to put an astronaut on the moon had numerous motivations. Many people thought it was a waste of money. Yet the space program has resulted in many inventions and technologies that improve our lives.

3. Prepare a working outline and a thesis statement for your own research paper.

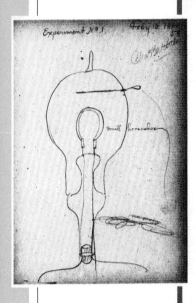

Getting Your Ideas Down on Paper

Think of the simple light bulb—something we take for granted. Yet the light bulb was once just an idea in the mind of Thomas Edison. To make his idea a reality, Edison had to do research, make plans, examine the research of others, and then carefully refine his work.

A research paper requires much the same effort. Even as you turn your outline and notes into a draft, you still need to experiment, ask new questions, and refine your ideas.

Going from Outlining to Drafting

From the structure you have given your outline, you will now be able to transform your piles of notes into a first draft. Give your outline another look, and be sure you're satisfied with the way in which each idea leads to the next. Then begin drafting. The chart on the next page, "Some Tips on Drafting," may be helpful.

Sources

Anderson, Norman D. and Walter R. Brown. *Ferris Wheels*. New York: Pantheon, 1983.

Fincher, Jack. "George Ferris Jr. and the Great Wheel of Fortune." *Smithsonian* July 1983.

Lee, William H. *Beautiful Scenes of the White City*. Chicago: Laird and Lee, 1894.

Notes

Admission 50 cents, the same as admission to fair. Still, 1.5 million rode it.
—Fincher, p. 14

Twenty-minute ride for 50 cents; two revolutions, six stops each time around; ran 8 A.M.–11 P.M.
—Anderson and Brown, p. 24

Lit by 3,000 electric bulbs at night, powered by generator in boiler house
—Anderson and Brown, p. 24

1. Set aside a couple of hours to begin writing. Find a quiet place where you won't be distracted.

2. Try to draft as smoothly and logically as possible without getting stalled on details. Don't worry about finding the "perfect" word or phrase; you can revise later.

3. Write at least one paragraph for each heading in your outline. Each paragraph should have a topic sentence and supporting details.

4. When you use data from a note card, write the number of that card near the data in the text to help you document the idea.

Drafting Tip

In your first draft, indicate the source of each borrowed idea by placing the author's name and the note card number in parentheses after that idea.

You don't have to include information from every note card in your draft. In fact, as the diagram shows, you are likely to develop the ideas from several note cards into one or two outline entries, and likewise into one or two ideas in your paper. As you put these ideas into your paper, identify the source of every borrowed idea, and try to use your own words wherever possible.

As you draft, use your outline as a "map" to help guide you in your writing. The outline should remind you of what comes before or after a particular idea. Furthermore, the outline should suggest the links, or transitions, you might use in your writing. After all, you have already begun linking ideas in your outline; now simply carry on that process, as the diagram below illustrates.

Outline

III. Specifics of Ferris Wheel
   A. Dimensions
   B. Built on principle of the bicycle wheel
   C. Riding
      1. Admission
      2. Hours
      3. Huge number of people riding
      4. Enthusiastic public response
IV. Early Criticism

Paragraph

A twenty-minute ride, or two revolutions with six stops each time around, cost 50 cents. The wheel ran from 8 A.M. to 11 P.M. At night, the wheel was lit by 3,000 electric light bulbs powered by a generator in the boiler house of the wheel (Anderson and Brown 24). One-and-one-half million people had ridden the wheel by Fair's end—a good number considering that the 50-cent fee was equal to admission (Fincher 14).

Handling Information

Now that you're ready to write your first draft, read the chart below for solutions to some common drafting problems.

Revising Tip

Reviewing the lessons on the parts of a sentence in Unit 11 in Grammar, Usage, and Mechanics, pages 449–459, may help you vary your sentence structure.

Solving Drafting Problems	
Problem	**Solution**
How can I overcome "writer's block" on my first draft?	Just begin writing and get the ideas down. Try writing for five minutes on whatever comes into your mind. Then, you'll be looser and ready to write your draft.
Do I have to write the first part of the paper first, the second part second, and so on?	Write any way that is easiest for you. If you write out of sequence, pay close attention to the transitions between sections as you revise.
What can I do with all these notes I have?	Set aside any note that duplicates another or is irrelevant to the main idea.
I have many notes on some aspects of my topic but few on others. What should I do?	Do more research, or look at your outline to see if you can write a good paper with the notes you now have. If so, revise your outline.
How can I avoid running out of time before I get very far into my writing?	Set aside at least three hours just for writing your paper. Eliminate distractions by going to a quiet place.
How can I best create transitions between my paragraphs?	Identify one major similarity or difference between the paragraphs. Try linking the paragraphs with a short phrase or sentence describing how they are similar or different.
What can I do to avoid being bogged down correcting spelling and grammar?	Ignore these problems until the next revision.

Writing Introductions and Conclusions

A good introduction should present your topic and approach. It should grab the attention of your readers and make them want to read on. Including an unusual anecdote or a quotation from an eyewitness can help you do this. Britta Waller begins her paper on the Ferris wheel with a quotation: "Ferris is a crackpot. He has wheels in his head."

Your conclusion should also be intriguing, but additionally it should alert the reader that you are wrapping up. You might return to your thesis statement and summarize your points. Or you might mention any new questions your paper raises. Britta concludes by recounting the "true achievement" of Ferris's magnificent wheel.

• ACTIVITIES •
Writer's Choice

The following are some writing options to help you apply what you have learned.

1. Based on the following outline entry and notes, write a few paragraphs on the subject of the elimination of yellow fever. Imagine that your audience is a high school U.S. history class and your purpose is to give them an interesting sidelight on the early 1900s.

    I. Eradication of yellow fever
      A. Walter Reed sent to Cuba
        1. Knows about Carlos Finlay's theories
        2. Sets up experiments
          a. Volunteer doctors and soldiers are intentionally infected and survive.
          b. Two others are infected accidentally and die.
          c. Experiments show disease is carried by mosquito.
      B. William Gorgas establishes mosquito control measures around Havana.

1881: Cuban physician Carlos Finlay suggests that a certain breed of mosquito carried the yellow fever disease.

1900: U.S. Army surgeon Walter Reed was sent to Cuba to investigate an epidemic of yellow fever among the U.S. troops there.

Reed's fellow doctors and a number of soldiers volunteered for rather unconventional experiments:
- Each was injected with yellow fever germs to study how the disease proceeds through the body.
- All those intentionally injected contracted the disease but survived.
- Two people who were infected accidentally came down with the disease and died.

Reed's experiments proved for certain that the disease was transmitted by the mosquito rather than by casual contact.

1905: Army physician William Gorgas developed and implemented measures to control mosquitoes, eliminating the disease as a major threat in Havana. These measures included spraying insecticide and draining pools of stagnant water where the mosquitoes bred.

Walter Reed and William Gorgas indirectly made the Panama Canal a reality. Their work enabled the elimination of yellow fever in the Canal Zone.

The identification of the source of yellow fever has rightfully been called one of the greatest achievements of modern medicine.

2. Prepare a first draft of your own research paper.

Giving Credit
Where Credit Is Due

While Ferris developed his wheel, others worked on some of the earliest automobiles. Yet while the Ferris wheel has remained about the same, the automobile has gone through amazing changes. The photo above and to the left shows Henry Ford's early Model T, while the one on the right shows a "car of the future." Suppose you're writing a research paper about cars. For what kinds of information must you cite, or document, your sources? Most people know that Ford was one of the auto's early developers. You won't have to cite such common knowledge in your paper. But for information not so widely known, such as features planned for future cars, you need to document the source.

Documenting Information

In a research paper you need to be quite careful to indicate the sources of the information you present—including all ideas, statements, quotes, and statistics that you take from your sources and that are not common knowledge. One reason for documenting your sources is to enable the reader to judge how believable or important a piece of information is by checking the source. Another reason for proper documentation is to avoid plagiarism, as discussed in Lesson 7.1, page 321.

But what information needs documentation? You should document your information whenever you use someone's exact words, or whenever you paraphrase a particular idea or series of ideas. You should also document any information that is not generally known or found in most books on the subject. Look at the chart below for tips on citing sources.

Documenting Your Information		
Information	**Citation?**	**Explanation**
"No single enterprise on the midway or the grounds proper approached it either in patronage or in wonderment."	Yes	Direct quotations reflect an author's opinion. Readers may want to check the source for bias.
The fair signified economic ambition, the rise of the city, and rapid change.	Yes	This is a paraphrase of another author's opinion or research.
Ironically, there was a focus on cultural enlightenment and achievement.	No	This is a paraphrase of general information found in many sources.
The Ferris wheel cost $400,000 to build and turned a total profit of $733,086.	Yes	Specific cost and profitability of Ferris's wheel are not common knowledge.
The 1893 Columbian Exposition commemorated the four hundredth anniversary of Columbus's historic voyage.	No	This is common knowledge that would appear in most sources on the fair.
Ferris's name was forever matched with later machines.	No	Most people are aware that such rides are referred to as Ferris wheels.

Formatting Citations Properly

You can cite your sources in one of three basic formats: parenthetical documentation, footnotes, or endnotes. Your teacher may have a preference and assign one style for your paper, but each format serves the same purpose—to tell where you obtained your information.

Place each citation as close as possible after the idea, statement, or quotation in the text, to let your reader know what is being cited. You should generally place the citation where a pause would naturally occur, such as at the end of a sentence or after a comma.

When you wrote your first draft, you included author names and note card numbers for all the material you used from the cards. Now simply replace this information with complete citations in parentheses, or with consecutive numbers for footnotes or endnotes. For the rest of the information needed in footnotes or endnotes, refer to your bibliography cards.

Parenthetical Documentation   One way to cite sources is to insert the author's name and a page reference in parentheses after the information from that author. Britta Waller uses this method. If the author is obvious from the text (for example, if the text reads "As Ferguson points out, . . ."), then you can merely insert the page number in parentheses. The chart below shows other forms of parenthetical documentation.

Examples of Parenthetical Documentation

1. (Fincher 110)
Used when the source has a sole author, and only one work by that person is used in the paper. In our model paper this note refers to page 110 of the magazine article by Jack Fincher. If no single author is listed for a book or other source, use the name of the editor.

2. (Anderson and Brown 18)
Used when the work cited has more than one author. If your source has three or more authors, just give the last name of the first author listed, followed by *et al.* ("and others"), such as (Lincoln et al. 151).

3. (*Dream City*)
When no author or editor is listed for the source, abbreviate the source's title for citation. This citation is for *The Dream City: A Portfolio of Photographic Views*. Since the book has no page numbers, *n.p.* is used in place of a page reference.

4. (Badger, *American Fair* 14)
When the paper uses more than one work by the same author, abbreviate the book's title, and insert it after the author's name. If our model paper had used two books by Reid Badger, the citation for his book *The Great American Fair* might be made as shown above.

5. (Lee; Anderson and Brown 26)
When you cite more than one source at the same place, include both sources, and separate them with a semicolon.

Footnotes   A footnote is a reference at the bottom of the text page that contains the information you are citing. You indicate the reference with a raised number, or superscript, and number notes consecutively throughout the paper. The footnote, unlike parenthetical documentation, contains the information from the bibliography card. Once you have cited a source, you can refer to it again in another footnote by using just the author's last name and the page reference.

Endnotes   You format endnotes similarly to footnotes. However, you put endnotes on a separate page at the end of your paper instead of on the page with the documented material. Type your endnotes double-spaced, and present them under the heading "Notes."

Examples of Footnote and Endnote Entries

1. **Book with one author**
   David F. Burg, *Chicago's White City of 1893* (Lexington: UP of Kentucky, 1976) xii.

2. **Book with more than one author**
   Norman D. Anderson and Walter R. Brown, *Ferris Wheels* (New York: Pantheon, 1983) 16.

3. **Magazine article**
   Kate Holliday, "Big Wheels of the Fun Business," *Popular Mechanics* Mar. 1969: 229.

4. **Encyclopedia article**
   "World's Columbian Exposition," *Encyclopedia Americana*, 1989 ed.

5. **Article by an author in a book with an editor**
   Bernard S. Finn, "Electricity," *1876: A Centennial Exhibition*, ed. Robert C. Post (Washington D.C.: Smithsonian, 1976) 63.

6. **Book with an editor but no author**
   Frank H. Norton, ed., *Frank Leslie's Illustrated Historical Register of the Centennial Exposition* (New York: Frank Leslie's Publishing House, 1877) 29.

7. **Newspaper article**
   Ida Louise Huxtable, "You Can't Go Home to Those Fairs Again," *New York Times,* 28 Oct. 1973: Section II, p. 27, Col. 1.

8. **Unsigned article**
   "Higher Aspects of the Columbian Exposition," *Dial*, 1 Nov. 1892: 263–65.

9. **Pamphlet with no specified author**
   A Week at the Fair Illustrating Exhibits and Wonders of the World's Columbian Exposition (Chicago: Rand McNally, 1893) 163.

Editing Tip

Remember to underline or italicize titles of books, periodicals, and pamphlets. For more information see Lesson 21.10 in Grammar, Usage, and Mechanics, pages 687–688.

Formatting Your List of Works Cited

Whether you cite your sources with parenthetical documentation, footnotes, or endnotes, your paper should include a complete list of the sources you used. This is your list of works cited, and, unlike your working bibliography, it contains only those sources that you use in your final version. While you may have consulted many additional sources for background and other general information, these sources shouldn't be included on this final list unless you use and cite ideas or data from the source in your paper.

From your bibliography cards, record all the publishing information about the source. Alphabetize the source according to the last name of the author or editor (or the first name listed, if there is more than one). If you use more than one work by the same author, you need not repeat the author's name for each entry; use a dash instead. If the source has no author or editor, alphabetize the entry by the title of the book or article. The proper bibliographic style for various sources is shown below.

Compiling a List of Works Cited	
Source	**Entry**
Book with Single Author	Badger, Reid. *The Great American Fair*. Chicago: Nelson-Hall, 1979.
Book with Multiple Authors	Anderson, Norman D. and Walter R. Brown. *Ferris Wheels*. New York: Pantheon, 1983.
Magazine Article	Fincher, Jack. "George Ferris Jr. and the Great Wheel of Fortune." *Smithsonian* July 1983: 109–112+.
Encyclopedia Article	"World's Columbian Exposition." *Encyclopedia Americana*, 1989 ed.
Newspaper Article	"The Rays Take in the Columbian Exposition." *Chicago Tribune* 26 July 1984, sec. 5: 2.

Student Model

Works Cited

Anderson, Norman D., and Walter R. Brown. *Ferris Wheels*. New York: Pantheon, 1983.

Badger, Reid. *The Great American Fair*. Chicago: Nelson-Hall, 1979.

Burg, David F. *Chicago's White City of 1893*. Lexington: UP Kentucky, 1976. ➡

For works with more than one author, reverse the name of the first author only.

Indent text that runs more than one line.

The Dream City: A Portfolio of Photographic Views. St. Louis:
N. D. Thompson, 1893.

Fincher, Jack. "George Ferris Jr. and the Great Wheel of
Fortune." *Smithsonian* July 1983: 109–112+.

Holliday, Kate. "Big Wheels of the Fun Business." *Popular
Mechanics* Mar. 1969: 144–146+.

Howells, William Dean. *Letters of an Altrurian Traveller (1893–
1894).* Gainesville: Scholars' Facsimiles and Reprints, 1961.

Lee, William H. *Beautiful Scenes of the White City.* Chicago:
Laird and Lee, 1894.

"World's Columbian Exposition." *Encyclopedia Americana.*
1989 ed.

> *When alphabetizing a work by its title, ignore the words* a, an, *and* the.

> *Include the edition of the encyclopedia.*

• ACTIVITIES •
Writer's Choice

The following are some writing options to help you apply what you have learned.

1. For each of the following pieces of information, tell whether you think source documentation is necessary and explain why:

- Many more calls can be handled by cellular mobile phone service than were handled by earlier systems.
- The first licenses to build and operate mobile telephone systems were granted in 1982.
- Many advances in telephone technology have taken place since Alexander Graham Bell invented the receiver in 1876.
- One author laments, "Cellular phone technology eliminates one more place— inside your own car—where you can be free from interruptions."
- Most Americans today cannot conceive of life without the telephone.
- As a car equipped with a phone travels from cell to cell, the call is transferred via computer from one transmitter and receiver to another without interrupting the call.

- Cellular phones are convenient for people such as sales agents who are often out of the office.

2. Write proper entries for a list of works cited for the following sources:

- an article from the 1990 edition of the *World Book Encyclopedia* on jet propulsion engines
- an article entitled "The Concorde Tests the Skies," written by Janet Feldman, which appeared on page 30 of *Newsweek* on August 14, 1975
- an article by John Simons entitled "Breakthroughs in Jet Technology," which appeared on pages 70–84 of the book *Aviation and Space*, edited by M. W. Wister and published in New York by Little, Brown in 1982
- a book written by Richard Samson entitled *Jet Engine Basics*, published by MIT Press in Boston in 1975

3. Prepare a working bibliography of the sources you are using in your research paper.

Making a Good Product Even Better

"Mr. Watson, come here. I want you!" said Alexander Graham Bell—the first sentence ever uttered over his new invention, the telephone. Yet despite this success, Bell continued to work on his invention and refine it so that it would communicate even better. Likewise, the first draft of your research paper will also "communicate" even better after you revise it.

Improving Your Paper

When you revise your first draft, you can improve your choice of words, your transitions, and most importantly, the way you present your ideas. The following chart may help you do these things.

Solving Revision Problems	
Problem	**Solution**
How can I give my first draft a clearer focus?	Review your thesis statement; delete or rewrite anything in the paper that doesn't support it.
How can I make my argument easier to follow?	Add transitions, rearrange, and add ideas to make the paper more coherent. Delete irrelevant information.
How can I make my paragraphs flow smoothly from one to another?	Add or change transitions between paragraphs; rearrange paragraphs in a more logical order.
What if my introduction doesn't connect well with the rest of the paper?	Add transitions or rewrite introduction to conform with the purpose and main idea.
What can I do if my sentences sound repetitive?	Vary sentence structure. Use precise, lively language. Find synonyms for repeated words.

Now take a look at some samples of the kind of revising you might need to do on your own research paper. First, look at the model below, which traces revision of two paragraphs. Consider the reasons behind the different revisions. Next, on page 338, follow the stages in the smaller-scale revision of one particular passage from another part of the same paper.

The Ferris wheel's ~~was very~~ popular*ity*. ~~This~~ was due to the ~~popularity of the Midway.~~ (The Midway provided (escape) both from ~~the pressure and pains of~~ real life and from the ^of^ culture ~~that was so~~ (overwhelming) ~~in~~ the rest of the Fair. Couples ^rushed^ ~~went~~ to be married at the top of the wheel, but the closest they got was the superintendent's office *on the ground below*. ~~Rumors were started in the~~ newspapers *started rumors* of the wheel losing parts that then hurtled to the ground below; ~~Other rumors~~ *or they* told of the mechanism locking in place, *trapping* ~~with~~ the wheel's passengers ~~trapped~~ up in the air with no help. ^As^ ~~T~~his never happened. Such publicity made the *gigantic toy* ~~wheel~~ only more popular. (Howells 25). "No single enterprise on the Midway or the grounds proper approached it either in patronage or in wonderment" (Fincher 114).

The wheel did have its critics.
Howells accused the wheel of being a mere money-making contrivance--an ex-

Change redundant sentence structures to make the paragraph more concise.

Does this change improve the paper? Why or why not?

Combine sentences that have the same subjects.

Why move this quotation?

Transition helps shift tone between paragraphs.

Draft sentence contains a basic fact, but the topic sentence isn't clear.

In an era hoping for a better world, grand engineering projects concentrated on building things other than weapons.

First revision sets off the topic sentence and explains the era, with the modern reader in mind. Supporting details add color and connect sentence ideas to the paper's topic.

The 1890s and early 1900s were marked by a general wish for a better world. Engineering projects focused on new marvels of iron and steel, such as the Ferris wheel, instead of weapons.

How does the choice of words and quotations improve this passage? What does revising the organization accomplish?

The 1890s and early 1900s were marked by a universal wish for a better world, and most of all, "a world without war." Steel and iron were shaped into engineering marvels, such as the Ferris wheel, rather than weapons.

Revising a Science Paper

When you write a research paper on a scientific subject, you need to pay particularly close attention to certain questions. Presenting scientific data often requires even more precision than presenting other kinds of information, so you need to double-check any data you cite. Make certain that you use the most up-to-date information possible. If your topic is very current, look for more journal, magazine, and newspaper articles for late-breaking developments, and rely more heavily on these sources. Be sure you use specialized terms precisely; you may even want to use direct quotations from sources.

If you are using the research of others to draw your own conclusions on a topic, you have to be sure that the research is valid. Look closely at your sources to be sure that they are free from possible bias and that they have made logical, convincing arguments. Also, look at your own argument to be sure it is logical and complete. Science papers deal in facts, but facts can be arranged in confusing or illogical ways. Think about ways your information could be misinterpreted, and revise to make your meaning clearer.

Drafting Tip

Many science papers are best organized in either causal or logical order. See Lesson 7.2, page 323, to review various methods of organization.

Checklist for Revising a Science Paper

1. Have I defined or explained technical terms adequately?

2. Have I used the latest information on the subject I can find?

3. Have all sources for quotations, theories, and technical information been credited properly?

4. Have I explained the scientific processes and reasoning so that an average reader can understand them?

5. Have I considered the validity of any opposing viewpoints? If those views contain important perspectives on my topic, have I mentioned them?

6. Have I considered any possible developments that may occur in the near future that may have an effect on my argument?

• ACTIVITIES •
Writer's Choice

The following are some writing activities to help you apply what you have learned.

1. Revise the following passages for clarity, coherence, and readability:

Passage A

Compact discs are made of plastic. They are coated with aluminum so that the signals can be read by a laser. Then the aluminum is coated in more plastic to protect the pits. Music is recorded on a compact disc in a series of minute pits of varying depths in an outward spiral. In the CD player a low-intensity laser is directed at the pits in their track. As the laser is alternately reflected or scattered off the pits, an optical sensor picks up these signals and converts the signals into sound impulses. Unlike long-playing records, which are played with styluses, the laser never touches the CD, so the CD doesn't wear down or scratch. Also, dust and fingerprints do not distort the laser beam. This results in almost no distortion in the playback. Not, surprisingly, CD recordings have become more popular than vinyl records.

Passage B

The first step for a spacecraft is to break away from Earth's gravity. This is a matter of speed, which is called the escape velocity. The craft ascends into interplanetary space.

A craft going 25,000 miles per hour is released from Earth's gravitational pull. Then no force works to keep the spacecraft up. Gravity from Earth and the Sun are still working to pull the craft down. As the craft gets farther from Earth, that planet's pull on it weakens. The gravity of the Sun takes over. The craft is pulled into a solar orbit.

To reach the planets then, a spacecraft must leave Earth at a speed greater than escape velocity. Much velocity is used up in getting away from Earth. There must be enough velocity for the spacecraft to escape Earth's gravity, and enough left over to speed the spacecraft to another planet. The extra velocity makes the spacecraft orbit the Sun at a different speed than Earth does.

2. Use what you have learned in this lesson to revise the paper you have been working on throughout this unit.

The Final Product

George W. G. Ferris's marvelous wheel was at last a reality. After much planning and research, after construction and testing, Ferris put the finishing touches on his wheel and opened it to the public. And his efforts truly paid off, as the Ferris wheel became a symbol of nineteenth-century technological ingenuity and the world-renowned centerpiece of Chicago's 1893 Columbian Exposition.

In the same way, after much planning, research, and writing, you are about to put the finishing touches on your paper. With these final touches you should have a complete and clean research paper, one ready for presentation to your teacher and classmates.

Preparing the Final Copy

After revising your draft, type or print a new copy of it with your corrections included. Then you can give your paper one final proofreading, checking citations, grammar, spelling, punctuation, and word use. The checklist below can help you catch any remaining problems or mistakes. For extra help review Lesson 2.10, pages 98–101, and Unit 9 in Grammar, Usage, and Mechanics, pages 377–400.

Final Copy Checklist

1. Have I organized my ideas clearly?

2. Have I explained or defined any words that may be unfamiliar to the reader?

3. Have I discussed my topic completely and fairly?

4. Have I corrected all grammar and spelling mistakes?

5. Have I documented my sources properly?

6. Have I considered the proper meaning(s) of the words I've used?

7. Have I spelled and capitalized everything correctly?

8. Have I prepared a neat and easy-to-read final copy?

Prewriting Tip

During the prewriting stage, you may want to refer to the Final Copy Checklist on this page to remind yourself of the kinds of details you will want to gather and document carefully.

Presenting the Complete Paper

Most research papers have a cover sheet, as shown here, containing the title of the paper as well as the writer's name and other identifying information. Your teacher may also ask you for other material to check the extent of your research and the construction of your paper. You may be asked to include a clean copy of your final outline. You can prepare this according to the structure discussed in Lesson 7.2, pages 322–323. If you type up your outline, do not include the introduction or conclusion.

Your teacher may ask you to include a summary statement. This is basically a brief restatement of your thesis statement, no more than two sentences long and inserted before the main body of your text. Your teacher may also ask you to include an annotated list of works cited, which is simply your final list of works cited, with each source followed by your own remarks on the source's content and usefulness.

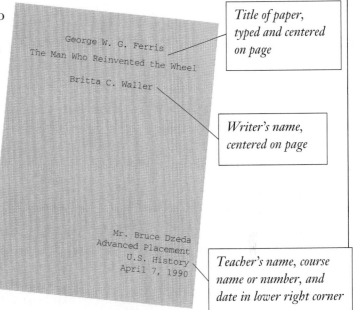

George W. G. Ferris
The Man Who Reinvented the Wheel

Britta C. Waller

Mr. Bruce Dzeda
Advanced Placement
U.S. History
April 7, 1990

Title of paper, typed and centered on page

Writer's name, centered on page

Teacher's name, course name or number, and date in lower right corner

---

• ACTIVITIES •
Writer's Choice

The following are some writing options to help you apply what you have learned.

1. Identify the grammatical mistakes in each of the following sentences, and correct them:

- Scientists should be sure that experiments do not merely reinforce his preconceived ideas.
- Henry Ford is aware of the European experiments in creating a "horseless carriage." He knew about them for many years when he began his work.
- Experiments in astronomy is difficult for people not having access to equipment.
- People are often unaware of the scientific advance that take place in the era they live in.

2. Edit the following entries for a final list of works cited. You may need to refer to Lesson

7.4, pages 330–335, to review the proper forms of different types of entries.

- Encyclopaedia Britannica, 1991 ed., Cardiovascular System Diseases and Disorders.
- Cooke, Alistair. Alistair Cooke's America. Alfred A. Knopf, New York: 1973
- John Molinari, Hurricane Prediction: Catching the Waves, Science News, 21 October 1989, p. 262

3. Read the research paper by Britta Waller on pages 342–347. Then write a summary statement, about two sentences long, explaining the topic and purpose of her paper.

4. Use what you have learned in this lesson to complete and present the final version of your own term paper.

GEORGE W. G. FERRIS
THE MAN WHO REINVENTED THE WHEEL

Britta C. Waller

"Ferris is a crackpot. He has wheels in his head."
(Anderson and Brown 16)

Why do you suppose Britta includes a quotation here?

Even officials of the famous World's Columbian Exhibition of 1893, such as the one quoted above, seemed to think that George Washington Gale Ferris's idea for an industrial monument to rival the Eiffel Tower was far-fetched, if not downright insane. Yet, when it was finally finished, Ferris's colossal wheel embodied the "can-do optimism" of the Exhibition (Fincher 109), America's industrial dominance, the American dream, and the flexibility of a capitalistic society. This paper will discuss turn-of-the-century America, how these times inspired the World's Columbian Exposition, and the birth, demise, and significance of the great Ferris wheel.

Is the thesis statement effective? Why or why not?

The 1890s and early 1900s were marked by a universal wish for a better world, and most of all, "a world without war" (Fincher 109). Steel and iron were shaped into engineering marvels, such as the Ferris wheel, rather than weapons. Chicago's World's Columbian Exposition of 1893 commemorated the 400th anniversary of Columbus's historic voyage and was the largest, most elaborate, and most magnificent World's Fair ever. The first international exposition was London's Great Exhibition of 1851, boasting Joseph Paxton's Crystal Palace—the first large scale iron and glass building and the ancestor of the modern skyscraper. The first American exposition was held in Philadelphia in 1876 to celebrate the country's centennial. However, it was the Paris Exhibition of 1889 that inspired the World's Columbian (Burg xii). Paris had produced the world-famous Eiffel Tower. America couldn't let Europe have all the limelight. In fact, this national rivalry was one of the prime moving forces behind the Fair. In addition, the Fair signified economic ambition, the rise of the city, and rapid progressive change (Badger 10). Ironically, there was a focus on cultural enlightenment and achievement. Buildings were in the "Greco-Roman-Oriental" style (Fincher 110). Under the direction of Chicago architect Daniel H. Burnham and landscape architect Frederick Law Olmsted, the ➡

Paper should be typed double-spaced, with one-inch margins on all sides.

Parenthetical documentation

nation's best sculptors, architects, painters, writers, and musicians joined with industrialists and inventors to put their best work into the Exposition. Its achievement in the arts far surpassed its historical significance: "We have put aside individual taste and have united in an effort to carry out the several parts of a design which . . . was dominated by one idea," wrote Professor Halsey C. Ives, the Chief of the Department of Fine Arts (*Dream City*). The dual nature—industry and culture combined—of the Fair was a direct reflection of the era. Henry Steele Commager called the decade of the 1890s a watershed in American history:

> On the one side lies an America predominantly agricultural; concerned with domestic problems; conforming, intellectually, at least, to the political, economic, and moral principles inherited from the 17th and 18th centuries. . . . On the other side lies the modern America, predominantly urban and industrial; inextricably involved in world economy and politics . . . experiencing profound changes in population, social institutions, economy, and technology; and trying to accommodate its traditional institutions and habits of thought to conditions new and in part alien (Burg xiii).

Set off any quotations longer than three lines by indenting the entire passage.

The cultural idealism of the Fair was embodied in its alternate title—"The White City," so named because of a substance called "staff" which covered many of the buildings. Composed of plaster of Paris and jute fibers, staff closely resembled white marble ("World's Columbian Exposition" 533). Author William Dean Howells praised the Fair as "the perfect embodiment of human ingenuity and Christian brotherhood—the ideal of Grecian democracy in industrial America" (vii–viii). Howells saw the Fair as a glimpse of the future of America, and as a departure from the "Age of Accumulation"—a term he used to denounce the period before World War I (xii).

Including the author's name in the text lets Britta use only the page number in the parenthetical note.

However, Howells's altruistic ideals were pushed aside in favor of the Midway Plaisance, and its Queen—the Ferris wheel.

Early in 1892, Ferris sat quietly at Burnham's planning session for the fabulous exposition. A tunnel and trestle engineer and bridge builder from Pittsburgh, Ferris was 33 years old, tall, slim, and pale, with a bushy black moustache and a "resolute face" (Fincher 110). Born the eighth child of a Nevada farmer, Ferris attended military school in Oakland, California, at age 16 and attended college at Rensselaer Polytechnic ➡

Institute (RPI) in Troy, New York. Graduating in 1881, Ferris
was said to have a great ability to meet a challenge. Burnham
told those who assembled at the planning session: "Mere big-
ness is not what is wanted. . . . something novel, original, daring and unique must be designed and built if American
engineers are to retain their prestige and standing" (Fincher
110). An evening soon after, Ferris sketched the design for his
famous amusement ride on a scrap of paper at a Chicago
restaurant. He determined all aspects of the wheel—size,
number of passengers, price of admission—in his original
sketch. He had "re-invented the wheel . . . big" (Fincher 110).

Ferris's wheel was 264 feet high and supported by two
140-foot pyramid-shaped steel towers (Burg 224). The wheel
was 26 stories high, taller than any building on the grounds. It
weighed, fully loaded, approximately 1,200 tons, or as much
as three Boeing 747s (Fincher 111–112). Thirty-six passenger
cars were suspended between two steel rims. Made of wood
and iron, paneled with plate glass windows, and furnished
with swivel chairs, the cars were approximately the size of
train passenger cars (Burg 224). The wheel had a total capacity
of 2,160 people (Lee).

The wheel was built on two 20-foot square, 35-foot deep
concrete blocks. Plans were approved by the end of 1892. The
thousands of parts needed for the steam-powered wheel were
built by five different steel companies. In late March of 1893,
five trains, each thirty cars long, brought all these parts to
Chicago (Anderson and Brown 18). The most crucial was the
huge axle—45½ feet long, 33 inches in diameter, weighing 46½
tons. Made by Bethlehem Iron Works of Bethlehem, Pennsylvania, the axle was the largest single piece of steel ever forged
in the United States (Lee; Anderson and Brown 18).

Ferris built his ride based on the principle of the bicycle
wheel. Heavy steel rods acted as the spokes and pulled
toward the axle to keep the wheel's shape. By using tension,
Ferris was able to build a lighter, stronger, and vastly larger
structure than was ever before possible (Anderson and
Brown 17).

A twenty-minute ride, or two revolutions with six stops
each time around, cost 50 cents. The wheel ran from 8 A.M. to
11 P.M. At night, the wheel was lit by 3,000 electric light bulbs
powered by a generator in the boiler house of the wheel
(Anderson and Brown 24). One-and-one-half-million people
had ridden the wheel by Fair's end—a good number considering that the 50-cent fee was equal to admission to the entire
Exposition (Fincher 114). One North Dakota farmboy wrote ➡

---

*Logical organization shows
how the combination of Ferris's
personality and the standards
set for the fair produced the
Ferris wheel.*

*What do you suppose is
the main purpose of this
sentence?*

*Interesting analogy about the
wheel's weight puts it in perspective for modern readers.*

*What kind of organization
does Britta use here? Why
might she have made this
particular choice?*

in a letter home: "Do whatever you have to do—even sell the kitchen stove—come to Chicago and ride the Ferris wheel!" (Anderson and Brown 26). A ride on the wheel, it was said, "may truly be called a round trip" (Lee).

Though an engineering milestone when completed, the wheel was not so well accepted in the early stages of its development. Burnham said it was not strong enough to withstand Lake Michigan winds, and even if it could, the public would be afraid to ride such a "rickety-looking contraption" (Fincher 112). Others doubted the wheel, too, but Ferris was finally allowed to build it if he could finance it. The Exposition had no better match for the Eiffel Tower. Ferris sold stock to wealthy Chicago businessmen (Fincher 112). The wheel cost $400,000 to build, and turned a total profit of $733,086 (Holliday 229).

What does this quotation contribute to the paragraph?

The Exposition was opened on May 1, 1893, by President Grover Cleveland, but the wheel was not completed. Work was done around the clock, but safety was still ensured. The wheel was powered by two 1,000-horsepower steam engines, one being held as a back-up (Anderson and Brown 21). It also had a huge air brake worked by two 10-foot steel bands which would tighten to stop the wheel in case it began to spin free (Fincher 111). With these features, the wheel was tested extensively. Wrote Ferris's partner and fellow RPI graduate William F. Gronau: "So perfect is the machinery that we did not feel the wheel move" (Fincher 114).

The Ferris wheel had its grand opening on Wednesday, June 21, 1893. Among the invited first riders were Mr. and Mrs. Ferris, the mayor of Chicago, and a 40-piece band, squeezed into one car (Anderson and Brown 23).

The Ferris wheel, and the Midway Plaisance where it was located, were both immediate successes. The Midway was a grand street of international displays and buildings meant to show the everyday life and oddities of all countries. The Midway was designed to "popularize" the Exposition, which it did very well, because many visitors enjoyed its atmosphere much more than the cultural attractions (Badger 109). Ironically, Jackson Park, the location of the Midway, not the cultural Court of Honor, became the entrance to the University of Chicago, or the "Grey City," as it was known at the time (Badger 90). One anonymous limerick showed the true, educational value of the Fair to the University:

> Oh, there were more Profs than students,
>   but then we didn't care;
> They spent their days in research work, ➡

> their evenings at the Fair.
> and life upon the Campus
> was one continual swing,
> We watched the Ferris wheel go round
> and didn't do a thing.
> (Badger 157)

The Ferris wheel's popularity was due to the escape the Midway provided, both from real life and the overwhelming culture of the rest of the Fair. "No single enterprise on the Midway or the grounds proper approached it either in patronage or in wonderment" (Badger 108). Couples rushed to be married at the top of the wheel, but the closest they got was the superintendent's office on the ground below. Newspapers started rumors of the wheel losing parts that then supposedly hurtled to the ground below; or they told of the mechanism locking in place, trapping the wheel's passengers up in the air with no help. As this never happened, such publicity made the gigantic toy only more popular (Fincher 114).

The wheel did have its critics. Howells accused the wheel of being a mere money-making contrivance—an exploitation of the visitors (Howells 25). Others said Ferris had plagiarized the idea for the wheel, and that American, Asian, and European history was filled with similar, if less complex, models. This is true, but it was the design that made Ferris's creation unique (Anderson and Brown 37–38).

Though not the first to build such rides, Ferris was forever associated with later machines. British engineer W. B. Basset sought to outdo Ferris's wheel in size and scope. American William Sullivan was also among those inspired by Ferris. Sullivan started the Eli Bridge Company in 1906 in Jacksonville, Illinois, largest current manufacturer of Ferris wheels. Sullivan, after riding the great wheel at the Exposition as many times as possible, capitalized on the commercial possibilities of the wheel. He made smaller, portable versions of about 45 feet in diameter which could be built in quantity (Anderson and Brown 41). George and Mary Tilyou wanted to buy Ferris's wheel and take it to their newly built Brooklyn amusement park—Coney Island, which was modeled after the Midway. The Tilyous couldn't afford the ride and instead built a 125-foot diameter "Wonder Wheel," which still stands. Though it wasn't the first or largest, as the signs claimed, Coney Island's Wonder Wheel established Ferris wheels and their many variations as a permanent fixture in modern American amusement parks (Fincher 117). ➡

Transitional sentence introduces the controversy surrounding the wheel.

Transition shows the connection between the original wheel and those that followed.

The criticism over the wheel's originality began the wheel's decline. Ferris's assets collapsed over lawsuits with the Exposition about the wheel's profits. During the winter of 1893–94, the wheel was left deserted. With a brief appearance at the North Clark Street Fair beginning in early 1895, the wheel regained some of its original standing, but it had simply lost its novelty. Neighbors in Clark Street campaigned to remove the wheel, ironically, complaining of its "undesirable industrialism" (Fincher 117). The wheel then appeared at the Louisiana Purchase Exposition of 1904 in Saint Louis and was still running perfectly. However, it remained unsuccessful. In 1906, following the Louisiana Exposition, the great wheel was brought tumbling down with 100 pounds of dynamite. The *Chicago Tribune* reported, "Within a few minutes, it was a tangled mass of steel and iron forty feet high" (Fincher 118). However, Ferris was not there to see its end. In November 1896, George W. G. Ferris had died unexpectedly in a Pittsburgh hospital at the age of 37. The cause was diagnosed as several different ailments, but mostly Ferris's death was due to depression over his potential bankruptcy and loss of hope (Fincher 118).

The true achievement of the Ferris wheel lay not in how long it stood, but in its combination of pleasurable enjoyment and industrial achievement. It symbolized the ideals of the World's Columbian Exposition. Moreover, the Ferris wheel signified the industrial advancement of the times and provided an escape in the peaceful period before World War I.

Story of wheel's demise is presented in chronological order.

What does Britta do in her conclusion?

Portfolio & Reflection

Summary

Key concepts in writing a research paper include the following:

• Prewriting for a research paper involves finding a topic, getting information, developing a working bibliography, taking notes, preparing a working outline, and formulating a thesis statement.

• Drafting means using your outline and notes as you write an introduction, body, and conclusion.

• Proper documentation includes citations for specific ideas from sources as well as a list of works cited.

• Careful revision and proofreading prepare a research paper for its audience.

Your Writer's Portfolio

Look over the research paper you prepared during this unit, and put it into your portfolio. Your paper should demonstrate that you have worked with the preceding concepts. In other words, the result of your research and your writing should be a research paper that does the following:

• has a topic that interests you and is neither too broad nor too narrow

• is kept on track by a strong thesis statement and a logical outline

• begins with an introduction that presents a topic and approach, and ends with a conclusion that wraps it all up

• contains proper citations for all sources

• reflects careful revision in its word choices, transitions, and ideas

• reflects careful proofreading

Reflection and Commentary

Write one page in which you demonstrate that you understand what this unit asked of you. Use your research paper as evidence while you consider the following numbered items. Respond to as many numbered items as possible. Label the page "Commentary on Research Paper Writing," and include it in your portfolio.

1. Was your topic interesting? Would you choose it again? Why or why not?
2. What were your best sources? What others would you use in future research?
3. How do you rate your note-taking skills? What did you learn about taking notes?
4. Did you revise your outline during your process? Does your paper follow your final outline? If not, which should you change, your paper or your outline?
5. Is your introduction engaging? How did you grab your readers' interest and make them want to know more?
6. How do you feel now about your research paper? What was the most important new technique you learned?

Feedback

If you had a chance to respond to the following comment by the writer of the model research paper in this unit, what would you say or ask?

In any piece of writing, I like the point where you finally understand an idea well enough that you can put it in your own words and then add your own ideas.

Britta Waller, Theodore Roosevelt High School, Kent, Ohio

Style Through Sentence Combining

Frank Stella, *Kastūra*, 1979

8 Style Through Sentence Combining

Playing the Game

In the tense, final moments of the state championship game you step up to the foul line and eye the basket carefully. You feel the ball, solid and familiar between your hands. The score is tied, and you can put the game on ice by doing what you've practiced thousands of times—shooting a single foul shot. Just like practice, you tell yourself. Take a deep breath and focus. You bounce the ball a time or two, spinning its seams beneath your fingertips. Then habit takes over, and you're locked on target, watching the ball loft toward the basket in a smooth, lovely arc. As it nests softly into the hoop, the crowd goes wild with joy.

Writing isn't always like that, of course. But practicing sentences, like practicing foul shots, can often help you in "clutch" situations. Why? Because skillful writing is partly a matter of habit, just like skillful shooting on the basketball court. The ability to write sentences smoothly frees your mind for other important tasks—like getting your ideas right.

Practice in Sentence Combining

This unit focuses on combining short sentences into longer, more complex ones. But remember that our goal is clear writing, not merely long sentences. Practice in sentence combining reveals your stylistic options, the "moves" you can make in the game of writing. Long sentences—like long shots on the basketball court—are not always good ones.

Regular practice in sentence combining enables you to find clear ways to express your ideas. In the game of writing, it's crucial to make good sentences consistently. Sentence combining can help you achieve that goal. By making you aware of writing choices, sentence combining also develops your writing style. As you try new sentence "moves" in the writing game, your personal style will emerge naturally.

Developing Your Style

One way to develop a personal style, as you already know, is by writing regularly in a journal. Such writing helps unlock your ideas and find your own voice as a writer. Sentence combining is a second approach that has worked for millions of students.

Sentence combining presents you with clusters of short sentences and invites you to express their meanings in more interesting ways. Here's an example:

Writing is a game.
It is full of challenges.
It requires regular practice.
It leads to personal rewards.

Scanning these sentences, you can probably see different ways of combining them into a longer, more complex statement. Basically, there are four strategies for combining: (1) deleting repeated words; (2) using connecting words; (3) rearranging words; and (4) changing the form of words. For example, take a look at one way of combining illustrated below:

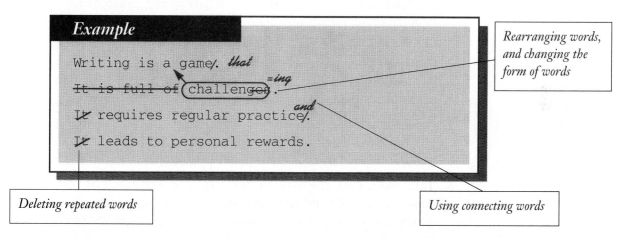

Example

Writing is a game. *that*
It is full of challenges. *=ing*
It requires regular practice. *and*
It leads to personal rewards.

Rearranging words, and changing the form of words

Deleting repeated words

Using connecting words

Notice that this editing produces sentence 1 below. Try reading it and the other sentences aloud, listening to differences in style.

1. Writing is a challenging game that requires regular practice and leads to personal rewards.
2. Writing, a game full of challenges, leads to personal rewards through regular practice.
3. Requiring regular practice, the challenging game of writing leads to personal rewards.
4. The challenges of the writing game require regular practice but lead to personal rewards.
5. Writing is a game that leads to personal rewards; overcoming its challenges, however, requires regular practice.

All of these sentences say basically the same thing, but they do so in different ways. In other words, each has a different emphasis. As a skilled writer, you choose the stylistic emphasis that best expresses your aims in the context of an emerging paragraph.

Sentence Combining Hints

Doing sentence combining is easy and fun. Here are some basic suggestions that have worked for other high school students—ones you might try as you explore style.

1. **Whisper sentences to yourself.** As you work with clusters of sentences, try doing them aloud. This process is faster than writing and helps you decide on a "best sentence" to write down.

2. **Work with a partner.** By trying out sentences on a partner—and hearing your partner's ideas—you often discover new, interesting ways to solve specific challenges. Don't be afraid to borrow ideas.

3. **Use context when choosing sentences.** Each paragraph has an emerging context—the sentences you have already combined. Reading this context aloud helps you decide on the best sentence option.

4. **Compare your sentences with those of other students.** Seeing how others have solved combining tasks broadens your awareness of sentence options. Keep asking yourself: Which do I prefer?

5. **Look for stylistic patterns in your writing.** Calculate your average words per sentence; study your sentence openers; listen to rhythms in your style. Try new patterns to stretch yourself.

6. **Take risks.** Learning to make clear, effective sentences also means taking risks and making mistakes. So, strange as it may sound, it actually makes sense to accept mistakes—even *welcome* them—as you combine sentences. After all, mistakes provide feedback for your language learning. As you learn from them, you develop an expressive style, a voice of personal authority. You come to know yourself as a writer.

As you can see, sentence combining involves skills of talking to yourself, making judgments, and holding what you say in short-term memory so that you can transcribe it. These are oral skills as much as writing skills. Good writers trust an "inner voice."

A Workshop on Style

Looking ahead in this unit, you will find two kinds of sentence combining. The exercises in sections 8.1 through 8.4 present clusters of short sentences, with spaces between the clusters. The exercises in section 8.5, drawn from literature selections in this book, are set up in an unclustered format.

Sections 8.1 to 8.4 give you practice in making descriptive, narrative, expository, and persuasive paragraphs. You can combine each cluster into a single sentence; but you can also leave a cluster partially combined—or combine clusters together. The idea, always, is to take risks and create the best sentences you can. Exercises on facing pages deal with the same topic or situation. Think of these exercises as "bookends" for the writing you will do. After you have combined sentences, your task is to connect the paragraphs into a longer essay or story. Doing so will help you transfer sentence-combining skills to your own writing.

Section 8.5 invites you to test your skills against those of a professional writer. As you do these unclustered exercises, you will need to figure out the ideas that logically belong together. After you have done the sentence combining, you can check your version against the author's original. By studying similarities and differences of the two passages, you will learn a great deal about your own style. Sometimes you will prefer the professional writer's sentences. Why, specifically, are they "better" than yours? But sometimes you will prefer your own style. Can you build on this writing skill, trying it out in your own stories and essays? Either way, you learn to write better.

Exploring Your Own Style

Of course, the whole point of sentence combining practice is to improve your revising and editing skills. Practice in sentence combining helps you see that sentences are flexible instruments of thought, not rigid structures cast in concrete. The simple fact that you feel confident in moving sentence parts around increases your control of the writing process. To acquire this sense of self-confidence—one based on your real competence in combining and revising sentences—you can try strategies like those shown below.

1. **Vary the length of your sentences.** Work for a rhythmic, interesting balance of long and short sentences, remembering that brevity often has dramatic force. Use this knowledge.

2. **Vary the structure of your sentences.** By using sentence openers on occasion—and by sometimes tucking information in the middle of a sentence—you can create stylistic interest.

3. **Use parallelism for emphasis.** Experiment with repeated items in a series—words, phrases, and clauses—to understand how structural patterns work and how you can use them to advantage.

4. **Use interruption for emphasis.** Colons, semicolons, dashes, commas, parentheses—all of these are useful tools in your stylistic toolkit; knowing how to use them well matters.

5. **Use unusual patterns for emphasis.** That you might sometimes reverse normal sentence patterns may never have occurred to you, but such a strategy can work—if you know how.

8.1 Description

Directions Combine each cluster of numbered items into one or more sentences. Combine clusters, if you wish.

1.1 Tony sat on the edge of a sofa.
1.2 The sofa was plush.
1.3 The sofa was mauve.
1.4 He waited for his date to appear.

2.1 The room felt like a funeral parlor.
2.2 The room looked like a funeral parlor.
2.3 This seemed only fitting.
2.4 Her father was a mortician.

3.1 A gas log burned in the fireplace.
3.2 Its burning was cheerless.
3.3 It bathed the room with warmth.
3.4 The warmth was antiseptic.

4.1 Next to it stood a TV console.
4.2 Its screen reflected the firelight.
4.3 The firelight was flickering.

5.1 Gold draperies extended along one wall.
5.2 The draperies were heavy.
5.3 They were like a dark shroud.
5.4 A painting depicted fading sunlight.
5.5 The sunlight was over an ocean shore.

6.1 The quietness of the room seemed eerie.
6.2 Its suggestions of death seemed eerie.
6.3 Its suggestions of dying seemed eerie.

7.1 In front of him was a marble table.
7.2 It had networks of veins.
7.3 It had networks of capillaries.
7.4 The networks were polished.

8.1 He traced its lines with his eye.
8.2 He listened to a mantle clock.

Writing Tip

In cluster 4 try changing *reflected* to *reflecting* as you combine. A connector like *with* may be useful in cluster 6.

Invitation So whom does Tony meet—Mom, Dad, or the family pet? Writing further description will help you link "First Date" to "Ready to Party."

Directions   Combine each cluster of numbered items into one or more sentences. Combine clusters, if you wish.

1.1 At school she was pretty.
1.2 Tonight she looked gorgeous.
1.3 Tonight she wore her hair pulled back.

2.1 She had olive skin.
2.2 She had facial features.
2.3 Her features were finely chiseled.

3.1 Her hair was combed past her ears.
3.2 Her hair was shoulder-length.
3.3 Her hair was black and lustrous.
3.4 Her eyes sparkled with laughter.
3.5 Her eyes were dark.

4.1 She wore earrings.
4.2 The earrings were gold loops.
4.3 She wore a denim jacket.
4.4 The jacket was over a red blouse.
4.5 She wore blue jeans.
4.6 The jeans were faded.

5.1 Even her boots looked ready for dancing.
5.2 The boots had pointed toes.
5.3 The dancing would be serious.

6.1 At school her image was low-key.
6.2 At school her image was conservative.
6.3 Tonight's outfit showed a personality.
6.4 The personality was outgoing.
6.5 The personality was fun-loving.

7.1 Tony felt awkward in his white shirt.
7.2 The white shirt was stiff.
7.3 He felt awkward in his sport coat.
7.4 He felt awkward in his slacks.
7.5 The slacks were carefully pressed.

Writing Tip

In clusters 1 and 6, try different connectors—*but, yet, however, while, although*—before settling on one; then check punctuation.

Invitation   Describe the scene you see happening *after* this scene. Then share your text—"First Date" plus "Ready to Party"—with a writing partner.

Exercise C: Student Teacher

Directions Combine each cluster of numbered items into one or more sentences. Combine clusters, if you wish.

1.1 The day was only half over.
1.2 The student teacher was frustrated.
1.3 She was completely discouraged.

2.1 Morning classes had not cooperated.
2.2 This was despite her best efforts.
2.3 This was despite her planning.
2.4 Her planning was careful.

3.1 Now her mouth was tense.
3.2 It sagged with fatigue.

4.1 Her desk looked like a disaster.
4.2 It was cluttered with announcements.
4.3 It was cluttered with office notes.
4.4 It was cluttered with tardy slips.
4.5 It was cluttered with late papers.
4.6 The disaster was educational.

5.1 A buzzer echoed in the hallway.
5.2 It signaled a class change.
5.3 She still had not found a planner.
5.4 It contained her lecture notes.

6.1 She wore a badge of resignation.
6.2 The resignation was weary.
6.3 She watched the room fill with students.
6.4 They wanted lunchtime to continue.

7.1 The clock's second hand swept toward twelve.
7.2 She searched for a friendly face.
7.3 The face might help her through the period.

8.1 It was there near the back of the room.
8.2 This was much to her surprise.
8.3 This was much to her relief.

Writing Tip

In cluster 4 try *cluttered* at the beginning, in the middle, and toward the end of the sentence. Which approach *doesn't* work?

Invitation Describe yourself as the person who saves the student teacher's day. Link this description to "Thunderstorm."

Exercise D: Thunderstorm

Directions   Combine each cluster of numbered items into one or more sentences. Combine clusters, if you wish.

1.1 The class moved to the windows.
1.2 The windows were half-open.
1.3 The class waited for the show to begin.

2.1 Dust had turned the sky beige.
2.2 The dust was windblown.
2.3 The dust swirled up from the west.

3.1 Above the hills were shades of gray.
3.2 The gray was the color of gunmetal.
3.3 The gray darkened to purple.
3.4 The purple was ominous.

4.1 Lightning splintered the horizon.
4.2 The horizon was turbulent.
4.3 Its flash was followed by a boom.
4.4 The boom was heavy.
4.5 The boom rumbled.
4.6 The boom was like boxcars.
4.7 The boxcars were in the train yard.

5.1 Then the wind came up.
5.2 The atmosphere seemed luminous.
5.3 Its luminescence was strange.

6.1 Trees swayed like dancers.
6.2 Trees jerked like dancers.
6.3 The dancers were frantic.
6.4 Rain began to fall in drops.
6.5 The drops were fat.

7.1 They splattered the concrete.
7.2 They punched craters in the earth.
7.3 The craters were tiny.
7.4 The earth was thirsty.
7.5 They washed the air clean.

Invitation   Describe what happens next in this classroom scene. Share the text—"Student Teacher" plus "Thunderstorm"—with a writing partner.

8.2 *Narration*

Exercise A: Waking Up

Directions Combine each cluster of numbered items into one or more sentences. Combine clusters, if you wish.

1.1 The alarm rang at 6:30 A.M.
1.2 It brought Gary out of bed.
1.3 He had slept only a few hours.

2.1 He had thrashed about.
2.2 He had been unable to sleep.
2.3 He was worried about an interview.
2.4 The interview was for employment.

3.1 Now he blinked heavily.
3.2 He leaned against squares of tile.
3.3 The squares were smooth.
3.4 The tile was in the shower.
3.5 He tried to wake himself.

4.1 Warm spray stung his back.
4.2 It prickled his shoulders.
4.3 He only wanted to close his eyes.
4.4 He only wanted to go back to bed.

5.1 His brain had become sludge.
5.2 The sludge was thick.
5.3 The sludge was viscous.

6.1 He worked shampoo into his hair.
6.2 He turned under the showerhead.
6.3 The showerhead was hissing.
6.4 He hoped to revive himself.

7.1 He finally shut off the shower.
7.2 Cold drops spattered his back.
7.3 The drain sucked at his feet.

8.1 Then he pulled a towel from the rack.
8.2 He wrapped it around his waist.
8.3 He stumbled forward to meet the day.

Writing Tip

In cluster 1 use a *who* connector, making sure that sentence 1.3 follows *Gary*. Use a pair of commas for this relative clause.

Invitation So what happens next? Narrate a transition from "Waking Up" to "Job Interview," perhaps using humor to build interest and tension.

Directions Combine each cluster of numbered items into one or more sentences. Combine clusters, if you wish.

1.1 The waiting area was noisy.
1.2 The waiting area was cramped.
1.3 The waiting area was poorly lit.
1.4 It looked like a large broom closet.

2.1 Gary sat with two other applicants.
2.3 He tried to relax.
2.4 His insides felt tense.

3.1 He touched his fingers to his face.
3.2 He noticed they were ice-cold.
3.3 This was a sure sign of nervousness.

4.1 His plan was to sell himself.
4.2 The selling would be straightforward.
4.3 It would be without arrogance.

5.1 He would emphasize his adaptability.
5.2 He would emphasize his friendliness.
5.3 He would emphasize his work habits.
5.4 His work habits were responsible.

6.1 The secretary called his number.
6.2 He wiped his palms dry.
6.3 He adjusted his new tie.
6.4 He arranged his face into a smile.
6.5 The smile was upbeat.

7.1 He strode into the interview room.
7.2 He told himself he had nothing to lose.

8.1 He shook hands with the interviewer.
8.2 He settled into an armchair.
8.3 He noticed his mismatched shoes.
8.4 One was light brown.
8.5 The other was black.

Writing Tip

In cluster 1 use *which* to create an adjective clause for sentence 1.4. For more on punctuating adjective clauses, see page 675.

Invitation Narrate an interesting conclusion for this story. Then share your text—"Waking Up" plus "Job Interview"—with a writing partner.

Directions Combine each cluster of numbered items into one or more sentences. Combine clusters, if you wish.

1.1 Sabrina lay on a blanket.
1.2 The blanket was in the back yard.
1.3 Her jacket was off.
1.4 Her sunglasses were on.

2.1 She had tried to study for an exam.
2.2 Last night's breakup was on her mind.
2.3 The breakup was sudden.

3.1 She had been sharing a pizza.
3.2 The pizza was after school.
3.3 She was with her boyfriend.
3.4 They had begun to argue.

4.1 Their voices grew louder.
4.2 Their voices grew more angry.
4.3 He had clenched a fist.
4.4 He had slammed it on the table.
4.5 This caused a stir in the restaurant.

5.1 He had leaned forward.
5.2 He had tried to hold her hand.
5.3 She had turned away.

6.1 Her rejection had been unexpected.
6.2 It had been a sharp blow.
6.3 The blow was to his pride.
6.4 His pride was masculine.

7.1 She had said he was immature.
7.2 He was unable to control his temper.

8.1 She had made her decision.
8.2 Her decision was not to see him again.
8.3 His apologies had been weak.
8.4 His apologies had been pathetic.

Invitation Narrate what you imagine Sabrina to be thinking about. Is she having second thoughts? Use your narration as a link to "The Spider."

Exercise D: The Spider

Directions Combine each cluster of numbered items into one or more sentences. Combine clusters, if you wish.

1.1 Spears cushioned her notebook.
1.2 The spears were grassy.
1.3 A spider moved up a page.
1.4 The spider was long-legged.

2.1 The spider hesitated.
2.2 It then changed direction.
2.3 It was threatened by a pencil.

3.1 Its legs scurried for safety.
3.2 Its legs were delicate.
3.3 Sabrina grabbed one.
3.4 She picked up the spider.
3.5 The spider was thrashing.

4.1 She was amused by its dance.
4.2 The dance was frantic.
4.3 She made a two-fingered vise.
4.4 She moved in for the kill.

5.1 Death hung merciless.
5.2 Death hung poised.
5.3 It was above the spider's scream.
5.4 The scream was silent.

6.1 The afternoon was breathless.
6.2 The afternoon was warm.
6.3 She thought about her boyfriend.
6.4 She considered her own impulsiveness.

7.1 Sabrina felt the sun's warmth.
7.2 It was on her back.
7.3 It was on her arms.
7.4 Sabrina rolled over on her side.
7.5 She smiled to herself.
7.6 She let the spider go.

Writing Tip

In clusters 4 and 7 try participial phrases to open the sentences. For more on participles, see pages 472–473.

Invitation Narrate a conclusion to this story. Then share your text—"Breakup" plus "The Spider"—with a writing partner.

8.3 Exposition

Exercise A: Dealing with Acne

Directions   Combine each cluster of numbered items into one or more sentences. Combine clusters, if you wish.

1.1 Acne is a common skin condition.
1.2 It is caused by oil glands.
1.3 Oil glands secrete too much sebum.
1.4 Sebum is a waxy lubricant.

2.1 Whiteheads result.
2.2 Excess sebum clogs the pores.
2.3 Excess sebum remains beneath the skin.

3.1 Plugs of sebum protrude above the skin.
3.2 Blackheads are the consequence.

4.1 Excess secretions cause red pimples.
4.2 Excess secretions invade other tissues.
4.3 Excess secretions inflame other tissues.

5.1 Simple steps can help you deal with acne.
5.2 They are mostly a matter of common sense.

6.1 Wash daily with soap and water.
6.2 Don't waste money on cleansers.
6.3 The cleansers are medicated.
6.4 Don't waste money on granular scrubs.

7.1 Use a drying lotion or cream.
7.2 This should contain benzoyl peroxide.

8.1 Wear your hair off your face.
8.2 This keeps it free of scalp oils.
8.3 Avoid hair dressings.
8.4 Hair dressings are greasy.

9.1 Don't pick at your face.
9.2 This increases inflammation.
9.3 This heightens your risk of pitting.
9.4 This heightens your risk of scarring.

Invitation   Introduce the hygiene advice in "Dealing with Acne" by explaining why people need to understand this skin condition.

Exercise B: Protecting Your Skin

Directions Combine each cluster of numbered items into one or more sentences. Combine clusters, if you wish.

1.1 Suntans may suggest good health.
1.2 They seriously damage your skin.
1.3 They destroy its elastic fibers.

2.1 Their consequence is premature aging.
2.2 No one wishes for the consequence.
2.3 This leaves skin dry and wrinkled.

3.1 Even less desirable are the health risks.
3.2 The risks include basal cell carcinoma.
3.3 The risks include malignant melanoma.

4.1 These skin cancers develop cumulatively.
4.2 These skin cancers develop irreversibly.
4.3 They are a result of sun exposure.

5.1 Early suntans can result in cancers.
5.2 Early sunburns can result in cancers.
5.3 The cancers are during adult years.

6.1 Many suntan salons promise safe tans.
6.2 They promise tans without burns.
6.3 They actually pose real health hazards.

7.1 Tanning booths use UVA radiation.
7.2 This penetrates the skin deeply.
7.3 This causes premature aging.
7.4 This increases susceptibility to cancers.

8.1 Protecting your skin requires something.
8.2 You reduce direct exposure to sunlight.
8.2 Use sunscreens rated at SPF 15 or higher.
8.4 Wear protective clothing in the sun.

9.1 Avoiding suntan salons is common sense.
9.2 It also saves you money.

Writing Tip

In clusters 2, 3, 4, 7, and 8, you can practice writing adjective clauses. For help on punctuating adjective clauses, see page 675.

Invitation Create a transition paragraph after "Dealing with Acne" that links to "Protecting Your Skin." Share your text with a writing partner.

Exercise C: Taking Notes

Directions Combine each cluster of numbered items into one or more sentences. Combine clusters, if you wish.

1.1 There are many systems for notetaking.
1.2 Two have proved popular with students.
1.3 The students dislike traditional plans.

2.1 One system develops a spider web of words.
2.2 The system is sometimes called "webbing."
2.3 The system is sometimes called "mapping."
2.4 The words are from the reading.

3.1 Responses to reading trigger words.
3.2 The responses are personal.
3.3 Words are jotted down as "webs of meaning."

4.1 These webs may not make sense to someone else.
4.2 The webs speak clearly to us.
4.3 We are their authors.
4.4 We know what they are trying to say.

5.1 A second system also uses personal meaning.
5.2 The system is popular.
5.3 It is called the "dialogue journal."

6.1 The journal consists of two facing pages.
6.2 One page is for notes in outline form.
6.3 The other is for thoughts about the notes.

7.1 The notes record information objectively.
7.2 The facing page processes the information.
7.3 It provides emotional reactions.
7.4 It makes summaries.
7.5 It gives examples.
7.6 It asks questions.

8.1 A basic principle underlies both systems.
8.2 We bring unique experiences to reading.
8.3 We take away personal meanings.

Invitation Develop a character sketch or dramatic incident that involves a student with poor study habits; use this sketch to introduce "Taking Notes."

Exercise D: Study Strategy

Directions   Combine each cluster of numbered items into one or more sentences. Combine clusters, if you wish.

1.1 Many students have trouble studying.
1.2 They have not discovered principles.
1.3 The principles make it easy and fun.
1.4 They therefore get discouraged.

2.1 One approach is to get an overview.
2.2 The approach works for many students.
2.3 This is by flipping through a text.
2.4 This is by skimming major headings.
2.5 This is by reading the chapter summary.

3.1 This overview is like a road map.
3.2 This overview provides "the big picture."
3.3 This overview triggers personal knowledge.
3.4 This overview leads to questions.

4.1 A person turns headings into questions.
4.2 Questions arouse a sense of curiosity.
4.3 Questions provide a focus for reading.
4.4 Reading will follow in a few moments.

5.1 Questions engage one's thinking processes.
5.2 They are a tool for preparing the mind.
5.3 The tool is indispensable.
5.4 The preparation is to remember ideas.

6.1 Many students make notes as they read.
6.2 The students are highly successful.
6.3 They jot down answers to questions.
6.4 They challenge the author.

7.1 These students are active readers.
7.2 The readers recite key points to themselves.
7.3 The readers discuss ideas with others.
7.4 The readers review their notes.
7.5 They cannot help but learn the material.

> ### Writing Tip
>
> In cluster 5 try *because* as a sentence opener; then try an appositive, with dashes, after the word *questions.* Choose the sentence you prefer.

Invitation   Write a conclusion for "Taking Notes" and "Study Strategy." Then share your text with a writing partner.

BENSON HIGH SCHOOL
546 N.E. 12th
PORTLAND, OR 97232

8.4   *Persuasion*

Exercise A: Diet Myths

Directions Combine each cluster of numbered items into one or more sentences. Combine clusters, if you wish.

1.1 Most Americans worry about their weight.
1.2 Our culture says that "thin is in."
1.3 Advertisers sell us images of bodies.
1.4 The bodies are lean and handsome.

2.1 Forty percent of us are on diets.
2.2 This is at any given moment.
2.3 We are trying to shed excess pounds.

3.1 Losing weight is a major industry.
3.2 Promoters make a variety of claims.
3.3 The promoters seek quick profits.
3.4 The claims are given wide circulation.

4.1 One such myth centers on grapefruit.
4.2 It is supposed to contain enzymes.
4.3 The enzymes burn fats away.

5.1 No scientific evidence supports these claims.
5.2 Dozens of diets are based on this myth.

6.1 A second myth centers on diet pills.
6.2 The pills are touted as "sure cures."
6.3 The cures are for weight loss.

7.1 Pills sometimes have short-term effects.
7.2 No evidence supports long-term weight loss.

8.1 A third myth centers on electric stimulators.
8.2 These claim to provide "passive exercise."
8.3 These claim to trim fat in specific areas.

9.1 Scientific studies show something.
9.2 Such devices provide no change in body weight.
9.3 Such devices provide no change in body fat.
9.4 Such devices do not improve muscle tone.

Writing Tip

In cluster 1 try rearranging sentences to achieve emphasis; in cluster 9 delete *something* and use *that* as a connector.

Invitation   To introduce "Diet Myths," find an actual advertisement (from a Sunday supplement magazine, perhaps) and make it part of your paragraph.

Directions Combine each cluster of numbered items into one or more sentences. Combine clusters, if you wish.

1.1 Some diet myths result from promoters.
1.2 Others seem to grow out of our folklore.
1.3 They are passed on by word of mouth.

2.1 There is a widely believed myth.
2.2 The stomach shrinks when you eat less.
2.3 This is simply untrue.
2.4 Your stomach cannot shrink.

3.1 Another myth is also quite common.
3.2 Potatoes are a fattening food.

4.1 A baked potato contains only 130 calories.
4.2 The potato is without butter.
4.3 The potato is without gravy.
4.4 The potato is without melted cheese.

5.1 Potatoes are a high-carbohydrate food.
5.2 The food has no fat or cholesterol.
5.3 The food has fewer calories than brown rice.

6.1 Yet another myth surrounds toast.
6.2 It is listed in many diets.
6.3 It may seem less fattening than bread.

7.1 Toasting bread removes only moisture.
7.2 It does not remove any calories.
7.3 This is contrary to popular belief.

8.1 A fourth myth concerns celery.
8.2 Some say it has "negative calories."
8.3 It takes so much work to chew celery.

9.1 Celery is a high-fiber vegetable.
9.2 It has only about six calories per stalk.
9.3 Chewing it does not use up extra calories.

Writing Tip

In either cluster 3 or 4, try dashes—as illustrated here—to achieve additional emphasis. In cluster 9 try *although* as an opener.

Invitation Draw conclusions from "Diet Myths" and "More Diet Myths" that will persuade your reader. Then share your text with a writing partner.

Directions   Combine each cluster of numbered items into one or more sentences. Combine clusters, if you wish.

1.1 Homolovi is an ancestral home.
1.2 Homolovi means "Place of the Mounds."
1.3 The home is for many Hopi people.
1.4 The Hopi live in the desert Southwest.

2.1 This area has been plundered by looters.
2.2 The area covers ten thousand acres in Arizona.
2.3 The area is protected by federal and state laws.
2.4 The looters are in search of pottery.
2.5 The pottery is Native American.

3.1 The "pothunters" use backhoes.
3.2 The "pothunters" use other machinery.
3.3 The "pothunters" leave a wake of destruction.

4.1 Hundreds of craters now scar the landscape.
4.2 Many buildings once stood there.
4.3 Two thousand people once lived there.
4.4 Two thousand people once worked there.
4.5 This was about 700 years ago.

5.1 The pothunters rip the land.
5.2 The pothunters gouge the land.
5.3 They destroy historical evidence.
5.4 The destruction is thoughtless.

6.1 Wealthy collectors support a black market.
6.2 The collectors are mainly from the United States.
6.3 The collectors are mainly from Japan.
6.4 The collectors are mainly from Germany.
6.5 The black market is flourishing.

7.1 Looters do the dirty work.
7.2 Private collectors are equally guilty.
7.3 They underwrite historical destruction.
7.4 They violate the heritage of Native Americans.

Writing Tip

In clusters 2 and 4 try *which* and *where* as connectors; in cluster 6 try a pair of dashes for stylistic emphasis.

Invitation   Should every culture have the right to record and document its own heritage? Make your case in a follow-up paragraph.

Exercise D: Black Market

Directions Combine each cluster of numbered items into one or more sentences. Combine clusters, if you wish.

1.1 Many Native Americans believe in spirits.
1.2 They deeply value ancient burial sites.
1.3 They deeply value ancestral dwellings.

2.1 They see the continuity in life.
2.2 They regard themselves as caretakers.
2.3 The caretakers have sacred duties.

3.1 Pots have significance to them.
3.2 Beads have significance to them.
3.3 Baskets have significance to them.
3.4 Projectile points have significance to them.
3.5 These objects help spirits find eternal peace.

4.1 Alaskan totem poles are cut up.
4.2 Alaskan totem poles are shipped overseas.
4.3 Native Americans shudder in disgust.

5.1 Someone tries to sell a Native American infant.
5.2 The Native American infant is mummified.
5.3 The price is $30,000.
5.4 Their jaws clench tight.

6.1 Anasazi pots bring nearly $100,000.
6.2 Anasazi baskets bring over $150,000.
6.3 They shake their heads sadly.

7.1 The black market angers Native Americans.
7.2 The market desecrates their past.
7.3 The market insults their values.
7.4 Their anger is understandable.

8.1 They look forward to a happier time.
8.2 Their heritage is accorded respect.
8.3 The black market collapses.
8.4 The market is now supported by looting.

Writing Tip

Try using *when* as an opener in clusters 4, 5, and 6. This effect is called *parallelism.*

Invitation Imagine finding an arrowhead while hiking. Does it go in your pocket? Write about the personal reasons behind your decision.

8.5   Literature Exercises

Directions   Scan the sentences below. Some come directly from *The Crystal Cave* by Mary Stewart. The numbered sentences are adapted from Stewart's original. Decide which of the numbered sentences belong together, and combine them in your own way. Then compare your sentences with the originals on page 153.

Next moment I stopped short, brought up by a shock which spilled the excitement through my bowels like water. Something had moved in the murk, just to my right.

1. I froze still.
2. I strained my eyes to see.
3. There was no movement.
4. I held my breath.
5. I listened.
6. There was no sound.
7. I flared my nostrils.
8. I tested the air round me.
9. My testing was cautious.
10. There was no animal or human smell.
11. I thought something.
12. The cave smelt of smoke.
13. The cave smelt of damp rock.
14. The cave smelt of the earth itself.
15. The cave had a scent.
16. The scent was musty.
17. The scent was queer.
18. I could not identify it.

I knew, without putting it into words, that had there been any other creature near me the air would have felt different, less empty. There was no one there.

19. I tried a word in Welsh.
20. My try was soft.
21. The word was "Greetings."
22. The whisper came back at me in an echo.
23. The whisper came back so quick.
24. I knew I was very near the wall of the cave.
25. Then it lost itself.
26. It was hissing in the roof.

Directions Scan the sentences below. Some come directly from *Of Wolves and Men* by Barry Lopez. The numbered sentences are adapted from Lopez's original. Decide which of the numbered sentences belong together, and combine them in your own way. Then compare your sentences with the originals on pages 266–267.

1. It is now late in the afternoon.
2. The wolf has stopped traveling.
3. He has lain down to sleep on cool earth.
4. The earth is beneath a rock outcropping.
5. Mosquitoes rest on his ears.
6. His ears flicker.
7. He begins to waken.
8. He rolls on his back.
9. He lies motionless.
10. His front legs are pointed toward the sky.
11. They are folded like wilted flowers.
12. His back legs are splayed.
13. His nose and tail are curved toward each other.
14. They are on one side of his body.

After a few moments he flops on his side, rises, stretches, and moves a few feet to inspect—minutely, delicately—a crevice in the rock outcropping and finds or doesn't find what draws him there. And then he ascends the rock face, bounding and balancing momentarily before bounding again, appearing slightly unsure of the process—but committed.

15. A few minutes pass.
16. He bolts suddenly into the woods.
17. He achieves full speed.
18. This is almost forty miles per hour.
19. This is for forty or fifty yards.
20. He begins to skid.
21. He begins to lunge at a lodgepole pine cone.
22. He trots away with it.
23. His head is erect.
24. His tail is erect.
25. His hips are slightly to one side.
26. They are out of line with his shoulders.
27. It is as though hindquarters were impatient with fore-quarters.
28. The cone is inert in his mouth.

Directions Scan the sentences below. Some come directly from *How the García Girls Lost Their Accents* by Julia Alvarez. The numbered sentences are adapted from Alvarez's original. Decide which of the numbered sentences belong together, and combine them in your own way. Then compare your sentences with the originals on pages 204–206.

"Go away," Yoyo wailed, but they both knew she was glad her mother was there, and needed only a moment's protest to save face.

1. Together they concocted a speech.
2. There were two brief pages of compliments.
3. The compliments were stale.
4. There were two brief pages of commonplaces.
5. The commonplaces were polite.
6. The commonplaces were on teachers.
7. It was a speech wrought by necessity.
8. It was a speech without much invention.
9. It was wrought by mother and daughter.
10. It was wrought late into the night.
11. It was wrought on one of the pads of paper.
12. Laura had once used the pads for her own inventions.
13. The speech was drafted.
14. Laura typed it up.
15. Yoyo stood by.
16. She corrected her mother's misnomers and mis-sayings.

Finally, her mother came up and pleaded with Yoyo to go down and reconcile with him [her father].

17. Yoyo found her father downstairs.
18. He was setting up a brand new typewriter.
19. The typewriter was on the kitchen table.
20. The typewriter was electric.
21. It was even better than her mother's.
22. He had outdone himself with all the extra features.
23. There was a plastic carrying case.
24. Yoyo's initials were decaled below the handle.
25. There was a brace to lift the paper upright while she typed.
26. There was an erase cartridge.
27. There was an automatic margin tab.
28. There was a plastic hood like a toaster cover.
29. The hood was to keep the dust away.

Directions   Scan the sentences below. Some come directly from *I Know Why the Caged Bird Sings* by Maya Angelou. The numbered sentences are adapted from Angelou's original. Decide which of the numbered sentences belong together, and combine them in your own way. Then compare your sentences with the originals on pages 44–45.

She took the bags from me and disappeared through the kitchen door. I looked around the room that I had never in my wildest fantasies imagined I would see.

1. Photographs leered from the walls.
2. Photographs threatened from the walls.
3. The photographs were browned.
4. The curtains pushed against themselves.
5. The curtains pushed against the wind.
6. The curtains were white.
7. The curtains were freshly done.
8. I wanted to gobble up the room entire.
9. I wanted to take it to Bailey.
10. He would help me analyze it.
11. He would help me enjoy it.

"Have a seat, Marguerite. Over there by the table." She carried a platter covered with a tea towel. Although she warned that she hadn't tried her hand at baking sweets for some time, I was certain that like everything else about her the cookies would be perfect.

12. They were wafers.
13. The wafers were flat.
14. The wafers were round.
15. They were slightly browned on the edges.
16. They were butter-yellow in the center.
17. They came with the cold lemonade.
18. They were sufficient for childhood's lifelong diet.
19. I remembered my manners.
20. I took nice little bites.
21. The bites were lady-like.
22. The bites were off the edges.
23. She said something.
24. She had made them expressly for me.
25. She had a few in the kitchen.
26. I could take them home to my brother.

Directions   Scan the sentences below. Some come directly from "Skeletons in the Attic" by Clara Spotted Elk. The numbered sentences are adapted from Spotted Elk's original. Decide which of the numbered sentences belong together, and combine them in your own way. Then compare your sentences with the originals on pages 306–307.

After a chance inquiry, a curator pulled out a drawer in one of the scores of cabinets that lined the attic. There were the jumbled bones of an Indian. "A Kiowa," he said.

1. We subsequently found 18,500 Indian remains.
2. Some consisted of a handful of bones.
3. Most were full skeletons.
4. They were stored in the Smithsonian's nooks.
5. They were stored in the Smithsonian's crannies.
6. Their storage was unceremonious.
7. Other museums also collect the bones.
8. Other individuals also collect the bones.
9. Other federal agencies also collect the bones.
10. The agencies include the National Park Service.
11. The bones are of Indian warriors.
12. The bones are of Indian women.
13. The bones are of Indian children.
14. Some are on display as attractions.
15. The attractions are for tourists.
16. The attractions are by the roadside.

It is estimated that another 600,000 Indian remains are secreted away in locations across the country.

17. The museum community defends these collections.
18. Forensic scientists defend these collections.
19. Their defense is vigorous.
20. The collections are grisly.
21. There are a few exceptions.
22. They refuse to return remains to the tribes.
23. The tribes wish to rebury them.
24. This is even when grave robbing has been documented.

They want to maintain adequate numbers of "specimens" for analysis and say they are dedicated to "the permanent curation of Indian skeletal remains."

Part 2

Grammar, Usage, and Mechanics

My family is ⌃a typical ~~of a family~~ ⌃of ~~in~~ the 1990s.
Both of my parents work, which means many of the
household responsibilitis⌃e are left to my brother
and ~~I~~. ⌃me We do them, of course⌃, even though we don't
like ~~it~~. ⌃the extra work Since ⌃everyone in my family is busy with⌃various activities,
it is unusual for all of us to be home at the
same time. ~~But~~ ⌃Occasionally though, we try to do
special things⌃together. My family is very close even if
we don't see each other ⌃very ~~all that~~ often.

TROUBLESHOOTER CHECKLIST

☐ Sentence Fragment

☐ Run-on Sentence

☐ Lack of Subject-Verb Agreement

☐ Lack of Pronoun-Antecedent Agreem[ent]

☑ Lack of Clear Pronoun Reference

☐ Shift in Pronoun

☐ Shift in Verb Tense

☐ Incorrect Verb Tense or Form

☐ Misplaced or Dangling Modifier

☐ Missing or Misplaced Possessive Apostr[ophe]

☑ Missing Commas with Nonessential Ele[ments]

☐ Missing Comma in a Series

Part 2 Grammar, Usage, and Mechanics

Unit 9 Troubleshooter

Research on thousands of student papers has identified the errors most frequently made by students and marked by teachers. This Troubleshooter is based on that research and is designed to help you correct these errors.

Use the Table of Contents below to locate quickly a lesson on a specific error. Your teacher may mark errors with the handwritten codes in the left-hand column.

9.1 Sentence Fragment

PROBLEM 1

Fragment that lacks a subject

frag   Sal put his best effort into his painting.
~~Hoped it would win a prize.~~

Solution
Sal put his best effort into his painting. He hoped it would win a prize.
Add a subject to the fragment to make it a complete sentence.

PROBLEM 2

Fragment that lacks a complete verb

frag   We heard a loud noise. The fire alarm across the street.

frag   The reviews are enthusiastic. The critics encouraging us to put on future shows.

Solution A
We heard a loud noise. The fire alarm across the street was wailing.

The reviews are enthusiastic. The critics are encouraging us to put on future shows.
Add a complete verb or a helping verb to make the sentence complete.

Solution B
We heard a loud noise—the fire alarm across the street.

The reviews are enthusiastic, with the critics encouraging us to put on future shows.
Combine the fragment with another sentence.

Fragment that is a subordinate clause

frag   Maria was relieved. (Because she found) (her notebook.)

frag   The restaurant is out of melon. (Which I) (wanted for dessert.)

Solution A
Maria was relieved because she found her notebook.

The restaurant is out of melon, which I wanted for dessert.
Combine the fragment with another sentence.

Solution B
Maria was relieved. She found her notebook.

The restaurant is out of melon. I wanted it for dessert.
Rewrite the fragment as a complete sentence, eliminating the subordinating conjunction or the relative pronoun and adding a subject or other words necessary to make a complete thought.

PROBLEM 4

Fragment that lacks both a subject and a verb

frag   Paul finally finished his homework. (At) (ten o'clock.)

Solution
Paul finally finished his homework at ten o'clock.
Combine the fragment with another sentence.

Need More Help?

If you need more help in avoiding sentence fragments, turn to 13.9, pages 500–502.

9.2   Run-on Sentence

PROBLEM 1

Comma splice—two main clauses separated only by a comma

run-on On vacation Luisa enjoys hiking in the mountains, Leon prefers swimming at the beach.

Solution A
On vacation Luisa enjoys hiking in the mountains. Leon prefers swimming at the beach.
Replace the comma with an end mark of punctuation, such as a period or a question mark, and begin the new sentence with a capital letter.

Solution B
On vacation Luisa enjoys hiking in the mountains; Leon prefers swimming at the beach.
Place a semicolon between the two main clauses.

Solution C
On vacation Luisa enjoys hiking in the mountains, but Leon prefers swimming at the beach.
Add a coordinating conjunction after the comma.

PROBLEM 2

Two main clauses with no punctuation between them

run-on Kim plays the guitar she writes music, too.

Solution A
Kim plays the guitar. She writes music, too.
Separate the main clauses with an end mark of punctuation, such as a period or a question mark, and begin the second sentence with a capital letter.

Solution B

Kim plays the guitar; she writes music, too.

Separate the main clauses with a semicolon.

Solution C

Kim plays the guitar, and she writes music, too.

Add a comma and a coordinating conjunction between the main clauses.

PROBLEM 3

Two main clauses with no comma before the coordinating conjunction

run-on Carla is planning to visit Yellowstone National Park next summer and her sister may join her.

run-on The main course was boring but the dessert was magnificent.

Solution

Carla is planning to visit Yellowstone National Park next summer, and her sister may join her.

The main course was boring, but the dessert was magnificent.

Add a comma before the coordinating conjunction to separate the two main clauses.

If you need more help in avoiding run-on sentences, turn to 13.10, pages 502–503.

9.3 Lack of Subject-Verb Agreement

PROBLEM 1

A subject that is separated from the verb by an intervening prepositional phrase

> *agr* The sound of the nightingales (fill) the air.
>
> *agr* The storms in winter (seems) severe.

Do not mistake the object of a preposition for the subject of a sentence.

Solution
The sound of the nightingales fills the air.

The storms in winter seem severe.
Ignore a prepositional phrase that comes between a subject and a verb. Make the verb agree with the subject, which is never the object of a preposition.

PROBLEM 2

A predicate nominative that differs in number from the subject

> *agr* Bicycle races (was) his passion.

Solution
Bicycle races were his passion.
Ignore the predicate nominative, and make the verb agree with the subject of the sentence.

PROBLEM 3

A subject that follows the verb

> *agr* Off the reef (lies) three sunken ships.
>
> *agr* Here (comes) the first three volunteers.

Solution
Off the reef lie three sunken ships.

Here come the first three volunteers.
In an inverted sentence look for the subject *after* the verb. Then make sure the verb agrees with the subject.

PROBLEM 4

A collective noun as the subject

agr   The chorus (sing) splendidly.

agr   The jury (disagrees) among themselves.

Solution A
The chorus sings splendidly.
If the collective noun refers to a group as a whole, use a singular verb.

Solution B
The jury disagree among themselves.
If the collective noun refers to each member of a group individually, use a plural verb.

PROBLEM 5

A noun of amount as the subject

agr   Ten months (are) the usual school year.

agr   Ten dimes (makes) a dollar.

Solution
Ten months is the usual school year.

Ten dimes make a dollar.
Determine whether the noun of amount refers to one unit and is therefore singular or whether it refers to a number of individual units and is therefore plural.

PROBLEM 6

A compound subject that is joined by and

agr   Oxygen and hydrogen (is) essential to life.

agr   Oil and vinegar (are) my favorite salad dressing.

Solution A
Oxygen and hydrogen are essential to life.
If the parts of the compound subject do not belong to one unit or if they refer to different people or things, use a plural verb.

Solution B
Oil and vinegar is my favorite salad dressing.
If the parts of the compound subject belong to one unit or if both parts refer to the same person or thing, use a singular verb.

PROBLEM 7

A compound subject that is joined by or or nor

agr   Neither hardships nor danger (deter) him.

agr   Either soup or sandwiches (makes) a good lunch.

Solution
Neither hardships nor danger deters him.

Either soup or sandwiches make a good lunch.
Make the verb agree with the subject that is closer to it.

PROBLEM 8

A compound subject that is preceded by many a, every, or each

agr   Every nook and cranny (were) searched.

Solution

Every nook and cranny was searched.

Use a singular verb when *many a*, *each*, or *every* precedes a compound subject.

PROBLEM 9

A subject that is separated from the verb by an intervening expression

agr   Carlos, as well as Dana, (love) baseball.

Certain expressions, such as *as well as*, *in addition to*, and *together with* do not change the number of the subject.

Solution

Carlos, as well as Dana, loves baseball.

Ignore an intervening expression between a subject and its verb. Make the verb agree with the subject.

PROBLEM 10

An indefinite pronoun as the subject

agr   Each of the climbers (carry) a rope.

Some indefinite pronouns are singular, some are plural, and some can be either singular or plural, depending upon the noun they refer to. (See page 563 for a list of indefinite pronouns.)

Solution

Each of the climbers carries a rope.

Determine whether the indefinite pronoun is singular or plural, and make the verb agree.

If you need more help with subject-verb agreement, turn to 16.1 through 16.7, pages 555–564.

9.4 Lack of Pronoun-Antecedent Agreement

PROBLEM 1

A singular antecedent that can be either male or female

ant   A good athlete must practice (his) routine daily.

ant   A parent and (his) child form a special bond.

Traditionally a masculine pronoun is used to refer to an antecedent that may be either male or female. This usage ignores or excludes females.

Solution A
A good athlete must practice his or her routine daily.

A parent and his or her child form a special bond.
Reword the sentence to use *he or she, him or her,* and so on.

Solution B
Good athletes must practice their routines daily.

Parents and their children form special bonds.
Reword the sentence so that both the antecedent and the pronoun are plural.

Solution C
Parents and children form a special bond.

Good athletes must practice routines daily.
Reword the sentence to eliminate the pronoun.

PROBLEM 2

A second-person pronoun that refers to a third-person antecedent

ant   Carlos and Jane love hiking because (you) benefit from vigorous exercise in peaceful, natural surroundings.

Be sure not to refer to an antecedent in the third person using the second-person pronoun *you*.

Solution A

Carlos and Jane love hiking because they benefit from vigorous exercise in peaceful, natural surroundings.

Use the appropriate third-person pronoun.

Solution B

Carlos and Jane love hiking because hikers benefit from vigorous exercise in peaceful, natural surroundings.

Use an appropriate noun instead of a pronoun.

PROBLEM 3

A singular indefinite pronoun as an antecedent

ant   Each of the women had (their) own goal.

ant   Neither of the men showed (their) surprise at the vote.

Each, everyone, either, neither, and *one* are singular and therefore require singular personal pronouns.

Solution

Each of the women had her own goal.

Neither of the men showed his surprise at the vote.

Don't be fooled by a prepositional phrase that contains a plural noun. Determine whether the indefinite pronoun antecedent is singular or plural, and make the noun agree.

If you need more help with pronoun-antecedent agreement, turn to 16.7, pages 563–564, and 17.5, pages 584–586.

9.5 Lack of Clear Pronoun Reference

PROBLEM 1

A pronoun reference that is weak or vague

ref The traffic was snarled, (which) was caused by an accident.

ref The room was stuffy and dimly lighted, and (that) made studying difficult.

ref Some astronomers think that black holes are very numerous, but (it) is difficult to prove.

Be sure that *this*, *that*, *which*, and *it* have a clear antecedent.

Solution A
The traffic was snarled in a massive tie-up, which was caused by an accident.
Rewrite the sentence, adding a clear antecedent for the pronoun.

Solution B
The room was stuffy and dimly lighted, and those conditions made studying difficult.

Some astronomers think that black holes are very numerous, but their theory is difficult to prove.
Rewrite the sentence, substituting a noun for the pronoun.

PROBLEM 2

A pronoun that refers to more than one antecedent

ref My sister always beats Susan at chess, but (she) still enjoys the game.

ref When the dancers performed for the children, (they) were pleased.

Solution A

My sister always beats Susan at chess, but Susan still enjoys the game.

Rewrite the sentence, substituting a noun for the pronoun.

Solution B

The children were pleased when the dancers performed.

Rewrite the sentence, making the antecedent of the pronoun clear.

PROBLEM 3

The indefinite use of you *or* they

ref   In Japan (you) go to school on Saturday mornings.

ref   In that school (they) have a fine music program.

Solution A

In Japan students go to school on Saturday mornings.

Rewrite the sentence, substituting a noun for the pronoun.

Solution B

That school has a fine music program.

Rewrite the sentence, eliminating the pronoun entirely.

If you need more help in making clear pronoun references, turn to 17.6, pages 588–590.

PROBLEM

An incorrect shift in person between two pronouns

pro   They are going to the international fair, where ⟨you⟩ can sample foods from many nations.

pro   I think life was easier when ⟨you⟩ had fewer possessions.

pro   After one runs a marathon, ⟨you⟩ are exhausted and exhilarated.

Incorrect pronoun shifts occur when a writer or speaker uses a pronoun in one person and then illogically shifts to a pronoun in another person.

Solution A

They are going to the international fair, where they can sample foods from many nations.

I think life was easier when I had fewer possessions.

After one runs a marathon, one is exhausted yet exhilarated.
Replace the incorrect pronoun with a pronoun that agrees with its antecedent.

Solution B

They are going to the international fair, where people can sample foods from many nations.

I think life was easier when people had fewer possessions.
Replace the incorrect pronoun with an appropriate noun.

If you need more help in eliminating incorrect pronoun shifts, turn to 17.5, page 585.

9.7 Shift in Verb Tense

PROBLEM 1

An unnecessary shift in tense

shift t Victor reads the newspaper and (noted) the sports scores.

shift t Nan arrived just as the play (begins).

When two or more events occur at the same time, be sure to use the same verb tense to describe each event.

Solution
Victor reads the newspaper and notes the sports scores.

Nan arrived just as the play began.
Use the same tense for both verbs.

PROBLEM 2

A lack of correct shift in tenses to show that one event precedes or follows another

shift t By the time the fire broke out, we (were) asleep for hours.

When events being described have occurred at different times, shift tenses to show that one event precedes or follows another.

Solution
By the time the fire broke out, we had been asleep for hours.
Shift from the past tense to the past perfect tense to indicate that one action began and ended before another past action began. Use the past perfect tense for the earlier of the two actions.

If you need more help with shifts in verb tenses, turn to 15.4, page 536, and 15.6, pages 540–541.

9.8 Incorrect Verb Tense or Form

PROBLEM 1

An incorrect or missing verb ending

tense Yesterday I (walk) four miles in the morning.

tense Have you ever (watch) a soccer match?

Solution
Yesterday I walked four miles in the morning.

Have you ever watched a soccer match?
Add *-ed* to a regular verb to form the past tense and the past participle.

PROBLEM 2

An improperly formed irregular verb

tense Mike (teared) his pants on a nail.

tense Angela has (sweeped) every room.

Irregular verbs form their past and past participle in some way other than by adding *-ed*. Memorize these forms, or look them up.

Solution
Mike tore his pants on a nail.

Angela has swept every room.
Use the correct past or past participle form of an irregular verb.

PROBLEM 3

Confusion between the past form and the past participle

tense Mr. Yei has often (spoke) about life in China.

Solution
Mr. Yei has often spoken about life in China.
Use the past participle form of an irregular verb, not the past form, when you use the auxiliary verb *have*.

PROBLEM 4

Improper use of the past participle

tense We (rung) the doorbell several times.

tense Jolene (swum) faster than anyone else on the team.

tense We (begun) the trip without much advance planning.

The past participle of an irregular verb cannot stand alone as a verb. It must be used with the auxiliary verb *have*.

Solution A
We have rung the doorbell several times.

Jolene has swum faster than anyone else on the team.

We have begun the trip without much advance planning.
Add the auxiliary verb *have* to the past participle to form a complete verb.

Solution B
We rang the doorbell several times.

Jolene swam faster than anyone else on the team.

We began the trip without much advance planning.
Replace the past participle with the past form of the verb.

Need More Help?

If you need more help with correct verb forms, turn to 15.1 and 15.2, pages 529–532.

9.9 Misplaced or Dangling Modifier

PROBLEM 1

A misplaced modifier

mod I got some fine pictures of the puppies with my new camera.

mod Dented and scratched, Marta found her bicycle.

mod We took a backpack on the train stuffed with sandwiches and fruit.

Modifiers that modify the wrong word or seem to modify more than one word in a sentence are called misplaced modifiers.

Solution

With my new camera I got some fine pictures of the puppies.

Marta found her bicycle dented and scratched.

We took a backpack stuffed with sandwiches and fruit on the train.

Move the misplaced phrase as close as possible to the word or words it modifies.

PROBLEM 2

The adverb only *misplaced*

mod Carlos only eats spaghetti with clam sauce.

The meaning of your sentence may be unclear if *only* is misplaced.

Solution

Only Carlos eats spaghetti with clam sauce.

Carlos eats only spaghetti with clam sauce.

Carlos eats spaghetti only with clam sauce.

Place the adverb *only* immediately before the word or group of words it modifies. Note that each time *only* is moved in the sentence, the meaning of the sentence changes.

PROBLEM 3

A dangling modifier

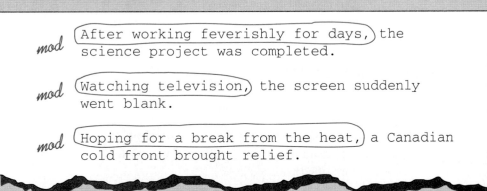

mod (After working feverishly for days,) the science project was completed.

mod (Watching television,) the screen suddenly went blank.

mod (Hoping for a break from the heat,) a Canadian cold front brought relief.

Dangling modifiers do not logically seem to modify any word in the sentence.

Solution

After working feverishly for days, Jan completed her science project.

Watching television, Yoshiko saw the screen suddenly go blank.

Hoping for a break from the heat, we were relieved when a Canadian cold front moved in.

Rewrite the sentence, adding a noun to which the dangling phrase clearly refers. Often you will have to add other words to complete the meaning of the sentence.

If you need more help with misplaced or dangling modifiers, turn to 18.7, pages 610–612.

9.10 Missing or Misplaced Possessive Apostrophe

PROBLEM 1

Singular nouns

poss The (waitress) wallet held that (days) tips.

Solution
The waitress's wallet held that day's tips.
Use an apostrophe and an *-s* to form the possessive of a singular noun, even one that ends in *-s*.

PROBLEM 2

Plural nouns ending in -s

poss The (soldiers) tents dotted the field.

Solution
The soldiers' tents dotted the field.
Use an apostrophe alone to form the possessive of a plural noun that ends in *-s*.

PROBLEM 3

Plural nouns not ending in -s

poss The (childrens) bookstore is on Broadway.

Solution
The children's bookstore is on Broadway.
Use an apostrophe and an *-s* to form the possessive of a plural noun that does not end in *-s*.

Pronouns

> *poss*   I found (somebodys) watch.
>
> *poss*   The best idea was (her's).

Solution A
I found somebody's watch.
Use an apostrophe and an *-s* to form the possessive of a singular indefinite pronoun.

Solution B
The best idea was hers.
Do not use an apostrophe with any of the possessive personal pronouns.

PROBLEM 5

Confusion between its *and* it's

> *poss*   The boat has slipped (it's) mooring.
>
> *poss*   (Its) a great day for a picnic.

The possessive of *it* is *its*. *It's* is the contraction of *it is*.

Solution
The boat has slipped its mooring.

It's a great day for a picnic.
Do not use an apostrophe to form the possessive of *it*. Use an apostrophe to form the contraction of *it is*.

If you need more help with apostrophes and possessives, turn to 17.1, page 578, and 21.11, pages 689–690.

Missing Commas with Nonessential Element

PROBLEM 1

Missing commas with nonessential participles, infinitives, and their phrases

com Claude watched⌒delighted⌒as Cheryl accepted the award.

com Marla⌒finishing her work⌒set out for a late afternoon jog.

com To repeat⌒the bus will leave promptly at five.

Solution

Claude watched, delighted, as Cheryl accepted the award.

Marla, finishing her work, set out for a late afternoon jog.

To repeat, the bus will leave promptly at five.

Determine whether the participle, infinitive, or phrase is truly not essential to the meaning of the sentence. If so, set off the phrase with commas.

PROBLEM 2

Missing commas with nonessential adjective clauses

com César⌒who is also a licensed pilot⌒is a certified scuba diver.

Solution

César, who is also a licensed pilot, is a certified scuba diver.

Determine whether the clause is truly not essential to the meaning of the sentence. If so, set off the clause with commas.

PROBLEM 3

Missing commas with nonessential appositives

> *com* Margaret Donelly⌒our letter carrier⌒is on vacation.

Solution
Margaret Donelly, our letter carrier, is on vacation.
Determine whether the appositive is truly not essential to the meaning of the sentence. If so, set off the appositive with commas.

PROBLEM 4

Missing commas with interjections and parenthetical expressions

> *com* Gosh⌒I enjoyed that game.
>
> *com* You know⌒of course⌒that the office is closed on Saturdays.

Solution
Gosh, I enjoyed that game.

You know, of course, that the office is closed on Saturdays.
Set off the interjection or parenthetical expression with commas.

Need More Help?

If you need more help with commas and nonessential elements, turn to 21.6, pages 674–676.

9.12   Missing Comma in a Series

PROBLEM

Missing comma in a series of words, phrases, or clauses

⌁ com   The garden was a riot of zinnias⌒hollyhocks⌒ marigolds⌒and lilies.

⌁ com   Reggie stopped⌒bent down⌒and picked up the quarter he had dropped.

⌁ com   Yuki ran down the street⌒around the corner⌒ and into the Murphys' garage.

⌁ com   We watched the kites soaring into the sky⌒ swooping back and forth⌒and gliding to earth.

⌁ com   Angela plays the guitar⌒Bill sings⌒and José accompanies them on the drums.

Solution
The garden was a riot of zinnias, hollyhocks, marigolds, and lilies.

Reggie stopped, bent down, and picked up the quarter he had dropped.

Yuki ran down the street, around the corner, and into the Murphys' garage.

We watched the kites soaring into the sky, swooping back and forth, and gliding to earth.

Angela plays the guitar, Bill sings, and José accompanies them on the drums.

When there are three or more elements in a series, use a comma after each element, including the element preceded by a conjunction.

Need More Help?

If you need more help with commas in a series, turn to 21.6, pages 673–674.

Unit 10 Parts of Speech

10.1 Nouns

A **noun** is a word that names a person, a place, a thing, or an idea.

PERSON	teacher, uncle, niece, sister-in-law
PLACE	star, garage, city, park
THING	paw, giraffe, bicycle, ice cream, doorknob
IDEA	democracy, fame, love, disappointment

A **concrete noun** names an object that occupies space or that can be recognized by any of the senses.

petal   smoke   cough   orange   nook

An **abstract noun** names an idea, a quality, or a characteristic.

motion   humor   quantity   tact   rudeness

Nouns can be singular or plural, depending upon whether they name *one* person, place, thing, or idea or *more than one*.

SINGULAR	boy, body, watch, wife, ox
PLURAL	boys, bodies, watches, wives, oxen

Nouns have a form to show possession, ownership, or the relationship between two nouns.

SINGULAR POSSESSIVE	PLURAL POSSESSIVE
the **car's** hood	the **cars'** hoods
a **baby's** bottle	the **babies'** bottles
the **dish's** pattern	the **dishes'** patterns
the **man's** idea	the **men's** idea

THING
ball

IDEA
sport

PERSON
player

PLACE
soccer field

Exercise 1

Identifying Nouns   On your paper list the twenty-five nouns that appear in the following literary passage.

Literature: In a New Country
   Hanging from a cord attached to the middle of the ceiling there was an electric bulb, low enough for an adult to reach and turn the black switch. I realized that this was our own electric light for us to turn on and off as we pleased. I pushed a chair under it and after some instruction from my mother proceeded to create lightning in the room by turning the switch as fast as I could. ➡

Next I discovered the bedsprings. When I sat on the bed it sank deliciously. Jumping on it in my stocking feet, I held my balance dangerously as I made the bed creak and the mattress bounce. The head and foot of the bed were made of iron scrollwork in loops and rosettes painted white.

From *Barrio Boy* by Ernesto Galarza

Exercise 2

Supplying Abstract and Concrete Nouns   For each concrete noun in items 1–5, write an abstract noun that names an idea with which the concrete noun can be associated. For each abstract noun in items 6–10, write a concrete noun that has the quality of the abstract noun.

SAMPLE ANSWERS   mechanic—deftness   taste—salt

1. bicycle
2. laughter
3. itch
4. home run
5. snow
6. haste
7. warmth
8. poverty
9. insight
10. sadness

Exercise 3

Completing Sentences with Nouns   On your paper complete each sentence by filling in the blanks with nouns. Be sure that your completed sentences make sense.

1. The _____ galloped by on her _____.
2. Two of her _____ waved their red _____.
3. The other _____ of her _____ cheered.
4. Her yellow _____ blew off her _____.
5. The _____ made her _____ fly wildly.

Proper and Common Nouns

A **proper noun** is the name of a particular person, place, thing, or idea.

A **common noun** is the general—not the particular—name of a person, place, thing, or idea.

Proper nouns are capitalized; common nouns are usually not capitalized.

PROPER NOUNS	
PERSON	Raul Julia, Uncle Peter, Emily Dickinson
PLACE	Mexico, Lake George, Grand Canyon
THING	Statue of Liberty, *Great Expectations,* Thanksgiving Day
IDEA	Romanticism, Baroque Age, Judaism

Exercise 4

Matching Proper Nouns with Common Nouns   Match the proper nouns on the left with the common nouns on the right.

1. Middle Ages
2. *Romeo and Juliet*
3. Cuba
4. *The Wizard of Oz*
5. Renoir
6. Rocky Mountains
7. Chicago Cubs
8. San Francisco
9. Nile River
10. Houston Space Center

a. city
b. mountains
c. building complex
d. team
e. painter
f. play
g. river
h. island
i. era
j. motion picture

Collective Nouns

A **collective noun** names a group.

family	(the) police	(the) senate	(a) gaggle (of geese)
team	(the) press	(an) audience	(the) board (of directors)

A collective noun is sometimes considered singular and sometimes considered plural. You consider a collective noun singular when you talk about a group as a whole. You consider a collective noun plural when you talk about the individual members of a group.

SINGULAR   The audience shouts its approval.
PLURAL   The audience have arrived in small groups.

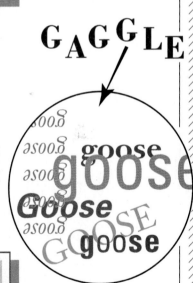

Exercise 5

Identifying Collective Nouns   On your paper list the five collective nouns in each of the following paragraphs:

Porgy and Bess
[1] The Metropolitan Opera's 1985 production of George Gershwin's *Porgy and Bess* had a chorus of seventy voices. [2] The cast included such noted opera stars as Grace Bumbry and ➡

Simon Estes. [3] The orchestra was conducted by James Levine. [4] The audience had bought their tickets well in advance for all sixteen performances. [5] The huge stage was filled with people representing the population of Catfish Row.

Animal Life in Africa

[1] In Africa a team of zoologists can observe many kinds of wild animals. [2] In a western forest one might see a family of chimpanzees. [3] In the eastern grasslands quiet watchers might spy a herd of roaming zebras. [4] In the northern desert a flock of ostriches is not an uncommon sight. [5] The African continent has an extraordinary collection of animal life.

Exercise 6: Sentence Writing

Creating Sentences with Nouns   Write five sentences about a shop in your town or neighborhood. Rely especially on concrete nouns to convey a vivid picture of the place.

Exercise 7: Review

Nouns   On your paper complete each sentence by filling in the twenty blanks with the kinds of nouns specified in *italic* typeface. Be sure that your completed sentences make sense.

Thanksgiving Day

The festive [1] *abstract* of the Thanksgiving [2] *concrete* filled our [3] *concrete*. My [4] *proper & concrete* told us the [5] *common* of the [6] *proper* who prepared the first Thanksgiving feast. All of the young [7] *common* listened. The table, set with our best [8] *concrete*, held steaming platters of [9] *concrete* and [10] *concrete*. For [11] *common* each of us had a generous [12] *common* of [13] *concrete*. After dinner we sat by the blazing [14] *concrete*, and [15] *proper & concrete* told us that it was President Lincoln who declared Thanksgiving an official holiday. Then we turned on the [16] *concrete* and watched [17] *proper & concrete.* Later that [18] *common* we agreed that we had had so much [19] *abstract* we wished that [20] *proper* came more than once a year.

In the following passage from *The Joy Luck Club*, Amy Tan uses nouns to convey the bustle and confusion that a California girl feels as she travels in a foreign country for the first time. Examine the passage closely, focusing especially on the italicized nouns.

> Before the *train* even comes to a *stop*, *people* are bringing down their *belongings* from above their *seats*. For a *moment* there is a dangerous *shower* of heavy *suitcases* laden with *gifts* to *relatives*, half-broken *boxes* wrapped in *miles* of *string* to keep the *contents* from spilling out, plastic *bags* filled with *yarn* and *vegetables* and *packages* of dried *mushrooms*, and camera *cases*. And then we are caught in a *stream* of *people* rushing, shoving, pushing us along, until we find ourselves in one of a dozen *lines* waiting to go through *customs*. I feel as if I were getting on the number 30 Stockton *bus* in *San Francisco*. I am in *China*, I remind myself. And somehow the *crowds* don't bother me. It feels right. I start pushing too.

Try to apply some of Amy Tan's writing techniques when you write and revise your own work:

1. Wherever possible, replace general words with precise concrete nouns. Notice that Tan does not merely say that the plastic bags are filled with *things*; instead, she mentions "*yarn* and *vegetables* and *packages* of dried *mushrooms*"—precise and concrete details that we can easily imagine.

2. Use proper nouns when appropriate to help make your writing more specific. Tan does not compare the scene with a crowded bus in any city; instead, she uses the proper noun "San Francisco."

3. Wherever possible, expand single nouns into longer groups of words that are more specific and detailed. For instance, Tan expands the noun *suitcases* into "heavy suitcases laden with gifts to relatives"; she expands *boxes* into "half-broken boxes wrapped in miles of string."

Practice these techniques by revising the following passage, using a separate sheet of paper. Pay particular attention to the italicized words.

> By seven o'clock on that snowy morning, the *park* was a scene of great activity. A *group* of *dogs* was racing across the *area*, putting *birds* to flight. Squirrels flicked their *tails* and scampered to *safety*. Along the *pathway*, the dog owners stamped their *feet* in snow and chatted about *things*.

10.2   Pronouns

A **pronoun** is a word that takes the place of a noun, a group of words acting as a noun, or another pronoun. The word or group of words that a pronoun refers to is called its **antecedent**.

When James Baldwin was fourteen years old, **he** became a preacher. [The pronoun *he* takes the place of the proper noun *James Baldwin*.]

When Georgia O'Keeffe and Alfred Stieglitz were married in 1924, **they** were **both** already famous artists. [The pronouns *they* and *both* take the place of the nouns *Georgia O'Keeffe* and *Alfred Stieglitz*.]

Although Georgia O'Keeffe **herself** was a painter, **her** husband was a photographer. [The pronouns *herself* and *her* take the place of the noun *Georgia O'Keeffe*.]

English has about seventy-five pronouns, which fall into one or more of the following categories: personal pronouns, reflexive and intensive pronouns, demonstrative pronouns, interrogative pronouns, relative pronouns, and indefinite pronouns.

Personal and Possessive Pronouns

A **personal pronoun** refers to a specific person or thing by indicating the person speaking (the first person), the person being addressed (the second person), or any other person or thing being discussed (the third person).

Personal pronouns also express number; they are either singular or plural.

Personal Pronouns		
	Singular	**Plural**
First Person	I, me	we, us
Second Person	you	you
Third Person	he, him	they, them
	she, her	
	it	

FIRST PERSON	**I** kept the dog. [*I* refers to the person speaking.]
SECOND PERSON	The dog was afraid of **you**. [*You* refers to the person being addressed.]
THIRD PERSON	**It** ran away from **them**. [*It* refers to the dog mentioned in the previous sentence. *Them* refers to the persons who are being discussed.]

Third-person pronouns express **gender.** *He* and *him* are masculine; *she* and *her* are feminine; *it* is neuter (neither masculine nor feminine).

The personal pronouns include several forms that indicate possession or ownership. These **possessive pronouns** take the place of the possessive forms of nouns.

Possessive Pronouns		
	Singular	**Plural**
First Person	my, mine	our, ours
Second Person	your, yours	your, yours
Third Person	his	their, theirs
	her, hers	
	its	

Some possessive forms are used before nouns. Other possessive forms can be used by themselves.

USED BEFORE A NOUN	Bring **your** bathing suit.
	Let's take **our** car.
USED ALONE	That bathing suit is **yours**.
	The car is **ours**.

Exercise 8

Using Personal and Possessive Pronouns   Improve the following paragraph by replacing the underlined words or groups of words with personal or possessive pronouns. Write your answers on your paper.

Isamu Noguchi, Sculptor

Isamu Noguchi is famous for [1] Noguchi's striking abstract sculptures. [2] These sculptures can be seen in museums everywhere. Noguchi's father was a Japanese poet, and [3] Noguchi's mother was an American writer. As a young man in Paris, Noguchi studied with the sculptor Constantin Brancusi, who encouraged [4] Noguchi to work in abstract forms. In the 1930s Noguchi settled in New York. Soon [5] Noguchi's spare and elegant sculptures were being exhibited, and many people went to see [6] the sculptures . One admirer, Martha Graham, invited [7] Noguchi to create sets for [8] Martha Graham's dance company. [9] Noguchi also designed sculpture gardens, as well as furniture and lamps. Noguchi's later interest in architectural forms and design is reflected in the monumental *Red Cube* (1968). [10] *Red Cube* stands outside the Marine Midland Building in New York.

Reflexive and Intensive Pronouns

Reflexive and intensive pronouns are formed by adding *-self* or *-selves* to certain of the personal and possessive pronouns.

Reflexive and Intensive Pronouns		
	Singular	**Plural**
First Person	myself	ourselves
Second Person	yourself	yourselves
Third Person	himself, herself, itself	themselves

A **reflexive pronoun** refers to a noun or another pronoun and indicates that the same person or thing is involved.

You outdid **yourself** when you wrote that song.

She always timed **herself** when jogging.

In dancing class we watch **ourselves** in the mirror.

An **intensive pronoun** adds emphasis to another noun or pronoun.

The team **itself** chose the captain.

Maria **herself** opened the door.

George and Pedro planned the party **themselves**.

Demonstrative Pronouns

A **demonstrative pronoun** points out specific persons, places, things, or ideas.

Demonstrative Pronouns		
Singular	this	that
Plural	these	those

This is your homeroom.   **That** will be your seat.
These are your classmates.   Carla's desk is cleaner than **those**.

Exercise 9

Using Reflexive, Intensive, and Demonstrative Pronouns
Supply the appropriate reflexive, intensive, or demonstrative pronoun for each blank. Write your answers on your paper.

An Orchestra Performance
1. He reminded _____ to watch the conductor's baton. ➡

2. The string, woodwind, brass, and percussion sections had prepared _____ during rehearsals.
3. Even the conductor _____ seemed nervous.
4. The air _____ seemed motionless in expectation.
5. We positioned _____ for the opening note.
6. Soon we found _____ listening anxiously for our cues.
7. _____ is a very moving piece.
8. We were so inspired by the occasion that our instruments seemed to play _____.
9. Afterward we all felt very proud of _____.
10. "Take _____," the concert manager said, handing several bouquets to the conductor.

Interrogative and Relative Pronouns

An **interrogative pronoun** is used to form questions.

who?   whom?   whose?   what?   which?

Who will lead the way?   **What** makes a good leader?
Whom would you choose?   **Which** of these paths is easiest?
Whose is the lightest pack?

The interrogative pronouns include the intensive forms *whoever, whomever, whichever,* and *whatever.*

Whoever could have made such a mistake?

A **relative pronoun** is used to begin a special subject-verb word group called a subordinate clause (see Unit 13).

who	whoever	which	that
whom	whomever	whichever	what
whose	whosoever	whatever	

The people **who** invented Monopoly were surprised by its success. [The relative pronoun *who* begins the subordinate clause *who invented Monopoly.*]

Dominoes is a game **that** many Texans play. [The relative pronoun *that* begins the subordinate clause *that many Texans play.*]

Exercise 10

Distinguishing Between Interrogative and Relative Pronouns   On your paper list the relative or interrogative pronoun that appears in each sentence, and label it as either a *relative* or an *interrogative* pronoun. ➡

Harriet Tubman, a Courageous Woman

1. Harriet Tubman, who was born a slave in 1820, became a leader of the antislavery movement.
2. Who would have guessed that she would become one of the most powerful speakers in the United States?
3. Tubman, whose maiden name was Araminta Greene, married a free black man named John Tubman.
4. She led more than three hundred fugitive slaves along the Underground Railroad, a secret route that led from the South to Canada.
5. Which of her many talents did she make use of during the Civil War?
6. She worked as a scout, spy, nurse, and laundress for the Union army, which fought to abolish slavery.
7. What did her fellow abolitionists call her?
8. Whatever she did, she lived up to her nickname, General Tubman.
9. Whom did she look after in the years following the Civil War?
10. She looked after orphans and old people, whom she loved dearly.

Some enjoyed the music.

Everyone went to the concert.

One got a crush on the lead singer.

Indefinite Pronouns

An **indefinite pronoun** refers to persons, places, or things in a more general way than a noun does.

> **Everyone** needs food. [The indefinite pronoun *everyone* refers to people in general.]

> Did you get **enough** to eat? [The indefinite pronoun *enough* does not indicate to what it specifically refers.]

> After two hamburgers he did not want **another**. [The indefinite pronoun *another* has the antecedent *hamburger*.]

Some Indefinite Pronouns				
all	each	many	nothing	somebody
another	either	most	one	someone
any	enough	much	other	something
anybody	everbody	neither	others	
anyone	everyone	nobody	plenty	
anything	everything	none	several	
both	few	no one	some	

Exercise 11: Sentence Writing

Using Pronouns Write ten sentences about a visit to a department store with a friend. Try to use pronouns from all the categories in this lesson.

Exercise 12: Review

Pronouns (a) On your paper list in order the twenty-five pronouns that appear in the following paragraph. (b) Identify each pronoun as *personal, possessive, reflexive* or *intensive, demonstrative, interrogative, relative,* or *indefinite*.

A Great Magician

¹Harry Houdini, a great magician who was born Ehrich Weiss, used a stage name borrowed from an earlier French magician called Houdin. ²Whereas many of Houdin's illusions were optical ones, those that made Harry Houdini famous were daring escapes from complex traps—most of them designed by Houdini himself. ³The most famous escape of all was the water-torture trick, in which Houdini, whose hands and feet were bound, was locked in the water-filled tank, only to emerge safe and free a moment later. ⁴Audiences would ask themselves, What does Houdini do to free himself? ⁵Wouldn't you wonder about this yourself? ⁶Actually Houdini created much of his magic by practicing yoga techniques, learning to survive on less oxygen than most of us need. ⁷Whose name is synonymous with magic? ⁸That is a question everyone can answer: it is Houdini.

10.3 Verbs

A **verb** is a word that expresses action or a state of being and is necessary to make a statement.

The violinists **begin.**	Rehearsals **are** important.
A flutist **entered** late.	The conductor **seems** enthusiastic.

The primary characteristic of a verb is its ability to express time—present, past, and future. Verbs express time by means of *tense* forms.

PRESENT TENSE	They **walk** home together.
PAST TENSE	They **walked** home together.
FUTURE TENSE	They **will walk** home together.

Exercise 13

Adding Verbs to Make Sentences On your paper write ten complete sentences by supplying a verb for each of the blanks in the items below.

The American Southwest

1. The Southwest _____ some of the most spectacular scenery in the country.
2. Deep canyons and tall mesas _____ the landscape.
3. Several Native American tribes _____ the Southwest: the Navaho, Hopi, Zuñi, and Pueblo make their home there.
4. Many Native Americans in the Southwest still _____ the customs of their ancestors.
5. Some ancient tribes _____ in houses made of adobe (sun-dried earth and straw).
6. Even today many people in the Southwest _____ their own adobe homes.
7. Navaho women still _____ rugs on handmade looms.
8. The Hopi people still _____ ancient rain dances.
9. The Native Americans of the Southwest _____ proud of their heritage.
10. Despite the intrusions of the modern world, many of their traditions _____ unchanged.

Action Verbs

An **action verb** tells what someone or something does.

Some action verbs express physical action; others express mental action.

PHYSICAL ACTION	In baseball the catcher often **signals** instructions to the pitcher.
MENTAL ACTION	A good catcher **understands** the technique of each batter.

A **transitive verb** is an action verb that is followed by a word or words that answer the question *what?* or *whom?*

Cats **see** their prey in the dark. [The action verb *see* is followed by the noun *prey*, which answers the question *see what?*]

An **intransitive verb** is an action verb that is *not* followed by a word that answers the question *what?* or *whom?*

Cats **see** well in the dark. [The action verb is followed by words that tell *how* and *when*.]

Recognizing Action Verbs   Write the action verbs that appear in each of the following sentences. Indicate whether each action verb is used as a *transitive* or an *intransitive verb*.

Sacajawea, an Intrepid Woman

1. After President Thomas Jefferson bought the Louisiana Territory from France, he arranged for its exploration.
2. In 1804 Meriwether Lewis and William Clark launched a search for an overland route to the Pacific Ocean.
3. Lewis and Clark hired a French-Canadian fur trapper, Toussaint Charbonneau, as guide and interpreter.
4. Charbonneau's wife, Sacajawea, a Shoshone of the Lehmi band, also joined the expedition.
5. With her linguistic skills Sacajawea helped Lewis and Clark's communication with Native American tribes.
6. Four years earlier hostile Native Americans had abducted Sacajawea and later sold her to Charbonneau.
7. In 1805 Lewis and Clark encountered a group of Shoshone, among them Sacajawea's brother, a chief.
8. He gave Lewis and Clark the horses they needed.
9. Sacajawea, her husband, and their infant son stayed with the expedition until Lewis and Clark reached the Pacific Coast.
10. Sacajawea and Charbonneau later returned to North Dakota, where some historians think Sacajawea died in 1812.

Creating Sentences with Action Verbs   Choose five of the action verbs that you identified in Exercise 14. For each verb write one sentence.

Linking Verbs

A **linking verb** links, or joins, the subject of a sentence (often a noun or pronoun) with a word or expression that identifies or describes the subject.

Be in all its forms—*am, is, are, was, were, will be, has been, was being*—is the most commonly used linking verb.

I **am** an athlete.	The players **are** fast.
Squash **is** an indoor sport.	They **were** hockey fans.

Several other verbs besides the forms of *be* can act as linking verbs:

Other Linking Verbs			
look	remain	seem	become
stay	grow	appear	sound
taste	smell	feel	

Exercise 16

Identifying Action and Linking Verbs   On your paper make a list of the ten verbs that appear in the following paragraph. Identify each verb as either *action* or *linking*.

The Statue of Liberty

[1]In 1884 France presented the United States with a gift as a dramatic gesture of friendship. [2]This spectacular gift was in the form of a huge copper statue. [3]Its official name is *Liberty Enlightening the World*. [4]Most people, however, know it simply as the Statue of Liberty. [5] The pieces of the statue arrived in the United States in 214 cases. [6] The French people donated the money for the construction of the statue. [7]Grateful, the people of the United States collected the funds for the massive granite and concrete pedestal. [8]This impressive monument found a permanent home on Liberty Island in New York Harbor. [9]At 151 feet and 1 inch high, it remains one of the largest statues in the world. [10] The monumental lady with the torch quickly became a symbol of American democracy.

Verb Phrases

The verb in a sentence may consist of more than one word. The words that accompany the main verb are called **auxiliary,** or helping, **verbs.** A **verb phrase** consists of a main verb and all its auxiliary, or helping, verbs.

Auxiliary Verbs			
Forms of *be*	am, is, are, was, were, being, been		
Forms of *have*	has, have, had		
Other auxiliaries	can, could	may, might	shall,	will,
	do, does, did	must	should	would

The most common auxiliary verbs are the forms of *be* and *have*.

We **are working.**   We **have worked.**   We **had been working.**

The other auxiliary verbs are not used primarily to express time:

I **should be leaving.**
Could he **have finished?**
Luisa **may** already **be waiting.**

Exercise 17

Identifying Verb Phrases   On your paper write each verb phrase that appears in each of the following sentences. (Five of the sentences have more than one verb phrase.) Put parentheses around the auxiliary verbs in each phrase.

Fats Waller, Great Jazz Musician

1. Fats Waller is regarded as one of the greatest jazz musicians of the twentieth century.
2. A versatile musician, he could compose, sing, and play several instruments with equal skill.
3. Fortunately, most of his music has been recorded.
4. Waller was already playing the piano at the age of six.
5. He had been taught by his mother, a musician herself.
6. Waller's father, a church deacon, had felt that his son should follow in his footsteps.
7. Nevertheless, young Waller was determined that his life would be dedicated to music.
8. By the age of sixteen, he was earning twenty-three dollars a week as a theater organist and had already written his first instrumental composition, "Boston Blues."
9. People must have been impressed with Waller's talents.
10. Can you believe that Waller's first song, "Squeeze Me," became a jazz classic?
11. A recording of the song by Louis Armstrong and Earl Hines had become popular by 1928.
12. By the beginning of the 1930s, Waller had become known not only as a major composer, bandleader, and jazz vocalist but also as the greatest jazz organist of his time.
13. By 1932 Waller had already composed the song that would become his most famous work, "Ain't Misbehavin'."
14. An earlier Waller song, "Honeysuckle Rose" (1928), has remained a favorite ever since.
15. It may not be widely recalled today that Waller was also known for several years as a successful radio performer.
16. By the mid-1930s Waller had become even more famous as a recording star for RCA Victor. ➡

17. At that time people were buying more records by Waller than by any other African-American musician.
18. *Ain't Misbehavin'*, a Broadway show with many of Waller's songs, was declared a hit in 1978, thirty-five years after Waller's death.
19. Those people who have seen *Ain't Misbehavin'* will surely never forget the experience.
20. Waller will always have a special place in American jazz.

Exercise 18: Sentence Writing

Creating Sentences with Vivid Verbs   Write five sentences about one of your favorite sports. Choose very specific action verbs and verb phrases to convey a vivid sense of the sport.

Exercise 19: Review

Verbs   On your paper complete each sentence in the following paragraph by supplying a verb. The kind of verb to use in each case is indicated in *italic* typeface. Be sure that your completed sentences make sense.

New York's World Trade Center

The massive World Trade Center in New York City [1] *linking verb* a city within a city. About fifty thousand people [2] *action verb* in its stores and offices, and another eighty thousand or so [3] *action verb* in and out each day. The center [4] *action verb* 110 stories in each of its twin towers, and another 6 levels [5] *action verb* underground. Its dozens of stores, from florists to drugstores, [6] *linking verb* attractive and busy. The stores often [7] *action verb* special services to their customers. Clients of the cleaners, for example, [8] *verb phrase* their clothes in large bags for protection on the subway. The enormous kitchens of the center [9] *verb phrase* as many as thirty thousand people each day. More than twenty restaurants [10] *action verb* inside the buildings. The vast complex even [11] *action verb* its own police station, with a force of thirty-nine officers. The manager's office [12] *linking verb* busy all the time. In fact, it [13] *action verb* over two hundred calls for assistance each day. Some people [14] *linking verb* too hot and [15] *action verb* a lower temperature. Others [16] *verb phrase* themselves out of their offices and [17] *action verb* spare keys. An ambulance [18] *verb phrase* outside the complex at all times in case of an emergency, and paramedics, with the latest ➡

in life-support equipment, [19] *verb phrase* the life of a seriously ill or injured person. With its impressive population and variety of services, the World Trade Center [20] *linking verb* a small city in the middle of New York City.

Writing Link

Here are guidelines for using verbs to crystallize poetic images:

1. Try to reduce a group of words to one action verb. For example, instead of writing "And let your hair fall loosely around your face," W. B. Yeats wrote, "And tumble out your hair."

2. Instead of beginning sentences with *there is* or *there were*, begin with a noun and follow up with a colorful action verb. Alfred, Lord Tennyson, for example, used the following image: "The long light shakes across the lake." How flat the picture would have been had Tennyson stated, "There was a long light shining across the lake."

3. Whenever possible, use action verbs rather than linking verbs. Christina Rossetti begins a poem with the question "Does the road wind uphill all the way?" The action verb "wind" is stronger than any linking verb. Compare the effect of Rossetti's line with "Is the road uphill all the way?"

4. Try to replace general verbs with more precise action verbs. Instead of writing "Old age should protest at close of day," Dylan Thomas wrote, "Old age should burn and rave at close of day." "Burn" and "rave" convey exactly how the poet felt a person who has led a long life should react to the approach of death.

Practice these techniques by revising the following passage. Pay particular attention to the italicized words.

Today *there was* a changed world. At some point very early in the morning, winter *went* and spring *was here*. When I *got up*, sunlight *was coming* through my window. My room *was light*, and my mood *became bright* to match it. I threw open the window and *gave the new season a greeting*. In response the mellow air *came in* and *made the room warm*.

10.4   Adjectives

An **adjective** is a word that modifies a noun or pronoun by limiting its meaning.

round window	**six** oranges	**that** hat	**adult** cat
romantic story	**many** ideas	**these** books	**Scottish** wool

Possessive pronouns, such as *our* and *his*, can be considered adjectives because they modify nouns in addition to acting in their usual function as pronouns: *our* book, *his* watch. Similarly, possessive nouns can be considered adjectives: *Julia's* dream.

Adjectives may be used in various positions in relation to the words they modify.

How **obedient** the poodle is!
That **obedient** poodle belongs to her.
The poodle is **obedient.**
The judges considered the poodle **obedient.**
The poodle, always **obedient,** waited by the door.

Many adjectives have different forms to indicate degree of comparison.

fastest
faster
fast

POSITIVE	COMPARATIVE	SUPERLATIVE
light	lighter	lightest
funny	funnier	funniest
practical	more practical	most practical

Exercise 20

Finding Adjectives   On your paper list the twenty adjectives that appear in the following passage, which describes a scene on a British heath during the last century. Count possessive pronouns as adjectives, but do not count the words *a, an,* and *the.*

Literature: A Long Road

Before him stretched the long, laborious road, dry, empty, and white. It was quite open to the heath on each side, and bisected that vast, dark surface. . . . The old man frequently stretched his eyes ahead to gaze over the tract that he had yet to traverse. At length he discerned, a long distance in front of him, a moving spot. . . . Its rate of advance was slow. . . . When he drew nearer he perceived it to be a . . . van, ordinary in shape, but singular in color. . . . The driver walked beside it; and, like his van, he was completely red.

From *The Return of the Native* by Thomas Hardy

Articles

Articles are the adjectives *a*, *an*, and *the*. *A* and *an* are called indefinite articles. *The* is called a definite article.

INDEFINITE	She found **a** ring.	They spotted **an** iceberg.
DEFINITE	She found **the** ring.	They spotted **the** iceberg.

Proper Adjectives

A **proper adjective** is formed from a proper noun and begins with a capital letter.

Rembrandt was a **Dutch** painter.
The **Berlin** Wall came down in 1989.

The following suffixes are often used to create proper adjectives: *-an*, *-ian*, *-n*, *-ese*, and *-ish*.

PROPER NOUNS	PROPER ADJECTIVES
Alaska	Alaskan
Queen Victoria	Victorian
Vietnam	Vietnamese
Denmark	Danish

Exercise 24: Review

Adjectives   On your paper write the twenty adjectives, including articles, that appear in the following paragraph.

Mayan Culture

[1]Recent discoveries have revealed new facts about the ancient Maya, who formed one of the oldest societies in Central America. [2]By A.D. 1000 they had already made impressive and original advancements in art and science. [3]Recently, at a site in northern Belize, fortunate archaeologists unearthed the unmistakable remains of an early civilization. [4]This discovery was remarkable and significant, for it pushed back the origins of Mayan culture to 2400 B.C.

In this passage from Rudolph Fisher's short story "Miss Cynthie," the title character, a woman from the rural South of the 1920s, has her first glimpse of the New York City neighborhood known as Harlem. Study the passage closely, focusing especially on the italicized adjectives.

They were traveling up Seventh Avenue now, and something was miraculously *different*. Not the road; that was as *broad* as ever, *wide*, *white*, *gleaming* in the sun. Not the houses; they were *lofty* still, *lordly*, *disdainful*, *supercilious*. Not the cars; they continued to race impatiently onward, *innumerable*, *precipitate*, *tumultuous*. Something else, something at once *obvious* and *subtle*, *insistent*, *pervasive*, *compelling*. . . . Not just a change of complexion. A completely *dissimilar* atmosphere. Sidewalks *teeming* with *leisurely* strollers, at once strangely *dark* and *bright*. Boys in *white* trousers, berets, and *green* shirts, with *slickened black* heads and *proud* swagger. *Bareheaded* girls in *crisp organdy* dresses, *purple*, *canary*, *gay scarlet*. And laughter, *abandoned strong Negro* laughter, some falling full on the ear, some not heard at all, yet sensed—the *warm* life-breath of the *tireless* carnival to which Harlem's heart quickens in summer.

Here are some of Fisher's techniques that you can apply when you write and revise your own work:

1. Try to use adjectives that will make nouns more specific. Fisher makes his nouns more specific by using adjectives that describe size ("broad," "wide," "lofty"), color ("white," "green," "black," "purple," "canary," "scarlet"), texture ("slickened," "crisp"), and other physical characteristics ("gleaming," "dark," "bright," "bareheaded," "strong," "warm"). These adjectives appeal to our senses.

2. Try to use adjectives that convey a consistent mood or atmosphere. Fisher wants to convey the lively, joyful mood of Harlem in summer, and he chooses adjectives that contribute to this mood ("gleaming," "innumerable," "precipitate," "tumultuous," "compelling," "proud," "gay," "abandoned," "strong," "warm," "tireless").

3. Try to choose adjectives for their sound as well as their meaning. Notice, for example, the repeated *l* sounds in "*l*ofty sti*ll*, *l*ord*l*y, disdainfu*l*, superci*l*ious." These sounds create a rolling effect that underscores the elegant sweep of the city houses that Miss Cynthie sees as she drives up the avenue.

Practice these techniques by revising the following passage on a separate sheet of paper. Improve the passage by adding adjectives in the places indicated by the carets (∧).

The ∧lights in the ∧theater dimmed, and the ∧crowd fell silent. Slowly the ∧curtain rose. A(n) ∧spotlight picked out a(n) ∧corner of the stage, where a(n) ∧actress dressed in ∧overalls and a(n) ∧hat sat quietly on a(n) ∧bench. Suddenly she began to sing, her ∧voice ringing out like chimes.

10.5 Adverbs

An **adverb** is a word that modifies a verb, an adjective, or another adverb by making its meaning more specific.

The following sentence illustrates the use of adverbs to modify an adjective *(odd)*, a verb *(become)*, and an adverb *(surprisingly)*:

Extremely odd styles **sometimes** become **rather** surprisingly popular.

Adverbs modify by answering the questions *when? where? how?* and *to what degree?*

I will call **tomorrow.**	Kim **carefully** polished the car.
His phone rings **often.**	We were **truly** sorry.
The speaker will stand **here.**	

Like adjectives, some adverbs have different forms to indicate degree of comparison.

POSITIVE	COMPARATIVE	SUPERLATIVE
runs **fast**	runs **faster**	runs **fastest**
works **carefully**	works **more carefully**	works **most carefully**
sees **well**	sees **better**	sees **best**

When an adverb modifies a verb, it may be placed in various positions in relation to the verb. When an adverb modifies an adjective or another adverb, it immediately precedes the modified word.

MODIFYING A VERB	**Finally** the storm is ending.
	The storm **finally** is ending.
	The storm is **finally** ending.
	The storm is ending **finally.**
MODIFYING AN ADJECTIVE	The snow was **quite** heavy.
MODIFYING AN ADVERB	It **almost** never snows this heavily.

Negative Words as Adverbs

The word *not* and the contraction *n't* are considered adverbs. Other negative words can function as adverbs of time and place.

The plane has **not** landed.	They have **hardly** boarded.
The plane is **nowhere** in sight.	I have **never** flown.

Exercise 25

Identifying Adverbs   Write the adverb(s) that appear in each sentence below. Then write the word or words each adverb modifies.

A Great Blues Singer

1. Bessie Smith is often considered a great blues singer.
2. She grew up in an extremely poor family in Chattanooga, Tennessee.
3. Hardly fourteen, she was already touring with Ma Rainey and her Rabbit Foot Minstrels.
4. Bessie Smith never sang songs matter-of-factly.
5. Jazz writers have called her style rhythmically adventurous.
6. In 1923 she began to make commercially successful records.
7. Louis Armstrong was one very famous jazz musician with whom she sang.
8. Her greatest fame probably came in the years from 1923 to 1928.
9. Her record *Nobody's Blues but Mine*, which covers the period from 1925 to 1927, remains popular today.
10. Bessie Smith died tragically in a car accident in 1937.

Exercise 26

Positioning Adverbs   (a) On your paper add an appropriate verb-modifying adverb to each of the following sentences. (b) Rewrite each sentence, placing the adverb in a different position.

SAMPLE   Track-and-field star Florence Griffith-Joyner accepted her gold medal.

ANSWER   (a) Track-and-field star Florence Griffith-Joyner proudly accepted her gold medal.
(b) Proudly, track-and-field star Florence Griffith-Joyner accepted her gold medal.

An Olympic Race

1. Another group of Olympic runners waited for their signal.
2. The starting shot rang out.
3. All eight racers leaped from their starting blocks.
4. The runner from Kenya began to lag.
5. The French contestant was pulling ahead of her.
6. The Kenyan runner exerted her last ounce of strength.
7. The two women were running neck and neck. ➡

8. The Kenyan spectators jumped to their feet as their favorite crossed the finish line.
9. To the strains of her national anthem, the Kenyan runner accepted the gold medal.
10. The French runner shook her opponent's hand.

Exercise 27: Sentence Writing

Following Models   A Tom Swifty is a sentence in which an adverb comments in a humorous way on an action or object mentioned in a quotation. Note the relationship between each adverb and quotation in the following examples:

"Will you hang up these wet clothes?" asked Ben dryly.

"I've never seen such flat land," said the farmer plainly.

(a) Write each of the following Tom Swifties on your paper, completing each with an adverb that comments in a humorous way on the quotation. (b) Write five Tom Swifties of your own, using the adverbs provided. Consult a dictionary if necessary.

1. "Please turn on the light," requested Sara _____.
2. "I need the sandpaper," said the carpenter _____.
3. "The temperature is rising," said the weather forecaster _____.
4. "Be careful with that knife!" warned Hiroshi _____.
5. "My arm is aching," complained the pitcher _____.
6. coldly
7. heavily
8. sourly
9. snappily
10. idly

Exercise 28: Review

Adverbs   On your paper write each of the twenty adverbs that appear in the following paragraph. Then write the word or words that each adverb modifies.

Hurricanes

[1]Hurricanes are severe storms with extremely strong winds. [2]Storms with this name are always limited to the northern Atlantic Ocean. [3]The same storm in the western Pacific Ocean is not called a hurricane; it is a typhoon. [4]In the Indian Ocean ➡

such a storm generally is known as a cyclone. [5]A hurricane is defined officially as a storm with winds of at least seventy-five miles an hour. [6]Such storms usually start in the North Atlantic and move westward. [7]Sometimes they progress northeastward from the Mexican coast. [8]They move at approximately ten miles an hour in the beginning and gradually gain speed. [9]A fully mature hurricane is almost circular. [10]Air pressure in its center, or eye, can be extremely low. [11]In the eye the air barely moves, the atmosphere seems strangely calm, and the sky often looks blue. [12]Clouds that swirl rapidly outside quickly bring violent winds and rain.

Writing Link

In this passage from Richard Wright's story "The Man Who Lived Underground," a man attempts a frantic escape. Notice how the italicized adverbs help clarify his actions and heighten the suspense:

> He dropped *instinctively* to his knees and his hands grasped the rim of the manhole. The siren seemed to hoot *directly* above him and with a wild gasp of exertion he snatched the cover *far enough off* to admit his body. . . . He dropped and was washed *violently* into an ocean of warm, leaping water. His head was battered against a wall and he wondered if this were death. *Frenziedly* his fingers clawed and sank into a crevice. He steadied himself and measured the strength of the current with his own muscular tension. He stood *slowly* in water that dashed past his knees with fearful velocity.

Try to apply some of Wright's techniques in using adverbs in your own writing:

1. Use adverbs to clarify actions or behavior. In Wright's sentences, for example, the adverb "instinctively" helps explain how the man jumps down the manhole.

2. Use adverbs to stress a point you are trying to make. Notice how Wright uses the adverb "directly" to stress his point about how close the siren is.

3. Choose adverbs that contribute to the mood or atmosphere you are trying to convey. Notice how the adverbs "violently" and "frenziedly" underscore the tense mood of the incident Wright is describing.

Apply these techniques by revising the following passage. On a separate sheet of paper, add adverbs in the places indicated by carets (∧).

> Melissa's interview with the personnel manager was ∧ dreadful. While Ms. Gonzalez sat ∧ in her padded armchair, Melissa was forced to hunch ∧ in a flimsy straight-backed chair. The personnel manager's questions were ∧ sharp and difficult, and she ∧ looked over Melissa's head as Melissa tried to answer.

10.6   Prepositions

A **preposition** is a word that shows the relationship of a noun or pronoun to some other word in a sentence.

The silverware is **inside** the cabinet.   [*Inside* shows the spatial relationship of the silverware and the cabinet.]

All the guests arrived **before** dinner.   [*Before* tells the time relationship between the guests' arrival and their dinner.]

He brought a gift **for** the host.   [*For* does not cover a spatial or time relationship, but it does relate *gift* and *host*.]

Olga had lunch **after** the meeting.   [*After* tells the time relationship between lunch and the meeting.]

Commonly Used Prepositions

aboard	beneath	in	regarding
about	beside	inside	since
above	besides	into	through
across	between	like	throughout
after	beyond	near	to
against	but*	of	toward
along	by	off	under
amid	concerning	on	underneath
among	despite	onto	until
around	down	opposite	unto
as	during	out	up
at	except	outside	upon
before	excepting	over	with
behind	for	past	within
below	from	pending	without

*meaning "except"

A **compound preposition** is a preposition that is made up of more than one word.

Compound Prepositions

according to	because of	next to
ahead of	by means of	on account of
along with	in addition to	on top of
apart from	in front of	out of
aside from	in spite of	owing to
as to	instead of	

Prepositions begin phrases that generally end with a noun or pronoun called the **object of the preposition.**

He drank a glass **of milk.**
She stood **in front of us.**
I ate some bread **with cheese.**
At the end the guests applauded.
According to her, they were **ahead of us.**

Exercise 29

Identifying Prepositions   On your paper list the prepositions that appear in each of the following sentences. Remember that some prepositions are made up of more than one word. (The numeral in parentheses at the end of each item indicates the number of prepositions in that sentence.)

A Great Jazz Musician

1. The great jazz musician Sonny Rollins was born in New York in 1920 to musical parents. (3)
2. Instead of the usual piano or violin, Rollins chose the tenor saxophone for his instrument. (2)
3. Like many jazz musicians he often improvised on themes within the music. (3)
4. His exceptional album *Moving Out* put him at the top of his profession. (2)
5. During the late fifties and into the sixties, his work became notable for its energy and daring. (3)
6. Rollins took music out of its usual locations and went beyond the usual limits of the saxophone. (3)
7. Sometimes he would play his saxophone outdoors instead of indoors. (1)
8. Another of his experiments involved making the sound from his saxophone bounce off walls and ceilings. (3)
9. Rollins continued experiments with music throughout the 1960s. (2)
10. In addition to his experimental work, Rollins played the music for the movie *Alfie.* (2)

Exercise 30: Sentence Writing

Creating Sentences with Prepositions   Choose five prepositions from the lists on page 426. Use each one in a sentence. Add adjectives and adverbs wherever necessary.

10.7 Conjunctions

A **conjunction** is a word that joins single words or groups of words.

Coordinating Conjunctions

A **coordinating conjunction** joins words or groups of words that have equal grammatical weight in a sentence.

Coordinating Conjunctions					
and	but	or	nor	for	yet

Two **and** two are four.
She is good at algebra **but** not at arithmetic.
We must leave now, **or** we will be late.
The bell rang, **yet** everyone remained seated.

Exercise 31

Identifying Coordinating Conjunctions   Write the coordinating conjunction that appears in each of the following sentences.

A Monument to Civil Rights

¹The civil rights leaders of the 1960s strove to win greater respect, dignity, and political freedom for African Americans. ²Martin Luther King Jr. was the most famous civil rights leader, but he was not the only person to participate in the struggle. ³Ordinary citizens, such as Rosa Parks, who refused to sit at the back of a segregated bus, contributed to the fight for justice and equality. ⁴Taunts did not deter the civil rights demonstrators, nor did physical abuse. ⁵A new monument in Alabama commemorates the famous heroes of the movement, yet it does not ignore its anonymous heroes. ⁶The monument is in the city of Montgomery, for it was there that many famous civil rights demonstrations took place. ⁷Made of smooth black granite, the monument is simple, yet it is remarkably powerful. ⁸Water flows gently over the flat surface of the granite stone and collects in a pool. ⁹The names of civil rights leaders or the dates of famous events in the struggle are engraved on the stone. ¹⁰The monument was designed by the Chinese-American architect Maya Lin, who is famous for her bold and austere monument to the veterans of the Vietnam War.

Correlative Conjunctions

Correlative conjunctions work in pairs to join words and groups of words of equal weight in a sentence.

Correlative Conjunctions		
both . . . and	just as . . . so	not only . . . but (also)
either . . . or	neither . . . nor	whether . . . or

Correlative conjunctions make the relationship between words or groups of words a little clearer than do coordinating conjunctions.

COORDINATING CONJUNCTIONS	CORRELATIVE CONJUNCTIONS
She **and** I were there.	**Both** she **and** I were there.
She **or** I can go.	**Either** she **or** I can go.
	Neither she **nor** I can go.
I met Jean **and** Ed.	I met **not only** Jean **but also** Ed.

Exercise 32

Identifying Correlative Conjunctions   On your paper write both parts of the correlative conjunctions that appear in the following sentences.

Weather Forecasting

1. Just as people are interested in the weather forecast today, so people thousands of years ago tried to predict weather conditions.
2. Methods of predicting the weather have grown not only more complicated but also more accurate.
3. Both modern and ancient cultures have looked to the sky for signs of change in the weather.
4. The predictions of the ancients, whether correct or incorrect, were based on very different methods from those of today.
5. Neither the seemingly essential thermometer nor the equally useful barometer was invented until a few hundred years ago.
6. Both the modern telegraph and the even more recent satellite have made it possible to exchange weather information more rapidly.
7. Satellites are used for early spotting not only of hurricanes but also of tornadoes.
8. Neither high-speed computers nor other advanced technological breakthroughs have revealed all we need to know to predict the weather accurately. ➡

9. The National Oceanic and Atmospheric Administration is responsible for both studying the weather and forecasting it.
10. Weather forecasting is an activity not only of government agencies but also of private companies.

Subordinating Conjunctions

A **subordinating conjunction** joins two clauses, or ideas, in such a way as to make one grammatically dependent upon the other.

The idea, or clause, that a subordinating conjunction introduces is said to be "subordinate," or dependent, because it cannot stand by itself as a complete sentence.

We raked the leaves **because** so many had fallen.
We raked the leaves **before** we had lunch.
Wherever the leaves had fallen, we raked them into piles.
When more leaves fall, we will rake again.

The father pushed the baby...

because

she could not push herself.

Common Subordinating Conjunctions			
after	as though	provided (that)	until
although	because	since	when
as	before	so long as	whenever
as far as	considering (that)	so that	where
as if	if	than	whereas
as long as	inasmuch as	though	wherever
as soon as	in order that	unless	while

Exercise 33

Identifying Subordinating Conjunctions   Write the subordinating conjunction that appears in each sentence below. Remember that some subordinating conjunctions are made up of more than one word.

The Art of Mural Painting

1. Although murals are found in many cultures around the world, they have always been a particularly important art form in Mexico.
2. Some of the murals painted by Mayan artists in ancient Mexico still survive, though many are in poor condition.
3. Before the Mexican painter Diego Rivera came on the scene, twentieth-century Mexican murals were relatively unknown. ➡

4. Rivera designed extraordinary murals in Mexico and the United States before he died in 1957.
5. Many of Rivera's murals depict scenes from Mexican history because Rivera believed that Mexicans are defined by their past.
6. After Rivera died, many Mexican-American muralists took up the style and themes of the late artist's work.
7. Mexican-American artists in Los Angeles are painting murals wherever they can find the space.
8. The muralists paint on public buildings so that their work can be enjoyed by many people.
9. If it is possible, the muralists use bright colors and bold, eye-catching designs.
10. As long as Hispanic culture continues to thrive in the United States, we will surely have many colorful and exciting murals to enjoy.

Conjunctive Adverbs

A **conjunctive adverb** is used to clarify the relationship between clauses of equal weight in a sentence.

Conjunctive adverbs are usually stronger and more precise than coordinating conjunctions.

| COORDINATING CONJUNCTION | Most people think of deserts as very hot places, **but** desert nights can be quite cool. |
| CONJUNCTIVE ADVERB | Most people think of deserts as very hot places; **however,** desert nights can be quite cool. |

There are many conjunctive adverbs, and they have several uses, as the following examples show:

TO REPLACE *AND*	also, besides, furthermore, moreover
TO REPLACE *BUT*	however, nevertheless, still, though
TO STATE A RESULT	consequently, therefore, so, thus
TO STATE EQUALITY	equally, likewise, similarly

Exercise 34

Identifying Conjunctive Adverbs   Each of the following sentences has one conjunctive adverb. Write that word on your paper. ➡

Toltec Civilization

1. The Toltec civilization of ancient Mexico was advanced in arts and architecture; moreover, it produced impressive stonework.
2. The Toltec religion at one time centered on Quetzalcoatl; consequently, this plumed serpent appeared in many legends and images.
3. Quetzalcoatl was the name of a deity; furthermore, it was the name of a legendary ruler.
4. Quetzalcoatl was identified with the planet Venus; likewise, he was associated with the wind.
5. Usually Quetzalcoatl was represented as a plumed serpent; however, he was often shown as the wind god.
6. The people wished to please Quetzalcoatl; therefore, they built circular temples, which presented no sharp obstacles to the wind.
7. There were many different religious ceremonies and rituals; moreover, people played a sacred ball game called *tlatchi* that resembled basketball.
8. The Toltec civilization expanded southward during the tenth century; therefore, the Toltecs dominated the Mayas of the Yucatan.
9. Other nomadic Mexican tribes conquered the Toltec Empire in the thirteenth century; thus, the Toltec civilization declined.
10. One of the new tribes, the Aztecs, soon built their own empire; consequently, art and science continued to flourish in Mexico.

Exercise 35: Sentence Writing

Creating Sentences with Conjunctions   Think of a day, either real or imagined, in which several interesting and varied events happened to you. Write several sentences about that day, using as many conjunctions as possible.

Exercise 36: Review

Conjunctions   On your paper replace the blank or blanks that appear in each of the following sentences with a conjunction that makes sense. The kind of conjunction to use is stated in parentheses at the end of each sentence. ➡

Modern Tunnel Construction

1. Modern tunnel building is a complicated process; _____, it is a very costly process, involving millions of dollars. (conjunctive adverb)

2. _____ a tunnel under a river costs considerably more than a bridge, it may have certain advantages. (subordinating conjunction)

3. _____ does it allow the unhindered passage of ships, _____ it is less vulnerable. (correlative conjunction)

4. A tunnel is a marvelous construction, _____ building it is extremely hazardous. (coordinating conjunction)

5. There are basically three ways to build a tunnel; _____, tunnels may be divided into three types. (conjunctive adverb)

6. A "true" tunnel is dug horizontally through earth _____ rock. (coordinating conjunction)

7. For the cut-and-cover tunnel a large ditch is dug, a tube is built in the ditch, _____ the tube is covered over. (coordinating conjunction)

8. _____ the first subway in the world, in London, _____ the first on the European continent, in Budapest, were built in this way. (correlative conjunction)

9. The trench tunnel involves a kind of cut-and-cover method used _____ the tunnel is dug underwater. (subordinating conjunction)

10. _____ a route is chosen for any tunnel, a careful geologic study is made of the type of earth and rock along the way. (subordinating conjunction)

Examine the following description of an important moment between Cress and her grandfather in Jessamyn West's story "Sixteen." Notice especially the effect of the italicized conjunctions.

> Cress sat down on the chair *and* put two squeamish fingers into the jar of gray ointment; *but* she could see far more sense to this than to any talking or being talked to. *If* they had brought her home from school *because* she was needed in helping to care for Grandpa, that she could understand—*but* not simply to be present at his death. What had death to do with her?
>
> She leaned over him, rubbing, *but* with eyes shut, dipping her fingers often into the gray grease. The rhythm of the rubbing, the warmth and closeness of the room, after the cold drive, had almost put her to sleep *when* the old man startled her by lifting a shaking hand to the bunch of yellow violets Edith had pinned to the shoulder of her dress *before* she left Woolman. She opened her eyes suddenly at his touch, *but* the old man said nothing, only stroked the violets awkwardly with a trembling forefinger.

Here are some of West's techniques that you can apply when you write and revise your work.

1. Notice West's frequent use of "but" to express contrast. The repeated appearance of the word subtly emphasizes the inner conflict that Cress is experiencing. In your own writing use coordinating conjunctions to express specific relationships between ideas. For example, use *or* to express alternatives, *for* to express a reason or cause and effect, and *but* or *yet* to express contrast.

2. Notice how West uses subordinating conjunctions to express the relationships between different ideas clearly and succinctly. In the third sentence the subordinating conjunctions "if" and "because" express reasons, whereas in the fifth sentence the conjunctions "when" and "before" establish the time of events. Note also how the conjunctions allow West to combine several ideas and clauses into one sentence. In your own writing make use of subordinating conjunctions to make clear the relationships between your ideas.

Apply these techniques by revising the following passage. Add conjunctions in the places indicated by carets (∧).

> ∧ I think of my late grandfather, what I remember is a proud ∧ determined ∧ stubborn man. ∧ he was an educated man ∧ literate in his native language ∧ he came to the United States from Italy in 1921, he had still not learned to speak more than a minimum of English ∧ he had lived here for more than sixty years. The cause was not lack of intelligence ∧ ability ∧ rather his fierce pride, ∧ a night school teacher had wounded that pride many years ago by criticizing my grandfather's English in class. ∧ that incident occurred, my grandfather refused to return to school to learn English. ∧ I came away learning something from this story, my lesson was that life calls on us to be proud ∧ humble also.

10.8 Interjections

An **interjection** is a word or phrase that expresses emotion or exclamation. An interjection has no grammatical connection to other words.

Oh, I didn't know that.   **Whew,** it's hot.
Ouch! That hurts!   **Why,** Stanley!

Exercise 37

Using Interjections   On your paper fill in the blank in each sentence below with an appropriate interjection from the following list:

wow	oops	ssh	ah	whew
well	psst	yipes	alas	ouch

1. _____ That was an amazing catch!
2. _____ I dropped the plate.
3. _____ you are here at last.
4. _____ The stove is hot!
5. _____ the concert is beginning.
6. _____ That was pretty close!
7. _____ it is finally over.
8. _____ come here a second, but do not let anyone see you.
9. _____ That is the wildest thing I have ever heard!
10. _____ It is pouring, and I forgot to shut the windows.

Grammar Workshop

Parts of Speech

Two orphaned sisters are the main characters of this novel, which is set in an impoverished town in Idaho sometime between the two world wars. In this passage the elder sister, Ruth, reminisces about the year when heavy snows nearly buried the village of Fingerbone. The passage has been annotated to show some of the parts of speech covered in this unit.

Literature Model

from HOUSEKEEPING
by Marilynne Robinson

Common noun

Proper noun

Adjective

Linking verb

Relative pronoun

Coordinating conjunction

Compound noun

Personal pronoun

It was a hard winter, too. The snow crested, finally, far above our heads. It drifted up our eaves on one side of the house. Some houses in Fingerbone simply fell from the weight of snow on their roofs, a source of grave and perpetual anxiety to my great-aunts, who were accustomed to a brick building, and to living below ground. Sometimes the sun would be warm enough to send a thick sheet of snow sliding off the roof, and sometimes the fir trees would shrug, and the snow would fall with surprisingly loud and earthy thuds, which would terrify my great-aunts. . . .

For some reason the lake was a source of particular pleasure to Fingerbone that year. It was frozen solid early and long. Several acres of it were swept, for people brought brooms to tend and expand it, till the cleared ice spread far across the lake. Sledders heaped snow on the shore into a precipitous chute that sent them sailing far across the ice. There were barrels on the shore for fires to be built in, and people brought boxes to sit on and planks and burlap bags to stand on around the barrels, and frankfurters to roast, and clothespins to clip frozen mittens to the lips of barrels. A number of dogs began to spend most of their time at the ice. They were young, leggy dogs, affable and proprietary, and exhilarated by the weather. They liked to play at retrieving bits of ice which sped fantastically fast and far across the lake. The dogs made a gallant and youthful ➡

joke of their own strength and speed, and flaunted an utter ——— Action verb
indifference to the safety of their limbs. Lucille and I took
our skates to school, so that we could go to the lake directly ——— Subordinating
and stay there through the twilight. Usually we would   conjunction
skate along the edge of the swept ice, tracing its shape, and
coming finally to its farthest edge, we would sit on the ——— Preposition
snow and look back at Fingerbone.
Possessive pronoun
   We felt giddily far from shore, though the lake was so
solid that winter that it would certainly have supported the
weight of the entire population of Fingerbone, past, pres- ——— Adverb
ent, and to come. Nevertheless, only we and the ice
sweepers went out so far, and only we stayed.

Grammar Workshop Exercise 1

Identifying Nouns   The following sentences elaborate on
ideas suggested by the passage from *Housekeeping*. On your
paper identify each of the nouns in these sentences. After each
noun write in parentheses *common*, *proper*, or *collective*, depending upon how the noun is used in the sentence.

SAMPLE   *Housekeeping* is about two sisters and their family.
ANSWER   *Housekeeping* (proper), sisters (common), family
            (collective)

1. The village of Fingerbone, Idaho, endured severe winters.
2. During a particularly bad winter Fingerbone was nearly
   buried by a fierce storm.
3. The snowfall was heavy, and temperatures were low.
4. Half of the roof was covered with snow.
5. According to Aunt Lily and Aunt Nona, the house might
   collapse from the weight.
6. The idea that the house could fall made the aunts nervous.
7. Lily and Nona were even startled by the noise made by
   huge clumps of falling snow.
8. A crowd of local residents gathered daily at Fingerbone
   Lake.
9. The lake froze early, well before Thanksgiving Day.
10. A team of sweepers cleared the snow from the icy surface.
11. People packed the snow into a steep chute for sledders
    to use.
12. The public enjoyed many activities on the ice.
13. One crowd of merrymakers roasted wieners.
14. Another group rode sleds down a snowy hill.
15. Gleefully, a pack of dogs scampered among the throng. ➡

16. Ruth and Lucille were among the throng of townspeople at the festivities.
17. After school the pair of girls went straight to the lake.
18. The sisters skated to the boundary of the swept ice.
19. Later the two skaters rested on a snowbank and looked at the village.
20. Ruth and her sister returned to their home after hours of fun.

Grammar Workshop Exercise 2

Using Pronouns Effectively The paragraph below elaborates on ideas suggested by a passage from *Housekeeping* that is not reprinted in this textbook. Rewrite each sentence in the paragraph, substituting pronouns for nouns when a pronoun would make good sense. Do not substitute a pronoun for a noun if the pronoun makes the sentence unclear.

¹Ruth and Ruth's sister, Lucille, lived in the small town of Fingerbone, Idaho. ²Ruth's and Lucille's grandfather was originally from the Midwest, but the grandfather had come to Idaho years ago and built the grandfather's home there. ³Ruth did not remember the grandfather, since the grandfather had died before Ruth was born. ⁴Ruth had been raised by Ruth's grandmother until the grandmother died. ⁵Then Ruth's great-aunts came to Fingerbone to take care of the two girls. ⁶The great-aunts were unfamiliar with rural life and did not really enjoy rural life. ⁷The great-aunts felt isolated in Fingerbone because of Fingerbone's small population. ⁸The heavy snowfall troubled the great-aunts, and the great-aunts also worried about the great-aunts' nieces. ⁹Ruth did not mind the harsh winter, since Ruth had lived in Fingerbone all Ruth's life. ¹⁰Ruth often took Ruth's ice skates with Ruth to school and afterward went to Fingerbone Lake to skate on Fingerbone Lake's frozen waters.

Grammar Workshop Exercise 3

Identifying Verbs and Verb Phrase The following sentences are adapted from the literary passage. Write on your paper any simple verbs and any verb phrases that appear in the sentences, and label them accordingly. ➡

SAMPLE	Ruth's great-aunts had lived in brick houses all their lives.
ANSWER	had lived—verb phrase

1. The snow had been falling for days.
2. It piled into drifts and covered the eaves of the house.
3. Finally the sun returned to the sky.
4. Sometimes the fir trees would shudder under a heavy load of snow.
5. A dense layer of snow often slid to the ground with an earthy thud.
6. Weeks of cold weather had frozen Fingerbone Lake to its depths.
7. There must have been a dozen children among the skaters.
8. Townspeople had cleared several acres of ice with their brooms.
9. After school Lucille and Ruth skated until twilight, and they would have stayed even later.
10. The boldest skaters, they would venture farther out than anyone else.

Grammar Workshop Exercise 4

Identifying Transitive and Intransitive Verbs   The following sentences contain verbs that appear in the passage from *Housekeeping*. For each item write *transitive* or *intransitive* on your paper, depending upon the way the italicized verb is used in the sentence.

SAMPLE	Mounds of snow *crested* as high as the windows.
ANSWER	intransitive

1. Snow *drifted* against the fence.
2. A child *fell* in the deep snow.
3. The howling blizzard *terrified* the small children.
4. Some neighbors *brought* snowshoes with them.
5. Children *heaped* snow into small hills to build igloos.
6. An expert skier *sped* through the countryside.
7. Ice skaters *flaunted* their skills before crowds.
8. They *skated* around the lake at dizzying speeds.
9. Toddlers *traced* patterns with their feet in the cold, sparkling snow.
10. The frozen lake *supported* hundreds of skaters.

Grammar Workshop Exercise 5

Identifying Adjectives   The following sentences are about Idaho. On your paper write the adjectives that appear in each sentence. Count pronouns and proper adjectives, but do not count the words *a*, *an*, and *the*. After each adjective write a dash and the word that the adjective modifies.

SAMPLE   Idaho is an unusual setting for a novel about ordinary life.

ANSWER   unusual—setting; ordinary—life

1. Few aspects of life in the state are unremarkable.
2. The lofty Rocky Mountains provide spectacular sights.
3. A large portion of Idaho remains a remote wilderness.
4. Its icy streams provide a suitable habitat for many varieties of trout.
5. The Native American peoples of the region were expert hunters of the mighty buffalo.
6. After the discovery of gold in the 1860s, many European settlers came to Idaho.
7. Hardy miners were prominent among these settlers in northern Idaho.
8. Because of the hostile landscape, life was difficult for most people.
9. Primitive conditions fostered a generous spirit of cooperation, however.
10. Today farming is a major industry in this large state.

Grammar Workshop Exercise 6

Expanding Sentences with Adjectives   The following sentences elaborate on ideas suggested by the passage from *Housekeeping*. Rewrite each sentence, adding adjectives in the places indicated by carets. Although there are no specific correct answers, you should base your choices on what you have learned from reading the passage.

SAMPLE   Temperatures were ∧, and a ∧ layer of snow blanketed the town.

ANSWER   Temperatures were low, and a thick layer of snow blanketed the town.

1. In the ∧ village the air was frosty and ∧.
2. The town of Fingerbone looked for a few days like a ∧ and ∧ wonderland. ➡

3. When the ∧ sun returned, ∧ neighbors dug paths from their homes.
4. Ruth's ∧ aunts worried about the ∧ roof.
5. Fingerbone Lake became a ∧ sheet of ice, ∧ for skating.
6. The ∧ townspeople took ∧ pleasure in the lake.
7. ∧ sledders built a ∧ chute of snow.
8. ∧ dogs raced across the ice at ∧ speeds.
9. Ruth and Lucille skated on the ∧ ice and looked back at the ∧ town.
10. Tired but ∧, the girls trudged home in the ∧ twilight.

Grammar Workshop Exercise 7

Identifying Adverbs   The following sentences are about ice-skating. On your paper write each adverb that appears in these sentences. After each adverb write a dash and the word that the adverb modifies.

SAMPLE   Skilled ice skaters twirl quite gracefully.
ANSWER   quite—gracefully; gracefully—twirl

1. Experienced skaters move rather rapidly on the ice.
2. Frequently they form special patterns, or figures.
3. In cold climates they often skate outside.
4. Sometimes they glide on frozen lakes and ponds.
5. Safety is very important for all skaters.
6. Wise skaters never skate alone.
7. Professional figure skaters generally perform indoors.
8. Special equipment mechanically creates the ice.
9. Have you ever seen a professional ice show?
10. The skaters dress beautifully and usually perform to music.

Grammar Workshop Exercise 8

Using Adverbs   Each of the following sentences is based on the information in the passage from *Housekeeping*. Rewrite each sentence, substituting an appropriate adverb for the preposi-tional phrase in italics. The adverb should express the same idea as the prepositional phrase.

SAMPLE   That year winter descended *with much harshness* on Fingerbone.
ANSWER   That year winter descended harshly on Fingerbone. ➡

1. The snow fell *in heavy masses* for many days.
2. *In a sudden motion* a heavy slab of snow slid from a tree.
3. Ruth's great-aunts looked *with anxiety* at their own snow-laden roof.
4. *To everyone's amazement* the dilapidated roof held up under the weight of the snow.
5. The villagers walked *with eagerness* to the frozen lake.
6. Some sledded *in a reckless way* down a steep chute of snow.
7. The dogs chased pieces of ice that slid *in a quick manner* across the frozen lake.
8. Dogs scampered *in an exuberant fashion* across the ice.
9. For hours Ruth and Lucille skated *with swiftness* on the frozen lake.
10. After twilight the girls returned home *in a weary manner*.

Grammar Workshop Exercise 9

Identifying Prepositions The following sentences are based on passages from *Housekeeping* not reprinted in this book. On your paper list the prepositions that appear in each sentence. Remember that some prepositions are made up of more than one word. (The numeral in parentheses at the end of each item indicates the number of prepositions the sentence contains.)

1. *Housekeeping* is about two orphaned sisters in Idaho. (2)
2. The novel is narrated by Ruth, one of the sisters. (2)
3. Ruth's grandmother brought order to the household through her insistence on strict attention to chores. (4)
4. After the death of Ruth's grandmother, Ruth's great-aunts came to Idaho and cared for the girls. (4)
5. The great-aunts came from Spokane, Washington, and were unfamiliar with life in a small town like Fingerbone. (4)
6. They moved to Fingerbone in spite of their preference for city life. (3)
7. During crises the aunts took refuge in the repetition of familiar chores. (3)
8. The normal needs of adolescents in the home caused too many changes in routine for the aunts' liking. (4)
9. They fled to the safety of a hotel and left Ruth's aunt, Sylvie, in charge as the girls' guardian. (4)
10. According to Sylvie, life is about change and surprises, not the dull tasks of housekeeping. (3)

Grammar Workshop Exercise 10

Using Prepositions   Each of the sentences below elaborates on the passage from *Housekeeping*. Rewrite each sentence, filling in the blanks with a preposition that completes the word or phrase in italics and makes sense in the sentence. In some cases there may be more than one preposition that makes sense.

SAMPLE   The cold spell lasted _____ *weeks*.

ANSWER   The cold spell lasted for weeks.

1. Because temperatures remained _____ *the freezing point*, Fingerbone Lake had turned to solid ice.
2. Townspeople _____ *brooms* steadily swept the snow from acres of ice.
3. They dumped snow from sleds into huge mounds _____ *the shore*.
4. Some villagers skated _____ *the frozen surface* almost to the far shore.
5. Sledders raced _____ *a steep hill* of snow.
6. People roasted meat _____ *barrels* on shore.
7. Frozen mittens were clipped _____ *clothespins* to the rims of the barrels.
8. Some of the townsfolk brought boxes to use _____ *chairs*.
9. Dogs scampered playfully _____ *the crowd*.
10. The lake assumed the aspect _____ *an impromptu festival*.

Grammar Workshop Exercise 11

Using Conjunctions   The following sentences tell more about Idaho, where *Housekeeping* is set. On your paper rewrite each sentence, filling in the blanks with appropriate conjunctions according to the directions in parentheses. Choose your conjunctions from the list below. There are more conjunctions listed than you will need.

CONJUNCTIONS

and	or	but	yet
neither . . . nor		not only . . . but also	
although	because	before	if	when	wherever

SAMPLE   Idaho is located in the Rocky Mountains, _____ like other western states it is very beautiful. (Add a coordinating conjunction.) ➡

ANSWER Idaho is located in the Rocky Mountains, and like other western states it is very beautiful.

1. _____ you go in Idaho, you are likely to find spectacular scenery. (Add a subordinating conjunction.)
2. _____ you visit the Snake River Canyon, be sure to see Shoshone Falls. (Add a subordinating conjunction.)
3. You might fish in one of Idaho's two thousand lakes in the summer _____ visit the state during the skiing season. (Add a coordinating conjunction.)
4. _____ Idaho is far from the coast, it has the cold winters typical of the American interior. (Add a subordinating conjunction.)
5. Winter temperatures often dip below freezing, _____ several feet of snow fall each year. (Add a coordinating conjunction.)
6. _____ Idaho is the thirteenth largest state in area, it is sparsely populated. (Add a subordinating conjunction.)
7. _____ Boise, Idaho's capital city, _____ the even smaller city of Twin Falls has a population of over 150,000. (Add a correlative conjunction.)
8. Native American tribes had inhabited Idaho for centuries _____ the first European explorers arrived in 1805. (Add a subordinating conjunction.)
9. _____ gold was discovered in Idaho in the 1860s, thousands of prospectors flocked to the state. (Add a subordinating conjunction.)
10. Today Idaho is famous for its potatoes, _____ few people know that it also has the largest silver mine in the nation. (Add a coordinating conjunction.)

Grammar Workshop Exercise 12

Review The following biography of Marilynne Robinson is followed by ten sentences. On your paper rewrite each sentence, filling in the blank with an appropriate word. Use the directions in parentheses as a guide. You will need to consult the biography in order to fill in some of the blanks properly.

Marilynne Robinson

Born in 1944, Marilynne Robinson is one of contemporary America's promising new writers. Her first novel, *Housekeeping* (published in 1981), was widely acclaimed for its poetic language, its vivid characterizations, and its keen understanding of human nature. Set in an isolated Rocky Mountain ➡

community in Idaho, *Housekeeping* earned Robinson the 1982 Ernest Hemingway Foundation Award for Best First Novel. The book was the basis of a critically acclaimed motion picture. Robinson is also the author of a nonfiction book called *Mother Country*. In addition, she has contributed several stories and articles to *Harper's* and other major magazines.

1. The _____ author Marilynne Robinson was born in 1944. (Add a proper adjective.)
2. Robinson _____ her novel *Housekeeping* in 1981. (Add an action verb.)
3. _____ *Housekeeping* was only a first novel, it received much critical attention. (Add a subordinating conjunction.)
4. *Housekeeping* takes place in a remote community in the _____ of Idaho. (Add a proper noun.)
5. The novel was praised for its _____ language. (Add an adjective.)
6. Critics also _____ applauded its finely drawn characters. (Add an adverb.)
7. *Housekeeping* _____ a winner of the Ernest Hemingway Foundation Award for Best First Novel. (Add a linking verb.)
8. The _____ based on the novel also won critical praise. (Add a common noun.)
9. Robinson has not yet published a second novel _____ has written a nonfiction work entitled *Mother Country*. (Add a coordinating conjunction.)
10. Some of Robinson's short stories have appeared _____ *Harper's*, the noted literary magazine. (Add a preposition.)

Proofreading   The following passage describes the artist Grandma Moses, whose painting appears on the opposite page. Rewrite the passage, correcting the errors in spelling, capitalization, punctuation, usage, and grammar. There are twenty-five errors in all.

Grandma Moses

[1]Anna Mary Robertson Moses (1860–1961), who was known as Grandma Moses, was born in Greenwich New York, to a family of Scottish and irish desent. [2]Remarkably, she did not begin painting until she was seventy seven. [3]During the last two decades of her life, Moses painted hundreds of scenes of rural northeastern farm life, She became perhaps the most famous folk painter in america.

[4]Encouraged by her father, Moses developed her talent for drawing, but had little time to pursue her interest in art. [5]She married a farmer, Thomas Salmon Moses and bore ten children. [6]She spent much of her life on a dairy farm in the tiny community of Eagle Bridge in upstate New york. [7]She began to paint seriously only after her arthrtis became so crippling that she could no longer work on the farm. [8]A few of her paintings on display at an Eagle Bridge drugstore were discovered by an art collector who happened to pass through town. [9]Somewhat taken aback by her sudden fame, Moses was scandalized when dealers began to offer large sums for paintings that she thought was worth only a few dollars.

[10]Moses paintings are remarkable for there harmony and detail. [11]Although she hadn't no formal training, Moses had a strong intuitive grasp of color, patern and design. [12]She recorded the landscapes and customs of her rural countryside with the sensitivity of a poet. [13]Every detail is carefully observed: the gray cast of the sky on a snowey morning, the steam rising from a locomotive, and the straining muscles of a horse pulling a sleigh.

[14]Moses's *Early Skating*, like the passage from Marilynne Robinson's novel "Housekeeping," captures the atmosphere of a small community on a Winter day. [15]Although the regional setting is different—the painting depicts new York, whereas the novel is set in idaho the mood is the same. [16]There is a playfulness about the two scenes of children cavorting on the ice. [17]There is also a feeling of isolation, as if these two small towns were seperated from the the outside world by time and winters snowy blanket.

Anna Mary Robertson ("Grandma") Moses, *Early Skating*, 1951

Unit 10 Review

Parts of Speech

Nouns and Pronouns

[pages 401–404, 405–411]

Identify each underlined word as **(a)** a common or a collective noun, **(b)** a proper noun, **(c)** a personal or a possessive pronoun, **(d)** a demonstrative, an intensive, or a reflexive pronoun, or **(e)** an interrogative, a relative, or an indefinite pronoun.

[1]I did [2]research on potatoes [3]myself. I learned [4]this: the first [5]people to cultivate the potato lived in [6]Peru over three thousand [7]years ago. [8]They took [9]advantage of [10]their fruitful [11]land. Occasionally a [12]group of scientists still goes to the [13]Andes to collect a [14]variety of specimens. [15]Who would have guessed [16]that this [17]vegetable was unknown to [18]everyone in [19]Europe until the [20]1530s?

Verbs

[pages 411–417]

Indicate whether each of the underlined verbs is **(a)** a transitive verb, **(b)** an intransitive verb, **(c)** a linking verb, or **(d)** a verb phrase.

It [21]is possible that if you [22]visited a cinema before 1967, you [23]might have seen a newsreel. Moviegoers [24]could watch newsreels decades before television [25]existed. Newsreels now [26]look primitive, but they [27]are the ancestors of TV news. Yesterday's viewer [28]was pleased to see events days after they occurred; today we [29]can witness news as it [30]happens.

Adjectives and Adverbs

[pages 418–420, 422–425]

Indicate whether each of the underlined words is **(a)** an adjective, **(b)** an article, **(c)** an adverb modifying a verb, **(d)** an adverb modifying an adjective or another adverb, or **(e)** a negative adverb.

Ray is learning [31]a second language. He has been reviewing the irregular [32]French verbs. Last week Kim lent him the [33]best book she had, and Ray found it much [34]clearer than his. Kim said, "Read the instructions [35]carefully. If you do [36]not skip anything, [37]the exercise should be [38]completely [39]clear. It [40]usually never pays to hurry."

Prepositions, Conjunctions, and Interjections

[pages 426–433, and 435]

Indicate whether each of the underlined words is used here as **(a)** a preposition, **(b)** a coordinating conjunction, **(c)** a part of a correlative conjunction, **(d)** a subordinating conjunction, or **(e)** an interjection.

[41]Well, perhaps the Gulf Stream was so named [42]because it comes [43]from the Gulf of Mexico. This current runs along the east coast [44]of North America [45]but long went undetected. [46]When ships sailed west [47]to New York rather than to Rhode Island, the trip took weeks longer. Benjamin Franklin knew that [48]neither distance nor climate caused this strange [49]and curious delay. He charted the current in 1769 [50]and dispelled the mystery.

Writing for Review

Write one paragraph on any subject. In your paragraph underline and identify at least one example of each of the following parts of speech: *noun, pronoun, verb, adjective, adverb, preposition,* and *conjunction.*

Unit 11 Parts of the Sentence

A **sentence** is a group of words expressing a complete thought.

Every sentence has two basic parts, a *subject* and a *predicate*.

11.1 Simple Subjects and Simple Predicates

The **simple subject** is the key noun or pronoun (or word or group of words acting as a noun) that tells what a sentence is about.

The **simple predicate** is the verb or verb phrase that expresses the essential thought about the subject of the sentence.

SIMPLE SUBJECT	SIMPLE PREDICATE
Dionne Warwick	will perform.
Owls	were hooting.
José Canseco	ran.
Things	change.

The simple subject is found by asking *who?* or *what?* about the verb.

11.2 Complete Subjects and Complete Predicates

In most sentences the meaning of the simple subject and the simple predicate is expanded or modified by the addition of other words and phrases.

The **complete subject** consists of the simple subject and all the words that modify it.

The **complete predicate** consists of the simple predicate and all the words that modify it or complete its meaning.

Whooooo ooooo

...was hooting in the night?

COMPLETE SUBJECT	COMPLETE PREDICATE
Talented Dionne Warwick	will perform her biggest hits.
Large owls with bright eyes	were hooting loudly in the dark forest.
The speedy José Canseco	ran all the way home from first base on a double.
Many things	change daily.

Identifying Subjects and Predicates Copy each of the following sentences, and draw a vertical line between the complete subject and the complete predicate. Then underline the simple subject once and the simple predicate twice.

SAMPLE ANSWER   An important <u>event</u> I <u>sparked</u> the civil rights movement in the United States.

Rosa Lee Parks, a Woman of Courage

[1]Rosa Lee Parks made history in Montgomery, Alabama, in 1955. [2]She boarded a bus there late one December day. [3]Parks took a seat at the front of the bus. [4]This action was illegal for an African-American person in Alabama at the time. [5]The angry driver ordered Parks to the back of the bus. [6]She courageously ignored his orders. [7]The police arrested Parks for her action. [8]The African-American community of Montgomery conducted a year-long boycott of the city buses in protest. [9]A Supreme Court decision in November 1956 made segregation on all public transportation illegal. [10]Many people consider Parks the catalyst of the modern civil rights movement.

11.3   Compound Subjects and Compound Predicates

A **compound subject** is made up of two or more simple subjects that are joined by a conjunction and have the same verb.

Tomatoes and **carrots** are colorful vegetables.
Neither the **tomato** nor the **pepper** grows underground.
Tomatoes, carrots, and **peppers** are healthful.

Exercise 2: Sentence Writing

Expanding Subjects (a) Write five sentences. In each one use a simple subject and a simple predicate. (b) Expand each sentence by making the subject compound.

SAMPLE ANSWER   **a.** John Hancock signed the Declaration of Independence.
    b. John Hancock and John Adams signed the Declaration of Independence.

A **compound predicate** (or **compound verb**) is made up of two or more verbs or verb phrases that are joined by a conjunction and have the same subject.

Horses **gallop** and **charge.**

Sea gulls **will glide** or **swoop** down to the ocean.

Nina **inserted** the film, **looked** through the viewfinder, and **snapped** the first photograph.

A sentence may have both a compound subject and a compound predicate.

    S   S   P   P

Butterflies and **hummingbirds dart** and **dip** in the air.

Exercise 3

Identifying Subjects and Predicates On your paper copy the following sentences. Then for each sentence underline the simple subject(s) once and the simple predicate(s) twice. Note that some subjects and predicates are compound.

Chief Joseph

1. The Nez Percé lived and flourished for centuries in the Northwest.
2. In 1877 the federal government ordered them away from their lands and assigned them to a reservation in Oregon.
3. The government wanted land for many new white settlers and their families.
4. The leader of the Nez Percé at the time was Chief Joseph, a wise and compassionate man.
5. Chief Joseph and the Nez Percé men, women, and children packed their belongings and left their homes.
6. During their journey a small group of Nez Percé encountered and killed several white settlers.
7. As a result of this incident, Chief Joseph and his advisers foresaw a long and bloody battle with the United States Army.
8. Chief Joseph therefore sought freedom for the Nez Percé in Canada.
9. He and his outnumbered people fought courageously but finally surrendered to the United States Army just thirty miles from the Canadian border.
10. The Nez Percé accepted land from the United States government on a reservation in Oklahoma and settled there in 1878.

11.4   Order of Subject and Predicate

In most sentences in English, the subject comes before the verb. There are exceptions, however, to this normal word order.

1. In the case of commands or requests, the subject *you* is not expressed; it is understood.

   [You] **Run**!   [You] **Give** it to me.   [You] Please **be** careful.

2. At times a sentence is written in **inverted order**—that is, with the predicate before the subject. This reversal of the usual order adds emphasis to the subject.

PREDICATE	SUBJECT
Across the field **galloped**	the three **horses.**
In the distance **ran**	a **river.**

3. When the word *there* or *here* begins a sentence and is followed by the verb *to be*, the subject follows the verb. (The sentence is in inverted order.) Remember that *there* and *here* are almost never the subject of a sentence.

PREDICATE	SUBJECT
There **is**	a **chill** in the air.
Here **are**	my **thoughts** on the subject.

Exercise 5

Recognizing the Order of Subject and Predicate   Copy each of the following sentences onto your paper. For each sentence draw a vertical line between the complete subject and the complete predicate, and label each. Then indicate with the letter *C* or *I* those sentences that are either a command (*C*) or written in inverted order (*I*). (Not all sentences will be labeled *C* or *I*.) ➡

                P

/ Look at that painting. **C**

       P   **S**

On the opposite wall is / another work of art. **I**

     P   **S**

There is / the loveliest statue in the museum. **I**

An African Art Exhibit

1. A visit to an African art exhibit can be an exciting and rewarding experience.
2. Many museums offer temporary shows in addition to their permanent collections.
3. Call ahead for information about special displays of African art.
4. There are fine examples of beadwork, basketry, woodwork, leatherwork, and metalwork.
5. In some museums are beautiful displays of African textiles.
6. Excellent craftsmanship is found in decorative ornaments and ceremonial objects.
7. Here is a Nigerian bronze sculpture of a priest-king.
8. This ancient civilization used sculptures of former kings in memorial rites for the dead.
9. Look at this elaborately carved ceremonial mask.
10. Dancers wore such masks as these at coronations and royal funerals.
11. There are still more African artifacts on display in the next room.
12. On the shelf to the left sits a seventeenth-century ivory bracelet from the kingdom of Benin.
13. Notice the intricate carvings of kings on the carefully preserved bracelet.
14. From the workshops of Benin came some of Africa's finest bronze figures.
15. Among the most ancient African art objects are terra-cotta figures nearly fifteen hundred years old.
16. Terra cotta is a kind of earthenware.
17. Superb bronze and terra-cotta heads were made in Nigeria in the thirteenth century.
18. There are even older examples of African art in the museum's exhibit.
19. Prehistoric cave paintings were discovered in the Tassili Plateau in the Sahara.
20. African people of today still create many such exquisite art objects.

11.5   Complements

A **complement** is a word or group of words that completes the meaning of a verb.

There are four kinds of complements: *direct objects, indirect objects, object complements,* and *subject complements.*

Direct Objects

A **direct object** answers the question *what?* or *whom?* after an action verb.

The subject of a sentence usually performs the action indicated by the verb. That action may be directed toward or received by someone or something—the direct object. Nouns, pronouns, or words acting as nouns may serve as direct objects. Only transitive verbs have direct objects.

Carlos served **dinner.** [Carlos served *what?*]

Marie admires **him** deeply. [Marie admires *whom?*]

The children contributed their **savings.** [The children contributed *what?*]

Carlos served a Mexican **dinner** and a fabulous **dessert.** [Carlos served *what?*]

Exercise 6

Identifying Direct Objects   On your paper write the action verb that appears in each of the following sentences. Then list any direct objects.

The First Cowboys
1. American cowboys copied the style of Mexican cowboys.
2. Historians see the Mexican vaqueros as the first real cowboys.
3. At all times of the year, the vaquero wore a floppy sombrero.
4. This large hat kept snow, rain, or sun off his face.
5. The American cowboy modeled his own hat on the Mexican sombrero.
6. During branding season the vaqueros roped cows with a sturdy riata.
7. Cowboys in America lassoed cows with a lariat (from the Spanish word *la riata*).
8. Mexican cowboys protected their shins and thighs from twigs and thorns with leather chaparejos. ➡

9. In a similar fashion American cowboys put leather chaps over their pants.
10. Cowboys throughout America owe a cultural debt to the vaqueros of Mexico.

Exercise 7: Sentence Writing

Creating Sentences with Direct Objects   Write five sentences describing how to make or do something. Use action verbs. Identify the *subject(s)*, *verb(s)*, and *direct object(s)* in each sentence.

Indirect Objects

An **indirect object** answers the question *to whom? for whom? to what?* or *for what?* after an action verb.

In most cases a sentence may have an indirect object only if it has a direct object. The indirect object will always come between the verb and the direct object.

Tyrone served his **sisters** dinner. [Tyrone served dinner *to whom?*]

Greta saved **him** a seat. [Greta saved a seat *for whom?*]

The children gave the worthy **charity** all their savings. [The children gave all their savings *to what?*]

Kim saved **Rosa** and **José** seats. [Kim saved seats *for whom?*]

Kim saved Rosa

a seat.

Kim saved Rosa.

Exercise 8

Identifying Indirect Objects   For each sentence write on your paper the direct object, and list any indirect object(s). (Not all sentences have an indirect object.)

Careers in Sports
1. Professional sports offer many interesting careers.
2. Television or radio sportscasters broadcast sporting events.
3. A good sports announcer gives fans play-by-play descriptions of the game.
4. The announcer tells them interesting anecdotes.
5. Newspaper writers and photographers also cover athletic competitions.
6. Newspapers in particular give sports much coverage. ➡

7. Teaching a sport may give a person much satisfaction.
8. Managers, coaches, and trainers all bring teams success.
9. Sports also give referees, umpires, and doctors jobs.
10. Athletic events even give hot-dog and peanut vendors work.

Object Complements

An **object complement** answers the question *what?* after a direct object. That is, it *completes* the meaning of the direct object by identifying or describing it.

Object complements occur only in sentences with direct objects and only in those sentences with the following action verbs or with similar verbs that have the general meaning of "make" or "consider":

appoint	elect	render	consider	name
choose	make	call	find	think

An object complement usually follows a direct object. It may be an adjective, a noun, or a pronoun.

Residents find the park **peaceful**. [adjective]
Critics call him a true **genius**. [noun]
My grandmother considers the property **hers**. [pronoun]
Katie appointed me **assistant, treasurer,** and **cook**. [nouns]

Exercise 9

Identifying Object Complements Write the object complement(s) that appear in the following sentences. (Not every sentence has an object complement.)

Musical Tastes
1. The Music Club has appointed Felipe president.
2. He finds that honor extraordinary.
3. One member, Maya, thinks Mozart the best composer.
4. Another member, Diane, considers Bach stupendous.
5. Felipe, Maya, and Diane make music a priority.
6. Diane calls Verdi a great composer and a musical genius.
7. Felipe likes chamber music better than opera.
8. Maya thinks opera sublime.
9. Diane names the basso singer Justino Díaz her favorite.
10. Maya finds the voice of Kiri Te Kanawa exquisite.

Subject Complements

A **subject complement** follows a subject and a linking verb and identifies or describes the subject.

There are two kinds of subject complements: *predicate nominatives* and *predicate adjectives.*

A **predicate nominative** is a noun or pronoun that follows a linking verb and points back to the subject to identify it further.

Sopranos are **singers.**

Clearly the star of the opera was **she.**

Predicate nominatives are usually found in sentences that contain forms of the linking verb *be.* A few other linking verbs (for example, *become* and *remain*) can be followed by a predicate nominative.

Julia became both a **musician** and an **actress.**
That experience remains a cherished **memory** for me.

A **predicate adjective** follows a linking verb and points back to the subject and further describes it.

Ballerinas are **graceful.**

Ballerinas must be extremely **dedicated.**

Predicate adjectives may follow any linking verb.

I felt completely **drained.**
Only a few marathoners appear **fresh** even now.
The water tasted **delicious.**
My friend Tanya looked **exhausted** but **happy.**

Exercise 10

Identifying Subject Complements   On your paper write all the subject complements that appear in the following sentences. Identify each as a *predicate nominative* or a *predicate adjective.* (Five sentences have more than one predicate nominative or predicate adjective.)

Japanese Flower Arrangements
[1]Flower arrangement is an ancient Japanese art. [2]This tradition grew popular in the sixth century. [3]Early flower arrangements were decorations for Buddhist temple altars. [4]Over the centuries the art of flower arrangement became increasingly refined. [5]Important features of Japanese floral ➡

arrangement are leaves, stems, and branches. ⁶The lines of the branches should be graceful and sleek. ⁷In Western countries blossoms are generally the only important features. ⁸The best Japanese floral arrangements look natural and colorful. ⁹A Japanese florist must be a designer and an artist. ¹⁰The art of Japanese flower arrangement is both appealing to viewers and satisfying to the creator.

Exercise 11: Sentence Writing

Writing Sentences with Complements   Write four sentences about a natural phenomenon, such as an eclipse, a thunderstorm, or a sunset. In each sentence use at least one of the four kinds of complements: direct object, indirect object, object complement, or subject complement. Label the complements for each sentence that you write.

Exercise 12: Review

Complements   On your paper write the complements that appear in the following sentences. Next to each complement write the kind of complement it is: *direct object, indirect object, object complement, predicate nominative,* or *predicate adjective.*

A Jazz Musician

1. Davenport, Iowa, was the home of the jazz musician Leon Bix Beiderbecke, who lived from 1903 to 1931.
2. Mississippi riverboats passing by Davenport gave Bix Beiderbecke the opportunity to hear jazz.
3. Bix Beiderbecke played two instruments, the cornet and the piano.
4. The cornet's sound is mellow and rich.
5. Bix Beiderbecke carried his cornet with him in a paper bag.
6. Louis Armstrong once met young Bix on a riverboat.
7. Beiderbecke's parents were conservative, wealthy Midwesterners.
8. They did not give Bix any financial assistance for his musical career.
9. Beiderbecke's reputation is still great in music circles today.
10. In fact, many musicians consider him a true classic of American jazz.

In this passage from *The Call of the Wild*, Jack London uses a variety of sentence patterns to create a lively, engaging prose rhythm:

> Buck's first day on the Dyea beach was like a nightmare. Every hour was filled with shock and surprise. He had been suddenly jerked from the heart of civilization and flung into the heart of things primordial. No lazy, sun-kissed life was this, with nothing to do but loaf and be bored. Here was neither peace, nor rest, nor a moment's safety.

Try to use London's techniques when you write and revise your work.

1.   Avoid monotony by varying the lengths of your sentences. In the passage above, London uses a compound predicate in the third sentence ("had been jerked" and "flung") and a compound subject in the last sentence ("peace," "rest," and "safety").

2.   Achieve sentence variety by occasionally varying word order. In the fourth sentence London writes, "No lazy, sun-kissed life was this" rather than "This was no lazy, sun-kissed life." Moreover, note in the last sentence that London uses inverted word order.

Revise the following passage, adapted from *The Call of the Wild*, combining ideas to expand the basic sentence patterns. Decide which sentence would be most effective in inverted order.

> Then an old wolf, gaunt and battle-scarred, came forward. Buck writhed his lips into the preliminary of a snarl. He sniffed noses with him. Whereupon the old wolf sat down. He pointed his nose at the moon. He broke out the long wolf howl. The others sat down. They howled. And now the call came to Buck in unmistakable accents. He, too, sat down. He howled. . . . And the story of Buck may well end here.

Grammar Workshop

Parts of the Sentence

A member of the Ibo tribe of eastern Nigeria, Chinua Achebe writes about his people in *Things Fall Apart*. Set in the Ibo village of Umuofia around the turn of the century, the novel chronicles the life of a proud young wrestler named Okonkwo. In this passage Okonkwo is just about to go to bed when he hears the town crier, who beats his metal drum and summons the men of the village to a meeting. The passage has been annotated to show some of the parts of the sentence covered in this unit.

Literature Model

from THINGS FALL APART

by Chinua Achebe

Okonkwo had just blown out the palm-oil lamp and stretched himself on his bamboo bed when he heard the *ogene* of the town crier piercing the still night air. *Gome, gome, gome, gome,* boomed the hollow metal. Then the crier gave his message, and at the end of it beat his instrument again. And this was the message. Every man of Umuofia was asked to gather at the market place tomorrow morning. Okonkwo wondered what was amiss, for he knew certainly that something was amiss. He had discerned a clear over-tone of tragedy in the crier's voice, and even now he could still hear it as it grew dimmer and dimmer in the distance.

The night was very quiet. It was always quiet except on moonlight nights. Darkness held a vague terror for these people, even the bravest among them. Children were warned not to whistle at night for fear of evil spirits. Dangerous animals became even more sinister and uncanny in the dark. A snake was never called by its name at night, because it would hear. It was called a string. And so on this particular night as the crier's voice was gradually swallowed up in the distance, silence returned to the world, a vibrant silence made more intense by the universal trill of a million million forest insects.

On a moonlight night it would be different. The happy voices of children playing in open fields would then be heard. And perhaps those not so young would be playing ➡

Annotations (left margin):
- Compound predicate
- Subject complement (predicate nominative)
- Subject complement (predicate adjective)
- Complete predicate
- Simple subject
- Simple predicate
- Complete subject

in pairs in less open places, and old men and women would remember their youth. As the Ibo say: "When the moon is shining the cripple becomes hungry for a walk." —— Direct object

Grammar Workshop Exercise 1

Writing Sentences with Complete Subjects and Complete Predicates   The following partial sentences draw on ideas in the passage from *Things Fall Apart*. Complete each sentence by writing on your paper either a complete subject or a complete predicate. Do not repeat the exact wording from the novel. Although there is no single right answer, your sentence should make sense within the context of the passage.

SAMPLE   The town crier _____.
ANSWER   The town crier beat his metal drum.

1. The voice of the crier _____.
2. _____ lay listening in the darkness.
3. The dark, moonless night _____.
4. Even the bravest villagers _____.
5. _____ roamed the jungle on dark nights.
6. A string _____.
7. _____ trilled in the darkness.
8. Moonlight _____.
9. _____ went outside in the moonlight.
10. Even the older people _____.

Grammar Workshop Exercise 2

Writing Sentences with Compound Subjects and Compound Predicates   Write on your paper a complete sentence answering each of the following questions about *Things Fall Apart*. Do not repeat the exact wording from the novel. Begin your sentence with the subject. When composing your answer, follow the directions in parentheses. Then underline and label the simple or compound subject and the simple or compound predicate. Finally, draw a line separating the complete subject from the complete predicate.

SAMPLE   What two kinds of nights had opposite effects on the people of Umuofia?
(Use a compound subject.) ➡

| COMPOUND SUBJECT   SIMPLE PREDICATE

ANSWER   Dark <u>nights</u> and moonlit <u>nights</u> | <u>had</u> opposite
                effects on the people of Umuofia.

1. What did Okonkwo do to prepare for sleep?
   (Use a compound predicate.)
2. What sounds made by the town crier broke the silence of
   the night?
   (Use a compound subject.)
3. What did Okonkwo do as the crier gave his message?
   (Use a compound predicate.)
4. What characteristics of the night made the crier's message
   all the more ominous to the villagers?
   (Use a compound subject.)
5. What things were troublesome on a dark night?
   (Use a compound subject.)
6. What did the villagers never do in the dark?
   (Use a compound predicate.)
7. What happened to the sound of the crier's voice?
   (Use a compound predicate.)
8. What did the villagers do on moonlit nights?
   (Use a compound predicate.)
9. What groups of villagers would go outside on a moonlit
   night?
   (Use a compound subject with three different nouns.)
10. Who would reminisce about the past?
    (Use a compound subject.)

Grammar Workshop Exercise 3

Writing Inverted Sentences   The following sentences
develop an image or idea suggested by the passage from *Things
Fall Apart*. On your paper rewrite each sentence in inverted
order, following the instructions in parentheses.

SAMPLE   A fear of darkness was in the hearts of the
                villagers.
                (Begin the sentence with *There was*.)
ANSWER   There was a fear of darkness in the hearts of the
                villagers.

1. Okonkwo lay on the bamboo bed.
   (Begin the sentence with *On the bed*.)
2. The town crier came down the road. ➡

(Begin the sentence with *Down the road.*)

3. Tragic overtones were in the crier's voice.
   (Begin the sentence with *There were.*)
4. Many a frightening creature was out and about on nights when the moon did not shine.
   (Begin the sentence with *There was.*)
5. Dangerous animals lurked in the darkness.
   (Begin the sentence with *In the darkness.*)
6. An evil spirit might be lurking within any shadow.
   (Begin the sentence with *Within any shadow.*)
7. The sound of the crier's drum faded into the distance.
   (Begin the sentence with *Into the distance.*)
8. Millions of insects were in the dark jungle.
   (Begin the sentence with *There were.*)
9. No children were playing outside on this moonless night.
   (Begin the sentence with *There were.*)
10. People of all ages appeared on a moonlit night.
    (Begin the sentence with *On a moonlit night.*)

Grammar Workshop Exercise 4

Writing Sentences with Predicate Nominatives and Predicate Adjectives   The pairs of words that follow are derived from the passage from *Things Fall Apart*. For each pair of words, write a sentence that uses the first word as the subject and the second word as a predicate adjective or a predicate nominative. Do not use Achebe's exact words, and be sure to add more than just a verb to the pair of words. After you have written the sentence, indicate whether the second word from the pair is acting as a *predicate adjective* or a *predicate nominative*.

SAMPLE   Umuofia, village
ANSWER   Umuofia was Okonkwo's village in Africa.
         predicate nominative

1. *Things Fall Apart*, novel
2. Nigeria, country
3. villagers, members
4. Okonkwo, wrestler
5. *ogene*, drum
6. sound, loud
7. message, worrisome
8. morning, time ➡

9. overtone, tragic
10. night, silent
11. people, fearful
12. spirits, threat
13. animals, danger
14. string, name
15. trill, persistent
16. silence, extreme
17. villagers, lively
18. children, happy
19. fields, playgrounds
20. elderly, thoughtful

Grammar Workshop Exercise 5

Writing Sentences with Direct and Indirect Objects
The following groups of words describe incidents related to
the passage from *Things Fall Apart.* Each word is labeled *S* (for
subject), *DO* (for *direct object*), or *IO* (for *indirect object*). On your
paper write a sentence using these words as those parts of the
sentence, but do not use the exact wording from the novel. Try
to add modifiers or prepositional phrases.

SAMPLE   lamp (S), Okonkwo (IO), light (DO)
ANSWER   A palm-oil lamp gave Okonkwo light at night.

1. town crier (S), drum (IO), thump (DO)
2. Okonkwo (S), sound (DO)
3. crier (S), instrument (DO)
4. crier (S), villagers (IO), message (DO)
5. Okonkwo (S), tragedy (DO)
6. darkness (S), townspeople (IO), feelings (DO)
7. whistle (S), trouble (DO)
8. distance (S), voice (DO)
9. trill (S), silence (DO)
10. moonlight (S), villagers (IO), courage (DO)

Grammar Workshop Exercise 6

Review The following sentences describe the life of Chinua
Achebe. Rewrite each sentence on your paper according to the
instructions that appear after each item. Make sure your
answers are complete sentences. ➡

Chinua Achebe

1. According to many critics, Chinua Achebe's works are insightful.
   (Add *and educational* to create a second predicate adjective.)
2. A member of the Ibo tribe of Nigeria, Achebe grew up in the village of Ogidi.
   (Add *and graduated from the University College at Ibadan* to expand the complete predicate.)
3. He spoke the Ibo language first.
   (Add *but learned English as a child* to expand the complete predicate.)
4. The fifth in a family of six children, Achebe was always a reader.
   (Add *eager* as a modifier of the subject complement.)
5. Achebe's mother insisted on the best education possible for the family's children.
   (Add *and father* to create a compound subject.)
6. From his experiences with African life have come Achebe's compelling themes.
   (Rewrite the sentence so that it begins with the complete subject.)
7. Many of his books give a sense of the effects of colonialism on African culture.
   (Add *readers* to the complete predicate so that it functions as an indirect object.)
8. Numerous examples of problems caused by colonial rule are in Achebe's works.
   (Rewrite the sentence so that it begins with *There are*.)
9. Over the years the popular Nigerian author has received many awards.
   (Add *and honorary doctorates* to create a second direct object.)
10. Chinua Achebe has become an important spokesperson for African people.
    (Add *and has been praised for his eloquent writings* to expand the complete predicate.)

Proofreading   The following passage describes the people and the art of Nigeria. (An example of Nigerian sculpture appears on the opposite page.) Rewrite the passage, correcting the errors in spelling, capitalization, punctuation, grammar, and usage. There are twenty-five errors in all.

The Art of Nigeria

[1] More than twice the size of California, Nigeria is the most populos nation in West Africa. [2] More then two hundred native tribes inhabit modern Nigeria. [3] The largest of these tribes are the Hausa and the Fulani, who live mainly in the north; the Yoruba, in the southwest; the Ibo, in the southeast; and the Ijo, on the southern coast. [4] Each group has it's own language, but the groups' common language is English, reflecting Nigeria's century-long domination by Great Britain. [5] Nigeria acheived its independance in 1960

[6] Nigeria is the home of many anchient cultures, some of which were established before the eigth century B.C. [7] These cultures produced some of Africas' most impresive art. [8] The Yoruba created magnifacent bronze sculptures. [9] The people of western Nigeria produced fine iveries.

[10] The Ijo who live in the warm and hummid region of the delta of the Niger River, are closely related to their neighbors, the Ibo. [11] The Ijo traditionaly venarated many gods, each of who was thought to control a particular facit of everyday life. [12] Although most Ijo people have converted to Christianity, some continue to practice the religion of their ancestors.

[13] The shrine that appears on the opposite page is typical of the sacred objects of the Ijo culture. [14] Made of highley polished wood, it depics a figure—possibly a tribal ancester—sitting on a throne. [15] Generally such an image was not displayed every day; rather, it was created for a special ritual, such as a mariage or a funeral.

[16] In recent years many nigerians have abandoned their native villages and migrated to large cities. [17] Those who remain in the country still live close to nature. [18] The Ibo villagers described by Chinua Achebe in "*Things Fall Apart*" are aware of every sound heard on a moonless night. [19] They attribute some of those sounds to animals and insects; they attribute others to the supernatural. [20] Sacred objects such as this shrine may have simbolized a bridge between the natural and the supernatural worlds.

6. The result was winning the Aztec capital Tenochtitlán through the overthrow of Emperor Montezuma. (1)
7. By 1521 Cortés's goals—finding gold, claiming Mexican lands, and conquering native tribes—were fulfilled. (3)
8. For several years Cortés was famous for controlling much of present-day Mexico. (1)
9. His trip to Spain in 1528 resulted in his receiving the title of marquis from Holy Roman Emperor Charles V. (1)
10. Cortés sailed back to Mexico in 1530 and engaged in ranching and mining. (2)

Exercise 8: Sentence Writing

Writing Sentences with Gerunds   Select five of the gerunds that you identified in Exercise 7, and write an original sentence for each one. Make sure you use the *-ing* word as a gerund, not as a present participle.

Infinitives and Infinitive Phrases

An **infinitive** is a verb form that is usually preceded by the word *to* and is used as a noun, an adjective, or an adverb.

When you use the word *to* before the base form of a verb, *to* is not a preposition but part of the infinitive form of the verb.

To stand can be uncomfortable. [infinitive as subject]

Infants first learn **to crawl**. [infinitive as direct object]

Her aim is **to walk**. [infinitive as predicate nominative]

Birds have an instinct **to fly**. [infinitive as adjective]

I am determined **to run**. [infinitive as adverb]

An **infinitive phrase** contains an infinitive plus any complements and modifiers.

We decided **to sail across the lake.**

They wanted **to drive slowly around the park.**

To run in a marathon someday is my secret ambition.

A triathlon requires athletes **to train diligently.**

To complete a triathlon is a success in itself.

Identifying Infinitives and Infinitive Phrases   Write the infinitive phrase that appears in each of the following sentences.

Mary Cassatt

1. Mary Cassatt was one of the foremost American artists to paint in the Impressionist style.
2. Cassatt grew up in Philadelphia and decided to study at the Pennsylvania Academy of the Fine Arts.
3. In 1868 she went to live in Paris.
4. The great French painter Edgar Degas began to influence her work.
5. Degas helped Cassatt to develop her precise and delicate style.
6. Cassatt often chose to paint portraits of mothers and children.
7. Degas invited Cassatt to exhibit paintings with other Impressionists.
8. Cassatt encouraged her American relatives and friends to purchase the paintings of the French Impressionists.
9. In so doing, Cassatt helped to influence a growing American interest in contemporary art.
10. Today art lovers are able to appreciate Cassatt's work for its own remarkable qualities.

Exercise 10: Sentence Writing

Using Infinitives   Jot down five action verbs. Then use each one in an infinitive phrase in an original sentence. Underline the infinitive phrases.

Exercise 11: Review

Verbal Phrases   On your paper write each of the verbal phrases that appears in the following sentences. Tell whether each is a participial phrase, a gerund phrase, or an infinitive phrase.

Elephants

1. Elephants have the distinction of being the largest land mammals.
2. Living in the tropical regions of Asia and Africa, they may reach a height of thirteen feet. ➡

3. Their tusks, weighing up to two hundred pounds each, can be more than ten feet long.
4. Their distinctive ears are huge, measuring up to forty-two inches in width.
5. They use their fingerlike trunks to pick up objects.
6. Elephants browse all day, feeding on leaves and tall grasses.
7. Elephants can learn to carry logs and to perform in circuses.
8. Training young elephants takes great skill.
9. It can be difficult to handle them, too.
10. Hunted for food and for ivory, elephants now must struggle for their survival.

Writing Link

Phrases can act as nouns, adjectives, or adverbs. This versatility allows writers to expand basic sentence patterns by adding precise description and detail. In addition, the placement of phrases in the sentence often allows writers to control the rhythm of their prose. Keep in mind the following techniques when you revise your writing:

1. Use prepositional phrases to add precise description and detail to your sentences. Notice that the underlined prepositional phrases in the following sentence from "Of Dry Goods and Black Bow Ties" by Yoshiko Uchida help the author's meaning come alive:

My father was impressed with these modest words from a man of such success. He accepted them with a sense of mission and from that day was committed to white shirts and black bow ties, and treated every customer, no matter how humble, with respect and courtesy.

Without the prepositional phrases Uchida's sentences would have been imprecise and flat. Try replacing "with respect and courtesy" with the adverb *well* to see the effectiveness of Uchida's phrase.

2. When you revise, see whether adding participial, infinitive, or appositive phrases improves the flow of your sentences or creates a dramatic effect. For example, in the following sentence from *Barrio Boy*, Ernesto Galarza uses the italicized appositive phrase to heighten the sense of tension and fright:

We stepped down into a frightening scene, *a huge barn filled with smoke and noise and the smell of burnt oil.*

Notice how much less dramatic the effect would be if "a frightening scene" were moved to the end of the sentence.

Apply these techniques in revising the sentence you just read from *Barrio Boy*. As your base use this opening:

We stepped down into a frightening scene. . . .

Add to it your own appositive, prepositional, participial, or infinitive phrases.

Grammar Workshop

Phrases

The passage in this workshop is taken from a recent novel by the Japanese-American writer Yoshiko Uchida. The novel tells the story of a young Japanese woman who arrives in San Francisco in 1917 to marry a man whom she has never met. Like many Japanese "picture brides" who came to the United States around the time of World War I, Hana Omiya faces an uncertain future. In this passage, taken from the opening scene of the novel, she contemplates her fate. The passage has been annotated to show many of the kinds of phrases covered in this unit.

Literature Model

from PICTURE BRIDE

by Yoshiko Uchida

Hana Omiya stood at the railing of the small ship that shuddered toward America in a turbulent November sea. She shivered as she pulled the folds of her silk kimono close to her throat and tightened the wool shawl about her shoulders.

She was thin and small, her dark eyes shadowed in her pale face, her black hair piled high in a pompadour that seemed too heavy for so slight a woman. She clung to the moist rail and breathed the damp salt air deep into her lungs. Her body seemed leaden and lifeless, as though it were simply the vehicle transporting her soul to a strange new life, and she longed with childlike intensity to be home again in Oka Village.

She longed to see the bright persimmon dotting the barren trees beside the thatched roof, to see the fields of golden rice stretching to the mountains where only last fall she had gathered plump white mushrooms, and to see once more the maple trees lacing their flaming colors through the green pine. If only she could see a familiar face, eat a meal without retching, walk on solid ground and stretch out at night on a *tatami* mat instead of in a hard narrow bunk. She thought now of seeking the warm shelter of her bunk but could not bear to face the relentless smell of fish that penetrated the lower decks. ➡

Prepositional phrase (adjective phrase)

Prepositional phrase (adverb phrase)

Infinitive phrase

Participial phrase (present participle)

Gerund phrase

Why did I ever leave Japan, she wondered bitterly. Why did I ever listen to my uncle? And yet she knew it was she herself who had begun the chain of events that placed her on this heaving ship. It was she who had first planted in her uncle's mind the thought that she would make a good wife for Taro Takeda, the lonely man who had gone to America to make his fortune in Oakland, California.

Grammar Workshop Exercise 1

Expanding Sentences with Prepositional Phrases The following sentences describe an imaginary journey on a boat. Read through the sentences quickly to get an idea of the scene, and then rewrite each sentence, adding a prepositional phrase— either an adjective phrase or an adverb phrase—to each sentence. You do not need to describe a Japanese immigrant heading toward America, as Yoshiko Uchida has done in her novel *Picture Bride*; you can imagine any scene that you wish.

SAMPLE   The voyage was long and tedious.
ANSWER   The voyage to the new land was long and tedious.

1. The ship rocked violently.
2. The boy watched the dark waves.
3. His hair was tossed.
4. He wore a long scarf.
5. The breeze flushed his cheeks.
6. He carried a small suitcase.
7. He was taking a long trip.
8. The previous night he had slept poorly.
9. The boy ate little.
10. Memories flooded his mind.
11. He felt intense longing.
12. He had left his family.
13. All his friends had stayed behind.
14. The ship was crowded.
15. Many people were traveling.
16. Some men sang songs.
17. Small children played games.
18. Young women chatted.
19. Sailors came and went.
20. The captain appeared only once.
21. The boy sat quietly.
22. He had a faraway look. ➡

23. The ship arrived late.
24. A man greeted the boy.
25. The boy's new life had begun.

Grammar Workshop Exercise 2

Expanding Sentences with Appositives   The following sentences describe Hana Omiya, the heroine of *Picture Bride*. Each sentence is followed by a group of words in parentheses. Rewrite each sentence, incorporating the words in parentheses so that they form an appositive or an appositive phrase. Use a comma or commas to set off the appositive or appositive phrase from the rest of the sentence.

SAMPLE   The ship sailed toward San Francisco.
            (a small steamer)

ANSWER   The ship, a small steamer, sailed toward
            San Francisco.

1. A solitary figure stood on the open deck.
   (a small woman with a shawl)
2. The woman was traveling to America.
   (Hana Omiya)
3. She had left her home and was traveling to meet her future husband. (a small village in Japan)
4. Her father had died, leaving four daughters and a wife behind. (a prosperous landowner)
5. Of the four sisters Hana was the only one without a husband. (the youngest)
6. Hana's mother was determined to find a match for her. (a practical woman)
7. The idea that Hana should go to America was suggested by another relative. (Uncle Oji)
8. Oji knew a Japanese man who had gone to California to seek his fortune.
   (Taro Takeda)
9. Taro Takeda had opened a small shop in Oakland.
   (the son of a friend of Oji's)
10. Oji said that Taro would make a good husband.
    (a hardworking and honest man)
11. Hana's dark eyes were fixed on the horizon.
    (a barely perceptible line of blue)
12. The bracing scene contrasted with her mood.
    (a heavy feeling of dread)
13. Familiar faces filled her mind. ➡

(now only distant memories)

14. She yearned to see not the ocean but the graceful persimmons and maples.
    (the trees of home)
15. The discomforts of the trip were becoming unbearable.
    (seasickness and unpleasant odors)
16. Even more unbearable was her fear.
    (a constant companion on the voyage)
17. Another land was to be her new home.
    (a country with strange people and an unfamiliar language)
18. A man unknown to her was to be her husband.
    (her companion for the rest of her life)
19. His picture offered few clues to his character.
    (a faded photograph)
20. She was overwhelmed by bitterness.
    (an emotion unfamiliar to her)

Grammar Workshop Exercise 3

Expanding Sentences with Participial Phrases   The following sentences relate to Hana Omiya and her life. Each sentence is followed by another sentence in parentheses. Combine the sentences, changing the sentence in parentheses into a participial phrase. Be sure to place the participial phrase close to the word that it modifies. Note that some of the sentences may be expanded in more than one way.

SAMPLE   Hana stood on the deck of the ship.
         (She was shivering in her thin clothes.)

ANSWER   Shivering in her thin clothes, Hana stood on the deck of the ship.

1. The woolen shawl offered little warmth.
   (The shawl was draped over her shoulders.)
2. Her silk kimono made her look like a bird.
   (Her kimono was fluttering in the wind.)
3. The sea air was damp and cheerless.
   (The air was rushing past her face.)
4. Hana recalled the warm colors of her village.
   (She was gazing absently at the sea.)
5. The memory of familiar faces haunted her.
   (The faces were filled with good will.)
6. She recalled the rice fields.
   (The rice fields were rustling in the breeze.)
7. She longed to see the orange persimmons. ➡

(The persimmons were hanging from the bare trees.)
8. Why was she going to America to marry a man?
(The man was unknown to her.)
9. Her uncle had described Taro as decent and hard working.
(Her uncle was speaking eagerly.)
10. Hana had decided to leave Japan.
(Hana had been longing for a different kind of life.)
11. Her sisters lived in big cities.
(Her sisters were married to merchants.)
12. Their lives were monotonous.
(Their lives were filled with routine.)
13. Hana did not want to be a bored wife.
(A bored wife is trapped in a dull marriage.)
14. At first Hana had looked forward to a new life.
(Her life would be filled with excitement.)
15. She dreaded the future now.
(She was plagued with uncertainty.)
16. She had reluctantly boarded the ship.
(She was leaving her family behind.)
17. Many passengers had stayed in their quarters.
(They were exhausted by the trip.)
18. Hana remained on the deck.
(She was not accompanied by even a single friend.)
19. She listened to some Russian travelers.
(The Russians were singing of home.)
20. The loneliness was as endless as the sea.
(The loneliness was stretching before her.)

Grammar Workshop Exercise 4

Writing Sentences with Gerund Phrases   The exercise that follows focuses on the lives of immigrants who came from Japan to the United States. Each item consists of a question followed by a phrase in parentheses that answers the question. For each item write a sentence that answers the question, using the words in parentheses as a gerund phrase. Note that some of the sentences may be reworded in several ways.

SAMPLE   What is painful? (leaving one's homeland)
ANSWER   Leaving one's homeland is painful.

1. In the late nineteenth century what was difficult in Japan? (earning a living)
2. What seemed like a good idea? (moving to the United States) ➡

3. What was a first step for many poor immigrants? (signing a work contract)
4. What was impossible for early Japanese immigrants? (becoming an American citizen)
5. What did many Japanese immigrants find practical? (living in California)
6. What was a common job for Japanese families who moved to California? (picking grapes)
7. What did many Japanese immigrants have to accept? (working for low wages)
8. What was a goal for many of them? (owning property)
9. How did many Japanese immigrants survive? (applying skills learned in their native land)
10. What did one Japanese immigrant begin doing? (growing rice on wasteland)
11. What is now an important industry in California? (cultivating rice)
12. How did other Japanese immigrants earn a living? (fishing for abalone, tuna, and sardines)
13. What enterprise did some Japanese families in California develop? (extracting salt from sea water)
14. How did many Japanese businessmen survive? (banding together in associations)
15. What was one goal of the associations? (lending money to members)
16. As more Japanese families arrived, what became a part of their lives? (maintaining a sense of their cultural heritage)
17. What became prevalent in many parts of the West? (segregating Japanese schools and communities)
18. What helped keep their heritage alive? (wearing traditional dress for special occasions)
19. What was one particularly important tradition? (practicing the ancient tea ceremony)
20. What was another means of preserving cultural ties? (singing traditional songs)

Grammar Workshop Exercise 5

Writing Sentences with Infinitive Phrases   The exercise that follows describes courtship practices of Japanese immigrants. Each of the items consists of a question followed by a phrase in parentheses that answers the question. For each item write a sentence that answers the question, using the words in parentheses as an infinitive phrase. ➡

1. What did many Japanese men want to do? (to get married)
2. What was difficult in the United States? (to find a Japanese bride)
3. What did some men return to Japan to do? (to seek a wife)
4. What did other men ask their parents in Japan to do? (to send them a suitable wife)
5. What did a friend usually agree to do? (to arrange the marriage)
6. What was the young wife forced to do? (to face her uncertain future with courage)
7. What did the wife need to do? (to travel to America alone)
8. What was wrenching for the picture brides? (to leave their families behind)
9. What did most wives expect to do in the United States? (to work hard)
10. What did most wives hope to do? (to find economic security)

Grammar Workshop Exercise 6

Review   Read the brief biography of Yoshiko Uchida. Then quickly scan the twenty sentences that follow it. Use the facts in the biography and the guidelines in parentheses to expand the twenty sentences. Be sure to place each phrase you add close to the word it modifies.

Yoshiko Uchida

Yoshiko Uchida was born in Alameda, California, in 1921. Her parents, seeking a better life, had moved to America several years before Uchida was born. Her mother, who was an amateur poet, taught Uchida to love words. As a child Uchida witnessed the struggles of many Japanese Americans. Many spoke little English, ran their own businesses, and earned a reputation as hard workers.

When Uchida was about to begin her final college exams, Japan attacked Pearl Harbor, and the United States entered World War II. Soon afterward the Uchidas, along with thousands of other Japanese-American families, were moved to relocation camps. At the camp at the Tanforan Race Track in California, Uchida's family lived in a horse stall; they spent ➡

five months there. Altogether Uchida spent three years in the grim, dusty camps.

After the war Uchida studied education and taught in a Philadelphia school. She later left her teaching job and traveled to Japan, where she collected folk tales and visited her ancestors' tombs. After learning a great deal about Japanese culture, she returned to California and dedicated herself to fiction. Uchida has written mostly for children; *Picture Bride* is her first novel for adults. It appeared in 1987.

1. Yoshiko Uchida was born in 1921. (Add an appositive phrase.)
2. Her parents came to America. (Add an infinitive phrase.)
3. Uchida's mother taught her to love words. (Add an appositive phrase.)
4. As a child Uchida observed many Japanese immigrants. (Add a participial phrase.)
5. Most of them knew few words. (Add an adjective phrase.)
6. Many of the immigrants earned a living. (Add a participial phrase.)
7. The immigrants earned a reputation. (At the end of the sentence, add the preposition *for* and a gerund phrase.)
8. The United States entered World War II. (Add an adverb phrase.)
9. When Pearl Harbor was attacked, Uchida was studying. (Add an adverb phrase.)
10. During the war the Uchidas were sent to the Tanforan Race Track. (Add an appositive phrase.)
11. Thousands were sent to the camps. (Add an adjective phrase.)
12. Uchida's entire family lived in a stall. (Add an adjective phrase.)
13. Uchida lived in the camps. (Add an adverb phrase.)
14. After the war Uchida studied. (Add an infinitive phrase.)
15. She taught school. (Add an adverb phrase.)
16. Later she decided to stop and travel to Japan. (Add a gerund or a gerund phrase.)
17. She went to Japan. (Add an infinitive phrase.)
18. After she returned, she made a decision. (Add an infinitive phrase.)
19. Most is written for children. (Add an adjective phrase.)
20. *Picture Bride* was published in 1987. (Add an appositive phrase.)

Proofreading   The following passage describes the artist Andō Hiroshige, whose work appears on the opposite page. Rewrite the passage, correcting the errors in spelling, capitalization, punctuation, grammar, and usage. There are twenty-five errors in all.

Andō Hiroshige

[1]Andō (or Ichiyū-sai) Hiroshige (1797–1858) was the son of a fire-brigade cheif. [2]His family was moderately wealthy and he was expected to follow in his fathers footsteps. [3]Early on, however, he abandoned his post with the fire brigade, and began to study painting.

[4]Unlike painters in Europe and America, japanese artists painted predetermined images according to Japans' strict rules of representation. [5]Hiroshege tried a number of pictorial themes, including portraiture and historcal painting, before finally settling on landscapes, birds, and flowers. [6]He focused on these themes throughout their life.

[7]Hiroshige made steady artistic progress, during which they expiremented with printmaking. [8]Began to make wood-block prints in a style called *ukiyo-e*, which, literaly translated, means "floating world." [9]These prints were inexpensively mass-produced for popular consumtion. [10]Craftspeople made the prints by following an artists instructions.

[11]The subject matter of the *ukiyo-e* prints included historical events; portraits of actors, beautiful young women, or wariors; and landscapes. [12]The prints were even used to teach children about japanese culture. [13]Countless numbers of such prints was made, enabling the populace to have art in their homes. [14]Although such prints were popular and inexpensive at the time, today they are quite valuable.

[15]*Compound of the Tenjin Shrine at Kameido* is a typical wood-block print made in the *ukiyo-e* style; Hiroshige may be the greatest exponint of this style. [16]Each color was applied with a seperate wood block. [17]Hiroshige was best known for his use of red and blue. [18]He combined plants, birds water, and figures crossing a bridge to create a subtly poetic atmosphere in an everyday scene.

[19]To the character in Uchidas' *Picture bride*, such an image would recall all things Japanese. [20]Its delicate design, decorative colors hanging leaves, and arched bridge would remind her of the World she had left behind.

Andō Hiroshige, _Compound of the Tenjin Shrine at Kameido,_ 1856

Unit 12 Review

Phrases

Identifying Phrases

[pages 469–477]

Tell whether the underlined phrase in each sentence is **(a)** a prepositional phrase, **(b)** an appositive phrase, **(c)** a participial phrase, **(d)** a gerund phrase, or **(e)** an infinitive phrase.

1. Ivory is a hard, white substance that comes <u>from tusks</u>.
2. The material is used <u>to make piano keys and decorative objects</u>.
3. <u>Carving ivory</u> is an ancient art.
4. Prehistoric carvings were found in Dordogne, <u>an area in southern France</u>.
5. <u>Using layers of ivory</u>, Greek sculptors created faces and hands.

Prepositional Phrases

[pages 469–470]

Tell whether the prepositional phrase in each sentence is acting as **(a)** an adjective or **(b)** an adverb.

6. Elephants in India have relatively small tusks.
7. The larger tusks of African elephants provide the best ivory.
8. These animals have long been hunted for their valuable tusks.
9. Today hunting elephants is generally forbidden by law.
10. Imitation ivory can be obtained from certain South American palm trees.

Gerund Phrases

[pages 474–475]

Tell whether the gerund phrase in each sentence is used as **(a)** a subject, **(b)** a direct object, **(c)** an object of a preposition, **(d)** a predicate nominative, or **(e)** an appositive.

11. Changing its identity is a common practice for a young insect.
12. Its goal becomes transforming itself into a different creature.
13. Metamorphosis, assuming a new form, is a dramatic process.
14. A butterfly begins crawling around as a fuzzy caterpillar.
15. After hiding for a while, a changed creature emerges from a cocoon.

Infinitive Phrases

[pages 475–476]

Tell whether the infinitive phrase in each sentence is used as **(a)** a noun, **(b)** an adjective, or **(c)** an adverb.

16. The Vikings were among the first Europeans to explore North America.
17. They began to send ships to North America in 1000.
18. Columbus, however, was the first European to establish permanent settlements in the Americas.
19. Columbus was unable to find his real destination, India.
20. To discover the "New World" was an unexpected development.

Writing for Review

Write a paragraph on any subject you choose. Include and underline at least one example of each kind of phrase: *prepositional*, *appositive*, *participial*, *gerund*, and *infinitive*.

Unit 13 Clauses and Sentence Structure

A **clause** is a group of words that has a subject and a predicate and is used as a part of a sentence.

There are two kinds of clauses: *main clauses*, also called *independent clauses*, and *subordinate clauses*, also called *dependent clauses*.

13.1 Main Clauses

A **main clause** has a subject and a predicate and can stand alone as a sentence.

Every sentence must have at least one main clause, and a sentence may have more than one main clause. Both of the clauses in the following example are main clauses because both can stand alone as a sentence:

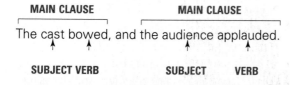

13.2 Subordinate Clauses

A **subordinate clause** has a subject and a predicate, but it cannot stand alone as a sentence.

A subordinate clause must be attached to a main clause in order for it to make sense. Subordinate clauses frequently begin with subordinating conjunctions or relative pronouns.

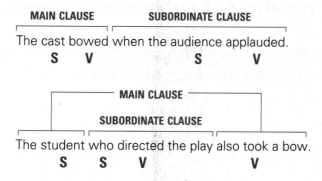

In the first example the subordinating conjunction *when* placed before *the audience applauded* creates a word group—*when the audience applauded*—that cannot stand alone as a main clause. Although the clause has a subject and a predicate, it does not express a complete thought.

In the second example the relative pronoun *who* begins a subordinate clause that comes between the subject and the verb of the main clause. *Who* also serves as the subject of the subordinate clause.

Exercise 1

Identifying Main and Subordinate Clauses   In each of the following sentences, the first clause appears in italics. On your paper indicate whether it is a *main clause* or a *subordinate clause*. (Remember that a subordinate clause cannot stand alone as a sentence.)

Romana Bañuelos, a United States Treasurer

[1]*Romana Acosta Bañuelos was treasurer of the United States from 1971 to 1974*, while Richard Nixon was President. [2]*Though many others have held this position*, Bañuelos was the first Mexican-American woman in such a high government post. [3]*Her signature became a familiar sight*, since the treasurer's name is printed on all paper currency. [4]*Because it involves a number of diverse tasks*, the job of treasurer is a challenging one. [5]*When Bañuelos was in office*, she wrote checks for all government agencies. [6]*Whenever currency became worn out*, she oversaw the destruction and replacement of the bills.

[7]*Bañuelos grew up in Mexico*, although she was born in Arizona. [8]*After she invested in a small tortilla stand in 1949*, the business grew into a five-million-dollar food company. [9]*Since her tortilla company had become such a success*, Bañuelos undertook another challenge. [10]*In 1964 she founded the Pan American National Bank of East Los Angeles*, which was the first bank in the United States run by a Mexican American.

13.3   Simple and Compound Sentences

A **simple sentence** has only one main clause and no subordinate clauses.

A simple sentence may have a compound subject or a compound predicate or both. The simple subject and the simple predicate may also be expanded in many other ways. Adjectives, adverbs, prepositional phrases, appositives, and verbal phrases may make some simple sentences seem anything but simple. Yet as long as the sentence has only one main clause, it remains a simple sentence.

> Bobcats stalk. [simple sentence]
>
> Bobcats and lynxes stalk. [simple sentence with compound subject]
>
> Bobcats stalk and pounce. [simple sentence with compound predicate]
>
> Bobcats and lynxes stalk and pounce. [simple sentence with compound subject and compound predicate]
>
> Bobcats silently stalk their prey during the night. [simple sentence expanded]

A **compound sentence** has two or more main clauses.

As the following examples show, each main clause of a compound sentence has its own subject and predicate. Notice that the main clauses of a compound sentence are usually joined by a comma and a coordinating conjunction, such as *and, but, or, nor, yet,* or *for*.

MAIN CLAUSE 1   **MAIN CLAUSE 2**
Bobcats stalk, and lynxes pursue.
   S   **V**   **S**   **V**

MAIN CLAUSE 1   **MAIN CLAUSE 2**   **MAIN CLAUSE 3**
Bobcats stalk, and lynxes pursue, but house cats slink.
   S   **V**   **S**   **V**   **S**   **V**

Two main clauses may also be joined by a semicolon to form a compound sentence.

MAIN CLAUSE 1
The frightened rabbit ran swiftly;

MAIN CLAUSE 2
the lynx followed at a close pace.

Exercise 2

Identifying Simple and Compound Sentences   Indicate whether each item is a *simple* or a *compound* sentence.

Climbing Mount Everest

1. Sir Edmund Hillary, a New Zealand mountain climber, and his Sherpa guide, Tenzing Norkay, were the first conquerors of Mount Everest. ➡

2. Hillary took photographs of Norkay at the summit, but none of Hillary were taken.
3. Norkay was already a well-known mountaineer, but Hillary's experience was limited to climbing in ice and snow in New Zealand.
4. Hillary, Norkay, and all the other members of the expedition looked for the easiest and safest route to the top of Mount Everest.
5. Today climbers look for greater challenges and choose the more difficult routes.
6. Hillary once traveled overland to the South Pole and also followed the Ganges River to its source.
7. The public and the media had shown considerable interest in Hillary.
8. Fame came with Hillary's successful ascent of Mount Everest, and afterward he raised money for the Sherpa people of Nepal.
9. They had helped Hillary, and in return he generously helped them.
10. Hillary gave lectures and raised funds for schools, hospitals, clinics, bridges, water pipelines, and airstrips in Nepal.

13.4 Complex and Compound-Complex Sentences

A **complex sentence** has one main clause and one or more subordinate clauses.

MAIN CLAUSE	SUBORDINATE CLAUSE

Some areas become deforested because people need wood for fuel.
   S   **V**   **S**   **V**

SUBORDINATE CLAUSE	MAIN CLAUSE

Because people need fuel, they cut down trees
       S   **V**   **S** **V**

SUBORDINATE CLAUSE

that had grown for many years.
  S   **V**

A **compound-complex sentence** has more than one main clause and at least one subordinate clause.

|MAIN CLAUSE| |MAIN CLAUSE|

Campers need fuel for cooking, but they should use a stove
  S   **V**   **S**   **V**

|SUBORDINATE CLAUSE|

that requires no wood.
  S   **V**

Exercise 3

Identifying Complex and Compound-Complex Sentences Write on your paper the subordinate clause that appears in each of the following sentences. Indicate whether each sentence is a *complex sentence* or a *compound-complex sentence*.

Energy Conservation

1. Because millions of energy-consuming devices are in use every day, energy conservation has become extremely important.
2. When builders construct new homes, they should install solar panels and other passive solar devices and as many energy-saving appliances as possible.
3. Although energy-efficient appliances cost more, their use results in savings for the owner, and the environment benefits, too.
4. Because legislators have enacted certain laws, all new cars must soon be energy-efficient.
5. When cars use less gas, the air is cleaner, and fewer people have trouble breathing.
6. While sulfur pollution is a threat to human health, it also damages lakes, wildlife, and buildings.
7. Although water power can generate electricity, hydroelectric dams may cause floods on farmland, in forests, and in wildlife areas.
8. We must always find ways of producing more goods, but at the same time we must reduce the amount of energy that we consume in producing those goods.
9. Conservation and solar power are the keys to a safe future, and so we must cautiously use the devices that cool, heat, and transport us.
10. Because our natural resources clearly cannot last forever, we must resolve as a nation to find better ways of conserving energy.

13.5   Adjective Clauses

An **adjective clause** is a subordinate clause that modifies a noun or a pronoun.

An adjective clause normally follows the word it modifies.

The hikers **who reached the peak** were overjoyed.

The trail, **which was rarely used,** had been a difficult one.

I forgot about the blisters **that covered my feet.**

The hiker **whom we appreciated most** carried the food.

Both relative pronouns (*who, whom, whose, that,* and *which*), and the subordinating conjunctions *where* and *when* may begin adjective clauses.

I will always remember the time **when I hiked to Pike's Peak.**
That is the spot **where we set up camp.**

Sometimes the relative pronoun is dropped at the beginning of an adjective clause.

Our camp was the spot **every hiker loved the most.** [The relative pronoun *that* has been omitted.]

An adjective clause is sometimes essential to a sentence; that is, it is needed to make the meaning of the sentence clear. This kind of adjective clause is called an *essential clause,* or a *restrictive clause.*

One characteristic **that most Native Americans had in common** was their love of dancing. [essential clause]

An adjective clause that is *not* needed to make the meaning of a sentence clear is called a *nonessential clause,* or a *nonrestrictive clause.* It adds information to a sentence, but the sentence would be perfectly logical without it. (Note that a nonessential clause must be set off with commas.)

The hikers, who were diverted by the natural splendor, arrived later in the day.

The Iroquois people of the East, **who were farmers,** thanked the spirits for the gift of food. [nonessential clause]

In the Southwest, **where water is scarce,** the Pueblo people performed rain dances. [nonessential clause]

That is usually used to introduce an essential clause, and *which* is used to begin a nonessential clause.

The Cheyenne hunted buffalo, **which supplied them with meat and skins for clothing and shelter.** [nonessential clause]

The animal **that was most important to the Cheyenne** was the buffalo. [essential clause]

Exercise 5

Identifying Adjective Clauses   On your paper write the adjective clause that appears in each of the following sentences. Then write the word that the clause modifies. (In one sentence the relative pronoun has been dropped.)

International Dances

1. The Pueblo rain dancers wore outfits with symbols that represented lightning, thunder, clouds, and rainbows.
2. In the eagle dance the dancers' movements are like those of the eagle, which swoops and dives for its food.
3. Chinese schoolchildren learn dances that require difficult head, wrist, and foot movements.
4. The Chinese ribbon dance, which has been performed for thousands of years, is often danced with red ribbons.
5. Red, which signifies happiness and good fortune in China, is the favorite ribbon color.
6. A lively dance that is very popular is the square dance.
7. Probably the best-known square dance is the Virginia reel, which became popular in George Washington's time.
8. Flamenco is a dance form the Gypsies in Spain invented.
9. A flamenco dancer, who is accompanied by a guitarist, typically wears bright and colorful clothing.
10. Folk dances often require steps that are difficult to learn.

Exercise 6

Recognizing Essential and Nonessential Clauses   For each sentence in the following pairs, write the adjective clause, and then identify it as an *essential* or a *nonessential clause*. ➡

Sacajuwea Hunter, Olympic Champion

1. **a.** Sacajuwea Hunter, who lost her legs at a very early age, competed in the 1984 Olympics.
   b. One young athlete who competed in the 1984 Olympics lost her legs at a very early age.
2. **a.** She was one of eight disabled women who competed in the eight-hundred-meter wheelchair exhibition race.
   b. Sacajuwea Hunter, who competed in the 1984 Olympics, was one of eight disabled women in the eight-hundred-meter wheelchair exhibition race.
3. **a.** Nearly one hundred thousand people watched the eight-hundred-meter wheelchair exhibition race, which was the first such event in Olympic history.
   b. An event that nearly one hundred thousand people watched was the eight-hundred-meter wheelchair exhibition race.
4. **a.** Bill Greene, who was Sacajuwea Hunter's special-education counselor, urged her to race.
   b. The man who was Sacajuwea Hunter's special-education counselor urged her to race.
5. **a.** Sacajuwea Hunter, who at fourteen was the youngest American in the 1984 Olympics, finished in fourth place overall.
   b. Sacajuwea Hunter was the youngest American athlete who competed in the 1984 Olympics.

13.6   Adverb Clauses

An **adverb clause** is a subordinate clause that modifies a verb, an adjective, or an adverb. It tells *when, where, how, why, to what extent,* or *under what conditions.*

> **Whenever it rains,** the river rises. [The adverb clause modifies the verb *rises.* It tells *when.*]

> The canoe is safe **as long as you remain seated.** [The adverb clause modifies the adjective *safe.* It tells *under what condition.*]

> You are paddling harder **than I am paddling.** [The adverb clause modifies the adverb *harder.* It tells *to what extent.*]

Subordinating conjunctions, such as those listed on page 430, introduce adverb clauses. Being familiar with those conjunctions will help you recognize adverb clauses. Remember also that an adverb clause may come either before or after the main clause. Notice that the adverb clause in the following example might also appear at the beginning of the sentence:

The river rises **whenever it rains**.

Occasionally words may be left out of an adverb clause. The omitted words can easily be supplied because they are understood, or implied. Such adverb clauses are described as *elliptical*.

You are paddling harder **than I [am paddling]**.
Paddling made me more tired **than [it made] him [tired]**.

Exercise 7

Identifying Adverb Clauses On your paper write the adverb clauses that appear in the following sentences. (Two sentences have more than one adverb clause.)

Yo-Yo Ma, an Outstanding Cellist

1. Yo-Yo Ma first played the cello on national television in 1962, although he was only seven years old at the time.
2. Because he had such talent, young Ma already played better than most adults play.
3. When Ma was only four, his father, a noted Chinese musician and teacher, gave his son cello lessons.
4. His father made a special cello from a viola, since a regular cello was too big for Ma at the time.
5. Once he was big enough, Ma switched to a regular cello.
6. After his family moved from Paris to New York, Ma studied at the Juilliard School of Music.
7. Wherever he played, Ma dazzled audiences with his deftness.
8. Ma continued on the cello while he worked on a degree in the humanities at Harvard University.
9. A highlight in his career came in 1978, when Ma received the highly respected Avery Fisher Prize for his musical talent.
10. Whenever Ma performs, fans can hardly imagine a cellist more talented than he.

13.7 Noun Clauses

A **noun clause** is a subordinate clause used as a noun.

You can use a noun clause as a subject, a direct object, an object of a preposition, or a predicate nominative.

NOUN

Campers enjoy the outdoors.
S

NOUN CLAUSE

Whoever camps enjoys the outdoors.
S

NOUN

Footgear affects hikers.
DO

NOUN CLAUSE

Footgear affects whoever walks often.
DO

In the preceding examples notice that each noun clause is an inseparable part of the sentence's main clause; the main clause is the entire sentence.

Here are some of the words that can be used to introduce noun clauses:

how	when	who, whom
that	where	whoever
what	which	whose
whatever	whichever	why

Here are additional examples of noun clauses:

I do not know **where my hiking boots are.** [direct object]

That is **why I did not join the others.** [predicate nominative]

We will make do with **whatever camping equipment we can borrow.** [object of a preposition]

Sometimes the relative pronoun may be dropped at the beginning of a noun clause.

I believe **we can have a great time outdoors.** [The relative pronoun *that* is omitted.]

Exercise 8

Identifying Noun Clauses   On your paper write the noun clauses that appear in each of the following sentences. (Two of the sentences have two noun clauses each. In one sentence the relative pronoun introducing the noun clause has been dropped.) ➡

The Importance of Police Dogs

1. Everyone knows dogs have a keen sense of smell.
2. What makes their sense of smell of great value is that people can train dogs to sniff out explosives.
3. Specially trained dogs search for whatever explosive device they can find.
4. What the dog finds may save whoever is in danger.
5. Do you believe that police dogs are valuable?
6. Whoever works with a police dog is trained along with the dog.
7. Many police officers say that police dogs make good partners.
8. Whoever says police dogs are vicious animals is misinformed.
9. That these dogs become aggressive upon command is true.
10. Police officers are appreciative of whatever help these dogs provide.

Exercise 9: Sentence Writing

Using Subordinate Clauses in Sentences   Write four original sentences. In the first use an adverb clause. In the second use an adjective clause. In the third use a noun clause as a subject. In the fourth use a noun clause as a direct object.

Exercise 10: Review

Clauses   On your paper write the subordinate clause that appears in each sentence. Then indicate whether the subordinate clause is (a) an *adverb clause*, (b) an *adjective clause*, or (c) a *noun clause*.

Sojourner Truth, a Crusader for Justice

[1]Sojourner Truth was a slave who was born in New York in the late eighteenth century. [2]Isabella is what she was called as a child. [3]Whoever has studied her life understands the importance of her work. [4]She fought against slavery wherever she went. [5]When an antislavery law was passed in New York in 1828, Isabella gained her freedom. [6]In 1843, after she took the name Sojourner Truth, she began a series of lecture tours throughout New England and the Midwest. [7]Her speeches expressed her strong belief that all people are equal. [8]She supported herself with proceeds from her biography, which was ➡

published in 1850. [9]Sojourner Truth campaigned for a state in the Midwest where freed slaves could have a land of their own. [10]Sojourner Truth was a woman whom everyone admired.

13.8 Four Kinds of Sentences

A **declarative sentence** makes a statement.

> An owl is hooting. I cannot see it.

A declarative sentence normally ends with a period. It is the type of sentence used most frequently in speaking and writing.

An **imperative sentence** gives a command or makes a request.

> Look at that bird.
> Please tell me what it is.

An imperative sentence usually ends with a period. The subject "you" is understood.

An **interrogative sentence** asks a question.

> What kind of bird is that?
> Is the hawk hunting for prey?

An interrogative sentence ends with a question mark.

An **exclamatory sentence** expresses strong emotion.

> Watch out for that hawk's sudden dive!
> What a powerful hunter the hawk is!

An exclamatory sentence ends with an exclamation point.

Exercise 11: Sentence Writing

Creating Four Kinds of Sentences   Write four sentences about a recent school event. Use one declarative, one imperative, one interrogative, and one exclamatory sentence.

13.9 Sentence Fragments

In general, avoid sentence fragments in your writing. A **sentence fragment** is an error that occurs when an incomplete sentence is punctuated as though it were a complete sentence.

When you check your work for sentence fragments, look for three things. First be alert for a group of words that lacks a subject. Then look for a group of words that lacks a verb, especially a group that contains a verbal rather than a complete verb. Finally, be careful that you have not punctuated a subordinate clause as a complete sentence.

Often you can correct a sentence fragment by joining it to an idea that comes before or after the fragment. Sometimes, however, you may need to add missing words to form a complete sentence.

FRAGMENT	Toshiko and Kenji are happy together. **Seem to be in love.** [lacks subject]
COMPLETE SENTENCE	Toshiko and Kenji are happy together, and they seem to be in love.
FRAGMENT	The two will marry. **Their new life together.** [lacks verb]
COMPLETE SENTENCE	The two will marry, and their new life together will begin.
FRAGMENT	They are planning an out-of-town wedding. **Many of their gifts arriving in the mail.** [lacks complete verb]
COMPLETE SENTENCE	They are planning an out-of-town wedding. Many of their gifts have been arriving in the mail.
FRAGMENT	On their honeymoon they will be traveling to Italy. **Which they both love.** [has subordinate clause only]
COMPLETE SENTENCE	On their honeymoon they will be traveling to Italy, which they both love.

Is missing her head

Greek,
Nike of Samothrace,
200–190 B.C.

Professional writers sometimes use sentence fragments to create a special effect—to add emphasis to what they are saying or to convey realistic dialogue. Remember that professionals use sentence fragments *carefully* and *intentionally*. In most of the writing you will do, however, including your writing for school, sentence fragments should be avoided.

Exercise 12

Identifying Sentence Fragments   Indicate on your paper whether each of the following numbered items is a *complete sentence* or a *sentence fragment.*

The Piñata Game
[1]In Mexico children often celebrate festivals and birthdays with parties. [2]By breaking a colorful piñata. [3]An earthenware or papier-mâché container covered with crepe-paper streamers. [4]A piñata is often shaped like an animal or a person. [5]Filled ➡

with nuts, candy, and small toys, it is hung by a rope from the ceiling. ⁶Or—if the party is outdoors—from a tree limb. ⁷The blindfolded children take turns hitting the piñata with a stick. ⁸Not always easy, because an adult raises and lowers the piñata with a rope. ⁹Finally, after many attempts, the break. ¹⁰Children rush to collect the treats scattered about.

Exercise 13: Sentence Writing

Correcting Sentence Fragments   Revise the preceding paragraph by correcting each fragment. Whenever possible, combine the fragments with other sentences in the paragraph.

13.10   Run-on Sentences

Avoid run-on sentences in your writing. A **run-on sentence** is two or more complete sentences written as though they were one sentence.

There are three basic kinds of run-on sentence.

1. A **comma splice,** probably the most common type of run-on sentence, occurs when two main clauses are separated by a comma rather than a period or a semicolon. To correct this type of run-on, replace the comma with a period (or other end mark of punctuation), and start the new sentence with a capital letter. You can also correct this error by adding a coordinating conjunction after the comma.

RUN-ON	Luis and Fredericka are going to Washington, D.C., with their school, they are very excited.
CORRECT	Luis and Fredericka are going to Washington, D.C., with their school**.** They are very excited.
CORRECT	Luis and Fredericka are going to Washington, D.C., with their school**, and** they are very excited.

2. Another kind of run-on sentence occurs when two main clauses are written with *no* punctuation between them. To correct this type of run-on, separate the main clauses with an end mark of punctuation or with a semicolon. Still another way to correct the error is to add a comma and a coordinating conjunction between the main clauses.

RUN-ON	They hope to see many famous sights the Lincoln Memorial will surely be among them.

CORRECT	They hope to see many famous sights; the Lincoln Memorial will surely be among them.
CORRECT	They hope to see many famous sights, **and** the Lincoln Memorial will surely be among them.

3. Still another kind of run-on sentence occurs when the comma is omitted before a coordinating conjunction joining two main clauses. To correct this error, simply add the comma before the coordinating conjunction.

RUN-ON	Fredericka and Luis will take notes for a written report on their Washington trip but they plan to have fun anyway.
CORRECT	Fredericka and Luis will take notes for a written report on their Washington trip, but they plan to have fun anyway.

Exercise 14

Correcting Run-on Sentences   Rewrite the following paragraph, correcting the run-on sentences. Watch for the three types of run-on errors. You may choose from among the several suggestions for correcting run-ons that you learned.

Animal Care in Zoos

[1]The earliest known zoo was established in Egypt around 1500 B.C. a half century later a Chinese emperor built a zoo that covered about fifteen hundred acres. [2]Today zoo facilities are limited and zoo keepers cannot have every animal on display year-round. [3]In the winter in colder climates, most birds must be brought indoors but zoo keepers cannot always keep each bird on view for the public. [4]Many visitors are surprised to see that some animals remain outside all year, penguins, polar bears, bison, and timber wolves are happy outdoors in wintertime. [5]Some animals are always indoors in northern areas, reptiles and small desert animals always have indoor displays. [6]Zoo keepers must provide indoor shelters for large animals such as elephants and giraffes how large those shelters must be! [7]Today zoologists understand much more about animal behavior and zoos are being designed that are similar to the animals' natural habitats. [8]Viewers can closely observe animals at animal parks, animals roam free. [9]Zoo kitchens keep a wide variety of foods and food supplements these are used to prepare meals that meet with each animal's nutritional needs. [10]Zoos contribute to wildlife conservation, they nurture species that are in danger of becoming extinct.

Sentence Completeness   Rewrite the following paragraph, correcting all sentence fragments and run-on sentences.

Chinese New Year

[1]The biggest and most popular of all Chinese festivals. [2]The Chinese New Year, an exciting and colorful holiday. [3]Falling anywhere between January 21 and February 19. [4]The New Year is celebrated by Chinese people all over the world, they parade through the streets and set off fireworks. [5]People pay visits to friends they wish them luck and prosperity with the greeting *kung-hsi fa-ts'ai*, which means "happy greetings, and may you gather wealth." [6]On the final day of the year, preparations are made for a great New Year's Eve supper. [7]All doors are sealed with paper strips and no one may leave or enter until the next morning. [8]Businesses are closed. [9]For days after the New Year begins. [10]Children receive presents of money in red envelopes adults give gifts to the poor.

In the following paragraph from "A Day's Pleasure," Hamlin Garland uses a variety of sentence types not only to capture the reader's interest but also to develop a pleasing rhythm and an appropriate mood of relaxation:

> They went into the little sitting room, so dainty and lovely to the farmer's wife, and as she sank into the easy chair she was faint and drowsy with the pleasure of it. She submitted to being brushed. She gave the baby into the hands of the Swedish girl, who washed its face and hands and sang it to sleep, while its mother sipped some tea. Through it all she lay back in her easy chair, not speaking a word, while the ache passed out of her back, and her hot, swollen head ceased to throb.

Notice how the structure of each of Garland's four sentences varies: compound-complex, simple, complex, compound-complex. Try to apply some of Garland's techniques when you write and revise your work:

1. Avoid using the same sentence structure repeatedly. A string of compound-complex sentences can be as monotonous as a series of choppy, simple sentences.

2. Use subordination not only to call attention to some ideas and downplay others but also to control the rhythm of your sentences. Garland, for example, subordinates many of the wife's actions ("as she sank"; "while its mother sipped"; "while the ache passed") and calls attention to her feelings and responses ("she was faint and drowsy"; "she submitted"; "she lay back"). Also, the alternation between main clauses and subordinate clauses gives the paragraph an appropriate mood of ease and tranquillity.

Apply these techniques in revising the following series of simple sentences adapted from "A Day's Pleasure." Decide which ideas should be subordinated, and try to use a variety of sentence structures.

> It grew warmer. They went on. A strong south wind arose. The dust settled upon the woman's shawl and hat. Her hair loosened and blew unkemptly about her face. The road led across the high, level prairie. It was quite smooth and dry but still jolted her. The pain in her back increased.

Grammar Workshop

Clauses and Sentence Structure

As Eudora Welty's novel *Delta Wedding* begins, young Laura McRaven is on her way from her home in Jackson, Mississippi, to Shellmound, the plantation where her cousin Dabney is to be married. It is Laura's first trip alone, and she savors every minute of it. The passage has been annotated to show the types of sentences and clauses covered in this unit.

Literature Model

from DELTA WEDDING

by Eudora Welty

The nickname of the train was the Yellow Dog. Its real name was the Yazoo-Delta. It was a mixed train. The day was the 10th of September, 1923—afternoon. Laura McRaven, who was nine years old, was on her first journey alone. She was going up from Jackson to visit her mother's people, the Fairchilds, at their plantation named Shellmound, at Fairchilds, Mississippi. . . .

In the passenger car every window was propped open with a stick of kindling wood. A breeze blew through, hot and then cool, fragrant of the woods and yellow flowers and of the train. The yellow butterflies flew in at any window, out at any other, and outdoors one of them could keep up with the train, which then seemed to be racing with a butterfly. Overhead a black lamp in which a circle of flowers had been cut out swung round and round on a chain as the car rocked from side to side, sending down dainty drifts of kerosene smell. The Dog was almost sure to reach Fairchilds before the lamp would be lighted by Mr. Terry Black, the conductor, who had promised her father to watch out for her. Laura had the seat facing the stove, but of course no fire was burning in it now. She sat leaning at the window, the light and the sooty air trying to make her close her eyes. Her ticket to Fairchilds was stuck up in her Madge Evans straw hat, in imitation of the drummer [salesman] across the aisle. Once the Dog stopped in the open fields and Laura saw the engineer, Mr. Doolittle, go ➡

Annotation labels:
- Simple sentence
- Complex sentence
- Compound-complex sentence
- Adverb clause
- Adjective clause
- Compound sentence

out and pick some specially fine goldenrod there—for whom, she could not know. Then the long September cry rang from the thousand unseen locusts, urgent at the open windows of the train. . . .

From the warm window sill the endless fields glowed like a hearth in firelight, and Laura, looking out, leaning on her elbows with her head between her hands, felt what an arriver in a land feels—that slow hard pounding in the breast.

— Noun clause

Grammar Workshop Exercise 1

Identifying Main and Subordinate Clauses   The following sentences are based on the passage from *Delta Wedding*. Each sentence contains a clause that appears in italics. On your paper indicate whether the italicized clause is a *main clause* or a *subordinate clause*.

1. *Although she was only nine years old*, Laura was traveling alone.
2. The conductor, *who was watching out for Laura*, would soon light the lamp.
3. *The ticket* that was stuck in Laura's hat *would take her to Fairchilds, Mississippi*.
4. Laura was traveling to Fairchilds *so that she could attend her cousin's wedding*.
5. *She would stay at her cousin's plantation*, which was named Shellmound.
6. Because it was a warm day, *all the windows of the train were propped open*.
7. *While the train moved along*, Laura sat quietly in her seat.
8. Laura could see the unlighted stove just opposite *where she sat*.
9. Laura saw a field of goldenrod *as she looked out the window*.
10. *After the engineer picked some goldenrod*, the train started up again.

Grammar Workshop Exercise 2

Identifying Compound, Complex, and Compound-Complex Sentences   The following sentences elaborate on ideas from the passage from *Delta Wedding*. On your paper ➡

indicate whether each sentence is *compound*, *complex*, or *compound-complex*.

1. The train's name was the *Yazoo-Delta*, but people called it the *Yellow Dog*.
2. It was September 10, 1923, and Laura McRaven was traveling by train to Fairchilds, Mississippi, where her cousin was getting married.
3. Laura, who was only nine years old, watched the countryside pass by.
4. Laura was enjoying the trip, for she was traveling alone for the first time.
5. The car of the train rocked gently as it hurried along, and the overhead lamp swung round and round.
6. The windows, which were held open with sticks of wood, let breezes into the cars.
7. The train had been traveling for a long time, yet the conductor had still not collected the tickets from Laura and the salesman across the aisle.
8. Because the day was warm, no fire burned in the stove.
9. Laura watched while the engineer picked some goldenrod, and she noticed that the flowers were especially fine.
10. Though she sat quietly, Laura could feel her heart pounding.

Grammar Workshop Exercise 3

Writing Sentences with Adjective Clauses   The sentences that follow elaborate on ideas from the passage from *Delta Wedding*. Rewrite each sentence, adding an adjective clause that answers the question in parentheses. Your clause must begin with a relative pronoun (see the list below), and it must contain a verb. Your sentence should make sense within the context of the passage; there may be more than one correct answer.

RELATIVE PRONOUNS   who   whom   whose   which   that

SAMPLE   The train was heading toward Fairchilds, Mississippi. (What was the name of the train?)

ANSWER   The train, whose name was the *Yazoo-Delta*, was heading toward Fairchilds, Mississippi.

1. Laura was traveling alone for the first time in her life. (How old was she?)
2. Laura was traveling from Jackson, Mississippi. (What was Jackson to Laura?) ➡

3. She was going to visit her mother's family. (Where did Laura's mother's family live?)
4. Laura's journey was taking place on a September afternoon. (What was the weather like?)
5. Laura felt very dressed up for her ride on the train. (What hat was she wearing?)
6. A breeze blew through the open windows. (What did the breeze smell like?)
7. Laura watched the yellow butterflies. (What did the butterflies do?)
8. A black lamp swung to the rhythm of the rocking car. (How was the lamp decorated?)
9. The lamp would probably not be lighted during the journey. (What odor did the lamp give off?)
10. The conductor would light the lamp later. (What was the conductor's name?)
11. Mr. Black had not yet collected the tickets. (What promise did he make?)
12. Laura sat in her seat. (Where was her seat?)
13. The air made her want to close her eyes. (What was the air like?)
14. Laura imitated the drummer, or traveling salesman. (Where was his ticket?)
15. Mr. Doolittle stopped the train. (What was Mr. Doolittle's job?)
16. The engineer picked some goldenrod. (What was the goldenrod like?)
17. Through the train's open windows Laura heard a cry. (From what did the cry come?)
18. Laura heard locusts. (Where were they?)
19. Laura gazed at the fields. (What did the fields look like?)
20. Laura was anxious for her journey to end. (How did she feel?)

Grammar Workshop Exercise 4

Writing Sentences with Adverb Clauses   The sentences that follow elaborate on ideas suggested by the passage from *Delta Wedding*. Rewrite each sentence, adding an adverb clause that answers the question in parentheses. Your clause must begin with one of the subordinating conjunctions listed below, and it must contain a subject and a verb. The sentence should make sense within the context of the passage; there may be more than one correct answer for each item. ➡

SAMPLE   Laura McRaven was traveling to Shellmound. (Why?)

ANSWER   Laura McRaven was traveling to Shellmound because her cousin Dabney was getting married.

1. It was an exciting day for Laura. (Why?)
2. Laura sat looking out the window. (When?)
3. Laura felt excited. (Why?)
4. Pieces of kindling were being used to keep the windows of the passenger car open. (Why?)
5. There were butterflies inside the car. (Why?)
6. Butterflies flew into the train. (Where?)
7. One butterfly flew alongside the train. (In what manner?)
8. The black lamp over Laura's head swung in circles on its chain. (Why?)
9. The conductor would finally light the lamp. (When?)
10. Laura's father had asked the conductor to promise to look after her. (When?)
11. A fire would be lighted in the stove opposite Laura. (Under what condition?)
12. Laura almost had to close her eyes. (Why?)
13. Laura put her ticket in her hat. (Why?)
14. The passengers would give the conductor their tickets. (When?)
15. The engineer stopped the train. (Why?)
16. Laura found the engineer's actions somewhat mysterious. (Why?)
17. Laura heard the locusts. (Why?)
18. The fields glowed in the daylight. (How?)
19. Laura's heart pounded. (When?)
20. Laura would see her mother's family. (When?)

Grammar Workshop Exercise 5

Identifying Noun Clauses   The following sentences describe the Mississippi Delta area, to which Laura McRaven was traveling. On your paper write the noun clauses that appear in the sentences. Two of the sentences have two noun clauses each. In one sentence the relative pronoun before the noun clause has been dropped. ➡

1. Does this book explain what the Mississippi Delta is?
2. Whoever has visited Mississippi is probably familiar with the area.
3. That the Mississippi River periodically floods its banks is the reason for the Mississippi Delta's existence.
4. What we now call the Mississippi Delta was formed by whatever deposits of silt the receding Mississippi River flood waters left behind.
5. You can easily understand why many farmers live in the Delta.
6. What attracts many farmers to the Delta is that the soil is so fertile.
7. Do you know what makes the Delta so famous?
8. One reason for the Delta's fame is that the area produces large crops of cotton.
9. You may also have read that large crops of soybeans are grown in the Delta.
10. I know visitors are also attracted by the area's many beautiful plantations.

Grammar Workshop Exercise 6

Writing Four Kinds of Sentences   On your paper identify each of the following sentences as *declarative*, *imperative*, *interrogative*, or *exclamatory*. Then rewrite each sentence in the form noted in parentheses.

SAMPLE   The engineer stopped the train. (Rewrite as an imperative sentence.)

ANSWER   declarative
             Engineer, please stop the train.

1. Was the train's official name the *Yazoo-Delta*? (Rewrite as a declarative sentence.)
2. We call the train the *Yellow Dog*. (Rewrite as an imperative sentence.)
3. The date was September 10, 1923. (Rewrite as an interrogative sentence.)
4. It was very warm that September day. (Rewrite as an exclamatory sentence.)
5. Were all the train windows open? (Rewrite as a declarative sentence.)
6. Will you open all the train windows? (Rewrite as an imperative sentence.) ➡

7. How delicate the butterflies were! (Rewrite as an interrogative sentence.)
8. Was Laura sitting across the aisle from the drummer? (Rewrite as an imperative sentence.)
9. Laura, put the ticket in your hat. (Rewrite as a declarative sentence.)
10. Laura liked the smell of the kerosene from the lamp. (Rewrite as an interrogative sentence.)
11. Cool breezes came from the woods nearby. (Rewrite as an interrogative sentence.)
12. How beautiful the goldenrod was! (Rewrite as a declarative sentence.)
13. Mr. Doolittle, please give her some goldenrod. (Rewrite as a declarative sentence.)
14. Mr. Doolittle stopped the train in order to pick some goldenrod. (Rewrite as an interrogative sentence.)
15. How loud the cries of the locusts were! (Rewrite as a declarative sentence.)
16. Did Laura look forward to seeing her cousins? (Rewrite as a declarative sentence.)
17. Laura's heart was pounding. (Rewrite as an exclamatory sentence.)
18. Mr. Black promised to look after Laura. (Rewrite as an imperative sentence.)
19. Laura's cousins were going to meet her train. (Rewrite as an interrogative sentence.)
20. Laura had a wonderful time. (Rewrite as an exclamatory sentence.)

Grammar Workshop Exercise 7

Correcting Sentence Fragments   The following paragraph describes Uncle Battle, another character from *Delta Wedding*. Revise the paragraph, correcting any sentence fragments. The fragments may be corrected by combining sentences, by adding words (such as a subject or a verb), or by changing the form of a verb.

SAMPLE   Laura arrived. Her cousins rushing out to meet her.
ANSWER   When Laura arrived, her cousins rushed out to meet her.

¹At Shellmound Laura so happy to see Uncle Battle again. ²A big man, her mother's brother. ³Always called all the children Skeeta. ⁴All of his children exactly like him. ⁵Wore tall ➡

boots that creaked when he stood up. **6**His hair always combed back over his brow. **7**At mealtime Uncle Battle always carving and serving the turkey. **8**Likely to drive off at any time of the day or night, without a moment's notice. **9**Because he needed to check to see that the plantation work was getting done. **10**Also to protect the plantation's workers from the sheriff.

Grammar Workshop Exercise 8

Correcting Run-on Sentences The following sentences elaborate on ideas suggested by the passage from *Delta Wedding*. On your paper revise each sentence, correcting any run-ons. Remember that run-on sentences may be corrected in more than one way. For the sentences that do not contain run-ons, write *correct*.

SAMPLE It was September 10, 1923, Laura McRaven was on her way to Fairchilds.

ANSWER It was September 10, 1923. Laura McRaven was on her way to Fairchilds.

ANSWER It was September 10, 1923, and Laura McRaven was on her way to Fairchilds.

1. Laura was only nine years old, nevertheless, she was traveling alone.
2. Laura's cousins lived at Fairchilds Laura was going to visit them.
3. The day was warm and butterflies flew in and out of the open windows.
4. The breeze kept changing, it would be hot for a while and then it would be cool.
5. Laura wanted to catch every detail of the countryside; however, the sooty air from the train's engine kept making her want to close her eyes.
6. Mr. Black was the conductor, Laura's father had asked him to watch out for Laura.
7. Laura wore a straw hat, she had stuck her ticket in it.
8. The train came to a halt and Mr. Doolittle went into the open fields.
9. Laura couldn't wait to get to Fairchilds she was anxious to see her mother's people.
10. Laura tried to stay calm, but her heart kept pounding.

Review The items that follow describe the life of Eudora Welty. Revise each item in the manner indicated in parentheses; there may be more than one correct answer.

SAMPLE Eudora Welty was born in Jackson, Mississippi, in 1909. She is well-known for her entertaining and insightful novels and short stories.
(Rewrite as a complex sentence.)

ANSWER Eudora Welty, who is well-known for her entertaining and insightful novels and short stories, was born in Jackson, Mississippi, in 1909.

Eudora Welty

1. There were always books around Welty's home. Because everyone in her family loved to read.
(Eliminate the sentence fragment.)
2. In 1926 and 1927 Welty attended Mississippi State College for Women she then went on to graduate from the University of Wisconsin.
(Eliminate the run-on by creating two sentences.)
3. Later Welty attended Columbia University. She studied advertising there.
(Combine the sentences by turning the second sentence into an adjective clause beginning with *where*.)
4. Welty's father died in 1931, and Welty returned to Jackson. Jackson is still her home today.
(Rewrite as a compound-complex sentence.)
5. Most of Welty's work focuses on southern rural life. She has traveled in the United States and Europe.
(Combine the sentences by turning the second sentence into an adverb clause beginning with *although*.)
6. Welty's themes include human relationships and the mystery of life. She often writes about people from small towns.
(Rewrite as a compound sentence.)
7. Some of her stories deal with change and love. Welty thinks these are important forces in human life.
(Combine the sentences by turning the second sentence into an adverb clause beginning with *since*.)
8. Welty's first book of short stories, *A Curtain of Green*, was published in 1941.
(Rewrite as an interrogative sentence.)
9. Her novella *The Robber Bridegroom* was published in 1942. It was later made into a successful Broadway play. ➡

(Rewrite as a complex sentence.)

10. *Delta Wedding* was Welty's first full-length novel. Published in 1946, five years after *A Curtain of Green* appeared. (Eliminate the sentence fragment.)

11. The novel shows a comfortable southern world. This world would soon change forever. (Rewrite as a complex sentence.)

12. Did Welty publish two collections of short stories between 1949 and 1955? (Rewrite as a declarative sentence.)

13. *The Golden Apples* (1949), her next book after *Delta Wedding*, contained seven related stories about a group of families in Mississippi. The lives of these families were intertwined. (Rewrite as a complex sentence.)

14. Like *The Robber Bridegroom*, Welty's novel *The Ponder Heart* (1954) has been turned into a play. *The Ponder Heart* has been called Welty's comic masterpiece. (Rewrite as a complex sentence.)

15. Welty published almost nothing between 1955 and 1970, but 1970 brought the publication of her novel *Losing Battles*. The novel presents humorous characters and situations. (Rewrite as a compound-complex sentence.)

16. Welty won the Pulitzer Prize in 1972 for her novel *The Optimist's Daughter*. This event further increased her popularity. (Combine the sentences by turning the first sentence into a noun clause beginning with *The fact that*.)

17. One reason for Welty's success is clear. Her fiction is often very humorous. (Combine the sentences by turning the second sentence into a noun clause beginning with *that*.)

18. Besides novels and short stories Welty has written several works of nonfiction. Including a collection of essays and an autobiography. (Eliminate the fragment by writing a complex sentence.)

19. Many readers pay special attention to Welty's gift for vivid detail. (Rewrite as an imperative sentence.)

20. Read Welty's works for her wry insights into human nature. (Rewrite as a declarative sentence.)

Grammar Workshop Exercise 10

Proofreading The following passage describes the artist Robert Duncan, whose painting appears on the opposite page. Rewrite the passage, correcting the errors in spelling, capitalization, punctuation, grammar, and usage. There are twenty-five errors in all.

Robert Duncan

[1]Robert Duncan was born in Salt lake City, Utah in 1952. [2]As a child he spent his Summers on his grandfather's ranch in Wyoming. [3]Beleiving that Duncan had talent, his grandmother gave the eleven-year old boy a set of oil paints and arranged for him too take art lessons. [4]Duncan continued to paint in high school. [5]Then studied art for a short time at the university of Utah. [6]Duncan, however, is largely self-taught, he has been painting full time since 1972. [7]He lives in Midway, Utah, with his wife and their six children. [8]Utahs citizens and rugged landscapes are frequent subjects in his paintings.

[9]Duncan derived his style from his study of traditional figuritive and landscape art. [10]He visited many museums in Europe and in the United States to study the techniques of various painters. [11]He was particlarly influenced by the work of realist painters from the turn of the century, such as John Singer Sargent. [12]Sargent, in turn, had been influenced by the Impressionists, who created their paintings with rapid strokes of pure color. [13]Duncans naturalistic settings and lose brushwork show his debt to realists such as Sargent and, indirectly, to the Impressionists. [14]Although his realistic style is at odds with many currants in modern art, it has won modest acclaim.

[15]In his paintings Duncan portrays many aspects of rural life, his goal is to show that all people are fundimentally the same. [16]Often painting outdoors to capture the natural light. [17]He depicts farms gardens, and country folk. [18]Children are among his favorite subjects Duncan's romantic and somewhat sentamental style is evidant in all of his paintings.

[19]*Mandy's Sunhat* shows Duncan's facility for depicting atmosphere and light. [20]Readers of Eudora Welty's "Delta Wedding" could easily believe that the girl in the painting is Laura McRaven. [21]The young heroine of Welty's novel. [22]One can imagine her stepping off the train and into the open feilds.

Robert Duncan, *Mandy's Sunhat,* 1988

Clauses and Sentence Structure

Clauses and the Sentences They Form

[pages 490–494]

Indicate whether each of the following sentences is (a) simple, (b) compound, (c) complex, or (d) compound-complex.

1. Fifteenth-century England had two kinds of timepieces, and their names remain with us.
2. Large clocks were placed in towers or homes and struck the hour.
3. The word *clock* comes from the Latin *clocca*, which means "bell."
4. Watches were smaller timepieces than clocks, and they had only hands and dials that indicated the hour.
5. Because a watch had no bell, one had to *watch* for the time.

Kinds of Clauses

[pages 489–499]

Identify the underlined clause in each sentence as (a) a main clause, (b) an adjective clause, (c) an adverb clause, or (d) a noun clause.

6. <u>Until the nineteenth century only the wealthy owned timepieces</u>.
7. Most of those <u>who needed to know the time</u> used sundials.
8. People assumed <u>that their stomach would alert them to mealtime</u>.
9. When clocks were placed on public buildings in North America in the 1770s, <u>they announced the hour to the country's cities and towns</u>.

10. <u>After cuckoo clocks arrived from Germany</u>, they became popular.

Kinds of Sentences

[page 500]

Identify each sentence as (a) declarative, (b) imperative, (c) interrogative, or (d) exclamatory.

11. Clockmakers began to mass-produce clocks in the 1800s.
12. What an important step forward that was!
13. As cities and businesses grew, punctuality became a fact of life.
14. Think about the importance of the following idea.
15. What time is it?

Sentence Completeness

[pages 500–504]

Identify each item as (a) a fragment, (b) a run-on, or (c) a complete sentence.

16. The growing importance of clocks, and punctuality in the 1840s.
17. People used the expression *on time*, and alarm clocks appeared.
18. Because grandfather clocks had become popular in the 1870s.
19. Time clocks appeared, the term *clock watcher* was coined.
20. The wristwatch appeared, and soon the pocket watch disappeared.

Writing for Review

Write a paragraph on a topic of your choice. Use at least one sentence of each type and a variety of clauses.

Diagraming Sentences

Diagraming is a method of showing the relationship of various words and parts of a sentence to the sentence as a whole.

14.1 Diagraming Simple Sentences

You begin to diagram a sentence by finding the simple subject. (Keep in mind that a sentence may have a compound subject.) After you have found the subject, find the action or linking verb that goes with it. Write the subject and the verb on a horizontal line. Separate them with a vertical line that bisects the horizontal line. This line indicates the division between the complete subject and the complete predicate.

Athletes train.

subject	action verb

Athletes	train

Adjectives and Adverbs

To diagram a simple sentence with adjectives and adverbs, follow the model diagram below.

A very good athlete must train extremely hard.

subject	action verb

adjective   adverb   adjective   adverb   adverb

athlete	must train

A   very   good   extremely   hard

Direct Objects and Indirect Objects

To diagram a simple sentence with an indirect object and a direct object, follow the model diagram below.

Coaches give players guidance.

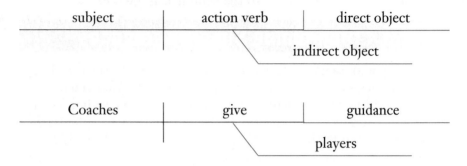

Object Complements

To diagram a simple sentence with a compound subject, a direct object, and an object complement, follow the model diagram below. If the simple subjects in a compound subject are connected by a conjunction, place the conjunction on a dotted vertical line between the subjects. If the simple subjects are connected by a correlative conjunction, such as *both . . . and* or *either . . . or*, place the first part of the conjunction on one side of the line and the second part on the other.

Coaches and players consider practice essential.

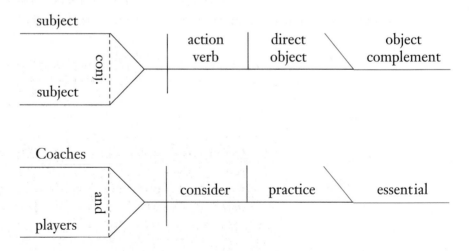

Subject Complements

To diagram a simple sentence with a subject complement (a predicate nominative or a predicate adjective), follow the model diagrams below.

Swimmers are athletes.

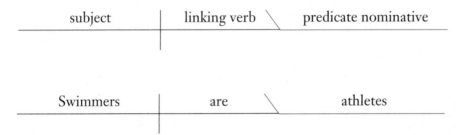

Gymnasts are strong and must be coordinated.

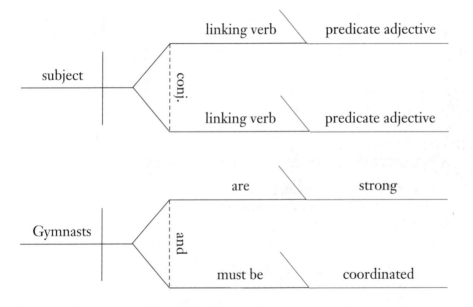

Exercise 1

Diagraming Simple Sentences   Using the preceding models as a guide, diagram the following sentences.
1. The muddy field was drying slowly.
2. A coach gave the players instructions.
3. The players and the coach considered the game critical.
4. It was the championship game.
5. The players were ready but felt nervous.

Prepositional Phrases

Place the preposition on a diagonal line that descends from the word the prepositional phrase modifies. Place the object of the preposition on a horizontal line that joins the diagonal. The diagonal line on which the preposition is placed should extend somewhat beyond the horizontal on which the object of the preposition is placed, forming a "tail."

Athletes of today set new records at every opportunity during a season.

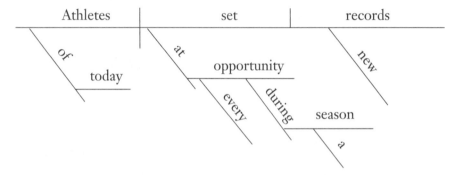

Appositives and Appositive Phrases

Place an appositive in parentheses after the noun or pronoun it identifies. Beneath it add any new words that modify the appositive. Any words that modify the noun or pronoun itself, and not the appositive, should be placed directly beneath the noun or pronoun.

The coach, a graduate of the school, preaches team spirit, an important ideal.

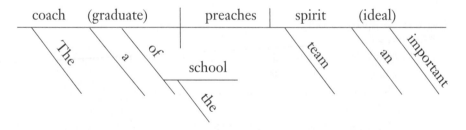

Participles and Participial Phrases

The line on which the participle is placed descends diagonally from the word the participle modifies and then extends to the right horizontally. The participle is written on the curve, as shown below. Add any modifiers and complements to the horizontal line in the same way that you would show the modifiers and complements of an action verb.

Stumbling, the quarterback fell, gracefully completing the pass in midair.

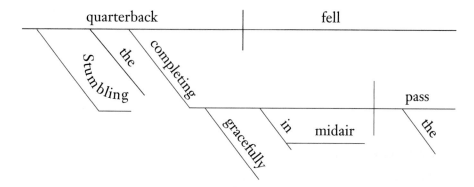

Gerunds and Gerund Phrases

Place a gerund on a "step," adding complements and modifiers in the usual way. Set the gerund or the gerund phrase on a "stilt," and position the stilt according to the role of the gerund. (Remember that a gerund can be a subject, a complement, an object of a preposition, or an appositive.)

Winning is one way of gaining confidence.

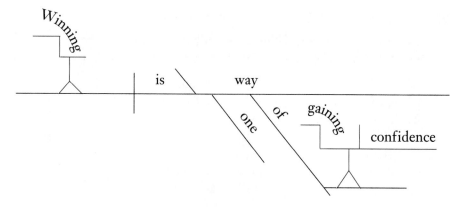

Infinitives and Infinitive Phrases as Adjectives or Adverbs

When an infinitive or an infinitive phrase is used as an adjective or an adverb, it is diagramed like a prepositional phrase.

Teams have a need to travel frequently.

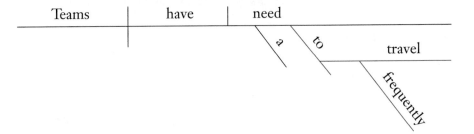

Infinitives and Infinitive Phrases as Nouns

When an infinitive or an infinitive phrase is used as a noun, it is diagramed like a prepositional phrase and then placed on a "stilt" in the subject or complement position.

To triumph is to taste glory.

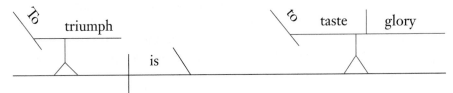

Exercise 2

Diagraming Simple Sentences with Phrases   Using the preceding models as a guide, diagram the following sentences.

1. People of that time knew nothing about the rest of the world.
2. My cousin Janet got her wish, a part in the play.
3. Thousands of leaves, falling gently, covered the damp sidewalk.
4. Watching television is one way of relaxing.
5. To write well means to think clearly.

Compound Sentences

Diagram each main clause separately. If the clauses are connected by a semicolon, use a vertical dotted line to connect the verbs of each main clause. If the main clauses are connected by a conjunction, place the conjunction on a solid horizontal line, and connect it to the verbs of each main clause by vertical dotted lines.

Athletes like to win, but they must also learn to lose.

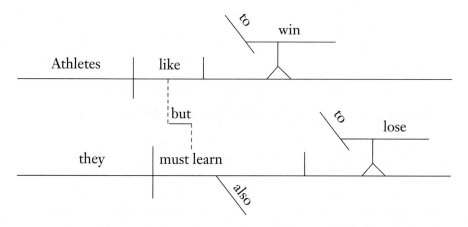

Complex Sentences with Adjective Clauses

Place the main clause in one diagram and the adjective clause beneath it in another diagram. Use a dotted line to connect the relative pronoun or other introductory word in the adjective clause to the modified noun or pronoun in the main clause.

The player whom you like won games that were close.

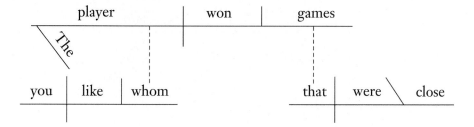

Complex Sentences with Adverb Clauses

Place the main clause in one diagram and the adverb clause beneath it in another diagram. Place the subordinating conjunction on a diagonal dotted line connecting the verb in the adverb clause to the modified verb, adjective, or adverb in the main clause.

Before a game begins, the coach gives encouragement.

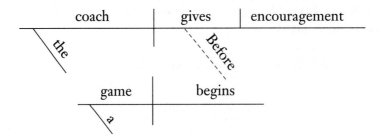

Complex Sentences with Noun Clauses

First decide what role the noun clause plays within the main clause. Is it the subject, direct object, predicate nominative, or object of a preposition? Then diagram the main clause, placing the noun clause on a "stilt" in the appropriate position. Place the introductory word of the clause in the position of the subject, object, or predicate nominative within the noun clause itself. If the introductory word merely begins the noun clause, place it on a line of its own above the verb in the subordinate clause, connecting it to the verb with a dotted vertical line.

NOUN CLAUSE AS SUBJECT

What the coach says is extremely important.

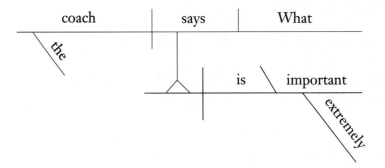

NOUN CLAUSE AS DIRECT OBJECT

The coach knows that the rival may win.

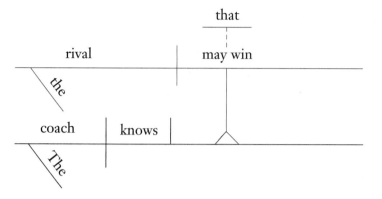

NOUN CLAUSE AS OBJECT OF A PREPOSITION

The coach assigns more practice to whoever needs it.

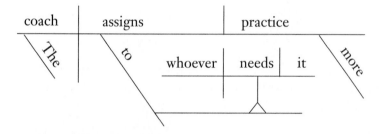

Exercise 3

Diagraming Sentences with Clauses   Using the preceding models as a guide, diagram the following sentences.

1. John is the oldest child, and Rebecca is the youngest.
2. The pilot who won last year's competition has sold his airplane.
3. Whenever Manolo remembers, he buys an extra newspaper for Juanito.
4. Whoever wins this game chooses the next one.
5. Everybody knows that Hefflemeyer is the greatest player.

Diagraming Sentences

   Study the sentences below and the accompanying diagram "skeletons." Next, number a separate sheet of paper from 1 to 20. Then show the place where each word in the sentence should appear in the diagram by matching the letter of each place with the number of the appropriate word. The main verb of each sentence has been placed in the diagram for you and therefore has not been numbered.

<u>Birds</u> can fly <u>efficiently</u> <u>because</u> <u>they</u> <u>have</u> <u>both</u> <u>warm</u> <u>blood</u>
  1   **2**   **3**   **4** **5** **6**   **7**   **8**
<u>and</u> <u>feathers</u>.
 9   **10**

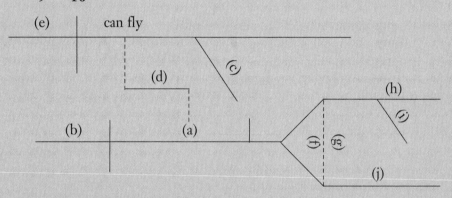

<u>Flying</u> <u>with</u> <u>stamina</u> requires <u>abundant</u> <u>energy</u> <u>that</u> <u>most</u>
 11   **12**   **13**   **14**   **15**   **16** **17**
<u>coldblooded</u> <u>creatures</u> <u>lack</u>.
   18   **19**   **20**

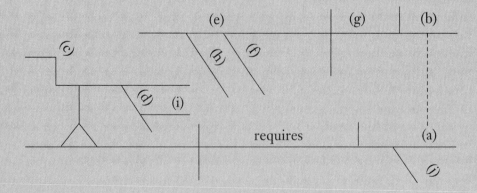

Unit 15 | Verb Tenses and Voice

15.1 Principal Parts of Verbs

All verbs have four **principal parts:** a *base form*, a *present participle*, a *simple past form*, and a *past participle*. All the verb tenses are formed from these principal parts.

Principal Parts of Verbs			
Base Form	**Present Participle**	**Past Form**	**Past Participle**
nail	nailing	nailed	nailed
talk	talking	talked	talked
ring	ringing	rang	rung
be	being	was, were	been
sit	sitting	sat	sat

The base form (except the base form of *be*) and the past form can be used by themselves as main verbs. To function as the simple predicate in a sentence, the present participle and the past participle must always be used with one or more auxiliary verbs.

Lions **roar.** [base or present form]
Lions **roared.** [past form]
Lions **are roaring.** [present participle with the auxiliary verb *are*]
Lions **have roared.** [past participle with the auxiliary verb *have*]

15.2 Regular and Irregular Verbs

A **regular verb** forms its past and past participle by adding -*ed* to the base form.

Principal Parts of Regular Verbs		
Base Form	**Past Form**	**Past Participle**
roar	roared	roared
talk	talked	talked

Some regular verbs undergo spelling changes when a suffix beginning with a vowel is added.

ruffle + **-ed** = ruffl**ed**   spy + **-ed** = sp**ied**   flop + **-ed** = flop**ped**

Regular and Irregular Verbs   **529**

An **irregular verb** forms its past and past participle in some way other than by adding -ed to the base form.

Principal Parts of Irregular Verbs		
Base Form	**Past Form**	**Past Participle**
be	was, were	been
beat	beat	beaten
become	became	become
begin	began	begun
bite	bit	bitten *or* bit
blow	blew	blown
break	broke	broken
bring	brought	brought
catch	caught	caught
choose	chose	chosen
come	came	come
do	did	done
draw	drew	drawn
drink	drank	drunk
drive	drove	driven
eat	ate	eaten
fall	fell	fallen
feel	felt	felt
find	found	found
fly	flew	flown
freeze	froze	frozen
get	got	got *or* gotten
give	gave	given
go	went	gone
grow	grew	grown
hang	hung *or* hanged	hung *or* hanged
have	had	had
know	knew	known
lay*	laid	laid
lead	led	led
lend	lent	lent
lie*	lay	lain
lose	lost	lost
put	put	put
ride	rode	ridden
ring	rang	rung
rise*	rose	risen
run	ran	run
say	said	said
see	saw	seen

*For more detailed instruction on *lay* versus *lie* and *raise* versus *rise,* see Unit 19.

Base Form	Past Form	Past Participle
set*	set	set
shrink	shrank *or* shrunk	shrunk *or* shrunken
sing	sang	sung
sink	sank *or* sunk	sunk
sit*	sat	sat
speak	spoke	spoken
spring	sprang *or* sprung	sprung
steal	stole	stolen
swim	swam	swum
take	took	taken
tear	tore	torn
tell	told	told
think	thought	thought
throw	threw	thrown
wear	wore	worn
win	won	won
write	wrote	written

* For more detailed instruction on *sit* versus *set,* see Unit 19.

Exercise 1

Supplying the Correct Principal Part   Complete each of the following sentences with the principal part of the verb that is indicated in parentheses.

Arthur Ashe, a Tennis Pioneer

1. Over the past two decades the name Arthur Ashe has _____ to signify athletic brilliance as well as personal integrity and grace. (past participle of come)
2. Ashe _____ interested in tennis when he was in elementary school in Richmond, Virginia. (past form of *grow*)
3. His athletic talent _____ the attention of a local physician, Dr. Robert ("Whirlwind") Johnson, who coached talented African-American youngsters to play for the U.S. Tennis Association. (past form of *draw*)
4. Before discovering Ashe, Dr. Johnson had _____ lessons to Althea Gibson, who became the first African American to win at Wimbledon. (past participle of *give*)
5. By the age of eighteen, Ashe had _____ to national prominence by winning the Junior Indoor Singles Championship in two consecutive years, 1960 and 1961. (past participle of *rise*)
6. While Ashe was _____ the University of California at Los Angeles on a tennis scholarship, he was coached by a former professional champion, Pancho Gonzales. (present participle of *attend*) ➡

7. After being named to the Davis Cup team in 1963, Ashe _____ both the singles and the doubles titles in the National Collegiate Athletic Association Championship of 1966. (past form of *win*)
8. Ashe's dream of reaching the highest levels of American tennis came true in 1968, when he _____ first place at the U.S. National Men's Singles Championship at the West Side Tennis Club in Forest Hills, New York. (past form of *take*)
9. By the end of 1968, Ashe had _____ all opponents in the Men's Singles competition of the first U.S. Open tournament. (past participle of *beat*)
10. By the time he retired from the professional tennis circuit, Arthur Ashe had _____ a dominant figure in a sport in which few African-American athletes had previously succeeded. (past participle of *become*)

15.3 Tense of Verbs

The **tenses** of a verb are the forms that help to show time.

There are six tenses in English: *present, past,* and *future* and *present perfect, past perfect,* and *future perfect.*

Present Tense

The present-tense form of a verb (excluding the third-person singular, which adds an *-s* or *-es*) is the same as the verb's base form. The one exception is the verb *be.*

	SINGULAR	PLURAL
FIRST PERSON	I **stay.**	We **stay.**
SECOND PERSON	You **stay.**	You **stay.**
THIRD PERSON	She, he, or it **stays.**	They **stay.**
	Jesse **stays.**	The children **stay.**

	SINGULAR	PLURAL
FIRST PERSON	I **am** sad.	We **are** sad.
SECOND PERSON	You **are** sad.	You **are** sad.
THIRD PERSON	She, he, or it **is** sad.	They **are** sad.
	Sheila **is** sad.	The players **are** sad.

The **present tense** expresses a constant, repeated, or habitual action or condition. It can also express a general truth.

The garden **grows** well in the summer. [not just this summer but every summer: a repeated action]

Helena **bakes** bread well. [always: a habitual action]

Gold **is** valuable. [a condition that is generally true]

The **present tense** can also express an action or condition that exists only now.

Jenny **feels** happy. [not always but just now]
I **see** a fly on the ceiling. [at this very moment]

The **present tense** is sometimes used in historical writing to express past events and, more often, in poetry, fiction, and reporting (especially in sports) to convey to the reader a sense of "being there."

In the stadium the fans suddenly **rise** to their feet with a roar.

The exhausted runner **seems** to stumble, but in a final spurt he **rushes** over the finish line and **wins.**

Exercise 2: Sentence Writing

Expressing the Present Tense in Sentences Write a sentence using each of the following verb forms. The content of your sentence should express the kind of present time indicated in parentheses.

SAMPLE   does (a repeated action)
ANSWER   He does his housecleaning on Saturday.

1. sleeps (a habitual action)
2. feel (just now)
3. is (generally true)
4. hopes (at this moment)
5. takes (constant action)

Past Tense

Use the **past tense** to express an action or condition that was started and completed in the past.

The orchestra **performed** well.
The musicians **seemed** pleased.

All regular and irregular verbs—except *be*—have just one past-tense form, such as *soared* or *began*. The word *be* has two past-tense forms: *was* and *were*.

	SINGULAR	PLURAL
FIRST PERSON	I **was** sad.	We **were** sad.
SECOND PERSON	You **were** sad.	You **were** sad.
THIRD PERSON	She, he, or it **was** sad.	They **were** sad.

Exercise 3: Sentence Writing

Expressing the Past Tense in Sentences Write a paragraph using the correct past tense of the following verbs:

1. feel   **3.** freeze   **5.** write
2. catch   **4.** eat

Future Tense

Use the **future tense** to express an action or condition that will occur in the future.

You form the future tense of any verb by using *shall* or *will* with the base form: *I shall study; you will go.*

> Roberta **will send** the telegram.
> I **shall practice** the piano tonight.

The following are other ways to express future time besides using *shall* or *will*:

1. Use *going to* with the present tense of *be* and the base form of a verb.

> Roberta **is *going to* send** the telegram.

2. Use *about to* with the present tense of *be* and the base form of the verb.

> Roberta **is *about to* send** the telegram.

3. Use the present tense with an adverb or an adverb phrase that shows future time.

> Roberta **leaves *tomorrow*.**
> Roberta **arrives *in the middle of next week*.**

about to...
shall
will
going to

Exercise 4

Using Expressions of Future Time Change each of the following sentences so that the verb is in the future tense. Try to use at least two other ways of expressing future time in addition to *shall* and *will*. ➡

> ### Japan's Classical Theater
> [1]Two classmates and I presented a cooperative report on the history of Japanese theater for our literature class. [2] There were three parts to the presentation. [3]First Kate spoke about the form of medieval theater called No. [4]She described the formality and beauty of No plays. [5] Then Miguel covered the history of Japan's Joruri puppet theater. [6]He focused on the extraordinary realism of the colorful and expressive Joruri puppets. [7]I was responsible for information on Kabuki theater. [8] I began with a description of the typical Kabuki stage, with its trapdoors and revolving platforms. [9]I explained the stylized and exaggerated movements of Kabuki actors. [10] The report concluded with a demonstration of Kabuki dance.

Exercise 5: Sentence Writing

Expressing Future Time in Sentences   Write five statements or predictions about the future. Your sentences may be as realistic or as imaginary as you wish. Remember to vary the ways in which you express future time.

SAMPLE ANSWER   Household robots are going to become a reality.

15.4   Perfect Tenses

Present Perfect Tense

Use the **present perfect tense** to express an action or condition that occurred at some *indefinite time* in the past.

You form the present perfect tense by using *has* or *have* with the past participle of a verb: *has stopped, have waited.**

She **has caught** the flu.
They **have brought** a present for us.

The present perfect can refer to completed action in past time only in an indefinite way. Adverbs such as *yesterday* cannot be added to make the time more specific.

Sophia **has completed** her project.
Jack **has wanted** to visit Mexico.

* Do not be confused by the term *present perfect;* this tense expresses past time. *Present* refers to the tense of the auxiliary verb *has* or *have.*

To be specific about completed past time, you would normally use the simple past tense.

> Sophia **completed** her project yesterday.
> Jack **wanted** to visit Mexico last summer.

The present perfect can also be used to communicate the idea that an action or a condition *began* in the past and *continues* into the present. This use is normally accompanied by adverbs of time or by adverb phrases.

> He **has worked every day** on his new book.
> The museum **has displayed** the exhibit **for months.**
> We **have kept** the dogs indoors **for a week.**

Past Perfect Tense

Use the **past perfect tense** to indicate that one past action or condition began *and* ended before another past action started.

You form the past perfect tense by using *had* with the past participle of a verb: *had loved, had written.*

> PAST PERFECT   PAST
> She **had been** the captain of the team before I **became** captain. [She was the captain; she stopped being captain; I became captain.]

>   PAST   PAST PERFECT
> Before I **slipped,** many other pedestrians **had slipped** in the same place. [They slipped; they finished slipping; I slipped.]

>   PAST PERFECT   PAST
> He **had** already **dried** the dishes by the time I **arrived.** [He dried the dishes; he finished drying the dishes; I arrived.]

Future Perfect Tense

Use the **future perfect tense** to express one future action or condition that will begin *and* end before another future event starts.

You form the future perfect tense by using *will have* or *shall have* with the past participle of a verb: *will have walked, shall have walked.*

> By summertime I **will have lived** here four months. [The four months will be over by the time another future event, the coming of summertime, occurs.]

> By the time the astronauts reach Jupiter, they **will have practiced** the maneuver many times.

Identifying the Perfect Tenses   On your paper write the perfect-tense verb that appears in each of the following sentences. Then identify the verb as *present perfect*, *past perfect*, or *future perfect*.

Reggae Music

1. Perhaps you have listened to a style of music known as reggae.
2. This intensely rhythmic music has been popular in Jamaica for some time.
3. Before he began to play music himself, the reggae star Bob Marley had been influenced by Jamaican and African folk music and American rhythm and blues.
4. Reggae had been performed in Jamaica for twenty years before it was heard in either the United States or Europe.
5. It has been popular in the United States since the 1970s.
6. The musical style had been known by various names— including rudie blues, ska, blue beat, and rock steady— before it took the name reggae.
7. Reggae music has gained international fame as a result of the two groups, Bob Marley and the Wailers and Toots and the Maytals.
8. By the time it became popular outside Jamaica, reggae had influenced such rock musicians as Eric Clapton, John Lennon, and the Police.
9. Even before Bob Marley died in 1981, his son Ziggy had begun to play.
10. By the time he completes his latest tour, Ziggy Marley will have performed in dozens of American cities.

Expressing the Present Perfect Tense in Sentences
(a) Rewrite each of the following sentences, changing the tense of the verb from past to present perfect. (b) Add appropriate adverbs or adverb phrases to each of your new sentences to communicate the idea that an action or condition began in the past and continues into the present.

SAMPLE   We wanted to go to Paris.
ANSWER   **a.** We have wanted to go to Paris.
         b. We have wanted to go to Paris for two years.

1. Lila gave piano lessons. ➡

2. My parents owned two dogs.
3. The trees were in bloom.
4. My friend wrote poetry.
5. The team played with determination.

15.5   Progressive and Emphatic Forms

Each of the six tenses has a **progressive** form that expresses a continuing action.

You make the progressive forms by using the appropriate tense of the verb *be* with the present participle of the main verb:

PRESENT PROGRESSIVE	They *are* reading.
PAST PROGRESSIVE	They *were* reading.
FUTURE PROGRESSIVE	They *will be* reading.
PRESENT PERFECT PROGRESSIVE	They *have been* reading.
PAST PERFECT PROGRESSIVE	They *had been* reading.
FUTURE PERFECT PROGRESSIVE	They *will have been* reading.

The present and past tenses have additional forms, called **emphatic,** that add special force, or emphasis, to the verb.

You make the emphatic forms by using *do, does,* or *did* with the base form of the verb.

PRESENT EMPHATIC	I *do* read the newspaper every day.
	Tony *does* read it every day.
PAST EMPHATIC	Inez *did* read the newspaper yesterday.

Exercise 8

Using the Progressive and Emphatic Forms   For each of the following sentences, replace the verb in parentheses with the progressive or the emphatic form of the verb that makes sense in the sentence.

The Modern Bicycle

1. Today more than seventy-five million Americans (ride) bicycles.
2. Over the years bicycling (gain) popularity as a form of both exercise and recreation.
3. Even before bicycles began to be widely used for transportation and exercise, numerous organizations already (work) to promote long-distance trips for experienced riders. ➡

4. Today the bicycle (provide) efficient transportation to and from work for many people.
5. Despite the dangers, many people (ride) bicycles in metropolitan areas.
6. Because of accidents involving bicyclists, safety rules (grow) increasingly important.
7. There is no doubt that bicyclists (find) it difficult to ride on busy streets.
8. We can predict that if environmental conditions don't improve, legislators (try) to pass laws to protect bicyclists.
9. Before the recession many cities (plan) to create bikeways, special lanes for bicyclists.
10. To ensure safety for all, new traffic laws (require) bicyclists to ride more carefully.

Exercise 9: Review

Understanding the Uses of the Verb Tenses   Explain the difference in meaning between the sentences in each of the pairs below. Name the tenses used in each sentence.

SAMPLE   **a.** Why was Gloria so secretive?
   b. Why has Gloria been so secretive?

ANSWER   In sentence *a* the action occurred and ended (past). In sentence *b* the action occurred in the past and is still continuing (present perfect).

1. **a.** Do you think that Anna is writing a birthday poem for the twins?
   b. Do you think that Anna has been writing a birthday poem for the twins?
2. **a.** Anna had finished the poem by the twins' birthday.
   b. Anna did finish the poem by the twins' birthday.
3. **a.** Michael was painting a picture for the twins before he left town on business.
   b. Michael had painted a picture for the twins before he left town on business.
4. **a.** The twins had been telling everyone not to make a fuss.
   b. The twins told everyone not to make a fuss.
5. **a.** Nonetheless, the twins' friends planned a surprise party.
   b. Nonetheless, the twins' friends were planning a surprise party.

15.6   Compatibility of Tenses

Do not shift, or change, tenses when two or more events occur at the same time.

INCORRECT   During the concert the pianist **forgot** the notes, and she **stops** in the middle of the piece. [The tense needlessly shifts from the past to the present.]

CORRECT   During the concert the pianist **forgot** the notes, and she **stopped** in the middle of the piece. [Now it is clear that both events happened at nearly the same time in the past.]

Shift tenses only to show that one event precedes or follows another.

INCORRECT   By the time we **arrived,** they **ate** dinner. [The two past-tense verbs give the mistaken impression that both events happened at the same time.]

CORRECT   By the time we **arrived,** they **had eaten** dinner. [The shift from the past tense (*arrived*) to the past perfect tense (*had eaten*) clearly indicates that they ate the dinner before we arrived.]

Exercise 11

Making Tenses Compatible First find the two verbs that appear in each of the following sentences. Then rewrite each sentence, making the second verb compatible with the first verb.

Maxine Hong Kingston: A Writer's Heritage

1. Maxine Hong Kingston was born in Stockton, California, in 1940, and she was speaking Cantonese as a child.
2. After she received several scholarships, she attends college at the University of California at Berkeley. ➡

3. Before she switched to English, Kingston studies engineering.
4. Kingston found out in college that she is not a reporter.
5. While she wrote her first book, Kingston supports herself with a full-time job.
6. When *The Woman Warrior: Memoirs of a Girlhood Among Ghosts* was published in 1976, reviewers praise its combination of autobiography, fiction, and history.
7. By the time I finished *The Woman Warrior*, I learned a great deal about her childhood.
8. Kingston published *China Men* four years after she was writing *The Woman Warrior*.
9. In *China Men* Kingston described her grandfather, who works on the transcontinental railroad in the early 1900s.
10. After I completed *The Woman Warrior*, I had decided to read *China Men* as well.

15.7 Voice of Verbs

An action verb is in the **active voice** when the subject of the sentence performs the action.

> The dog **pleased** the child.

An action verb is in the **passive voice** when its action is performed on the subject.

> The child **was pleased** by the dog.

The woman petted the cat.

Generally the active voice is stronger, but there are times when the passive voice is preferred or, in fact, necessary. If you do not want to call attention to the performer or if you do not know who the performer is, use the passive voice, as in the following examples:

> The dinner **was ruined.** [You may not want to identify the culprit.]

> The manuscript **was stolen.** [You may not know who the culprit is.]

The cat was petted by the woman.

You form the passive voice by using a form of the auxiliary verb *be* with the past participle of the verb. The tense of a passive verb is determined by the tense of the auxiliary verb.

> The child **is pleased** by the dog. [present tense, passive voice]

> The child **was pleased** by the dog. [past tense, passive voice]

> The child **will be pleased** by the dog. [future tense, passive voice]

Changing the Voice of Verbs   In each of the following sentences, change the active voice to the passive or the passive voice to the active.

Explorer Robots

1. The explorer robot has been brought to us by new technology.
2. Human beings operate some of these robots.
3. Areas that are dangerous to people have been explored by these robots.
4. NASA can test some explorer robots.
5. Marine biologists expect explorer robots to do underwater research.
6. Endurance superior to that of humans is offered by these robots.
7. Therefore, explorer robots can maintain underwater equipment.
8. Pictures of Mars were relayed to Earth by planetary explorer robots.
9. Engineers have designed some explorer robots to help the handicapped.
10. Scientists predict a great future for explorer robots.

Read the following passage, and examine the italicized passive-voice verbs. Notice how the use of the passive voice makes the passage flat and awkward.

> Two willow sticks *had been taken* by the boy and his father, and they carefully *were split*. The willow was dry and very light but not very strong. The boy's father's pocket knife *was taken* by the boy's father, the blade's sharpness *was tested* by him with his thumb, and the sticks *were split* in half.

Now read the passage as the author Simon J. Ortiz actually wrote it in his story "The Way You See Horses." Notice how much better the passage reads because Ortiz avoids any unnecessary use of the passive voice.

> The boy and his father *had taken* two willow sticks and carefully *split* them. The willow was dry and very light but not very strong. The boy's father *took* his pocket knife, *tested* the blade's sharpness with his thumb, and *split* the sticks in half.

Consider the following reasons for using the active voice whenever possible:

1. The active voice clearly identifies the performer of an action. In the first passage we cannot be sure who splits the sticks (first sentence) and who splits them in half again (last sentence). By contrast, it is clear who performs these actions in Ortiz's version.

2. The active voice makes a passage more vivid and immediate, and it focuses the reader's attention on the *doer* of the action. It is easier to form a vivid picture of the characters in Ortiz's story if their actions are described in the active voice. If their actions are described in the passive voice, their actions—even their personalities— seem vague and dull.

3. Using the active voice cuts down on wordiness. Notice that Ortiz's original version is about 10 percent less wordy than the other version.

On a separate sheet of paper, revise the following passage by putting the verbs in the active voice. The adapted passage, which has been rewritten in the passive voice, is from "The Way You See Horses."

> The strips were knotted together by the boy's father, and then a bit of string was cut by him and the tail was tied to the bottom of the kite. "Now let's see what we have here," was said by the father grandly. . . . The fragile-looking plastic-bag-and-willow-stick kite was handed by him to the boy. It was held in his hands by the boy, and it was looked over by him.

Usage Workshop

Verb Tenses and Voice

The following literary passage is taken from *Black Boy*, Richard Wright's autobiography. Born in Natchez, Mississippi, in 1908, Wright grew up poor, neglected, and hungry. In this passage he describes a happy memory: the abundant meals that his Aunt Maggie served at her home in Arkansas. The passage has been annotated to show some of the kinds of verbs covered in this unit.

Literature Model

from BLACK BOY: A RECORD OF CHILDHOOD AND YOUTH

by Richard Wright

Passive voice —

Active voice —

Past tense of an irregular verb —

Present tense of an irregular verb —

Past progressive form —

... At mealtime Aunt Maggie's table was so loaded with food that I could scarcely believe it was real. It took me some time to get used to the idea of there being enough to eat; I felt that if I ate enough there would not be anything left for another time. When I first sat down at Aunt Maggie's table, I could not eat until I had asked:

"Can I eat all I want?"

"Eat as much as you like," Uncle Hoskins said.

I did not believe him. I ate until my stomach hurt, but even then I did not want to get up from the table.

"Your eyes are bigger than your stomach," my mother said.

"Let him eat all he wants to and get used to food," Uncle Hoskins said.

When supper was over I saw that there were many biscuits piled high upon the bread platter, an astonishing and unbelievable sight to me. Though the biscuits were right before my eyes, and though there was more flour in the kitchen, I was apprehensive lest there be no bread for breakfast in the morning. I was afraid that somehow the biscuits might disappear during the night, while I was sleeping. I did not want to wake up in the morning, as I had so often in the past, feeling hungry and knowing that there was no food in the house. So, surreptitiously, I took ➡

some of the biscuits from the platter and slipped them into my pocket, not to eat, but to keep as a bulwark against any possible attack of hunger. Even after I had got used to seeing the table loaded with food at each meal, I still stole bread and put it into my pockets. In washing my clothes my mother found the gummy wads and scolded me to break me of the habit; I stopped hiding the bread in my pockets and hid it about the house, in corners, behind dressers. I did not break the habit of stealing and hoarding bread until my faith that food would be forthcoming at each meal had been somewhat established.

Past perfect tense

Past tense of a regular verb

Usage Workshop Exercise 1

Identifying Principal Parts The following sentences elaborate on ideas suggested by the passage from *Black Boy*. Each sentence contains an italicized verb in one of four forms: (a) the base form, (b) the past form, (c) the present participle, or (d) the past participle. At the end of the sentence is a second verb in parentheses. First, identify the form of the verb in italics. Then rewrite the sentence, substituting the verb in parentheses for the italicized verb. In the rewritten sentence be sure the new verb is in the same form as the original verb.

SAMPLE   The family *dined* at Aunt Maggie's. (eat)
ANSWER   past form; The family ate at Aunt Maggie's.

1. At home in Mississippi, food had often *seemed* scarce. (be)
2. Young Wright *had* the acute, daily ache of hunger. (feel)
3. Then Wright and his mother *traveled* to his aunt's home in Arkansas. (come)
4. They are *visiting* Wright's Aunt Maggie and Uncle Hoskins today. (see)
5. The kindly pair *welcome* them into their home. (take)
6. Later Wright was *devouring* an abundant dinner. (eat)
7. Aunt Maggie *carried* a lavish platter of hot biscuits to the table. (bring)
8. Wright had *grown* fearful that the biscuits would disappear before breakfast. (become)
9. He was even *concealing* extra food in his pocket. (hide)
10. For many days he *feared* that every full meal might be his last. (think)

Using the Present, Past, and Future Tenses   The following sentences are based on passages from *Black Boy* that are not reprinted in this textbook. On your paper rewrite each sentence, changing the tense of the italicized verb according to the directions in parentheses. Use only the present, past, and future tenses; with the exception of *will* to express the future tense, do not use any helping verbs.

SAMPLE	Wright's mother *will bring* her son to Arkansas. (Change to the present tense.)
ANSWER	Wright's mother brings her son to Arkansas.

1. On the train to Elaine, Arkansas, Wright *will become* aware of racism and segregation. (Change to the present tense.)
2. In those days blacks and whites *ride* in separate sections of the train. (Change to the past tense.)
3. The naive youngster *wanted* a peek at the whites' part of the train. (Change to the present tense.)
4. His mother *says*, "Quit talking foolishness!" (Change to the past tense.)
5. The travelers *went* to Aunt Maggie and Uncle Hoskins's home to live. (Change to the future tense.)
6. Uncle Hoskins *owned* a prosperous business in town. (Change to the present tense.)
7. Aunt Maggie *will have* plenty of food on the dinner table. (Change to the past tense.)
8. Soon a major calamity *will break* Wright's mood of contentment. (Change to the present tense.)
9. Some white people in town, envious of Uncle Hoskins's success, *murder* him one night. (Change to the past tense.)
10. Aunt Maggie, Wright, and Wright's mother *flee* to safety in another town. (Change to the future tense.)

Using the Perfect Tenses   Each of the following sentences is based on events in Richard Wright's *Black Boy*. On your paper rewrite each sentence, adding the appropriate form of the italicized verb in the place indicated by the caret. Write the verb in the tense indicated in parentheses, using the past participle of the main verb and the appropriate form of the helping verb *have*. ➡

SAMPLE	Before he arrived in Arkansas, Wright ∧ in Mississippi and Tennessee. (past perfect tense of *reside*)
ANSWER	Before he arrived in Arkansas, Wright had resided in Mississippi and Tennessee.

1. By the time he became a teen-ager, Wright ∧ in several southern states. (past perfect tense of *live*)
2. Wright ∧ the age of four before he moved from his grand-parents' home near Natchez, Mississippi. (past perfect tense of *reach*)
3. A fire nearly destroyed the Wright home soon after Richard's grandmother ∧ ill. (past perfect tense of *fall*)
4. The fire ∧ through several rooms before Wright fled to safety. (past perfect tense of *tear*)
5. When the adults at last put out the blaze, nearly half the house ∧ down. (past perfect tense of *burn*)
6. Wright ∧ to Arkansas to live with his aunt and uncle. (present perfect tense of *come*)
7. Before he arrived at his aunt's home, Wright ∧ in Memphis, Tennessee. (past perfect tense of *live*)
8. His mother ∧ against exhaustion and despair before she decided to leave Memphis. (past perfect tense of *struggle*)
9. Her meager wages ∧ her almost no money for food. (present perfect tense of *leave*)
10. Now that his mother ∧ Wright to his aunt's home, he is finally getting enough to eat. (present perfect tense of *bring*)
11. Because he ∧ constant hunger, at first he eats until his stomach hurts. (present perfect tense of *know*)
12. After he ∧ a meal, he hides bread in his pockets. (present perfect tense of *finish*)
13. His mother often finds gummy wads of bread in the clothes that she ∧. (present perfect tense of *wash*)
14. She realizes what he ∧ and scolds him. (present perfect tense of *do*)
15. In spite of her criticism, she understands why he ∧ the bread. (present perfect tense of *steal*)
16. During his short life he ∧ great hardship and misery. (present perfect tense of *endure*)
17. In a month or so Wright ∧ the habit. (future perfect tense of *break*)
18. By then he ∧ more confident that food will always be available. (future perfect tense of *become*)
19. Violence tears the family apart the night after envious whites ∧ Uncle Hoskins. (present perfect tense of *murder*) ➡

20. By the following morning mother and son ∧ to safety in a nearby town. (future perfect tense of *flee*)

Using the Progressive and Emphatic Forms   Each of the following sentences is based on events in Richard Wright's *Black Boy*. On your paper rewrite each sentence, adding the appropriate form of the italicized verb in the place indicated by the caret. Write the verb in the form indicated in parentheses. Use the present participle of the main verb and the appropriate tense of the auxiliary verb *be* or the base form of the main verb and the appropriate form of *do*.

SAMPLE   The writer ∧ about the meaning of his life. (present progressive form of *think*)

ANSWER   The writer is thinking about the meaning of his life.

1. A train trip to Arkansas in 1917 ∧ Wright about the realities of the Jim Crow laws that limited the rights of African Americans. (past emphatic form of *teach*)
2. He wonders why whites and blacks ∧ in separate sections of the train. (present progressive form of *sit*)
3. During the train ride to Arkansas, Wright ∧ about his grandmother's life as a slave before the Civil War. (present progressive form of *ask*)
4. Tonight young Wright ∧ in the home of his Uncle Hoskins. (future progressive form of *sleep*)
5. Although startled at first by all the food served by his Aunt Maggie, eventually Wright ∧ to Hoskins's home. (past emphatic form of *adjust*)
6. Envious men in town ∧ Uncle Hoskins's life. (past progressive form of *threaten*)
7. One night Aunt Maggie ∧ for Uncle Hoskins's return when a tall boy knocked on the door. (past progressive form of *wait*)
8. The threat ∧ a reality: Uncle Hoskins was murdered. (past emphatic form of *become*)
9. Weeks later a regiment of black soldiers ∧ with rifles on their shoulders. (future progressive form of *parade*)
10. Soon these troops ∧ in World War I. (future progressive form of *fight*)

Making Tenses Compatible The following sentences elaborate on events in the passage from *Black Boy*. On your paper rewrite each sentence, changing the tense of the italicized verb so that the tenses are compatible.

SAMPLE   Before Wright came to his aunt's home in Arkansas, he *lived* in Memphis.

ANSWER   Before Wright came to his aunt's home in Arkansas, he had lived in Memphis.

1. Aunt Maggie was married to Uncle Hoskins, who *runs* a thriving business in Arkansas.
2. In Memphis Wright *is eating* poorly, but at Aunt Maggie's he ate well.
3. He *sits* shyly at the table when Aunt Maggie brought out the first meal.
4. Aunt Maggie was a fine cook, and she *sets* a variety of savory foods on the table.
5. As Wright *bites* into a biscuit, he recalled his many hungry times.
6. The others had not yet finished their first portion when Wright *takes* a second helping.
7. After his meals Wright *puts* some extra food into a pocket or hid it in the house.
8. Wright's mother *finds* wads of bread when she washed his clothes.
9. Wright controlled his urge to hoard food only after he *becomes* certain of his next meal.
10. In his years in Memphis, Wright *is failing* to gain weight, but in Arkansas, at Aunt Maggie's table, he never went hungry.

Voice of Verbs The following sentences are about Richard Wright and *Black Boy*. First, identify each sentence as being in either the *passive voice* or the *active voice*. Then rewrite each sentence, changing the active voice to the passive or the passive voice to the active.

SAMPLE   *Black Boy* was written by Richard Wright.
ANSWER   passive voice; Richard Wright wrote *Black Boy*. ➡

1. The events in *Black Boy* are recounted by the author with fury and eloquence.
2. The Civil War ended slavery in the United States.
3. Little was done by society about the plight of African Americans.
4. *Black Boy* was written by Richard Wright as a story of protest.
5. His forceful voice has inspired generations of African Americans.

Usage Workshop Exercise 7

Review   The following sentences describe the life and literary achievements of the author Richard Wright. Rewrite each sentence, following the directions in parentheses.

SAMPLE   Richard Wright portrayed his childhood in the rural South and also writes about urban American life. (Change the second verb to make the tenses compatible.)

ANSWER   Richard Wright portrayed his childhood in the rural South and also wrote about urban American life.

Richard Wright

1. Richard Wright was born in a rural region of Mississippi, where his grandparents were slaves before the Civil War.
   (Change the second verb to the past perfect tense.)
2. Wright lived in Memphis when his father abandoned the family to a life of great poverty.
   (Change the first verb to the past progressive form.)
3. After he had spent time with relatives in Arkansas and Mississippi, Wright had returned to Memphis.
   (Change the second verb to the past tense.)
4. In Memphis Wright worked as a postal clerk when he decided to become a writer.
   (Change the first verb to the past progressive form.)
5. He reads several books that stimulated his interest in becoming a writer.
   (Change the first verb to make the tenses compatible.)
6. The American author H. L. Mencken wrote one of those books.
   (Rewrite the sentence in the passive voice.) ➡

7. Financial aid was given to the budding author by the Federal Writers' Project, a government assistance program.
(Rewrite the sentence in the active voice.)

8. Before he moved to New York City in 1937, Wright lived for a time in Chicago.
(Change the second verb to the past perfect tense.)

9. Wright first wins attention with *Uncle Tom's Children*, a collection of short works of fiction that appeared in 1938.
(Correct the error caused by the use of the present tense.)

10. Two years later he published his popular novel *Native Son*.
(Rewrite the sentence in the passive voice.)

11. *Native Son* was adapted for the Broadway stage by the noted director Orson Welles.
(Rewrite the sentence in the active voice.)

12. Eventually Hollywood turned *Native Son* into a film drama.
(Change the verb to the past emphatic form.)

13. When an Argentine film version of *Native Son* appeared in 1951, Wright himself plays the main character, Bigger Thomas.
(Correct the error caused by the use of the present tense.)

14. An American studio recently released a film adaptation of *Native Son*.
(Change the verb to the present perfect tense.)

15. In fact, the video store in my neighborhood stocks the 1986 version of *Native Son*.
(Change the verb to the present emphatic form.)

16. In 1995 *Black Boy*, Wright's famous autobiography, celebrates its fiftieth anniversary.
(Change the verb to the future progressive form.)

17. Meanwhile, literary scholars continue their study of Wright's achievements.
(Change the verb to the present progressive form.)

18. The poet Margaret Walker wrote a book-length assessment of Wright's contributions to American literature.
(Change the verb to the present perfect tense.)

19. Many critics praise Wright's brilliant depiction of both rural and urban environments.
(Change the verb to the present progressive form.)

20. American readers will most likely enjoy Wright's works for a long time.
(Change the verb to the future progressive form.)

Proofreading   The following passage describes the artist William H. Johnson, whose painting appears on the opposite page. Rewrite the passage, correcting the errors in spelling, capitalization, punctuation, grammar, and usage. There are twenty-five errors in all.

William H. Johnson

[1] One of the most inovative artists of the Harlem Renaissance, William H. Johnson (1901–1970) is born in Florence, South Carolina. [2] One day one of his elementry-school teachers discovered on Johnson's desk a peice of paper with a remarkable likeness of herself. [3] From then on his teachers and his family encourage Johnson to paint.

[4] When he was seventeen, Johnson moved to Harlem, a neighborhood in New York City. [5] Three years later he accepted into the prestigious National academy of Design, where he won several Awards. [6] In 1926 he left for Paris. [7] He spent twelve years altogether in Europe, (nine of them in Scandinavia). [8] There he studied art, and met the danish woman who became his wife. [9] His painting was influenced by the highly expresive works of Edvard Munch, a Norwegian painter and Vincent van Gogh.

[10] Johnson once described himself as "one who is at the same time . . . a primitive and a cultured painter". [11] When he returned to the United States, he refined his hybred style. [12] Using vivid colors and a deliberatly primitive technique, he painted scenes of contemporary African-American life. [13] Poor farm workers, city dwellers, soldiers, convicts, musicians, and preachers appears often in his work. [14] The heightened colors and the strong emotional tone of his paintings shows the influence of the European school of painting known as Expressionism.

[15] Soon after World War II ended, Johnson was hospitilized for a nervous disorder. [16] Tragically, his last years was spent in mental institutions. [17] Despite his careers premature end, his works have continued to be exhibited and praized.

[18] A relatively early portrait, *Jim* is painted in a realistic style that Johnson later abandoned. [19] The vivid colors and lose brush strokes are reminiscent of Expressionist techniques. [20] It is not hard to imagine the young Richard Wright as the boy in Johnson's painting. [21] The gaze in Jims eyes suggests an inner turmoil that seems akin to the physical and spiritual hunger that Wright felt as a boy.

William H. Johnson, *Jim*, 1930

Verb Tenses and Voice

Principal Parts of Verbs

[page 529]

1. In which of the following items is the underlined participle used correctly to form a complete sentence?

   a. The steamboat <u>traveling</u> down the Mississippi River.
   b. The passengers <u>been</u> on the deck for hours.
   c. Steamboats were <u>docking</u> at Hannibal when Mark Twain was a boy.

Regular and Irregular Verbs

[pages 529–532]

For each item indicate the set of principal parts that is correct. (Each set should include the <u>base form</u>, the <u>past form</u>, and the <u>past participle</u>.)

2. a. blow, blowed, blewn
   b. bite, bit, bitten
   c. drive, drived, driven
3. a. freeze, froze, frozen
   b. beat, beated, beat
   c. steal, stoled, stolen

Tense of Verbs

[pages 532–540]

Indicate whether the underlined verb in each sentence is in the (a) present tense, (b) past tense, (c) future or future perfect tense, (d) present perfect tense, or (e) past perfect tense.

4. Since the 1950s American poetry <u>has undergone</u> a great change.

5. Beat poets of the 1950s <u>wrote</u> a new type of poetry.
6. By 1956 they <u>had attracted</u> national attention.
7. For many years to come, poetry <u>will display</u> the influence of these poets.

Compatibility of Tenses

[pages 540–541]

8. In which of the following sentences are the tenses compatible?

   a. Clara had been working for the company for three years when she received a promotion.
   b. When her supervisor complimented her on a job well done, Clara thanks him.
   c. By the time Clara told her friends the good news, they already heard about it.

Voice of Verbs

[pages 541–542]

Indicate whether the verb in each sentence is in (a) the active voice or (b) the passive voice.

9. Airplanes have been tested by daring pilots.
10. Airplane crashes are not as common today as they were in the past.

Writing for Review

Write a paragraph relating an incident that you remember from your childhood. Be sure the verbs in all your sentences are used correctly.

Subject-Verb Agreement

A verb must agree with its subject in person and number.

With most verbs the only change in form to indicate agreement occurs in the present tense. An -*s* (or -*es*) is added to the base form of the verb when its subject is third-person singular. The linking verb *be* changes in both the present and the past tense.

SINGULAR	PLURAL
She **speaks**.	They **speak**.
He **is** there.	They **are** there.
It **was** sweet.	They **were** sweet.

In verb phrases the auxiliary verbs *be, have,* and *do* change in form to show agreement with third-person subjects.

SINGULAR	PLURAL
She **is reading**.	They **are reading**.
She **has seen** a movie.	They **have seen** a movie.
Does he **stay** here?	**Do** they **stay** here?

16.1 Intervening Prepositional Phrases

Do not mistake a word in a prepositional phrase for the subject of a sentence.

The simple subject is never within a prepositional phrase. Make sure the verb agrees with the actual subject and not with the object of a preposition.

The ***taste*** of the cherries **surprises** us. [The subject, *taste*, is singular; *of the cherries* is a prepositional phrase; therefore, the verb, *surprises*, is singular.]

The ***spices*** in the food **are** interesting. [The subject, *spices*, is plural; *in the food* is a prepositional phrase; therefore, the verb, *are*, is plural.]

ALONG
THE
ROAD

The signs signal us to yield.

Exercise 1

Making Subjects and Verbs Agree When Prepositional Phrases Intervene   Find the simple subject in each of the following sentences. Then write on your paper the form of the verb indicated in parentheses that agrees with the subject of each sentence. ➡

Barbara Jordan: A Texas Congresswoman

1. Barbara Jordan's years in the U.S. Congress (has/have) given her a unique perspective on American politics.
2. Over thirty years ago this distinguished graduate of two universities (was/were) first attracted to politics.
3. Jordan, despite many setbacks and difficulties, (has/have) achieved many of her goals.
4. A public speaker with Jordan's exceptional talents (is/are) rare.
5. Politicians from every state (was/were) impressed with Barbara Jordan's address at the 1976 Democratic National Convention.
6. Perhaps Jordan's extraordinary abilities in public speaking (was/were) encouraged by her father, a Baptist minister.
7. African-American women, in Jordan's opinion, (needs/need) to make their voices heard in government.
8. Jordan's reputation in political circles (was/were) enhanced by her strong role in the congressional hearings about the impeachment of President Richard Nixon.
9. Jordan, in spite of her popularity among Texas voters, (was/were) planning by 1978 to leave politics for a teaching career.
10. Barbara Jordan's place in history books clearly (seems/seem) secure.

16.2   Agreement with Linking Verbs

Do not be confused by a predicate nominative that is different in number from the subject. Only the subject affects the number of the linking verb.

> The lightest **crate** **is** two tons. [The singular verb, *is*, agrees with the singular subject, *crate*, not with the predicate nominative, *tons*.]

> Recent **studies** on the behavior of wild animals **are** his topic for the day. [The plural verb, *are*, agrees with the plural subject, *studies*, not with the predicate nominative, *topic*.]

Exercise 2

Making Linking Verbs Agree with Their Subjects   Find the simple subject or subjects in each of the following sentences. Then write on your paper the form of the verb in parentheses that agrees with the subject of each sentence. ➡

Our Endangered Forests and Wildlife

1. The growing threat to America's wild animals (is/are) a national problem.
2. Wildlife (remains/remain) a rich and vital part of our national heritage.
3. Research on plant and animal life (is/are) the means of much scientific discovery.
4. Not long ago our forest land (was/were) millions of acres more extensive.
5. By the 1990s the result of deforestation (was/were) high numbers of endangered species.
6. The cost of deforestation (is/are) years of floods and damaging soil erosion.
7. The long-term effects of excessive hunting and fishing (poses/pose) another problem.
8. The destructive results (is/are) a disturbance of the balance of nature.
9. Protected lands (seem/seems) the only hope for wildlife.
10. Efforts by government and private citizens (seems/seem) the solution.

16.3   Agreement in Inverted Sentences

In an **inverted sentence**—a sentence in which the subject follows the verb—take care in locating the simple subject, and make sure that the verb agrees with the subject.

Inverted sentences often begin with prepositional phrases. Do not mistake the object of the preposition for the subject.

	V **S**
SINGULAR	In the jungle **roars** the *lion.*

	V **S**
PLURAL	In the jungle **roar** the *lions.*

	V **S**
SINGULAR	In a large cage at the zoo **rests** a noble *lion.*

	V **S**
PLURAL	In a large cage at the zoo **rest** two noble *lions.*

In inverted sentences beginning with *there* or *here,* look for the subject after the verb. The word *there* or *here* is almost never the subject of a sentence.

	V	S
SINGULAR	There **is** a *lion* in the jungle.	

	V	S
	Here **goes** the *ambulance.*	

	V	S
PLURAL	There **are** *lions* in the jungle.	

	V	S
	Here **go** the two *ambulances.*	

In questions an auxiliary verb may come before the subject. Look for the subject between the auxiliary verb and the main verb.

	V	S	V
SINGULAR	**Does** that *lion* **live** in the jungle?		

	V	S	V
PLURAL	**Do** those *jungles* **contain** lions?		

Exercise 3

Making Subjects and Verbs Agree in Inverted Sentences
Find the simple subject in each of the following sentences. Then write on your paper the form of the verb in parentheses that agrees with the subject of each sentence.

Dining Out

1. There (is/are) three excellent and unusual restaurants in my neighborhood.
2. In the window of one of the restaurants (hangs/hang) an interesting menu.
3. Over the door of another (swings/swing) an old and elaborate sign.
4. Outside the third (stands/stand) two statues representing a waiter and a waitress.
5. (Does/Do) the restaurant owners ever cook and bake?
6. (Is/Are) expert chefs brought in to create mouthwatering specialties to please the demanding clientele?
7. There (is/are) a pleasant decor in all three of these restaurants.
8. Into the restaurants (crowds/crowd) the hungry customers.
9. Here (comes/come) the people who want to eat before they go to the theater.
10. There (gathers/gather) the people waiting to be seated.

16.4   Agreement with Special Subjects

Collective Nouns

A **collective noun** names a group. Consider a collective noun singular when it refers to a group as a whole. Consider a collective noun plural when it refers to each member of a group individually.

SINGULAR	His *family* **arrives**.
PLURAL	His *family* **are** well.

SINGULAR	The *committee* **decides.**
PLURAL	The *committee* **sign** their names.

Special Nouns

Certain nouns that end in -*s*, such as *mumps*, *measles*, and *mathematics*, take singular verbs.

SINGULAR	*Mumps* **is** a disease.

Certain other nouns that end in -*s*, such as *scissors*, *pants*, *binoculars*, and *eyeglasses*, take plural verbs.

PLURAL	The *scissors* **were** sharp.
	Your *eyeglasses* **need** cleaning.

Many nouns that end in -*ics* may be singular or plural, depending upon their meaning.

SINGULAR	*Statistics* **is** an interesting subject. [one subject of interest]
PLURAL	*Statistics* **show** that women live longer than men. [more than one application of this particular field of study]

Nouns of Amount

When a noun of amount refers to a total that is considered as one unit, it is singular. When it refers to a number of individual units, it is plural.

SINGULAR	Three *dollars* **is** not too much for that book. [one amount]
PLURAL	Three *dollars* **are** on the table. [three individual bills]

SINGULAR	Ten *years* **is** a decade. [one unit of time]
PLURAL	Ten *years* **have passed.** [ten individual periods of time]

players is a team.

Five players are on the court.

Titles

A title is always singular, even if a noun within the title is plural.

> **SINGULAR** ***Great Expectations* is** one of the best-loved novels in English literature.

Exercise 4

Making Verbs Agree with Special Subjects Find the subject in each sentence, and write on your paper the form of the verb in parentheses that agrees with the subject.

Roberto Clemente, a Baseball Hero

1. The first baseball team to hire Roberto Clemente (was/were) the Santurce Cangrejeros of Puerto Rico.
2. When Clemente became a professional ballplayer with the Pittsburgh Pirates in 1954, fifty thousand dollars (was/were) considered a princely salary.
3. Clemente's family (was/were) proud of his career.
4. Roberto Clemente's impressive offensive and defensive statistics (shows/show) that he was a versatile player.
5. Professional athletics (is/are) a demanding field.
6. Clemente's eighteen years in major-league baseball (is/are) considered a long career.
7. Five hours (is/are) a long time for a professional baseball game to last.
8. On December 31, 1972, his team (was/were) shocked to hear that Clemente had died in a plane crash while taking supplies to earthquake victims in Nicaragua.
9. Sometimes a professional athlete's second family (is/are) his or her teammates.
10. Our class agrees that *Homers* (is/are) an appropriate title for a biography of Roberto Clemente.

16.5   Agreement with Compound Subjects

Compound Subjects Joined by And

A compound subject that is joined by *and* or *both . . . and* is plural unless its parts belong to one unit or they both refer to the same person or thing.

PLURAL	The *lion* and the *tiger* **are roaring**.
	Both *skiing* and *skating* **are** fun.
SINGULAR	***Peanut butter*** and ***jelly*** **is** a favorite combination. [Compound subject is one unit.]
	His *friend* and *companion* **accompanies** him. [One person is both friend and companion.]

Compound Subjects Joined by Or or Nor

With compound subjects joined by *or* or *nor* (or by *either . . . or* or *neither . . . nor*), the verb always agrees with the subject nearer the verb.

PLURAL	*Neither* the *lion* nor the *tigers* **are roaring**.
SINGULAR	*Either* the *lion* or the *tiger* **is roaring**.
	Neither the *lions* nor the *tiger* **roars**.

Many a, Every, *and* Each *with Compound Subjects*

When *many a*, *every*, or *each* precedes a compound subject, the subject is considered singular.

SINGULAR	*Many a* ***giraffe*** and ***elephant*** **lives** in the nature preserve.
	Every ***chair, bench,*** and ***table*** **was taken**.
	Each lion and *tiger* **is roaring**.

16.6 Intervening Expressions

Certain expressions, such as *accompanied by*, *as well as*, *in addition to*, *plus*, and *together with*, introduce phrases that modify the subject but do not change its number. Although their meaning is similar to that of *and*, these expressions do not create compound subjects.

If a singular subject is linked to another noun by an intervening expression, such as *accompanied by*, the subject is still considered singular.

SINGULAR	The ***pianist,*** as well as the guitarist, the saxophonist, and the lead singer, **is** late.
	Sleet, in addition to snow, **is expected** tomorrow.
	Sports, together with band, **is** the most popular extracurricular activity.

Making Verbs Agree with Their Subjects   On your paper
write the appropriate form of each verb in parentheses.

Leontyne Price, Opera Star

1. The opera expert and the casual listener (agrees/agree)
   that Leontyne Price is one of the greatest living sopranos.
2. The president of the college Price attended in Ohio, as
   well as her friends and relatives in Mississippi, (was/were)
   influential in her decision to pursue a career in music.
3. When Price undertook four demanding years of formal
   training in New York, neither her talents nor her ambition
   (was/were) lacking.
4. Before she became a star, both Ira Gershwin and Virgil
   Thomson (was/were) impressed by Price's singing.
5. Price's longtime friend and adviser, vocal coach Florence
   Page Kimball, (feels/feel) that Price's finest role was that of
   Bess in Gershwin's *Porgy and Bess*.
6. Neither Price's performance in *The Magic Flute* nor her triumphs in Verdi's operas (has/have) given me as much pleasure as her singing in *Madame Butterfly*.
7. Fortunately, neither serious illnesses nor stage fright
   (has/have) interrupted Price's long career.
8. To be a successful singer like Price, talent, together with
   perseverance, (is/are) required.
9. Every note, gesture, and facial expression (is/are) crucial to
   the success of a performance.
10. Many a performer and audience member (feels/feel) excited
    when the lights in a theater dim.

Creating Sentences with Compound Subjects   Write
five sentences, each using one of the following items as the
compound subject. Make the compound subject agree with a
present-tense verb.

1. bread and butter
2. neither the players nor the coach
3. both the climate and the geography of the South
4. Aunt Susan or Uncle Harold
5. many a cat and dog

16.7   Indefinite Pronouns as Subjects

A verb must agree in number with an indefinite pronoun subject.

Indefinite pronouns can be divided into three groups, as shown in the following chart:

Indefinite Pronouns				
ALWAYS SINGULAR	each either neither one	everyone everybody everything no one	nobody nothing anyone anybody	anything someone somebody something	
ALWAYS PLURAL	several	few	both	many	
SINGULAR OR PLURAL	some	all	any	most	none

SINGULAR	***Everybody* is** going to the rodeo. ***No one*** in the audience **looks** upset. ***Something*** in the kitchen **smells** good.
PLURAL	***Both*** of the children **are** in school this morning. ***Many*** of the books **were** donated to the library.

A pronoun from the group labeled singular or plural can be either singular or plural, depending upon the noun to which it refers.

SINGULAR	***Some*** of the dessert **is** left. [*Some* refers to *dessert*, a singular noun.]
PLURAL	***Some*** of the commuters **were caught** in the rainstorm. [*Some* refers to *commuters*, a plural noun.]

Exercise 7: Sentence Writing

Making Verbs Agree with Indefinite Pronoun Subjects
Write five sentences, each using one of the following indefinite pronouns as the subject. Make each subject agree with a present-tense verb.

SAMPLE   One
ANSWER   One of my friends owns a ten-speed bike.

1. each   **4.** both
2. many   **5.** neither
3. few

Exercise 8: Sentence Writing

Creating Sentences with Indefinite Pronoun Subjects
For each indefinite pronoun listed below, write two sentences, using the pronoun as the subject of both sentences. In the first sentence of each pair, use a singular present-tense verb. In the second sentence use a plural present-tense verb.

SAMPLE   Some
ANSWER   Some of the work is not finished.
            Some of the books are on the shelf.

1. none   **4.** all
2. any   **5.** some
3. most

Exercise 9: Review

Subject-Verb Agreement   The following paragraph contains ten errors in subject-verb agreement. Locate the sentences with errors, and rewrite those sentences, using the verb form that agrees with the subject. (Not every sentence contains an error.)

Popular Music

¹Many people in the cities of Los Angeles, Miami, and New York enjoys several kinds of popular music. ²While a family in a Jamaican neighborhood in Brooklyn probably listen to reggae music together, a Dominican family in Miami probably like merengue. ³Many a New Yorker, whether young or old, like jazz and blues. ⁴Cuban Americans as well as people from Puerto Rico dances to the brassy music known as salsa. ⁵The syncopated rhythms of calypso music is popular among people who come from Trinidad. ⁶Very popular in the Hispanic communities of Los Angeles is Mexican folk songs called *rancheras*. ⁷From the recording studios come one new popular hit after another. ⁸Usually thousands of dollars are the sum needed to record a new song. ⁹In many American cities neither the Motown tunes of the 1960s nor rock-and-roll have gone out of style. ¹⁰Ask whether your family or friends enjoy a special kind of music.

While many decisions you make in revising your writing are matters of style, many others are matters of usage. For example, most readers expect writers to adhere to the rules of subject-verb agreement, and they lose respect for writers who do not. Keep these guidelines in mind as you revise your work:

1. Be alert to prepositional phrases and other expressions that fall between a subject and its verb. Mentally block them out when you check for agreement.

> "Young woman," she said, "do you deny that all this *nonsense* with the eggs and the telephone calls *is* an attempt to entangle my nephew into matrimony?"
>
> Shirley Jackson, "About Two Nice People"

2. When you check for agreement in inverted sentences, remember that the subject follows the verb.

> As smooth as your forehead
> *Are* the *gulch* and the *bramble*.
> Gabriela Mistral, "Serenity"

3. Remember that some indefinite pronouns are always singular, some are always plural, and a few may be used in either a singular or a plural sense. Be careful about subject-verb agreement when subjects are indefinite pronouns.

> Inside the lodge there are many Indians. *Some sit* on benches around the walls; *others dance* in the center of the floor around a drum. *Nobody seems* to notice me.
> Thomas S. Whitecloud, *Blue Winds, Dancing*

Apply these techniques to the following sentences. On a separate sheet of paper, rewrite the paragraph, filling each blank with a verb in the present tense.

> The boy with black eyes _____ over the rim of the canyon into the valley below. Everything _____ pale, as if the hot midday sun had bleached the colors from the landscape. The boy stands with arms upraised and throws a stone over the cliff. "One, two, three," _____ the boy as the stone falls, and on "four" he hears it clatter on the rocks. Then he remembers that in one of his pockets _____ the carving of the bird he had finished the night before. As polished as river rocks _____ his bird, and as white as sunlight. Quickly, without thinking, the boy from Wide Ruins _____ the bird and _____ it over the cliff. There _____ a brief flash of white, and the bird is gone. Nobody, not even the boy, _____ whether it hits the ground.

Usage Workshop

Subject-Verb Agreement

Simin Daneshvar is from Iran, and her novel *Savushun* describes the fortunes of an Iranian family at the time of the Second World War. The chief characters of the novel are a sensitive young woman named Zari and her husband, Yusof, a landowner. In this passage Zari spends a quiet afternoon in her garden with her twin daughters. The passage has been annotated to show some examples of subject-verb agreement covered in this unit.

Literature Model

from SAVUSHUN
by Simin Daneshvar
translated from the Persian
by M. R. Ghanoonparvar

Agreement between a singular pronoun subject and a singular past form of *be*

An inverted sentence with agreement between an indefinite pronoun subject (referring to the plural noun *flowers*) and the plural past form of *be*

An inverted sentence with agreement between a plural noun subject and the plural past form of *be*

Agreement between a compound noun subject and the plural past form of *be*

Agreement between a singular noun subject and a singular past form of *be*

Ten days had passed since Yusof had left for the winter pastures, and the weather in the garden wasn't much better than where he was. Summer always hurried in like this, chasing away spring. It was afternoon and Gholam was sprinkling water on the patio in front of the house. Zari, carrying gardening clippers, was looking for flowers to pick. But there were none worth picking in the garden. Mina and Marjan, chirping like birds, followed their mother from one bush to another. By the stream around the patio there were some cockscombs so wilted and dusty that not even an old hen would have looked at them twice. By another stream, the faces and heads of the snapdragons were all covered with dust. Some more humble plants were straining to close their eyes and sleep as the sun set. The only hope was for the tuberoses, which Gholam claimed would "blossom when there is a full moon." The orange-blossom petals had dried up completely and, under the trees, looked like dried and shriveled brown stars. How one missed winter, when the narcissuses opened at the edge of the streams, and gave their reflections to the passing water as a memento. The water flowed on, losing the reflections, pouring into the pool without a witness. One could only hear its current. And when spring came, the ➡

white and purple violets gracefully greeted the passing water without promise or memento.

Making Subjects and Verbs Agree When Prepositional Phrases Intervene Each of the following sentences describes characteristics of the Persian garden. On your paper rewrite each sentence, following the directions in parentheses. In some cases you will need to change the form of the verb to make the sentence correct; in other cases the verb will remain the same.

SAMPLE For Persians an image of paradise is created by gardens. (Change *an image* to *images*.)

ANSWER For Persians images of paradise are created by gardens.

1. The scene on ancient Persian pottery often depicts garden images. (Change *scene* to *scenes*.)
2. A pool of water usually plays a prominent role in these scenes. (Change *A pool* to *Pools*.)
3. Often, too, the patterns on Persian rugs suggest a garden. (Change *Persian rugs* to *a Persian rug*.)
4. Persian gardens throughout the years have been laid out in four sections. (Change *the years* to *time*.)
5. Pavilions of cypress trees were often built at the center of the garden. (Change *Pavilions* to *A pavilion*.)
6. In Iran some gardens still follow this plan. (Move the prepositional phrase so that it comes directly after the subject.)
7. The pool in such a garden is still an important feature. (Change *such a garden* to *these gardens*.)
8. Sometimes streams from nearby areas supply the water for these pools. (Change *nearby areas* to *a nearby spring*.)
9. In some seasons water is provided by sloping tunnels called *qanat* lines. (Move the first prepositional phrase so that it comes directly after the subject.)
10. The length of the *qanat* line varies considerably. (Change *line* to *lines*.)
11. Beneath the surface *qanat* lines connect the valleys to the snow-capped mountains. (Move the first prepositional phrase so that it comes directly after the subject.)
12. Owners of gardens rent the channel for a certain length of time. (Change *gardens* to *a garden*.) ➡

13. From the mountains melting snow thus becomes a source of water. (Move the first prepositional phrase so that it comes directly after the subject.)
14. Varieties of roses dominate Persian gardens. (Change *Varieties* to *A variety.*)
15. A rose with deep aroma has been used in many interesting ways. (Change *A rose* to *Roses.*)
16. Gardeners of certain roses press petals to make fragrant rosewater. (Change *Gardeners* to *A gardener.*)
17. A flavoring from the rose is used in a variety of desserts. (Change *the rose* to *roses.*)
18. The song of a nightingale makes a garden even more delightful. (Change *song* to *songs.*)
19. A common sight in Persian gardens is brightly colored tulips. (Change *A common sight* to *Common sights.*)
20. A plane tree of huge proportions often provides shade for the garden. (Change *A plane tree* to *Plane trees.*)

Usage Workshop Exercise 2

Writing Sentences with Intervening Prepositional Phrases   The following sentences describe an imaginary garden. Rewrite each sentence, adding an appropriate prepositional phrase in the place indicated by the caret and choosing the correct form of the verb in parentheses.

SAMPLE   The flower garden ∧ (is/are) beautiful.
ANSWER   The flower garden behind my grandmother's house is beautiful.

1. Flowers ∧ (offers/offer) a spectacle of color throughout the growing season.
2. Fragrant roses ∧ (delights/delight) all who behold them.
3. Lilacs ∧ (is/are) a charming sight.
4. The rich soil ∧ (nourishes/nourish) the flowers.
5. A birdbath ∧ (attracts/attract) robins and sparrows.
6. A vegetable garden ∧ (is/are) practical but not necessarily beautiful.
7. Vegetables ∧ (enhances/enhance) one's diet.
8. Surplus crops ∧ (is/are) frozen, dried, or canned.
9. A small herb garden ∧ (provides/provide) fresh seasonings for cooking.
10. Daily watering ∧ (is/are) a must when rainfall is scarce.

Making Linking Verbs Agree with Their Subject   Each of the following sentences describes the scene from the passage from *Savushun*. On your paper rewrite each sentence, following the directions in parentheses. If necessary, change the number of the linking verb.

SAMPLE   Gardens in Iran are retreats from the dry
              countryside. (Change *retreats* to *a retreat*.)
ANSWER   Gardens in Iran are a retreat from the dry
              countryside.

1. Usually Zari's garden is a beautiful sight. (Change *garden* to *flowers*.)
2. Today, however, the main feature of the garden is a cluster of wilted flowers. (Change *a cluster* to *clusters*.)
3. An orange-blossom petal has become a shriveled jumble. (Change *An orange-blossom petal* to *Orange-blossom petals*.)
4. The streams are mirrors for the drooping blossoms. (Change *mirrors* to *a mirror*.)
5. The garden tool is a useless device on such a day. (Change *tool* to *clippers*.)
6. The only animals in the parched garden are birds. (Change *animals* to *surprising sight*.)
7. In winter a flowering plant is a welcome sight. (Change *a flowering plant* to *flowering plants*.)
8. In spring one image of loveliness is the violet. (Change *the violet* to *violets*.)
9. Water is the key to survival for these fragile plants. (Change *key to* to *means of*.)
10. Irrigation systems are the best solution for dry areas. (Change *Irrigation systems* to *An irrigation system*.)

Making Subjects and Verbs Agree in Inverted Sentences
Each of the following sentences elaborates on an idea suggested by the passage from *Savushun*. First, write each sentence on your paper, choosing the correct form of the verb in parentheses. Then rewrite each sentence in inverted order, making adjustments to the form of the verb.

SAMPLE   The hot sun (beats/beat) upon the dry plants.
ANSWER   The hot sun beats upon the dry plants.
              Upon the dry plants beats the hot sun. ➡

1. The clippers (is/are) in Zari's hand.
2. The gardener (stands/stand) among some bushes.
3. A gently curving stream (flows/flow) between the towering trees.
4. Some wilted cockscombs (droops/droop) by the side of the stream.
5. Crumbling orange-blossom petals (lies/lie) in the dry dust.
6. The colorful snapdragons (blooms/bloom) near another stream.
7. The limp blossoms (bends/bend) toward the parched earth.
8. The refreshing water (flows/flow) onto the thirsty plants.
9. New growth (comes/come) with frequent waterings.
10. The white tuberose (appears/appear) on cool moonlit nights.

Usage Workshop Exercise 5

Making Verbs Agree with Special Subjects   The following sentences are about a panel discussion on the occupation of Iran during the Second World War by Great Britain and the Soviet Union. First, find the subject in each sentence, and then write on your paper the form of the verb in parentheses that agrees with the subject.

SAMPLE   A panel of experts (prepares/prepare) for discussions of various aspects of the occupation of Iran.

ANSWER   prepare

1. Because mumps (is/are) spreading throughout the community, some students will miss the discussion.
2. Binoculars (helps/help) those in the back of the large auditorium to see the speakers.
3. *The Effects of Allied Occupation on Iran* (is/are) a book recommended by one of the speakers.
4. First, the audience (learns/learn) about the German influence in Iran at the beginning of World War II.
5. The panel then (discusses/discuss) among themselves the British and Soviet control of Iran in the early 1940s.
6. The group at the podium (disagrees/disagree) about whether that occupation was necessary.
7. Five years (was/were) the length of the Allied occupation of Iran. ➡

8. Our class next (hears/hear) about the economic and social problems in Iran at the time.
9. Thirty thousand (was/were) the approximate number of troops provided by the United States when it joined the occupation in 1942.
10. Statistics (shows/show) that the years of occupation were difficult for Iran.

Usage Workshop Exercise 6

Making Verbs Agree with Compound Subjects   Each of the following sentences elaborates on an idea suggested by the passage from *Savushun*. On your paper rewrite each sentence, following the directions in parentheses and making any necessary adjustments to the form of the verb.

SAMPLE   Every flower needs water. (Add *and shrub* to the complete subject.)

ANSWER   Every flower and shrub needs water.

1. Mina scampers from bush to bush. (Add *and her sister* to the complete subject.)
2. Zari and the girls look for flowers. (Delete *and the girls* from the complete subject.)
3. Every cockscomb droops. (Add *and orange blossom* to the complete subject.)
4. Many a violet has faded. (Add *and narcissus* to the complete subject.)
5. Each stem withers. (Add *and blossom* to the complete subject.)
6. Zari and Gholam tend the garden. (Delete *and Gholam* from the complete subject.)
7. The stream and the pond supply water for the garden. (Delete *and the pond* from the complete subject.)
8. Many a dried leaf floats on the still water. (Add *and petal* to the complete subject.)
9. The spring and the winter bring fresh foliage. (Delete *and the winter* from the complete subject.)
10. Now Zari and her children want only the safe return of Yusof. (Delete *and her children* from the complete subject.)

Making Subjects and Verbs Agree When Expressions Intervene The following sentences describe the situation and characters in *Savushun*. Rewrite each sentence, correcting any errors in subject-verb agreement. If the sentence contains no errors, write *correct*.

1. In the novel *Savushun* a British army, as well as Soviet troops, occupy Iran.
2. The troops, plus a poor harvest, causes a food shortage.
3. Yusof, as well as Zari, is sympathetic to the hungry nomads and peasants.
4. A tribal leader, accompanied by his brother, bring Yusof news of the peasants' hardships.
5. The peasant population, plus its sheep, is starving.
6. Yusof, accompanied by servants, have gone to his pastures.
7. Yusof, in addition to his foreman, visits the herdsmen.
8. Zari, together with Yusof's sister, give food to the poor.
9. Bread, as well as dates, are taken by Zari to hospitals.
10. Famine, together with disease, cause death everywhere.

Making Verbs Agree with Indefinite Pronoun Subjects The following sentences describe gardens around the city of Shiraz, the setting of *Savushun*. Rewrite each sentence, replacing the indefinite pronoun in italics with the pronoun in parentheses. If necessary, change the number of the verb.

SAMPLE *Many* of Iran's historic sites are near Shiraz.
(One)

ANSWER One of Iran's historic sites is near Shiraz.

1. *Most* of the sites, such as the tombs of the ancient poets Hafiz and Sadi, feature gardens.
(A few)
2. *Both* of these poets are revered in Muslim cultures.
(Each)
3. *Either* of their tombs attracts numerous visitors.
(Both)
4. *Most* in Iran are familiar with the poems of Hafiz.
(Everyone) ➡

5. *Many* enjoy reading his verse in a nearby garden.
   (Anybody)
6. *Several* of the older gardens have vanished entirely.
   (Some)
7. *Each* of the area's palaces was decorated with mirrored tile.
   (Many)
8. *All* are able to imagine the beauty of the palaces.
   (Someone)
9. *Few* of the ancient gardens have been fully restored.
   (Several)
10. *Some* of the renovation of the Rose Garden is complete.
    (Most)

Usage Workshop Exercise 9

Review   The following sentences describe the life and achievements of Simin Daneshvar [sē mēn´ dä´nesh vär´]. For each sentence write the appropriate form of the verb in parentheses.

Simin Daneshvar

1. Simin Daneshvar, as well as her husband, (figures/figure) prominently among contemporary Iranian writers.
2. Daneshvar, along with other Iranian writers, (criticizes/criticize) the lack of freedom in her homeland.
3. Studies at Tehran University (was/were) the foundation for her doctorate in Persian literature.
4. Daneshvar's lectures at Tehran University (has/have) exposed many scholars to her ideas.
5. All of Iran's social classes (is/are) represented in her fiction.
6. Among the greatest influences on her works (was/were) the American author O. Henry.
7. *The Quenched Fire* (1948) and *A City as Paradise* (1961) (deals/deal) with women's roles in society.
8. None of the stories in *The Quenched Fire* (has/have) been reprinted because the author was dissatisfied with the work.
9. In Daneshvar's most widely read novel, *Savushun* (1969), the descriptions of suffering (composes/compose) a portrait of the effects of war on common people.
10. Daneshvar's works (is/are) a realistic depiction of social problems in her country.

Proofreading   The following passage describes manuscript illumination; an example by an anonymous Persian artist appears on the opposite page. Rewrite the passage, correcting the errors in spelling, capitalization, punctuation, grammar, and usage. There are twenty-five errors in all.

Persian Illuminated Manuscripts

[1]Illustrated, or illuminated, books was one of the highest art forms in the Islamic world. [2]From the tenth through the sixteenth centuries, manuscript painting was highly cherished for it celebrated the beauty and the power of the written word. [3]Because in Islam books were considered to be the embodiment of devine revelation, they was treated with reverence. [4]Moreover, written Arabic lends itself to exquisite calligraphy, a type of stylized handwriting.

[5]In persia and other Middle eastern countries the teachings of the sixth-century prophet Mohammed were often illustrated. [6]Similarly, many literary manuscripts was illustrated in the sixteenth century. [7]The illustration on the opposite page dates from that time. [8]It is taken from a book entitled *Mantiq at-Tayr (Language of the Birds)*, which was written by Farid-Al-Din 'Attar. [9]The image is quite small and carefully painted. [10]Parts of the painting is covered with gold leaf, which was used to brighten the scene. [11]Gold represented the earthly manifestation of divine light. [12]The imaje is a rich brocade that represents the idealized realm of the birds. [13]The birds theirselves represent creatures of the heavens.

[14]At the upper right is the figure of a man. [15]This here figure can be interpreted in two ways—as a guardian of the birds sanctuary or as a representation of the human threat to that world. [16]The painting, however, mirror the poem in reflecting an ideal word rather than an actual world. [17]Therefore, peace and harmony predominate.

[18]Garden-related themes appears in many Persian literary classics. [19]The richly varied colors, and textures that exists in Nature can be found not only in Persia's art but in it's architecture and in the many complex decorative designs that pervade persian culture. [20]In the illumination on the opposite page, the colorful garden is a haven for birds. [21]In Simin Daneshvars novel "Savushun," the colors and sounds of the garden calls up visions of natural beauty.

Habib Allah, *Mantiq at-Tayr (Language of the Birds),* **c. 1600**

Unit 16 Review

Subject-Verb Agreement

Directions: For sentences 1–20 indicate the verb that agrees with its subject.

Agreement with Intervening Prepositional Phrases

[pages 555–556]

1. A butterfly with unusual migratory habits **(a)** is / **(b)** are of great interest to scientists.
2. A trait of monarch butterflies **(a)** is / **(b)** are migrating for many miles.
3. Other species of this insect also **(a)** embarks / **(b)** embark on long voyages.
4. Flights of the large sulphur butterfly **(a)** has / **(b)** have been recorded by ships far out at sea.

Agreement with Linking Verbs

[pages 556–557]

5. One factor influencing butterfly distribution **(a)** is / **(b)** are geographical barriers.
6. A butterfly's adult life span **(a)** is / **(b)** are approximately thirty days.
7. Butterflies **(a)** is / **(b)** are a kind of insect found on all continents except Antarctica.
8. The wide, colorful wings of a butterfly **(a)** is / **(b)** are one characteristic that distinguishes it from a moth.

Agreement in Inverted Sentences

[pages 557–558]

9. There **(a)** is / **(b)** are many illustrations of butterflies in my encyclopedia.
10. **(a)** Does / **(b)** Do your encyclopedia illustrate metamorphosis?
11. Here **(a)** is / **(b)** are a detailed drawing.

12. In this section **(a)** is / **(b)** are the illustrations you want.

Agreement with Special and Compound Subjects

[pages 559–561]

13. To a lepidopterist a hundred butterflies or a single moth **(a)** is / **(b)** are significant.
14. A team at the college **(a)** has / **(b)** have been studying butterflies.
15. Two years **(a)** is / **(b)** are how long the research project will last.
16. Every man and woman on the team **(a)** believes / **(b)** believe in the project.

Agreement with Intervening Expressions and Indefinite Pronoun Subjects

[pages 561–564]

17. Almost all of these insects **(a)** has / **(b)** have some means of protection from enemies.
18. Protective coloration, as well as spiny larvae, **(a)** is / **(b)** are characteristic of many butterflies.
19. The monarch butterfly, in addition to the pipe vine swallowtail, **(a)** has / **(b)** have a bitter taste.
20. Neither of these butterflies **(a)** makes / **(b)** make a tempting meal for a hungry bird.

Writing for Review

Write a short description on a subject of your choice. Include compound subjects and intervening phrases.

Unit 17 — Using Pronouns Correctly

17.1   Case of Personal Pronouns

Pronouns that are used to refer to persons or things are called **personal** pronouns.

Personal pronouns have three **cases,** or forms, called **nominative, objective,** and **possessive.** The case of a personal pronoun depends upon the pronoun's function in a sentence (whether it is a subject, a complement, or an object of a preposition).

Personal Pronouns			
Case	**Singular Pronouns**	**Plural Pronouns**	**Function in Sentence**
NOMINATIVE	I, you, she, he, it	we, you, they	subject or predicate nominative
OBJECTIVE	me, you, her, him, it	us, you, them	direct object, indirect object, or object of preposition
POSSESSIVE	my, mine, your, yours, her, hers, his, its	our, ours, your, yours, their, theirs	replacement for possessive noun(s)

You can avoid errors with the case of personal pronouns if you keep the following rules in mind:

1. Be sure to use the nominative case for a personal pronoun in a compound subject.

> Paul and **I** play the guitar.
> **She** and **I** sing duets.

2. Be sure to use the objective case for a personal pronoun in a compound object.

> Paul's sister accompanies Paul and **her.**
> This is between you and **me.**
> The tickets are for the Yangs and **us.**

Hint: When you have to choose the correct pronoun in a sentence with a compound subject or object, try saying the sentence aloud without the conjunction and the other subject or object.

3. Use the nominative case of a personal pronoun after a form of the linking verb *be*.

> The best guitar player is **he.**
> The best singer in the show was **she.**
> I hope a future star will be **I.**

This rule is changing now, especially in speaking. In informal speech people often use the objective case after a form of the linking verb *be*; they say, *It's me*, and *It was her*. Some authorities even recommend using the objective case in informal writing in order to avoid sounding pretentious. To be strictly correct, however, use the nominative case after the linking verb *be*, at least in formal writing.

4. Be careful not to spell possessive pronouns with apostrophes.

> This sheet music is **hers.**
> The instruments are **theirs.**

It's is a contraction for *it is*. Do not confuse *it's* with the possessive pronoun *its*.

> **It's** a great day for an outdoor concert.
> Bring me the guitar and **its** case.

5. Be sure to use possessive pronouns before gerunds (*-ing* forms used as nouns).

> **Your** dancing bothers me.
> He wasn't pleased by **my** complaining to him.

Exercise 1

Choosing the Correct Case Form   For each of the following sentences, choose the correct personal pronoun from the pair in parentheses.

Phillis Wheatley, Poet

1. When you and (I/me) think of African-American poets, there is one we often forget: Phillis Wheatley, who was born in Africa in 1753.
2. Wheatley was kidnapped by slave traders when she was eight, and the traders and (she/her) sailed to Boston, where she was sold to a rich tailor named John Wheatley.
3. (He/Him) and his wife, Susannah, welcomed Phillis into their home and treated her as if she were (theirs/their's). ➡

4. Susannah Wheatley took great interest in Phillis's education, and it was (she/her) who taught Phillis how to read and write in English.
5. John Wheatley encouraged Susannah and (she/her) in their studies, and Phillis Wheatley soon began to write poems in English.
6. In 1772 (he/him) and Susannah sent Phillis to England, for they hoped that her going would improve her health, which had never been good.
7. The king of England wished to meet with Wheatley, for (she/her) and her poems were much admired.
8. (Its/It's) sad, for it was (she/her) who had to cancel the meeting: Susannah had taken ill, and Phillis had to return to Boston.
9. George Washington was so impressed with Wheatley's poems that he invited her to his headquarters and praised both the poems and (she/her).
10. My knowledge of Phillis Wheatley has increased by (me/my) reading about her in the library.

17.2   Pronouns with and as Appositives

Use the nominative case for a pronoun that is in apposition to a subject or a predicate nominative.

The judges, **she** and **Mrs. Chiu,** will have a difficult task. [*Judges* is the subject of the sentence.]

The winners were the pianists, **Linda** and **he.** [*Pianists* is the predicate nominative.]

Use the objective case for a pronoun that is in apposition to a direct object, an indirect object, or an object of a preposition.

The audience cheered their favorite performers, **Darnell** and **her.** [*Performers* is the direct object.]

The director gave the stage crew, **Lee** and **him,** special thanks. [*Stage crew* is the indirect object.]

The judges explained the rules to both groups, **them** and **us.** [*Groups* is the object of the preposition *to.*]

When a pronoun is followed by an appositive, choose the case of the pronoun that would be correct if the appositive were omitted.

We violinists hope one day to play in a concert hall. [*We* is the correct form because *we* is the subject of the sentence.]

The music teacher handed the scores to **us musicians**. [*Us* is the correct form because *us* is the object of the preposition *to*.]

Hint: When you are choosing the correct pronoun, it is often helpful to say the sentence aloud without the appositive.

Exercise 2

Using Pronouns Correctly with and as Appositives For each of the following sentences, choose the correct personal pronoun from the pair in parentheses.

The Game of Golf

1. The first lecturers, Anna and (I/me), explained that golf was popularized by the Scottish king James IV and his granddaughter, Mary.
2. The two of them, James IV and (she/her), helped to introduce the game to sports enthusiasts in England and France.
3. (We/Us) Americans often claim that golf was played here in colonial times, but there is little evidence to support this.
4. Two very successful contemporary golfers, Nancy Lopez and (he/him), earn top salaries.
5. The winners of the U.S. Open, Hale Irwin and (she/her), played masterfully.

Exercise 3

Using Pronouns Correctly with and as Appositives For each sentence in the following paragraph, choose the correct pronoun from the pair in parentheses.

Making a Movie

[1]The writers, Lawrence Kasdan and (she/her), were willing to revise the script. [2]The director worked well with the leads, Harrison Ford and (she/her). [3]The two cinematographers, Gordon Willis and (him/he), were both efficient and creative. [4](We/Us) young actors were lucky to work with such a fine team. [5]There is no question that working on this film had a positive effect on (we/us) beginners.

17.3   Pronouns After *Than* and *As*

In elliptical adverb clauses using *than* and *as,* choose the case of the pronoun that you would use if the missing words were fully expressed.

> You use a brush more skillfully than **I.** [The nominative pronoun *I* is the subject of the incomplete adverb clause *than I use a brush.*]

> The logic of the problem puzzled Jennifer as much as **me.** [The objective pronoun *me* is the direct object of the incomplete adverb clause *as much as it puzzled me.*]

Exercise 4: Sentence Writing

Using Pronouns After *Than* and *As*   Expand each of the following expressions into a complex sentence containing an elliptical adverb clause. End each sentence with a personal pronoun other than *you* or *it.*

SAMPLE   more nervous than
ANSWER   No one at the audition last night was more nervous than I.

1. frightened than
2. as pleased as
3. more curious than
4. less than
5. as much as

17.4   *Who* and *Whom* in Questions and Subordinate Clauses

Use the nominative pronoun *who* for subjects.

> **Who** won the contest? [*Who* is the subject of the verb *won.*]
> Tell me **who** is in your class. [*Who* is the subject of the noun clause *who is in your class.*]

In questions with an interrupting expression such as *did you say* or *do you think,* it is often helpful to drop the interrupting phrase to determine whether to use *who* or *whom.*

> **Who** do you think will emcee the show? [Think: *Who* will emcee the show? *Who* is the subject of the verb *will emcee.*]

Use the objective pronoun *whom* for the direct or indirect object of a verb or verbal or for the object of a preposition.

Whom are you introducing first? [*Whom* is the direct object of the verb *are introducing*.]

Whom did you say Maria invited to the party? [*Whom* is the direct object of the verb *invited*.]

They told him **whom** he could invite to the show. [*Whom* is the direct object of the verb *could invite* in the noun clause *whom he could invite to the show*.]

Theodore Roosevelt is a president about **whom** I have read quite a bit. [*Whom* is the object of the preposition *about* in the adjective clause *about whom I have read quite a bit*.]

In informal speech people generally use *who* in place of *whom* in sentences like this one: *Who did you tell?* In writing and in formal speaking situations, however, people are expected to make the distinctions between *who* and *whom*.

direct object

Maria invited **them** to the party.
Maria invited **whom** to the party?

Exercise 5

Choosing *Who* or *Whom*   For each of the following sentences, choose the correct pronoun from the pair in parentheses.

Learning About Holography

1. (Who/Whom) did you say gave you the passes to the Museum of Holography?
2. Setsuko Ishii is the holographic artist about (who/whom) I've been reading.
3. Setsuko Ishii, (who/whom) many consider one of Japan's top holographic artists, has put together an exhibit at the museum.
4. The director of the museum, (who/whom) our teacher knows, will show us a twenty-minute film on holography.
5. The director introduced us to several artists (who/whom) he said would be represented in future exhibitions.

Exercise 6

Choosing *Who* or *Whom*   For each of the following sentences, choose the correct pronoun from the pair in parentheses.

George Washington Carver, Scientist

1. (Who/Whom) would you say changed forever the way we look at the lowly peanut? ➡

2. George Washington Carver, (who/whom) many consider one of the best scientists of his day, developed hundreds of products from peanuts.
3. Carver, (who/whom) many still admire today, was born on a Missouri plantation in 1861 and left home when he was ten years old.
4. He was accepted by a college in Kansas, but he was barred from attending by faculty members (who/whom) were prejudiced.
5. Carver was later admitted to Simpson College in Iowa and paid his way by ironing laundry for students (who/whom) were attending the college.
6. Carver, (who/whom) every student of agriculture has studied, made several important discoveries about plants.
7. Booker T. Washington, a scientist (who/whom) Carver greatly respected, invited Carver to work at the Tuskegee Institute in Alabama.
8. Carver, (who/whom) Washington believed to be hard working and imaginative, eventually came up with more than three hundred products derived from peanuts, including peanut butter, ink, shampoo, vinegar, and a coffee substitute.
9. For (who/whom) did Carver develop these products?
10. Carver developed them for poor southern farmers, about (who/whom) he was greatly concerned.

Exercise 7

Using *Who* or *Whom* in Sentences   On your paper complete the following paragraph by filling each blank with *who* or *whom.*

Mary Cassatt, an American Painter

¹Mary Cassatt, _____ many students of art admire, was a successful nineteenth-century American painter who spent much of her time in France. ²Her friends, _____ included Edgar Degas, were some of the great French Impressionists. ³Degas, _____ we know primarily for his paintings of ballerinas, greatly influenced Cassatt. ⁴Cassatt also encouraged American collectors to purchase the art of the Impressionists, _____ she considered very important. ⁵_____ are some other American artists influenced by the European Impressionists?

17.5　Pronoun-Antecedent Agreement

An **antecedent** is the word or group of words to which a pronoun refers or that a pronoun replaces. All pronouns must agree with their antecedents in number, gender, and person.

Agreement in Number and Gender

A pronoun must agree with its antecedent in number (singular or plural) and gender (masculine, feminine, or neuter).

A pronoun's antecedent may be a noun, another pronoun, or a phrase or clause acting as a noun. In the following examples the pronouns appear in bold type and their antecedents in bold italic type. Notice how they agree in both number and gender:

> ***Helen Keller*** did not let blindness and deafness prevent **her** from graduating *cum laude* from Radcliffe College. [singular feminine pronoun]

> ***Helen Keller*** and ***Robert Smithdas*** overcame double handicaps to earn **their** college degrees. [plural pronoun]

> ***Octavio Paz*** is one of the greatest poets of **his** era. [singular masculine pronoun]

> ***Walt Whitman*** and ***Emily Dickinson*** are also famous for **their** poetry. [plural pronoun]

> The ***horseshoe crab,*** despite **its** name, is not a true crab but is related to the spider. [singular neuter pronoun]

> ***Oysters*** and ***clams*** are becoming endangered because of oil spills near **their** breeding grounds. [plural pronoun]

Traditionally a masculine pronoun is used when the gender of the antecedent is not known or may be either masculine or feminine.

> An ***author*** must capture **his** readers' interest.

This rule touches on an area of controversy and changing language, however. Although some people still prefer the traditional use of the masculine pronoun, others today prefer to use a more gender-neutral expression. If you do not wish to use a masculine pronoun when the antecedent may be feminine, you can frequently reword the sentence in one of three ways: (1) by using *he or she*, *his or her,* and so forth, (2) by using a plural pronoun, or (3) by eliminating the pronoun.

> An ***author*** must capture **his or her** readers' interest.
> ***Authors*** must capture **their** readers' interest.
> ***Authors*** must capture readers' interest. [no pronoun]

Agreement in Person

A pronoun must agree in person with its antecedent.

Most problems with agreement in person arise when the second-person pronoun *you* is used incorrectly to refer to an antecedent in the third person. Either change *you* to an appropriate third-person pronoun, or replace it with a suitable noun.

POOR	Suki and James are going to visit the Everglades, where ~~you~~ can see storks and alligators.
BETTER	Suki and James are going to visit the Everglades, where **they** can see storks and alligators.
BETTER	Suki and James are going to visit the Everglades, where **tourists** can see storks and alligators.

When the antecedent of a pronoun is another pronoun, be sure that the two pronouns agree in person. Avoid unnecessary shifts from *they* to *you*, *I* to *you*, or *one* to *you*.

POOR	**They** often visit New Orleans, where ~~you~~ can enjoy French cooking.
BETTER	**They** often visit New Orleans, where **they** can enjoy French cooking.
POOR	**I** hiked on trails that amazed ~~you~~ with their beauty.
BETTER	**I** hiked on trails that amazed **me** with their beauty.

Exercise 8

Making Pronouns and Antecedents Agree   On your paper complete the following sentences by filling each blank with an appropriate possessive pronoun. Also write the antecedent for each pronoun that you supply.

Sarah Winnemucca, a Piute Spokeswoman
[1]Sarah Winnemucca, the daughter of a Piute chief, was taken by _____ grandfather to California in 1850. [2]Some years later, after she had learned English and Spanish, she moved to Nevada and worked for a stagecoach agent and _____ wife and family. [3]When several bands of Piutes were forced off their ancestral land in the 1860s, Winnemucca served as _____ interpreter. [4]After lecturing in the East about the plight of her people, she moved to the town of Vancouver and taught in one of _____ schools for Native Americans. [5]Winnemucca's book *Life Among the Piutes* was a great success, and it has added to _____ understanding as Americans of an important chapter in Native American history.

Making Pronouns and Antecedents Agree   In each of the following sentences, find the personal pronoun and its antecedent. If there is an error in agreement, revise the sentence in one or more ways to correct the problem. If there is no error, write *correct*.

Ethnic Cuisines

1. A cook who likes unusual food is in luck these days, for they can find plenty of ethnic recipes and special ingredients.
2. A lover of Japanese food can prepare their own shrimp or vegetable tempura.
3. Even an amateur chef can make their own pasta at home, using an electric or hand-cranked machine.
4. A person who is partial to Mexican food can concoct their own hot sauce with tomatoes, onions, and hot green peppers.
5. Shoppers can visit ethnic grocery shops, where they can purchase many hard-to-get ingredients, such as dried Chinese mushrooms, tortilla mix, collard greens, juniper berries, pine nuts, and litchi nuts.

Making Pronouns and Antecedents Agree in Person
Rewrite each of the following items, eliminating the inappropriate use of *you* by substituting a third-person pronoun or a suitable noun.

José Feliciano: A Success Story

1. Blind people face more obstacles than the sighted, for you must be unusually self-reliant and persevering.
2. José Feliciano is a highly respected blind musician. He grew up in Puerto Rico, where you had to struggle hard to get ahead.
3. When Feliciano was five, he and his family moved to New York, where you hoped to find better opportunities.
4. From his idol, Ray Charles, Feliciano learned that blind people can succeed in the music business. You must learn to expect setbacks and disappointment, however.
5. Feliciano's fans praise his skillful guitar playing. They say that you expect nothing less than the best from this disciplined musician.

Agreement with Indefinite Pronoun Antecedents

In general, use a singular personal pronoun when the antecedent is a singular indefinite pronoun, and use a plural personal pronoun when the antecedent is a plural indefinite pronoun. (See page 563 for a list of singular and plural indefinite pronouns.)

> **Each** of the boys must buy **his** own uniform.
> **One** of the women has **her** own diving equipment.
> **Many** of the students bring **their** lunch to school.

Notice that the plural nouns in the prepositional phrases—*of the boys, of the women*—do not affect the number of the personal pronouns. *His* and *her* are singular because *each* and *one*, their antecedents, are singular. In speaking, however, people often use the plural pronoun *their*.

> **INFORMAL** **Neither** of the boys bought **their** own uniforms.

When no gender is specified, writers traditionally make a masculine pronoun agree with an indefinite antecedent.

> **Everyone** must buy **his** own uniform.

This rule, again, is one that is experiencing a change, because some people today prefer a more gender-neutral wording. If you do not want to use a masculine pronoun when the indefinite pronoun may refer to a female, try rewording your sentence. You might substitute a plural indefinite pronoun for the singular one or eliminate the personal pronoun entirely. (Although some people use two pronouns, many writers consider such wording awkward.)

> **All** must buy **their** own uniforms.
> **Everyone** must buy a uniform. [no pronoun]

Exercise 11

Making Pronouns Agree with Indefinite Pronoun Antecedents   On your paper indicate which of the following sentences are correct. Then revise each of the incorrect sentences to make it correct. In some cases you will need to change a single word to make a sentence correct; in others you may wish to revise the entire sentence.

Native American Medicine

1. Many of the Native American tribes relied on their shaman, or medicine man, to treat anyone who became ill.
2. All of the herbs in the shaman's collection had special curative powers of its own.
3. Many in the Dakota tribe drank powdered skunk-cabbage roots to relieve his asthma. ➡

4. Each of the women in the Cheyenne tribe would gather their own stock of wild mint, which was used to treat nausea.
5. Everybody searched for natural remedies for their illnesses; the Cree people chewed the cones of the spruce tree to soothe sore throats.
6. Among the Kiowa anybody with dandruff knew that their scalp should be washed with soaproot.
7. Some of the Utes treated his cuts and bruises with a salve made from the yarrow plant.
8. Many who lived on the frontier owed his life to natural cures.
9. Some of the pioneers ended their bouts with scurvy by eating wild garlic, a plant coveted by many Native American tribes.
10. Today few of our doctors question the curative powers of Native American medicines, and their respect for the shaman's remedies continues to grow.

17.6 Clear Pronoun Reference

Make sure that the antecedent of a pronoun is clearly stated and that a pronoun cannot possibly refer to more than one antecedent.

Vague Pronoun Reference

Do not use the pronouns *this, that, which,* and *it* without a clearly stated antecedent.

VAGUE	She is an excellent singer, and **this** was evident in the performance last night. [What showed in the performance? Her talent showed, but *talent* is not specifically mentioned.]
CLEAR	She is an excellent singer, and **her talent** was evident in the performance last night.
VAGUE	Last week our garage burned, **which** started from a kerosene heater. [What started from a kerosene heater? A fire started, but the word *fire* is not mentioned.]
CLEAR	Last week a fire, **which** started from a kerosene heater, burned our garage.

VAGUE	The Supreme Court is deliberating on the question of the death penalty, and **it** will have a great impact on the nation. [What will have a great impact? The Supreme Court's decision will, but *its decision* has not been specifically mentioned.]
CLEAR	The Supreme Court is deliberating on the question of the death penalty, and **its decision** will have a great impact on the nation.

Ambiguous Pronoun Reference

If a pronoun seems to refer to more than one antecedent, either reword the sentence to make the antecedent clear, or eliminate the pronoun.

UNCLEAR ANTECEDENT	When the tickets slipped between the reports, **they** were lost. [Which word is the antecedent of *they?* Were the tickets or the reports lost?]
CLEAR ANTECEDENT	The tickets were lost when **they** slipped between the reports.
NO PRONOUN	When the tickets slipped between the reports, **the tickets** were lost.

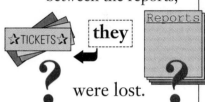

When the tickets slipped between the reports, **they** were lost.

Indefinite Use of Pronouns

Avoid the indefinite use of the pronouns *you* and *they.*

INDEFINITE	In Japan **you** bow after saying hello.
CLEAR	In Japan **people** bow after saying hello.

INDEFINITE	In some countries **they** take a nap after lunch.
CLEAR	In some countries **people** take a nap after lunch.

Exercise 12

Making Pronoun Reference Clear   On your paper rewrite each of the following sentences, making sure that all pronoun references are clearly stated.

1. The governor told the mayor that she would win by a landslide.
2. When the mayor thanked the governor, she was happy.
3. People who wish to vote must do so before 7:00 P.M., for after that you are turned away. ➡

4. Some citizens charged that the elections had been fixed, and it angered the officials.
5. The newspaper's editors criticized the politicians, and they argued for full disclosure of the facts.
6. The activists said that some politicians in the city had accepted bribes; this was a scandal.
7. Eric's father was mayor of the city, which gave him considerable social status.
8. When the newspapers disclosed the mayor's actions, it caused a great decline in his prestige.
9. The city council member told the newspaper reporter that he had manipulated the coverage of the election.
10. The early election returns pleased the senator, which had been widely predicted.

Exercise 13: Review

Pronoun Usage   Rewrite each of the following sentences by eliminating any mistakes in the use of pronouns. Each sentence has one error.

Sports Jargon
1. Sportscasters and us use sports jargon frequently.
2. More than one ordinary word changes it's meaning when applied to sports.
3. Anyone who watches tennis knows that you call an unreturned serve an ace.
4. The same word is used in golf, which refers to a hole in one.
5. In baseball a bean ball is a pitch thrown so near a batter's head that your head is in danger of being hit.
6. The batter must watch each ball carefully and determine it's speed and position.
7. We watched Roger Clemens pitch three shutouts in a row, and him pitching so well seemed almost miraculous to us.
8. My friends and me are familiar with the word *eagle*.
9. No one was more surprised than me to learn that in golf the word *eagle* means "two strokes under par."
10. I know sports, but it was her who first made me especially aware of sports jargon.

In the following excerpt from *Great Expectations* by Charles Dickens, the narrator, Pip, is discussing two other characters, Mr. Jaggers and Mr. Pocket. Note the many masculine pronouns. Try to see how Dickens avoids unclear pronoun references.

> My guardian took me into *his* room, and while *he* lunched, standing, from a sandwich-box and a pocket flask of sherry (*he* seemed to bully *his* very sandwich as *he* ate it), informed me what arrangements *he* had made for me. I was to go to "Barnard's Inn," to young Mr. Pocket's rooms, where a bed had been sent in for my accommodation; I was to remain with young Mr. Pocket until Monday; on Monday I was to go with *him* to *his* father's house on a visit, that I might try how I liked it.

If Dickens had written "I was to remain with him" instead of "I was to remain with *young Mr. Pocket*," readers might have wondered whether Pip was to remain with his guardian or with Mr. Pocket. Dickens avoided confusion and kept the pronoun references clear by simply referring to Mr. Pocket by name in the middle of the second sentence. When you revise sentences containing many pronouns, pause to make sure that each pronoun has a clear antecedent. If some references are confusing, rephrase the sentence, or replace some of the pronouns with the nouns to which they refer.

Apply these techniques in revising the following passage adapted from *Great Expectations*. Eliminate the confusion by making the unclear pronoun references clear.

> I found Miss Havisham and Estella; she [was] seated on a settee near the fire, and the other on a cushion at her feet. She was knitting, and Miss Havisham was looking on.

Usage Workshop

Using Pronouns Correctly

In this passage from *The Old Man and the Sea*, an aging Cuban fisherman named Santiago sets out for his day's work after eighty-four days without a catch. A young boy named Manolín has come to see him off. The passage has been annotated to show examples of the kinds of pronouns covered in this unit.

Literature Model

from THE OLD MAN AND THE SEA

by Ernest Hemingway

Pronoun in the possessive case

Pronoun *them* in the objective case used as a direct object. The pronoun agrees in number with its antecedent, *boats*.

Pronoun in the nominative case used as a subject

Pronoun in the nominative case used as a subject. The pronoun agrees in gender and number with its antecedent, *the old man*.

The boy was back now with the sardines and the two baits wrapped in a newspaper and they went down the trail to the skiff, feeling the pebbled sand under their feet, and lifted the skiff and slid her into the water.

"Good luck old man."

"Good luck," the old man said. He fitted the rope lashings of the oars onto the thole pins and, leaning forward against the thrust of the blades in the water, he began to row out of the harbor in the dark. There were other boats from the other beaches going out to sea and the old man heard the dip and push of their oars even though he could not see them now the moon was below the hills.

Sometimes someone would speak in a boat. But most of the boats were silent except for the dip of the oars. They spread apart after they were out of the mouth of the harbor and each one headed for the part of the ocean where he hoped to find fish. The old man knew he was going far out and he left the smell of the land behind and rowed out into the clean early morning smell of the ocean. He saw the phosphorescence of the Gulf weed in the water as he rowed over the part of the ocean that the fishermen called the great well because there was a sudden deep of seven hundred fathoms where all sorts of fish congregated because of the swirl the current made against the steep walls of the floor of the ocean. Here there were concentrations of shrimp and bait fish and sometimes schools of squid in the deepest holes and these rose close to the ➡

surface at night where all the wandering fish fed on them.

In the dark the old man could feel the morning coming and as he rowed he heard the trembling sound as flying fish left the water and the hissing that their stiff set wings made as they soared away in the darkness. He was very fond of flying fish as they were his principal friends on the ocean. He was sorry for the birds, especially the small delicate dark terns that were always flying and looking and almost never finding, and he thought, the birds have a harder life than we do except for the robber birds and the heavy strong ones. Why did they make birds so delicate and fine as those sea swallows when the ocean can be so cruel? She is kind and very beautiful. But she can be so cruel and it comes so suddenly and such birds that fly, dipping and hunting, with their small sad voices are made too delicately for the sea.

He always thought of the sea as *la mar* which is what people call her in Spanish when they love her. Sometimes those who love her say bad things of her but they are always said as though she were a woman.

Pronoun in the objective case used as the object of a preposition

Pronoun *they* in the nominative case used as a subject. The pronoun agrees with its antecedent, the irregular plural *fish*.

The pronoun *who* in the nominative case used as the subject of *love*

Usage Workshop Exercise 1

Choosing the Correct Pronoun Case   The following sentences give background information on the passage from *The Old Man and the Sea*. For each sentence determine whether the italicized pronoun is used correctly. If it is not, write the pronoun as it should appear. If it is used properly, write *correct*.

SAMPLE   Although the old man had been fishing for weeks, *him* finding nothing had not discouraged him.

ANSWER   his

1. The boy and Santiago had worked together for many years, but now *their* fishing together had ended.
2. The boy's parents disapproved of *him* working with an unlucky old fisherman.
3. It was *him* who had brought supper the previous night for the old man and himself.
4. Forgetting his parents, the boy had decided, "It is *us* who will eat supper together this evening."
5. Martin, the owner of a restaurant, had given the supper to Santiago and *he*.
6. Santiago once had a wife, whose picture he had removed from his wall since *it's* being hung there made him sad. ➡

7. The religious pictures in his shack were also *hers;* they and his bed were his few possessions.
8. Santiago never dreamed of the boy and *her,* though he loved them.
9. Santiago stood by the boat with the other fishermen as the fishermen and *him* prepared to leave.
10. By *him* fitting the ropes onto the thole pins, the old man secured the boat's oars.
11. Other fishermen were near, and Santiago could hear them rowing although he could not see their boats or *them.*
12. It was *him* who would catch a fish so huge that it would astonish the other fishermen.
13. The ocean suddenly became deep, and *it's* current made a deep swirl over the well in the ocean floor.
14. Santiago seemed to realize the ocean was beautiful, but the ocean was also cruel to wildlife and men like *he.*
15. The old man watched the terns and thought, "The gulls and terns have a harder life than *me.*"
16. He also pitied the sea swallows, and the sad voices he heard were *their's.*
17. Santiago heard many flying fish, and it was *they* that he regarded as his principal friends at sea.
18. Santiago landed a huge marlin, but *it's* size was a challenge.
19. After sharks bit the marlin's head, Santiago thought that the fish was now *theirs'* and his.
20. The boy might have reflected, "The struggle of Santiago and *I* against nature is unending."

Usage Workshop Exercise 2

Using Pronouns Correctly with and as Appositives

The following sentences are based on passages from *The Old Man and the Sea* that are not reprinted in this textbook. For each sentence determine whether the italicized pronoun appears in the proper form. If it does not, write the pronoun as it should appear. If the pronoun is used properly, write *correct.*

1. The restaurant owner sometimes fed the two fishermen, the boy and *he.*
2. The two early risers, Santiago and *him,* quietly left the hut and went to the boat.
3. Joe DiMaggio was a great athlete; apparently Santiago's idols were two baseball players, Dick Sisler and *him.*
4. While at sea Santiago caught a dolphin with two fish in its ➡

stomach; such catches, *they* and a tuna, were his only food.

5. Santiago loved the terns and watched two groups of birds, *they* and the swallows, while he fished.

6. Santiago hooked a marlin that attracted sharks; he had to contend with two powerful species, the marlin and *them*.

7. The other fishermen, the boy and *them*, were saddened by the sight of Santiago's poor marlin.

8. The boy might have decided, "Now we will again be partners, Santiago and *me*."

9. The boy thought, "The villagers, the other fishermen and *me*, have never seen such a fish."

10. Tourists showed interest in the fish, but no onlookers, not *them* or the fishermen, could fully understand Santiago's experience.

Usage Workshop Exercise 3

Using Pronouns After *Than* and *As*   The following sentences are based on passages from *The Old Man and the Sea.* Each sentence contains an italicized word or group of words. Rewrite each sentence, substituting the correct pronoun for the words in italics.

SAMPLE   Santiago was more patient than *most fishermen.*
ANSWER   Santiago was more patient than they.

1. Still, the other fishermen caught more fish than *Santiago*.
2. They did not even go as far out as *the old man.*
3. The boy might have concluded, "Santiago is braver than *the other fishermen.*"
4. Not caring as much for the other fishermen as he did for Santiago, the boy helped Santiago more than *the others*.
5. The old man rowed as steadily as *the younger fishermen.*
6. Later Santiago would seem to vow to the marlin, "You are not as strong as *Santiago.*"
7. Although the sea could be cruel to humans, Santiago reflected that it seemed more cruel to birds than to *his fellow human beings.*
8. The sea swallows searched as hard for food as *the terns.*
9. Watching its ceaseless waves, Santiago wondered whether anything was as cruel as *the ocean.*
10. Yet, did he love anything else as much as *the ocean?*

Choosing *Who* or *Whom*   The following sentences describe the history of Cuba, the setting of *The Old Man and the Sea* and Hemingway's home for many years. For each sentence choose the correct pronoun from the pair in parentheses.

1. When Columbus reached Cuba in 1492, he found the Taino, (who/whom) he discovered were farmers.
2. (Who/Whom) did the Spanish Crown appoint to conquer Cuba?
3. The island's mountains offered refuge for the natives, (who/whom) the Spanish treated harshly.
4. The Taino population, to (who/whom) European diseases proved deadly, became greatly reduced.
5. African slaves, (who/whom) the Spaniards wished to use for mining gold, were imported in 1524.
6. The slaves (who/whom) the plantation owners bought toiled long hours in sugar-cane and coffee fields.
7. Hernán Cortés, (who/whom) we know conquered Mexico, used Cuba as a base.
8. (Who/Whom) did you say established Havana as an important port?
9. Ports like Havana offered recreation for sailors, (who/whom) the natives entertained with African drums and Spanish guitars.
10. At sea many dangers threatened these sailors, (who/whom) pirates attacked regularly for their ships' gold.
11. Tobacco growers, (who/whom) the Spanish government regulated, rebelled unsuccessfully as early as 1717.
12. (Who/Whom) did you say told you that *criollos* are people of Spanish descent?
13. In Haiti slaves (who/whom) the American Revolution inspired rebelled and set up a free republic.
14. Cuban slaves, (who/whom) the government freed in 1880, revolted several times between 1812 and 1840.
15. Chinese laborers, (who/whom) nervous landowners recruited, added a new ethnic group to the Cuban population.
16. Cubans, (who/whom) Indian, Spanish, African, and Chinese cultures have influenced, share a colorful heritage.
17. In 1895 revolutionary armies (who/whom) were led by José Martí demanded Cuba's independence from Spain.
18. American investors, to (who/whom) an independent Cuba would be profitable, rejoiced when America aided ➡

the revolutionaries.

19. Cuban independence in 1898 attracted the attention of American businessmen, (who/whom) invested heavily in Cuba for nearly sixty years.
20. Nonetheless, peasant classes, to (who/whom) fishermen like Santiago belonged, continued to live in poverty.

Usage Workshop Exercise 5

Making Pronouns and Antecedents Agree   Each of the following sentences about terns contains an example of pronoun-antecedent agreement. Rewrite each sentence according to the directions in parentheses, changing the pronouns if necessary. In some cases you will also have to change the form of the verb and other words in the sentence.

SAMPLE   The fairy tern gets its name from its delicate beauty. (Change *The fairy tern* to *Fairy terns*.)

ANSWER   Fairy terns get their name from their delicate beauty.

1. These sea birds make tropical and semitropical islands their habitat. (Change *These sea birds* to *This sea bird*.)
2. The male tern grooms the female's face as part of his courtship. (Change *The male* to *Male terns*.)
3. As people watch the terns, their wonder at the birds' behavior increases. (Change *people* to *we*.)
4. Because females build no nest, their eggs appear in odd, even unsuitable, places. (Change *females* to *the female*.)
5. The mother often lays her egg on the edge of a roof or in the fork of a tree. (Change *mother* to *mothers*.)
6. Both of the parent birds take their turn tending the egg. (Change *Both* to *Each*.)
7. Fairy tern eggs hatch thirty-four days after they are laid. (Change *Fairy tern eggs* to *A fairy tern egg*.)
8. Many of the parents leave their young untended for hours while they search for food. (Change *Many* to *Some*.)
9. A flying fish sometimes finds itself in the throat of a hungry tern. (Change *A flying fish* to *Flying fish*.)
10. Chicks may fall to the ground while their parents are gone. (Change *Chicks* to *A chick*.)

Making Pronouns and Antecedents Agree   The following sentences are about Hemingway's characters. Each sentence contains an example of pronoun-antecedent agreement. Rewrite the sentences according to the directions in parentheses, changing the pronouns if necessary. In some cases you will also have to change the verb.

SAMPLE   Sports enthusiasts have compared their true experiences to Santiago's fictional one. (Change *Sports enthusiasts* to *A sports enthusiast.*)

ANSWER   A sports enthusiast has compared his true experiences to Santiago's fictional one.

1. Cuban fishermen have described their own struggles with a large fish. (Change *Cuban fishermen* to *A Cuban fisherman.*)
2. In these stories a marlin has fought as long as fifteen hours before it was caught. (Change *a marlin* to *a few marlins.*)
3. Two of Hemingway's skippers have stated their ideas about the true identity of Santiago. (Change *Two* to *Each.*)
4. Are some of the real people who found their way into Hemingway's fiction famous? (Change *some* to *any.*)
5. In fact, readers find themselves drawn to Hemingway's characters because of their realism. (Change *readers* to *we.*)
6. Have all of Hemingway's wives seen reflections of themselves in his female characters? (Change *all* to *each.*)
7. Any veteran of war might recognize his or her own feelings in Hemingway's soldiers. (Change *Any veteran* to *Veterans.*)
8. All people must fight personal obstacles to maintain their self-respect. (Change *All people* to *Everyone.*)
9. Hemingway characters show their valor amidst violence. (Change *Hemingway characters* to *A Hemingway character.*)
10. The stories, with their familiar conflicts, help us understand real life. (Change *The stories* to *Each story.*)

Review   Each of the following sentences describes aspects of Hemingway's life and work. For each sentence choose the proper pronoun from the pair in parentheses and write it on your paper. ➡

Ernest Hemingway

1. Ernest Hemingway, (who/whom) we know was one of America's finest writers, was born in Illinois in 1899.
2. Hemingway's numerous sports activities were balanced by (him/his) playing the cello and writing for his school newspaper.
3. His father was an outdoorsman, and the two of them, (he/him) and Ernest, often took fishing trips to Michigan.
4. It was (he/him) who discouraged Hemingway from enlisting in the army when the United States entered World War I.
5. While driving an ambulance in the war, Hemingway received a wound that might have killed a man who was weaker than (he/him).
6. In Paris after the war, Hemingway met F. Scott Fitzgerald and Gertrude Stein, both of (who/whom) influenced him.
7. These young writers, Fitzgerald and (he/him), were part of what Stein called the Lost Generation.
8. A friendship also grew up between the writer Sherwood Anderson and (he/him).
9. The Lost Generation writers found the politics and morality of (its/their) society destroyed by war.
10. (Who/Whom) would you say is the most admirable character in *The Sun Also Rises*, Hemingway's first novel?
11. Several pieces of Hemingway's writing found (its/their) way onto the movie screen.
12. Everybody has (his/their) favorite Hemingway novel.
13. Hemingway, (who/whom) many know was a journalist, wrote in a spare, unemotional style.
14. He and his third wife bought a home in Cuba in 1940; the couple, Ernest and (she/her), entertained many celebrities.
15. Some of these celebrities remember these adventures they had with Hemingway—for example, (their/them) watching bullfights in Spain and hunting in Africa.
16. This life style appealed less to Hemingway's third wife than to (he/him), and the marriage failed.
17. His wartime experience as an ambulance driver and as a news correspondent had (its/their) own profound effects on Hemingway's fiction.
18. Hemingway, (who/whom) Cuba fascinated, stayed in this tropical country even after Castro gained control in 1958.
19. *The Old Man and the Sea*, a best seller in 1952, led to (his/him) winning the Pulitzer and Nobel prizes.
20. In the years following Hemingway's death in 1961, the novel has retained (its/it's) immense popularity.

Proofreading   The following passage describes the artist Winslow Homer, whose painting appears on the opposite page. Rewrite the passage, correcting the errors in spelling, capitalization, punctuation, grammar, and usage. There are twenty-five errors in all.

Winslow Homer

[1]Winslow Homer (1836–1910 was one of America's finest watercolorists. [2]Born in Boston, Massachusets, him, along with his family, moved to the town of cambridge when he was six. [3]Growing up with his two brothers in the country, Homer learned to love the outdoors. [4]This interest in nature preoccupied him for much of his life.

[5]For the first seventen years of his long career Honer supported hisself by doing illustrations for periodicals, including *Ballou's Pictorial* and *Harper's Weekly*. [6]During the Civil war he was sent by *Harper's Weekly* to the front lines in Virginia, where he made many illustrations of battle scenes.

[7]Homer's training in illustration enables him to depict dramatic scenes naturally and unsentimentally. [8]With his masterful draftsmanship he was able to create a clear and honest record of landscapes and people as he saw it.

[9]After the War Homer began to exibit his paintings, which was very well received. [10]In his late thirties he began making watercolors directly from nature. [11]His watercolors are forceful, direct, and saturated with pure color. [12]Later in life she began to paint large and powerful canvases of the sea. [13]No American painter is more closely associated with scenes of the sea than him.

[14]*Palm Trees, Nassau* is charateristic of Homer's late watercolors. [15]The casual observer may see an apparently simple nature scene, but on closer scrutiny you can see the tension between the calm setting and the coming storm. [16]The trees bend in the rising wind, clouds scud acros the sky, and a red flag possibly signaling an oncoming hurricane) flutters near the lighthouse.

[17]*The Old Man and The Sea* is about an old cuban fisherman whom is confronted with the great power of nature. [18]In the passage from the novel reprinted in this textbook, Hemingway hints at the seas ominous power. [19]He writes, "She is kind and very beautiful. But she can be so cruel and it comes so suddenly." [20]Homers watercolor also evokes this insight.

Winslow Homer, *Palm Trees, Nassau,* **1898**

Using Pronouns Correctly

Using Personal Pronouns

[pages 577–581]

Indicate the correct personal pronoun in each sentence.

1. Two of the busiest people are my sister and **(a)** I / **(b)** me.
2. The fees are split between the two proprietors of the business, Mrs. Chin and **(a)** she / **(b)** her.
3. A neighbor asked Victor and **(a)** he / **(b)** him to walk her dog.
4. The dog was bigger than **(a)** they / **(b)** them.

Who *and* Whom

[pages 581–583]

Indicate the correct pronoun in each sentence.

5. The actor **(a)** who / **(b)** whom you admired won an award.
6. I wonder **(a)** who / **(b)** whom our substitute teacher will be.

Pronoun-Antecedent Agreement in Number and Gender

[page 584]

Indicate the correct pronoun.

7. The newest driver obtained **(a)** their / **(b)** her job last week.

Agreement in Person

[pages 585–586]

8. In which sentence does the pronoun agree in person with its antecedent?

a. Kim and Maria are going to Florida, where you can swim in the ocean.
b. After Bill and Patsy visited Mexico, they studied Spanish.

Agreement with Indefinite Pronoun Antecedents

[pages 587–588]

9. In which sentence is the agreement between pronouns correct?

a. Each of the critics expressed their opinions about the play.
b. Both of the critics published their reviews in the local paper.
c. Neither of the critics liked having their words quoted.

Clear Pronoun Reference

[pages 588–590]

10. In which sentence is the pronoun reference clear?

a. When the reporters met the politicians, they were polite.
b. The politicians answered the reporters' questions, which pleased the reporters.
c. One politician amused the crowd with a funny anecdote that was quoted in the newspaper the next day.

Writing for Review

Write a paragraph describing what your family does on Thanksgiving. Use a variety of personal and indefinite pronouns.

Unit 18 Using Modifiers Correctly

18.1 The Three Degrees of Comparison

Most adjectives and adverbs have three degrees: the positive, or base, form; the comparative form; and the superlative form.

The **positive** form of a modifier cannot be used to make a comparison. (This form appears as the entry word in a dictionary.)

The **comparative** form of a modifier shows two things being compared.

The **superlative** form of a modifier shows three or more things being compared.

swift

She ran **swiftly.**

POSITIVE	My cousin is **tall.**
	The cat ran **swiftly.**
COMPARATIVE	My cousin is **taller** than I am.
	My dog ran **more swiftly** than the cat.
SUPERLATIVE	Of the three cousins Paula is **tallest.**
	I ran **most swiftly** of all.

The following rules will guide you in forming the comparative and superlative degrees of adjectives and adverbs:

In general, for one-syllable modifiers add *-er* to form the comparative and *-est* to form the superlative.

swifter

green, green**er**, green**est**
The neighbor's grass always looks **greener** than ours.

loud, loud**er**, loud**est**
That sonic boom is the **loudest** noise I've ever heard.

She ran **more swiftly.**

fast, fast**er**, fast**est**
Her hair grows **faster** than mine.

In some cases adding *-er* and *-est* requires spelling changes.

big, bi**gger,** bi**ggest**
hot, ho**tter,** ho**ttest**
true, tru**er,** tru**est**
wry, wr**ier,** wr**iest**

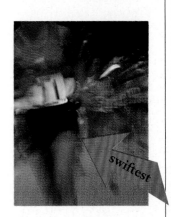

swiftest

With some one-syllable modifiers it may sound more natural to use *more* and *most.*

just, **more** just, **most** just
Of the three, that judge's ruling was the **most just** of all.

She ran **most swiftly** of all.

For most two-syllable adjectives add -*er* to form the comparative and -*est* to form the superlative.

> ugly, ugl**ier,** ugl**iest**
> Your mask is **uglier** than mine.
> That is the **ugliest** mask I've ever seen.

If -*er* and -*est* sound awkward with a two-syllable adjective, use *more* and *most*.

> afraid, **more** afraid, **most** afraid
> No one is **more afraid** of spiders than I am.

For adverbs ending in -*ly*, always use *more* and *most* to form the comparative and superlative degrees.

> clearly, **more** clearly, **most** clearly
> Lewis gives directions **more clearly** than most people.
> This candidate explains his views the **most clearly** of all.

For modifiers of three or more syllables, always use *more* and *most* to form the comparative and superlative degrees.

> attractive, **more** attractive, **most** attractive
> I think red looks **more attractive** on you than on me.

Less and *least,* the opposite of *more* and *most,* can also be used with most modifiers to show comparison.

> Are prepared foods **less economical** than fresh foods?
> I think cabbage is the **least appetizing** of all vegetables.

18.2 Irregular Comparisons

A few modifiers form their comparative and superlative degrees irregularly. It is most helpful simply to memorize their forms.

Modifiers with Irregular Forms of Comparison		
Positive	**Comparative**	**Superlative**
good	better	(the) best
well	better	(the) best
bad	worse	(the) worst
badly	worse	(the) worst
ill	worse	(the) worst
far (distance)	farther	(the) farthest
far (degree, time)	further	(the) furthest
little (amount)	less	(the) least
many	more	(the) most
much	more	(the) most

Exercise 1

Making Correct Comparisons   Complete the following sentences with the correct degree of comparison of the modifier in parentheses. (The positive degree is used in two of the sentences.)

SAMPLE   Of all the planets, which one is _____ the sun? (near)

ANSWER   nearest

Our Solar System

1. Our solar system is only a _____ part of the Milky Way. (tiny)
2. The planets are _____ than any other natural object in our solar system except the sun. (large)
3. Jupiter is the _____ planet in our solar system. (big)
4. Venus is _____ to Earth than Mars is. (close)
5. Mercury is a _____ planet. (small)
6. The _____ planet from the sun is Pluto. (distant)
7. Of all the descriptions of the motion of the planets, that of the seventeenth-century astronomer Johann Kepler is the _____. (accurate)
8. The _____ objects in our solar system are drifting particles called interplanetary dust. (minute)
9. Some asteroids—small, planetlike objects—have diameters _____ than 120 miles. (great)
10. A comet, with its bright head and glowing tail, is one of the _____ astronomical sights you will ever see. (dazzling)

Exercise 2

Making Correct Comparisons   Complete the following sentences with the correct degree of comparison of the modifier in parentheses.

SAMPLE   *The Joy Luck Club* is one of the _____ novels I ever read. (interesting)

ANSWER   most interesting

Amy Tan and The Joy Luck Club

1. *The Joy Luck Club* is an entertaining book, and it is _____ to read than many other contemporary novels. (easy)
2. The novel is by Amy Tan, perhaps the _____ voice in contemporary Asian-American fiction. (lively) ➡

3. In the book the members of the Joy Luck Club do many things, but their _____ activity is playing mah-jongg. (important)
4. Though she is _____ experienced than the other club members, June Woo is asked to join the mah-jongg game. (little)
5. The club members, who are June's aunts, are _____ than June and observe traditional Chinese customs. (old)
6. June is _____ to be with her friends than she is to be playing games with her aging aunts. (happy)
7. The aunts are the _____ of all when they are reminiscing about their years in China. (content)
8. China seems even _____ away for June than it does for her aunts, for whom China is a distant memory. (far)
9. Eventually, though, June learns that the _____ decision of all would be to abandon her Chinese heritage completely. (bad)
10. From all the aspects of her Chinese heritage, June learns to accept only the _____. (good)

Exercise 3: Sentence Writing

Creating Sentences That Make Comparisons   Select five of the irregular modifiers from the list on page 604. Write a sentence for each, using the positive and comparative degrees of the modifier. Underline each modifier.

SAMPLE   little
ANSWER   Add just a <u>little</u> salt to the water, even <u>less</u> than a teaspoonful.

18.3   Double Comparisons

Do not make a double comparison by using both -*er* or -*est* and *more* or *most*.

INCORRECT   A redwood grows ~~more~~ taller than an oak.
CORRECT   A redwood grows taller than an oak.

INCORRECT   Aunt Rosa is my ~~most~~ kindest aunt.
CORRECT   Aunt Rosa is my kindest aunt.

Correcting Double Comparisons   Rewrite each of the following sentences, correcting the double comparison.

Thomas Edison, Inventor

1. Many people believe that Thomas Alva Edison was the world's most best inventor.
2. Some people consider him even more greater than Leonardo da Vinci.
3. The phonograph and the electric light are probably his most usefulest creations.
4. Edison was most happiest with his phonograph.
5. But he was most proudest of his work on the electric light.
6. Electric light is certainly more safer than candlelight.
7. Edison also took others' inventions, such as the telephone and the typewriter, and made them more better.
8. As a boy Edison was more curiouser than other children.
9. He worked more harder and longer than his peers.
10. Historians agree that Edison was one of the most fruitfulest inventors of modern times.

18.4   Incomplete Comparisons

Do not make an incomplete or unclear comparison by omitting *other* or *else* when you compare one member of a group with another.

UNCLEAR	Mercury is closer to the sun than any planet.
CLEAR	Mercury is closer to the sun than any **other** planet.
UNCLEAR	My aunt has more pets than anyone.
CLEAR	My aunt has more pets than anyone **else.**

Be sure your comparisons are between like things.

UNCLEAR	The grace of a basketball player is more obvious than a baseball player. [The grace of a basketball player is being compared illogically with everything about a baseball player.]
CLEAR	The grace of a basketball player is more obvious than **that of a baseball player.**
CLEAR	The grace of a basketball player is more obvious than a **baseball player's.**

UNCLEAR	The claws of a lion are sharper than a cat.
CLEAR	The claws of a lion are sharper than **those of a cat**.
CLEAR	The claws of a lion are sharper than **a cat's**.

Exercise 5

Making Complete Comparisons   Rewrite the following sentences to correct the incomplete comparison in each.

Native American Dwellings

[1] Native American homes were just as varied as today. [2] The buffalo-skin dwellings of the Plains tribes were more portable than the Wichita. [3] The design of the tepees of the Plains tribes was perhaps more ingenious than any design. [4] Women were responsible for erecting the tepees, and they could do this faster than anyone. [5] Many people think that the tepee was more beautiful than any Native American dwelling. [6] The lodges of the Pawnees were warmer and sturdier than the Plains tribes. [7] Because the Pawnees did not move frequently, their homes were less portable than Native American dwellings. [8] The Pueblos of New Mexico were probably cooler than anyone, for they lived in well-insulated buildings made of clay. [9] Pueblo dwellings were several stories high, like many city dwellers today. [10] If I could, I would rather live in a tepee than any place.

18.5   *Good* or *Well; Bad* or *Badly*

Always use *good* as an adjective. *Well* may be used as an adverb of manner telling how ably something is done or as an adjective meaning "in good health."

Blue is a **good** color for you. [adjective]
You look **good** in blue. [adjective after a linking verb]
You dress **well.** [adverb of manner]
Aren't you feeling **well?** [adjective meaning "in good health"]

Always use *bad* as an adjective. Therefore, *bad* is used after a linking verb. Use *badly* as an adverb. *Badly* almost always follows an action verb.

That was a **bad** idea. [adjective]
The milk tasted **bad.** [adjective following a linking verb]
I feel **bad** about your moving to another state. [adjective following a linking verb]
The faucet is leaking **badly.** [adverb following an action verb]

Exercise 6

Choosing the Correct Modifier On your paper complete the following sentences correctly by filling each blank with *good, well, bad,* or *badly.*

Taking a Hike

1. No one can hike _____ without comfortable hiking shoes.
2. Improper equipment can make a hiker or camper feel _____ .
3. _____ planning is absolutely essential for a long and difficult hike.
4. A hike that is _____ planned will not be enjoyable and may be unpleasant.
5. Locating a _____ trail is one important aspect of planning a hike.
6. A hiker who is not feeling _____ can become a serious problem on the trail.
7. Hikers feel _____ if they cannot keep up with their companions.
8. If a hike begins _____, the hikers may become discouraged and decide to turn back.
9. The views along the Appalachian Trail look as _____ as the views that one sees in the Rocky Mountains.
10. Hikers should know their capabilities _____ before they start off on an ambitious hike.

Don't never use double negatives!

18.6   Double Negatives

In general, do not use a **double negative,** two negative words in the same clause. Use only one negative word to express a negative idea.

INCORRECT	I don't have ~~no~~ stereo equipment.
CORRECT	I do**n't** have **any** stereo equipment.
INCORRECT	We have~~n't~~ seen no concerts this year.
CORRECT	We have**n't** seen **any** concerts this year.
CORRECT	We have seen **no** concerts this year.
INCORRECT	My parrot ~~never~~ says nothing.
CORRECT	My parrot **never** says **anything.**
CORRECT	My parrot says **nothing.**

Avoiding Double Negatives On your paper rewrite the following sentences, eliminating the double negative in each. (Most sentences can be corrected in more than one way.)

Camping Tips

1. When our family goes camping, we like to find a site where there isn't no one around.
2. Don't never pitch your tent on sloping ground, for you will be very uncomfortable.
3. Nobody should never forget to dig a trench around the tent, in case it rains during the night.
4. Can't none of them help us pitch our tent?
5. It's best never to leave no food in your tent, for animals may be attracted to it.
6. One time my sister and I discovered a raccoon in our tent, and after that we didn't leave nothing edible inside.
7. In some wilderness areas campers aren't allowed to build no fires, and they must cook all their meals on a portable stove.
8. Some campers bring canned food along, but we don't bring none, because it is too heavy to carry.
9. My parents always pack dried food because it is light and doesn't never spoil.
10. When it is time to break camp, no one should leave no trash on the ground.

18.7   Misplaced and Dangling Modifiers

Place modifiers as close as possible to the words they modify in order to make the meaning of the sentence clear.

Misplaced modifiers modify the wrong word, or they seem to modify more than one word in a sentence. To correct a sentence with a misplaced modifier, move the modifier as close as possible to the word it modifies.

Soaring over the edge of the cliff, the photographer captured the eagle.

MISPLACED **Soaring over the edge of the cliff,** the photographer captured the eagle. [participial phrase incorrectly modifying *photographer*]

CLEAR The photographer captured the eagle **soaring over the edge of the cliff**. [participial phrase correctly modifying *eagle*]

| MISPLACED | He easily spotted the eagle **with his high-powered binoculars.** [prepositional phrase incorrectly modifying eagle] |
| CLEAR | **With his high-powered binoculars** he easily spotted the eagle. [prepositional phrase correctly modifying *he*] |

Dangling modifiers seem logically to modify no word at all. To correct a sentence with a dangling modifier, you must supply a word the dangling phrase can sensibly modify.

DANGLING	**Working all night long,** the fire was extinguished. [participial phrase logically modifying no word in the sentence]
CLEAR	**Working all night long,** fire fighters extinguished the fire. [participial phrase modifying *fire fighters*]
DANGLING	**After a valiant effort** the blaze was still raging uncontrollably. [prepositional phrase logically modifying no word in the sentence]
CLEAR	**After a valiant effort** the fire fighters still faced a blaze that was raging uncontrollably. [prepositional phrase modifying *fire fighters*]
DANGLING	**Sleeping soundly,** the raucous alarm startled me into consciousness. [participial phrase logically modifying no word in the sentence]
CLEAR	**Sleeping soundly,** I sprang into consciousness at the sound of the raucous alarm. [participial phrase modifying *I*]

Place the adverb *only* immediately before the word or group of words it modifies.

If *only* is not positioned correctly in a sentence, the meaning of the sentence may be unclear.

UNCLEAR	Dan **only** has art on Monday. [Does Dan have only one class on Monday, or does he have no class on any day but Monday? Or is Dan the only person (in a group) who has one class on Monday?]
CLEAR	Dan has **only** art on Monday. [He has no other class.]
CLEAR	Dan has art **only** on Monday. [He does not have art on any other day.]
CLEAR	**Only** Dan has art on Monday. [No other person has art on Monday.]

Exercise 8

Correcting Misplaced and Dangling Modifiers On your paper rewrite the following sentences, correcting the misplaced or dangling modifiers in each.

1. Walking along the shore, a shell cut Mr. Chin's foot.
2. In a great hurry the buzzer rang as Gustavo ran to the door.
3. Winston takes Sabah out on dates and no one else because she is only his girlfriend.
4. At the end of the block, Michael and Alicia discovered a hundred-dollar bill rounding the corner.
5. Yogurt sundaes were served to all the children smothered in granola.
6. Only a fire destroyed Kazuo's house, and the chimney was left standing.
7. Sleeping too late, the train had already left.
8. In the red dress the policeman arrested the woman.
9. We bought a stuffed bear from the vendor with fuzzy pink fur.
10. Howling at the moon, William saw a dog.

Exercise 9

Correcting Misplaced and Dangling Modifiers On your paper rewrite the following sentences, correcting the misplaced or dangling modifiers in each.

Going to the Circus

[1]The Barnum and Bailey circus is a big event, for it comes only to our town once a year. [2]Julio and I arrived early and took our seats inside the tent in high spirits. [3]Dimming the lights, the elephants lumbered into the ring. [4]Swinging their great trunks, the trainers marched the elephants in a circle. [5]On a tightrope high above the ring, we watched the acrobat walk steadily and fearlessly. [6]Three lions were released from a cage growling fiercely. [7]The clown pretended that he had been attacked by the lions, but one girl only in the audience screamed. [8]Galloping around the ring, a woman in a blue sequined dress waved to the crowd on horseback. [9]Julio watched nervously as the trapeze artists leaped through the air clutching his seat. [10]Under the stars our hearts were content as we walked home.

Modifiers   The following paragraph contains ten errors in the use of modifiers. Rewrite the paragraph, correcting the errors.

Ted Williams, Home-Run Ace

[1] Ted Williams is considered one of the most finest baseball players of all time. [2] At the age of seventeen, the San Diego Padres was the team he joined. [3] By 1939 he was playing good enough to start with the Boston Red Sox. [4] From that time until his retirement in 1960, Ted Williams only played baseball with the Red Sox; he never played for no other team. [5] Williams was one of baseball's all-time most greatest hitters. [6] His batting average was higher than most other players. [7] He hit especially good in 1941, when he had a .406 batting average. [8] Williams did not do so bad in 1942 either. [9] In both 1941 and 1942 he hit more home runs than any player in the league.

Modifiers   On your paper rewrite any of the following sentences in which there are errors in the use of modifiers, correcting the errors in your revision. Write *correct* for each sentence that does not contain any errors.

Famous Comic Strips

1. In 1897 the first comic strip appeared in the *New York Journal*, called "The Yellow Kid."
2. The next comic strip to come along was "The Katzenjammer Kids," whose prankster stars, Hans and Fritz, usually behaved bad.
3. Hans and Fritz never gave the Captain and Momma no peace.
4. In "Mutt and Jeff," a strip that started in 1908, Mutt is always more taller than Jeff.
5. "Mutt and Jeff" was one of the most early strips to appear in the newspaper in color.
6. All the comic strips in the early years depended upon slapstick more than any form of comedy.
7. Based on real-life people, the cartoonist of "The Gumps" drew popular characters.
8. The character Andy Gump had a mustache, but he didn't have no chin.
9. First appearing in 1919, Frank King sometimes drew innovative backgrounds for his "Gasoline Alley" strip. ➡

10. People liked this strip good, especially after the character Uncle Walt adopted little Skeezix.
11. Before "Gasoline Alley" there had been no comic strip in which the characters grew up and aged.
12. Although full of crusading political content, "Little Orphan Annie" also told a good story.
13. The eyes of Little Orphan Annie are larger than most people.
14. For its first ten years the "Thimble Theatre" comic didn't have no Popeye in it.
15. "Blondie" was more widely circulated than any comic strip.
16. Dagwood, Blondie's husband, only made huge sandwiches when he raided the refrigerator; he never made an average-sized sandwich.
17. In his pursuit of such bizarre criminals as Flattop and Eighty-eight Keys, a yellow hat and square jaw were the trademarks of the cartoon detective Dick Tracy.
18. In "Peanuts" Pigpen is more dirtier than his friends Charlie Brown, Lucy, and Linus.
19. "We have met the enemy, and he is us," said the comic-strip opossum Pogo in a famous comment on the ecological crisis.
20. In spite of its sometimes controversial political remarks, Garry Trudeau won a Pulitzer Prize for his "Doonesbury" strip.

Good writers are careful about the clear use and placement of modifiers. Notice, for example, the italicized modifiers in the following passage from Alice Walker's story "The Flowers":

> *Turning her back on the rusty boards of her family's sharecropper cabin*, Myop walked along the fence till it ran into the stream made by the spring. Around the spring, *where the family got drinking water*, silver ferns and wildflowers grew.

Now consider how this passage would sound with a dangling participial phrase in the first sentence and a misplaced adjective clause in the second sentence. The passage would be awkward and confusing.

> *Turning her back on the rusty boards of her family's sharecropper cabin*, the fence was walked along till it ran into the stream made by the spring. *Where the family got drinking water*, silver ferns and wildflowers grew around the spring.

When you write and revise your own work, keep these guidelines in mind:

1. Avoid dangling modifiers by making sure you include the word or phrase being modified. In the second passage above, the italicized participial phrase dangles because the noun it modifies was omitted. In contrast, Walker's version includes the name *Myop*, the noun being modified.

2. Check to see whether moving a modifier or moving other words in the sentence will make your meaning clearer. For example, compare the second sentence of each passage above. Notice how much clearer Walker's version is, because she puts the clause "where the family got drinking water" near the noun it modifies, *spring*.

Apply both of these rules in revising the following passage, which contains misplaced and dangling modifiers. Write your revision of the passage on a separate sheet of paper.

> Alice Walker grew up in rural Georgia, born to a family of sharecroppers. In the South she later taught literature at several universities and then worked as an editor of *Ms.*, the well-known magazine for women, in New York City. After producing several volumes of poetry and fiction, Walker's novel *The Color Purple* won a 1983 Pulitzer Prize.

Usage Workshop

Using Modifiers Correctly

The passage in this workshop is taken from _An American Childhood_, a memoir by Annie Dillard. In it Dillard recalls her fascination with books describing the pleasures and perils of rock collecting, one of her hobbies as a child. The passage has been annotated to show the kinds of modifiers covered in this unit.

Literature Model

from AN AMERICAN CHILDHOOD
by Annie Dillard

People who collected rocks called themselves "rock-hounds." In the worst of cases, they called their children "pebble pups." Rockhounds seemed to be **wild** and obsessive amateurs, my kind of people, who had stepped aside from the rush of things to devote themselves to folly. . . .

Some rockhounds had **recently** taken up scuba diving. These people dove down into "brawling mountain streams" with tanks on their backs to look for crystals underwater, or to pan for gold. The gold panning was especially **good** under boulders in rapids.

One book included a photograph of a mild-looking hobbyist in his basement workshop: he sawed chunks of Utah wonderstone into wavy, landscapy-looking slabs suitable for wall hangings. Here was a photograph of rockhounds in the field: two men on a steep desert hillside delightedly smash a flat rock to bits with two hammers. Far below stands a woman in a dress and sensible shoes, doing nothing. Here is their campsite: a sagging black pyramidal tent pitched on the desert floor. A Studebaker fender nudges the foreground. The very hazards of field collecting tempted me: "tramping for miles over rough country," facing cold, heat, rain, cactus, rough lava, insects, rattlesnakes, scorpions, and glaring alkali flats. Collectors fell over boulders and damaged crystals. Their ballpoint pens ran out of ink. . . .

Getting back home alive **only** aggravated their problems. If you bring home five hundred pounds of rocks from an ➡

Positive form of the adjective wild

Positive form of the adverb recently

Correct use of good

Correctly placed prepositional phrase modifying men

Correct placement of the adverb only

average collecting trip, what do you do with them? Splay them attractively about the garden, one book suggested lamely. Give them away. Hold yard sales. One collector left five tons of rough rock in his yard when he moved. . . .

On the other hand, rock collecting had unique rewards. For example, the thinner you sliced your specimens when you sawed them up, the more specimens you had. In this way you could multiply your collection without leaving home.

— Comparative form of the adverb *thin*

Usage Workshop Exercise 1

Making Correct Comparisons The following sentences are about rock collecting. For each sentence, write on your paper the proper comparative or superlative form of the modifier in parentheses.

SAMPLE Rock collecting is _____ in some areas than in others. (easy)

ANSWER easier

1. Rock hunting in areas where the ground is already broken, such as quarries and building sites, is _____ than hunting in areas with unbroken ground. (simple)
2. Some rock hunters gather rocks at a local site, whereas others travel _____ than that for specimens. (far)
3. One of the _____ practices to engage in while rock hunting is trespassing on private property. (bad)
4. One of the _____ and most dangerous things a rock hunter can do is hunt alone on a steep rock wall. (silly)
5. Of the rock hunter's various tools, a rock hammer is the _____ implement for loosening solid rock. (good)
6. To loosen individual crystals, a chisel works _____ than a pocketknife. (good)
7. Museum specimens are often larger and _____ than those kept by amateur rock collectors. (impressive)
8. Minerals can be identified _____ than rocks because the atoms in minerals are arranged in a regular pattern, resulting in the formation of crystals. (quickly)
9. Rocks and minerals cannot always be identified simply by looking at them; _____ testing is often required. (far)
10. Of the various testing methods, the one that is probably used _____ is the streak test. (frequently)

Correcting Double Comparisons   The following sentences are based on passages from *An American Childhood* that are not reprinted in this textbook. Rewrite the sentences, correcting any errors of double comparison. If a sentence contains no errors, write *correct*.

SAMPLE	To outsiders no one seems more crazier than rockhounds.
ANSWER	To outsiders no one seems crazier than rockhounds.

1. The young Annie Dillard liked nothing more better than the natural sciences.
2. She was more curiouser about rocks than she was about stamps or coins.
3. To Dillard rock hunting seemed like the most liveliest of hobbies.
4. The books she read showed rockhounds hunting for specimens in the most wildest places imaginable.
5. Although Dillard obtained her own specimens by less ruggeder methods, she still found the rocks' secrets intriguing.
6. Some plain-looking rocks, when scratched on a rough surface, created streaks of color more brighter than greasepaint.
7. Even the dullest rocks, when cracked open, might reveal lovely crystals inside.
8. Of the rocks in Dillard's collection, the most prettiest was a red one called cinnabar.
9. Many minerals have strange names, but chalcopyrite (a brassy yellow mineral) was the most hardest for Dillard to pronounce.
10. Dillard longed to possess rocks with names even odder than that of chalcopyrite: sillimanite and agaty potch, for example.

Correcting Incomplete Comparisons   The following sentences are about minerals and gemstones. Rewrite the sentences, correcting any errors of incomplete comparison. Some of the sentences can be revised in more than one way. If a sentence contains no errors, write *correct*. ➡

SAMPLE	The value of a diamond is far greater than a ruby.
ANSWER	The value of a diamond is far greater than that of a ruby.

1. On the Mohs scale, which lists minerals by their hardness, the mineral talc is softer than any mineral.
2. Quartz, a mineral that can cut glass, is much harder than talc.
3. Diamonds, among the world's most valuable minerals, are harder than anything in nature.
4. The facets, or flat surfaces, of a diamond are different from an amethyst.
5. Among beryls, which come in different colors, green is more valuable than any color.
6. Green beryls are called emeralds, and the value of some emeralds is higher than some diamonds.
7. The emeralds from Colombia are finer than those supplied by any South American country.
8. More fine rubies are found in Southeast Asia than anywhere.
9. The appearance of many synthetic rubies is very close to natural rubies.
10. Unlike most other gemstones, pearls are not minerals but an organic material.

Usage Workshop Exercise 4

Choosing the Correct Modifier   The following sentences are based on passages from *An American Childhood* not reprinted in this textbook. For each sentence choose the correct form of the modifier in parentheses, and write it on your paper. Then indicate whether the modifier you have chosen is being used as an *adjective* or an *adverb*.

SAMPLE	To the young Annie Dillard few hobbies seemed as (good/well) as rock collecting.
ANSWER	good—adjective

1. Dillard obtained the first rocks in her collection from a newspaper boy whom she did not know very (good/well).
2. The newspaper boy had received the rocks as a gift from a (good/well) customer named Mr. Downey.
3. Mr. Downey, an avid rock hunter and collector, could no longer maintain his collection because his health was failing (bad/badly). ➡

4. He had not been feeling (good/well) for several months and decided to give the collection to his newspaper boy, one of the few young people he knew.
5. The newspaper boy felt (bad/badly) because he did not have enough time to devote to the rock collection, and eventually he decided to give it to Dillard.
6. Some of the rocks were attractive; others did not look too (good/well).
7. The fact that he could identify only two stalagmites made the newspaper boy feel (bad/badly) about his right to the collection.
8. Dillard herself was not informed (good/well) about the rocks and minerals when she first accepted the collection.
9. Had someone tested her on the names of Mr. Downey's rocks, Dillard would have done quite (bad/badly).
10. It was (good/well) that Dillard was able to borrow and read several books about rocks and minerals.

Usage Workshop Exercise 5

Correcting Double Negatives   The following sentences are about precious metals. Rewrite the sentences, eliminating any double negatives. Most of the sentences can be corrected in more than one way.

SAMPLE   Finding precious metals isn't no easy task.
ANSWER   Finding precious metals is no easy task.

1. Gold is a very malleable metal; if you hammer it, it won't never break.
2. Because there isn't no more malleable metal, people began using gold for jewelry thousands of years ago.
3. In addition, nobody never has to worry that gold will tarnish, as many other metals do.
4. You can't make no jewelry out of pure gold, however, for it is too soft.
5. Pure gold is hardly never found; usually it is combined with another metal.
6. For centuries there wasn't nothing more valuable than gold, and many people tried to obtain it.
7. Silver was also deemed valuable, but there wasn't no interest in platinum until recently. ➡

8. In medieval times alchemists tried to create gold from other substances, but no one could make none of it.
9. Few early European explorers of the Americas hadn't never heard about the gold of the Inca and the Aztec.
10. Most prospectors who hunted for gold in nineteenth-century America never had no scientific training.

Usage Workshop Exercise 6

Correcting Misplaced Modifiers   The following sentences elaborate on ideas suggested by the passage from *An American Childhood.* Rewrite the sentences, correcting each misplaced modifier by shifting it or the term it modifies to a position that makes the meaning clearer. If a sentence has no errors, write *correct*.

SAMPLE   Dillard tried to identify unfamiliar rocks consulting books and visiting local museum displays.

ANSWER   Consulting books and visiting local museum displays, Dillard tried to identify unfamiliar rocks.

1. Rockhounds seem eccentric to conventional people, having an unusual obsession.
2. Everyday activities seem unimportant to adventurous rockhounds with their dull routines.
3. Divers find some of the most interesting specimens in mountain streams using scuba-diving equipment.
4. Rockhounds often pan for gold in streams leaving no opportunity unexplored.
5. Some hobbyists might find enough gold to turn a tidy profit in the water.
6. Browsing through a book, Annie Dillard noticed a strange photograph of a rockhound.
7. The picture showed a hobbyist sawing a chunk of wonderstone in his workshop destined for use as a wall hanging.
8. Lugging home hundreds of pounds of rock, the question of practicality gnaws at the hobbyist.
9. The rockhound now begins to search for ideas about unloading his bounty in books.
10. One idea is to sell the specimens to friends occupying too much space.

Correcting Dangling Modifiers   The following sentences elaborate on ideas suggested by the passage from *An American Childhood*. Rewrite the sentences, correcting each dangling modifier by adding appropriate information based on the passage. Reword the sentence if necessary. If a sentence has no errors, write *correct*.

SAMPLE   Finding rock collectors wildly impractical, their hobby was attractive.

ANSWER   Finding rock collectors wildly impractical, Dillard was attracted to their hobby.

1. Calling themselves "rockhounds," rock collectors sometimes called their children "pebble pups."
2. Pausing to reflect, rock hunting began to seem like a wild obsession to Dillard.
3. Strapping on their heavy tanks, the hunt for rock crystals in mountain streams began.
4. After studying the photographs and reading the anecdotes in books about rock collecting, Dillard decided the hobby was both artistic and adventurous.
5. Sawed into wavy slabs by one hobbyist, its suitability for wall hangings was achieved.
6. After climbing a steep desert hillside, the flat rock was joyfully smashed with two hammers.
7. Pitched in the desert, a black tent served as the rockhounds' flimsy refuge from the elements.
8. Hunting for unusual rock specimens in wild and isolated places, minor problems like running out of ink constantly arose.
9. After moving to a new home, five tons of rock remained in the yard of the rockhound's old house.
10. Tramping for miles over rough country, their ballpoint pens ran out of ink.

Review   Read the following biography of Annie Dillard. Then rewrite the sentences below it, correcting any errors in the use of modifiers. If you need additional information in order to complete any of your sentences, consult the biography. ➡

Annie Dillard

Born and raised in Pittsburgh, Annie Dillard fell in love with nature when, at the age of ten, she discovered *The Field Book of Ponds and Streams* at a local library. Always a fine scholar, Dillard was an honor-society member at Hollins College. For her master's degree she wrote a paper on Henry David Thoreau, the famous American nature writer to whom she is often compared. Dillard's journal of a year spent alone in rural Virginia became the basis for *Pilgrim at Tinker Creek*, which earned her the 1975 Pulitzer Prize. This vivid and introspective exploration of the natural world remains Dillard's best-known work. She has also published a volume of poetry and several more works of nonfiction, including her fine autobiography, *An American Childhood* (1987). Despite her success, Dillard claims to dislike writing because it takes her away from the great outdoors.

1. Writing vividly about the world of nature and her own experiences, Annie Dillard's books have enjoyed great popularity.
2. Some readers and critics consider her writings about nature as powerful as the classic American author Henry David Thoreau.
3. Born in Pittsburgh, her youth is described vividly in the book *An American Childhood*, an autobiography published in 1987.
4. As a child Dillard was an avid reader and almost never had no trouble with her schoolwork.
5. She later did good at Hollins College in Virginia and was elected to the school's honor society.
6. After spending a year in rural Virginia, her journal of that period was expanded into her acclaimed best seller *Pilgrim at Tinker Creek*.
7. *Pilgrim at Tinker Creek* is probably more popular than any book by Dillard.
8. In fact, although it was Dillard's first book, *Pilgrim at Tinker Creek* won her the 1975 Pulitzer Prize as the year's most finest work of nonfiction.
9. Dillard has only published a single volume of poetry.
10. Cooped up in her office, writing often keeps Dillard away from the natural world she loves.

Proofreading The following passage describes the artist Georgia O'Keeffe, whose painting appears on the opposite page. Rewrite the passage, correcting the errors in spelling, capitalization, punctuation, and the use of modifiers. There are twenty-five errors in all.

Georgia O'Keeffe

¹Born in 1887 in Sun Prairie Wisconsin, art was an early love of Georgia O'Keeffe's. ²She began studing art while still in her teens. ³In 1909 she worked in Chicago as an advertising illustrator but she resumed her art studies in 1912. ⁴O'Keeffe first worked as a teacher for the public school system in Amarillo Texas. ⁵She then taught art at the University of Virginia, and later returned to Texas to head the art department at West Texas State normal College.

⁶Although she had been painting good for some years, O'Keefe did not produce her first important works until 1915. ⁷They were large charcoal drawings based on elements in nature showing great promise. ⁸These works were seen and admired by the photographer and gallery owner Alfred Stieglitz. ⁹O'Keeffe's first exhibition was in 1916 at one of Stieglitz's galleries in New York city. ¹⁰Eight years later O'Keeffe and Stieglitz were married. ¹¹Every year until her husband's death in 1946, O'Keeffe had an exhibit at one of Stieglitz's galleries.

¹²After visiting New Mexico in 1929, the dessert landscape became O'Keeffe's main subject. ¹³She was more happier painting there than anywhere. ¹⁴After her husband's death she made Abiquiu, New Mexico her permanant home.

¹⁵O'Keeffe belonged to the first generation of American abstract artists, and drew on her American roots in particular the vast landscape of the arid Southwest) more than many of her compatriots. ¹⁶Unlike them, she was not greatly influenced by no european art. ¹⁷O'Keeffe often used large, simple forms that combined both soft and vivid colors. ¹⁸In many of her works, she exaggeratted the size or scale of an object.

¹⁹O'Keeffe painted some of the more dramatic landscapes in all America. ²⁰In *From the White Place* she used subdued tones and masive shapes to capture the dry, sun-bleached cliffs of northern New Mexico. ²¹A setting such as this would perhaps be attractive, to the kinds of rockhounds described by Annie Dillard.

Georgia O'Keeffe, *From the White Place,* **1940**

Using Modifiers Correctly

The Three Degrees of Comparison

[pages 603–606]

Choose the correct modifier.

1. Hydrogen is (a) <u>lighter</u> / (b) <u>more light</u> than oxygen.
2. Of the three books I liked *Rebecca* (a) <u>better</u> / (b) <u>best</u>.
3. Amanda is the (a) <u>secretivest</u> / (b) <u>most secretive</u> person I know.

Double and Incomplete Comparisons

[pages 606–608]

Indicate the correct comparison.

4. The groceries were (a) <u>heavier</u> / (b) <u>more heavier</u> than I expected.
5. Al eats more than (a) <u>anyone</u> / (b) <u>anyone else</u> I know.
6. Sometimes I think his capacity for food is greater than a (a) <u>lion's</u> / (b) <u>lion</u>.
7. The crocuses bloomed earlier than (a) <u>any</u> / (b) <u>any other</u> flowers.
8. There is no (a) <u>better</u> / (b) <u>more better</u> sign of spring!

Using Good *or* Well, Bad *or* Badly

[pages 608–609]

Indicate the modifier that is used correctly.

9. I felt (a) <u>good</u> / (b) <u>well</u> enough to play.
10. Carlos felt (a) <u>bad</u> / (b) <u>badly</u> about losing.
11. The pitcher threw so (a) <u>good</u> / (b) <u>well</u> that the crowd cheered.

12. The visiting team played (a) <u>bad</u> / (b) <u>badly</u>.
13. You played (a) <u>good</u> / (b) <u>well</u>.

Double Negatives

[pages 609–610]

Indicate the correct usage.

14. I have (a) <u>never eaten</u> / (b) <u>eaten</u> no sushi.
15. I don't see (a) <u>no</u> / (b) <u>any</u> other solution.
16. He hasn't chopped (a) <u>no</u> / (b) <u>any</u> wood.

Misplaced and Dangling Modifiers

[pages 610–612]

Choose the correct sentence.

17. a. Watching television, boredom soon set in.
    b. Watching television, we became bored.
18. a. In the vase I rearranged the tulips.
    b. I rearranged the tulips in the vase.
19. a. Yuki only has piano lessons on Thursdays.
    b. Yuki has piano lessons only on Thursdays.
20. a. Using a charcoal sliver, I drew a sketch of a German shepherd dog.
    b. I drew a sketch of a German shepherd dog using a charcoal sliver.

Writing for Review

Write a paragraph in which you compare two things, such as winter and summer. Use modifiers in making the comparisons.

Unit 19 Usage Glossary

The glossary that follows presents some particularly troublesome matters of preferred usage. The glossary will give you guidance, for example, in choosing between two words that are often confused. It will also make you aware of certain words and expressions that you should avoid when speaking or writing for school or business.

a, an   Use the article *a* when the word that follows begins with a consonant sound, including a sounded *h*: *a poem, a house*. Use *an* when the word that follows begins with a vowel sound or an unsounded *h*: *an apple, an heirloom*. Use *a* before a word that begins with the "yew" sound: *a European, a unit*.

a lot, alot   This expression is always written as two words and means "a large amount." Some authorities suggest avoiding it altogether in formal English.

> **A lot** of snow fell last night.

a while, awhile   *A while* is made up of an article and a noun. *In* and *for* often come before *a while*, forming a prepositional phrase. *Awhile* is an adverb.

> We'll stop in **a while.**
> We'll stop for **a while.**
> We'll stop **awhile** before hiking to the top of the mountain.

accept, except   *Accept* is a verb that means "to receive" or "to agree to." *Except* is a preposition or a verb. As a preposition it means "but."

> Eric will **accept** the trophy for the team.
> Alanna will not **accept** defeat.
> Everyone will be at the ceremony **except** the captain. [preposition]

affect, effect   *Affect* is a verb that means "to cause a change in; to influence." *Effect* may be a noun or a verb. As a noun it means "result." As a verb it means "to bring about or accomplish."

> The mayor's policies have **affected** every city agency.

> The mayor's policies have had a good **effect** on every agency. [noun meaning "result"]

> The mayor has been able to **effect** his goals in every city agency. [verb meaning "to bring about"]

ain't *Ain't* is unacceptable in speaking and writing unless you are quoting somebody's exact words. Instead, use *I am not; she is not; he is not;* and so on.

all ready, already The two words *all ready* mean "completely ready." *Already* is an adverb that means "before or by this time."

> The band was **all ready** to play its last number, but the fans were **already** leaving the stadium.

all right, alright Always write this expression as two words. Although the expression is often seen in print as one word, most language authorities prefer *all right*.

> She was sick yesterday, but today she feels **all right**.

all the farther, all the faster These are regional expressions. Use *as far as* and *as fast as* in writing.

> We drove **as far as** we could during daylight hours.

> I'm pedaling this bike **as fast as** I can.

all together, altogether Use *all together* to mean "in a group." Use the adverb *altogether* to mean "completely" or "on the whole."

> For the holidays our family will be **all together** at my grand-mother's house.

> My grandmother is **altogether** delighted to have us with her.

Exercise 1

Making Usage Choices For each of the following sentences, choose the correct word or expression from the pair in parentheses.

San Francisco

1. When gold was discovered in California in 1848, miners seeking their fortune traveled there (all the faster/as fast as) they could.
2. Although most prospectors found no gold, some of them discovered that staying on in California as ranchers or farmers was quite (all right/alright).
3. As a city San Francisco has everything residents could want (except/accept) a sunny climate, for it is often rainy and foggy.
4. In 1906 a terrible earthquake and fire destroyed much of San Francisco, but by 1916 the city had recovered and was (all ready/already) for a major cultural exposition. ➡

5. There are (a lot/alot) of people of Chinese ancestry in San Francisco.
6. About thirty-six thousand of them live in (a/an) area known as Chinatown.
7. The buildings in this district, many of which echo traditional Chinese architectural styles, create a picturesque (affect/effect).
8. Many visitors spend quite (a while/awhile) browsing in the shops on Grant Avenue, Chinatown's main thoroughfare.
9. There (ain't/is not) another Chinese community in the entire Western Hemisphere that is as large as San Francisco's Chinatown.
10. At first the Chinese families who immigrated to San Francisco lived (all together/altogether) in Chinatown, but now many of them have resettled in other parts of the city.

amount, number   *Amount* and *number* both refer to quantity. Use *amount* when referring to nouns that cannot be counted. Use *number* when referring to nouns that can be counted.

> Fort Knox contains a vast **amount** of gold.
> Fort Knox contains a large **number** of gold bars.

bad, badly   See Unit 18.

being as, being that   These expressions are sometimes used instead of *because* or *since* in informal conversation. In formal speaking and writing always use *because* or *since*.

> **Because** their car broke down, they could not get here.
> **Since** they did not call, we assumed they were not coming.

beside, besides   *Beside* means "at the side of." *Besides* means "in addition to."

> Katrina sat **beside** her mother at the table.
> **Besides** yogurt and fruit they had homemade muffins.

between, among   In general, use *between* to compare one person or thing with one other person or thing or with an entire group.

> What is the difference **between** Seattle and Portland? [Two cities are compared.]

> What was the difference **between** Pavlova and other ballet dancers? [One dancer is compared with an entire group of dancers.]

In general, use *among* to show a relationship in which more than two persons or things are considered as a group.

> The committee members were arguing **among** themselves.
> You are **among** friends.

borrow, lend, loan *Borrow* and *lend* have opposite meanings. *Borrow* is a verb meaning "to take something with the understanding that it must be returned." *Lend* is a verb meaning "to give something with the understanding that it will be returned." *Loan* is a noun. It may be used as a verb, but most authorities prefer *lend*.

> May I **borrow** ten dollars till payday? [verb]
> Will you **lend** me some money? [verb]
> Did the bank give you a **loan?** [noun]

bring, take Use *bring* to mean "to carry from a distant place to a closer one." Use *take* to mean the opposite: "to carry from a nearby place to a more distant one."

> Will you **bring** me some perfume when you come back from Paris?

> Don't forget to **take** your passport when you go to Europe.

can, may *Can* indicates the ability to do something. *May* indicates permission to do something or the possibility of doing it.

> You **can** make hot chocolate by dissolving cocoa in warm milk.
> You **may** have a cup of hot chocolate before going to sleep.

can't hardly, can't scarcely These terms are considered double negatives, because *hardly* and *scarcely* by themselves have a negative meaning. Therefore, avoid using *hardly* and *scarcely* with *not* or *-n't*.

> Eduardo **can hardly** tell the twins apart.
> The driver **can scarcely** see through the dense fog.

could of, might of, must of, should of, would of After the words *could, might, must, should,* or *would,* one should use another verb form, not the preposition *of.* Use the helping verb *have* after *could, might, must, should,* or *would.*

> Some historians say that the United States **could have** prevented the stock market crash of 1929.

> The country **might have** avoided the Great Depression that followed.

Making Usage Choices   For each of the following sentences, choose the correct word or expression from the pair in parentheses.

Kansas City

1. The Missouri River flows (between/among) Kansas City, Missouri, and Kansas City, Kansas.
2. If you look at a map, you (can/may) see that the Missouri River forms part of the boundary between Kansas and Missouri.
3. A large (amount/number) of Native Americans belonging to the Osage tribe once lived in the area that is now Kansas City.
4. Pioneers who settled in the area called the Native Americans living there Osage (being as/because) they could not pronounce the tribe's real name, Wazhazhe, which means "We Are the People."
5. (Beside/Besides) the Osage tribe, the Kansa, Otoe, and Missouri tribes lived in the area where Kansas City now stands.
6. Until the late nineteenth century visitors to Kansas City (could of/could have) seen several Native American tribes living around the town.
7. One (can scarcely/can't scarcely) exaggerate the importance of the role played by Native American tribes in the history of Kansas City.
8. Visitors to Old Shawnee, a restored mission near Kansas City, should bring their cameras or (borrow/loan) one from a friend.
9. Years ago Native Americans would (bring/take) furs to nearby Fort Osage and exchange them for manufactured goods.
10. In the 1870s the federal government resettled many Native Americans from Kansas on reservations in Oklahoma, and many historians claim that the plan was carried out (bad/badly).

different from, different than   The expression *different from* is generally preferred to *different than*.

The sport of cross-country skiing is very **different from** downhill skiing.

doesn't, don't   *Doesn't* is a shortened form of *does not*, which is used with *he, she, it,* and all singular nouns. *Don't* is a shortened form of *do not*, which is used with *I, you, we, they,* and all plural nouns. Authorities usually discourage the use of contractions in formal writing.

> Our state **doesn't** allow people to drive before the age of seventeen.

> Some foreign countries **don't** require their citizens to attend school.

emigrate, immigrate   Use *emigrate* to mean "to go from one country to another to live." Use *immigrate* to mean "to come to a country to settle there." Use *from* with *emigrate* and *to* or *into* with *immigrate.*

> Mr. Roh **emigrated** from South Korea.
> He **immigrated** to the United States.

farther, further   *Farther* should be used in reference to physical distance. *Further* should be used in reference to degree or time.

> San Antonio is **farther** south than Dallas.
> She did not question him **further.**

fewer, less   Use *fewer* when referring to nouns that can be counted. Use *less* when referring to nouns that cannot be counted. *Less* may also be used with figures that are seen as single amounts or single quantities.

> **Fewer** students have enrolled in physics this year than last year.

> This year there is **less** interest in physics among the students.

> We traveled to New York City in **less** than two hours. [*Two* is treated as a single period of time, not as individual hours.]

> It cost **less** than twenty dollars to go by train. [The amount of money is treated as a single sum, not as individual dollars.]

good, well   See Unit 18.

had of   Do not use *of* between *had* and a past participle.

> I wish I **had received** this information earlier.

hanged, hung   Use *hanged* when you mean "to put to death by hanging." Use *hung* in all other instances.

> The state of New Hampshire **hanged** three convicts between 1900 and 1950.

> The teacher **hung** the bulletin board above her desk.

in, into   Use *in* to mean "inside" or "within" and *into* to indicate movement or direction from the outside to a point within. The preposition *in* suggests a fixed location within a particular area or place. The preposition *into* suggests movement within or between locations.

> Jeanine was sitting outdoors **in** a lawn chair.
> When it got too hot, she went **into** the house.

irregardless, regardless   Use *regardless*. The prefix *ir-* and the suffix *-less* both have negative meanings. When used together, they produce a double negative, which is incorrect.

> **Regardless** of what the critics said, I liked the movie.

Exercise 3

Making Usage Choices   For each of the following sentences, choose the correct word or expression from the pair in parentheses.

San Antonio

1. During its early history San Antonio, now part of the state of Texas, was under the control of no (fewer/less) than six different countries.
2. Many people who first settled in San Antonio (emigrated/immigrated) from Spain.
3. The beautiful Spanish mission San José in San Antonio still looks (good/well) after many years.
4. Any group visiting San Antonio (don't/doesn't) want to miss seeing the old fort called Alamo.
5. To see the Alamo, the site of the famous battle between Texas and Mexico, you must go (in/into) the center of San Antonio.
6. Perhaps if the Texas garrison (had/had of) been larger, it could have withstood the Mexican attack.
7. (Irregardless/Regardless) of their defeat at the Alamo, the Texans went on to win the war against Mexico.
8. Officials (hanged/hung) the flag of the independent Republic of Texas in buildings in San Antonio from 1836 to 1845.
9. During the 1800s pioneers flocked to Texas, pushing the frontier (farther/further) west.
10. The modern city of San Antonio is quite different (from/than) the original Spanish settlement founded hundreds of years ago.

this kind, these kinds   *Kind* is singular. Therefore, the singular form *this* or *that* modifies *kind*. *This* and *that* should also be used with *sort* and *type* (*this type, that type, this sort, that sort*). *Kinds* is plural. Therefore, the plural form *these* or *those* modifies *kinds*. Also use *these* and *those* with the plural nouns *sorts* and *types*.

> **This kind** of bulb should be used in your lamp.
> **These kinds** of lamps are very attractive.
> **This sort** of food is found in many ethnic cuisines.
> **These sorts** of foods are nutritious.

lay, lie   *Lay* means "to put" or "to place"; it takes a direct object. *Lie* means "to recline" or "to be positioned"; it never takes an object.

> **Lay** your coat on the bed.
> I am going to **lie** in the sun now.

Problems arise particularly in using the principal parts of these verbs. Notice, for example, that the past tense of *lie* is *lay*. Learn all the principal parts of these verbs.

BASIC FORM	lay	lie
PRESENT PARTICIPLE	laying	lying
PAST FORM	laid	lay
PAST PARTICIPLE	laid	lain

> She **laid** her coat on the bed.
> I **lay** in the sun too long and got sunburned.

learn, teach   *Learn* means "to receive knowledge," and *teach* means "to give knowledge."

> Jon **learned** to play the piano at the age of ten.
> Mrs. Ramos **teaches** us American history.

leave, let   *Leave* means "to go away," and *let* means "to allow" or "to permit."

> When you **leave** next week, I will miss you.
> Please **let** me use your dictionary.

like, as   *Like* is a preposition and introduces a prepositional phrase. *As* is a subordinating conjunction and introduces a subordinate clause. Many authorities say that it is incorrect to use *like* before a clause.

> Phil plays baseball **like** a professional.

> Teresa is confident, **as** I am, that everything will go well on the expedition.

loose, lose   The adjective *loose* means "free," "not firmly attached," or "not fitting tightly." The verb *lose* means "to have no longer," "to misplace," or "to fail to win."

> That ring is so **loose** you are sure to **lose** it.
> Which team do you think will **lose** the game?

passed, past   *Passed* is the past form and the past participle of the verb *to pass*. *Past* may be an adjective, a preposition, an adverb, or a noun.

> We **passed** your house on the way to school. [verb]

> Chris had a cold this **past** week. [adjective]

> We drove **past** your house last Sunday. [preposition]

> What time did you drive **past?** [adverb]

> Louise's grandmother always tells wonderful stories about her **past.** [noun]

precede, proceed   *Precede* means "to go or come before." *Proceed* means "to continue" or "to move along."

> Our car **preceded** the homecoming parade as the parade **proceeded** through town.

raise, rise   The verb *raise* means "to cause to move upward"; it always takes an object. The verb *rise* means "to go up"; it is intransitive and does not take an object.

> **Raise** your hand if you know the answer.
> The rocket will **rise** from the launching pad at 9:01 A.M.

reason is because   *Because* means "for the reason that." Therefore, do not use *because* after *reason is*. Use *that* after *reason is,* or use *because* alone.

> The **reason** I am tired is that I did not sleep last night.
> I am tired **because** I did not sleep last night.

Exercise 4

Making Usage Choices   For each of the following sentences, choose the correct word or expression from the pair in parentheses.

New York City

1. New York, the most populous city in the United States, (lies/lays) near the mouth of the Hudson River in the southeastern corner of New York State. ➡

Set!

Now sit!

2. The reason New York is often called a melting pot is (because/that) many ethnic groups have settled there.

3. At the American Museum of Immigration near the Statue of Liberty, exhibits (teach/learn) visitors about the contributions made by people from many cultures who immigrated to the United States.

4. Also, the federal government now (lets/leaves) people visit Ellis Island, where nearly twelve million immigrants entered the country between 1892 and 1954.

5. If you wish to learn more about ethnic America, (like/as) our class did, you can visit the Hispanic Society of America, Japan House, and the Museum of the American Indian.

6. You can admire works by African-American artists at the Studio Museum in Harlem and then (precede/proceed) to the Schomburg Center, a library for the study of African-American culture.

7. At the Metropolitan Museum of Art, visitors can stroll (past/passed) an Egyptian temple and many exhibits of African and Asian art.

8. In Chinatown, near a large red-brick apartment building that (rises/raises) high above the street, is a bronze statue of Confucius, the venerable Chinese philosopher.

9. Tourists and New Yorkers alike enjoy visiting (these kinds/this kind) of places to learn more about our country's multicultural heritage.

10. As it was in the past, New York is still a city in which people of many races and ethnic backgrounds can live together and not (lose/loose) their cultural identity.

respectfully, respectively   *Respectfully* means "with respect." *Respectively* means "in the order named."

The audience listened **respectfully** as the poet spoke.

Phoenix and Phoenixville are, **respectively,** in Arizona and Pennsylvania.

says, said   *Says* is the third-person singular of the verb *say*. *Said* is the past tense of *say*. Be careful not to use *says* for *said*.

At dinner last night Nelson **said** that he wasn't hungry.
He always **says** that, but he eats everything anyway.

sit, set   *Sit* means "to place oneself in a sitting position." *Sit* rarely takes an object. *Set* means "to place" or "to put" and usually takes an object.

Set is also an intransitive verb, when it is used with *sun* to mean "the sun is going down" or "the sun is sinking below the horizon." When *set* is used in this way, it does not take an object.

> Grandpa likes to **sit** on the porch.
> Lian **set** the pots on the stove after the sun **set**.

than, then   *Than* is a conjunction used to introduce the second element in a comparison; it also shows exception.

> Elsa is taller **than** Isabel.
> Our visitor was none other **than** Uncle Al!

Then is an adverb that means "at that time," "soon afterward," "the time mentioned," "at another time," "for that reason," or "in that case."

> My grandmother was a young girl **then.**
> Marguerite finished the book and **then** turned out the light.
> By **then** the party was almost over.
> If it rains, **then** we cannot go.

this here, that there   Avoid using *here* and *there* after *this* and *that*. Use *this* and *that* alone.

> All of us want to read **this** magazine.
> Have you heard **that** story?

where at   Do not use *at* after *where*.

> **Where** is Valley Forge?

who, whom   See Unit 17.

Exercise 5

Making Usage Choices   For each of the following sentences, choose the correct word or expression from the pair in parentheses.

Santa Fe

1. Santa Fe, New Mexico, has more sites of historic interest (than/then) most American cities.
2. Tourists in Santa Fe can explore the narrow, winding streets and (than/then) visit museums that display Native American crafts.
3. In summer audiences (set/sit) in the open-air theater of the Santa Fe Opera.
4. (This/This here) opera house is one of the most famous in the world. ➡

5. Audiences listen (respectfully/respectively) as some of the world's greatest opera singers perform.
6. Pueblo Indians and Spanish colonists were, (respectfully/respectively), the first groups to reside in the Santa Fe area.
7. Many of the early Spaniards (who/whom) we know about in this area came to search for fabulous riches.
8. These early Spaniards reported hearing of a man who (said/says) he had seen seven cities of gold in the area.
9. Santa Fe is the place (where the historic Santa Fe Trail ended/where the historic Santa Fe Trail ended at).
10. (This/This here) trail was used by pioneers traveling west during the 1800s.

Exercise 6: Review

Usage (Part 1) For each of the following sentences, choose the correct word or expression from the pair in parentheses.

New Orleans

1. New Orleans, Louisiana, has (a/an) average elevation of one foot above sea level.
2. (A lot/Alot) of levees were constructed along the banks of the Mississippi River to prevent flooding.
3. The Mississippi River flows through Baton Rouge and then (precedes/proceeds) southeast to New Orleans.
4. New Orleans (ain't/is not) only a shipping center.
5. (Being that/Because) New Orleans is picturesque, many people enjoy vacationing there.
6. The temperature in the winter months (doesn't/don't) drop below freezing very often.
7. French and Spanish colonists (preceded/proceeded) Americans in settling New Orleans.
8. Many people from Italy (emigrated/immigrated) to New Orleans.
9. In New Orleans restaurants customers can choose (among/between) French and Creole cuisine.
10. Most visitors enjoy strolling through the streets of the historic French Quarter for quite (a while/awhile), taking in the beautiful architecture.
11. No skyscrapers (raise/rise) above the low skyline of the French Quarter.
12. Visitors need walk no (farther/further) than Basin and Bourbon streets to hear jazz. ➡

13. A large (number/amount) of visitors attend concerts at music halls like the famous Preservation Hall.
14. Visitors crowd (in/into) this small hall whenever jazz is being played.
15. In Preservation Hall fans (set/sit) their coats on their laps as they (set/sit) on the crowded wooden benches.
16. Here musicians play jazz (like/as) it was played in the early 1900s.
17. This style of jazz is quite (different from/different than) the style of modern jazz.
18. By February of each year, the citizens of New Orleans are (all ready/already) to hold their famous Mardi Gras festival.
19. During Mardi Gras the city (can scarcely/can't scarcely) accommodate its many visitors.
20. During this celebration it is (all right/alright) to take a vacation from work, dress in elaborate costumes, and take part in carnivals and parades.

Exercise 7: Review

Usage (Part 2)   For each of the following sentences, choose the correct word or expression from the pair in parentheses.

Boston

1. Boston is an (all together/altogether) special place.
2. If it were more centrally located, Boston (might have/ might of) been the nation's capital.
3. New York City and Philadelphia were, (respectively/ respectfully), the first and second capitals of the United States.
4. In 1773 Bostonians who would not (accept/except) King George III's taxes dumped many pounds of tea into Boston Harbor.
5. They wanted independence from England (bad/badly).
6. They (set/sit) several demands before the English king.
7. The government of the city of Boston has (hanged/hung) plaques at historic sites.
8. Beacon Hill, more (than/then) any other area in Boston, is known for its beauty and historic importance.
9. Boston is a very accessible city. The reason is (because/that) it has an efficient transit system.
10. If you want to get from the suburbs to the city center, just go (in/into) the nearest station of the rapid transit system, and you'll be there in no time. ➡

11. Be sure to (bring/take) a raincoat if you come to Boston in the fall, for it is often stormy.
12. A visitor can tour the Boston Museum of Fine Arts and (then/than) visit the Metropolitan Boston Arts Center.
13. Boston abounds in (this kind/these kinds) of cultural centers.
14. After the Charles River has (passed/past) through the city, it empties into Boston Harbor.
15. People can picnic in the parks (beside/besides) the river.
16. A visitor who likes to walk (can/may) follow the Freedom Trail to many of Boston's historic sites.
17. Along the one-and-a-half-mile-long trail are no (less/fewer) than fifteen historic sites.
18. Guide books will (learn/teach) the visitor about places on the trail.
19. The visitor will not (lose/loose) the way because the trail is well marked.
20. Time spent in Boston (can't hardly/can hardly) be forgotten.

Exercise 8: Review

Usage (Part 3) For each of the following sentences, choose the correct word or expression from the pair in parentheses.

Seattle

1. Recently a report (said/says) that Seattle, Washington, is one of America's most attractive cities.
2. (Irregardless/Regardless) of whether or not people choose to live in Seattle, most agree it is a beautiful place.
3. Many tourists (who/whom) the Century 21 Exposition attracted in 1962 later returned to Seattle to live.
4. Seattle is known as the Emerald City, a name (borrowed/loaned) from *The Wizard of Oz*.
5. The city of Seattle (lays/lies) near the Pacific Ocean.
6. (This/This here) location made Seattle a gateway to the Far East.
7. Many Japanese were (between/among) Seattle's early settlers.
8. Other early settlers (emigrated/immigrated) from Scandinavia.
9. A glance at the beautiful Cascade Mountains east of Seattle can easily (raise/rise) one's spirits.
10. This is the mountain range (where Mount Saint Helens is located/where Mount Saint Helens is located at).

Usage (Part 4)   For each of the following sentences, choose the correct word or expression from the pair in parentheses.

Atlanta

 1. (Leave/Let) us go to Atlanta, Georgia.
 2. Atlanta is a larger city (than/then) Birmingham, Alabama.
 3. Today's Atlanta is very (different from/different than) the city portrayed in *Gone with the Wind.*
 4. Traces of the Old South (can't hardly/can hardly) be found in Atlanta.
 5. A devastated city after the Civil War, Atlanta is more than (alright/all right) now.
 6. Other cities seeking Atlanta's success have done (like/as) Atlanta has.
 7. Because of its location, Atlanta is (all ready/already) well situated as a transportation crossroads.
 8. By promoting itself (good/well), Atlanta attracted national corporations and federal government offices.
 9. Some visitors who (could have/could of) seen the *Cyclorama*, a depiction of the Battle of Atlanta and one of the three largest paintings in the world, (passed/past) it up.
10. Many of those who see the painting agree that its (affect/effect) is striking.

Usage Workshop

Usage Glossary

The following quotations, which relate to the themes of friendship and love, have been annotated to show usage items covered in this unit.

Literature Models

QUOTATIONS ABOUT FRIENDSHIP AND LOVE

The relative pronoun *who* in the nominative case because it is the subject of a clause

He who has a thousand friends has not a friend to spare.
And he who has one enemy will meet him everywhere.

From *Sentences* by Ali Ibn-Abi-Talib (seventh century),
translated from the Arabic

Can used to suggest ability

To me, fair friend, you never can be old. . . .

From Sonnet 104 by William Shakespeare

The preposition *into* used to suggest movement from outside to inside

The preposition *in* used to mean "inside"

I breathed a song into the air,
It fell to earth, I knew not where. . . .
And the song, from beginning to end,
I found again in the heart of a friend.

From "The Arrow and the Song" by Henry Wadsworth Longfellow

Except used as a preposition meaning "but"

"Every man's his own friend." "Except sometimes some people are nobody's enemies but their own."

From *Oliver Twist* by Charles Dickens

Like, a preposition, used to introduce a prepositional phrase

For there is no friend like a sister
In calm or stormy weather;
To cheer one on the tedious way,
To fetch one if one goes astray. . . .

From "Goblin Market" by Christina Rossetti

May used to suggest possibility

The process of falling in love at first sight is as final as it is swift . . . , but the growth of true friendship may be a life-long affair.

From *The Country of the Pointed Firs* by Sarah Orne Jewett ➡

Only solitary men know the full joys of friendship. Others have their family; but to a solitary and an exile his friends are everything.

From *Shadows on the Rock* by Willa Cather

The articles *a* used before a word beginning with a consonant and *an* used before a word beginning with a vowel

We have fewer friends than we imagine, but more than we know.

From *The Book of Friends* by Hugo von Hofmannsthal, translated from the German by Mary Hottinger and Tania and James Stern

Fewer used to refer to something that can be counted

Among those whom I like or admire, I can find no common denominator, but among those whom I love, I can: all of them make me laugh.

From *The Dyer's Hand* by W. H. Auden

The relative pronoun *whom* in the objective case because it is a direct object

"Love, Umi, means something very different from 'falling in love,' " Daddyji said. "It's not an act but a lifelong process. . . ."

From *The Ledge Between the Streams* by Ved Mehta

Different from rather than *different than*

Usage Workshop Exercise 1

Making Usage Choices   These sentences describe friendships between famous artists. For each item choose the correct word or expression in parentheses, and write it on your paper.

1. Though very (different from/different than) each other in temperament, the Dutch painter Vincent van Gogh and the French painter Paul Gauguin were close friends.
2. The French artist Edgar Degas noted the similarities (between/among) his drawing style and that of his friend, the American artist Mary Cassatt.
3. (Beside/Besides) Degas, Cassatt was also friendly with several other Impressionists.
4. (Being as/Since) Berthe Morisot's close friend, fellow French painter Edouard Manet, so admired one of her paintings, she gave it to him as a gift.
5. The friendship may have influenced Morisot's work more (than/then) it influenced that of Manet.
6. Spanish artist Pablo Picasso and French artist Georges Braque had a great (affect/effect) on each other's work.
7. They are known as the founders of Cubism, which was an (all together/altogether) new style of art for its time.
8. In the 1920s the Russian artist Wassily Kandinsky and ➡

the Swiss artist Paul Klee were colleagues at the Bauhaus, a school of architecture and design in Berlin, (where they taught painting/where they taught painting at).

9. An artistic friendship between two Americans, the painter Georgia O'Keeffe and the photographer Alfred Stieglitz, (preceded/proceeded) their marriage.

10. Stieglitz (hanged/hung) O'Keeffe's paintings in his gallery.

Usage Workshop Exercise 2

Making Usage Choices The following sentences describe friendships between famous writers. Choose the correct word or expression in parentheses, and write it on your paper.

1. In Rome in the first century B.C., the poet Virgil was supported, (like/as) his friend and fellow poet Horace was, by the patron Maecenas.
2. (This/This here) article says that the writers Edith Wharton and Henry James were friends.
3. The authors Gustave Flaubert and Ivan Turgenev exchanged letters faithfully for two decades; (this kind/these kinds) of long-term correspondence is now rare.
4. Flaubert and Turgenev had (all ready/already) published some of their most famous novels when they met in 1863.
5. *Madame Bovary* and *Fathers and Sons*, by Flaubert and Turgenev (respectfully/respectively), remain classics.
6. Herman Melville befriended his fellow American writer Nathaniel Hawthorne, (who/whom) he greatly admired.
7. During these authors' lifetime, Hawthorne's works were more widely read (than/then) Melville's.
8. The novelists Joseph Conrad and Ford Madox Ford collaborated on two novels that are (all right/alright).
9. In the course of their friendship, the American poets Elizabeth Bishop and Marianne Moore (must of/must have) enjoyed each other's lively wit and humor.
10. The poet Joseph Brodsky received much support from his fellow Russian poet Anna Akhmatova before he was forced to (immigrate/emigrate) to the United States.

Usage Workshop Exercise 3

Making Usage Choices The following sentences describe famous fictional friendships and romances. For each sentence ➡

choose the correct word or expression in parentheses, and write it on your paper.

1. In Arthur Conan Doyle's works Sherlock Holmes investigates a great (amount/number) of criminal cases.
2. Horatio tells his dear friend Hamlet, one of Shakespeare's tragic heroes, that he has seen a ghost of Hamlet's father (raise/rise) from the dead.
3. Romeo and Juliet, Shakespeare's famous young lovers, (can't/can't hardly) bear to be apart from each other.
4. By the end of Jane Austen's novel *Pride and Prejudice*, Elizabeth Bennet thinks she had (passed/past) judgment on Mr. Darcy much too quickly.
5. In Emily Brontë's novel *Wuthering Heights*, Cathy's brother, who feels (bad/badly) about her impending marriage to Heathcliff, tries to prevent the match and causes a tragedy.
6. In Tolstoy's novel *War and Peace* Prince Andrei and Pierre are devoted friends, (irregardless/regardless) of their opposing personalities.
7. Huckleberry Finn and Tom Sawyer have (a lot/alot) of adventures together in Mark Twain's novels.
8. At the outset of Herman Melville's *Moby-Dick*, Ishmael is terrified when he finds that he is (laying/lying) beside the bizarre-looking Queequeg in their shared hotel room, but they later become close friends.
9. Unhappy at school, the orphan Jane Eyre, Charlotte Brontë's heroine, finds comfort for (a while/awhile) in a friendship with the sweet but sickly Helen Burns.
10. Although Cervantes's character Don Quixote (looses/loses) touch with reality, his squire and friend Sancho Panza maintains common sense.

Usage Workshop Exercise 4

Making Usage Choices   The following sentences describe relationships from mythology and folklore. For each sentence choose the correct word or expression in parentheses, and write it on your paper.

1. In Homer's *Iliad* Achilles (borrows/lends/loans) his armor to his dear friend Patroclus, who lacks armor of his own, but Patroclus is nevertheless killed in battle.
2. Because Orpheus cannot (accept/except) the death of Eurydice, he enters the underworld to try to retrieve her. ➡

3. In a tale told by Ovid, the parents of Pyramus and Thisbe tell the young lovers they (cannot/may not) marry.
4. The reason Pyramus stabs himself is (that/because) he believes a lioness has killed Thisbe.
5. Orestes, with his friend Pylades, goes (in/into) the palace of Clytemnestra to avenge Orestes' father's death.
6. In Greek legend Damon and Pythias are willing to die for each other, (a/an) honorable trait that has made them symbols of true friendship.
7. Some versions of Arthurian legend say that King Arthur (should have/should of) been less trusting of Sir Lancelot.
8. Lancelot secretly loves Arthur's wife, Guinevere, so Arthur will not (leave/let) him remain in the kingdom.
9. Hansel and Gretel, of the Grimms' fairy tale, venture (farther/further) into the forest than they should.
10. Robin Hood, as well as his companions Little John and Friar Tuck, (doesn't/don't) believe that stealing from the rich to give to the poor is wrong.

Usage Workshop Exercise 5

Making Usage Choices   The following sentences describe collaborations in science. For each sentence choose the correct word or expression in parentheses, and write it on your paper.

1. In 1903 the inventors Orville and Wilbur Wright altered aviation history with the first sustained flight; its distance was (fewer/less) than 150 feet.
2. The French chemist Marie Curie, working (beside/besides) her husband, Pierre Curie, discovered the element radium.
3. The Curies' work caused scientists to (raise/rise) their hopes about treating certain medical problems.
4. The Swiss psychologist Carl Jung and the Austrian founder of psychoanalysis, Sigmund Freud, had a brief association that worked (good/well) for both of them.
5. Jung (might of/might have) supported Freud's ideas initially, but he later disputed many of Freud's doctrines.
6. The discovery of the DNA double helix by James D. Watson and Francis H. C. Crick advanced (farther/further) our understanding of biology.
7. Their discovery, in turn, spurred a great (amount/number) of research into the role of DNA in the human body.
8. The anthropologists Louis and Mary Leakey and the team of Don Johanson and Tom Gray, working in Tanzania and ➡

Ethiopia (respectfully/respectively), made astounding archaeological discoveries.

9. The first lunar landing succeeded through cooperation (between/among) the astronauts Neil Armstrong, Buzz Aldrin, and Michael Collins of the *Apollo 11* spaceflight.

10. *Apollo 11* was one of sixteen Apollo space missions (all together/altogether).

Usage Workshop Exercise 6

Review   The following sentences provide information about the authors of the quotations in this workshop. For each sentence choose the correct word or expression in parentheses, and write it on your paper.

1. Ali Ibn-Abi-Talib, (who/whom) was married to Mohammed's daughter, became a leader of Islam.

2. If you could (bring/take) only one writer's works to a desert island, the plays of William Shakespeare might suffice.

3. In narrative poems such as *Hiawatha* and *The Courtship of Miles Standish*, Henry Wadsworth Longfellow explored the events and folklore of the American (passed/past).

4. It (can/may) be fair to say that Charles Dickens ranks among the most popular English writers of all time.

5. Christina Rossetti, (like/as) her brother Dante Gabriel Rossetti, was an English poet known for vivid imagery.

6. The stories and novels of Sarah Orne Jewett give readers a sense of lingering (a while/awhile) in the countryside of the author's native Maine.

7. Her childhood in Nebraska had a great (affect/effect) on Willa Cather, whose novels often portray the lives of immigrant settlers in the Midwest.

8. Hugo von Hofmannsthal, an Austrian writer, wrote (fewer/less) lyric poems as he grew older.

9. The poet W. H. Auden (emigrated/immigrated) from England in 1939 and became an American citizen.

10. Although the Indian-born author Ved Mehta had become completely blind by the age of three, he (preceded/proceeded) to excel in college and in his profession.

Proofreading The following passage describes the artist John Singer Sargent, whose painting is reproduced on the opposite page. Rewrite the passage, correcting any errors in spelling, capitalization, punctuation, grammar, and usage. There are twenty-five errors in all.

John Singer Sargent

[1]The portrait and landscape painter John singer Sargent (1856–1925) was born in Italy. [2]His father, a physician and his mother, an amatuer painter, were wealthy new Englanders; they spent much of their time in Europe, however. [3]Educated in Florence and Paris, the young Sargent was said to "look like a German, speak like an Englishman, and paint like a spaniard. [4]Some of his early work resemble that of Diego Velázquez, the great seventeenth-century Spanish master.

[5]Sargent began his studies in Florence at the age of fourteen, and moved to Paris four years later. [6]In Paris he discovered that he prefered to paint directly on the canvass without making preliminery sketches. [7]His early work betrays the influence of Edgar Degas and of James whistler, the american painter renowned for his careful compositions and sensitive brushwork.

[8]When he was twenty, Sargent made his first trip to the United States. [9]Despite his youth and relative inexperience, he became instantly popular and his portraits were in great demand in Boston and new York. [10]He quickly made a name for himself in London as well moving there permenently in 1884.

[11]In London Sargent cultivated influential friends, among who were the painter Edwin Abbey and the writer Henry James. [12]Sargents taste for aristocratic life are reflected in his portraits of upper-class Britons and Americans. [13]Although it appears that Sargent tossed off these portraits rapidly, he often labored over them until he acheived the affect he wanted.

[14]As the art world turned increasingly toward modernism and abstraction, Sargent's realistic style gradually fell out of favor. [15]His great talent as a painter, however, was never challenged. [16]His painting "Carnation, Lily, Lily, Rose" shows his extraordinary technique. [17]Sargent, who painted the scene in the open air, could work on the picture for only a few minutes each day—when the waning light was perfect. [18]This here painting echoes the love and friendship expressed in the quotations that appear in this workshop.

John Singer Sargent, *Carnation, Lily, Lily, Rose*, 1885–86

Unit 19 Review

Usage Glossary

Preferred Usage

[pages 627–649]

Indicate the usage that is preferred in each sentence.

1. The baseball game will start in **(a)** <u>a while</u> / **(b)** <u>awhile</u>.
2. A misanthrope is a person who exhibits **(a)** <u>a</u> / **(b)** <u>an</u> universal dislike of other human beings.
3. **(a)** <u>Irregardless</u> / **(b)** <u>Regardless</u> of the rain, the parade will go on.
4. The toys were divided **(a)** <u>between</u> / **(b)** <u>among</u> the four children.
5. **(a)** <u>A lot</u> / **(b)** <u>Alot</u> of people visit the Smithsonian Institution.
6. I would like to **(a)** <u>borrow</u> / **(b)** <u>loan</u> your book about the history of flight.
7. Barry and Rachel plan to **(a)** <u>accept</u> / **(b)** <u>except</u> the invitation to the party.
8. The health code states that workers **(a)** <u>can</u> / **(b)** <u>may</u> eat only in designated areas.
9. There were **(a)** <u>fewer</u> / **(b)** <u>less</u> questions on this week's current-events quiz than on last week's quiz.
10. The new seat-belt law **(a)** <u>affects</u> / **(b)** <u>effects</u> everyone who travels by car.
11. Remember to **(a)** <u>bring</u> / **(b)** <u>take</u> your hat with you when you leave the restaurant.
12. The audience is so noisy that I **(a)** <u>can scarcely</u> / **(b)** <u>can't scarcely</u> hear the speaker.
13. I never feel comfortable in **(a)** <u>this kind</u> / **(b)** <u>these kinds</u> of sandal.
14. The crew of the jumbo jet was **(a)** <u>all ready</u> / **(b)** <u>already</u> for the flight.
15. The music at the rock concert was **(a)** <u>all together</u> / **(b)** <u>altogether</u> too loud.
16. **(a)** <u>Being that</u> / **(b)** <u>Because</u> you were ill, you will need to take a makeup test next Thursday.
17. Bluegrass music is **(a)** <u>different from</u> / **(b)** <u>different than</u> country music.
18. Has it ever been hotter **(a)** <u>than</u> / **(b)** <u>then</u> 120 degrees Fahrenheit in Nevada?
19. Cynthia **(a)** <u>doesn't</u> / **(b)** <u>don't</u> study hard enough.
20. Maura **(a)** <u>could have</u> / **(b)** <u>could of</u> visited Canada last summer, but she decided to take a job instead.

Writing for Review

Demonstrate your knowledge of the distinction between the words in each of the following pairs by writing a sentence using each word.

emigrate, immigrate   hanged, hung
farther, further   lay, lie

Unit 20 Capitalization

20.1 Capitalization of Sentences

Capitalize the first word of every sentence, including the first word of a direct quotation that is a complete sentence.

> **O**ne of the first computers was large enough to fill a two-car garage.

> Henry Ford said, "**T**hinking is the hardest work there is, which is the probable reason why so few engage in it."

Capitalize the first word of a sentence in parentheses that stands by itself. Do not capitalize a sentence within parentheses that is contained within another sentence.

> Games can be tools for learning about computers. (**M**any programmers think that programming itself is the best game of all.)

> They were looking for software (**t**hey hoped to buy no more than three or four programs) that they could use in writing reports.

Do not capitalize the first word of a quotation that cannot stand as a complete sentence.

> Although astronauts must learn how to use computers, experts say most astronauts are "**c**omputer users, not computer wizards."

Do not capitalize an indirect quotation. An **indirect quotation** gives the meaning of an original statement without repeating it word for word. It is often introduced by the word *that*.

> This letter from a computer camp states that **s**wimming, hiking, and archery will be offered this summer.

Capitals form the top of Greek columns.

Exercise 1

Capitalizing Sentences   Rewrite correctly any of the following sentences that have one or more errors in capitalization. Write the word *correct* if a sentence has no errors.

Words to Ponder

1. the great Indian leader Mohandas Gandhi said, "civilization is the encouragement of differences."
2. The Chinese-American novelist Maxine Hong Kingston remarked, "you can be a writer at any time. you don't have to worry about talent." ➡

3. Eleanor Roosevelt wrote, "No one can make you feel inferior without your consent."
4. the civil rights leader Dr. Martin Luther King Jr. wrote that nonviolence is a powerful weapon. (he described nonviolence as a "sword that heals.")
5. The Russian-born sculptor Louise Nevelson said, "I never liked the middle ground—the most boring place in the world."
6. the Spanish philosopher and statesman José Ortega y Gasset wrote, "living is a constant process of deciding what we are going to do."
7. The Native American poet Simon J. Ortiz answered the question "why do you write?" by saying, "Your children will not survive unless you tell them something about them."
8. Albert Einstein wrote that Imagination is more important than knowledge.
9. The American abolitionist Frederick Douglass wrote, "if there is no struggle, there is no progress."
10. Margaret Mead (She was an anthropologist) wrote, "today's children are the first generation to grow up in a world that has the power to destroy itself."

20.2   Capitalization of Proper Nouns

Capitalize a proper noun.

Do not capitalize a common noun unless it is the first word of a sentence.

In proper nouns composed of several words, remember to capitalize only the important words. Do not capitalize articles, coordinating conjunctions, and prepositions of fewer than five letters.

1. Names of individuals

Seiji **O**zawa	**S**equoya
Sally **R**ide	**S**teffi **G**raf
Mother **T**eresa	**J**esse **J**ackson

2. Titles of individuals

Capitalize titles used before a proper name and titles used in direct address.

Dr. Henry Ramirez	**C**hief Sitting Bull
Princess Caroline	**P**rime **M**inister John Major

Pope John Paul II   Senator Dole
Congresswoman Schroeder   Aye, aye, Captain. [direct address]

In general, do not capitalize titles that follow a proper name or are used alone. Most writers, however, capitalize *president* when referring to the current president of the United States.

Lawton Chiles, the governor of Florida, met with the President last evening at the White House.

In general, capitalize a title that describes a family relationship when it is used with or in place of a proper name.

Have you met Aunt Flora?   *but*   Have you met my aunt?
Please ask Grandfather.   your grandfather's business
What did you say, Mother?   What did my mother say?
After a moment Mother spoke.

3. **Names of ethnic groups, national groups, and languages**

Native Americans   Italian
Laotians   Swahili
Mexicans   Japanese
Scots   Latin

4. **Names of organizations, institutions, political parties and their members, and firms**

Food and Drug Administration
Girl Scouts of America
Utah State University
the Congress
the Democratic party
a Republican
Bank of America
General Electric

The word *party* is not capitalized. Do not capitalize common nouns such as *court* or *university* unless they are part of a proper noun.

She was appointed judge of the First District Court.
Mr. Tavares was a witness in traffic court.
He became interested in science at the university.

5. **Names of monuments, bridges, and buildings**

Eiffel Tower
Vietnam Veterans Memorial
World Trade Center
Golden Gate Bridge
the Parthenon
Sears Tower

The World Trade Center

is a center of commerce

6. Trade names

Chevrolet	**C**heerios
Kleenex	**F**riskies cat food

7. Names of documents, awards, and laws

the **C**onstitution	**P**ulitzer **P**rize
Fifth **A**mendment	a **G**rammy
Emancipation **P**roclamation	**B**ill of **R**ights

8. Geographical terms

Capitalize the names of continents, countries, states, counties, and cities, as well as the names of specific bodies of water, topographical features, regions, and streets.

Asia	**L**ake **H**uron
Africa	**B**iscayne **B**ay
Mexico	**G**rand **C**anyon
Virginia	**B**lue **R**idge **M**ountains
Oregon	**C**ape **C**od
Dade **C**ounty	the **S**ahara
Dallas	**M**iddle **E**ast
Atlantic **O**cean	**S**outhern **H**emisphere
Mississippi **R**iver	**M**ain **S**treet

9. Names of planets and other heavenly bodies

Pluto	the constellation **S**corpio
Mars	**N**orth **S**tar
the **B**ig **D**ipper	the **M**ilky **W**ay

Do not capitalize the words *sun* and *moon*. *Earth* is capitalized only when it is used in conjunction with the names of the other planets. It is never capitalized when used with the definite article *the*.

Venus and **M**ars are **E**arth's closest planetary neighbors.
The astronauts took many photographs of the **e**arth.

10. Compass points

Capitalize the words *north*, *east*, *south*, and *west* when they refer to a specific area of the country or the world or when they are part of a proper name. Do not capitalize them when they merely indicate direction.

the **N**orth	*but*	**n**orth of Forty-second Street
the **W**est **C**oast		the **w**est **c**oast of Africa
South **P**acific		**s**outh of Bangor

11. **Names of ships, planes, trains, and spacecraft**

USS **C**onstitution   **S**pirit of **S**t. Louis
Challenger   **Y**ankee **C**lipper

12. **Names of most historical events, eras, and calendar items**

Reconstruction   **W**ashington's **B**irthday
Middle **A**ges   **L**abor **D**ay
Ming **D**ynasty   **W**orld **W**ar **II**

Do not capitalize a historical period when it refers to a general span of time.

the **t**wenties
the **t**enth **c**entury

Capitalize the days of the week and the months of the year, but do not capitalize the names of the seasons (*spring, summer, autumn, fall, winter*).

We met on a **M**onday in **M**arch; it was the first day of **s**pring.

13. **Religious terms**

Capitalize names of deities, religions and their denominations and adherents, words referring to a supreme deity, and religious books and events.

Allah   **M**uslims
God   **K**oran
Christianity   **N**ew **T**estament
Russian **O**rthodox   the **A**lmighty
Protestants   **H**anukkah
Jews   the **S**econd **C**oming

14. **Names of school courses**

Capitalize only those school courses that are the name of a language or the title of a specific course. Do not capitalize the name of a subject.

Spanish   *but*   **g**eography
Music 101   **m**usic

15. **Titles of works**

the **O**dyssey   [epic poem]
"**T**he **G**ift of the **M**agi"   [story]
the **L**os **A**ngeles **T**imes   [newspaper]
"**H**ome on the **R**ange"   [song]

Capitalize articles (*a*, *an*, and *the*) at the beginning of a title only when they are part of the title itself. It is common practice not to capitalize (or italicize) articles preceding the title of a newspaper or a periodical. Do not capitalize (or italicize) the word *magazine* unless it is part of the title of a periodical.

"**T**he Fifty-first Dragon"   **t**he *Christian Science Monitor*
"**A** Marriage Proposal"   a *Newsweek* **m**agazine

Exercise 2

Capitalizing Proper Nouns   Rewrite the following sentences correctly, adding or dropping capital letters as necessary.

Early Settlers in America

1. Early in the Seventeenth Century king george I of England gave a trading company the right to send settlers to live in north america.
2. The settlers, among them captain John Smith, set sail in the Company's ships, the *godspeed*, the *discovery*, and the *sarah constant*.
3. After crossing the atlantic ocean, the Settlers founded jamestown, Virginia, the first permanent British settlement in north america.
4. In 1619 a ship owned by holland brought the first africans to the colonies in america.
5. The pilgrims, a group of English puritans, landed a good distance North of Virginia, in present-day massachusetts, in december of 1620.
6. Squanto, a native american, helped the pilgrims survive their first harsh Winter in a new land in the Settlement named plymouth.
7. Wall street in New York city is named after a wall built in 1653 by colonists from holland who feared an attack by the British.
8. In 1681 william penn, the English quaker leader, together with a group of quakers, founded the City of Philadelphia on the Delaware river.
9. In philadelphia members of all Religious groups were allowed to worship god and interpret the bible in their own way.
10. In 1704 the first issue of a successful colonial newspaper, the *boston newsletter*, was printed.

20.3 Capitalization of Proper Adjectives

Capitalize proper adjectives (adjectives formed from proper nouns).

Most proper adjectives fit into the following categories:

1. **Adjectives formed from names of people**

   Napoleonic era   **J**acksonian ideals
   Victorian customs   **M**arxist revolutionary
   Georgian architecture   **D**ickensian character

2. **Adjectives formed from place names and names of national, ethnic, and religious groups**

   Chinese acupuncture   **I**sraeli dances
   African languages   **N**orwegian accent
   Hispanic studies   **B**uddhist temple

Many proper nouns do not undergo a change in form when they are used as adjectives.

   United **N**ations calendar   **T**hanksgiving dinner
   New **O**rleans cooking   **P**assover meal
   Beethoven sonata   **M**onday night

Exercise 3

Capitalizing Proper Adjectives and Proper Nouns
Rewrite the following sentences correctly, adding or dropping capital letters as necessary.

The Triumph of Kathleen Battle

1. Kathleen Battle, a talented contemporary american Opera singer, is celebrated for the purity of her voice.
2. Born in the City of Cleveland, Ohio, she studied at the College Conservatory of music at the university of Cincinnati.
3. In addition to being one of the favorite Sopranos at the Metropolitan Opera House in New York city, she has won ovations in many european Opera Houses.
4. Battle is best known for her roles in mozart operas, including *the magic flute*.
5. She has worked closely in many Concerts and on many Musical Recordings with James Levine, a well-known Conductor.
6. In 1988 Battle sang in New York's central park with the italian star luciano Pavarotti. ➡

7. Later that year she traveled to the far east and sang in Tokyo with the spanish opera star Placido Domingo.
8. One of her greatest triumphs was her role in *antony and cleopatra*, an opera based on a shakespearean play.
9. Years ago it was difficult for african-American singers to win major roles in opera, but Battle, Leontyne price, and Jessye norman have begun to change that.
10. My aunt Julia says that Battle's recording of spirituals is so outstanding that she is sure it will win a grammy.

Summary of Capitalization Rules	
Capitalize	**Do Not Capitalize**
She gave us thirty pages of reading for homework. (**S**he said we needed to do it.)	For homework (**s**he said we needed to catch up) she gave us thirty pages of reading.
He said, "**L**et me drive."	He said that **h**e would drive.
Then **F**ather smiled at me.	My **f**ather wants to retire.
Captain **A**hab	The **c**aptain paced the deck.
Texas **S**tate **U**niversity	a **u**niversity in Texas
Lawrence **H**all of **S**cience	the **s**cience **m**useum in town
Prell shampoo; **I**vory soap	Bring **s**oap and **s**hampoo.
Bill of **R**ights	an animal **b**ill of **r**ights
Pacific **O**cean; **G**hirardelli **S**quare; **S**anta **C**lara **A**venue	the **s**quare where the two **a**venues meet near the **o**cean
Neptune; **M**ercury; **E**arth	**s**un; **p**lanets; the **e**arth
the **K**orean **W**ar	the **w**ar in the Middle East
the **B**ible; **H**alloween	**s**acred **b**ook; **h**olidays
Russian; **E**nglish Literature I	**f**oreign **l**anguage; **l**iterature

Exercise 4: Sentence Writing

Writing a Dialogue Write several sentences of imagined dialogue between you and a friend about a country you would like to visit and the sights you would like to see.

Capitalization   Write the letter of the one item that is correctly capitalized in each of the following pairs.

1. **a.** James Baldwin wrote, "one cannot deny the humanity of another without diminishing one's own."
   b. James Baldwin wrote, "One cannot deny the humanity of another without diminishing one's own."
2. **a.** university of California
   b. University of California
3. **a.** General George Patton
   b. general George Patton
4. **a.** The English stage actress Rachel Kempson is the mother of Vanessa and Lynn Redgrave.
   b. The English stage actress Rachel Kempson is the Mother of Vanessa and Lynn Redgrave.
5. **a.** Georgia O'Keeffe's painting *New York night* is done mostly in dark colors.
   b. Georgia O'Keeffe's painting *New York Night* is done mostly in dark colors.
6. **a.** *A Raisin In The Sun*
   b. *A Raisin in the Sun*
7. **a.** European History I and physics
   b. European History I and Physics
8. **a.** a Buddhist temple
   b. a buddhist temple
9. **a.** I wished that summer would not quickly fade.
   b. I wished that Summer would not quickly fade.
10. **a.** West of the Colorado River
    b. west of the Colorado River

Georgia O'Keeffe's
New York Night.

New York at night.

Mechanics Workshop

Capitalization

Immortalized in Garrison Keillor's radio show *A Prairie Home Companion*, the town of Lake Wobegon is so true to life that it seems a mistake that no map of Minnesota shows it. Keillor's book *Lake Wobegon Days* grew out of the radio show. In this passage from the book, Keillor describes some of the sights in this little town, whose population is 942. The passage has been annotated to show some of the rules of capitalization covered in this unit.

Literature Model

from LAKE WOBEGON DAYS
by Garrison Keillor

Place names —

Compass point, not capitalized —

Proper adjective —

First word of a sentence —

Name of a firm —

Title not capitalized because not followed directly by an individual's name —

Trade name —

First word of a full sentence in quotation marks —

The town of Lake Wobegon, Minnesota, lies on the shore against Adams Hill, looking east across the blue-green water to the dark woods. From the south, the highway aims for the lake, bends hard left by the magnificent concrete Grecian grain silos, and eases over a leg of the hill past the SLOW CHILDREN sign, bringing the traveler in on Main Street toward the town's one traffic light, which is almost always green. A few surviving elms shade the street. Along the ragged dirt path between the asphalt and the grass, a child slowly walks to Ralph's Grocery, kicking an asphalt chunk ahead of him. It is a chunk that after four blocks he is now mesmerized by, to which he is completely dedicated. At Bunsen Motors, the sidewalk begins. . . . The boy kicks the chunk at the curb, once, twice, then lofts it over the curb and sidewalk across the concrete to the island of Pure Oil pumps. He jumps three times on the Bunsen bell hose, making three dings back in the dark garage. The mayor of Lake Wobegon, Clint Bunsen, peers out from the grease pit, under a black Ford pickup.

Incorporated under the laws of Minnesota but omitted from the map due to the incompetence of surveyors, first named "New Albion" by New Englanders who thought it would become the Boston of the west, taking its ultimate name from an Indian phrase that means either "Here we ➡

are!" or "We sat all day in the rain waiting for [you]," Lake Wobegon is the seat of tiny Mist County, the "phantom county in the heart of the heartland" (Dibbley, *My Minnesota*), founded by Unitarian missionaries and Yankee promoters, then found by Norwegian Lutherans who straggled in from the west, having headed first to Lake Agassiz in what is now North Dakota, a lake that turned out to be prehistoric, and by German Catholics, who, bound for Clay County, had stopped a little short, having misread their map, but refused to admit it.

A town with few scenic wonders such as towering pines or high mountains but with some fine people of whom some are over six feet tall, its highest point is the gold ball on the flagpole atop the Norge Co-op grain elevator south of town on the Great Northern spur, from which Mr. Tollefson can see all of Mist County when he climbs up to raise the flag on national holidays, including Norwegian Independence Day, when the blue cross of Norway is flown. (No flag of Germany has appeared in public since 1917.) Next highest is the water tower, then the boulder on the hill, followed by the cross on the spire of Our Lady, then the spire of Lake Wobegon Lutheran (Christian Synod), the Central Building (three stories), the high school flagpole, . . . etc.

Annotations (right margin):
- Book title
- Name of a religious group
- General time period, not capitalized
- Name of a holiday
- First word of a sentence in parentheses that stands by itself
- Name of a building

Mechanics Workshop Exercise 1

Capitalizing Sentences   Rewrite the following sentences, which are based on information from passages of *Lake Wobegon Days* that are not included in this textbook. Correct any errors in capitalization. If a sentence has no errors, write *correct*.

1. the imaginary town of Lake Wobegon has been called "The little town that time forgot and decades cannot improve."
2. Keillor claims the town is not on any map because of surveying errors. (it is supposedly in central Minnesota.)
3. Keillor states that One early explorer thought Lake Wobegon was the headwaters of the Mississippi River.
4. A statue of an unknown Norwegian (the town was largely settled by Scandinavians) is a major landmark.
5. The town also displays an old stone carved with Viking runes. (runes are ancient alphabetical symbols.)
6. An early settler from Boston complained that no civilized society could find comfort or nurture in Lake Wobegon. ➡

7. later she said, "Providence has led us here."
8. The young woman (She had come west as a missionary) soon married a French trapper and opened a hotel.
9. In his broadcasts Keillor said, "that's the news from Lake Wobegon, where all the women are strong, all the men are good-looking, and all the children above average."
10. he also described the residents of Lake Wobegon as "Skeptical of progress."

Mechanics Workshop Exercise 2

Capitalizing Proper Nouns   The following sentences provide information about Minnesota, the location of the fictional Lake Wobegon. Rewrite the sentences, correcting any errors in capitalization. If a sentence has no errors, write *correct*.

1. The french, who settled Canada during the reign of king Louis XIV, explored Minnesota in the Seventeenth Century.
2. In 1825 Norwegian quakers crossed the atlantic Ocean on the *restauration*, a ship smaller than the *mayflower*.
3. The Norwegians were attracted to Minnesota's lakes.
4. The swedes, who also came in large numbers, were predominantly lutherans, followers of martin Luther.
5. Many Irishmen worked for the Saint Paul and pacific railroad company, which advertised in the *St. Paul Daily press*.
6. Their leader archbishop John Ireland served in the civil war and became a friend of president Theodore Roosevelt's.
7. Bad harvests after the napoleonic wars and advertisements for workers on the Northern pacific railway spurred German immigration after 1815.
8. Several tribes of native americans were already living in what was then called the northwest territory.
9. Among them were the dakota, a branch of the sioux.
10. The United States bureau of the census estimates that over thirty-five thousand native americans still live in minnesota.

Mechanics Workshop Exercise 3

Capitalizing Proper Adjectives and Proper Nouns
The following sentences describe some famous Minnesotans. Rewrite each sentence, correcting any errors in capitalization. If a sentence has no errors, write *correct*. ➡

1. Though lake wobegon characters seem ordinary, many famous americans, both real and imaginary, have minnesota roots.
2. Sinclair Lewis, a nobel prize winner, set his novel *babbitt* in a town that resembled his birthplace, sauk Centre.
3. Charles Lindbergh, a minnesota native of swedish descent, made the first solo flight across the atlantic ocean.
4. The Mayo Clinic founders, Drs. Charles and William Mayo, established their famous hospital in Minnesota.
5. The Minnesota-born actress and singer Judy Garland won worldwide popularity as Dorothy in *The Wizard of Oz*.
6. Ole Rölvaag, a Minnesotan of scandinavian ancestry, wrote novels about pioneers in the dakotas.
7. Eugene McCarthy, who was a united states senator from Minnesota, sought the democratic party's nomination for President in 1968.
8. John S. Pillsbury, a founder of pillsbury, a food-products company, served as a republican Governor of Minnesota for three terms.
9. The minnesota-born author F. Scott Fitzgerald depicted the decaying morality of society in the years following world war I.
10. The paul bunyan and hiawatha legends, both based on fictional heroes, are set in the minnesota frontier.

Mechanics Workshop Exercise 4

Review Rewrite the following sentences, which provide biographical information about Garrison Keillor. Correct any errors in capitalization.

Garrison Keillor

1. Garrison Keillor was born in 1942 in Anoka county, Minnesota, to parents of scottish descent.
2. After finishing High School, he entered the University of Minnesota. (he earned a degree in english in 1966.)
3. Keillor had written earlier for the *Anoka herald*, and he became Editor of the literary magazine at the University.
4. Keillor went East to New York after college, hoping to work as a journalist, but soon returned to minnesota.
5. in 1974 he sold a story about the Grand ole Opry to the *New Yorker* for six thousand dollars (More money than he had ever seen).
6. He began hosting *a Prairie Home Companion*, a radio ➡

show about a fictional town named lake Wobegon, for the public Radio Station in Minnesota.

7. Keillor has said that one of his Great-Uncles, Uncle Lew (his Grandma's brother), inspired some of the show's homespun characters.

8. The imaginary sponsors for the humorous show were Raw bits Cereal and a pet shop called Bertha's kitty boutique.

9. Chet atkins (He is a country guitarist and Keillor's friend) has said, "that man's voice just mesmerizes people."

10. Keillor's book *Lake Wobegon days* grew out of the radio program. (it became an immediate Best seller in 1985.)

Mechanics Workshop Exercise 5

Proofreading   The following passage describes the artist Grant Wood, whose painting appears on the opposite page. Rewrite the passage, correcting the errors in spelling, capital-ization, punctuation, grammar, and usage. There are twenty-five errors in all.

Grant Wood

¹Grant Wood (1892–1941) was born on a farm outside the small town of anamosa Iowa. ²He studied at the Handicraft Guild in Minneapolis and at the Art institute of Chicago. ³Before he began military service in 1918, he worked as a schoolteacher, an interior decorater and a metalworker. ⁴After World war I ended, he returned to iowa to teach art.

⁵Wood made several trips to Europe over the next decade and he studied at a parisian art school. ⁶His european travels reflected his discontent with american art, and his early works recall those of the french painters of the late nineteenth century. ⁷Later Wood had a change of heart and began to con-centrate on American subjects. ⁸By the 1930s he, along with thomas Hart Benton and John Steuart Curry, was ranked as one of Americas' great regional painters.

⁹Wood is best known for his portrayals of the land and the people of the midwest. ¹⁰His pictures are finely detailed and stylized, his lanscapes are reduced to round shapes and his peo-ple are witty caricatures. ¹¹His technique was influenced by the lush and detailed paintings of the flemish masters. ¹²Curiously, he was also influenced by the stylized pattern on his mother's dishes. ¹³His best-known work, "American gothic," is typical of his mature style. ¹⁴The panting, which depicts a man hold-ing a pitchfork and standing with his wife in front of there ➡

house, was completed in 1930.

[15]Wood painted very slowly and produced relatively few major works during his lifetime. [16]*Stone City, Iowa,* the painting on this page, reveals both his skill as an artist and his reverance for the rural countryside. [17]Wood's gently ironic realism is like that of Garrison Keillor. [18]Both Wood and Keillor poke fun at the obsesive orderliness—both physical and moral of the people who live in the small towns of the Midwest. [19]Yet they do so with respect and tenderness.

Grant Wood, *Stone City, Iowa,* **1930**

Capitalization

Read the following passages, paying attention especially to the underlined text. Then, for each numbered item below, choose the word or group of words that shows the correct capitalization for that underlined item.

Ursula LeGuin is an author of [1]fantasy and science fiction. A native of [2]berkeley, california, she writes books for adults and young people. The Taoist principles of the [3]chinese philosopher lao-tse have greatly influenced her work. For the Earthsea trilogy she received many awards, including [4]the hugo award. "Clarity and simplicity," she has said, [5]"are permanent virtues in a narrative."

1. **a.** Fantasy and Science Fiction
   b. fantasy and science fiction
2. **a.** Berkeley, California
   b. berkeley, california
3. **a.** Chinese Philosopher Lao-Tse
   b. Chinese philosopher Lao-Tse
4. **a.** the Hugo Award
   b. The Hugo Award
   c. the Hugo award
5. **a.** "Are
   b. "are

In my sixth-period class, [6]introduction to music appreciation, I learned about the history of the Spanish guitar. Developed in medieval Spain from Oriental models, the Spanish guitar traveled [7]northeast to other sections of [8]europe during the [9]seventeenth century. During the last two centuries the [10]spanish musician andrés segovia and other great virtuosos have proved the guitar an important classical instrument.

6. **a.** introduction to music appreciation
   b. Introduction to Music Appreciation
   c. introduction to Music Appreciation
7. **a.** northeast
   b. Northeast
8. **a.** europe
   b. Europe
9. **a.** Seventeenth century
   b. seventeenth century
   c. Seventeenth Century
10. **a.** Spanish musician Andrés Segovia
    b. spanish musician Andrés Segovia
    c. Spanish Musician Andrés Segovia

Writing for Review

Write a paragraph in which you use several different proper nouns, proper adjectives, titles, and quotations.

Unit 21 Punctuation, Abbreviations, and Numbers

21.1 The Period

Use a period at the end of a declarative sentence and at the end of a polite command.

DECLARATIVE SENTENCE   Track practice is held twice a week.
POLITE COMMAND   Please sign up for two track events.

21.2 The Exclamation Point

Use an exclamation point to show strong feeling and indicate a forceful command.

Oh, no!   Look out!
What lovely weather!   Wake up!

21.3 The Question Mark

Use a question mark to indicate a direct question.

Who would like a part-time job?
Which call should I answer first?

Do not place a question mark after an indirect question (one that has been reworded so that it is part of a declarative sentence).

He asked whether I needed a work permit.

Exercise 1

Using End Punctuation   Rewrite the following sentences correctly, adding periods, exclamation points, and question marks where they are needed.

First Aid

1. Don't you think that everyone should learn about first aid
2. First aid is the immediate medical care given to an ill or injured person
3. Oh, if only people realized the importance of first aid So many lives could be saved ➡

4. An instruction manual by John S. Kelly, published by the U.S. Bureau of Mines, has useful information about first aid Will you get it from the library

5. The primary goals of first aid are to treat serious injuries, prevent infection, and make the injured or ill person as comfortable as possible

6. If you come upon an injured person, try to send for medical help right away Don't panic Try to stay calm

7. Are you the person best qualified to take charge If two of you know first aid, decide which one has more experience and training The other one can assist

8. If people are crowding the injured person, make them stand at a distance

9. Once you have sent for help and the patient is lying still, ask yourself which injuries require immediate attention and which are less critical

10. Because an injured person may have broken bones or internal injuries, move someone only if it is absolutely necessary

21.4   The Colon

Colons to Introduce

1. Lists

Use a colon to introduce a list, especially after a statement that uses such words as *these*, *the following*, or *as follows*.

> The science test on Friday will cover **these** areas: the circulatory system, the digestive system, and the nervous system.

> To get to my house, follow **these** directions: (1) Drive north on Ashby Avenue. (2) After you pass the Claremont Hotel, take the first left, which will be Tunnel Road. (3) At the second stop sign turn right onto Peralta Road. (4) Look for 248 Peralta, a brown shingled house with an oak tree in front.

Do not use a colon to introduce a list if the list immediately follows a verb or a preposition.

> The best nonanimal sources of protein **are** soybeans, wheat germ, brewer's yeast, nuts, seeds, and whole grains. [The list follows the verb *are*.]

> My sister likes to top her hamburger **with** lettuce, tomato, mustard, ketchup, and relish. [The list follows the preposition *with*.]

2. Illustrations or restatements

Use a colon to introduce material that illustrates, explains, or restates the preceding material.

> I often wish that my parents had had more than one child: they worry too much about me.

A complete sentence following a colon is generally not capitalized.

Colons Before Quotations

Use a colon to introduce a long or formal quotation. A formal quotation is often preceded by such words as *this, these, the following,* or *as follows.*

> Mrs. Hopkins asked the class to write an essay on **the following** traditional saying from the Hausa tribe of Africa: "It is the rainy season that gives wealth."

Poetry quotations of more than one line and prose quotations of more than four or five lines are generally written below the introductory statement and indented on the page.

> In his long poem *The Other Pioneers* Roberto Félix Salazar describes some of this nation's early settlers:
>
> > Now I must write
> > Of those of mine who rode these plains
> > Long years before the Saxon and the Irish came.

Other Uses of Colons

Use a colon between the hour and the minute of the precise time, between the chapter and the verse in biblical references, and after the salutation of a business letter.

12:30 A.M.	Genesis 7:20–24	Sir:
4:00 P.M.	Ruth 1:16–18	Dear Ms. Snow:

Exercise 2

Using the Colon   Rewrite the following sentences correctly, adding colons where they are needed. For the sentence that does not need a colon, write *correct.* Remember that colons are not needed when a list immediately follows a verb or a preposition.

The Game of Chess

1. Many people enjoy playing these board games chess, checkers, and pachisi. ➡

2. Chess may have spread from place to place in the following order India, Persia, and Spain.

3. There are several board games that resemble chess checkers, the Japanese game go, and Chinese checkers.

4. In chess each player has the following playing pieces one king, one queen, two bishops, two knights, two rooks, and eight pawns.

5. The qualities essential to a good chess player are a good memory, a quick mind, and foresight.

6. In some ways chess is like war it pits two "armies" against each other.

7. The *Encyclopaedia Britannica* notes that chess players use strategies of attack and defense aimed at the surrender of the opponent's king. The encyclopedia continues as follows "Nevertheless, the game is only a rather limited simulation of war or, in Freudian terms, a sublimation of that aggressive impulse."

8. The Old Testament has the following to say about war

> They shall beat their swords into plowshares
> and their spears into pruning-hooks:
> nation shall not lift up sword against nation,
> neither shall they learn war anymore.
> —Isaiah 2 4

9. A regional chess tournament typically takes place on a three-day weekend, with two rounds each day at the following times round 1 occurs from 1100 A.M. to 100 P.M. and round 2 from 500 P.M. to 730 P.M.

10. In addition to the type of chess that most people play, here are some other types blindfold chess, lightning chess, postal chess, and computer chess.

The arch bridge is one of the oldest types of bridges **, and** many early examples were constructed of stone

21.5   The Semicolon

Semicolons to Separate Main Clauses

Use a semicolon to separate main clauses that are not joined by a coordinating conjunction (*and, but, or, nor, yet,* and *for*).

Paul Robeson was an excellent singer and actor, **and** he was also a talented football player.

Paul Robeson was an excellent singer and actor; he was also a talented football player.

Use a semicolon to separate main clauses joined by a conjunctive adverb (such as *however, therefore, nevertheless, moreover, furthermore,* and *subsequently*) or by an expression such as *for example* or *that is.*

In general, a conjunctive adverb or an expression such as *for example* is followed by a comma.

> Robeson appeared in many plays and musicals; for example, he starred in *Othello* and *Porgy and Bess.*

> Robeson appeared in *Show Boat* in 1926; subsequently, he acted in the films *Jericho* and *Song of Freedom.*

Semicolons and Commas

Use a semicolon to separate the items in a series when the items contain commas.

> Some of the powerful African kingdoms that flourished before the sixteenth century were Kush, which dominated the eastern Sudan; Karanga, which was located around Zimbabwe in southern Africa; Ghana, Mali, and Songhai, which successively controlled the Niger River in West Africa; and Benin, which had its center in what is now Nigeria.

Use a semicolon to separate two main clauses joined by a coordinating conjunction when the clauses already contain several commas.

> The rule of Mansa Musa, the Moslem emperor of the African kingdom of Mali from 1312 to 1337, is remembered for military success, trade expansion, and Moslem scholarship; but this period is probably most noteworthy as a golden age of peace and prosperity.

Exercise 3

Using the Semicolon   Rewrite the following sentences correctly, adding semicolons where they are needed.

Louise Nevelson, Sculptor

1. The sculptor Louise Nevelson lived in a number of places in Europe and the United States, including Kiev, U.S.S.R., Rockland, Maine, Munich, Germany, and New York City.
2. At the age of five, Nevelson moved to Rockland with her family, she lived there for fifteen years.
3. Nevelson's family name was Berliawsky, at the age of twenty she married Charles Nevelson and moved to New York. ➡

4. Nevelson studied art under Hans Hofmann, the abstract painter who used primary colors in explosive contrasts, she also studied with the muralist Diego Rivera.
5. Many artists are not willing to struggle however, Louise Nevelson worked for years without money or fame.
6. Nevelson's first one-woman sculpture show was in 1940 after that she became world renowned.
7. Nevelson made sculptures with found objects her artworks were large and intricate.
8. Nevelson used many materials in her sculptures nevertheless, her wooden assemblages in black and white are the best known.
9. A pioneer in environmental art, Nevelson created walls of framed sculptures her large-scale works sometimes take up an entire room.
10. Nevelson's art was influenced by multimedia sculpture along with Cubism and Surrealism in addition, the art of Africa and pre-Columbian America affected her work.

21.6 The Comma

As you study the rules for comma usage, keep in mind that to *separate* elements means to place a comma between two equal elements. To *set off* an element means to put commas before and after it.

Commas and Compound Sentences

Use commas between the main clauses in a compound sentence.

Place a comma before a coordinating conjunction (*and, but, or, nor, yet,* or *for*) that joins two main clauses.

I am not going to the concert, for I am too busy.

Many of the prospectors searched for years, but others struck gold immediately, and some became quite rich.

You may omit the comma between very short main clauses that are connected by a coordinating conjunction unless the comma is needed to avoid confusion.

Mara washed the dishes and Jim dried them. [clear]

We visited Miami and the Everglades are next. [confusing]

We visited Miami, and the Everglades are next. [clear]

Commas in a Series

Use commas to separate three or more words, phrases, or clauses in a series.

> A chair, a table, and a sofa were the room's only furnishings.
>
> It was a sunny, hot, humid day in July.
>
> The cat ran out of the house, across the lawn, and down the street.
>
> I rounded third, headed for home, and slid in safely.
>
> Read carefully, take good notes, and outline the chapter.

No commas are necessary when all of the items are connected by conjunctions.

> It was a sunny and hot and humid day in July.

Nouns that are used in pairs (*thunder and lightning, table and chairs, bread and butter*) are usually considered single units and should not be separated by commas. If such pairs appear with other nouns or groups of nouns in a series, they must be set off from the other items in the series.

> My favorite breakfast is bacon and eggs, toast, and milk.

Commas and Coordinate Adjectives

Place a comma between coordinate adjectives that precede a noun.

Coordinate adjectives modify a noun equally. To determine whether adjectives are coordinate, try to reverse their order or put the word *and* between them. If the sentence still sounds natural, the adjectives are coordinate.

> Pepper is a good, obedient, gentle dog.

Do not use a comma between adjectives preceding a noun if they sound unnatural with their order reversed or with *and* between them. In general, adjectives that describe size, shape, age, and material do not need commas between them.

> Jelani grew up in a small white frame house.

Commas may be needed between some of the adjectives in a series but not between others.

> I like to read in our bright, cozy family room.

In the preceding sentence *and* would sound natural between *bright* and *cozy*, but it would not sound natural between *cozy* and *family*.

Using the Comma (Part 1) Rewrite the following sentences correctly, adding commas where they are needed. For the sentence that needs no comma, write *correct*.

Arthur Schomburg, Collector

1. Arthur Schomburg led a long active productive life.
2. He grew up in Puerto Rico studied in the Virgin Islands and came to the United States in 1891.
3. Schomburg was an author and historian but he is best known as a collector of literature about African-American culture.
4. Schomburg was also an important figure in the literary artistic and musical movement known as the Harlem Renaissance.
5. Schomburg collected over ten thousand books and manuscripts and pamphlets about Africans and African Americans.
6. The Carnegie Corporation bought his collection donated it to the New York Public Library and named it in Schomburg's honor.
7. The Schomburg Collection has a wide reputation for it has more books on African-American history and literature than any other library in North America.
8. The collection is housed in a tall modern brick building in the neighborhood of Harlem in New York City.
9. Many people who use the collection are students of African-American history literature art or music.
10. You may find that your own local library has a collection of books about African-American culture or that a nearby historical society has some information about local African-American families.

Commas and Nonessential Elements

1. Participles, infinitives, and their phrases

Use commas to set off participles, infinitives, and their phrases if they are not essential to the meaning of the sentence.

> She watched, puzzled, as the man in the yellow hat drove away.

> A customer, complaining loudly, stepped up to the counter.

> I have no idea, to be honest, what you would like for a graduation present.

Do not set off participles, infinitives, and their phrases if they are essential to the meaning of the sentence.

> The man standing by the door is my father. [The participial phrase tells *which* man.]

> She went to medical school to become a doctor. [The infinitive phrase tells *why*.]

> To become a doctor had been her goal for years. [The infinitive phrase is used as the subject of the sentence.]

2. Adjective clauses

Use commas to set off a nonessential adjective clause.

A nonessential (nonrestrictive) clause can be considered an extra clause because it gives additional information about a noun. Because an extra clause adds to the basic meaning of a sentence, it is set off by commas.

> Atlanta, which is the capital of Georgia, is the transportation center of the Southeast. [*Which is the capital of Georgia* is a nonessential clause.]

Do not set off an essential adjective clause. Because an essential (restrictive) clause gives necessary information about a noun, it is needed to convey the exact meaning of the sentence.

> People who are afraid of heights do not like to look down from balconies or terraces. [*Who are afraid of heights* is an essential clause.]

3. Appositives

Use commas to set off an appositive if it is not essential to the meaning of a sentence.

A nonessential (nonrestrictive) appositive can be considered an extra appositive; it calls for commas.

> Nelson Mandela, a leader of the African National Congress, was freed from a South African prison in 1990.

> My mother lives in Escondido, a town near San Diego in southern California.

A nonessential (nonrestrictive) appositive is sometimes placed before the noun or pronoun to which it refers.

> An insurance executive, Charles Ives wrote music in his spare time. [The appositive, *An insurance executive*, precedes the subject of the sentence, *Charles Ives*.]

An essential (restrictive) appositive gives necessary information about a noun and is not set off.

The word *fiesta* came into English from Spanish. [The appositive, *fiesta*, is needed to identify *word*.]

Commas with Interjections, Parenthetical Expressions, and Conjunctive Adverbs

Use commas to set off interjections (such as *oh* and *well*), parenthetical expressions (such as *on the contrary, on the other hand, in fact, by the way, to be exact*, and *after all*), and conjunctive adverbs (such as *however, moreover*, and *consequently*).

Well, we'd better be going home.
Oh, I don't know.
We have to leave, unfortunately.
Last night, on the other hand, we could have stayed longer.
We said we'd be home early; consequently, we must leave now.
You might want to come with us, however.

Exercise 5

Using the Comma (Part 2)   Rewrite the following sentences correctly, adding commas where they are needed. For the sentence that needs no commas, write *correct*.

Sequoya and the Cherokee Language

1. Most Native American languages before the eighteenth century were not written down; consequently it was difficult for people to learn them.
2. A Cherokee Sequoya saw the need for a way of writing down his language.
3. The Cherokees who had no system of writing thought that writing was the privilege of certain people.
4. Like many other Native American groups in fact the Cherokees used smoke and drum signals to communicate with people some distance away.
5. Sequoya having considered the idea for some time realized how valuable a written language would be.
6. He had been hurt in a hunting accident; therefore he had the leisure to think about a writing system.
7. Sequoya a skilled silversmith began to draw marks on twigs and stones.
8. People who once laughed at Sequoya's dream began to change their mind about him. ➡

9. Sequoya produced the first Cherokee alphabet making it possible for his tribe to write messages and record its history.
10. Sequoya who had been successful despite the doubts of others was sent to Washington, D.C., in 1828 to represent the Cherokees.

Commas and Introductory Phrases

1. Prepositional phrases

Use a comma after a short introductory prepositional phrase only if the sentence would be misread without the comma.

> To those outside, the house appeared deserted. [comma needed to prevent misreading]

> At the last moment we decided not to go. [comma not needed]

Use a comma after a long prepositional phrase or after the final phrase in a succession of phrases.

> On the precipitously steep and rocky cliff, the mountain climbers carefully found their footholds.

> On the afternoon of the day of the game, we made a banner.

Do not use a comma if the phrase is immediately followed by a verb.

> On the stone above the front door of the building was the date.

2. Participles and participial phrases

Use commas to set off introductory participles and participial phrases.

> Purring, the kitten curled up in my lap.
> Sitting in a tree, my little sister called down to us.

Commas and Adverb Clauses

Use commas to set off all introductory adverb clauses.

Use commas to set off internal adverb clauses that interrupt the flow of a sentence.

> Although I like country music, I did not want to hear his entire record collection.

> Until she arrived, I thought that no one was coming.

> Evan, after he thought about it awhile, agreed with our idea.

In general, do not set off an adverb clause at the end of a sentence unless the clause is parenthetical or the sentence would be misread without the comma.

Commas and Antithetical Phrases

Use commas to set off an antithetical phrase.

An **antithetical phrase** uses a word such as *not* or *unlike* to qualify what precedes it.

You, not I, deserve this honor.
Bicycles, unlike cars, cause no pollution.

Exercise 6

Using the Comma (Part 3) Rewrite the following sentences correctly, adding commas where they are needed. If a sentence is correct, write *correct*.

I. M. Pei

1. To most people the name I. M. Pei means good taste and quality of design.
2. Among contemporary architects throughout the world Pei's name is unquestionably one of the best known and most respected.
3. Because his firm has frequently combined a beautiful and practical design with an affordable budget Pei is considered a gifted architect.
4. Among Pei's most successful designs are the East Building of the National Gallery of Art in Washington, D.C., and the pyramidal entrance to the Louvre in Paris.
5. Architects unlike artists must seek to harmonize a building's appearance with its purpose.
6. After a series of problems with the John Hancock Tower in Boston Pei's firm lost some business.
7. Pei and his staff gradually regained their hands-on reputation after the problems with the John Hancock Tower were resolved.
8. For a resort hotel in mainland China not on Taiwan Pei created a design that pleased everyone.
9. Having been born in China Pei was happy to design a structure for his native land.
10. Although Pei has become highly successful as an architect he continues to welcome new challenges.

Commas with Titles, Addresses, and Numbers

1. Titles of people

Use commas to set off titles when they follow a person's name.

> Alan Wong, M.D.
> Maureen O'Connor, mayor of San Diego
> Jorge Gonzalez, Ph.D., will speak on Thursday.

2. Addresses, geographical terms, and dates

Use commas to separate the various parts of an address, a geographical term, or a date.

> Anaheim, California, is the home of Disneyland.

> During the summer my address will be 90 Sherwick Road, New Bedford, Massachusetts 02745, and my sister's address will be the same.

> Friday, March 15, 1985, was the day I got my driver's license.

Use the following forms for letter writing.

> 90 Sherwick Road
> New Bedford, MA 02745
> July 7, 1992

Do not use commas if only the month and the day or only the month and the year are given.

> October 31
> September 1986

3. References

Use commas to set off the parts of a reference that direct the reader to the exact source.

> Odysseus becomes reunited with his son Telemachus in the *Odyssey*, Book 16, lines 177–219.

> Please find three examples of extended metaphor in Act IV, Scene i, of Shakespeare's *Romeo and Juliet*.

Commas and Direct Address

Use commas to set off words or names used in direct address.

> Nathaniel, do you know where Kathleen is?
> I can order the book for you, sir, if you like.
> Thank you for the ride, Mrs. Salerno.

Commas and Tag Questions

Use commas to set off a tag question.

A tag question (such as *shouldn't I?* or *have you?*) emphasizes an implied answer to the statement preceding it.

> You've already seen this film, haven't you?
> You won't repeat this, will you?

Commas in Letter Writing

Place a comma after the salutation of an informal letter and after the closing of all letters.

> Dear Dolores,   Very truly yours,

Misuse of Commas

In general, do not use a comma before a conjunction that connects a compound predicate composed of only two verbs or verb phrases.

> **INCORRECT** She started the car, and drove down the hill.
> **CORRECT** She started the car and drove down the hill.

The same rule applies to other compound elements:

> **INCORRECT** The adults playing softball, and the children playing soccer argued in the field. [compound subject]
> **CORRECT** The adults playing softball and the children playing soccer argued in the field.

Do not use only a comma to join two main clauses that are not part of a series. A sentence with this error is called a *run-on sentence* (or a *comma splice* or *comma fault*). Use a coordinating conjunction with the comma, or use a semicolon.

> **INCORRECT** John Wayne worked in Hollywood for almost fifty years, he made more than two hundred films.
> **CORRECT** John Wayne worked in Hollywood for almost fifty years, and he made more than two hundred films.

Do not use a comma between a subject and its verb or between a verb and its complement.

> **INCORRECT** What you do with your money, is your business.
> **CORRECT** What you do with your money is your business.

> **INCORRECT** For the overnight camping trip you will need, a sleeping bag, a towel, soap, and a toothbrush.
> **CORRECT** For the overnight camping trip you will need a sleeping bag, a towel, soap, and a toothbrush.

Using the Comma (Part 4) Rewrite the following letter, adding commas where they are needed. (Twenty commas are needed altogether.)

> 1516 Evergreen Road
> Bonita California 92002
> October 5 1992

Dear Belinda

　Your mother has told me that you would like some advice about a good diet. She wrote that you want to lose about twenty pounds. I hope that she has misunderstood your goal Belinda because you would be quite thin if you lost that much weight wouldn't you?

　I have enclosed a copy of an article about diet and weight loss that was published in the May 6 1991 issue of *News in America* page 22. Ruth Smith M.D. the author is a specialist in nutrition. In November 1990 I heard Dr. Smith speak at a conference in Washington D.C. and I have a great deal of respect for her knowledge. You will read this article carefully won't you?

　I am looking forward to visiting your family at Thanksgiving. I haven't seen any of you since I was in San Diego on May 14 1989 for a convention. When I visit this year I hope we'll be able to spend some time together Belinda.

> Love
> Aunt Miriam

21.7　The Dash

　On a typewriter indicate the dash with two hyphens (--). Do not place a comma, semicolon, colon, or period before or after a dash.

Dashes to Signal Change

Use a dash to indicate an abrupt break or change in thought within a sentence.

> A small stand sells sugar loaves—the gift to bring when invited to dinner—sugar for the mint tea and for the sweet pastry, so flaky and light, that they bake.
>
> Anaïs Nin

Dashes to Emphasize

Use a dash to set off and emphasize supplemental information or parenthetical comments.

> It was a shiny new car—the first he had ever owned.

> A shiny new car—the first he had ever owned—was his most prized possession.

21.8 Parentheses

Use parentheses to set off supplemental material.

Commas and dashes are also used to set off supplemental material; the difference between the three marks of punctuation is one of degree. Use commas to set off supplemental material that is closely related to the rest of the sentence. Use parentheses to set off supplemental material that is not important enough to be considered part of the main statement. Use dashes to set off and emphasize material that interrupts the main statement.

> Many contemporary women's fashions (business suits and low heels) show the influence of Gabrielle "Coco" Chanel (1883–1971).

A complete sentence within parentheses is not capitalized and needs no period if it is contained within another sentence. If a sentence in parentheses is not contained within another sentence (if it stands by itself), both a capital letter and a period are needed.

> The unisex trend (it still seems to be popular) was started by Chanel, who wore a man's trench coat.

> Chanel introduced the world's most famous perfume, Chanel No. 5. (This scent is still in great demand.)

Parentheses with Other Marks of Punctuation

1. With a comma, semicolon, or colon

Always place a comma, semicolon, or colon *after* the closing parenthesis.

> Despite the simple clothes that Chanel designed and wore (the little black dress became her uniform), she became fabulously wealthy.

> In the early 1950s fashionable women wore long skirts with cinched waists and high heels (the Dior look); Chanel helped to change all that.

2. With a question mark or an exclamation point

Place a question mark or an exclamation point *inside* the parentheses if it is part of the parenthetical expression.

> Chanel believed that simplicity and practicality were more important than obviously expensive, complicated-looking clothes (who would not agree today**?).**

> Chanel exerted little influence on fashion during World War II (1939–1945), but she reopened her fashion house in 1954 (when she was seventy**!).**

Place a question mark or an exclamation point *outside* the parentheses if it is part of the entire sentence.

> Did you know that Chanel introduced many of today's fashion classics (sweaters, costume jewelry, sling-back shoes**)?**

> How amazed I was to find out that it was Chanel who made a suntan fashionable (in the 1930s**)!**

Exercise 8

Using the Dash and Parentheses Rewrite the following sentences correctly, adding dashes and parentheses where they are needed. Use the marks of punctuation indicated in parentheses at the end of each sentence. Remember that a dash is used to show emphasis or an interruption in thought, whereas parentheses are used to set off supplemental material.

1. Roger he was a frail boy and never tried out for sports had an inordinate love for baseball. (dashes)
2. Amarillo from the Spanish word for "yellow" is a town in the Texas Panhandle. (parentheses)
3. It was a stormy December night, and the snow heavy, wet, and as thick as porridge was falling steadily. (dashes)
4. That song is it by Handel or Mozart? always reminds me of Paula, for she used to play it constantly when we were in college together. (parentheses)
5. He was aggressive, overbearing, and mean, and who would have thought it possible! completely devoted to his dachshund. (parentheses)
6. Anorexia can have serious even tragic consequences if not treated properly. (dashes)
7. Some people I am not one of them think that Elvis Presley was a devastatingly handsome man. (parentheses)
8. Do you believe in love at first sight forgive the cliché? (parentheses) ➡

9. It was an extraordinary feat: she threw the javelin 245 feet about 75 meters! (parentheses)
10. Otis was an Air Force pilot during the Persian Gulf War the war against Iraq, which occurred in 1991. (parentheses)

21.9 Quotation Marks

Quotation Marks for Direct Quotations

Use quotation marks to enclose a direct quotation.

Place quotation marks around the quotation only, not around purely introductory or explanatory remarks. Generally separate such remarks from the actual quotation with a comma.

> A famous poster asks, "What if they gave a war and nobody came?"

> A Pawnee poem reminds us of "the sacredness of things."

Do not use a comma after a quotation that ends with an exclamation point or a question mark.

> "What is the question?" Gertrude Stein asked.

(For the use of colons to introduce quotations, see p. 669.)

When a quotation is interrupted by explanatory words such as *he said* or *she wrote*, use two sets of quotation marks.

Separate each part of the quotation from the interrupting phrase with marks of punctuation before and after the interrupting phrase. If the second part of the quotation is a complete sentence, begin it with a capital letter.

> "Over increasingly large areas of the United States," wrote Rachel Carson, "spring now comes unheralded by the return of the birds."

> "It wasn't just that Babe Ruth hit more home runs than anybody else," said Red Smith. "He hit them better, higher, and farther."

Do not use quotation marks in an indirect quotation (a quotation that does not repeat a person's exact words).

> **ORIGINAL QUOTATION**   "Dance is life at its most glorious moment," said Pearl Lang.

INDIRECT QUOTATION   Pearl Lang said that dance is life's most glorious moment.

Use single quotation marks around a quotation within a quotation.

> President John F. Kennedy said, "I am one person who can truthfully say, 'I got my job through the *New York Times.*'"

In writing dialogue, begin a new paragraph and use a new set of quotation marks every time the speaker changes.

> He looked at me proudly. "Was it so hard to do, Daughter?"
> "Not so hard as I thought." I pinned the brooch on my dress.
> "I'll wear it always," I said. "I'll keep it forever."
> "Mama will be glad, Katrin."
>
> Kathryn Forbes

Quotation Marks with Titles of Short Works

Use quotation marks to enclose titles of short works, such as short stories, short poems, essays, newspaper and magazine articles, book chapters, songs, and single episodes of a television series.

> "The Legend of Sleepy Hollow" [short story]
> "The Raven" [poem]
> "On the Duty of Civil Disobedience" [essay]
> "Steven Spielberg's Newest Film" [newspaper article]
> "The 1980s in America" [chapter]
> "If I Had a Hammer" [song]
> "Division of the Spoils" [episode in a television series]

(For the use of italics with titles of longer works, see p. 687.)

Quotation Marks with Unusual Expressions

Use quotation marks to enclose unfamiliar slang and other unusual or original expressions.

> My cousin uses the expression "the cat's meow" to describe something she likes.

Quotation Marks with Other Marks of Punctuation

1. With a comma or a period

Always place a comma or a period *inside* closing quotation marks.

"The frog does not drink up the pond in which it lives," states a Native American proverb.

Henry David Thoreau humorously advises, "Beware of all enterprises that require new clothes."

2. With a semicolon or a colon

Always place a semicolon or a colon *outside* closing quotation marks.

Her father said, "We cannot go"; her mother said, "Perhaps we can go next year"; her elder brother just shrugged his shoulders.

This is what I think of Lady Ōtomo's poem "My Heart, Thinking": it is romantic and powerful.

3. With a question mark or an exclamation point

Place the question mark or the exclamation point *inside* the closing quotation marks when it is part of the quotation.

A famous sonnet by Shakespeare begins with these words: "Shall I compare thee to a summer's day?"

She said, "I never want to hear from you again!"

Place the question mark or the exclamation point *outside* the closing quotation marks when it is part of the entire sentence.

I've finally memorized all of "Paul Revere's Ride"!
Why do you keep saying, "I'm sorry"?

If both the sentence and the quotation at the end of the sentence need a question mark (or an exclamation point), use only one punctuation mark, and place it *inside* the quotation marks.

When did he ask, "Would you like to go to the movies?"

Exercise 9

Using Quotation Marks   Rewrite the following sentences correctly, adding quotation marks where they are needed. For the sentences that need no changes, write *correct*.

Gabriela Mistral, a Prize-Winning Poet

1. When Chilean poet Gabriela Mistral received the Nobel Prize for Literature in 1945, the Swedish Academy said that Mistral had almost become a legend.
2. The poem Close to Me, which appears in Gabriela Mistral's first book, *Despair*, is a lullaby that is sung by a mother to a young child. ➡

3. The refrain, *sleep close to me!* appears at the end of each verse of the poem.
4. In his introduction to a collection of Mistral's poems, the African-American poet Langston Hughes implies that her language is simple and direct.
5. Even when she sings the commonplace in life, writes critic A. Ortiz-Vargas, there is always a restraint, a dignity in her tone.
6. Ortiz-Vargas goes on to say, Sometimes her song soars high as on eagle wings, but more often it is rooted in the fertile region of her own heart.
7. Ortiz-Vargas writes, There is never any gaiety in her poetry—nor lightness—for her emotions are always ardently passionate; many other critics agree with his view.
8. The phrase *a cry from the heart* could be used to describe many of Mistral's verses.
9. Do you know Mistral's powerful poem about motherhood, Song of Virgo?
10. In his introduction to *Selected Poems of Gabriela Mistral,* Langston Hughes writes: Mildred Adams wrote, Gabriela's clarity and precision, her passion and that characteristic which can only be called her nobility of soul are accepted as ideals.

21.10   Italics (Underlining)

Italic type is a special slanted type that is used in printing. (*This is printed in italics.*) Indicate italics on a typewriter or with handwriting by underlining. (This is underlined.)

Italics with Titles

Italicize (underline) titles of books, lengthy poems, plays, films and television series, paintings and sculptures, and long musical compositions. Also italicize the names of newspapers and magazines, ships, trains, airplanes, and spacecraft.

Great Expectations [book]	*Snow-Bound* [long poem]
Romeo and Juliet [play]	*Gone with the Wind* [film]
Nova [television series]	*Starry Night* [painting]
The Thinker [sculpture]	*Grand Canyon Suite* [musical work]
Sports Illustrated [magazine]	the *Oakland Tribune* [newspaper]
U.S.S. *Enterprise** [ship]	*Spirit of St. Louis* [airplane]
Orient Express [train]	*Columbia* [spacecraft]

*Do not italicize abbreviations such as U.S.S. that precede the name of a ship.

Italicize (underline) and capitalize articles (*a, an, the*) written at the beginning of a title only when they are part of the title itself. It is common practice not to italicize (underline) the article preceding the title of a newspaper or a magazine. Do not italicize the word *magazine* unless it is part of the title of a periodical.

A Light in the Attic	but	a *National Geographic* magazine
The Red Badge of Courage		the *Chicago Tribune*

Italics with Foreign Words

Italicize (underline) foreign words and expressions that are not used frequently in English.

The motto of the U.S. Marine Corps is **semper fidelis** ("always faithful").

Do not italicize a foreign word or expression that is commonly used in English.

I eat **croissants** for breakfast.

Italics with Words and Other Items Used to Represent Themselves

Italicize (underline) words, letters, and numerals used to represent themselves.

His typewriter did not have the numeral **1**, so he used a small **l** in its place.

She was too superstitious to say the number aloud, so she handed the elevator operator a piece of paper on which she had written **13**.

Replace all of the number signs (**#**'s) with the word **number**.

Exercise 10

Using Italics   Rewrite the following sentences correctly, underlining the parts that should be italicized.

Women in the Olympics

1. In the book Golden Girls by Carli Laklan, you will find information about the many women who have won Olympic medals.
2. The ancient Greeks based the first Olympics on the concept of arete, which means "excellence in every area of life—physical, moral, and intellectual." ➡

3. The author of Golden Girls notes that the earliest games featured just one event, the stade, a two-hundred-yard footrace; the English word stadium comes from the Greek word stade.
4. The word Olympics comes from Olympia, the name of the Greek city where the first Olympic games were held in 776 B.C.
5. Sonja Henie, who won three gold medals in figure skating at three successive Olympic games, gained recognition as a movie star with her first film, One in a Million.
6. Peggy Fleming won a gold medal in figure skating at the 1968 Grenoble Olympics; she skated to Tchaikovsky's Pathétique.
7. With the financial backing of the publishers of the Chicago Tribune, Gertrude Ederle, who had won the gold medal for swimming in 1924, became the first woman to swim the English Channel in 1926; the French tug the Alsace followed her with a jazz band on board "to keep up her spirits."
8. Wilma Rudolph, who overcame serious illnesses in childhood, was the first American woman to win three gold medals in track and field; she later became a commentator for the radio series Olympic Odyssey.
9. After the 1984 Olympics gold-medal winners Florence Griffith-Joyner and Jackie Joyner-Kersee were featured in Time, Life, Newsweek, the New York Times, and Sports Illustrated.
10. Many of the Olympic gold medalists have been on television series ranging from What's My Line? to Evening Magazine.

21.11 The Apostrophe

Apostrophes with Possessives

1. Pronouns

Use an apostrophe and -*s* for the possessive of a singular indefinite pronoun.

Do not use an apostrophe with other possessive pronouns.

everybody**'s** problem	*but*	**its** owner
each other**'s** parents		**whose** talents

2. Singular nouns

Use an apostrophe and -*s* to form the possessive of a singular noun, even one that ends in -*s*.

the woman's team	San Francisco's earthquake
the class's election	Robert Burns's poetry
the princess's career	Cape Hatteras's beauty
the box's lettering	Groucho Marx's biography

There are some exceptions to this rule, however. To form the possessive of ancient proper nouns that end in -*es* or -*is*, the name *Jesus*, and expressions with words such as *appearance* and *conscience*, just add an apostrophe.

Euripedes' plays	Jesus' teachings
Acropolis' structure	for appearance' sake

3. Plural nouns ending in -*s*

Use an apostrophe alone to form the possessive of a plural noun that ends in -*s*.

the countries' treaty	the Joneses' picnic

4. Plural nouns not ending in -*s*

Use an apostrophe and -*s* to form the possessive of a plural noun that does not end in -*s*.

women's clubs	Women's Bar Association

5. Compound nouns

Put only the last word of a compound noun in the possessive form.

my sister-in-law's office
the court-martial's effect
the Vice President's responsibilities
the chief of staff's order

6. Joint possession versus individual possession

If two or more persons (or partners in a company) possess something jointly, use the possessive form for the last person named.

Claude and Louise's children
Johnson and Johnson's baby-care products
Abbott and Costello's antics

If two or more persons (or companies) possess an item (or items) individually, put each one's name in the possessive form.

Tina Turner's and the Rolling Stones' songs
Chrysler's and the American Motor Company's cars

7. Expressions of time and money

Use a possessive form to express amounts of money or time that modify a noun.

The modifier can also be expressed as a hyphenated adjective. In that case, no possessive form is used.

one dollar**'s** increase	*but*	a one-dollar increase
five minutes**'** drive		a five-minute drive
ten days**'** wait		a ten-day wait

Apostrophes in Contractions

Use an apostrophe in place of letters omitted in contractions.

A **contraction** is a single word made up of two words that have been combined by omitting letters. Common contractions combine a subject and a verb or a verb and an adverb.

you**'**d	*formed from*	you had, you would
you**'**re		you are
who**'**s		who is, who has
it**'**s		it is, it has
won**'**t		will not

Use an apostrophe in place of the omitted numerals of a particular year.

the class of **'**94   the **'**92 campaign

Apostrophes with Special Plurals

Use an apostrophe and -*s* to form the plural of letters, numerals, symbols, and words used to represent themselves.

Italicize (underline) the letter, numeral, symbol, or word but not the apostrophe and the -*s*.

Your *e***'s** look like *I***'s**, and your *5***'s** look like *S***'s**.
She told me to replace the *henceforth***'s** with *therefore***'s**.

Exercise 11

Using the Apostrophe   Rewrite the following sentences correctly, adding an apostrophe or an apostrophe and -*s* wherever necessary.

Women and Literature
[1]Imagine that you were making a list of writers names for a new encyclopedia about female authors. [2]Under the *as* ➡

youd include Louisa May Alcott, whos best known for *Little Women*, and Isabel Allende, author of *The House of the Spirits*. [3]Maya Angelou, who wrote *I Know Why the Caged Bird Sings*, would surely be on everyones list. [4]The *b*s would include the names of Toni Cade Bambara and Gwendolyn Brooks. [5]Both Bambaras novels and Brooks poems focus on the lives of African Americans and on womens issues. [6]Nikki Giovanni is a poet whod be listed under the *g*s; her books include *Black Feeling* and *My House*. [7]At least five twentieth-century authors names would be listed under the *m*s: Carson McCullers, Edna St. Vincent Millay, Margaret Mitchell, Marianne Moore, and Toni Morrison. [8]Millays and Moores names would be found on anyones list of talented poets; McCullers and Morrisons names are familiar to lovers of prose. [9]Most people don't know that Margaret Mitchells *Gone with the Wind* took ten years labor to write; it was finally published in 36. [10]In the entry about the novelist Katherine Anne Porter, youd want to mention Porters great-great-grandfathers name: Daniel Boone.

21.12 The Hyphen

Hyphens with Prefixes

A hyphen is not ordinarily used to join a prefix to a word. There are a few exceptions, however. If you are in doubt about using a hyphen, consult a dictionary. You should also keep in mind the following guidelines:

Use a hyphen after any prefix joined to a proper noun or a proper adjective. Use a hyphen after the prefixes *all-*, *ex-* (meaning "former"), and *self-* joined to any noun or adjective.

> mid-Atlantic
> all-city
> ex-coach
> self-confidence

Use a hyphen after the prefix *anti-* when it joins a word beginning with *i-*. Also use a hyphen after the prefix *vice-*, except in *vice president*.

> anti-intellectual
> vice-mayor

The offensive end re-covered the ball.

Use a hyphen to avoid confusion between words beginning with *re-* that look alike but are different in meaning and pronunciation.

re-cover the couch	*but*	recover the ball
re-store those cans		restore your confidence
re-lease the car		release the brake

Hyphens in Compound Adjectives

Use a hyphen in a compound adjective that precedes a noun.

In general, a compound adjective that follows a noun is not hyphenated.

dark-green eyes	*but*	Her eyes are dark green.
a fifteen-year-old aunt		His aunt is fifteen years old.
a well-liked reporter		That reporter is well liked.

An expression made up of an adverb ending in -*ly* and an adjective is not hyphenated.

a nicely behaved dog	a fairly close race
a slightly rusted exterior	a hastily written report

Hyphens in Numbers

1. Compound numbers

Hyphenate any spelled-out cardinal or ordinal compound number up to ninety-nine or ninety-ninth.

sixty-four	sixty-fourth
eighty-two	eighty-second

2. Fractions used as adjectives

Hyphenate a fraction used as an adjective (but not one used as a noun).

one-eighth teaspoon	*but*	one eighth of a teaspoon
one-quarter cup		one quarter of a cup
one-half pound		one half of a pound

3. Connected numerals

Hyphenate two numerals to indicate a span.

pages 30-56	1986-1990

Hyphens to Divide Words at the End of a Line

Words are generally divided between syllables or pronounceable parts. Because it is frequently difficult to determine where a word should be divided, check your dictionary.

In general, if a word contains two consonants occurring between two vowels or if it contains a double consonant, divide the word between the two consonants.

foun-tain   struc-ture
lin-ger   sup-per
profes-sor   tomor-row

If a suffix has been added to a complete word that ends in two consonants, divide the word after the two consonants.

kick-ing   point-less
meaning-ful   strong-est

Exercise 12

Using the Hyphen   Hyphens must be added to five of the following sentences. Rewrite those sentences, adding the hyphens where they are needed. Then make a list of all the italicized words, showing where each would be divided if it had to be broken at the end of a line.

Sally Ride, Astronaut

1. Sally Ride was thirty one in 1983 when she became the first American woman to *orbit* the earth.
2. She was also the *youngest* American astronaut to go into orbit.
3. At Swarthmore College, where she did her undergraduate work, Sally Ride won a national tennis tournament for *college* students.
4. Astronaut Ride received her *doctorate* from Stanford University.
5. Dr. Ride said that one third of the *scientists* at NASA are women.
6. A thirty four year old Russian woman, Svetlana Savitskaya, *orbited* the earth about eight months before Dr. Ride.
7. Astronauts are *resourceful*, self confident, healthy, highly educated, and experienced in their special fields of study.
8. By the year 2000 spaceflight may become *common*; within your lifetime thousands may be taking trips into space every year.
9. Ex astronauts such as John Glenn and Neil Armstrong were viewed as all American heroes for years after their space *missions*.
10. Astronaut trainees must learn to live in an almost *weightless*, low gravity environment.

21.13 Abbreviations

Abbreviations are shortened forms of words. Abbreviations save space and time and prevent unnecessary wordiness. For instance, *M.D.* is more concise and easier to write than *Medical Doctor.* Most abbreviations take periods. If you are unsure of how to write an abbreviation, consult a dictionary.

Use only one period if an abbreviation occurs at the end of a sentence that would ordinarily take a period of its own.

If an abbreviation occurs at the end of a sentence that ends with a question mark or an exclamation point, use the period *and* the second mark of punctuation.

Gerry left at 8 **A.M.**   Did she leave at 8 **A.M.?**

Capitalization of Abbreviations

Capitalize abbreviations of proper nouns.

109-46 Queens **Blvd.**   **Rev.** Jesse Jackson
Shreveport, **La.**   **U.S.** Congress

Abbreviations of organizations and government agencies are often formed from the initial letters of the complete name. Such abbreviations omit periods.

YWCA   CORE   IRS
NASA   UNICEF   CBS

State names used in addressing mail may be abbreviated as shown in the following list. The official ZIP-code form consists of two capital letters with no periods.

Alabama	**Ala.**	**AL**	Kansas	**Kans.**	**KS**
Alaska		**AK**	Kentucky	**Ky.**	**KY**
Arizona	**Ariz.**	**AZ**	Louisiana	**La.**	**LA**
Arkansas	**Ark.**	**AR**	Maine		**ME**
California	**Calif.**	**CA**	Maryland	**Md.**	**MD**
Colorado	**Colo.**	**CO**	Massachusetts	**Mass.**	**MA**
Connecticut	**Conn.**	**CT**	Michigan	**Mich.**	**MI**
Delaware	**Del.**	**DE**	Minnesota	**Minn.**	**MN**
Florida	**Fla.**	**FL**	Mississippi	**Miss.**	**MS**
Georgia	**Ga.**	**GA**	Missouri	**Mo.**	**MO**
Hawaii		**HI**	Montana	**Mont.**	**MT**
Idaho		**ID**	Nebraska	**Nebr.**	**NB**
Illinois	**Ill.**	**IL**	Nevada	**Nev.**	**NV**
Indiana	**Ind.**	**IN**	New Hampshire	**N.H.**	**NH**
Iowa		**IA**	New Jersey	**N.J.**	**NJ**

New Mexico	**N.Mex.**	**NM**	South Dakota	**S.Dak.**	**SD**
New York	**N.Y.**	**NY**	Tennessee	**Tenn.**	**TN**
North Carolina	**N.C.**	**NC**	Texas	**Tex.**	**TX**
North Dakota	**N.Dak.**	**ND**	Utah		**UT**
Ohio		**OH**	Vermont	**Vt.**	**VT**
Oklahoma	**Okla.**	**OK**	Virginia	**Va.**	**VA**
Oregon	**Oreg.**	**OR**	Washington	**Wash.**	**WA**
Pennsylvania	**Pa.**	**PA**	West Virginia	**W.Va.**	**WV**
Rhode Island	**R.I.**	**RI**	Wisconsin	**Wis.**	**WI**
South Carolina	**S.C.**	**SC**	Wyoming	**Wyo.**	**WY**

Capitalize the following abbreviations related to dates and times:

A.D. (*anno Domini*), "in the year of the Lord" (since the birth of Christ); place before the date: **A.D.** 5

B.C. (before Christ); place after the date: 1000 **B.C.**

B.C.E. (before the common era); place after the date: 164 **B.C.E.**

C.E. (common era); place after the date: 66 **C.E.**

A.M. (*ante meridiem*), "before noon"

P.M. (*post meridiem*), "after noon"

Abbreviations of Titles of People

Use abbreviations for some personal titles.

Titles such as *Mrs., Mr.,* and *Jr.* and those indicating professions and academic degrees (*Dr., M.A., B.S.*) are almost always abbreviated. Titles of government and military officials and members of the clergy are frequently abbreviated when used before a full name.

Mrs. Bush	**Sen.** Nancy Kassebaum
Desi Arnaz **Jr.**	**Gen.** Colin Powell
Dr. Rosalyn Ying	Myron Greene, **D.D.S.**

Abbreviations of Units of Measure

Abbreviate units of measure used with numerals in technical or scientific writing but not in ordinary prose.

Ken Griffey **Sr.** and Ken Griffey **Jr.**

The abbreviations that follow stand for both plural and singular units:

ENGLISH SYSTEM

ft.	foot	**mi.**	mile	**tbsp.**	tablespoon
gal.	gallon	**oz.**	ounce	**tsp.**	teaspoon
in.	inch	**pt.**	pint	**yd.**	yard
lb.	pound	**qt.**	quart		

METRIC SYSTEM

cg	centigram	**l**	liter	
cl	centiliter	**m**	meter	
cm	centimeter	**mg**	milligram	
g	gram	**ml**	milliliter	
kg	kilogram	**mm**	millimeter	
km	kilometer			

Exercise 13

Using Abbreviations   Write the abbreviations for the italicized words or phrases in the following sentences.

1. Secretary of State William Seward purchased Alaska from Russia in *anno Domini* 1867.
2. *Senator* Bob Graham is the junior senator from Florida.
3. Many students attended summer school from 10:00 *ante meridiem* to 3:00 *post meridiem*.
4. The ZIP code for Waco, *Texas*, is 77005.
5. The *Internal Revenue Service* is responsible for collecting federal taxes.
6. W. E. B. Du Bois founded the *National Association for the Advancement of Colored People* in 1909.
7. The Greek philosopher Aristotle lived in the fourth century *before Christ*.
8. *Doctor* Mary Walker, an army surgeon, won the Congressional Medal of Honor for her work with wounded soldiers during the American Civil War.
9. The architect's plans indicated that the garden would be 40 *feet* by 23 *feet* (12 *meters* by 7 *meters*).
10. *Saint* Louis, Missouri, is located on the Mississippi River.

21.14   Numbers and Numerals

In nontechnical writing some numbers are spelled out, and some are expressed in figures. Numbers expressed in figures are called *numerals*.

Numbers Spelled Out

In general, spell out cardinal and ordinal numbers that can be written in one or two words.

Spell out any number that occurs at the beginning of a sentence.

New Hampshire is one of the original **thirteen** states.
There are **twenty-seven** students in the class.
Alaska was the **forty-ninth** state to join the Union.
Sixteen hundred fifteen delegates attended.

Numerals

In general, use numerals to express numbers that would be written in more than two words.

Mount Mitchell, the highest mountain in the eastern United States, is **6,684** feet tall.

In 1790 the total population of the United States (according to the first census) was **3,929,214.**

In 1984 Joe W. Kittinger covered **3,535** miles in eighty-three hours and fifty-three minutes, setting a record for balloon flight.

Very large numbers are often written as a numeral followed by the word *million* or *billion*.

The surface area of the earth is close to **197 million** square miles.

If related numbers appear in the same sentence and some can be written out while others should appear as numerals, use all numerals.

Edgar ranked **65th** in the class; his brother ranked **119th.**

1. Money, decimals, and percentages

Use numerals to express amounts of money, decimals, and percentages.

$897 million	**1.2** kilograms
$3.50	**5** percent

Amounts of money that can be expressed in one or two words, however, should be spelled out.

forty-five cents
two thousand dollars

2. Dates and time

Use numerals to express the year and day in a date and to express the precise time with the abbreviations A.M. and P.M.

The Soviet Union launched *Sputnik I,* the first manufactured satellite to orbit the earth, on October **4, 1957.**

She went to the meeting at **4:15 P.M.**

Spell out expressions of time that do not use the abbreviation A.M. or P.M.

> She set her alarm clock for **five** o'clock.

To express a century when the word *century* is used, spell out the number. Likewise, to express a decade when the century is clear from the context, spell out the number.

> In the **twentieth** century the nation experienced the greatest economic depression of its history.

> The Great Depression of the **thirties** was a severe national economic crisis.

When a century and a decade are expressed as a single unit, use numerals followed by an -*s*.

> In the **1930s** the federal government developed many new programs to ease the crisis.

3. Addresses

Use numerals for numbered streets and avenues over ten and for all house, apartment, and room numbers. Spell out numbered streets and avenues of ten or under.

> **1654** West **66th** Street   **4** North Main Street
> Apartment **8C**   Room **3**
> **30** East **15th** Street   **20 Second** Avenue

4. References

Use numerals to express page, line, act, and scene numbers and the like.

> Look on pages **20** and **59** for information about Pablo Casals.
> Read lines **1–80** in Book **I** of the *Iliad*.
> We rehearsed Act **2,** Scenes **3** and **4,** of the play.

Exercise 14

Using Numbers and Numerals   Write out the following sentences, making any necessary changes in the use of numbers and numerals.

Althea Gibson, Tennis Star

[1]In 1957, the year she turned 30, Althea Gibson became the 1st African-American tennis player to win the championship in the annual tennis tournament at Wimbledon in England. [2]Gibson traveled three thousand five hundred miles from her home in New York City to Wimbledon, but the distance ➡

that she traveled from being a 13-year-old high school dropout to a renowned tennis champion was even greater. [3]Gibson was born on a farm in South Carolina on August twenty-fifth, 1927; she was the oldest of 5 children. [4]For many years she lived with her family at 135 West 143rd Street in Harlem, and she spent her free time playing basketball at the One Hundred Thirty-fourth Street Boys Club with a team called the Mysterious 5. [5]When she was a lanky girl of fifteen (she would eventually be five feet eleven inches tall), she started taking tennis lessons from a 1-armed coach named Fred Johnson. [6]In 1947, when Gibson was 19, she played in 9 tournaments and won the singles title in each one. [7]Through the late 40s and early 50s, Gibson concentrated on both her tennis and her education. [8]She went back to high school, finishing 10th in her class, and then went to college, graduating in 1953 at the age of twenty-five. [9]49 minutes was all the time it took Gibson to win the championship at Wimbledon in 1957. [10]After Wimbledon she won a one-hundred-thousand-dollar contract to play exhibition tennis matches and, in 1960, the women's professional singles title; she later became a professional golfer.

Exercise 15: Review

Punctuation, Abbreviations, and Numbers   On your paper rewrite the following sentences, correcting the errors in punctuation, abbreviations, and numbers. There may be several errors in each sentence.

Shopping in a Bookstore

1. In the travel section of Campbells Bookshop, I looked at books about Kenya Switzerland and Mexico.
2. While I looked at travel books Jane and Rafael wandered into other sections.
3. Jane went to the literature section for she wanted a copy of Wuthering Heights.
4. On her way Jane spied a book of quotations with an attractive bright red cover.
5. Picking it up she thumbed through the thick white pages.
6. Then her eye fell on a familiar saying Ask me no questions and Ill tell you no lies.
7. Oh she said to herself. I didn't know that Oliver Goldsmith first wrote that line in his play She Stoops to Conquer.
8. Rafael in the meantime hurried to the record videotape and audiocassette section. ➡

9. A music student he was hoping to find a videotape of Mozarts Magic Flute.
10. May I help you? inquired Mrs Kato a sales clerk.
11. Rafael who wanted to browse first thanked her and then headed for the neatly arranged video packages.
12. Mozarts opera was not on the shelf but Rafael found twenty one copies of a new release, James Galway Plays Mostly Mozart.
13. With all out enthusiasm he grabbed a copy paid for the tape and came looking for me.
14. Having found the travel books I wanted I had moved to the humor section to find a birthday present for my brother.
15. Rafael suggested James Thurbers Fables for Our Time.
16. I especially like The Unicorn in the Garden he said referring to his favorite fable. Then he added your brother will like it.
17. Jane arrived next, having bought Wuthering Heights and the book of quotations.
18. I have no self restraint she explained. I wish I could buy out the whole store.
19. Laughing I admitted that I had found no fewer than thirty six books I would have liked to buy.
20. With our arms laden with the purchases we had made we left the bookstore and headed for the post office where I mailed the Thurber book to my brother in Saint Louis.

Mechanics Workshop

Punctuation

In *Arctic Dreams* Barry Lopez describes the landscapes of the north and the people and animals who live there. In the following passages, which have been annotated to show some of the rules of punctuation covered in this unit, he describes the Arctic's most magnificent creature: the polar bear.

Literature Model

from ARCTIC DREAMS
by Barry Lopez

Colon to introduce a sentence that explains the preceding material

The polar bear is a creature of arctic edges: he hunts the ice margins, the surface of the water, and the continental shore. The ice bear, he is called. His world forms beneath him in the days of shortening light, and then falls away in the spring.

Commas to separate elements in a series

❦

Comma to separate two main clauses joined by a coordinating conjunction

Polar bears vary in size, and their weights can change dramatically during the year. (Very large polar bears may stand 12 feet on their hind legs and weigh 2000 pounds. The number of 12- and 13-foot bears weighing 2200 or 2400 pounds that have been reported, however, says more about unadjusted scales, stretched hides, and wishful exaggeration than about polar bears.) Bears eat prodigiously in the spring, lightly in late summer, and lightly or not at all (in the case of denning females) during the winter. An adult male might weigh between 550 and 1700 pounds and measure 75 to 100 inches from tip of nose to tip of tail.

Parentheses to set off supplemental material

❦

Hyphen in a compound adjective preceding a noun

The Polar Eskimos of northwest Greenland call the polar bear *pisugtooq*, the great wanderer. On the basis of mark-and-recapture studies and radio- tracking information, scientists have determined that individual bears wander largely within a local area; but some, indeed, are long-distance travelers. A polar bear tagged in Svalbard, for example, showed up a year later near Nanortalik, Greenland, 2000 miles to the southwest. Another bear, a female, traveled a straight-line distance of 205 miles in ➡

Semicolon to separate two main clauses

Period at the end of a declarative sentence

two days. Polar bears have also been found far afield in unlikely places, at the crest of Mount Newton in Svalbard, for example, 6600 feet above sea level, or 30 miles inland on the Greenland ice cap. An American crew on the ice island Alpha saw a female and her cub at 84°N in December 1957.

❧

Thor Larsen, a biologist who has observed polar bears in Svalbard for more than fifteen years, when I asked him about their hunting behavior, said, "Cats. They are like big cats." Fast? "It is absolutely unbelievable how fast they are—oh, do they come fast." Shrewd? "Yes. They are making judgments at every point about what to do. And they are patient."

Commas to set off a nonrestrictive appositive

Quotation marks for dialogue

Dash to mark an abrupt break

Question mark to indicate a direct question

Mechanics Workshop Exercise 1

Using End Punctuation   The following sentences are about the Arctic. Rewrite each sentence, correcting any errors in end punctuation. If a sentence contains no errors, write *correct*.

1. How is the arctic region commonly defined.
2. Geographers describe it as the region around the North Pole lying north of the Arctic Circle.
3. The Arctic can also be defined as the area north of the tree line, which is the area where trees cannot grow.
4. How the Arctic has always fascinated people?
5. People wonder who first reached the North Pole?
6. Robert E. Peary attained this goal on April 6, 1909.
7. Can you imagine a blizzard that, in Peary's words, "surpasses in fury the sandstorms of the Sahara."
8. Imagine an immense, ice-covered ocean?
9. Water temperatures in the Arctic remain near the freezing point of salt water—about 29 degrees Fahrenheit or minus 1.7 degrees Celsius?
10. "On this great frozen Sahara of the North," wrote Peary, "the wind never ceases to blow."

Mechanics Workshop Exercise 2

Using Colons and Semicolons   The following sentences are about the Arctic. Rewrite each sentence, correcting any errors in the use of colons and semicolons. If a sentence contains no errors, write *correct*. ➡

SAMPLE	Arctic winters are cold and long: summers are cool and short.
ANSWER	Arctic winters are cold and long; summers are cool and short.

1. The Arctic includes parts of the following regions; Greenland, Canada, Alaska, Russia, Finland, Sweden, and Norway.
2. Some geographers include Iceland in the Arctic: others, however, exclude it from the region.
3. These minerals have been discovered in the Arctic; gold, tin, nickel, copper, and coal.
4. The climate is harsh: nevertheless, the Arctic is home to a variety of animals and plants.
5. Two features of the area are permafrost and lack of rainfall.

Mechanics Workshop Exercise 3

Using the Comma (Part 1)   The following sentences are about the Arctic. For each sentence add the material in parentheses in the place indicated by the caret. If the material in parentheses is *not* essential to the meaning of the sentence, add commas. If it is essential, do not add commas.

SAMPLE	The Arctic ∧ is home to many animals. (a region of extreme cold)
ANSWER	The Arctic, a region of extreme cold, is home to many animals.

1. Caribou ∧ migrate in huge herds. (similar to reindeer)
2. ∧ the caribou might not seem threatened. (No)
3. ∧ this animal has, however, been overhunted. (As a prime resource for the peoples of the Arctic)
4. Caribou are prized for their meat ∧. (which is extremely nutritious)
5. Another arctic animal ∧ is the musk ox. (that lives on the tundra)
6. ∧ musk oxen can easily withstand the bitter chill of the Arctic. (Wrapped in their dense wool)
7. Snowshoe hares ∧ seek the protection of the taiga, the forests of the far north. (unlike musk oxen)
8. The taiga is also the habitat of the hare's archenemy ∧. (the lynx)
9. In 1986 ∧ Fred Buemmer estimated that fifteen thousand polar bears remained in the Arctic. (the writer) ➡

10. A remarkable sight is polar bears hunting their favorite prey ʌ. (the harp seal)

Mechanics Workshop Exercise 4

Using the Comma (Part 2)   The following sentences describe Arctic animals. Rewrite each sentence correctly, adding or deleting commas where necessary.

1. Arctic animals have two major defenses against the harsh pervasive cold.
2. Voracious eating helps animals to stay warm and insulation minimizes heat loss.
3. A seventy-pound sea otter for example can eat fifteen pounds of food each day.
4. An otter's typical diet includes sea urchins mollusks and fish.
5. Life is feast or famine for wolves; consequently a single meal may be 25 percent of a wolf's body weight.
6. Fur, and fat, and feathers shield arctic animals from the intense cold.
7. The musk ox's long, glossy skirt of coarse, guard hair is its most striking feature.
8. Musk oxen will in fact seek shelter during severely cold weather, but their thick fur provides such excellent insulation that they routinely endure extremes of minus forty degrees Fahrenheit in the open air for prolonged periods.
9. Nature insulates many animals, but leaves humans unprotected.
10. For warmth the Inuit dress in animal skins; indeed they have long copied the animals' survival strategies.

Mechanics Workshop Exercise 5

Using the Dash and Parentheses   The following sentences are about arctic exploration. Rewrite each sentence correctly, adding dashes or parentheses where needed. Use the marks of punctuation indicated in parentheses at the end of each sentence.

SAMPLE	Eric the Red he was a Norse chieftain explored Greenland in the tenth century. (parentheses)
ANSWER	Eric the Red (he was a Norse chieftain) explored Greenland in the tenth century. ➡

1. The Dutch navigator Willem Barents a sea is named for him led a mission of exploration in 1597. (dashes)
2. Barents's arctic expedition the first in recorded history set out to survive a winter in the far north. (dashes)
3. The Dutch were looking for a Northeast Passage a northern route from Europe to the Pacific. (dash)
4. Vitus Bering the strait between Asia and North America bears his name was a Dane in service to Russia during the eighteenth century. (parentheses)
5. The strait usually frozen from October to June is a mere fifty-five miles wide. (parentheses)

Mechanics Workshop Exercise 6

Using Quotation Marks and Italics   The following sentences are about *Arctic Dreams*. Rewrite each sentence correctly, adding quotation marks or italics (underlining) where necessary. For the sentences that contain no errors, write *correct*.

1. In his book Arctic Dreams Barry Lopez describes his first encounter with a narwhal.
2. According to Chapter Four of the book, entitled Lancaster Sound, narwhals are very mysterious.
3. "We know more about the rings of Saturn, Lopez writes, than we know about the narwhal.
4. The scientific name of this small whale consists of two Greek words: monodon monoceros.
5. The first part of this name literally means "one tooth, and the second part means one horn."

Mechanics Workshop Exercise 7

Using the Apostrophe   The following sentences are about Barry Lopez's book *Of Wolves and Men*. Rewrite each sentence correctly, adding or deleting apostrophes where necessary. If a sentence has no errors, write *correct*.

1. Another of Barry Lopez major books is entitled *Of Wolves and Men*.
2. In this widely acclaimed work Lopez studies wolve's behavior. ➡

3. Minnesota's and Canada's wolves have drastically declined in numbers, Lopez reports.
4. Wolves are so shy that you might not spot one even after three months stay in the north woods.
5. Its surprising how many myths feature wolves as major characters.

Mechanics Workshop Exercise 8

Review The following sentences are about Barry Lopez. Rewrite each sentence, correcting all errors in punctuation. For a sentence that contains no errors, write *correct*.

Barry Lopez

1. Barry Lopez one of Americas' foremost writers on nature was born in 1945.
2. Soon after his graduation from the University of Notre Dame (in 1966), Lopez became a full-time writer.
3. Isn't it ironic that Lopez said, "I never thought I would be able to make a living as a writer?"
4. "Arctic Dreams" a celebration of animals and people in the frozen north was published in 1986, it earned the Francis Fuller Victor Award in nonfiction from the Oregon Institute of Literary Arts, in 1987.
5. Among the animals Lopez describes are these; polar bears, narwhals, musk oxen and caribou.
6. Arctic Dreams—the work won a National Book Award explores human being's relationship with the landscape.
7. Like the nature writer, Peter Matthiessen, with whom he has been compared), Lopez of course has traveled widely in search of material for his books.
8. Splendidly detailed Lopez' books convey impressive amounts of carefully researched information.
9. In an interview, Lopez once stated, "Writers work with metaphors.
10. It is legitimate to ask whether the natural world has ever had a more thorough and eloquent chronicler than Barry Lopez?

Proofreading   The following passage describes the artist Rockwell Kent, whose painting appears on the opposite page. Rewrite the passage, correcting the errors in spelling, capitalization, punctuation, usage, and grammar. There are twenty-five errors in all.

Rockwell Kent

1 Rockwell Kent (1882–1971) was born in Tarrytown Heights a small town on the Hudson River North of New York City. **2** He studied architecture at Columbia University, and painting at the New york School of Art. **3** He was strongly influenced by three of his teachers; William Chase, Robert Henri and Abbott Thayer. **4** These men, all prominent realists portrayed American life with a clear and unsentimental eye.

5 When he was in his early 20s Kent developed a strong interest in the landscape and the people of the Arctic and the Antarctic. **6** Like many other young men of his time Kent had become interested in Alaska and the Yukon by reading the novels of Jack London. **7** Like London, Kent lived an adventurous life, spending much of his time in the harsh, cold climates that he loved. **8** He trapped lobsters in Maine, sailed through treacherous waters off the tip of South America and lived in the hinterlands of Alaska, Newfoundland, and Greenland.

9 Kent was also a gifted writer. **10** He wrote and illustrated several books, including *Wilderness* (1920), which describes his travels through Alaska and *Voyaging Southward from The Strait of Magellan* (1924), which tells of his seafaring adventures in South America. **11** Kent received wide praise for the powerful wood engravings that appeared in the books he illustrated during the 1920's and 1930s. **12** He developed a boldly graphic style that used strong but simple patterns and decorative designs. **13** His interest in simplicity and stylized forms is apparent in *The Trapper* which depicts a solitary man trudging through the snow in a bleak landscape.

14 Kent would have been the ideal illustrater for Barry Lopez' *Arctic Dreams*. **15** (the book was published in 1886, 15 years after Kents death). **16** Both men felt a deep affinity for the harsh landscape of the Arctic and the struggles endured by its inhabitants. **17** Lopez writes in *Arctic Dreams,* "i came to believe that people's desires and aspirations were as much a part of the land as the wind, solitery animals, and the bright fields of stone and tundra." **18** Kent probably would have agreed.

Rockwell Kent, *The Trapper,* 1921

Unit 21 Review

Punctuation, Abbreviation, and Numbers

Read the following passages, noting the underlined text. Then, in each numbered item below, choose the word or group of words for which the punctuation and treatment of numbers are correct as they are used in the passage.

Gordon Parks, the noted [1]photographer is also an artist, [2]a filmmaker an author and a painter. He has written [3]3 autobiographical novels (including [4]"The Learning Tree"), poetry, and [5]essays he has also composed [6]music and produced films. Now Parks says [7]that "there are many things he still wants to [8]do. I just want [9]the time, he said, [10]to do them carefully and with joy."

1. **a.** photographer,
   b. photographer
   c. "photographer"
2. **a.** a filmmaker, an author
   b. a filmmaker, an author,
3. **a.** three
   b. 3
4. **a.** *The Learning Tree*),
   b. "The Learning Tree"),
   c. The Learning Tree,)
5. **a.** essays, he
   b. essays. he
   c. essays; he
   d. essays; He
6. **a.** music, and
   b. music and
7. **a.** that "there
   b. "that there
   c. that there
8. **a.** do. "I
   b. do." I
   c. do. I
9. **a.** the time, he said
   b. the time," he said
   c. the time. he said

10. **a.** "to do
    b. to do

On [11]Monday April 15 1991 I tried out for a [12]play the first play I had ever auditioned for. It was one of Tennessee [13]Williams [14]best [15]"The Glass Menagerie" I was flattered to be [16]considered however, I was nervous about the audition. My acting teacher gave me the following [17]advice "Lose yourself in the character." At the audition I took a [18]long deep [19]breath and then the director told me to begin. Did you know that I got the role of Laura [20]Wingfield

11. **a.** Monday April 15, 1991
    b. Monday, April 15, 1991,
    c. Monday, April 15, 1991
12. **a.** play—
    b. play:
13. **a.** William's
    b. Williams's
    c. Williams'
14. **a.** best
    b. best:
    c. best,
15. **a.** "The Glass Menagerie".
    b. *The Glass Menagerie*.
    c. "The Glass Menagerie."
16. **a.** considered;
    b. considered,
17. **a.** advice,
    b. advice:
    c. advice—
18. **a.** long,
    b. long
19. **a.** breath
    b. breath,
20. **a.** Wingfield.
    b. Wingfield?
    c. Wingfield!

Part 3

Resources and Skills

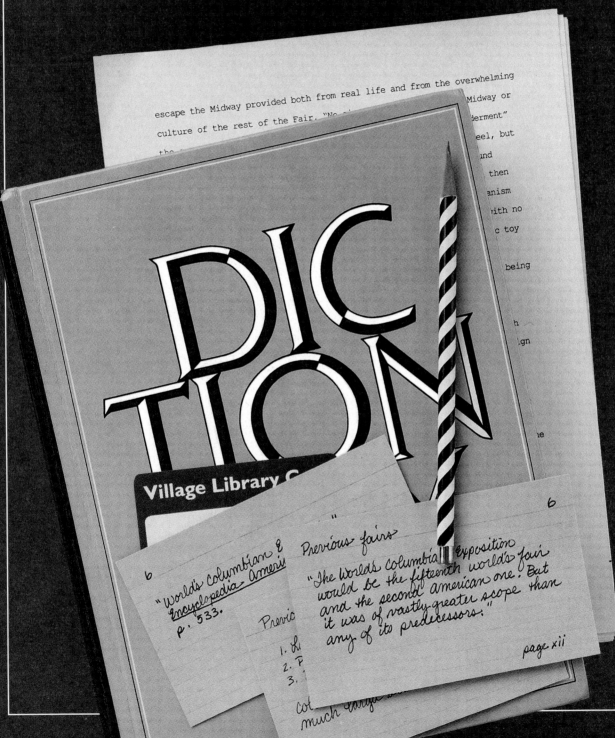

Part 3 Resources and Skills

Unit 22 | Sources of English Words

22.1 | English in Our Time

Fifteen or twenty years ago, the following news item probably wouldn't have made much sense to most Americans. Can you imagine why?

> Muslim fundamentalists in Iran took to the streets today to support a conservative ayatollah's call for a renewed commitment to the Islamic revolution.
>
> Meanwhile, in Israel, Palestinian leaders urged support for the intifada being waged in the West Bank and Gaza.

The words *ayatollah*[1] (referring to a Muslim religious leader) and *intifada* (*struggle*) were unknown to most English-speaking people two decades ago. These words come from Arabic, a language with which few Americans are familiar. Yet by 1990 these words were routinely used in both broadcast and print news. How did these words find their way into English?

1 Words from Arabic and from African and Native American languages are given in their English spellings throughout the unit.

A Living Language

Like all extant languages, English is continually changing. The adoption of foreign words into English vocabulary, called borrowing, is anything but a new phenomenon. In fact, it's been going on from the time the language first began to take shape around A.D. 450. English has been borrowing words from conquerors and conquered, missionaries, trading partners, immigrants, and a variety of other sources.

So when events in the Middle East commanded the world's attention during the latter part of the twentieth century, English simply borrowed the words it needed to describe what was happening in that region of the world. The more often such words were used, the less "foreign" they sounded. Eventually, these borrowed words came to be used routinely in speech and writing.

Borrowed vocabulary from foreign languages is not the only source of new words in English. As fresh ideas evolve and innovative technologies are developed, new English words are created to describe them. These words may be words borrowed from other languages, existing words taking on new meanings, acronyms, blends, compounds, or newly coined words, as the following examples and the chart show.

Kwanza   (borrowing from Swahili: seven-day African-American cultural festival)

rap   (old word, meaning to knock quickly, taking on a new meaning: a form of music)

AIDS   (acronym for *a*cquired *i*mmune *d*eficiency *s*yndrome)

exercycle   (blend of existing words: exercise + bicycle)

skateboard   (compound of existing words)

cellulite   (new word for fatty deposits on the hips and thighs, coined in 1971)

In the next four lessons you'll be introduced to some of the history and mechanisms that have shaped and continue to influence the language we use. Whether the words we speak are borrowed or created, they illustrate a vital feature of English—adaptability. English is alive.

Some Recent Additions to the English Vocabulary

Borrowed Words
- perestroika (Russian: restructuring)
- contra (Spanish: literally "against"—rebel guerrilla fighter)
- satay (Thai: skewered grilled meat)

Old Words, New Meanings
- scan (to transfer words and images into electronic files)
- mouse (hand-operated device for controlling movement on a computer screen)

Acronyms
- MIRV (*m*ultiple *i*ndependently targeted *r*eentry *v*ehicle— a missile with two or more warheads)

Blends
- modem (modulator/demodulator—device for transferring computer files from one computer location to another via telephone lines)

Compounds
- virtual reality (lifelike computer simulation of the real world)
- laser disc (grooveless disc on which digital data is stored and replayed by a laser beam scanning the surface)

Exercise 1

Skim the contents of several popular magazines, such as news, personality, and special-interest magazines. Look for words that you think are in the process of being assimilated into English. These might be words from foreign languages (often italicized) or words that have been created, or adapted from existing words, to name new ideas, technologies, events, consumer goods, and so on. Make a list of the words *you* find, and define each one.

Eponyms
Making History

Have you ever wondered why men, boys, and sometimes whole groups of people are called *guys*? Well, here's the story. Guy Fawkes was an English traitor who plotted to murder the king. Fawkes was hanged for his treason in 1606, but each year on November 5 (Guy Fawkes Day), the British burn a straw figure of Guy Fawkes in effigy. Originally, any ragged or odd-looking men—men who resembled Fawkes's straw effigy—were called *guys*. Today the word refers to men, boys, or people in general.

François Boucher, *Madame de Pompadour* (detail), 1756

Guy Fawkes is an eponym. An eponym is a person whose name is the source for the name of someone or something. William Penn, for example, is the eponym for Pennsylvania. Madame de Pompadour (pictured at the right) gave her name to a hairstyle.

Some people have become eponyms because of their inventions or achievements. The Ferris wheel is named for George W. G. Ferris, who invented this popular ride. Louis Pasteur gave his name to pasteurization—the process of sterilizing milk and other bacteria-rich liquids.

Other people have become eponyms because their names were associated with a certain thing. Jules Léotard, for example, was a nineteenth-century French circus performer whose costume included a form-fitting body stocking—what we today call a leotard. Similarly, Samuel Maverick was a Texas cattle rancher who, unlike his fellow ranchers, refused to brand his cattle. These unbranded cattle became known as *mavericks,* and the word *maverick* has now come to mean anyone who refuses to go along with the group.

Eponymous Explorations

Look at the list of definitions on the left, and match them with their eponyms on the right.

1. A wind instrument	**A.** Rudolf Diesel
2. A type of car engine	**B.** Adolphe Sax
3. A temperature scale	**C.** George Pullman
4. A railroad sleeping car	**D.** James Watt
5. A unit of electricity	**E.** Gabriel Fahrenheit

The year is A.D. 449, and throughout the British Isles the apprehensive mood of the Celtic people is reflected in the low, gray clouds of the winter sky. The Roman legions that have enforced the rule of law in this distant outpost of the Empire have withdrawn back to Rome in what will prove to be a futile effort to repel invading barbarians from the north. The once-invincible Empire is collapsing.

Meanwhile, poised for attack just across the English Channel are three fierce Germanic tribes—the Angles, the Saxons, and the Jutes. The Celts enlisted the aid of these tribes to fight off the Picts and Scots, who attacked the Celts from the west and the north (the areas we now know as Ireland and Scotland). The Germanic warriors have routed the Picts and Scots but now will turn on their Celtic hosts, driving the Celts into the mountains of what are today Wales and Scotland. A new culture will take root on the island of Britain, and its principal language will be Anglo-Saxon, or Old English.

Emissaries from the Pope

Almost as soon as Old English was established, it began to change. Many of the language changes were due to foreign influences. Both Celtic and Anglo-Saxon already had been influenced by Latin because of the dominance of the Roman Empire. That influence increased during the sixth century when Pope Gregory, the spiritual leader of the Roman Catholic church, sent missionaries to Britain to convert the Anglo-Saxons to Christianity.

Latin into English		
Latin	**Old English**	**Modern English**
schola	scōl	school
magister	magister	master
altare	altar	altar
candela	candel	candle
vinum	wīn	wine
cuppa	cuppe	cup
templum	tempel	temple

The monks opened schools where they taught Latin to the Anglo-Saxon people. In addition, religious services were routinely conducted in Latin. Most written texts were also in Latin. As you might expect, many Latin words, especially those pertaining to school and religion, became part of the Anglo-Saxon vocabulary.

Invaders from the North

Starting around 800 the conquering Anglo-Saxons were given a taste of their own military medicine. Vikings from the Scandinavian countries to the north began raiding Engla Land (Land of the Angles) much as the Angles, Saxons, and Jutes had invaded Britain four hundred years earlier. This sporadic warfare continued for over two hundred years. By the eleventh century, many Norse had settled in Engla Land, and again English underwent change with the addition of Scandinavian words.

Significantly, the Scandinavians contributed three Danish words: the personal pronouns *they*, *their*, and *them*. This is an unusual case of one language borrowing pronouns from another language. Generally, pronouns are firmly entrenched in a language, and the native forms are not readily displaced.

Scandinavian into English		
Old Norse	**Middle English**	**Modern English**
kalla	callen	call
sæti	sete	seat
skinn	skin	skin
skȳ	sky	sky
bāthir	bothe	both
deyja	dien	die
fēlagi	felawe	fellow

Exercise 2

Each of the following words from modern English was originally borrowed from either Latin or a Scandinavian language. Use a dictionary to discover the origin of each word. Give its Latin or Scandinavian form as well as its Old or Middle English form.

1. discipline
2. low
3. skull
4. priest
5. Sabbath
6. take

Spoonerisms

Time Wounds All Heels

Have you ever made some unintentionally humorous or embarrassing slip of the tongue, such as telling someone to "ship up or shape out" when you meant to say "shape up or ship out"? Well, if that's the case, you're in good company.

At the turn of this century, an English clergyman and educator named William Spooner (pictured at right) acquired a reputation for habitually making such humorous blunders. It seems the Reverend Spooner's brain anticipated what his tongue was about to say, and he would often transpose the sounds from one word to another.

For example, once when steering a prominent member of his congregation away from a reserved pew, he supposedly offered this assistance: "Let me sew you to another sheet." And much to the amusement of his congregation, when Spooner was delivering a sermon about half-formed wishes, he announced, "We all know what it is to have a half-warmed fish within us." The Reverend Spooner became so notorious for these linguistic bungles that people began calling them spoonerisms.

Everyone makes such slips now and then. The technical term for this normal process is metathesis. Other practitioners of the art besides Spooner include the meteorologist who forecast "rain and slow, followed by sneet" and the radio announcer who, while describing the audience at a world championship bout at Madison Square Garden, informed his listeners, "I see the beautiful Mrs. DePuyster Van Courtland looking gorgeous in her stunning white gownless evening strap."

Scrambled Sayings

Unscramble the following spoonerisms.

1. Is the bean dizzy?
2. a blushing crow
3. You have tasted a whole worm.
4. Someone is occupewing my pie.
5. a well-boiled icicle

22.3　A Conquerer from France

The English weren't the only people to be harassed by Scandinavian warriors. Coastal areas of France were also attacked and settled. The French called the invaders *Normans*, the Old French word for "Northmen." The region of France settled by the Normans became known as Normandy.

In 1066 the seventh Duke of Normandy, William the Conqueror (pictured at right), was embroiled in a dispute for succession to the English throne. The dispute ended when William defeated King Harold II, at the Battle of Hastings. William became king, and the Norman Conquest, as William's victory came to be called, altered the English language.

Parlez-vous français?

Because the conquering Normans were from France, French became the language of the aristocracy in England. The working classes still spoke English, but after several decades of French rule, English was borrowing liberally from the French language. Words relating to religion, the arts and sciences, military affairs, social life, clothing, manners, and food were taken from French.

The vocabulary of food provides an interesting example of how social class influenced the development of English. Farmers and herders were part of the working class, so the names of the animals they tended are

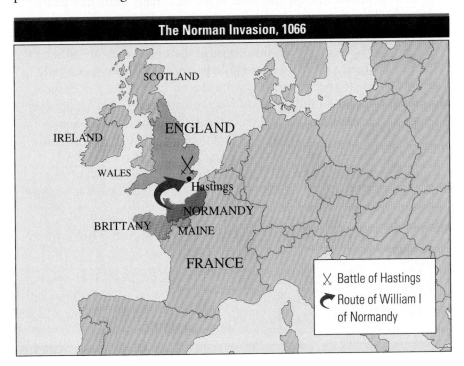

The Norman Invasion, 1066

SCOTLAND

IRELAND

ENGLAND

WALES

Hastings

NORMANDY

BRITTANY　MAINE

FRANCE

✕ Battle of Hastings

↪ Route of William I of Normandy

from Old and Middle English: *cou (cow), cealf (calf), sceap (sheep), deor (deer),* and *swin (swine).* When these animals were prepared as elaborate dishes for the nobility, their names shifted from English to Old and Middle French: *buef (beef), veel (veal), moton (mutton), veneison (venison),* and *porc (pork).*

English Borrowings from French	
Social Life	peasant (paisant), court (court)
Food	roast (rostir), sausage (saussiche)
Government	authority (auctorité), constable (conestable)
Housing	palace (palais), tower (tor)
Religion	chaplain (chapelain), saint (saint)
Arts and Sciences	music (musique), medicine (medicine)
Military	charge (chargier), powder (poudre)

Plague and War

During the fourteenth century a terrible plague, known as the Black Death, swept across Europe and Asia. Some historians think that nearly one fourth of the European and Asian population died from bubonic plague during this period.

In England the plague left businesses in the towns without sufficient workers. Eventually, these jobs were filled by peasants, who spoke only English, because no proper aristocrat was about to become a tradesperson. In addition, the Hundred Years' War, which began in 1337, between England and France, caused French culture to decline in favor. Soon French became a language studied only in school. English, with significant French influence, was again the principal language of England.

Exercise 3

Look up these words in a dictionary. Write the Old or Middle French word from which each of the following English words was derived.

1. bacon
2. porch
3. castle
4. boil
5. prayer
6. judge
7. gentle
8. courage
9. lieutenant

Puns and Tom Swifties

Ever Seen a Horse Fly?

Remember when you were a kid and loved to tell silly riddles like "What's black and white and red (read) all over?" (a newspaper). This riddle is an example of a pun, or a play on words.

Shakespeare loved puns. So did Lewis Carroll, author of *Alice in Wonderland*. Here's how Mock Turtle describes his education to Alice:

"I only took the regular course."
"What was that?" enquired Alice.
"Reeling and Writhing, of course, to begin with," the Mock Turtle replied; "and then the different branches of Arithmetic—Ambition, Distraction, Uglification, and Derision."

The puns in this passage are double-sound puns—words that sound very similar to other words. Homophone puns are based on different words that sound the same, such as *red* and *read*. Homograph puns are based on words that are spelled and pronounced the same but have different meanings. Benjamin Franklin used this type of pun when, after signing the Declaration of Independence, he told the gathering of revolutionaries, "We must all hang together or, most assuredly, we shall all hang separately!"

Some of the funniest puns are "Tom Swifties." In the Tom Swift stories, created by Edward Stratemeyer, Tom and his cronies never just plain said anything—they said it *happily* or *hurriedly* or *speedily* or in some other adverbial way. The humor in Tom Swifties occurs when the adverb describing how something is said forms a pun on what the speaker is saying, for example: "I love pancakes," said Tom flippantly.

"Try This Game," Said Tom Playfully

Match each quotation with a punning adverb below.

1. "These cherries aren't quite ripe," said Tom _____.
2. "This tire needs repair," said Tom _____.
3. "My dog just had puppies," said Tom _____.
4. "Come in out of the rain," said Tom _____.
5. "We studied the body's circulatory system," said Tom _____.

A. literally **B.** tartly **C.** dryly **D.** vainly **E.** flatly

Throughout its early history, English acquired most of its new words from invaders and conquerors. By the Middle Ages, however, trade had led to peaceful contacts with distant cultures whose languages further enriched the English word bank.

algebra   cipher   sugar

When traders came back from the Middle East, their cargoes of exotic imports included sugar. In Middle English sugar was called *sucre*, from the Arabic *sukkar*. Arabic was also the source of the name for the mathematical discipline of algebra, *al-jabr*; and for the numeral cipher, from the Arabic *sifr*. Later, commercial contacts with Spain added *vanilla (vainilla)*, *brocade (brocado)*, and *embargo (embargar)* to the English vocabulary.

Cultural Exchange

The exchange of goods between nations led inevitably to an exchange of culture. For example, William Shakespeare's *The Merchant of Venice*

Some English Borrowed Words		
Language	**Word**	**Date into English**
French	shanty (chantier)	1822
	depot (dépôt)	1795
Dutch	cookie (koekje)	1786
	snoop (snoepen)	1832
German	quartz (quarz)	1631
	nix (nichts)	1789
Yiddish	bagel (beygel)	1932
	klutz (klotz)	1960
Italian	ravioli (ravioli)	1611
	piano (pianoforte)	1803
Algonquian	hominy (rockahominy)	1629
	caucus (caucauasu)	1763
Spanish	alligator (el legarto)	1568
	cannibal (canibal)	1553

(1597) was based on a story written by the Italian author Giovanni Fiorentino. In contrast, Shakespeare's *Othello* (1604), adapted from an Italian story by Cinthio, was itself adapted in 1887 by Italian composer Giuseppe Verdi for his opera *Otello*. Such cultural exchanges, particularly in the field of music, led to cultural word borrowings by English. From Italian, English borrowed *stanza (stanza)*, *studio (studio)*, and *violin (violino)*.

Settling North America

As English-speaking people settled North America, contact with Native Americans soon added new words to the settlers' vocabularies. From both the Natick and Narraganset languages came *squash (askootasquash)* and from the Natick came *moccasin (mokussin)*. The chart below shows additional borrowings from Native American languages.

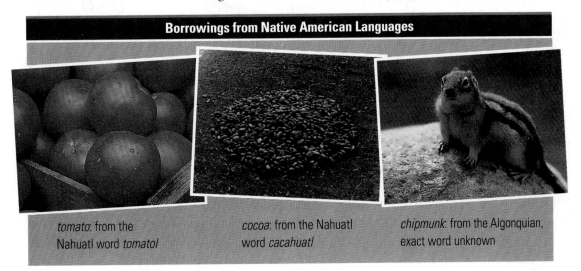

Borrowings from Native American Languages

tomato: from the Nahuatl word *tomatl*

cocoa: from the Nahuatl word *cacahuatl*

chipmunk: from the Algonquian, exact word unknown

Native American languages were just one influence on the English settlers' speech. The Spanish who settled in what is now the southwestern United States added *corral (corral)* and *rodeo (rodear)*. The Dutch contributed *bakery (bakkerij)* and *sleigh (slee)*. And Africans brought to America in the slave trade added *gumbo* (from the Bantu *gombo*) and *banjo* (from the Kimbundu *mbanza*).

Exercise 4

Look up the following words in a dictionary. From what language was each word borrowed?

1. cole slaw   **3.** delicatessen   **5.** moose

2. afghan   **4.** lariat   **6.** tycoon

Euphemisms

Burt's Gone West

Well," said the young man with a sigh, "Burt bought the farm this morning. Who would have thought the old guy would cash in his chips so soon? His wife's been checking out a few resting places in the memorial park. We'll all be pushing up daisies soon enough."

No, this young man isn't talking about real-estate transactions, a poker game, or gardening. He's talking about death, an unpleasant subject that most people would just as soon avoid mentioning. When people talk about it, they often employ euphemisms to soften this unpleasant fact of life.

A euphemism is an agreeable or neutral word or phrase used in place of another word or phrase that is considered harsh, insensitive, or offensive. People have created euphemisms to cover a wide variety of subjects, especially anything having to do with the human body. The concern to avoid mention of the human body was taken to absurd lengths during the Victorian era.

The Victorian era, named for Queen Victoria of England, was characterized by extreme modesty and propriety. For example, not only was it considered indecent to display one's legs, it was even thought improper to say the word *leg*. Instead, Victorians said *limb*.

Belly was another Victorian no-no. Much preferred were *tummy* and *breadbasket*. And at the dinner table, no proper Victorian, eyeing the roast chicken, would dream of shocking the other diners by requesting a breast or a thigh. *White meat* and *dark meat* became the accepted euphemisms.

> DO ALL OF YOUR FROGS CROAK AT NIGHT?
>
> CLUMSY'S BAIT SHOP
>
> NO,....A LOT OF THEM PASS AWAY RIGHT HERE IN THE SUN.
>
> CLUMSY'S BAIT SHOP

Euphemistically Speaking

Try to match the words on the left with their euphemisms on the right.

1. fire
2. dirty
3. retreat
4. spying
5. poor

A. intelligence gathering
B. terminate
C. underprivileged
D. strategic withdrawal
E. unhygienic

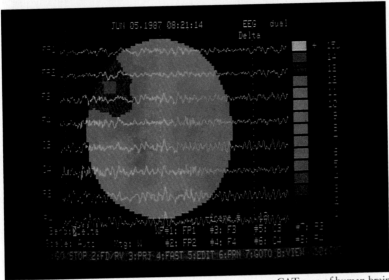

CAT scan of human brain

Do you know what a CAT scan is? A hard drive? How about a quasar, a simulcast, or an enkephalin? All of these words are fairly recent additions to the English vocabulary, made necessary by the advance of science and technology and the need to name and describe new things, ideas, and concepts. As the world changes, so does English. New words are invented to name and describe space exploration, computers, medical science, social movements—any new aspect of any people's culture.

Compounds and Blends

These new words arise through a variety of methods. Some are compounds, such as *meltdown*, which describes the uncontrollable burning of the fuel rods in a malfunctioning nuclear reactor. Another new compound is *cross-training*, a physical workout that combines several different types of exercise, such as running, swimming, weight lifting, and rowing.

Blending, another way new words are formed, occurs when parts of two or more words are blended into one. *Simulcast*, the process of broadcasting a program simultaneously on radio and television, is a blend of *simultaneous* and *broadcast*. *Jazzercise*, a popular form of aerobic dance, is a blend of *jazz* and *exercise*.

Acronyms

Acronyms are yet another way new words enter English. *CD*, for example, stands for *c*ompact *d*isc, thin, round, silver-colored disks that contain laser-etched, digitally coded music and information. In 1963,

New Words in English			
	Word	**Date**	**Source**
Compounds and Blends	hands-on	1969	hands + on
	launch pad	1958	launch + pad
	Medicare	1955	medical + care
Acronyms	VCR	ca. 1971	*video*cassette *r*ecorder
	RV	ca. 1980s	*r*ecreational *v*ehicle
	laser	1957	*l*ight *a*mplification by *s*timulated *e*mission of *r*adiation
Existing Words, New Meanings	aerobic	1967	From "requiring air or free oxygen"; exercise that increases oxygen intake
	network	1940	From "interconnecting wires"; group of interconnected individuals who exchange

when the U.S. Postal Service wanted to speed up delivery, they urged that all mail include a *ZIP* code, for *z*one *i*mprovement *p*lan.

Existing Words with New Meanings

Around the time of World War II, military scientists working with radar discovered short radio waves that travel in straight lines. They called this particular type of radio wave a microwave. Today, however, say *microwave* and most people assume you mean a small oven that cooks food quickly using microwave radiation. The word has taken on a new meaning.

Launder is another such example. It has always meant "to wash in water." Today it also means "to 'cleanse' money obtained from illegal or disreputable sources." Similarly, *rap* once meant "to knock." Today, *rap* is a style of music based on rhymed verses spoken to a particular beat.

Exercise 5

Make a list of new words you and your friends use in casual conversation. Most, if not all, of these words will be slang, but chances are they have their roots in other words. Which are completely new creations? Compounds or blends? Are any acronyms? Are any existing words with new meanings?

Slang

Awesome, Daddy-O!

The scene: Lou's Short Orders Deluxe on a rainy Sunday in 1952. A woman walks in and seats herself at the counter. After a quick glance at the menu, she tells the waitress she'd like two scrambled eggs on toast and some coffee. The waitress turns to the kitchen and yells, "Adam and Eve on a raft—wreck 'em—and a cup of jamoch!"

A young man who's already ordered toast and orange juice decides he'd like a couple of eggs as well. The waitress sighs and shouts to the cook, "Make that toast cackle!" A mother orders a hamburger for her daughter—"Hitch old Dobbin to a bun!" the waitress calls out.

Such colorful and inventive language was once part of the atmosphere in every American diner. The words and phrases are slang, popular, informal, faddish, and nonstandard speech. The use of slang is probably as old as language itself, but early examples of slang are difficult to document because most slang has a very brief life span. What is popular today is often long forgotten by tomorrow.

Consider a case in point. When you're leaving a party today, you might say "Catch you later" or "I'm outta here." In the 1960s you would have said "Let's split"; in the 1940s, "Let's amscray" (pig Latin for "scram"). And in the Roaring Twenties, the popular expression was "Twenty-three skiddoo!" A few years from now, the expression will change again. That's the nature of slang.

Generations of Slang

How have slang expressions changed over the years? You can find out by conducting a slang survey. First make a list of popular slang expressions you and your friends use. Assign each word to a category—such as "used when leaving," "means up-to-the-minute," and so on. Ask your parents for comparable expressions from their youth. Then do the same with your grandparents or any individuals who are, say, seventy or eighty years old. Share the results of the survey with your classmates.

Slang

1920
the cat's meow
anything desirable

1940
mess around
to kill time, hang out

1950
dig
to understand

1960
groovy
wonderful

1970
far out
great, wonderful

1980
excellent
first-rate

?

Unit 23 Library Resources

23.1   Arrangement of a Library

Although the word *library* comes from *liber*, the Latin word for "book," modern libraries offer many resources in addition to books. Knowing how a typical library is organized can help you open up a wealth of information.

Stacks The stacks, or shelves, hold fiction and nonfiction books. Fiction books are works of the imagination, such as novels and short-story collections. Nonfiction books, which are fact based rather than imaginative, include books about such subjects as science, history, and philosophy.

Circulation Desk A librarian or assistant librarian helps you check out books that you intend to remove from the library. When you have questions, someone at the circulation desk usually can help answer them.

Catalogs Both the card catalog and computer catalog contain information about books in the library and give their location.

Young Adult and Children's Section Fiction and nonfiction books for younger readers are often grouped in a separate part of the library.

Audio-Visual Materials Records, audiocassettes, compact discs, videos, and slides are usually grouped in a separate area of the library. Ask a librarian which audio-visual materials you can check out.

Reference The reference area holds encyclopedias, dictionaries, almanacs, atlases, and other reference materials. Some libraries have a reference librarian to help answer questions and locate specific information. Most reference materials cannot be checked out.

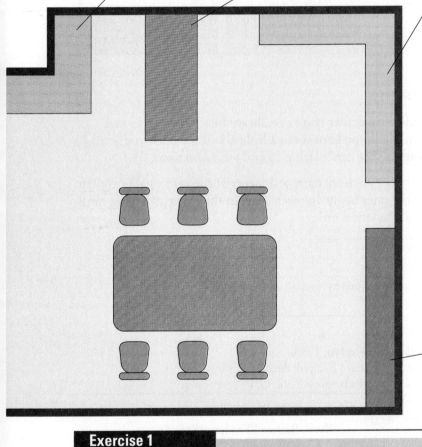

Newspapers and Periodicals Newspapers, and periodicals, which include magazines and journals, are published on a regular schedule. Current issues of newspapers and periodicals are kept in a general reading area. The *Readers' Guide to Periodical Literature,* an index that can help you locate specific articles, is kept in either the periodical or reference area.

Exercise 1

In which section of the library might you find these items?

1. *Newsweek* (a magazine)
2. *Hammond Contemporary World Atlas*
3. *The Phantom of the Opera* (an audiocassette of the musical)
4. *All Quiet on the Western Front* (a novel)
5. *Encyclopedia of Baseball*

When you are searching for information about a particular subject, first decide which resource will provide the information you need. If you are conducting research for a paper, you might want to begin with more general types of resources, such as encyclopedias and dictionaries, and then refer to more specific books, articles, and tapes later.

Identify
your resource as specifically as possible—by subject, title, or author.

▶

Look up
your resource in the card catalog or in the *Reader's Guide to Periodical Literature.*

▶

Find
your resource in the stacks or in the young adult, audio-visual, reference, or periodical section.

▶

Check out
your resource at the circulation desk, unless the material is restricted to in-library use only.

Using Catalogs

Trying to find a particular book in a library filled with books may seem overwhelming. If you know even a little about the book you want, however, you can use the card catalog to find what you need.

Card Catalog   The deep, narrow drawers of the card catalog contain cards similar to the ones below for each book in the library. Catalog cards are arranged in alphabetical order.

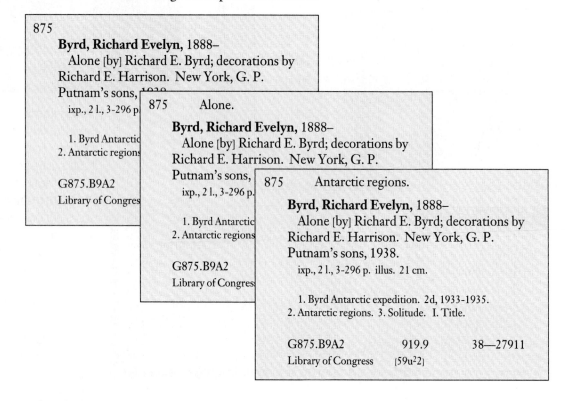

875

Byrd, Richard Evelyn, 1888–
    Alone [by] Richard E. Byrd; decorations by
Richard E. Harrison. New York, G. P.
Putnam's sons, 1938.
    ixp., 2 l., 3-296 p.

    1. Byrd Antarctic
    2. Antarctic regions

  G875.B9A2
  Library of Congress

875   Alone.

Byrd, Richard Evelyn, 1888–
    Alone [by] Richard E. Byrd; decorations by
Richard E. Harrison. New York, G. P.
Putnam's sons,
    ixp., 2 l., 3-296 p.

    1. Byrd Antarctic
    2. Antarctic regions

  G875.B9A2
  Library of Congress

875   Antarctic regions.

Byrd, Richard Evelyn, 1888–
    Alone [by] Richard E. Byrd; decorations by
Richard E. Harrison. New York, G. P.
Putnam's sons, 1938.
    ixp., 2 l., 3-296 p. illus. 21 cm.

    1. Byrd Antarctic expedition. 2d, 1933-1935.
    2. Antarctic regions. 3. Solitude. I. Title.

  G875.B9A2   919.9   38—27911
  Library of Congress   [59u^{2}2]

A call number is printed in the upper left-hand corner of each card in the catalog. This number is also printed on the spine of the book. Because library books are arranged on the shelves by call numbers, knowing the exact call number allows you to locate a book easily.

Most fiction books have two cards: an author card and a title card. Nonfiction books usually have three cards in the catalog: an author card, a title card, and a subject card. Some books will also have cross-reference cards, such as the examples below. Some libraries arrange subject cards separately in a subject index. In that case author and title cards are together in an author/title index.

See cards direct you to other ways a subject is listed in that particular library.

See card

> Antarctic expeditions.
>
> see
>
> Antarctic regions.

See also card

> Antarctic regions. See also
>
> South Pole

See also cards lead you to other possible subject headings or related subjects.

Computer Catalog   Some libraries have a computer catalog that contains the same information as a card catalog. Computer catalogs have separate ways to search for authors, titles, and subjects. For example, if you were looking for *The Good Earth* by Pearl S. Buck, you might enter *good earth* under the title search. You would then see a list of all the books that the library owns with titles that begin with the words *good earth*. Each item would be numbered; for more detailed information you would enter the item number of the book you want. The example at right shows the first listing among the four possible listings for *good earth*. Follow the on-screen prompts to operate the computer catalog, or ask a librarian to help you with the computer, if you need assistance.

```
Buck, Pearl S. (Pearl Sydenstricker), 1892-1973.
   The good earth / Pearl S. Buck. -- New York :
   The John Day Company, c1931.
   375 p. ; 22 cm.
   Spec copy: signed by the author.

LOCATION:  Olin Library
CALL NUMBER:  PS3503 U198 G65 1931
   Not charged out.  If not on shelf, ask at
   Circulation Desk.
LOCATION:  Special Collections (non-circulating)
CALL NUMBER:  PS3503 U198 G65 1931
```

Call numbers and circulation information are included in computer catalog listings. Some computer catalogs are connected to printers so that you can print out listings.

Understanding Classification Systems

Once you have found the information you need in the catalog, you are ready to look for a specific book in a particular section of the library, often in the stacks. All libraries use a system to categorize their collections and physically organize their materials. Most libraries use either the Dewey Decimal System or the Library of Congress Classification.

Dewey Decimal System   In 1876 librarian Melvil Dewey created a system that groups books into ten broad categories based on general areas of thought and study. In a library using the Dewey Decimal System, books are shelved according to the following categories.

Dewey Decimal System			
Category Numbers	Major Category	Examples of Subcategories	Sample Book Titles
000–099	General works	Encyclopedias, bibliographies	*The Lifetime Reading Plan* *The Cambridge Encyclopedia of China*
100–199	Philosophy	Ethics, psychology	*The Senses of Animals and Men* *Sleep and Dreams*
200–299	Religion	Theology, mythology	*Greek Gods and Heroes* *What Is Islam?*
300–399	Social sciences	Sociology, education	*Society and Change* *World Perspectives in Education*
400–499	Language	Dictionaries, foreign languages	*A Hog on Ice and Other Curious Expressions* *The Story of English*
500–599	Sciences	Chemistry, astronomy, math	*From Zero to Infinity* *How to Make and Use a Telescope*
600–699	Technology	Medicine, engineering	*How Things Work* *The Artificial Heart*
700–799	Arts	Painting, music, theater, sports	*Women Artists* *African Roots of Jazz*
800–899	Literature	Poetry, plays, essays	*Life with Father* *A Street in Bronzeville*
900–999	History and geography	Ancient history, biography, travel	*Isaac Newton: Reluctant Genius* *A History of Mexico*

These general categories contain subcategories—the more specific the topic, the more specific the classification number. Additional categories are indicated by adding a decimal and more numbers. For example, look at the Dewey Decimal number below for *The Ultimate Skateboard Book.*

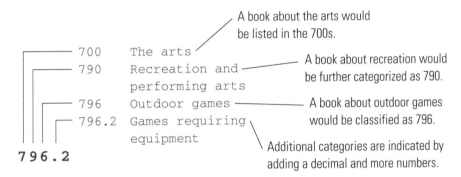

A book about the arts would be listed in the 700s.

700   The arts

790   Recreation and performing arts

A book about recreation would be further categorized as 790.

796   Outdoor games

A book about outdoor games would be classified as 796.

796.2   Games requiring equipment

Additional categories are indicated by adding a decimal and more numbers.

796.2

Books are shelved by Dewey Decimal number and then by author. For instance, two books about African-American society would both be filed in the 301.45 section, but a book by W. E. B. Du Bois would appear before a book by Henry Louis Gates.

Many libraries that use the Dewey Decimal System do not assign classification numbers to fiction books. Instead, the first line of the call number is either an *F* or *Fic* to indicate a fictional work, and the second line contains the first three letters of the author's last name. Fiction works are organized alphabetically on the shelves by authors' last names. If a library has more than one book by the same author, those books are also alphabetized by title.

Library of Congress Classification   Some libraries use the Library of Congress Classification, or LC. This system divides books into twenty-one general categories; each category is assigned a letter, as shown in the chart on the next page. Many libraries with a large number of books that cover a vast number of subjects use the LC.

Like the Dewey Decimal System the LC has subcategories, identified by additional letters and numbers. Study the following LC call number for the book *Planets* by Carl Sagan.

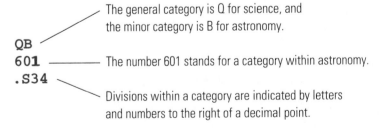

The general category is Q for science, and the minor category is B for astronomy.

QB

601   The number 601 stands for a category within astronomy.

.S34

Divisions within a category are indicated by letters and numbers to the right of a decimal point.

Library of Congress Classification System			
Category Letter	Major Category	Category Letter	Major Category
A	General works	N	Fine arts
B	Philosophy, psychology, religion	P	Language and literature
		Q	Science
C–F	History	R	Medicine
G	Geography, anthropology, recreation	S	Agriculture
		T	Technology
H	Social sciences	U	Military science
J	Political science	V	Naval science
K	Law	Z	Bibliography and library science
L	Education		
M	Music		

Special Sections Special categories of books, such as reference, biography, and oversize, are often grouped in separate sections. Letters above the call number indicate that a book is in a special section. For example, a *B* denotes a biography. The call number on the catalog card matches the number on the spine of the book.

R or *Ref* identifies a reference book. You would find a book having this Dewey Decimal number in the reference area.

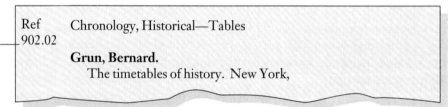

Ref 902.02 Chronology, Historical—Tables

Grun, Bernard.
The timetables of history. New York,

Checking the Shelves

Once you have the call number of a resource, you are ready to continue your investigation in the stacks or in a special section.

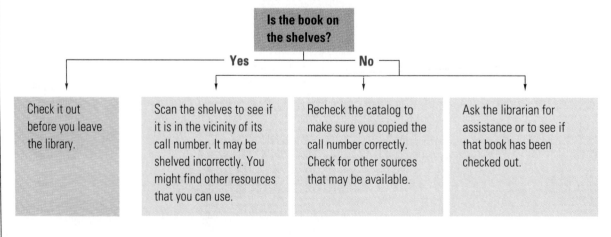

Is the book on the shelves?

— Yes — No —

Check it out before you leave the library.

Scan the shelves to see if it is in the vicinity of its call number. It may be shelved incorrectly. You might find other resources that you can use.

Recheck the catalog to make sure you copied the call number correctly. Check for other sources that may be available.

Ask the librarian for assistance or to see if that book has been checked out.

Use the card catalog or computer catalog to find a book for each of the following topics. List the author, title, call number, and publication date of the books you find.

1. How to speed-read
2. Astronomy
3. Stand-up comedy
4. Indonesia
5. General background information for stage crews
6. Inventors
7. Trends in twentieth-century Japanese literature
8. Family life in Mexico
9. A book by Margaret Mead
10. A collection of letters
11. A book by Paule Marshall
12. Robots
13. A history of soldiers
14. Korean folk tales
15. The economy of Nigeria
16. A book on the American Civil War by Shelby Foote
17. A trip through China
18. Mathematics and numbers
19. Sensory perception
20. Great speeches

23.3 Using a Periodicals Index

Looking at newspapers and periodicals can be especially helpful if you are studying current events. Newspapers and periodicals, such as magazines and journals, provide the best source of up-to-date information.

Locating Periodicals and Newspapers

Recent issues of magazines, journals, and sometimes newspapers are often kept on open shelves in a reading area. Back issues of newspapers are usually stored on microforms, which are small photographs of printed pages. Reproduced on either microfilm (filmstrips) or microfiche (film cards), microforms can be viewed on a special machine that enlarges the photographs so they can be read. Some of these viewing machines also allow you to make photocopies. Back issues of magazines are either bound in hardback volumes, grouped by month or year, or stored on microforms.

Using the Readers' Guide

Special reference books called indexes help you find the most recent periodicals information. One widely used index of periodicals is the *Readers' Guide to Periodical Literature*. Articles from over 175 magazines are indexed by author and subject. Paperback editions of this index are published every two weeks, larger paperback editions covering a three-month period are published quarterly, and hardbound volumes of all a year's entries are issued annually. The following annotated excerpts from the *Readers' Guide* show you how to read the information in the index.

Subject heading

Article title and title enhancement

Magazine citation

***See also* cross-reference**

Author of article

BASEBALL RECORDS
Henderson steals way into baseball history by topping
Lou Brock. il pors *Jet* 80:46–7 My 20 '91
Wizard of Whiff, Sultan of Swipe [N. Ryan's no-hitter
and R. Henderson's 939th stolen base]. W. Shapiro.
il por *Time* 137:55 My 13 '91
BASEBALL THROWING
See also
Pitching (Baseball)
BASEMENTS
Waterproofing
See Waterproofing
BASES (MILITARY) *See* Military bases
BASHFULNESS IN CHILDREN
The bold and the bashful. G. Cowley il *Newsweek* 117
Special Issue: 24–5+ Summ '91

The magazine citation tells you exactly where the article can be found. It lists the name, volume, page numbers, and date of the periodical in which the article appears.

***See* cross-reference**

Subheading

Author entry

BASS TOURNAMENTS *See* Fishing—Competitions
BATAVIA (N. Y.)
Social conditions
Back to Batavia. B. Kauffman. *The American Scholar*
60:223–33 Spr '91
BATCH FILES (COMPUTER SCIENCE)
Serve up better-looking, more useful batch files.
C. DeVoney. *PC Computing* 4:182 Ap '91
BATES, KAREN GRIGSBY
Are you my mother? il *Essence* 21:49–50+ Ap '91
BATHROOMS
The bathroom. il *Good Housekeeping* 212:180 Ap '91
Lively bath in the treetops. il *Southern Living* 26:126
Ap '91

Using the excerpts from the *Readers' Guide* on the opposite page, answer the following questions.

1. Who is the author of the article about computer batch files?
2. Where in the *Readers' Guide* would articles about bass tournaments be listed?
3. Which magazine contains an article by Karen Grigsby Bates?
4. Under what subject heading would you look for articles about waterproofing a basement?
5. Who are the subjects of the article entitled "Wizard of Whiff, Sultan of Swipe," listed under the heading "Baseball Records"?
6. In which magazine would you find an article about Batavia, New York?
7. On which page in *Good Housekeeping* does an article about bathrooms appear?
8. What is the title of G. Cowley's article about bashfulness in children?
9. Which magazine features an article about the breaking of Lou Brock's baseball record?
10. How many articles about bathrooms are listed in this edition of the *Readers' Guide?*

23.4 Using Reference Works

Knowing what library materials are available and how to use them can help you find information quickly and easily for class assignments and research papers. If you want to track down specific details, such as names, dates, or other facts, or if you just want to satisfy your curiosity about something, most research begins in the reference area.

General Reference Works

You probably know about and use many general reference works, such as encyclopedias, almanacs, and atlases. When conducting research, ask a librarian about specialized reference works, such as specialized encyclopedias and various literary reference works, that might provide more detailed information.

An encyclopedia yearbook, a separate volume in a set of encyclopedias, contains the most recently available information for the year prior to the yearbook's publication. Yearbooks contain current information, such as annual chronologies, obituaries, and in-depth articles on political, cultural, and social events, not included in the regular volumes of the encyclopedia.

Using General Reference Works to Answer Questions		
Question	**Where to Look for an Answer**	**Examples of Sources to Check**
Were any Civil War battles fought in Indiana?	**Encyclopedias** include general information on a variety of topics.	• *Grolier Encyclopedia* • *World Book Encyclopedia* • *Encyclopaedia Britannica*
Who were the recipients of Pulitzer Prizes in letters for fiction and for general nonfiction in 1989?	**Almanacs and yearbooks** provide statistics, lists, and detailed information on recent issues.	• *Information Please Almanac* • *Guinness Book of World Records*
What is the coldest month of the year in Lima, Peru?	**Atlases** are collections of maps. They often include special maps on climate, land use, history, and other features.	• *Hammond Contemporary World Atlas* • *Times Atlas of World History* • *Cambridge Atlas of Astronomy*
Where was Ernest Hemingway born?	**Biographical reference works** include short life histories of noteworthy individuals, both living and deceased.	• *Webster's Biographical Dictionary* • *Current Biography* • *Dictionary of American Biography*

Specialized Reference Works

Literary reference works provide information both about writers and about their work. Literary criticism or biographical information on authors is collected in several different sources, such as the *Literary Criticism Series* and *Contemporary Authors*. Books of quotations, such as Bartlett's *Familiar Quotations*, index well-known sayings. If you know the first line of a poem or even just part of a title, poetry indexes, such as *Granger's Index to Poetry*, can help you find a specific poem.

A library's collection of news clippings, pamphlets, and brochures on current events and topics is called the vertical file. This material is arranged alphabetically by subject and is usually stored by the library in a set of file cabinets.

Parts of a Book

Using all parts of a book, not just the main text, can help you determine whether a book has the information you need. Some information, including the introduction, table of contents, copyright page, and title page, is found in the front of a book, before the main text. The pages after the main text contain other useful sources, such as the appendix, glossary, bibliography, and index.

Using a Book Effectively

Questions	Where to Look for an Answer
Does this book have more than one author?	The **title page** contains the complete book title, edition number, and names of authors or editors.
Will this book contain information about developments in this field during 1990?	The **copyright page** tells when a book was first published and when it was updated.
Will this book contain information on my topic?	The **table of contents** identifies the main topics covered in the book.
Was the author intending to thoroughly inform, persuade, or briefly analyze?	The **introduction, preface,** or **foreword** indicates the author's purpose in writing the book.
Will I be able to trace any of the quotations cited by this author to their original sources?	The **bibliography** lists information sources for material covered in the book.
Would this be a good source of visuals I could adapt and re-create to use in an oral presentation?	The **appendix** contains additional information, such as maps, charts, tables, illustrations, or graphs.
If this book is highly technical, will I be able to easily understand the terms used?	The **glossary** alphabetically lists special or unfamiliar terms used in the book.
Have the individuals I am researching been written about in this book? If so, how much is written about them?	The **index** lists alphabetically all people, places, events, and significant topics covered in the book.

Exercise 4

Use this textbook or the reference works in your school library to answer the following questions.

1. How many composition units are in this book?
2. How many pages are in the index of this book?
3. Who won the Academy Award for best actress in 1988?
4. Were Herod and Herod Antipas the same person? Explain your answer.
5. Where is Mount Kilimanjaro?
6. What are Guatemala's chief crops?
7. Who wrote the poem "The Waste Land"?
8. Who was the first person recorded as running one mile in less than four minutes?
9. Which planet was the most recently discovered?
10. When did Henry "Hank" Aaron retire as a baseball player?

Using Dictionaries

24.1 General Dictionaries

"The first time I ever read the dictionary," mused comedian Steven Wright, "I thought it was a poem about everything." Wright was joking, but he does have a point. Through its alphabetical listing of words with their definitions, called entries, dictionaries can tell you about almost everything. Most dictionaries fall into one of the categories below.

Unabridged Dictionaries
250,000 or more entries

Characteristics
- Extensive word histories
- Detailed definitions
- May be in several volumes
- Found mostly in libraries

Examples
- *Random House Dictionary of the English Language*
- *Webster's Third New International Dictionary*

College Dictionaries
About 150,000 entries

Characteristics
- Detailed enough to answer most questions on spelling or definitions
- Widely used in schools, homes, and businesses

Examples
- *Random House Webster's College Dictionary*
- *American Heritage Dictionary of the English Language*
- *Webster's New World Dictionary*

School Dictionaries
90,000 or fewer entries

Characteristics
- Definitions based on students' backgrounds
- Emphasizes common words

Examples
- *Macmillan Dictionary*
- *Webster's School Dictionary*

The Organization of Entries

With many entries to search through, how do you find the one you want? Guide words, the first and last words listed on the page, can help you locate entries much more quickly than if you simply browse. The sample dictionary page opposite shows the organization of word entries and how to use guide words and the pronunciation key.

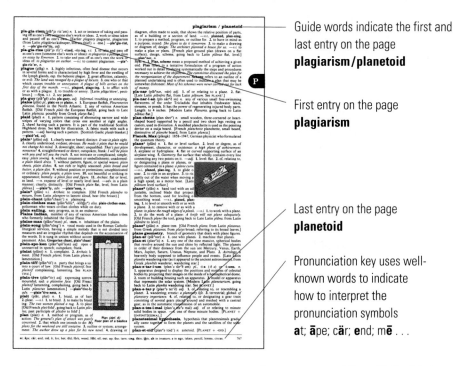

Guide words indicate the first and last entry on the page
plagiarism/planetoid

First entry on the page
plagiarism

Last entry on the page
planetoid

Pronunciation key uses well-known words to indicate how to interpret the pronunciation symbols
at; **ā**pe; **c**är; **e**nd; m**ē** . . .

If you do not know how to spell a word, you can usually still find it in a dictionary if you try to sound it out. You may also want to look at the tips for improving your spelling presented in Unit 26. The following tips suggest other ways of finding unfamiliar words.

Tips on Finding Unfamiliar Words

1. Consider whether the word contains silent consonants. They might appear at or near the beginning of a word, such as *k* in *knife,* and *h* in *rhyme.* Silent consonants may also appear in the middle of a word, such as *b* in *debt,* and *gh* in *night.*

2. Consider alternative spellings of consonants. For example, the *sh* sound can be spelled several ways, as in these words: *ocean, tissue, election, chandelier, special, conscious,* and *sugar.*

3. Consider alternative spellings of vowels. Some vowel sounds are formed by combinations of vowels, such as the *ā* sound in *paid, suede, eight, obey,* and *break.*

4. Check a larger dictionary. Even if you have the right spelling in mind, a school dictionary may not contain the word you need. If you can't find the word in a college or unabridged dictionary, try the above tips again.

The Main Entries

The main part of a dictionary consists of word entries and their definitions. Other information is given as well. The entry for *forbid* on the next page shows some of the main information in an entry.

The entry word is listed first.

The pronunciation is indicated by symbols.

Inflected forms, such as past tense and past participle for a verb, are sometimes listed.

The part or parts of speech that the word takes are indicated.

The etymology explains the history of a word.

for·bid (fər bid′, fôr-) **-bade** (-bad′, -bād′) or **-bad** (-bad′), **bid·den** or *(archaic)* **-bid**, **-bid·ding**, *v.t.* **1.a.** to command (someone) not to do something; refuse to allow: *I forbid you to go out.* **b.** to prohibit (something); ban: *to forbid the wearing of makeup.* **2.** to command to keep away from; bar or exclude from: *I forbid you the car.* **3.** to stand in the way of or make impossible; hinder; prevent: *The snowstorm forbids air travel.* [Old English *forbēodan* to prohibit, restrain.]

Syn. 1. Forbid, prohibit mean to order that something not be done. **Forbid** suggests a direct command from an authority who expects to be obeyed: *The airline forbids smoking on takeoff and landing.* **Prohibit** implies a legal order, as by statute, or a less arbitrary command: *The law prohibits smoking on the subways.*

Syllabication The entry word indicates how to divide, or hyphenate, a word of more than one syllable. Notice how *for·bid* is divided by the dot. A word entry may also indicate when a word is a solid compound, such as *folklore*, a hyphenated compound, such as *follow-up* when used as a noun or an adjective, or two words, such as *folk tale.*

Synonyms When an entry includes synonyms, words with similiar meanings, it often also includes examples to help you distinguish between the meanings. Compare the synonyms *forbid* and *prohibit* in the example above.

Homographs Words that are spelled the same but have different meanings and histories are called homographs. They are listed separately and identified by small, raised numerals after the word. If pronunciation varies between different homographs, these pronunciations are noted in the entry. Two separate entries are listed below for *meal.*

Some homographs, like meal[1] and meal[2], have the same pronunciations.

Notice the different etymologies for these homographs.

meal[1] (mēl), *n.* **1.** the food served and eaten at one time or occasion. **2.** one such regular time or occasion for eating. [bef. 900; ME *mel*, OE *mǣl* measure, fixed time, occasion, meal, c. OFris *mel* (meal)time, OHG *māl*, ON *māl*. Go *mēl* time, hour] —**meal′ less,** *adj.*

meal[2] (mēl), *n.* **1.** a coarse, unsifted powder ground from the edible seeds of any grain: *barley meal.* **2.** any ground or powdery substance, as of nuts or seeds. [bef. 900; ME *mele*, OE *melu*, c. OFris *mele*, OS, OHG *melo*, ON *mjǫl*; akin to Go *malan*, L *molere* to grind; cf. MILL[1]] —**meal′ less,** *adj.*

de·pre·ci·ate (di prē′ shē āt′), *v.*, **-at·ed, -at·ing.** —*v.t.* **1.** to reduce the purchasing value of (money). **2.** to lessen the value or price of. **3.** to claim depreciation on (a property) for tax purposes. **4.** to represent as of little value or merit; belittle. —*v.i.* **5.** to decline in value. [1640–50; < LL *dēprētiātus* undervalued, ptp. of *dēpretiāre* (in ML sp. *dēpreciāre*) = L *dē-* DE- + *-pretiāre*, der. of *pretium* PRICE + *-ātus* -ATE¹] —**de·pre′ci·at′ing·ly,** *adv.* —**de·pre′ci·a′tor,** *n.* —**Usage.** See DEPRECATE.

Cross-references direct you to other main entries for information that may help you understand a word's meaning and when to use it.

dep·re·cate (dep′ ri kāt′), *v.t.,* **-cat·ed, -cat·ing.** . . . —**Usage.** The most current sense of DEPRECATE is "to express disapproval of." In a sense development still occasionally criticized, DEPRECATE has come to be synonymous with the similar but etymologically unrelated word DEPRECIATE in the sense "belittle": *The author deprecated the importance of his work.* In *self-* compounds, DEPRECATE has almost totally replaced DEPRECIATE in modern usage: *She charmed the audience with a self-deprecating account of her career.*

Usage information explains the differences between the uses of certain words.

Cross-references   The entry for *depreciate* lists a cross-reference to *deprecate.* The usage information for *deprecate* shows you that *depreciate* and *deprecate* sometimes have the same meaning; however, *deprecate* has almost totally replaced *depreciate* in certain situations.

Usage Information   Some definitions may be preceded by usage labels. These labels indicate when to use a particular definition of a word. For example, the label "baseball" appears before a definition of the term *hit-and-run.* The label tells you that the definition that follows is used only when describing a baseball play. The following chart describes different kinds of usage information.

Usage Information in Dictionary Entries		
Type of Information	**Description**	**Example**
Capitalization	Indicates when a word or a particular meaning of a word needs to be capitalized	**southeast** . . . **3. the Southeast.** southeastern part of the United States.
Out-of-date usage	Labels words as obsolete—no longer used—or archaic—once used commonly but now used only in special contexts	**quick** . . . **1.** *Archaic.* living; alive.
Special field usage	Indicates with subject labels a definition that is restricted to a particular study or area of reference	**fly**² . . . **8.** *Baseball.* to hit a fly ball.
Regional usage	Indicates how a word is used in a certain geographical area	**tonic** . . . **5.** *Chiefly Eastern New Eng.* soda pop.
Usage note	Provides general guides for using (or not using) words in particular situations	**scorcher** . . . **2.** *Informal.* an extremely hot day.

Other Information in Dictionaries

In addition to a greater number of word entries, some larger dictionaries include separate biography and geography sections. A biography section alphabetically lists names of important people and provides brief details about them. Names of cities, countries, and other geographical areas and information about them are alphabetically listed in the geography section. These sections usually appear at the back of the dictionary, after the main entries.

Exercise 1

Use a school or college dictionary to answer the following questions.

1. Who was Ho Chi Minh?
2. How is the word *passerine* hyphenated?
3. What is the plural of *hero*?
4. What are the guide words for the page on which *hakim* is listed?
5. What does *try* mean in the game of rugby?
6. What are the origins of the two homographs of *fair*?
7. What synonyms are given for *fashion*?
8. Is *Draconian* always capitalized? Explain your answer.
9. Does the word *queue* rhyme with *me* or with *you*?
10. What is the origin of *cantaloupe*?

24.2   Thesauruses

One special type of dictionary is a collection of synonyms, also known as a thesaurus. Such a book can help a writer choose just the right word in a given context. Even though a thesaurus is a type of dictionary, it is used in the opposite way from most dictionaries. You usually refer to a dictionary to find the meaning of a certain word. You refer to a thesaurus when you know the meaning you want to convey but need to find a specific word to express it.

Thesaurus Formats

The best-known thesaurus is *Roget's*, first developed by a British doctor, Peter Mark Roget, in 1852. Roget organized large lists of words into broad categories, such as *color* and *honor*. He then developed an index to the categories. This original thesaurus format is still used. To use this type of thesaurus, you would first check the index. You would then refer to one of the lists of possible synonyms given in the index.

Dictionary-style Entries

A dictionary-style thesaurus, which organizes words alphabetically rather than in categories, is also widely used. In the dictionary format each word entry is followed by several synonyms and cross-references to related major categories. A major category includes nouns, verbs, adjectives, and adverbs all related to one main idea. Most major category entries also include cross-references to antonyms. The following entry for the major category *generality* shows the main parts of a thesaurus entry.

Major categories appear in boldfaced, capital letters.

GENERALITY

Nouns—**1,** generality, generalization; universality, broadness, collectivity; average; catholicity, catholicism; miscellany, miscellaneousness; prevalence; DISPERSION.

2, everyone, everybody [and his brother]; all hands, all the world and his wife; anybody. *Colloq.,* whole kit and caboodle. *Slang,* the works.

Verbs— be general, prevail, be going about; generalize, render general.

Adjectives—general, generic, collective; broad, comprehensive, sweeping; encyclopedic, widespread, dispersed; universal, catholic, common, all-inclusive, worldwide; ecumenical; transcendental; prevalent, prevailing, rife, epidemic, besetting; all over, covered with; every, all; unspecified, impersonal; customary (see HABIT).

Adverbs—generally, in general, generally speaking; always, for better or worse; for the most part, in the long run; whatever, whatsoever; to a man, one and all, all told.

Antonym, see SPECIALITY.

In this thesaurus synonyms are listed by part of speech.

Cross-references to other major categories appear in capital letters.

Antonyms can be located by referring to the cross-reference at the end of an entry.

Exercise 2

Using a thesaurus, find one synonym for each word below. Then find one antonym for each word listed below. Finally, write an original sentence to illustrate the meaning of either the synonym or antonym for each word listed. You may wish to check the exact meaning of each word in a dictionary before you use it in a sentence.

1. ability (noun)
2. defeat (verb)
3. modesty (noun)
4. move (verb)
5. strong (adjective)
6. fear (noun)
7. courtesy (noun)
8. difficult (adjective)
9. growth (noun)
10. talk (verb)

Vocabulary

25.1   Building Vocabulary

With Marcie's helpful tips whispered in her ear, Peppermint Patty might yet develop a stronger vocabulary. Like any student, the better she understands words and their meanings, the better equipped she will be to communicate with others.

Developing Your Vocabulary

You probably hear or read at least one new word a day, while listening in classes at school, reading books or magazines, or listening to news broadcasts. What do you do when you come across a word you don't know? Rather than skipping over or tuning out an unfamiliar word, you can develop strategies for learning and remembering new words you encounter. The first step, however, is to become aware of new words. Only then is it possible to discover their meanings and practice using them. The following steps suggest ways to strengthen your vocabulary.

Steps in Learning and Remembering a New Word

1. **Notice** new words while reading or listening. You might want to keep a new-word journal in which you record unfamiliar words and their meanings.

2. **Understand** the meaning of a new word by studying the context—the surrounding words that are familiar—or checking a dictionary, or doing both.

3. **Verify** your understanding of a word with someone else. A teacher or a friend may be able to tell you if you correctly understand the meaning of a word.

4. **Use** the new word in your speaking and writing. For one week, try to use the new word at least once a day. You might want to double-check the meaning to be sure you're using the word appropriately.

You might also want to study vocabulary with someone—a friend or a small group of classmates. Then you can share your journals, agree to use new words with each other, and help each other figure out the meanings of some items. Your teachers will support you in your efforts. The chart below suggests a few ways to increase your vocabulary, both on your own and with other people.

Tips for Discovering New Words
1. Read extensively in a variety of areas. The more time you spend reading quality material, the more new words you are certain to encounter.
2. Use a thesaurus. Especially when you write, challenge yourself to use new vocabulary. Try to replace "worn out" verbs, such as forms of the verb *to be,* with vivid verbs.
3. Play word games. There are many word games on the market that can be challenging and fun, but you might enjoy inventing a game of your own.

Learning from Context

An unfamiliar word nearly always appears among other words that are familiar to you. These surrounding words provide the context of the new word. Thinking about the meaning of the rest of the phrase, sentence, paragraph, or passage and analyzing how the unknown word fits into that meaning helps you figure out the meaning of the new word.

Analyzing Specific Clues   Writers often supply clues that help you figure out the meanings of unfamiliar words. Notice how the sentence structure provides clues to the meaning of *mélange*.

> Our last talent show had a *mélange* of acts: classical vocalists, jugglers, gymnasts, tap dancers, and performance artists.

The colon tells you that examples of the acts follow. Because the examples are diverse, you might guess that *mélange* means "a mixture." In the following sentence, clue words can help you determine the meaning of *impediment.*

> The Postal Service allows no *impediment,* such as bad weather, to prevent the delivery of mail.

The clue phrase is *such as.* Bad weather is an example of an impediment. You can figure out that the Postal Service does not let any obstacle, like bad weather, get in its way. *Impediment* means "obstacle."

The chart on the next page describes different types of context clues and the specific clue words that help you interpret them. In the "Example" column, the clue words are in bold type. The unfamiliar words and the words that indicate a definition are in italics.

Interpreting Clue Words		
Type of Context Clue	**Clue Words**	**Example**
Definition: The meaning of the unfamiliar word is stated in the sentence.	that is in other words or also known as which means	The lecturer was *verbose;* **in other words,** he was *long-winded.*
Example: The meaning of the unfamiliar word is explained through one familiar case.	like for example such as for instance including	The paramedic quickly checked Amy's *vital signs,* **including** her *pulse rate and body temperature.*
Comparison: The unfamiliar word is similar to a familiar word or phrase.	also likewise similarly resembling identical	Joan's friend testified to her *veracity;* **likewise,** her teacher said Joan's *honesty* was evident to all who knew her.
Contrast: The unfamiliar word is the opposite of a familiar word or phrase.	but on the other hand on the contrary unlike however	Rachel is always *punctual,* **unlike** Brendan, who is usually *late.*
Cause and effect: The unfamiliar word describes a cause in a sentence in which the effects are understood.	because since therefore as a result consequently	Maria felt the stranger was being *intrusive* **because** he *asked too many personal questions.*

Analyzing the General Context   What if the context of an unfamiliar word has no specific clue words? You can still interpret unfamiliar words when the context clues are more general. After figuring out the part of speech of the unfamiliar word, you can try to figure out the idea of the word from supporting and contrasting details, as shown in the following examples.

> Because your friend Jesse was reading a book about the field of *ornithology,* she went to the library to view some of John James Audubon's famous drawings of birds.

How can you figure out the meaning of *ornithology?* You know from the passage that ornithology is a field of study. You also know that Jesse wanted to look at drawings of birds while she was reading about that subject. Therefore, you might deduce that *ornithology* is the study of birds.

The satellite was 670 miles from Earth at its apogee but only 260 miles away at its perigee.

What are the meanings of *apogee* and *perigee*? You know these two words are nouns since they are both objects of a preposition in a prepositional phrase. The particular measurements cited must be significant. You might guess that the *apogee* is the farthest point away from Earth in the satellite's orbit, while the *perigee* is the closest point.

You can see that being a good word detective helps you figure out unfamiliar words. Paying attention to all the surrounding details and to the general tone of a passage can help you learn many new words. If you carefully examine the context, you can often wait until a more convenient time to consult a dictionary or a more knowledgeable source. Checking to see if you guessed correctly, however, is a good habit to form.

Exercise 1

Each of the following passages contains an italicized word that may be unfamiliar to you. Determine the meaning by examining the context, looking for the different types of context clues described in the chart on page 748. Write the italicized word and its meaning. Then indicate the strategy used in each case by writing either *definition*, *example*, *comparison*, *contrast*, or *cause and effect*. Check your work in a dictionary afterward to see how close you came to figuring out the word meanings.

1. Like the other volunteers, Gayle did not expect payment for her *gratis* performance at the community center.
2. Copper is highly *malleable*, that is, easily shaped.
3. The first day of winter was *balmy*, and the days that followed were similarly mild.
4. Because this room is so small, you don't need a *stentorian* voice to be heard.
5. The village was *enshrouded*, or covered, in a thick fog.
6. Although Eduardo is an *immaculate* housekeeper, his twin sister, Mercedes, is an untidy person.
7. Michael's *acrophobia* was intense; likewise, his father also had an overwhelming fear of heights.
8. *Contiguous* countries, such as the United States and Canada, usually have border patrols.
9. Before the accident my car bumper was perfectly *symmetrical*; however, it is now uneven.
10. Teresa joined a *philately* club because she enjoyed looking at stamps from different countries.

25.2   Recognizing Parts of a Word

Another way to understand words is by analyzing their parts. The main part of a word is its root. When this is a complete word, it is called a base word. A root can be thought of as the "spine" of the word: it gives the word its backbone of meaning. It is often combined with a prefix (a part attached to the beginning), a suffix (a part attached to the end), or another root. Prefixes and suffixes often change the direction of a word's meaning. Look at the following example.

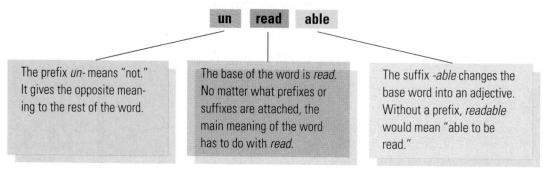

The prefix *un-* means "not." It gives the opposite meaning to the rest of the word.

The base of the word is *read*. No matter what prefixes or suffixes are attached, the main meaning of the word has to do with *read*.

The suffix *-able* changes the base word into an adjective. Without a prefix, *readable* would mean "able to be read."

Analyzing its parts, you can see that the word *unreadable* means "not able to be read."

Word Roots

While prefixes and suffixes can change a word's meaning, remember that the root gives the word its central meaning. The following words have the same root.

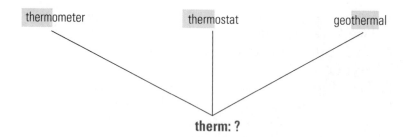

You may know that a meter is a unit of measure and that a thermometer measures heat. You may also know that *static* can mean "motionless" and that a thermostat is a device that keeps the amount of heat steady. Finally, you may know that *geo* means "earth" and that *geothermal* means "related to heat produced by the earth." Since all three words in the graph above concern heat and contain the root *therm*, you can infer that *therm* has something to do with heat. If you didn't know the meaning of one of the words above, you could begin to figure it out by using what you know about *therm*. The table opposite shows some words that share roots.

Analyzing Word Roots		
Words	**Meanings**	**Roots**
animate unanimous	having life being of one mind	*anima* means "mind" or "life"
anarchy archives	without government government records	*arch* means "rule" or "govern"
beneficial benevolent	good, helpful inclined to do good	*ben* means "good"
recede proceed	go back, yield again go forward	*ced* means "go"
contradict dedicate	to say the opposite of to say when giving	*dic* and *dict* mean "say" or "speak"
facsimile factory	a thing made similar to another a place where things are made	*fac* and *fact* mean "make"
general generate	affecting whole class to start or create	*gen* means "class" or "origin"
hydrant dehydrate	a large pipe used to draw water to remove water	*hydr* means "water"
manuscript manual	document written by hand done by hands	*man* means "hand"
portable porter	capable of being carried one who carries	*port* means "carry"
science omniscient	knowledge about the natural world knowing everything	*sci* means "know"
stringent unrestricted	binding, severe not bound, free	*string* and *strict* mean "bind"
traction extract	friction when pulling across a surface to pull out	*trac* means "draw" or "pull"
vivacious revive	full of life, lively bring back to life	*viv* means "live" or "alive"

Prefixes

Prefixes are syllables attached before a root to alter or enhance its meaning. Though the English language does not contain as many prefixes as suffixes, prefixes are still important tools for understanding and learning new words.

A prefix can sometimes completely change the meaning of a word. For example, the prefix *un-* gives the opposite meaning to any word to which it is attached. The following chart shows other valuable prefixes and their meanings. Notice that some prefixes have more than one meaning and that sometimes several different prefixes can convey the same meaning.

Analyzing Prefixes		
Words	**Meanings**	**Prefixes**
circumstance circumference circumvent	surrounding conditions distance around a circle avoid by going around	*circum-* means "around" or "about"
demote deduction	move down in rank conclusion drawn from reasoning	*de-* means "from" or "down"
disapprove disassociate	to not approve to not associate	*dis-* means "not"
hypersensitive hyperbole	overly sensitive much exaggeration	*hyper-* means "excessive"
illegal immortal insignificant irresponsible	not legal not mortal not significant not responsible	*il-*, *im-*, *in-*, and *ir-* mean "not"
misspell misogamy	spell badly hatred of marriage	*mis-* means "do badly" or "hate"
precede premonition	go before to warn in advance	*pre-* means "before"
submarine subhuman	beneath the ocean less than human	*sub-* means "beneath" or "less than"

Suffixes

Suffixes have their own meanings and can be added to the ends of base words to create new words with new meanings. Besides having specific meanings, however, suffixes also have grammatical functions. For example, the suffix *-ness* means "state of," "act of," or "quality of." In addition to creating a new meaning, this suffix also turns the base word *deaf*, which is an adjective, into an abstract noun. Therefore, *deafness* is a noun meaning "the state, act, or quality of being deaf." As you study the chart at the top of the next page, notice that the spelling of the root may change when a suffix is added.

Analyzing Suffixes			
Words	Meanings	Suffixes	Part of Speech Formed
movable peaceable visible	able to be moved capable of peace able to be seen	*-able* and *-ible* mean "capable of" or "able to be"	Adjective
occupant dependent	one who occupies one who depends	*-ant* and *-ent* mean "one who does an action"	Concrete noun
quicken moisten deepen	cause to be quick make moist make deep	*-en* means "to become"	Verb
parenthood childhood	state of being a parent state of being a child	*-hood* means "condition" or "state"	Abstract noun
dentist scientist	one who fixes teeth one who special- izes in science	*-ist* means "one who"	Concrete noun
evenly closely slowly	in an even manner in a close manner in a slow way	*-ly* means "in the manner or way mentioned"	Adverb
joyous courageous	full of joy full of courage	*-ous* means "full of"	Adjective
suspension civilization	state of being suspended state of being civil	*-sion* and *-tion* mean "the state of being something"	Abstract noun

Exercise 2

Copy the words below onto a separate sheet of paper. Then draw one line under the prefix in each of the words. Circle the root or the base word. Draw two lines under the suffix. Then write the meaning of the original word.

1. unfriendly
2. procession
3. dissatisfy
4. incredible
5. transmission
6. circumnavigation
7. incorruptible
8. omnivorous
9. repentance
10. intermediation

Unit 26 Spelling

26.1 Improving Your Spelling

One of your goals as a writer is to clearly communicate your ideas to your audience. But if your writing is filled with misspelled words, your ideas may be lost. Using correct spelling in your writing will enable your readers to focus on what you have to say and understand your ideas more easily.

You can improve your spelling—and in turn help make your writing understood—in several ways. First, you can learn some basic rules that will help you spell correctly. Second, you can pay attention to the new words you encounter and learn to spell them.

Basic Spelling Rules

The following rules, examples, and exceptions will help you master the spellings of many words.

Spelling *ie* and *ei* Many writers find the rules for certain combinations of letters, like *ie* and *ei*, difficult to remember. One helpful learning strategy is to develop a rhyme to remember a rule, like the following rhyme for the *ie* and *ei* rule.

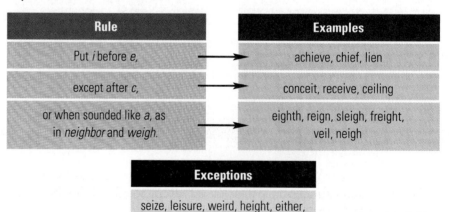

Rule	Examples
Put *i* before *e*,	achieve, chief, lien
except after *c*,	conceit, receive, ceiling
or when sounded like *a*, as in *neighbor* and *weigh*.	eighth, reign, sleigh, freight, veil, neigh

Exceptions
seize, leisure, weird, height, either, forfeit, protein

Spelling *-cede*, *-ceed*, and *-sede* Because various letters in the English spelling system are sometimes pronounced the same way, it is often easy to make slight spelling errors between two different letters. The similarity of pronunciation between *c* and *s* accounts for the confusion in spelling words ending in *-cede*, *-ceed*, and *-sede*. Because there are only four exceptions, however, you should be able to memorize them.

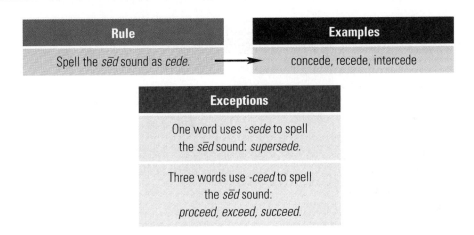

Rule	Examples
Spell the *sēd* sound as *cede*.	concede, recede, intercede

Exceptions
One word uses *-sede* to spell the *sēd* sound: *supersede*.
Three words use *-ceed* to spell the *sēd* sound: *proceed, exceed, succeed*.

Spelling Unstressed Vowels   Notice the vowel sound in the second syllable of the word *or-i-gin*. This is the unstressed vowel sound, and it can be spelled several ways. Dictionary respellings use the schwa symbol (ə) to indicate it. To help spell words with unstressed vowels correctly, try thinking of a related word in which the syllable containing the vowel sound is stressed. The chart below shows examples of this process.

Spelling Unstressed Vowels		
Unknown Spelling	**Related Word**	**Word Spelled Correctly**
leg_l	le**gal**ity	legal
fant_sy	fan**tas**tic	fantasy
host_le	hos**til**ity	hostile
opp_site	op**pose**	opposite

Adding Prefixes   When adding a prefix to a word, keep the original spelling of the word. If the prefix forms a double letter, keep both letters.

dis- + appear = disappear   ir- + regular = irregular
mis- + direct = misdirect   co- + operate = cooperate

Suffixes and the Silent e   Many English words end in a silent letter *e*. When adding a suffix, sometimes the *e* is dropped. The following chart shows when to keep and when to drop the *e*.

Adding Suffixes to Words with Silent *e*	
Rule	**Examples**
When adding a suffix that begins with a consonant to a word that ends in silent *e*, keep the *e*. **Common exceptions**	place + -ment = placement rare + -ly = rarely *awe + -ful = awful* *judge + -ment = judgment* ➡

Adding Suffixes to Words with Silent *e* (continued)	
Rule	**Examples**
When adding a suffix that begins with a vowel or *y* to a word that ends in silent *e*, usually drop the *e*. **Common exceptions**	excite + -able = excitable shine + -y = shiny *mile + -age = mileage*
When adding a suffix that begins with *a* or *o* to a word that ends in *ce* or *ge*, keep the *e* so the word will retain the soft *c* or *g* sound.	change + -able = changeable trace + -able = traceable
When adding a suffix that begins with a vowel to a word that ends in *ee* or *oe*, keep the *e*.	agree + -able = agreeable see + -ing = seeing canoe + -ing = canoeing

Suffixes and the Final *y* When adding a suffix to a word that ends in a consonant + *y*, change the *y* to *i*. Do not change the *y* to *i* when the suffix begins with *i*.

try + -ed = tried   copy + -ing = copying

When adding a suffix to a word that ends in a vowel + *y*, keep the *y*.

joy + -ous = joyous   convey + -ed = conveyed
boy + -ish = boyish   play + -ing = playing

Doubling the Final Consonant When adding a suffix to a word, you sometimes need to double the final consonant before adding the suffix. You double the consonant when adding a suffix that begins with a vowel to a word that ends in a single consonant preceded by a single vowel, if the original word

- is a one-syllable word
  dip + -ing = dipping   stop + -age = stoppage

- has an accent on the last syllable and the accent remains there after the suffix is added
  occur + -ence = occurrence   repel + -ing = repelling

- is a prefixed word based on a one-syllable word
  reset + -ing = resetting

Based on the preceding rule, you would not double the final consonant when

- the accent is not on the last syllable
  develop + -ing = developing

- the accent shifts when the suffix is added
  refer + -ence = reference

- the final consonant is preceded by two vowels
  train + -ing = training

- the final consonant is preceded by another consonant
  remind + -er = reminder

- the word ends in a consonant and the suffix begins with a consonant
  reck + -less = reckless

Adding -ly   When adding *-ly* to a word that ends in a single *l*, keep the *l*. When the word ends in a double *l*, drop one *l*. When the word ends in a consonant + *le*, drop the *le*.

real + -ly = really   dull + -ly = dully   terrible + -ly = terribly

Adding -ness   When adding *-ness* to a word that ends in *n*, keep the *n*.

sullen + -ness = sullenness   keen + -ness = keenness

Forming Compound Words   When joining a word that ends in a consonant to a word that begins with a consonant, keep both consonants.

after + noon = afternoon   key + board = keyboard

Forming Plurals   English nouns form plurals in many ways. Most nouns simply add *s*. The following chart shows other ways of forming plural nouns and some common exceptions to the patterns.

General Rules for Plurals		
If the Noun Ends In	**Then Generally**	**Example**
ch, s, sh, x, or *z*	add *-es*	wish → wishes crutch → crutches
a consonant + *y*	change *y* to *i* and add *-es*	cannery → canneries baby → babies
a vowel + *y*	add *-s*	day → days key → keys
a vowel + *o*	add *-s*	studio → studios stereo → stereos
a consonant + *o* **Common exceptions**	generally add *-es* but sometimes add *-s*	potato → potatoes cargo → cargoes *silo → silos halo → halos*
f or *ff* **Common exceptions**	add *-s* change *f* to *v* and add *-es*	reef → reefs *leaf → leaves*
lf	change *f* to *v* and add *-es*	half → halves wolf → wolves
fe	change *f* to *v* and add *-s*	life → lives knife → knives

A few plurals are exceptions to the rules listed on the previous page or present some other special problem, but they are easy to remember. The following chart lists these plurals and some examples.

Special Rules for Plurals	
Special Case	**Examples**
To form the plural of proper names, add either -s or -es.	D'Amico → D'Amicos Sanchez → Sanchezes
To form the plural of one-word compound nouns, follow the general rules for plurals.	penknife → penknives blackberry → blackberries
To form the plural of hyphenated compound nouns or compound nouns of more than one word, generally make the most important word plural.	father-in-law → fathers-in-law attorney general → attorneys general
Some nouns have irregular forms. These nouns do not follow any rules.	man → men ox → oxen
Some nouns have the same singular and plural form.	series → series deer → deer

Learning to Spell New Words

As you read, note unfamiliar words that you meet as well as words that you recognize but that look hard to spell. As you write, pay attention to any words that you have difficulty spelling. Then try the simple process shown below to learn to spell those words.

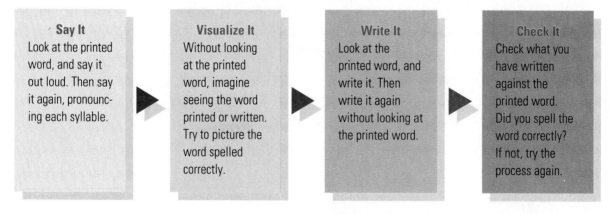

Say It
Look at the printed word, and say it out loud. Then say it again, pronouncing each syllable.

Visualize It
Without looking at the printed word, imagine seeing the word printed or written. Try to picture the word spelled correctly.

Write It
Look at the printed word, and write it. Then write it again without looking at the printed word.

Check It
Check what you have written against the printed word. Did you spell the word correctly? If not, try the process again.

Remember that the dictionary is a source for finding the correct spelling of words. You might ask, How can I look up a word if I don't know how to spell it? Typically you will be able to spell enough of a word to find it in the dictionary. If you don't find a word in the first place you look, think of other probable spellings. Once you have located the correct spelling of a word, use the process described above to learn the word.

In each group of words, find the one word that is misspelled. Write the word correctly. Cite the rule that applies to the spelling of the word. If the word is an exception to a rule, note that as well.

1. biege, conceit, thief
2. exceed, supercede, accede
3. definite, editor, abdumen
4. enjoiment, daily, carriage
5. truly, arguement, brownness

26.2 Spelling Difficult Words

Clearly, some words are more difficult to spell than others. As you have learned, not all words follow basic spelling rules. But you can learn to spell even the most difficult words.

One very useful strategy for learning difficult words is to develop a personal word list. What words are especially difficult for you? What words do you frequently misspell? Include those words in your personal word list. Study the words, using the four-step process you learned in Lesson 26.1, page 758.

Another helpful strategy for learning to spell difficult words involves developing memory devices. For example, if you have trouble remembering how many *e*'s are in the word *cemetery*, you might think of how we get there with *e*'s (ease). Puns, like this one, can help you remember how to spell difficult words.

Frequently Misspelled Words

Following is a list of words that many people often misspell. Which words on the list do you have difficulty spelling?

Words Often Misspelled			
absence	arctic	cafeteria	commercial
accidentally	attendant	canceled	complexion
accommodate	ballet	canoe	concede
adviser	beautiful	catastrophe	conscientious
alcohol	benefited	cemetery	convenient
allot	buffet	changeable	definite
all right	bureau	choir	deodorant
answer	business	colonel	descend ➡

Words Often Misspelled (continued)

discipline	hippopotamus	occasion	rhythm
disease	humorous	original	schedule
efficiency	hygiene	pageant	separate
eligible	immediate	pamphlet	sincerely
embarrass	incidentally	parallel	succeed
environment	jewelry	pastime	sufficient
essential	laboratory	permanent	supersede
exceed	leisure	pharmacy	technique
familiarize	library	physical	technology
fascinating	license	physician	theory
February	maintenance	pneumonia	traffic
foreign	mischievous	precede	truly
forty	misspell	preferable	unanimous
funeral	molasses	proceed	usually
genius	muscle	receipt	vacuum
government	necessary	recognize	variety
guarantee	neighborhood	recommend	versatile
height	niece	restaurant	Wednesday

Easily Confused Words

Some words are easily confused because they contain similar sounds. Other confusing words are homophones, words that have the same pronunciation but different meanings and spellings. Study the following list of easily confused words. Are there any words on the list that you confuse?

Words Often Confused

affect	to influence; to act upon
	I'm sure that sad movie will affect her mood.
effect	a result
	What effect did the punishment have on him?
altogether	entirely
	Mom is altogether pleased with my report.
all together	everyone in one place
	We waited all together at the bus stop.
capital	a city that is the seat of government
	On our trip we stopped in Jefferson City, the capital of Missouri.
capital	wealth
	The company invested its capital.
capitol	a building in which a legislature meets
	In the capitol we observed the Senate in session. ➡

formally	politely; officially; according to custom or rule
	Because our visitor was so important, we addressed him formally.
formerly	previously
	The principal was formerly a teacher.
holy	sacred
	Religious travelers make pilgrimages to holy places.
holey	having holes
	You should probably stop wearing that holey jacket.
wholly	completely; fully
	I am wholly satisfied with your story.
its	possessive pronoun
	The United States celebrated its bicentennial in 1976.
it's	contraction of *it is*
	It's not about winning; it's about fair play.
lose	to misplace; to drop
	Did you lose your assignment on the way to school?
loose	free; not confined; not tight
	My clothes are loose since I lost ten pounds.
passed	moved through; elapsed; completed satisfactorily
	I passed you in the hall several times today.
past	the time before the present; gone by; ended; over
	You can't change the past.
stationary	fixed; unmoving
	For a moment the plane appeared stationary in the sky.
stationery	writing paper and envelopes
	Rhonda wrote me a letter on hot pink stationery.
than	in comparison with
	You studied harder today than I have ever seen you study.
then	at that time; next
	He did his chores, and then he played a computer game.

Exercise 2

For each sentence below, determine which word in parentheses correctly completes the sentence.

1. The ambulance (passed, past) us.
2. Our teacher was (formerly, formally) a stock broker.
3. (Its, It's) beginning to snow.
4. (Then, Than) what do you do?
5. I always seem to (loose, lose) my keys.

Unit 27 Study Skills

27.1   Taking Notes in Class

Taking notes on classroom lectures and teachers' directions gives you a written record of important information for later use. In addition, taking notes makes you think about the information you're receiving. As a result, you learn more. Taking notes helps you do the following:

- organize ideas
- recognize relationships among different topics
- evaluate information
- identify points you find confusing

Many students take notes in the form of an outline. After each main idea the details supporting that idea are listed and indented below it. For more information on outline form, see Lesson 7.2 in Composition, pages 322–325. The chart below lists other suggestions on how to take class notes.

Tips on Taking Notes

1. Write down only key words and phrases. Focusing on main points allows you to continue to listen while you write.

2. Underline or star main ideas. Highlighting the most important points makes reviewing easier.

3. Revise your notes after class. Clarifying your organization and adding details makes your notes more complete.

4. Keep your notes in a folder or notebook. Having a separate folder for each class helps you keep your notes organized.

Organize your notes by class, date, and topic for easy reference.

To save time, use symbols and numerals instead of words.

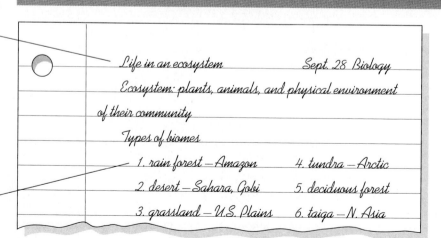

Life in an ecosystem   Sept. 28 Biology

Ecosystem: plants, animals, and physical environment

of their community

Types of biomes

   1. rain forest – Amazon   4. tundra – Arctic

   2. desert – Sahara, Gobi   5. deciduous forest

   3. grassland – U.S. Plains   6. taiga – N. Asia

Exercise 1

Watch a television program or listen to a radio broadcast, and take notes on what you observe and hear. You might choose a talk show, a news program, a documentary, or even a drama or play. The point is to practice your note-taking skills by recording as best you can what happens during the program.

Exercise 2

In a small group have one student read aloud from an encyclopedia article for five minutes. Other students in the group should take notes as the student reads. After the reading, the students taking notes should compare notes. What can you learn from your classmates about how to take good notes?

27.2   Studying Outside of Class

Your teacher usually determines what learning activities happen in class. Outside of class, though, you're responsible for allocating your study time and learning material. The first step in studying efficiently is to learn to manage your study time.

Using Study Time Wisely

By preparing yourself to study and organizing your work, you can make the most effective use of your time. Following are some suggestions to help you use your study time well.

Divide large assignments into smaller tasks. Reading four pages of a textbook each night is easier than trying to read twenty pages every fifth night.

Select a place to study. By using the same place for studying each day, you will begin to associate that place with studying.

Make a monthly assignment calendar. By writing down due dates, test dates, and notes about tasks to complete, you can see at a glance what work you need to do and when.

Gather necessary materials. If possible, leave study supplies such as pencils and a dictionary at your study place.

When you sit down to study, follow these tips to help you make the best use of your study time.

Tips on Studying Effectively
1. Focus on one assignment at a time. Try to stay on your task until you accomplish your goal.
2. Take short breaks after reaching a goal. Stretching, walking, or having a light snack can help keep you alert.
3. Write down questions about what you are studying. This gives you a written record of what to ask your teacher or classmates.
4. Review material before stopping. Even a short review will greatly increase the amount of material that you remember.

Reading Efficiently

Reading is probably the most important way of learning information. Whether you're looking for the year Simón Bolívar was born, trying to analyze his personality, or reviewing his accomplishments, you're reading. In each case, however, you're reading in a different way. The following chart shows you three different styles of reading and when you might use them.

Hints on Using Three Reading Styles		
Style	**Description**	**Purpose**
Skimming	Glancing over the text to identify main ideas by reading chapter and lesson titles, words in bold or italic type, and topic sentences	• Previewing material before a study session • Reviewing before a test • Deciding whether a book covers a subject you're interested in
Scanning	Glancing over the text in search of specific information by looking for key words	• Reviewing key terms • Looking for a detail to support an opinion • Searching a book to see if it covers a particular topic
In-depth Reading	Reading over the text carefully to absorb new ideas and facts	• Learning the material for the first time • Evaluating the information presented • Preparing to explain the information to someone else

The following text shows the information that you might learn in reading the passage in three different ways.

The Quran According to a Muslim tradition, the angel Gabriel revealed divine messages to Muhammad over a 22-year period. Faithful Muslims wrote down or memorized these messages, but they were not compiled into one written collection until after Muhammad died. Then his successor, Abu Bakr, ordered Muslims to retrieve these messages from wherever they could be found, from the ribs of palm-leaves and tablets of white stone and from the breasts of men. It took 20 years before the messages were compiled into the holy book of Islam, the Quran, whose name means recital. For all Muslims, the Quran is the final authority in matters of faith and practice.

Written in Arabic, the Quran is believed to contain God's message as revealed to Muhammad. This message is expressed in stories, legends, and poems. Some of the stories—such as Noah's ark and Jonah in the belly of the whale—are variations of those found in the Bible.

▓▓▓	**Skimming**
────	**Scanning**
═══	**In-depth reading**

Using the SQ3R Method

One way to increase your efficiency when studying material for the first time is to follow a five-step process known as the SQ3R method. The steps are described below.

Survey	**Question**	**Read**	**Record**	**Review**
Preview the material by skimming. Read heads, highlighted terms, and the first sentence of each paragraph. Look at all pictures and graphs.	Ask questions about the material. Your questions might begin with *who, what, when, where, why,* and *how.*	Read the selection carefully. Identify the main idea of each section. Take notes, and add questions to your list.	Write answers to your questions without looking at the text. Make brief notes about additional main ideas or facts.	Check your answers in the text. Continue to study the text until you can answer all questions correctly.

You can apply the SQ3R method to studying any subject. If you use the method regularly, it will become a habit. You may find that this habit brings several benefits, including the following:

- You remember more of what you read.
- You develop specific questions about information that is unclear.
- You are better prepared for class discussions and lectures.

Evaluating What You Read

The more you think about what you read, the better you will remember it. Hence, if you get in the habit of evaluating material as you read it, you will find that you learn it better.

Identifying Facts and Opinions   Most of what you read includes both facts and opinions. A fact is a statement that can be verified or proved true. How do you prove something is true? One way is through direct experience—something you saw or experienced yourself. If someone says it is raining outside, you can step outside and see for yourself.

Proof also might come from an authoritative source, such as a reference book or an expert on the subject. Did the Inca emperor Pachacuti come to power in 1438? You could check the date in an encyclopedia.

An opinion is a personal judgment. Since opinions are expressions of someone's beliefs or feelings, they cannot be proved true or false. While people generally can agree on facts, they often disagree about opinions. Opinions are most convincing when supported by evidence.

The following chart shows examples of facts and opinions. Learning how to distinguish between them will help you evaluate what you read.

Distinguishing Between Facts and Opinions	
Statement	**Fact or Opinion**
1. Computers now do much of the assembly line work that formerly was performed by factory workers.	Fact: Examining factories over the last twenty years would verify this statement.
2. Computerized manufacturing is bad because it causes people to lose their jobs.	Opinion: Computerized manufacturing may actually cause some unemployment, but whether it is good or bad is a value judgment.
3. Many kinds of vegetation and wildlife live in areas known as wetlands.	Fact: You could check this statement by reading studies done by biologists or visiting a wetland yourself.
4. The federal government should protect wetlands from pollution.	Opinion: Facts could be used to support or oppose this statement, but the statement is an opinion. People often disagree on the proper role of the federal government.

Interpreting Figurative Language   Writers use figurative language to make their texts more interesting and to express their ideas more clearly. Figurative language is a word or phrase used in an imaginative way rather than in a literal sense. You will see figurative language most often in novels, short stories, poems, and advertising. The text below includes several examples of figurative language.

> The dancers, clad in silks of green and blue, took their positions as the curtain rose. The music floated softly upward from somewhere below the stage and gathered like mist about their feet. As the melody swelled, their frozen forms melted into a celebration of movement. They swept across the floor, colorful rivers seeking their own paths along the barren landscape of the stage.

The dancers were not so cold they were actually "frozen." Rather, they were motionless as if they were frozen.

Describing how the dancers would "melt" into "rivers" suggests the dancers' graceful, fluid movements.

Exercise 3

Read a newspaper article, an editorial or a column, and identify ten statements in the piece as either facts or opinions. Then decide whether the writer presents any facts to support the statements that are opinions. Share your comments with your class, and decide whether or not newspapers report mostly facts or mostly opinions.

Exercise 4

Select a short passage from a novel or short story that uses figurative language. Rewrite the passage, changing the figurative language to literal language. Which style is more effective—the figurative or literal? Why?

Exercise 5

Find a three- or four-paragraph passage in a history or science textbook. Rewrite the passage, expressing the same information but using figurative language.

27.3   Learning from Graphics

Read the following sentence quickly: In 1990 the proportion of American women in the labor force was 63 percent among women aged 16–24, 74 percent among women aged 25–54, 45 percent among women aged 55–64, and 8 percent among women aged 65 and over. Did you grasp all of that? Probably not. The mass of numbers in the sentence makes the information difficult to comprehend at a glance. To present numbers and other facts that are difficult to communicate clearly in sentences, writers often use charts, tables, graphs, and maps. The rest of this lesson will give you tips on how to interpret each of these types of visuals.

Tables

Tables separate information into categories so you can compare information easily. The following table shows the percentage of women in the work force in seven countries in 1990. Notice how much more easily you can pick out information from the chart than from the first sentence in the above paragraph.

Across the top of the chart and down the left-hand side are the categories of information in the chart.

Compare information across columns. Among which age group were the most women in the labor force in Japan?

Compare information between rows. In which country was the percentage of women workers aged 55–64 highest in 1990?

| Percentage of Women in the Work Force, 1990 | | | |
16–24 Years Old	25–54 Years Old	55–64 Years Old	65+ Years Old
United States	63	74	45	8
Canada	66	76	36	4
France	34	73	31	2
Italy	41	49	10	2
Japan	45	64	47	16
Sweden	68	91	66	5
United Kingdom	73	73	37	3

To find out what percentage of Japanese women aged 25–54 were in the work force in 1990, you would first read down the left-hand column in the table to find Japan. Then you would read across the top of the table until you reached the age group "25–54." Moving down the column of numbers to the row even with Japan, you would see that 64 percent of Japanese women between the ages of 25 and 54 were in the work force in 1990.

Bar Graphs

In bar graphs each quantity is shown as a bar. The length of the bar reflects the amount. Because the bars are separate and distinct, writers often use bar graphs to compare quantities. In this bar graph, the consumption of vegetable protein in five world regions (horizontal axis) is compared using the measurement of grams per head per day (vertical axis). The bars provide a quick way to see who consumes the most and the least vegetable protein.

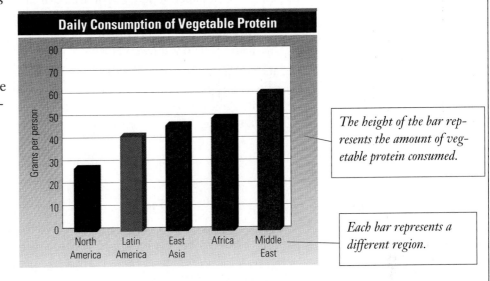

The height of the bar represents the amount of vegetable protein consumed.

Each bar represents a different region.

In the bar graph shown here, the bars run vertically. In many bar graphs the bars run horizontally. In these, the vertical axis indicates the categories being compared, and the horizontal axis indicates the quantities being compared.

Flow Charts

Flow charts show the steps in a process. Arrows connect the steps to show how one flows into the next. For example, a flow chart might show the steps a bill goes through in becoming a law or the stages in the life of a frog. The flow chart below shows the selection process for a Supreme Court justice.

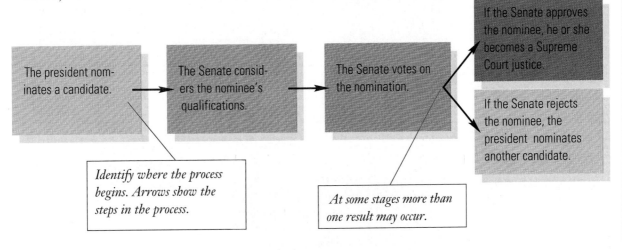

Identify where the process begins. Arrows show the steps in the process.

At some stages more than one result may occur.

Cluster Diagrams

Another way to show the relationship among ideas is through a cluster diagram. To create a cluster diagram, first write your main topic in the center of a piece of paper. Then, as you think of ideas related to it, write those. Connect each new idea with the ones related to it.

Cluster diagrams are a great method of connecting ideas you learn in class. The diagram below shows a cluster diagram about South American rain forests. Notice how the diagram shows the relationships among ideas.

The central idea is listed in the center of the diagram.

Each new idea creates the possibility of another cluster.

If you expanded the diagram, what ideas might you add?

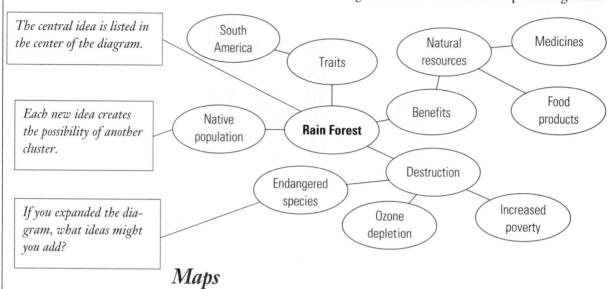

South America

Traits

Natural resources — Medicines

Native population

Rain Forest

Benefits — Food products

Endangered species

Destruction

Ozone depletion

Increased poverty

Maps

ITALY 500 B.C.

ALPS

ETRURIA

Rome

LATIUM

APENNINES

TIBER RIVER

ADRIATIC SEA

TYRRHENIAN SEA

Strait of Messina

SICILY

AFRICA

N

Greeks
Etruscans
Latins

0   50   100 miles
0 50 100 kilometers

12°E   16°E

42°N

38°N

A blue line on a land-mass indicates a river.

Why would you use a map such as this one?

Using the color key, you can determine that the Greeks occupied most of southern Italy.

Maps are a representation of a portion of the earth. Political maps show features that are created by or reflect the culture of people, such as countries, cities, or roads. Physical maps show the natural features of the earth, such as mountains, rivers, and plains. This map shows both political and physical features.

Political and physical maps usually show large land areas: the world, a country, a state, a city. Maps can also show smaller areas: the houses in a neighborhood, the buildings on a college campus, or the location of rooms in a building. Architects use a type of map, a floor plan, to help them visualize their ideas. Below is an example of a floor plan that you might see in a history book. It shows the layout of a palace built in Morocco about one thousand years ago.

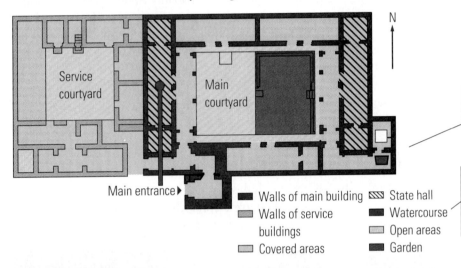

Service courtyard

Main courtyard

N

Main entrance ▶

Walls of main building
Walls of service buildings
Covered areas
State hall
Watercourse
Open areas
Garden

Breaks in the lines used to show walls indicate doors or windows.

Different colors and patterns distinguish separate areas and their uses.

Exercise 6

Create a table showing the increase in the number of female scientists between 1970 and 1986.

In 1970 around 23 percent of social scientists were women. About 17 percent of mathematical scientists and about 14 percent of natural scientists were women. Among physicians 10 percent were women. Only 2 percent of engineers were women. By 1986 women constituted 46 percent of social scientists, 36 percent of mathematical scientists, 23 percent of natural scientists, 18 percent of physicians, and 6 percent of engineers.

Exercise 7

In a group of four to six students, develop a cluster diagram. One student should choose a broad subject and write it down. Members of the group should take turns adding ideas to the diagram. Once you've filled the page, analyze the connections, and discuss their meanings.

Taking Tests

28.1   Classroom Tests

How do you get ready for a test? You probably review your textbook, class notes, and any assignments you have done. Learning the material is the most important step in preparing for a test. In addition, though, you can get ready for a test by learning how to answer the types of questions that you will see on the test.

This lesson will show you some strategies for answering different types of objective test items. An objective test item is one that asks for very specific information about material that you have studied.

Multiple-Choice Items

A multiple-choice item includes an incomplete sentence or a question, and several responses. You are to pick the response that best completes the sentence or answers the question. Consider the following tips.

Tips on Answering Multiple-Choice Items

1. Read the item carefully. You need to know what information you are looking for.

2. Read all the responses. Even if the first one seems right, a later response may be better.

3. Eliminate any responses that are clearly incorrect. This helps you focus your attention on the responses that might be correct.

4. Be cautious about responses that contain absolute words—*always, never, all,* or *none.* Since most statements have exceptions, absolute statements are often incorrect.

Here is an example of a multiple-choice question. In this case you are given a statement with a missing word. You are to choose the response that, when placed in the blank, will make the statement correct.

Though the stories were written by Arab writers, a does not complete the sentence correctly.

The sentence structure indicates that the answer is a female, so b and d are incorrect. The correct answer is c.

```
In The Thousand and One Nights, _____
prevents her execution by telling tales of
high adventure to her husband.

a. an Arab writer      c. Scheherazade
b. Sinbad              d. an unnamed man
```

Here is another multiple-choice item. This one is phrased as a question. You are to select the best answer to the question.

> Which of the following statements
> concerning the book *Native Son* is accurate?
>
> a. It was written by Richard Wright.
> b. It takes place in the North.
> c. It is a work of fiction.
> d. all of the above

Though a sounds correct, read all of the responses before answering.

Select this response only if you are sure that at least two of the responses are correct. In this case, d is correct.

True-False Items

A true-false item asks you to decide whether a statement is true or not. Many true-false items include some information that is true and some that is false. If any part of a statement is false, the entire statement is considered false. For the answer to be true, the entire statement must be true. Look at the statement on word usage below. Why is it false?

> The word *affect* is usually a verb meaning
> "to influence," and the word *effect* is
> always a noun meaning "the result."

The first part of this sentence is true, but the second is not because "effect" can also be a verb meaning "to cause." The correct answer is false.

Short-Answer Items

Short-answer items ask for specific information. Therefore, they are usually best answered with precisely phrased complete sentences. Note also that since these items may ask you to supply several pieces of information, your answers to these items may be worth more than those you provide to other questions. For example, look at the following question, which might appear on an earth science test.

> Why is soil erosion viewed as both helpful
> and harmful to people?

The question above asks you for more than a list of the effects of soil erosion. In your answer you should clearly distinguish between effects of soil erosion that are viewed as helpful and those that are viewed as harmful. Soil erosion is seen as helpful because it breaks up rocks and earth, moving rich soil to valleys and the mouths of rivers. Erosion is seen as harmful because it often strips farmland of valuable topsoil and threatens crop production.

Fill-in Items

Fill-in items usually consist of a sentence with one or more blanks for you to fill in. The number of blank spaces provided often indicates the number of words needed in the response. Your answer should make the statement true and also grammatically correct. Consequently, rereading the statement with your answer included will help you check whether your choice is correct. Try to answer the fill-in question below.

> In our solar system, the first three
> planets in order from the sun are _____,
> _____, and _____.

Notice that the order of the planets is important. The only correct answer is Mer-cury, Venus, and Earth.

On some tests you might be given a list of words from which to choose your answers. If so, complete the ones you're sure of first. If answers from the list can be used only once, cross them off as you use them. As you reduce the number of possible answers, you increase your chances of finding the correct answers to the harder items. For example, assume that you can answer the first two items below, but not the third.

> 1. Astronomers believe that the sun is a
>   star in the _____ galaxy.
> 2. The _____ revolves around the earth
>   about once a month.
> 3. The second closest star to the earth is
>   _____.
>
> Milky Way   moon
> Andromeda   Alpha Centauri
> quasar

After answering *Milky Way* for the first item and *moon* for the second, only three possible responses remain. Since the structure of the sentence suggests that the correct answer is the name of a star, and star names are capitalized, you can eliminate *quasar*. You now need to choose between only two answers, which improves your chances of choosing correctly. What is the correct answer? *Alpha Centauri.*

Matching Items

Fill-in items with the responses given are similar to matching items. However, instead of writing in the word, you write down the letter or number of the correct response. In matching items you have two sets or lists of items and must match those in the first column or group to those in the second. Reading the directions carefully helps you know what type of match you should make. Some common matches are

- terms and their definitions
- events and the dates they occurred
- causes and their effects
- chemical elements and their symbols

Whatever the subject, compare the lists. Do they include the same number of items? Will every item be used exactly once? If so, you can cross out each one as it is used. Just as you used the process of elimination to help you with fill-ins, you can use it again here. In the following example match each country with its capital. Each city is used only once.

```
1. _____  Japan            a. New Delhi
2. _____  Uruguay          b. London
3. _____  India            c. Montevideo
4. _____  Great Britain    d. Cairo
5. _____  Egypt            e. Tokyo
```

As with other test items, answer the ones you know well first. Note, however, that if each response is used only once, you'll have to make two changes if you change an answer.

Time Management

Tests usually last one class period or less. Since the time is limited, you need to use it efficiently. The chart below gives a few suggestions for using your time wisely.

Tips for Allocating Time During a Test

1. Spend the first few minutes preparing. Reading the directions carefully will help you answer items appropriately.

2. Answer the items you know well. Skipping difficult items will allow you to respond to all of the items you know.

3. Return to the difficult items. Using the strategies learned in this lesson, give the best answers you can.

4. Spend the last few minutes reviewing your answers. Taking time to check your answers will help prevent simple mistakes.

Exercise 1

Read the passage below, and use the test-taking strategies in this lesson to help you complete the items that follow.

Over the centuries Japan's Kabuki theater has grown and flourished. Continuing a tradition that historians have traced back to the 1600s, Kabuki plays are still performed in Japan to large audiences. Kabuki theater seems to have originated as a new form of drama to satisfy the lavish and melodramatic tastes of a new social class in Tokugawa Japan.

When the lower and middle classes of society began to increase in the urban centers, they sought new forms of entertainment. The name *kabuki* means "to lean in the direction of fashion," reflecting Kabuki theater's popular origins.

Kabuki dramatizes subjects ranging from historical events to daily life. With elaborate costumes, exaggerated movements, and amazing special effects (including snowstorms and fires), Kabuki theater is a spectacular event. Sometimes the stories make fun of political figures. During the 1600s government officials banned some performances they felt were too controversial. If anything, this censorship seems to have made Kabuki all the more popular.

1. Which of the following is true of Kabuki theater?
   a. It is an old art form.
   b. It can be controversial.
   c. It is still performed today.
   d. all of the above

2. True or False: Kabuki has a name appropriate to its origins.

3. Like many popular films today, Kabuki theater makes spectacular use of elaborate staging and _____ _____, such as snowstorms and fires.

4. How did the government's ban on certain political plays affect public opinion of Kabuki?

5. For each effect in the following list, choose the cause from which that effect most directly resulted.

   a. bans on Kabuki by the government
   b. increase in the popularity of Kabuki
   c. desire for a new form of drama
   ___ rise of a new social class
   ___ ridicule of political figures
   ___ censorship of performances

28.2   Standardized Tests

To compare large numbers of students, schools often give standardized tests, tests that have been given to similar groups of students around the country. By studying these test results, experts develop standards of performance. Most standardized tests fall into one of three categories:

- Ability tests evaluate general learning skills, such as how well you can read, write, or use logic.
- Achievement tests evaluate knowledge in specific content areas, such as how much you know about biology or world history.
- Aptitude tests evaluate individual talents and interests, such as whether you prefer working in groups or alone.

Standardized tests contain several types of items. Becoming familiar with the kinds of questions most often used on standardized tests will improve your chances of scoring well.

Reading Comprehension Items

How well you understand what you read is measured by reading comprehension items. These items usually include a long passage about a literature, social studies, or science topic, and several questions about the passage. You should be able to answer all of the questions, based on the information in the passage. These questions often require you to

- identify main ideas
- recognize details supporting main ideas
- figure out information that is not stated in the passage

The last type of item, also known as an inference item, requires you to come to a conclusion that is based on the information in the passage but is not explicitly expressed. As you read the following passage and the items that follow it, notice the suggestions for how to respond to the items.

> Siddharta Gautama, the founder of Buddhism, began his life as a Kshatriya prince. Born the son of a prince in northern India around 566 B.C., Gautama was raised in luxury. As a young man he continued to live a sheltered life, shielded from sickness and poverty. Tradition states that one day Gautama's charioteer drove him around his estates, and for the first time Gautama saw sickness, old age, and death. Shocked at these scenes of misery, Gautama decided to find out why people suffered and how suffering could be ended. At the age of 29, he left his wife and newborn son and wandered throughout India in what is known as the Great Renunciation.

```
1.Which sentence best summarizes the most
  important information in this passage?

a. Gautama was raised in luxury in India.
b. Gautama was born around 566 B.C.
c. Gautama left home at the age of 29.
d. Gautama wanted to know why people suffered.

2.Based on this passage, Gautama seemed to be

a. proud of his achievements
b. concerned about others
c. angry about his family's situation
d. eager to meet other people
```

Vocabulary Items

Standardized tests often evaluate your vocabulary knowledge through varieties of multiple-choice items. Sometimes you may be asked to complete a sentence by filling in the meaning of a word, as in the item below.

```
A preliminary step is taken _____.

a. before any other step in a process
b. during the most important stage of a
   process
c. after all other steps in a process are
   completed
d. only when necessary to complete a process
e. only if the first step of a process fails
```

One tip for completing vocabulary items is to analyze the parts of an unknown word. See Unit 25, pages 746–749, for more information on how to build your vocabulary. Notice that the word *preliminary* begins with the letters *pre-*. If you recall other words that begin with these letters, such as *precede, preface, prepare*, you may realize that *pre-* often means "first" or "early." Using this knowledge, you might correctly determine that the answer is *a*.

A different type of vocabulary item, an analogy, tests your ability to analyze the relationships between words, not just your understanding of the meanings of words. Consider the words *healthy* and *robust*. What is the relationship between them? They are synonyms, words that have the same meaning. Now examine the pairs of words at the top of the next page. Which pair has the same relationship as *healthy* and *robust*?

```
Healthy is to robust as

a. sociable is to disagreeable
b. haughty is to arrogant
c. mumble is to mouth
d. student is to teacher
e. gaggle is to goose
```

> *"Sociable" is the opposite of "disagreeable." "Haughty" and "arrogant" are synonyms. Mumble is something you do with your mouth. A student learns from a teacher. A "gaggle" is a collection of geese.*

None of the choices listed has anything to do with being healthy. However, the relationship between each pair of words is different. Only in *b* are the words synonyms. Hence, *b* is the correct answer.

Some analogy items are shown in a different format. Each pair of words is separated by a colon, with a double colon used after the first pair. However, this format still requires you to choose the pair of words with the same relationship as the first. What is the relationship below?

```
carpenter : hammer::

a. swimmer : athlete
b. hospital : doctor
c. waiter : tray
d. inept : awkward
e. inane : ridiculous
```

One strategy for answering analogy items is to create a simple sentence in your mind that states the relationship between the first pair of words—for example, A carpenter uses a hammer. Then try each pair of words in that sentence. For *a* you would come up with the statement, A swimmer uses an athlete. Since this sentence makes no sense, you could conclude that the relationship between *swimmer* and *athlete* is not the same as the relationship between *carpenter* and *hammer*. After trying each pair of words in the sentence, you would find that *c* makes the most sense.

Grammar, Usage, and Mechanics Items

Standardized tests often include sections evaluating your ability to recognize and use standard English. Items may ask you to find grammatical errors in sentences, point out misused words, or choose the best way to correct an awkward or incorrect sentence.

English usage items often show a sentence with several underlined and lettered sections. As you read the sentence, decide if one of the underlined parts contains an error, and mark the corresponding letter on your answer sheet. If the sentence contains no error, mark that choice; it usually follows the sentence. Examine the following item.

The error is in b; "I" should be "me."

> The competition between Michelle and I
>   a   b
> became more intense as the school year
>   c   d
> progressed. no error
>   e

Some usage questions test your knowledge of homonyms, words that sound alike but have different spellings and meanings. Given a list of phrases that contain homonyms, you might be asked to find the one item with a word used incorrectly or the one item with no errors. In the following example find the response in which all words are used correctly.

> a. a heard of cattle
> b. a jury of your peers
> c. a steal beam
> d. to much sun

The only phrase in which all words are used correctly is b.

Correction items ask you to correct a mistake as well as to recognize it. Usually only one part of the given sentence is underlined. Each response is a possible correction. You have to choose the response that best corrects the error in the sentence. Often one of the choices will look identical to the underlined section. Choose it if you feel the sentence contains no error. Here is an example of a sentence correction item.

As you read the sentence, decide if the underlined words are incorrect.

> Ms. Hasan is the best of the two candidates
> running for mayor.
>
> a. is the best of the two
> b. is the more better of
> c. is the very best of
> d. is the better of

"Best" should be used only in discussing three or more, so a and c are incorrect. "More better" is incorrect usage. The best response is d.

Test-taking Strategies

Certain test-taking strategies will help you as you take a test. The chart on the next page lists some strategies you might use.

Exercise 2

Use the test-taking strategies described in this lesson to help you complete the following items.

1. Choose the phrase that best completes this sentence:
   A transatlantic message is one that _____.
   a. travels under a body of water
   b. goes across the ocean
   c. is sent by passengers on a ship
   d. is always about navigation

2. Find the pair of words with the same relationship as the given pair.
   player : team : :
   a. conductor : baton   d. soldier : army
   b. engineer : bridge   e. cat : Siamese
   c. United States : country

3. Where is the error in the following sentence?

   Our teacher <u>was pleased</u> that <u>all of us</u> <u>have passed</u> the exam,
                a   **b**   **c**
   and <u>we were happy</u> that the test was over. <u>no error</u>
       d   **e**

4. Which item includes a word that is used incorrectly?
   a. a strong ally   c. the capital building
   b. gives good advice   d. the bare facts

5. Correct the underlined section in the following sentence.
   I wanted to remind her that the party starts at seven o'clock, but she <u>had already went</u> out the door.
   a. had already went   c. had went
   b. had went already   d. had already gone

Listening and Speaking

29.1   Listening with a Purpose

Did you ever play the telephone game? In a group of people, one person whispers a story to his or her neighbor. That person repeats the story to the next person, who tells the next person, and so on. The final person then tells the story aloud. After several retellings the story has usually changed in unpredictable ways, to the amusement of everyone in the group. With better listening skills, people would repeat the story more accurately and enjoy the telephone game less. However, at least they would learn and gain more from what they heard.

Listening in Class

Next to reading, listening is probably the most important skill you have for learning new information. Study the chart below to gain tips on how to listen effectively in class.

Tips for Effective Listening

1. Think about what you hear. Sorting out the main ideas in your mind helps you identify the points to remember.

2. Write down the important information. This gives you a written record of what you learned.

3. Notice verbal clues. Clues such as "another reason" or "in summary" help you organize the information you are hearing.

4. Listen for helpful information your teacher offers. Your teacher might indicate what material is most important or will appear on a test.

5. Organize your thoughts and notes after class. This gives you a chance to fill in missing information while the material is still fresh in your mind.

Interpreting Vocal Clues   How your teacher says something may also give you clues about what information is important. To emphasize a point, a teacher might speak more quickly and loudly because he or she is excited. On the other hand, another teacher might speak more slowly and quietly in order to add emphasis to each word.

Interpreting Nonverbal Signs   Teachers also may communicate nonverbally. For example, a teacher might emphasize a key point with an emphatic gesture or a change in facial expression.

Listening to Television and Radio

Outside of class, you may listen to news programs, documentaries, and talk shows that provide information about current events. As you listen, you should also develop your skill at evaluating what you hear. Is this information true? What perspective does it represent? Who would disagree with this? The chart below presents some statements you might hear on a typical news report along with questions to ask about each.

Evaluating News Statements	
Sample Statement	**Questions to Ask**
1. An unidentified source close to the president said there will not be a summit on peace this fall.	Why wouldn't the source give his or her name? Is the source unable to back up the information?
2. Statistics gathered by a Washington-based research group show that high-fat foods may not harm most people's health.	Who was the research group? Who paid the group to conduct the research? Have other research groups challenged their findings?
3. A popular supermarket tabloid has published a story linking the governor to a ring of drug smugglers.	Is a supermarket tabloid believable? Do the news reporters seem to take the story seriously?
4. A radical political organization today vowed to continue its illegal protests.	Who considers this organization radical? Why are its protests illegal?
5. The candidate today charged that her opponent failed to be on hand for thirty roll-call votes.	Is thirty votes many to miss or a low number? Were these votes important? Were any of the votes close?

Exercise 1

Choose a partner, and prepare an interview. Each person should role-play someone famous. The partners should take turns interviewing each other for fifteen minutes. Then each student should introduce his or her partner's character to the class. The person interviewed will evaluate how well the partner listened by noting how accurate the introduction was.

Exercise 2

Follow a nightly newscast for one week. Keep a journal of the topics covered and the questions that you thought of as you listened. In a class discussion explain how the stories developed during the week and whether or not any of your questions were eventually answered. Write a two-page report summarizing the experience.

29.2　Speaking Effectively

Speaking effectively involves more than responding to a question with correct information or reacting to another's statement. It involves using the type of communication most appropriate to the situation—and different situations call for different types of communication. You probably already adjust your speaking style to match your situation. However, to be sure you're doing this appropriately, review the chart below. The chart can also help you better understand the differences between informal, semiformal, and formal communication.

Types of Speaking Situations		
Type	**Traits**	**Examples**
Informal	• Involves little planning or preparation • Often covers many topics • Much interaction among speakers	conversations introductions
Semiformal	• Involves some preparation by the speaker • Covers a subject chosen for a specific purpose • Moderate interaction between speaker and audience	class discussions announcements
Formal	• Involves extensive preparation by the speaker • Covers a specific topic and purpose • Interaction between speaker and audience limited and controlled	class report graduation speech dramatic reading

Preparing Spoken Comments

Just as you practice a dance routine before a recital or important plays before a game, you need to practice spoken comments before you give them. In general, the more formal the speaking situation is, the more you should prepare for it. To help you speak effectively, follow the steps outlined in the flow chart on the facing page. You may notice that preparing a speech is similar to preparing a piece of writing.

Prewriting	Drafting	Revising	Practicing	Presenting
• Find an appropriate topic. • Consider what your audience knows and how much time you have to speak. Do any necessary research.	• Organize your ideas by writing a preliminary outline. • Identify your main ideas and supporting information. • Put your outline on note cards.	• Review the organization of information. • Improve word choices. • Add transitions.	• Read the speech aloud. • Critique your delivery. • Time your speech.	• Be organized. • Deliver your speech in a clear, strong voice.

Presenting Yourself and Your Ideas

Many speakers, from students to experienced politicians, get nervous before delivering a speech. Here are a few tips to help you remain calm.

Tips for Relaxing

1. Writing the word *relax* several places in your note cards will remind you to take it easy.

2. Taking a deep breath before you begin will help you calm down.

3. Speaking to one person in your audience at a time will help you speak in a normal tone of voice.

In addition to staying relaxed, you want to deliver a speech that will capture the attention of your listeners. Here are a few suggestions for how to speak effectively.

Tips for Effective Speaking

1. Pause after each important point. This gives people time to take in what you've said.

2. Use gestures to help explain your material. By pointing to a place on a map or using your hands to show the size of a fish you caught, you help your audience visualize what you are discussing.

3. Look people in the eye. Making eye contact with individuals in your audience helps you keep your audience's attention.

4. Vary the tone and pitch of your voice. Letting your voice rise and fall naturally and get louder and softer will make your speech sound more conversational.

When you deliver a speech, you are doing the talking. However, your audience is also communicating with you. With practice you can read the signals the audience is sending you and then adapt your speech. Following are suggestions about how to interpret audience signals.

Communicating with Your Audience	
Audience Signals	Speaker Response
1. People are staring out the window or fidgeting in their chairs.	People are probably getting bored. Try to use a more emotional or exciting tone of voice.
2. People are frowning or appear to be asking each other questions.	People might be confused. Try to review key points, using new examples.
3. People are leaning forward in their chairs and appear to be struggling to hear you.	People may be unable to hear. Besides speaking more loudly, scan the room for other sources of noise, such as fans, that can be reduced.
4. People are attentive, smiling, and nodding their heads in an affirmative manner.	People are listening closely. Keep doing just what you've been doing.

Exercise 3

With a group of four or five classmates, analyze the following topics (or develop more topics on your own) as possible subjects for a three-minute speech. Decide how the topics can be narrowed, what your class would like to hear, and how much research the topics would require.

- women in sports
- fairy tales and nursery rhymes in history
- minority roles in World War II
- high school course requirements

Exercise 4

Choose one of the topics you discussed in Exercise 3, and prepare a speech on it. In small groups each student should prepare and deliver part of his or her speech. Other members of the group should make suggestions on how to improve the presentation. Use these suggestions to help you practice and deliver your speech to the entire class.

29.3   Working in Groups

As a member of a group, you need certain skills that you don't use when working alone. For example, group work requires more communication skills, more organizational skills, and more interpersonal skills than does working alone. However, group work has several advantages. The members of a group can

- benefit from the special skills and knowledge of each member
- work together to accomplish tasks that one person could not do alone
- get feedback on their ideas and proposals

Because of these advantages, you may often find yourself part of a group. You might be part of a group that is doing a science research experiment, reviewing for a social studies test, or trying to raise money for a school project.

Roles in Groups

In a group every member has a role to play. Each member is partially responsible for the successful functioning of the group. However, two people in a group usually have special roles to play, the chairperson and the recorder. The various roles of group members are described below.

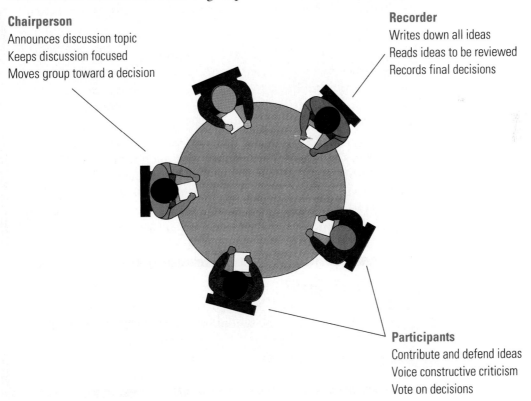

Chairperson
Announces discussion topic
Keeps discussion focused
Moves group toward a decision

Recorder
Writes down all ideas
Reads ideas to be reviewed
Records final decisions

Participants
Contribute and defend ideas
Voice constructive criticism
Vote on decisions

Group Procedures

Certain procedures will help any group to stay on its task and function more smoothly. For example, if everyone follows common courtesy, such as not interrupting one another, the group will function better. Below are additional suggestions to help a group work well.

Tips for Working in a Group

1. Listen to other group members. You may want to jot down suggestions, examples, and other comments made by people in the group.

2. Help members stay on track. When the discussion is wandering, say something like, "I think we should remember that our goal is . . . ."

3. Criticize ideas, not individuals. Focus on supporting or opposing ideas rather than people.

4. Accept criticism of your ideas from others. Assume that everyone in the group is trying to help. They are not trying to belittle you.

5. Encourage quiet members to participate. Pull people in with phrases such as "You've been quiet. What do you think of this idea?"

Exercise 5

Working in a group of five or six students, decide the following issue: What is the most crucial problem facing high school students today? Select a chairperson and a recorder for your group. In addition, select an observer, a person to keep track of how well the group is functioning. The observer should notice if everyone is participating, if people are being courteous, if the group is staying focused, and so on.

After thirty minutes of discussion, ask the observer to evaluate the group. Then write a summary of your own evaluation of the group experience. Discuss such items as your feelings of comfort or anxiety in the group and whether or not you think you'd enjoy a career that requires much group work.

Exercise 6

Attend a meeting of the school board, city council, or some type of committee. Write a one-page summary evaluating how well the group worked together.

Index

B

Bad, badly, 608
Baker, Russell, 178
Bar graphs, 769
Barnes, Jim, 87
Barrio Boy (Galarza),
    401–402Base words, 750
Being as, being that, 629
Beside, besides, 629
Bessone, Lisa Twyman, 166–170
Between, among, 629
Bible
    capitalization, 658
    references to, 669
Bibliography, 739
    final, 333, 334–335
    working, 319, 333
Bibliography cards, kinds of, 319
Biography, 34–37. *See also*
    Autobiography
Biography section, in dictionary,
    744
*Black Boy: A Record of Childhood
    and Youth* (Wright),
    544–545
Blends, 714, 725, 726
Bodanis, David, 220
Book, parts of a, 738–739
Borrow, lend, loan, 630
Borrowed words, 714, 716, 717,
    720, 722
Bradbury, Ray, 140
Brainstorming, 23, 59, 73, 78,
    81, 107, 119, 139, 141, 147,
    173, 179, 194, 225, 227, 259,
    271, 301, 311
Bridges, capitalizing names of, 653
Bring, take, 630
Brooks, Gwendolyn, 4, 5, 6, 7, 9,
    33
Buildings, capitalizing names of,
    653
Business letters, 669

C

Calendar items, capitalizing
    names of, 655
Call of the Wild, The (London),
    459

Can, may, 630
Can't hardly, can't scarcely, 630
Capitalization
    of abbreviations, 695–696
    of articles in titles of works,
      656, 688
    of compass points, 654
    Mechanics Workshop for,
      660–665
    of proper adjectives, 419, 657
    of proper nouns, 402–403,
      652–656
    of sentences, 651
    summary of capitalization rules,
      658
Card catalog, 728, 730–731
Case Study feature
    in fantasy writing, 124–128
    in feature writing, 54–58
    in letter writing, 4–8
    in movie reviews, 276–280
    in nature writing, 214–218
    in sportswriting, 166–170
Cause-and-effect diagram, 291
Cause-and-effect organization,
    86, 88, 226, 234, 338
    as context clue, 748
Cause-and-effect writing,
    232–235, 274. *See also*
    Expository writing
    eliminating errors in, 291
    literature model in, 232
    revising, 234
    thesis statement in, 233
    transitions for, 91
Characters, 108
    in descriptive writing, 146, 147,
      148–151
    in expository writing, 253
    in narratives, 172, 175
Charts, in prewriting, 25, 35, 49,
    229, 230, 261, 303
Chavez, Lorenzo, 54–58
Chronological order, 86, 174,
    272
"Circling Hand, The" (Kincaid),
    172
Circulation desk, 728
Cisneros, Sandra, 4–8, 9, 82
Civics, writing topics in, 63, 105,
    293
Claim
    reaffirming, in persuasive

    writing, 284
    stating central, in persuasive
      writing, 283
Classification in expository writ-
    ing, 236–239, 274
    definition of, 236–237
    drafting, 237, 238
    literature model in, 236
    planning, 237
    revising, 238
Classroom tests. *See* Tests
Clauses
    adjective, 494–495, 525, 675
    adverb, 496–497, 526, 581, 677
    definition of, 489
    Grammar Workshop for,
      506–516
    main, 489
    noun, 497–498, 526–527
    subordinate, 409, 489–490, 581
Clustering, 16, 19, 52, 109, 141,
    770
Coherence, in paragraphs,
    90–92, 96
Collaborative learning. *See*
    Cooperative Learning
Collecting, in prewriting, 65
Collective nouns, 403
    and subject-verb agreement,
      383, 559
Collier, Eugenia, 197
Colons
    in biblical references, 669
    in expressions of time, 669
    to introduce, 668–669, 747
    parentheses with, 682
    quotation marks with, 686
    before quotations, 669
    after salutation of business
      letter, 669
Comet (Sagan and Druyan), 232
Commas
    with addresses, 679
    with adverb clauses, 677–678
    with antithetical phrases, 678
    to avoid confusion, 672
    in compound sentences, 491,
      502, 503, 672
    with conjunctive adverbs, 676
    and coordinate adjectives, 673
    with geographical terms, 679
    with interjections, 399, 676
    in letter writing, 680

Copyright page, 739
Correlative conjunctions, 429
  diagraming, 520
*Could of, might of, must of, should
  of, would of,* 630
Criteria, 51, 121, 163, 211, 273,
  313
Critical analysis
  of biography, 34–37
  of character descriptions,
    148–150
  characters in, 108
  explaining theme in, 106–109
    comparing and contrasting
    myths in, 260–263
  of movie, 276–280, 302–305
  plot in, 108
  in reader-response journal,
    30–32
  sentence combining in,
    370–374
  setting in, 108
Critical Thinking. *See* Thinking
  Skills
Cross-curricular writing topics.
  See Writing across the
  curriculum
Cross-references, in dictionaries,
  743
Crystal Cave, The (Stewart), 134,
  152–158

D

Daneshvar, Simin, 566
Dangling modifiers, 395,
  610–611, 615
Dashes
  for emphasis, 682
  to signal change, 681
Dates
  abbreviations for, 696
  commas in, 679
  numerals for, 698–699
Day, David, 240–241
"Day's Pleasure, A" (Garland),
  505
Declarative sentences, 500, 667
Definite article, 419
Definitions
  as context clues, 748
  in expository writing, 215

guidelines for writing personal,
  236
Delta Wedding (Welty), 506–507
Demonstrative pronouns, 408
Descriptive writing, 144, 160
  analysis of character
    descriptions, 148–151
  Case Study in fantasy writing,
    124–128
  connotation of words in,
    136–137, 164
  creating an overall impression
    in, 131–133, 164
  describing an imaginary person
    in, 144–147, 164
  describing an imaginary place
    in, 141–143, 164
  descriptive language in,
    136–139 164
  drafting, 127, 162
  editing, 163
  explaining theme in, 106–109
  mood in, 131
  portfolio in, 164
  presenting, 163–164
  prewriting, 126, 160–161
  revising, 128, 162–163
  sentence combining in,
    354–357
  spatial organization in, 133
  suspense writing in, 195
  topic sentence in, 131, 132
  transitions in, 134
Desert Exile (Uchida), 71
Details
  in a character description, 149
  checking for, in revising, 132,
    142, 150, 163
  creating mood with, 142
  in creating suspense, 194
  in expository writing, 218, 224–
    227
  in a feature article, 252
  in a news story, 244
  ordering, 80, 86–89
  in a personal essay, 20
  in a screen play, 129
  supporting, 80, 132, 224–226
Dewey decimal system, 732–733
Diagraming sentences, 519–528
Diagrams, 103, 245, 256
  in comparing and contrasting,
    240, 241, 242

in planning classification, 237
Dialogue, 180–183
  developing, 181–182
  editing, 181, 211
  in narratives, 180–183, 210
  prewriting, 182
  uses of, 180
  writing, 105, 182, 183
Dickens, Charles, 591
Dictionary
  biography section in, 744
  cross-references in, 743
  geography section in, 744
  guide words in, 740–741
  homographs in, 742
  main entries, 741–743
  organization of entries in,
    740–741
  syllabication in, 742
  synonyms in, 742
  usage information in, 743
  using, 758
Different from, different than, 631
Dillard, Annie, 616–617
Direct address, commas to set off
  words or names in, 679
Direct objects, 454
  diagraming, 520
  noun clause as, 497, 527
Direct quotations, quotation
  marks for, 684–685
Documentation, 330–335. *See
  also* Bibliography; Footnotes
  in research paper, 319–321
  parenthetical, 332
Documents, capitalizing names
  of, 654
Doesn't, don't, 632
Doomsday Book of Animals, The
  (Day), 241
Double comparisons, 606–607
Double negatives, 609
Drafting, 61, 122
  in classification, 238
  coherent paragraphs in, 90–92,
    93
  in descriptive writing, 127, 162
  in expository writing, 217–218,
    222, 272–273
  in feature articles, 57, 251–252
  in narrative writing, 209–210
  ordering details in, 80, 86–89
  in personal writing, 49–51

Drafting *(continued)*
 in persuasive writing, 312–313
 in a research paper, 326–329
 revising, 128
 in suspense writing, 194
 topic sentence in, 80
 turning prewriting into a
  paragraph, 78–80, 81
 unified paragraphs in, 82–85
 in the writing process, 119–120
Druyan, Ann, 232

E

Each, compound subjects joined
 by, 384–385, 561
Editing, 61, 122. *See also*
 Proofreading; Revising;
 Troubleshooter
 in comparison-contrast writing,
  242
 in descriptive writing, 163
 dialogue, 181, 211
 in an essay answer, 258
 in expository writing, 274
 labels for graphics, 245
 marking draft in, 100
 in narrative writing, 211–212
 in personal writing, 51–52
 in persuasive writing, 313–314
 for sense, 98–99, 101
 in a sports narrative, 170
 in the writing process, 121
Editorials, 298–301
 appealing to audience, 300
 choosing an issue for, 299
 literature model for, 298
 prewriting, 299
 summing up, 300
Effect, affect, 627, 760
Either/or thinking, eliminating,
 291
Elliptical adverb clause, 581
Emigrate, immigrate, 632
Emphatic forms of verb, 538
English language
 acronyms in, 725, 726
 borrowed words in, 714, 716,
  717, 722
 eponyms in, 715
 euphemisms in, 724
 formal versus informal, 72

French words in, 719–720
history of, 713–714, 716–717,
 719–720, 722–723, 725–726
Latin words in, 716
puns in, 721
Scandinavian words in, 717
slang in, 727
spoonerisms in, 718
Tom Swifties in, 721
Eponyms, 715
Eras, capitalizing names of, 655
Essay question answers, 254–
 259
 and clues in questions, 255
 drafting, 255, 257
 editing, 257, 258
 literature model for , 254
 organizing information for, 256
 revising, 255, 257, 258
 time management in, 257
Essays, 222. *See also* Critical
 analysis; Expository writing
Essential clauses, 494
Ethnic groups, capitalizing
 names of, 653
Euphemisms, 724
Every, compound subjects joined
 by, 384–385, 561
Evidence
 assessing accuracy of, in
  persuasive writing, 287–288
 assessing relevance of, in
  persuasive writing, 288
 defining, in persuasive writing,
  286
 explaining, as claim support,
  284
 identifying supporting, 283
 selecting, in persuasive writing,
  289
Examples
 adding, to paragraph, 84
 as context clues, 748
 transitions for, 91
Except, accept, 627
Exclamation point, 500
 to end exclamatory sentence,
  500, 667
 parenthesis with, 683
 quotation marks with, 686
Exclamatory sentences, 500, 667
Expository writing, 270
 adding detail in, 224–227

answering essay questions,
 254–259
Case Study in nature writing,
 214–218
cause and effect in, 222,
 226–228, 232–235, 274
classification in, 222, 236–239,
 274
comparing and contrasting,
 217, 222, 240–243, 274
comparing and contrasting
 myths in, 260–263
conclusion in, 230, 234
definition in, 222, 234–236
drafting, 217–218, 222,
 272–273
editing, 274
essay tests as, 246–250, 259
explaining and informing in,
 220–223
feature article, 248–253, 274
graphics in, 244–247
identifying audience, 221–223
introduction in, 230, 234
literature models in, 220, 224,
 228, 232, 236, 241, 249, 250,
 252, 254
mixing strategies in, 216
nature of, 221
news articles as, 242–244
portfolio in, 274
presenting, 274
prewriting, 221, 228–230,
 270–272
process explanation in,
 222–224, 228–231, 274
revising, 218, 273–274
sentence combining in, 362–365
varieties of, 222
External conflicts, 177

F

Facts
 adding, to paragraph, 84
 anecdotes based on, 185
 distinguishing between
  opinions and, 766
 getting, for news article, 243
Fantasy writing, Case Study in,
 124–128
Farther, further, 632

L

Lake Wobegon Days (Keillor), 660–661
Languages, capitalizing names of, 653
Latin, words from, 716
Laws, capitalizing names of, 654
Lay, lie, 634
Leads
　for feature article, 251, 253
　writing effective, 243
Learn, teach, 634
Learning log. *See* Journal Activity
Leave, let, 634
LeGuin, Ursula K., 145
Lend, loan, borrow, 630
L'Engle, Madeleine, 136
Less, fewer, 632
Let, leave, 634
Letters
　apostrophe to form plural of, 691
　as letters, 688
Letter writing
　Case Study in, 4–8
　commas in, 680
　hints for, 9
Lewis, Anthony, 288
Library
　arrangement of, 728–729
　checking the shelves in, 734
　classification systems in, 732–734
　general reference works in, 737–738
　locating books and other resources in, 730–731
　locating periodicals and newspapers in, 735–736
　Readers' Guide to Periodical Literature in, 736
　specialized reference works in, 738
　using, 74
　using parts of book, 738–739
Library of Congress classification, 733–734
Lie, lay, 634
Life map, 23
Life of Langston Hughes, Volume II, The (Rampersad), 184

Light Elements (Stone), 224
Like, as, 634
Limerick, 28, 29
Limiting words, 291, 294–295
Line graphs, 245
Linking verbs, 413–414
　nominative case after, 578
　subject-verb agreement with, 556
Listening. *See also* Speaking
　in class, 782
　to television and radio, 783
　with a purpose, 782
Listing, 13, 31, 66, 79, 120, 131, 141, 178, 190, 215, 217, 223, 229, 299
Lists, colon to introduce, 668
Literature, writing about. *See* Writing About Literature
Literature, writing topics in, 129, 171, 199, 219, 229, 263, 281, 305. *See also* Critical analysis
　in reader-response journal, 30–33
　about biography, 34–36
Literature models. *See also* Literature selections; Workshop literature
　Anne Frank: The Diary of a Young Girl (Frank), 14
　"Circling Hand, The" (Kincaid), 172
　Comet (Sagan and Druyan), 232
　Crystal Cave, The (Stewart), 134
　Desert Exile (Uchida), 71
　Doomsday Book of Animals, The (Day), 241
　"For the Love of Loons" (Hubbell), 236
　Growing Up (Baker), 178
　Hannah's Daughters (Gallagher), 76
　House Made of Dawn (Momaday), 92
　House on Mango Street, The (Cisneros), 82
　In Search of Our Mothers' Gardens (Walker), 62
　It Was on Fire When I Lay Down on It (Fulghum), 18
　Kareem (Abdul-Jabbar), 24
　Life of Langston Hughes, Volume II, The (Rampersad), 184

Light Elements (Stone), 224
　"Man and Daughter in the Cold" (Updike), 198
　"Marigolds" (Collier), 197
　Martian Chronicles, The (Bradbury), 140
　"Merchants of Death" (Lewis), 288
　"My People," (Hughes), 26
　Names, The (Momaday), 10
　"On Native Ground" (Barnes), 87
　Return of the King, The (Tolkien), 130–131
　Rubber Legs and White Tail-Hairs (McManus), 228
　"Searching for Medicinal Wealth in Amazonia" (Jackson), 249, 252
　Season Ticket (Angell), 190
　Secret House, The (Bodanis), 220
　"Sisters Under the Skin" (McDonough), 292
　"Song of the Open Road" (Nash), 27
　Straight Dope, The (Adams), 254
　"Sunday" (Llosa), 193
　Tehanu: The Last Book of Earthsea (LeGuin), 145
　"View of the Woods, A" (O'Connor), 79
　"Winking at Steroids in Sports" (*New York Times*), 298
　Wrinkle in Time, A (L'Engle), 136
Literature selections. *See also* Literature models; Workshop literature
　Crystal Cave, The (Stewart), 152–158
　How the García Girls Lost Their Accents (Alvarez), 200–206
　I Know Why the Caged Bird Sings (Angelou), 38–46
　Kitchen God's Wife, The (Tan), 110–116
　Of Wolves and Men (Lopez), 264–268
　questions about, 46, 116, 158, 206, 268, 308
　"Skeletons in the Attic" (Spotted Elk), 306–308
Llosa, Mario Vargas, 193

Nouns
  abstract, 401
  collective, 383, 403, 559
  common, 402–403
  concrete, 401, 405
  definition of, 401
  as direct object, 454
  gerund as, 474
  infinitives and infinitive phrases
    as, 524
  as object complement, 456
  as predicate nominative, 457
  proper, 402–403, 405, 652–657,
    690, 695
  special, and subject-verb
    agreement, 559
  using precise, 137, 139, 405
  verbals as, 472
Noun clauses, 497–500
  diagraming, 526–527
Nouns of amount, and subject-
  verb agreement, 383, 559
Number, amount, 629
Number, pronoun-antecedent
  agreement in, 584
Numbers
  apostrophe to form plural of,
    691
  hyphens in, 693
  as numbers, 688
  spelling out, 697–698
Numerals, 697, 698–699

O

Object complements, 456
  diagraming, 520
Object of the preposition, 427
  noun clause as, 497–498, 527
Objective case, for personal
    pronouns, 577–578,
    581–582
Objective tests, 772–775
Objects
  direct, 454–455, 497, 520, 527
  indirect, 455, 520
O'Connor, Flannery, 79
Of Wolves and Men (Lopez),
    264–268
Old Man and the Sea, The
    (Hemingway), 592–593
"Old Mary" (Brooks), 33

On Assignment, 9, 59, 129, 171,
    219, 281
"On Native Ground" (Barnes),
    87
Open Assignments, 25, 29, 33,
    37, 69, 73, 77, 81, 85, 89,
    93, 101, 105, 109, 135, 139,
    143, 147, 151, 175, 183,
    187, 195, 199, 227, 231,
    239, 243, 247, 253, 259,
    263, 285, 289, 293, 297,
    301, 305
Open-market forums, 104
Opinions, distinguishing
    between facts and, 766
Or, compound subjects joined
    by, 384, 561
Oral histories, 76
Oral presentations, 104
Organization
  cause-and-effect, 86, 88, 226,
    227, 234
  chronological, 86, 174, 209,
    272
  effect-to-cause pattern, 227
  importance, 86, 88, 162
  logical, 162, 245, 338
  spatial, 86, 87, 133, 135, 162
Organizations
  abbreviations of, 695
  capitalizing names of, 653
Ortiz, Simon J., 543
Outline, 322–323
  for autobiographical sketch, 25
  for class notes, 762
  for essay test, 259
  for research paper, 322–323,
    326–327
  in writing process, 80
Overgeneralizations, avoiding,
    294–295

P

Paragraphs
  adding examples or incidents
    to, 84
  adding facts and statistics to, 84
  definition of, 78
  pronouns in, 92
  repetitions in, 92
  revising, 94–97

  structure of, 78
  supporting details in, 83–84
  synonyms in, 92
  topic sentence in, 82–83
  transitions in, 91
  writing coherent, 90–92
  in writing process, 79–80
Parentheses
  capitalization of first word of
    sentence in, 651
  with other marks of
    punctuation, 682–683
  to set off supplemental
    material, 682
Parenthetical documentation,
    332
Parenthetical expressions, com-
    mas with, 399
Participial phrases, 473, 477
  commas to set off, 473, 677
  diagraming, 523
Participles, 472
  commas to set off, 677
  diagraming, 523
  past, 472
  present, 472
Parts of speech, Grammar
    Workshop for, 436–446
Passed, past, 635, 761
Passive voice, of verb, 541, 543
Past participles, 472
  confusion between past form
    and, 392
  improper use of, 393
Past, passed, 635, 761
Past perfect tense, 536
Past tense, 533–534
Peer editing, 100, 163, 211, 227,
    247, 281, 283
Periodicals, locating, in library,
    729, 735–736
Periodicals indexes, using,
    735–736
Periods
  with abbreviations, 695
  to end declarative sentence,
    500, 667
  to end imperative sentence,
    500, 667
  quotation marks with, 685–
    686
Person, pronoun-antecedent
    agreement in, 585

Acknowledgments *(continued from page iv)*

Text

4 Sandra Cisneros, courtesy of Susan Bergholz Literary Services. **5** From *Blacks* by Gwendolyn Brooks. Copyright © November 1991 by Third World Press, Chicago. **10** Copyright © 1976 by N. Scott Momaday. All rights reserved. Printed in the United States of America. **14** From *Anne Frank: The Diary of a Young Girl* by Anne Frank. Copyright © 1967 by Doubleday & Company, Inc. **18** From *It Was on Fire When I Lay Down on It* by Robert Fulghum. Copyright © 1988, 1989 by Robert Fulghum. Reprinted by permission of Villard Books, a division of Random House, Inc. **24** From *Kareem* by Kareem Abdul-Jabbar, with Mignon McCarthy. Copyright © 1990 by Kareem Abdul-Jabbar. Reprinted by permission of Random House, Inc. **26** From *Selected Poems* by Langston Hughes. Copyright 1926 by Alfred A. Knopf, Inc., and renewed 1954 by Langston Hughes. Reprinted by permission of the publisher. **27** From *Verses from 1929 On* by Ogden Nash. Copyright 1932 by Ogden Nash. First appeared in the *New Yorker*. By permission of Little, Brown and Company. **28** From *Lots of Limericks: Light, Lusty, and Lasting*. Copyright © 1961 by Louis Untermeyer. Published by Doubleday & Company, Inc. (l); From *Cricket Songs*, Japanese haiku translated by Harry Behn. © 1964 by Harry Behn. Reprinted by permission of Marian Reiner (r). **32** "Reflection" from *A Light in the Attic* by Shel Silverstein. Copyright © 1981 by Shel Silverstein. Reprinted by permission of HarperCollins Publishers. **33** From *The Adventures of Huckleberry Finn* by Mark Twain. Copyright © 1948. Published by Holt, Rinehart and Winston with permission from Harper and Row (l); From *Blacks*, published by The David Company, © by Gwendolyn Brooks in 1987 (r). **37** From *The Autobiography of Malcolm X* by Alex Haley. Copyright © 1965 by Grove Press. **38** From *I Know Why the Caged Bird Sings* by Maya Angelou. Copyright © 1969 by Maya Angelou. Reprinted by permission of Random House, Inc. **55** Reprinted by permission. **56** Reprinted with permission of G.K Hall, an imprint of Macmillan Publishing Company, from *Spanish Surnames in the Southwestern United States* by Richard Donovon Woods and Grace Alvarez-Altman. Copyright © 1978 by Richard Donovon Woods and Grace Alvarez-Altman. **58** Reprinted by permission of *Vista*. **62** From *In Search of Our Mothers' Gardens* by Alice Walker. Copyright © 1983, 1982, 1981, 1980, 1979, 1977, 1976, 1975, 1974, 1973, 1972, 1971, 1970, 1967 by Alice Walker. All rights reserved. Published by Harcourt Brace Jovanovich. **71** From *Desert Exile: The Uprooting of a Japanese American Family*, by Yoshiko Uchida. Copyright © 1982 by Yoshiko Uchida. Published by University of Washington Press. **76** From *Hannah's Daughters: Six Generations of an American Family 1876–1976* by Dorothy Gallagher. Copyright © 1976 by Dorothy Gallagher. Published by Thomas Y. Crowell. **79** Excerpt from "A View of the Woods" from *The Complete Stories* by Flannery O'Connor. Copyright © 1957, 1965 by the Estate of Flannery O'Connor. Reprinted by permission of Farrar, Straus & Giroux, Inc. **82** Copyright © by Sandra Cisneros 1989. From "My Name" published in *The House on Mango Street*. Published in the United States by Vintage Books, a division of Random House, Inc., New York, and distributed in Canada by Random House of Canada Limited, Toronto. Originally published, in somewhat different form, by Arte Publico Press in 1984 and revised in 1989. Reprinted by permission of Susan Bergholz Literary Services, New York. **87** From *I Tell You Now:*

Autobiographical Essays by Native American Writers, edited by Brian Swann and Arnold Krupat. Copyright © 1987 by the University of Nebraska Press. **92** Excerpt from *House Made of Dawn* by N. Scott Momaday. Copyright © 1966, 1967, 1968 by N. Scott Momaday. Reprinted by permission of HarperCollins Publishers. **109** From *I Am a Black Woman*, published by Wm. Morrow & Co., 1970, by permission of the author. **110** Reprinted by permission of The Putnam Publishing Group from *The Kitchen God's Wife* by Amy Tan. Copyright © 1991 by Amy Tan. **127, 128** Gary Ross and Anne Spielberg, courtesy of Creative Artist Agency. **131** From *The Return of The King* by J. R. R. Tolkien. Copyright © renewed 1983 by Christopher R. Tolkien, Michael H. R. Tolkien, John F. R. Tolkien and Priscilla M. A. R. Tolkien. Reprinted by permission of Houghton Mifflin Company. All rights reserved. **134** From *The Crystal Cave* by Mary Stewart. Copyright © 1970 by Mary Stewart. **136** Excerpt from *A Wrinkle in Time* by Madeleine L'Engle. Copyright © 1962 and renewal copyright © 1990 by Madeleine L'Engle Franklin. Reprinted by permission of Farrar, Straus & Giroux, Inc. **140** Reprinted by permission of Don Congdon Associates, Inc. Copyright © 1949, renewed 1977 by Ray Bradbury. **145** Reprinted with the permission of Atheneum, an imprint of the Macmillan Publishing Company. From *Tehanu: The Last Book of Earthsea*, by Ursula K. LeGuin. Copyright © 1990 by the Inter-Vivos Trust for the LeGuin Children. **151** From *Ancient, My Enemy* by R. Gordon Dickson. Copyright © 1969 by Doubleday & Company, Inc. **152** From *The Crystal Cave* by Mary Stewart. Copyright © 1970 by Mary Stewart. Reprinted with permission by William Morrow & Company, Inc. **169** Reprinted courtesy of *Sports Illustrated* from the July 2, 1990, issue. Copyright © 1990, The Time Inc. Magazine Company. "Salute to an Amazing Ironman" by Lisa Twyman Bessone. All Rights Reserved. **172** Excerpt from "The Circling Hand" from *Annie John* by Jamaica Kincaid. Copyright © 1983, 1984, 1985 by Jamaica Kincaid. Reprinted by permission of Farrar, Straus & Giroux, Inc. **178** Reprinted from *Growing Up* by Russell Baker © 1983. Used with permission of Contemporary Books, Inc., Chicago. **182** From *Merlyn's Pen: The National Magazine of Student Writing*, October/November 1990, Vol. VI, No. 1. Reprinted by permission of *Merlyn's Pen*. **184** From *The Life of Langston Hughes Volume II: 1941–1967, I Dream A World* by Arnold Rampersad. Copyright © 1988 by Arnold Rampersad. Oxford University Press, Inc. **186** From *Merlyn's Pen: The National Magazine of Student Writing*, April/May 1989, Vol. 4, No. 4. Reprinted by permission of *Merlyn's Pen*. **193** From *Contemporary Latin American Short Stories* edited by Pat McNees Mancini. Copyright © 1974 by CBS Publications, The Consumer Publishing Division of CBS Inc. Published by Ballantine Books. **195** From *Elements of Literature Fourth Course*. Copyright © 1989 by Holt, Rinehart and Winston, Inc. **199** From *Franz Kafka: The Complete Stories* by Franz Kafka, edited by Nahum N. Glatzer. Copyright 1946, 1947, 1948, 1949, 1954 1958, 1971 by Schocken Books Inc. Reprinted by permission of Schocken Books, published by Pantheon Books, a division of Random House, Inc. **200** Copyright © by Julia Alvarez 1991 from *How the García Girls Lost Their Accents*, Algonquin Books of Chapel Hill. First published in *The Writer's Craft*, 2nd ed., ScottForesman Co., 1988. Also published in *Unholy Alliances: New Fiction by Women*, Cleis Press, 1988. Reprinted by permission of Susan Bergholz Literary Services, New York. **217, 218** Theresa Larkin, courtesy of *Audubon* magazine. **220** From *The Secret House* by David Bodanis. Copyright © 1986 by David Bodanis. Reprinted by permission of Simon &

Schuster. **224** From *Light Elements: Essays in Science from Gravity to Levity* by Judith Stone. Copyright © 1991 by Judith Stone. Published by Ballantine Books. **228** From *Rubber Legs and White Tail-Hairs* by Patrick F. McManus. Copyright © 1987 by Patrick F. McManus. Reprinted by permission of Henry Holt and Company, Inc. **232** Copyright © 1985 Carl Sagan and Ann Druyan. All rights reserved. Reprinted by permission of the author. **236** From "For the Love of Loons" by Sue Hubbell. Copyright © *Smithsonian*. Published March 1989. Reprinted with permission of Darhansoff & Verrill Literary Agency. **241** From *The Doomsday Book of Animals: A Natural History of Vanished Species* by David Day. Copyright © 1981 by London Editions/David Day. Published by the Viking Press. **244** Text: Jeffrey Brune/© 1991 *Discover* Magazine. **249** From "Searching for Medicinal Wealth in Amazonia" by Donald Dale Jackson. Copyright © Smithsonian. Published February 1989. **254** From *The Straight Dope* by Cecil Adams. Copyright © 1984. Published by Chicago Review Press. **264** Reprinted with permission of Charles Scribner's Sons, an imprint of Macmillan Publishing Company, from *Of Wolves and Men* by Barry Lopez. Copyright © 1978 Barry Holstun Lopez. **277** Melanie McFarland, courtesy of *New Expressions* magazine. **288** Copyright © 1988 by The New York Times Company. Reprinted by permission. **292** Copyright © 1988 by The New York Times Company. Reprinted by permission. **298** Copyright © 1988 by The New York Times Company. Reprinted by permission. **304** © Copyrighted July 5, 1991, Chicago Tribune company, all rights reserved, used with permission. **306** Copyright © 1989 by The New York Times Company. Reprinted by permission. **342** From *The Concord Review*, Spring 1991, Volume Three, Number Three. Copyright © 1991 by The Concord Review, P.O. Box 661, Concord, Massachusetts 01742. Reprinted with permission. **402** Excerpt from *Barrio Boy* by Ernesto Galarza. Copyright © 1971 by University of Notre Dame Press. Reprinted by permission. **405** Excerpt from *The Joy Luck Club* by Amy Tan. Reprinted by permission of The Putnam Publishing Group. Copyright © 1989 by Amy Tan. **421** "Miss Cynthie" by Rudolph Fisher, published in STORY MAGAZINE, June 1933. **425** Excerpts from "The Man Who Lived Underground" from *Eight Men* by Richard Wright. Copyright © 1944 by Richard Wright. Reprinted by permission of Paul R. Reynolds, Inc. **434** Excerpt from "Sixteen" from *Cress Delahanty* by Jessamyn West. Reprinted by permission of Harcourt Brace Jovanovich, Inc. Copyright 1946, 1974 by Jessamyn West. **436** Excerpt from *Housekeeping* by Marilynne Robinson. Copyright © 1980 by Marilynne Robinson. Reprinted by permission of Farrar, Straus & Giroux, Inc. **460** Excerpt from *Things Fall Apart* by Chinua Achebe. Copyright © 1959 by Chinua Achebe. Reprinted by permission of William Heinemann Limited. **478** Excerpt from *Picture Bride* by Yoshiko Uchida. Reprinted by permission of Northland Publishing. **505** Excerpt from *A Son of the Middle Border* by Hamlin Garland. Reprinted with the permission of Macmillan Publishing Company. Copyright © 1917 by Hamlin Garland, renewed by Mary I. Lord and Constance G. Williams. **506** Excerpt from *Delta Wedding* by Eudora Welty. Reprinted by permission of Harcourt Brace Jovanovich, Inc. Copyright © 1945, 1946, 1973 by Eudora Welty. **544** Excerpt from *Black Boy* by Richard Wright. Copyright © 1937, 1942, 1944, 1945 by Richard Wright; copyright © renewed by Ellen Wright. Reprinted by permission of HarperCollins Publishers, Inc. **565** Excerpt from "Serenity/ Sauvidades" from *Selected Poems of Gabriela Mistral*, edited and translated by Doris Dana. Copyright © 1961, 1964, 1970, 1971 by Doris Dana. Reprinted by permission of Joan Daves Agency. **566** Excerpt from *Savushan* by Simin Daneshvar. Reprinted by permission of Mage Publishers. **592** Excerpt from *The Old Man and the Sea* by Ernest Hemingway. Reprinted with permission of Charles Scribner's Sons, an imprint of Macmillan Publishing Company. Copyright 1952 by Ernest Hemingway; renewal copyright 1980 by Mary Hemingway. **616** Excerpts from *An American Childhood* by Annie Dillard. Copyright © 1987 by Annie Dillard. Reprinted by permission of HarperCollins Publishers Inc. **660** Excerpts from *Lake Wobegon Days* by Garrison Keillor. Copyright © 1985 by Garrison Keillor. Used by permission of Viking Penguin, a division of Penguin Books USA, Inc. **702** Excerpts from *Arctic Dreams* by Barry Lopez. Reprinted with permission of Charles Scribner's Sons, an imprint of Macmillan Publishing Company. Copyright © 1986 by Barry Lopez.

Photos

AR=Art Resource, New York; EF=Eric Futran; RJB=Ralph J. Brunke; SB=Stock Boston, Inc.; SK=Stephen Kennedy; TIB=The Image Bank, Chicago.

Front cover Joan Miró, *Chiffres et constellations en amoureux de sa femme*, 1941, gouache on paper, 45.8 x 38.2 cm, Gift of Mrs. Gilbert W. Chapman © 1992 The Art Institute of Chicago. Photo by RJB. **1** © 1992 The Art Institute of Chicago. Photo by RJB. **3** © The Pace Gallery. **4** © John Dyer 1991. **5** RJB. **6** RJB (t); © David Muench (b). **7** RJB; **8** © John Dyer 1991 (t); RJB (b). **9** EF (t, b). **10** © The Estate of John Lennon, 1989. **14** © AFF/ AFS Amsterdam, the Netherlands. **16** RJB. **17** Private Collection. **21** © Boston Athenæum. **22** U.S. SPACE CAMP® Photo. **26** © D. Taylor/H. Armstrong Roberts. **29** Courtesy Fundación Rufino Tamayo/AR. **31** *Lord of the Flies* courtesy of Castlerock Entertainment/Columbia Pictures (t); EF (b). **34** UPI/ Bettmann Newsphotos. **36** © Ron Tom, Globe Photos. **37** EF (l); RJB (r). **39** © 1991 Bequest of Maxim Karolik. Courtesy, Museum of Fine Arts, Boston. **41** Courtesy Bernice Steinbaum Gallery, New York. **43** Courtesy of the Evans-Tibbs Collection, Washington, D.C. **46** Courtesy of the collection of the B. R. Brazeal Family, Atlanta, Georgia. **53** *Family Blackboard*, 1989, by Jane Ash Poitras. Courtesy of The Heard Museum, Phoenix, Arizona. **54** Jeff Williams. **55** Courtesy Carmen Chavez (tl); Courtesy Lorenzo Chavez (tc, tr); EF (b). **56** Jeff Williams (t); EF (b). **57** © Manuel Chavez/*The Houston Post*. **58** EF. **59** EF. **60** © Nippon Television Network, Japan. **64** © Matthew Naythons/SB. **69** © The Museum of Fine Arts, Houston. Museum purchase with funds provided by the Museum Collectors. **72** EF. **73** © 1985 The Estate of Keith Haring. **74** Private Collection. **76** © Dorothy Gallagher/The Estate of Hannah Lambertson Nesbitt. **80** The Metropolitan Museum of Art, Gift of Frederic H. Hatch, 1926. **81** Collection of the Chase Manhattan Bank, N.A. **83** The Bridgeman Art Library Ltd./AR. **87** SCALA/AR. **89** Iran, late 12th-, early 13th-century. Ceramic 3 3/8 x 8 1/2". The Brooklyn Museum 86.227.61. Gift of the Ernest Erickson Foundation. **93** Carl Van Vechten Gallery of Fine Arts, Fisk University, Nashville, Tennessee. **94** *The Far Side* © 1990 Universal Press Syndicate. Reprinted with permission. **102** © The Peninsula Outlook. **104** © Bob Daemmrich/The Image Works. **108** ©1981 Paramount Pictures Corporation. All Rights Reserved. **109** Beatrice Whitney Van Ness (American, 1888–1981). *Summer Sunlight*, circa 1936.

Oil on canvas. National Museum of Women in the Arts. Gift of Wallace and Wilhelmina Holladay. **111** © Tomie Arai 1988. **116** Courtesy Bluett and Sons, London/Bridgeman Art Library, London. **117** EF (l, r). **123** © James C. Christensen, Courtesy of The Greenwich Workshop, Inc., Trumbull, Connecticut. **124** John Dougan. **125** EF. **126** Photofest. **129** Albright-Knox Art Gallery, Buffalo, New York. **130** © Frank Siteman/SB. **133** © Budd Symes (l, c); © Superstock (r). **134** © Nancy Thill. **135** Courtesy of Koplin Gallery, Santa Monica, California. **139** Marc Chagall. *Paris Through the Window*. 1913. Oil on canvas, 53 1/2 x 55 3/4". Solomon R. Guggenheim Museum, New York. Gift, Solomon R. Guggenheim, 1937. Photo: David Heald. Copyright Solomon R. Guggenheim Foundation, New York. **142** © 1989 Masahiro Sano/The Stock Market. **144** Courtesy Holly Solomon Gallery, New York. **147** Courtesy Walter Gruen, Mexico City. **148** © David Wenzel. **154** National Gallery of Art, Washington,Widener Collection. **157** Giraudon/AR. **159** EF (t); RJB (b). **165** The Frick Collection, New York. **166** EF. **168** EF (l,r). **169** © Rick Browne/SB (t); EF (b). **170** © Tracy Frankel 1989 (t); RJB (c); © Mario Ruiz (b). **171** RJB. **173** © Bob Daemmrich/SB. **176** Photofest. **179** Courtesy of the artist and J. Cacciola Gallery. **180** *Calvin and Hobbes* © 1985 Universal Press Syndicate. Reprinted with permission. **187** Courtesy Frumkin/Adams Gallery, New York. Private Collection. **188** © Nicholas Foster/TIB. **191** Courtesy Washburn Gallery, New York. **192** Grant Wood, *Death on Ridge Road*, 1935 oil on Masonite, 32 x 39" Collection Williams College Museum of Art, Williamstown, Massachusetts. Gift of Cole Porter, 47.1.3. **193** EF. **195** © Patricia Gonzalez. **196** © 1991 Sherry Rayn Barnett/Michael Ochs Archives. **203** Courtesy the Chapingo Chapel of the National School of Agriculture and the Instituto Nacional de Bellas Artes, Mexico. **205** © 1990 Thames and Hudson, Ltd., London. Photo by David Lavendar. **207** EF (t, b). **213** Van Gogh, Vincent. *The Starry Night*. (1889) Oil on canvas, 29 x 36 1/4". Collection, The Museum of Modern Art, New York. Acquired through the Lillie P. Bliss Bequest. **214** David Smart. **215** © Art Wolfe. **216** David Smart. **217** © Charles C. Place. **218** David Smart (t, b). **219** © Catherine Karnow 1991. **220** RJB. **223** © Don Beatty 1984. **224** © Obremski/TIB. **232** © NASA. **233** © Scott Anger/Gamma Liaison. **235** Courtesy of the Evans-Tibbs Collection, Washington, D.C. **239** © Reprinted with permission from Clear Light Publishers from *Old Father Story Teller* by Pablita Velarde. ISBN 940666-10-3. **243** 1991 Spaulding Collection. Courtesy, Museum of Fine Arts, Boston. **244** © Andrew Christie/© 1991 *Discover* Magazine. **248** © Mike Mazzaschi/SB (l); Mark J. Plotkin/Conservation International (r). **253** © Jake Rajs/TIB. **254** © Slug Signorino. **265** Nancy Schutt © 1988. **267** Courtesy of the Thomas Burke Memorial Washington State Museum, Catalog Number 2.5E 1543. Photo by Eduardo Calderon. **269** RJB (t); EF (b). **275** © Lili Lakich and Museum of Neon Art 1981. **276** Scott Raffe (t, c, b). **277** Photofest (l, c, r); EF (b). **278** EF (t); Photofest (l, r); © 1985 Universal City/Photofest (c). **279** © 1989 Courtesy Tri-Star Pictures (tl); © 1987 Courtesy Columbia Pictures (tr); EF (b). **280** Scott Raffe. **280–281** RJB. **281** © Morray Alcosser/TIB. **282** © Camera Five. **285** © 1991 Field Museum of Natural History, Chicago, Neg # A 108764 c, Cat. # 8258. **286** © Julie Houck/SB. **289** Oppenheim, Méret. *Object*. (1936) Fur-covered cup, saucer, and spoon; cup 4 3/8" diameter; saucer 9 3/8"

diameter; spoon, 8" long; overall height 2 7/8". Collection, The Museum of Modern Art, New York. Purchase. **290** © L. Roberts/H. Armstrong Roberts. **294** *For Better or Worse* © 1990 Lynn Johnston. Reprinted with permission of Universal Press Syndicate. **296** SCALA/AR. **297** Picasso, Pablo. *Two Acrobats with a Dog*. Paris, spring 1905. Gouache on cardboard, 41 1/2 x 29 1/2". Collection, The Museum of Modern Art, New York. Gift of Mr. and Mrs. William A. M. Burden. **302** Photofest. **307** Collection New York State Museum. Photo by Peter T. Furst. **309** EF (t); RJB (b). **315** © Bob Adelman. **316** Chicago Historical Society. ICHi-1893. **317** © P. and G. Bowater/TIB. **322** SK. **326** Courtesy of the U.S. Department of the Interior, National Park Service, Edison National Historic Site, West Orange, New Jersey. **330** © Photoworld 1991/FPG International (l); Courtesy of General Motors Corp. (r). **336** The Bettman Archive. **349** Stella, Frank. *Kastura*. (1979) Oil on epoxy on aluminum, wire mesh, 9' x 7'8" x 30" (292.1 x 233.7 x 76.2cm). Collection, The Museum of Modern Art, New York. Acquired through the Mr. and Mrs. Victor Ganz, Mr. and Mrs. Donald H. Peters and Mr. and Mrs. Charles Zadok Funds. **401** © Janeart Ltd./TIB. **410** © Bob Daemmrich/SB. **418** © The Telegraph Colour Library/FPG International. **430** © Steve Woit/SB. **447** Anna Mary Robertson Moses (Grandma Moses) 1860–1961 *Early Skating*. (1951) tempera or oil on masonite 17 7/8 x 24" The Brooklyn Museum 83.122.1. Bequest of R. Thorton Wilson. **455** © Shawn Weimer 1991/Lifestyles (t); © Kent Fleming 1991/Lifestyles (b). **467** The Metropolitan Museum of Art, The Michael C. Rockefeller Memorial Collection, Gift of the Matthew T. Mellon Foundation, 1960. **487** The Metropolitan Museum of Art, Rogers Fund, 1936. (JP 2517). **501** Giraudon/AR. **517** © Robert Duncan; **532** ©The Estate of Harold Edgerton. Courtesy of Palm Press, Inc. **541** © Don Smetzer//TSW. **553** National Museum of American Art, Washington, D.C./AR. **559** © Jerry Wachter/F.O.S. **575** The Metropolitan Museum of Art, Fletcher Fund, 1963. (63.210.11). **601** The Metropolitan Museum of Art, Amelia B. Lazarus Fund, 1910. **603** © Benn Mitchell/TIB (t); © David Brownell/TIB (c); © Janeart Ltd./TIB (b). **607** © E. James T. Flynn. **625** Courtesy of The Phillips Collection, Washington, D.C. **649** Tate Gallery, London/AR. **653** ©Steve Elmore/ TSW-Click/Chicago Ltd. **659** © NAA-Thomas C. Woods Memorial Collection, Sheldon Memorial Art Gallery, University of Nebraska—Lincoln (t); © Joseph Pobereskin/TSW (b). **665** Joslyn Art Museum, Omaha, Nebraska. **682** © Gino Beghe Encore Art Prints, New York. **692** © Elyse Lewin/TIB. **694** © Chuck Solomon/F.O.S. **709** Rockwell Kent. *The Trapper*. 1921. Oil on canvas. 34 x 44". Collection of Whitney Museum of American Art. Purchase 31.258. **715** The Bridgeman Art Library Ltd./AR. **716** The Bettman Archive. **717** The Bettman Archive. **718** © The Hulton-Deutsch Collection, London. **719** The Bettman Archive. **721** Courtesy of The Lilly Library, Indiana University, Bloomington, Indiana. **723** © 1987 Jon Feingersh/SB (l); © Robert Frerck/Odyssey Productions (c); © Andre Gallant/TIB (r). **724** By permission of Johnny Hart and Creators Syndicate, Inc. **725** © Jay Freis/TIB. **726** © 1990 Bill Horsman/SB. **728** SK (t, b). **729** SK. **740** RJB. **746** © PEANUTS reprinted by permission of UFS, Inc. **763** SK. **771** © 1986 Courtesy of Collier, Macmillan Publishers, London. Photo by RJB.

Picture Research by Ligature, Inc.